P9-EDR-844

Books by Richard J. Barnet:

ROOTS OF WAR: THE MEN & INSTITUTIONS
BEHIND U.S. FOREIGN POLICY
THE ECONOMY OF DEATH
INTERVENTION AND REVOLUTION
WHO WANTS DISARMAMENT?

Global Reach

THE POWER OF THE

MULTINATIONAL CORPORATIONS

Richard J. Barnet   Ronald E. Müller

SIMON AND SCHUSTER   NEW YORK

Portions of this book appeared originally in *The New Yorker*.

Copyright © 1974 by Richard J. Barnet and Ronald E. Müller
All rights reserved
including the right of reproduction
in whole or in part in any form
A Touchstone Book
Published by Simon and Schuster
A Division of Gulf & Western Corporation
Simon & Schuster Building, Rockefeller Center
1230 Avenue of the Americas, New York, New York 10020

ISBN 0-671-21835-2
ISBN 0-671-22104-3 Pbk.
Library of Congress Catalog Card Number 74-2794
Designed by Jack Jaget
Manufactured in the United States of America

4 5 6 7 8 9 10 11

Acknowledgments

The authors wish to express their special thanks to Joseph D. Collins, Michael P. Moffitt, David H. Moore, and Susan Berner for their original and dedicated work in the preparation of the research for this book.

The following have carried out indispensable research for various parts of this study: Marcos Arruda, Richard C. Barnett, Susan Berner, Bruce DeCastro, David Dyer, Paula Echeverria, Jacques Ganzler, Fred Goff (and NACLA–West Coast), Robin Hahnel, Suraj Kanowa, Sandra Kelly, Jesus Montañes, Hugo Valladares, and Jeff Zinnsmeyer.

We have benefited greatly from comments or suggestions from the following: Eqbal Ahmad, David Apter, Helmut Arndt, Orlando Arraujo, Jack Baranson, Ann Barnet, Nancy Barrett, Barbara Bick, Sergio Bitar, Jack Blum, Nicholas Bruck, Robb Burlage, Martin Carnoy, Bettina Connor, Ana deKarpf, Guido DiTella, Arthur Domike, Joan Ronder Domike, José Epstein, Max Flores, Ricardo French-Davis, Celso Furtado, Peter Gabriel, Walter Goldstein, William Henderson, Jr., Birgitta Hessel, Jorge Katz, Helen Kramer, Saul Landau, Roger Lesser, Jerome Levinson, Michael Maccoby, Harry Magdoff, Lewis McCoy, Susan McKnight, Hector Melo, Ignacio Millán, Robert Eric Miller, Nancy Mills, Gabriel Misas, Richard Morgenstern, Hans Morgenthau, Cynthia Taft Morris, Paul Neville, Francisco Otero, Marcus Raskin, James Ridgeway, Steve Roday, Leonard Rodberg, Paul Rosenstein-Rodan, Gert Rosenthal, Stanford G. Ross, Herbert Schiller, John Sinclair, Elliot Stein, Jr., Paul Streeten, Osvaldo Sunkel, Stanley S. Surrey, Paul Sweezy, Frank Tamagna, Oliver Thorold, Father Gene Tolland, Louis Turner, Victor Urquidi, Constantine

Vaitsos, Carlos Villarroel, Howard Wachtel, Albert Watterston, James
Weaver, Peter Weiss, Stanley Weiss, Rolando Weissman, Charles K.
Wilber, Miguel Wionczek, and William Wipfler.

We are grateful for the dedicated help we have had on the manu-
script, particularly from Susan Berner, and from Dee Albert, Beth
Barnet, Mary Brock, Sherry Cramer, Irma Dodd, Laurie Ann Kaye,
Ruthanne Müller, Tina Smith, Margot White, and the staffs of the
Institute for Policy Studies and the Department of Economics, The
American University.

The intellectual debt to the pioneering work of the late Stephen
Hymer is acknowledged with gratitude and sadness.

Our thanks go also to our editor, Alice Mayhew, for her great help
and her devotion to the manuscript.

Needless to say, all are absolved from any responsibility for the
ways in which we have made use of their help.

Note to the Reader

The subject matter of this book is both global and controversial. Global corporations operate everywhere. They cross the frontiers of academic disciplines as easily as they cross national frontiers. Any serious attempt to understand what they are doing or the meaning of what they are doing involves a journey into politics, sociology, and psychology as well as economics. Because they are bold, powerful, and new, they elicit strong opinions of all sorts. We have arrived at ours after sifting a mass of widely scattered materials. Any reader who wishes to explore our data or reasoning in greater detail than appears in the text should consult the extensive notes at the back. The general reader should not feel burdened by them.

Contents

9

PART

1

The World Managers

1

The men who run the global corporations are the first in history with the organization, technology, money, and ideology to make a credible try at managing the world as an integrated unit. The global visionary of earlier days was either a self-deceiver or a mystic. When Alexander the Great wept by the riverbank because there were no more worlds to conquer, his distress rested on nothing more substantial than the ignorance of his mapmaker. As the boundaries of the known world expanded, a succession of kings, generals, and assorted strong men tried to establish empires of ever more colossal scale, but none succeeded in making a lasting public reality out of private fantasies. The Napoleonic system, Hitler's Thousand Year Reich, the British Empire, and the Pax Americana left their traces, but none managed to create anything approaching a global organization for administering the planet that could last even a generation. The world, it seems, cannot be run by military occupation, though the dream persists.

The managers of the world's corporate giants proclaim their faith that where conquest has failed, business can succeed. "In the forties Wendell Willkie spoke about 'One World,' " says IBM's Jacques G. Maisonrouge. "In the seventies we are inexorably pushed toward it." Aurelio Peccei, a director of Fiat and organizer of the Club of Rome, states flatly that the global corporation "is the most powerful agent for the internationalization of human society." "Working through great corporations that straddle the earth," says George Ball, former Under Secretary of State and chairman of Lehman Brothers International, "men are able

13

for the first time to utilize world resources with an efficiency dictated by the objective logic of profit." The global corporation is ushering in a genuine world economy, or what business consultant Peter Drucker calls a "global shopping center," and it is accomplishing this, according to Jacques Maisonrouge, "simply by doing its 'thing,' by doing what came naturally in the pursuit of its legitimate business objectives."

The global corporation is the first institution in human history dedicated to centralized planning on a world scale. Because its primary purpose is to organize and to integrate economic activity around the world in such a way as to maximize global profit, the global corporation is an organic structure in which each part is expected to serve the whole. Thus in the end it measures its successes and its failures not by the balance sheet of an individual subsidiary, or the suitability of particular products, or its social impact in a particular country, but by the growth in global profits and global market shares. Its fundamental assumption is that the growth of the whole enhances the welfare of all the parts. Its fundamental claim is efficiency.

Under the threat of intercontinental rocketry and the global ecological crisis that hangs over all air-breathing creatures, the logic of global planning has become irresistible. Our generation, the first to discover that the resources of the planet may not last forever, has a particular reverence for efficiency. The global corporations, as Maisonrouge puts it, make possible the "use of world resources with a maximum of efficiency and a minimum of waste . . . on a global scale." Rising out of the post–World War II technological explosion which has transformed man's view of time, space, and scale, global corporations are making a bid for political acceptance beyond anything ever before accorded a business organization. The first entrepreneurial class with the practical potential to operate a planetary enterprise now aspires to become global managers.

"For business purposes," says the president of the IBM World Trade Corporation, "the boundaries that separate one nation from another are no more real than the equator. They are merely convenient demarcations of ethnic, linguistic, and cultural entities. They do not define business requirements or consumer trends. Once management understands and accepts this world economy, its view of the marketplace—and its planning—necessarily expand. The world outside the home country is no longer viewed as series of disconnected customers and prospects for its products, but as an extension of a single market."

The rise of the planetary enterprise is producing an organizational revolution as profound in its implications for modern man as the Industrial Revolution and the rise of the nation-state itself. The growth rate of global corporations in recent years is so spectacular that it is now easy to assemble an array of dazzling statistics. If we compare the annual sales of corporations with the gross national product of countries for 1973, we discover that GM is bigger than Switzerland, Pakistan, and South Africa; that Royal Dutch Shell is bigger than Iran, Venezuela, and Turkey; and that Goodyear Tire is bigger than Saudi Arabia. The average growth rate of the most successful global corporations is two to three times that of most advanced industrial countries, including the United States. It is estimated that global corporations already have more than $200 billion in physical assets under their control. But size is only one component of power. In international affairs Mao's dictum that political power grows out of the barrel of a gun shocks no one. To those who question their power, corporate statesmen like to point out that, like the Pope, they have no divisions at their command. The sources of their extraordinary power are to be found elsewhere—the power to transform the world political economy and in so doing transform the historic role of the nation-state. This power comes not from the barrel of a gun but from control of the means of creating wealth on a worldwide scale. In the process of developing a new world, the managers of firms like GM, IBM, Pepsico, GE, Pfizer, Shell, Volkswagen, Exxon, and a few hundred others are making daily business decisions which have more impact than those of most sovereign governments on where people live; what work, if any, they will do; what they will eat, drink, and wear; what sorts of knowledge schools and universities will encourage; and what kind of society their children will inherit.

Indeed, the most revolutionary aspect of the planetary enterprise is not its size but its worldview. The managers of the global corporations are seeking to put into practice a theory of human organization that will profoundly alter the nation-state system around which society has been organized for over 400 years. What they are demanding in essence is the right to transcend the nation-state, and in the process, to transform it. "I have long dreamed of buying an island owned by no nation," says Carl A. Gerstacker, chairman of the Dow Chemical Company, "and of establishing the World Headquarters of the Dow company on the truly neutral ground of such an island, beholden to no nation or society. If we were located on such truly neutral ground we could then really operate in the United States as U.S. citizens, in Japan as Japanese citizens and in Brazil as Brazilians rather than being governed in prime by the laws of the United States. . . . We could even pay any natives handsomely to move elsewhere."

A company spokesman for a principal competitor of Dow, Union Carbide, agrees: "It is not proper for an international corporation to put the welfare of any country in which it does business above that of any other." As Charles P. Kindleberger, one of the leading U.S. authorities on international economics, puts it, "The international corporation has no country to which it owes more loyalty than any other, nor any country where it feels completely at home." The global interests of the world company are, as the British financial writer and Member of Parliament Christopher Tugendhat has pointed out, separate and distinct from the interests of every government, including its own government of origin. Although, in terms of management and ownership, all global corporations are either American, British, Dutch, German, French, Swiss, Italian, Canadian, Swedish, or Japanese (most, of course, are American), in outlook and loyalty they are becoming companies without a country.

It is not hard to understand, however, why American corporate giants, even those whose presidents must still make do with an office in a Park Avenue skyscraper instead of a Pacific island, feel that they have outgrown the American Dream. The top 298 U.S.-based global corporations studied by the Department of Commerce earn 40 percent of their entire net profits outside the United States. A 1972 study by Business International Corporation, a service organization for global corporations, shows that 122 of the top U.S.-based multinational corporations had a higher rate of profits from abroad than from domestic operations. In the office-equipment field, for example, the overseas profit for 1971 was 25.6 percent, compared with domestic profits of 9.2 percent. The average reported profit of the pharmaceutical industry from foreign operations was 22.4 percent as against 15.5 percent from operations in the United States. The food industry reported profits from overseas of 16.7 percent as compared with U.S. profits of 11.5 percent. (Extraordinarily high profit on relatively low overseas investment is not uncommon. In 1972, for example, United Brands reported a 72.1 percent return on net assets, Parker Pen 51.2 percent, Exxon 52.5 percent.) By 1973, America's seven largest banks were obtaining 40 percent of their total profits from abroad, up from 23 percent in 1971.

Department of Commerce surveys show that dependence of the leading U.S.-based corporations on foreign profits has been growing at an accelerating rate since 1964. In the last ten years it has been substantially easier to make profits abroad than in the U.S. economy. The result has been that U.S. corporations have been shifting more and more of their total assets abroad: about one-third of the total assets of the chemical industry, about 40 percent of the total assets of the consumer-goods industry, about 75 percent of those of the electrical industry, about one-third of the assets of the pharmaceutical industry are now located outside the United States. Of the more than $100 billion invested worldwide by the U.S. petroleum industry, roughly half is to be found beyond American shores. Over 30 percent of U.S. imports and exports are bought and sold by 187 U.S.-based multinational corporations through their foreign subsidiaries. It is estimated by the British financial analyst Hugh Stephenson that by the mid-1970's, 90 percent of overseas sales of U.S.-based corporations "will be manufactured abroad by American-owned and controlled subsidiaries." "Investment abroad is investment in America" is the new slogan of the global corporations.

2

The popular term for the planetary enterprise is "multinational corporation." In this book we shall seek to avoid it, because it suggests a degree of internationalization of management, to say nothing of stock ownership, which is not accurate. A study of the 1,851 top managers of the leading U.S. companies with large overseas payrolls and foreign sales conducted a few years ago by Kenneth Simmonds reveals that only 1.6 percent of these high-level executives were non-Americans. It is well known that non-Americans hold no more than insignificant amounts of the stock of these enterprises.

More important, the term is inadequate because it fails to capture that aspect of the contemporary world business which is most revolutionary. Businessmen have been venturing abroad a long time—at least since the Phoenicians started selling glass to their Mediterranean neighbors. Some of the great trading companies like the sixteenth-century British Company of Merchants Adventurers antedated the modern nation-state. Each of the great nineteenth-century empires—the British, the French, the Dutch, and even the Danish—served as a protector for private trading organizations which roamed the earth looking for the markets and raw-material sources on which the unprecedented comforts of the Victorian Age depended. Nor could it be said that doing business abroad is a new departure for Americans. At the turn of the century, American firms, such as the Singer Sewing Machine Company, were already playing such an important role in the British economy that the book *The American Invaders* was assured an apoplectic reception in the City when a London publisher brought it out in 1902. Ford has had an assembly plant in Europe since 1911, and the great oil companies have been operating on a near-global scale since the early days of the century.

What makes the global corporation unique is that unlike corporations of even a few years ago, it no longer views overseas factories and markets as adjuncts to its home operations. Instead, as Maisonrouge puts it, the global corporation views the world as "one economic unit." Basic to this view, he points out, "is a need to plan, organize, and manage on a global scale." It is this holistic vision of the earth, in comparison with which "internationalism" seems parochial indeed, that sets the men who have designed the planetary corporation apart from the generations of traders and international entrepreneurs who preceded them.

The power of the global corporation derives from its unique capacity to use finance, technology, and advanced marketing skills to integrate production on a worldwide scale and thus to realize the ancient capitalist dream of One Great Market. This cosmopolitan vision stands as a direct challenge to traditional nationalism. Indeed, the world's leading corporate managers now see the nation-state, once the midwife of the Industrial Revolution, as the chief obstacle to planetary development. "The political boundaries of nation-states," declares William I. Spencer, president of the First National City Corporation, which does busi-

ness in 90 countries, "are too narrow and constricted to define
the scope and sweep of modern business." For George Ball the
world corporation "is planning and acting well in advance of the
world's political ideas" because it is "a modern concept, designed
to meet modern requirements." The nation-state, unfortunately,
"is a very old-fashioned idea and badly adapted to our present
complex world." A true world economy, says John J. Powers,
president of Pfizer, echoing Ball, "is no idealistic pipe dream but
a hard-headed prediction: it is a role into which we are being
pushed by the imperatives of our own technology." Even more
blunt an attack on the nation-state comes from Maisonrouge of
IBM. "The world's political structures are completely obsolete.
They have not changed in at least a hundred years and are woe-
fully out of tune with technological progress." The "critical issue
of our time," says Maisonrouge, is the "conceptual conflict between the search for global optimization of resources and the
independence of nation-states." Business International warns its
corporate clients in a 1967 Research Report: ". . . the nation
state is becoming obsolete: tomorrow . . . it will in any meaningful sense be dead—and so will the corporation that remains
essentially national."

A little more than a generation after the withering of the
wartime dream of world brotherhood—"Globaloney," in Clare
Boothe Luce's epitaph for Wendell Willkie's "One World"—a
new breed of globalists have launched an attack on the nation-
state more radical than anything proposed by World Federalists,
U.N. enthusiasts, or other apostles of "woolly-headed internationalism" who traditionally cause dismay in boardrooms and country
clubs. The men who run the global corporations, aware that
ideologies, like crackers, travel well only if skillfully packaged,
are putting great energy into marketing a new gospel of peace
and plenty, which has more potential to change the face of the
earth than even the merchandising miracles that have brought
Holiday Inns and Pepsi-Cola bottling plants to Moscow and
Pollo Frito Kentucky to Latin America. Jacques Maisonrouge
likes to point out that "Down with Borders," a revolutionary
student slogan of the 1968 Paris university uprising—in which
some of his children were involved—is also a welcome slogan at
IBM.

The new generation of planetary visionaries, unlike globalists of earlier days, come to their prophetic calling not by way of poetic imagination, transcendental philosophy, or Oriental mysticism but by solid careers in electrical circuitry, soap, mayonnaise, and aspirin. But they proclaim the heavenly city of the global corporation with the zeal of a Savonarola. For Roy Ash, the former head of Litton Industries, later Nixon's budget director and chief consultant in managerial matters, the world corporation represents a "transcendental unity." It is the wave of the future, "for nothing can stop an idea whose time has come." Men like Ash know that their vision of a world without borders is the most important product they have to sell, for the extraordinary role they are proposing to play in human affairs challenges what Arnold Toynbee calls "mankind's major religion, the cult of sovereignty." What we need, Pfizer's president, John J. Powers, told a business gathering some years ago, is "philosophers in action" to explain "the promise of the world corporation." David Rockefeller, chairman of the Chase Manhattan Bank, calls for a massive public relations campaign to dispel the dangerous "suspicions" about the corporate giants that lurk in minds not yet able to grasp an idea whose time has come.

The rhapsodic tone which the new globalists have developed in their celebration of the global corporation as "the instrument of world development," "the only force for peace," "the most powerful agent for the internationalization of human society," or, in the words of Dean Courtney Brown of the Columbia Business School, the "prologue to a new world symphony" is no doubt attributable in part to the salesman's traditional weakness for puffing. But more important, the hard sell of the global corporation, now being promoted in hundreds of industry speeches and industry-sponsored studies and by elaborate lobbying activities, such as that of the Emergency Committee for American Trade, reflects deep and growing customer resistance on many levels.

The managers of the global corporations keep telling one another that there can be no integrated world economy without radical transformations in the "obsolete" nation-state; but however progressive a notion this may be, those who depend on the old-fashioned structures for their careers, livelihood, or inspiration are not easily convinced. The executives who run the global corporations have persuaded themselves that they are far ahead of politicians in global planning because political managers are prisoners of geography. As much as the mayor of Minneapolis or Milan or São Paulo may aspire to a planetary vision, his career depends upon what happens within his territorial domain. Rulers of nations exhibit a similar parochialism for the same reasons. They are jealous of their sovereign prerogatives and do not wish to share, much less abdicate, decision-making power over what happens within their territory.

The new globalists are well aware of the problem. "Corporations that buy, sell, and produce abroad," says George Ball, "do have the power to affect the lives of people and nations in a manner that necessarily challenges the prerogatives and responsibilities of political authority. How can a national government make an economic plan with any confidence if a board of directors meeting 5,000 miles away can by altering its pattern of purchasing and production affect in a major way the country's economic life?" But the World Manager's answer to the charge of being a political usurper is not to deny the extraordinary power he seeks to exercise in human affairs but to rationalize it.

David Rockefeller has called for a "crusade for understanding" to explain why global corporations should have freer rein to move goods, capital, and technology around the world without the interference of nation-states; but such a crusade calls for the public relations campaign of the century. Perhaps the logic of One World has never been so apparent to so many, yet the twentieth century is above all the age of nationalism. There has been no idea in history for which greater numbers of human beings have died, and most of the corpses have been added to the heap in this century. The continuing struggle for national identity is the unifying political theme of our time. The imperial architects of Germany, Italy, and Japan; the guerrilla leaders of liberation movements, Tito, Ho, Castro; and those who are still fighting to free Africa from colonial rule have all been sustained by the power of nationalism. "The nation-state will not wither away," the chairman of Unilever, one of the earliest and largest world corporations, predicts. A "positive role" will have to be found for it.

3

Any enterprise with a planetary appetite is bound to gather a global collection of enemies. Basically, they fall into three dis-

tinct groups. The first includes those whose economic interests
are adversely affected by the rise of the world corporation. In the
United States the most seriously damaged member of this group
is organized labor. To the UAW and the AFL-CIO the "prologue
to a new world symphony" looks like nothing more than an up-
dated version of the "runaway shop." Singer Sewing Machine,
one of the earliest international companies, has in recent years
reduced its main U.S. plant in New Jersey from 10,000 employees
to 2,000. General Instruments recently cut its New England
labor force by 3,000 and increased its force in Taiwan by almost
5,000. This process shows no sign of stopping. The global corporations claim that the effect of internationalization of production is a net increase in jobs, because the stimulation of new industry is greater than the job displacement in older industry. We
shall look at this question of job displacement in detail in Part III;
but whether one reads union studies or industry studies, the fact
is indisputable that thousands of U.S. workers are losing jobs
because of plant relocation. That other workers in other places
may be getting jobs in the process is small comfort to the unemployed.

The discomfort is sufficiently acute that organized labor has
mounted a campaign to pass frankly punitive legislation designed
to discourage foreign investment, principally the Hartke-Burke
bill. Organized labor is hostile to the world corporation not only
because it employs cheap labor under what can only be described
as sweatshop conditions (60 percent of the male workers of Hong
Kong work seven days a week for about a dollar a day), but also
because the mobility of the global enterprise robs labor of its
traditional bargaining weapons. (Companies now deliberately
duplicate production facilities so that they can shift from one to
another in the event of labor trouble.)

Some older domestic industries in the United States such as
shoes and textiles continue to fight the world without borders
because they are dependent upon such borders to protect them
from devastating foreign competition. The motto of the growing
band of neoprotectionists is "Up with Borders"—the opposite of
the one that may unite revolutionary students and IBM executives. In poor countries, national industries threatened with either
absorption by the global giants or lethal competition also form
part of the protectionist coalition.

But the torrent of articles, exposés, and impassioned speeches on the global companies, particularly in the underdeveloped countries, is a reflection of a second group of enemies, who are motivated as much by political feelings as by economic interest. The disclosures of ITT's efforts to bring down the Allende government in Chile have confirmed widespread fears that the global corporations not only have too much power but that they abuse that power. There is increasing concern around the world that global corporations are in a position to dominate governments, dislocate national economies, and upset world currency flows. Corporate managers have such power to shift capital, develop (or suppress) technology, and mold public moods and appetites that even the most powerful governments worry about their ability to control them. Whether the global corporation should be welcomed, barred, or fitted with a legal straitjacket is shaping up as a prime political issue in virtually all developing countries and increasingly in the more industrialized nations as well.

Potential members of the second group include officials and bureaucrats in the largest developed countries who are beginning to see the worldwide corporate attack on "irrational nationalism" as a direct challenge to their own power. It is one thing to be against "irrational nationalism" in Guatemala, where what is presumably meant is expropriation of bananas. It is something else again when U.S. officials themselves become the target. Although the U.S. Government has yet to focus on the challenge which the power of the global corporation poses to its own power (in such policy areas as anti-trust, taxation, pollution control, and energy, for example), there are even now a few hints of irritation from government bureaucrats over the high-handedness of the corporate giants. The series of governmental investigations of the global corporations around the world, by the U.S. Senate Foreign Relations and Finance committees, the European Economic Community, the United Nations, the Canadian and Swedish governments, among others, attests to the growing fears of politicians that in a world without borders dominated by global corporations they may lose the capacity to govern. The Council of the Americas, a mutual-support association of the 200 principal U.S.-based corporations operating in Latin America, devoted its 1972 annual meeting to the theme of anticorporatism and how business must "explain itself" better. A similar concern dominated the 1972 White House Conference on the Industrial World Ahead 1990. David Rockefeller shocked bankers at the Detroit Economic Club by pointing out that, according to a recent poll, three out of five students believe that "big business has taken the reins of government away from the Congress and Administration." Rockefeller's poll is corroborated by a University of Michigan survey which reveals that 59 percent of all Americans think that "the Government is run by a few big interests looking out for themselves." Opinion Research Corporation reports that "53% of the people feel business is doing very little in pollution control while only 10% think it is doing a great deal."

The attitude of young people around the world toward the global corporation is a cause of particular concern. "If I were asked to describe the current stereotype of the corporation held by the young," says Jacques Maisonrouge in a speech he has delivered on more than one occasion, "I would be compelled to say:

> A corporation is a business structure whose sole reason for existence is the earning of profits by manufacturing products for as little as possible and selling them for as much as possible. It does not matter whether the product does good or evil; what counts is that it be consumed—in ever-increasing quantities. Since everything the corporation does has, as its ultimate goal, the creation of profit, it offers its workers no deep personal satisfactions, no feeling of contributing anything worthwhile to society, no true meaning to their activities. Go to work for a corporation and you are, through good salaries and various fringe benefits, installed as a faceless link in the lengthening chain—completing the circle by becoming one more consumer of all that junk. And, like all circles, the whole structure signifies nothing.

"America's Growing Anti-Business Mood," as *Business Week* calls it, threatens what the World Managers seek above all: public acceptance of the global corporation as the most effective and rational force to develop and distribute the resources of the world. In short, political legitimacy.

The confrontation between the multinational corporation and its enemies promises to influence the shape of human society in the last third of the century more than any other political drama

of our time. To survive and to grow, certainly to fulfill its promise to create a rational, integrated world economy, the global
corporation must forge a new global consensus on the most fundamental questions of political life: What kind of social and
economic development meets the needs of twentieth-century
man? What is a just social order? What is "freedom," "justice,"
or "need" in a world in which 4 billion inhabitants are struggling
for food, water, and air? What does "efficiency" or "growth" or
"rationality" mean in such a world?

And in the end they must answer the 1970's version of the
same question that has confronted every new elite aspiring to
political leadership and social management: by what right do a
self-selected group of druggists, biscuit makers, and computer
designers become the architects of the new world? To establish
their political legitimacy, the aspiring World Managers must be
able to demonstrate that the maximization of global profits is
compatible with human survival.

For more than three years we have been trying to answer these
questions for ourselves. We have examined the claims of the
World Managers in their writings, in their own commissioned
studies, and in numerous personal interviews with some of the
leading corporate executives in the United States and Europe.
We have also looked closely at the case against them. We have
benefited from the explosion of academic analysis on what has,
lately, become a fashionable topic of university study. We have
studied both their financial, political, and diplomatic operations
and some of their plans for our collective future.

Our conclusions about the impact of global corporations are
based on what they do rather than on what they say. In this book
we try to assess what their current operations and future plans
mean in the daily lives of ourselves and our children—not only
in the United States but in the rest of the world. Does the rise of
the World Managers offer a new golden age or a new form of
imperial domination? Is the global corporation mankind's best
hope for producing and distributing the riches of the earth, as the
World Managers contend—or, as their critics argue, is their
vaunted rational integrated world economy a recipe for a new
stage in authoritarian politics, an international class war of huge
proportions, and, ultimately, ecological suicide?

2

From Globaloney to the Global Shopping Center

1

The global corporation is transforming the world political economy through its increasing control over three fundamental resources of economic life: the technology of production, finance capital, and marketing. The internationalization of production means simply that more and more of the world's goods and services (Gross World Product) are being produced in more and more countries and that the production process increasingly ignores national frontiers. A watch or a car or even a shirt may include various components produced in widely scattered places. Some observers, such as Professor Howard Perlmutter of the Wharton School, estimate that by 1985, 200 to 300 global corporations will control 80 percent of all productive assets of the non-Communist world. Even the more modest predictions are staggering. Judd Polk, senior economist of the U.S. Chamber of Commerce, calculates that by the turn of the century a few hundred global companies will own productive assets in excess of $4 trillion, or about 54 percent of everything worth owning for the creation of wealth.

Industry has transcended geography. One indication of this is that some of the largest U.S. corporations and banks such as Gillette, Woolworth's, Pfizer, Mobil, IBM, Coca-Cola, and the First National City Bank earn more than 50 percent of their profits overseas. But it is important to understand that the rise of the global corporation is far more than the overseas expansion of U.S.

26

corporations. As we shall see in later chapters, the U.S.-owned-and-managed global corporations have transcended their own country in interest, outlook and strategy.

Global corporations are neither an American invention nor an American phenomenon. Among the earliest were Unilever (British-Dutch) and Shell (British). Non-U.S. global corporations already own more than 700 major manufacturing enterprises in the United States. Holders of Sinclair Oil credit cards had a graphic illustration of this trend when they received a letter from British Petroleum informing them that it was taking over Sinclair's gasoline stations in the United States. (BP also controls about 50 percent of the known oil reserves on Alaska's North Slope.) According to the studies of Stephen Hymer, Robert Rowthorn, and Rainer Hellman, European companies were by 1967 increasing their investment in U.S. industry at a faster rate than American companies were acquiring investment in Europe. Today many famous American brand names in the supermarket, such as Good Humor, are owned by foreign companies.

While U.S. firms still hold a commanding lead in the internationalization of production and the development of the global market, the world corporation is far more than an American challenge. Japan- and West Europe–based global companies have expanded aggressively in such traditional U.S. economic preserves as Brazil. U.S. world production figures illustrate the sharp decline in the American domination of the global market. In 1953 the United States was responsible for 69.8 percent of the world motor-vehicle production; by 1968 the U.S. share of the total was down to 37.9 percent. Twenty years ago the United States produced 75 percent of all television sets in the world; now U.S. companies produce less than 25 percent, and as of 1973 only a few black-and-white sets were still being made in the United States. The same trend exists in many other big industries, including crude steel, plastics, cargo ships, and synthetic rubber. But despite the increasing concern in the United States about "foreign penetration" of the U.S. economy by Arab sheiks and Japanese firms, U.S. companies are far in the lead in the race to control the new global economy.

The revolutionary aspect of international production is that widely dispersed productive facilities can, thanks to such innovations as containerized shipping and satellite communications, be integrated into what is, conceptually, a global factory without geographical ties. Before its product reaches the consumer, it will bear the stamp of several lands: the capital of one, the natural resources of another, and the labor of a third. Massey-Ferguson, a Canadian-based global company, assembles French-made transmissions, Mexican-made axles, and British-made engines in a Detroit plant for the Canadian market. Ford now supplies the U.S. market in part from its Canadian and Brazilian plants. Volkswagen has begun to supply the German market from its Mexican plant.

The internationalization of finance capital is as crucial to this global process as the internationalization of production. Global corporations can borrow money almost anywhere in the world. Dollars, despite the patriotic slogans on the bills, have no nationality. In the 1960's the Eurodollar market, now estimated at $100 billion, was developed. This first transnational money market, one of the most important innovations of modern capitalism, was originally the creation of a Soviet bank. During the same period, the international loan syndicate and the international bank consortium appeared on the scene. Typical of such consortiums is a joint venture called Orion Bank, organized by Chase Manhattan, National Westminster (U.K.), the Royal Bank of Canada, the Westdeutsche Landesbank Girozentral, Credito Italiano and Nikko Securities of Japan. At the same time, U.S. banks have enormously increased their overseas operations. In 1972, the First National City Bank, the world's first bank to earn more than $200 million in a single year, earned $109 million of it from its foreign operations. Global industrial corporations are also establishing their own financial arms. The Dow Bank, started by the global petrochemical firm, is now the sixth-largest bank of Switzerland.

Two days before President Nixon announced on August 15, 1971, his new economic policy to strengthen the dollar, Donald G. Robbins, Jr., the chief financial officer for Singer, added to the flood of unwanted dollars by selling $20 million for Swiss francs and British pounds. Since many other multinational companies were also shifting currencies, they were, *Newsweek* concluded, "the prime force behind the whole currency crisis." James Meigs, economist for the Argus Research Corporation, is more explicit: "If you want to find all those evil speculators, don't look for them on the Orient Express. They're on the 5:15 to Larchmont." A

1973 Senate Finance Committee report put the point this way:

> It is beyond dispute that the persons and institutions operating in these markets have the resources with which to generate international monetary crises of the sort that have plagued the major central banks in recent years . . . $268 billion, all managed by private persons and traded in private markets virtually uncontrolled by official institutions anywhere . . . more than twice the total of all international reserves held by all central banks and international monetary institutions in the world. . . .

Through the increasing use of centralized, computerized cash-management systems, global corporations are in a unique position to play the world capital and currency markets, arranging where possible to "lead" their Accounts Payable (i.e., make early payment) where currencies are on the rise and "lag" their Accounts Receivable (i.e., delay payment) where the currency is likely to weaken. Because of their size and power they are able to attract local finance capital, particularly from poor countries. Their attractiveness as an investment has the effect of preempting scarce local funds which might have been available to finance locally controlled projects.

The introduction of the global payroll has produced dramatic changes in world labor markets. The essential strategy of the global corporation is based on the international division of labor. Top management continues to be recruited from rich countries; workers increasingly come from low-wage areas. For a world corporation it is an ideal combination. While automation continues to reduce the amount of labor relative to capital use in the manufacturing process, wage differentials are becoming more critical in maintaining competitive profit margins as between the global corporations themselves. Thus, a few years ago only the most labor-intensive industries would go abroad looking for cheap help. Today Fairchild Camera, Texas Instruments, and Motorola have settled in Hong Kong to take advantage of the $1-a-day, seven-day-working-week conditions there. Timex and Bulova make an increasing share of their watches in Taiwan, where they share a union-free labor pool with RCA, Admiral, Zenith, and a large number of other corporations. Kodak imports its top seller, the "Instamatic," from Germany. Polaroid is now the only major camera being manufactured in the United States. European

companies are also moving to Southeast Asia. Rollei, having fig-
ured out that wages make up 60 percent of the cost of the modern
complex camera and that wages are six times higher in Germany
than in Singapore, has built a huge factory in that "heavenly city
of the global corporations," as Singapore's Foreign Minister recently billed his industrious little island. (It is heavenly in large
part because the government guarantees freedom from union
trouble for a given number of years if the foreign companies will
agree to make a minimum dollar investment.)

U.S. companies are licensing production of the video recorder,
the next potential consumer best seller in the electronics field, to
Europe and the Far East, and it is unlikely that this innovation
developed by CBS and other U.S. companies will ever be manufactured in commercial quantities on American soil. Having
found that what were once highly skilled jobs can now be rou-
tinized and subcontracted to low-wage areas, U.S. companies are
now making components in Mexico, sometimes within a mile
of the border, and importing the finished product into the U.S.
market. The ability of global companies to shift production from
one facility to another perhaps thousands of miles away is already having a crucial impact on organized labor around the
world. Later in the book we shall explore the question whether
the internationalization of organized labor movements can proceed fast enough to cope with management's efforts to exploit
the international division of labor.

Finally, to create a Global Shopping Center it has been necessary to create what Ernest Dichter, the architect of Exxon's "Put
a tiger in your tank" campaign, calls "the world customer." Writing in the *Harvard Business Review*, he observes that companies
with "foresight to capitalize on international opportunities" must
understand that "cultural anthropology will be an important tool
of competititve marketing." The advertising firm McCann-Erickson, which now has offices in 47 countries, recently sent a detailed
questionnaire to professors of Latin American studies seeking
for their clients such useful information as the eating habits of
campesinos and the consumption patterns of the new urban
middle-class family. Only when the corporate manager is aware
of the similarities and differences in the hopes, fears, and desires
of human beings in different parts of the world can he tailor his
product and his sales pitch to influence and direct the "world

revolution of human expectations." The development of new markets, Dichter points out, depends upon knowing that "only one Frenchman out of three brushes his teeth" or "four out of five Germans change their shirts but once a week." It is equally vital to know enough of the local culture to be able to take advantage of or to shape local tastes and customs. Dichter reports that a toothpaste company tried unsuccessfully to adapt its U.S. advertising campaign to France: or "Threatening Frenchmen that if they didn't brush their teeth regularly, they would develop cavities or would not find a lover, failed to impress." A more seductive approach emphasizing that brushing teeth is "chic" and "modern" succeeded after company anthropologists decided that Frenchmen feel guilty about "overindulging in bathing or toiletries." U.S. toilet-tissue manufacturers have also found a way to overcome cultural resistance to their product. For example, in West Germany many families, despite rising affluence, still think newspapers will do. "The advertising approach, then," says Dichter, "has to deal much more with providing absolution and selling the concept that good quality toilet tissue is a part of modern life." As Pfizer's John J. Powers puts it, global corporations are "agents of change, socially, economically and culturally."

Lee S. Bickmore, former chairman of the National Biscuit Company, believes the key to the global market is "the tendency for people all over the world to adopt the same tastes and same consumption habits," and he has some ideas to help that process along. Some time ago, he told *Forbes:* "Why, we plan someday to advertise all over the world. We might spend, say, $8 million for an advertisement on a communications satellite system. It might reach 359 million people. So what we are doing now is establishing the availability of our products in retail outlets all over the world." When we interviewed him four years later, he was talking of reaching 2 billion munchers someday. In projecting the Ritz Crackers box on TV screens around the world, he emphasized that his company is selling more than crackers. "We are selling a concept."

The challenge of the Global Shopping Center, as the World Managers see it, is at once to retail old needs to new customers and to create new needs for old customers. Thus the rising middle class in Latin America is a key target for established products such as automobiles. With population growth declining in the industrial world and its highways already choked, market expansion in the developed nations is slowing down. (This does not mean that more cars will not be sold each year, but it does mean that the rate of increase will be more modest than the managers of growth industries are willing to accept.) But in countries like Brazil and Mexico, each year thousands of people in the middle class are beginning to have sufficient income to discover that they cannot exist without a car. "Latin America must be our market," a top Fiat executive told us. "We cannot trust the Arabs. God knows what we could get from the Africans. Latin America is still the best place," he insisted, despite the fact that several Fiat managers have been kidnapped in Latin America and the head of Fiat in Argentina was assassinated by revolutionaries.

In the developed world, the problem is different. There established companies compete for greater shares of a relatively stable market through innovation and advertising. Companies such as the Big Three auto makers, the big television producers, and the big computer makers compete with one another, contrary to the model of perfect competition celebrated in classical economic theory, not by seeking to undercut one another in price, but by means of what economists call oligopolistic competition. Oligopolies are rather like clubs. (All it takes to be a member is to be of sufficient size.) In any industry a handful of companies compete for ever-larger shares of the market according to certain well-established but unstated rules. The principal rule is that price competition, except on very limited occasions, is an antisocial practice to be strictly avoided, since it threatens to destroy the whole club. Once started, the process of retaliatory price cuts has a way of spiraling out of control. Similarly, the products offered by members are more or less identical; introducing radically new technology is considered unsporting. Thus the essential interchangeability of Fords, Chevrolets, and Plymouths; RCA's, Zeniths and Hitachis.

Occasionally, a small company such as the Haloid Company, which invented xerography, will gain admittance to the club by bringing off a significant technological breakthrough. But while the managers of high-technology industries confidently predict new technological revolutions around the corner and like to twit doubters by pointing out that the U.S. Commissioner of Patents resigned in 1883 because there was nothing left to be invented, oligopolists seldom challenge one another to a technology race. Instead they compete in the less volatile arenas of cost cutting (through automation and the removal of factories to low-wage areas) and product differentiation (beating out the competition by means of more attractive and convenient packaging and more arresting advertising). Hertz and Avis cars are identical, but many Americans liked the idea of patronizing the "underdog" during Avis's famous "We try harder" campaign—despite the fact that during much of that campaign Avis was owned by ITT, one of the giants of them all. Product differentiation is a strategy for distinguishing a company's product from its competitors in order to increase its share of the market at minimum cost. Since a dollar in advertising is likely to have a quicker payoff than a dollar invested in the product itself—how much better than a Camel can you make a Chesterfield?—the "breakthroughs" in consumer products tend to be trivial changes tailored to advertising campaigns. This generally means an escalation in what might be called the make-believe-reality ratio in the marketing of new products. General Foods has recently discovered that your family dog has "three life periods" for which three different kinds of dog food, all conveniently made by GF, are essential. Its success depends wholly upon how much guilt can be generated by the prospect of feeding middle-aged-dog food to senescent hounds.

The most important integrating effect of global marketing techniques is the creation of what Daniel Boorstin calls the "consumption community"—a bond transcending race, geography, and tradition based on eating, drinking, smoking, wearing, and driving identical things. An internationally placed advertisement for *Time* magazine suggests the extraordinary political impact of this development:

> *Time*'s 24 million readers [throughout the world] are apt to have more in common with each other than with many of their own countrymen. High income, good education, responsible positions in business, government and the professions. The readers constitute an international community of the affluent and the influential. . . .

2

The driving force behind oligopolistic competition is a compulsion toward growth; corporate expansion, which Charles G. Mortimer of General Foods calls "a law of nature," is the essential strategy for maintaining or increasing market shares. From the perspective of General Foods, the cry to limit growth from environmentalists, from "zero-growth" economists, from people who feel crowded on the highways or drowned in goods, is "unnatural"; "bigness" is "a great force for good." Robert W. Johnson, a recent chairman of Johnson & Johnson pharmaceuticals, also believes that "a nation as well as a business that does not grow will go back to the Dark Ages. The price of lethargy is slavery." Oligopolists cannot seek a comfortable plateau on which to rest. For the management of global oligopolies, the alternatives are to maintain, or preferably to wrest, an ever-larger share of the market from the other club members or to face a vote of no confidence from the stock market.

Almost by definition, a company with sufficient resources to integrate its activities on a global scale is an oligopoly. Thus IBM controls about 40 percent of the world computer market. Seven oil companies, known as the "seven sisters," control over two-thirds of the world's oil and natural-gas supply; the top three U.S.-based auto makers have captured well over 50 percent of the world market. Ford, General Motors, National Biscuit, Du Pont, Dow, Bayer all enjoy an oligopolistic position in the U.S. market. Each makes literally hundreds of products which only a few other giants can match. In the underdeveloped countries, as we shall see, the oligopolistic position of a few companies is even more dramatic. In Chile, for example, in the late 1960's 22 global firms controlled over 50 percent of seven crucial industries, and all but three were monopolies or oligopolies.

In the business world, as in government bureaucracy, invention is the mother of necessity. When corporations push technology in the inexorable pursuit of growth, it is not a matter of choice; it is a law of life. The campaign to integrate the world into a Global Factory, Global Money Market, and Global Shopping Center was virtually inescapable once the integrating technologies of the past generation were developed. When top executives of the largest corporations discovered that they could manage a world enterprise divided into coordinated "profit centers" in the comfort of a Boeing 707, the rise of the corporate jet set was assured.

Indeed, the spectacular growth of the global corporation and international air travel are simultaneous phenomena of the early 1960's. Today the top managers of these corporations are in constant motion. In the preparation of this book we interviewed the top executives of some of the leading global corporations. Virtually all were either leaving for or returning from an inspection trip abroad. Henry Ford makes four major world trips each year. Jacques Maisonrouge, who still travels on a French passport, spends several months of the year away from his Paris office. José de Cubas, president of Westinghouse World Corporation, was delighted to learn at his retirement banquet that he had logged the equivalent of thirty-nine orbits of the earth in the line of duty. Before his retirement as chief of General Electric, Fred Borch took his successor to visit GE operations around the world in what has come to be the corporate equivalent of the state visit. One of the main functions of the executive vice-president for executive development of Exxon (formerly Standard Oil of New Jersey when it was merely the world's largest oil company) is to route the top 250 executives on their continuing odyssey across the earth. He showed us the "executive deployment" chart for the coming month which he had prepared with all the care of a military operation. It appears that only the Strategic Air Command takes greater care to keep some of its top brass airborne at all times.

The communications satellite makes it possible for the top corporate executive to "think globally" in the comfort of his office. Telephone connections from New York to Santiago or Peking are excellent. The satellite, as television viewers of President Nixon's trip to China will recall, makes it possible to have a clear conversation with anyone, anywhere. Indeed, corporate executives in underdeveloped countries in Latin America and Africa often have the frustrating experience of being able to hear the boss in New York perfectly but not the customer at the other end of a barely functioning local phone. A company such as IBM now has the technology to link its laboratories around the world. "With the magic of today's communications technologies," says Maisonrouge, "we were able to set up a network between the United States and Europe and by use of facsimile equipment, could transmit not only messages but drawings as well. An engineer in our laboratory in Poughkeepsie, New York, can talk with and jointly design circuits with an engineer in Hursley, England, transmitting designs back and forth as they work."

But even more important than hardware in the development of the global market are the new techniques of centralized management that have been developed in the last few years. Richard Eells of Columbia University has made something of a study of what he calls "corporate intelligence" (it is less than exhaustive research, since corporations are on the whole better at keeping their secrets than governments). Global companies, he finds, have a "communications strategy . . . not dissimilar to many of the strategies used by nation-states." Their political power stems in large part from the "valuable information flow" which they can generate on a worldwide basis. The economic analyst of Ford, for example, whose job in part is to predict when currency devaluations will take place, maintains a complete library on key national officials in the countries where Ford operates, much as the CIA amasses similar sorts of data to help in making political predictions. He tries, as he explained to a *Fortune* interviewer, to get "into the skin of financial bureaucrats" to decide when or whether they will devalue the local currency. He claims to have accurately predicted key currency decisions in 69 out of 75 monetary crises.

The advanced computer now makes it possible to handle enormous quantities of information from widely diverse places. The availability of a tool that can assemble global data has created, to use John Kenneth Galbraith's term, the "technological imperative" for global programming. In the same way, the sheer availability of a global market has led to the development of esoteric techniques for manipulating the market for maximum profitability. Tax lawyers have perfected the Liechtenstein, Bahama, Cayman, Panama, and New Hebrides tax haven. (A General Motors subsidiary is incorporated in Luxembourg.) Such corporations are often little more than a gold plaque engraved with the corporate name on the wall of a sleepy, palm-shaded office, but the fiction that the gold plaque is the real home of an important part of Nestlé's worldwide operations, to give one example, has magical power to save millions of dollars in corporate income taxes. The simple expedient of selling to one's own wholly owned subsidiary at an absurdly high price where local taxes are high or at a bargain where taxes are low can do wonders for global profit maximization—which is, after all, the prime goal of corporate planning and the ultimate test of its success or failure.

3

The rise of the global corporation has been sparked by two fundamental tenets of the modern business faith: the cult of bigness and the science of centralization. The ultimate success of the Global Shopping Center will depend upon whether these basic notions can be marketed in an increasingly skeptical world. No effort is being spared in the attempt. "It has been abundantly proved," says Carl Gerstacker, "that size is often a gigantic advantage, and often, for certain tasks, a necessity. The problems of our times will require greater, bigger organizations than we now have, rather than smaller ones, for their solution. . . . We must cast aside our outmoded notions of size and our fear of bigness."

At each stage of the Industrial Revolution, bigness has served the growth of business as both ideology and weapon. As economist Stephen Hymer points out, just as the corner grocery store became uneconomic when technology made the national food chain possible, the national corporation is now no match for a globally integrated enterprise. At each stage, entrepreneurs have used the growth of the previous stage to overcome not only competition from less adaptable businessmen but also psychological resistance from the public. When the "chain stores," as they used to be termed with some suspicion, invaded the territory of the local butcher and grocer and eventually put them out of business, customers had to be convinced that they were not merely a convenience but represented an advance in civilization. So too the global corporation, with its wholesale attack on the way nation-states customarily do business, will have to battle traditional notions about how corporations and nations should behave and what power each should wield.

But even the most sacrosanct ideas and habits that have stood in the way of economic growth have had a poor survival record. When, as the great economic historian R. H. Tawney pointed out, fledgling capitalists of the Middle Ages discovered that charging interest on money was too profitable to be a sin, the Church modified its attitude toward usury, and the modern banking industry was born. The struggle for political legitimacy is the most important task that faces the global corporation, and the development of a compelling ideology is its most important product.

Organizational growth is as elusive a subject as human growth itself. In 1927 R. D. McKenzie, in an essay called "The Concept of Dominance and World Organization," developed the interesting theory that the "spatial distribution of human beings and institutions is not accidental . . . but represents a dynamic functional interrelationship in which the units are organized around centers or points of dominance." In other words, organizations, like human beings, reveal "an ongoing tendency toward a more specialized and refined relation between the center of dominance and the subordinated integrated parts." This is an almost perfect description of the growth pattern of the world corporation. McKenzie predicted thirty years before the explosion of the multinationals that the development of communications would transform the world "from the small undifferentiated, symmetrical unit of spatial distribution into the highly centralized and specialized axiated pattern" that in fact characterizes the contemporary world. The ability to monitor and to control at a distance has greatly accelerated the process of centralization and specialization that began with the Industrial Revolution. Throughout the world, great metropolitan centers have been created through the annexation of formerly independent surrounding communities. McKenzie describes the beginning of the process in Tokyo a hundred years ago:

> The pre-railroad city was a loose federation of villages clustered around the shogun's castle, now the imperial palace. The villages were connected by narrow winding roads which in course of time became lined with small shops of every description. On the advent of the railroad in 1872 and the construction of the big central depot, a new center of specialized activity commenced to develop. . . . In a word, Tokio is rapidly assuming the structure of any Western city of its size. All the "districts" normal to a city of two millions are emerging in Tokio. Population is rapidly being segregated according to income, and the domestic economy is yielding to the factory. The shuttling process of workers and shoppers in and out from periphery to center is increasing apace.

The process of oligopolistic competition itself promotes big-

ness. The "American Challenge" dramatized by Jean-Jacques Servan-Schreiber a few years ago was nothing more than the buy-up
by U.S. firms of actual or potential European competitors to protect their oligopolistic advantage. By the late 1960's, U.S.-based
companies controlled two-thirds of the photographic-film-paper,
farm-machinery, and telecommunications industries of France.
In Europe as a whole, according to Servan-Schreiber, U.S.-based
firms produced 80 percent of the computers, 95 percent of the
integrated circuits, 50 percent of the semiconductors, and 15 percent of consumer electronic products. While U.S.-based companies controlled less than 5 percent of Europe's business as a
whole, they were well on their way to controlling the most advanced and dynamic sectors of the European economies, leaving
the laundries, restaurants, and utilities to the natives.

The European governments launched a counterattack, which
stemmed somewhat the American Challenge but produced ever-
greater concentration of wealth and power in fewer and fewer
hands in the process. The weapon hastily brought up to stop
the American corporate invasion was the government-inspired
merger. In England the Industrial Reorganization Corporation
blocked attempts by General Foods and SKF (the formerly
Swedish ballbearing giant) to acquire British companies and fos-
tered mergers, sometimes by putting up large blocks of government capital, in more than twenty industries. Its biggest project
was the creation of two British giants, the British Leyland Motor
Company and International Computers, Ltd., to counter the U.S.
giants in these fields. In France the state planning agency has
been encouraging concentration of the nation's largest industries.
By 1970 two companies, Usinor and Wendel-Sidelor, accounted
for two-thirds of France's crude-steel production. Banks, electrical
companies, and chemical and computer industries were also
merged under government direction. The same process is going
on in Germany, Italy, and Austria.

The partnership of government and big business has reached
new heights in Japan. The great trading corporations and official
ministries are so intertwined that only a sophisticated legal mind
can discern where one leaves off and the other begins. Indeed,
U.S. business literature employs the code term "Japan, Inc." to
describe the complex competition from the East.

The U.S. global manager, despite his traditional suspicion of

government and his extravagant faith in the ability of businessmen to serve the public interest better than politicians, is now
asking Washington to step up official support of U.S. business
abroad to counter the advantages that national governments afford his foreign competitors. Fred Borch, former chairman of the
board of General Electric, told the National Foreign Trade Convention in late 1972 that "our government must recognize and
accept—as the Japanese and European governments have long
ago—that business and its employees are practically the sole
source of national income" and that government must now have
a "positive" attitude toward business that will "promote the corporation's ability to grow. . . . The Congress and the Administration must screen every legislative proposal in terms of its impact
on U.S. international competitiveness." The response to the response to the American Challenge is a growing demand in the
United States for a much tighter coordination between national
policy and corporate policy. The enduring result of the American
Challenge may well be a profoundly important organizational
trade-off: the rest of the industrial world imports the global corporation and the United States imports the corporate state.

4

Advances in the science of centralization made the global corporation possible, and sophisticated coordination at the world-
headquarters level remains its chief distinguishing characteristic.
Jack N. Behrman, a former Assistant Secretary of Commerce and
a leading academic analyst of global corporations, suggests that
the most important criterion for determining whether a corporation should be called multinational is "centralization of policy
and the integration of key operations among the affiliates." The
world corporation has taken the eighteenth-century economic
dicta about comparative cost advantages and division of labor
and applied them on a global scale for the maximization of profits. The nineteenth-century British economist David Ricardo, in
his famous example which has supported an entire industry of
economics textbooks, pointed out that it was to the advantage of
pastoral Britain to exchange wool with wine-producing Portugal
rather than to try to produce both itself. The multinational corporation owns the modern equivalent of both wineries and wool fac-

tories and in effect derives a double "comparative advantage" by arranging to trade with itself.

To put it most simply, each part of the global enterprise does what it does best and cheapest. Each contributes that part to the total enterprise which top management determines to be most rational. It makes sense for General Electric to ship components to Singapore, where they can be assembled at 30 cents an hour, rather than produce them in the Ashland, Massachusetts, plant for $3.40 an hour. Between 1957 and 1967 GE built 61 plants overseas. A number of these moves followed closely upon strikes and other labor difficulties, which government authorities in Singapore and Hong Kong can arrange to avoid for their corporate guests. Where one locates a factory depends, of course, upon many factors, including not only comparative wages, tariffs, taxes, and transportation costs, but the political and labor-relations climate as well. It is the ability of the World Managers to weigh all these factors and to coordinate decisions on pricing, financial flows, marketing, tax minimization, research and development, and political intelligence on a global level that gives the world corporation its peculiar advantage and extraordinary power. Omer Voss, executive vice-president of International Harvester, puts it:

> When you have a joint venture in Turkey, with engines from Germany, a chassis from the U.S. together with a local sourcing of components, you just have to be centralized. You'd probably have to call us centralized as far as design, product development, purchasing, and financing are concerned.

Heads of global companies, like Albert A. Thornbrough of Massey-Ferguson, use words like "rationalization," "commonization," "uniformity," "standardization," and "quality control," which sound better than "centralization." ITT has a world payroll of 425,000 employees in 70 countries. The body is international, but the brain is in New York. As a *Fortune* magazine portrait of the company noted:

> Geneen [Harold S. Geneen, the ITT chairman] eliminated much of the autonomy of ITT's operating managers and replaced it with a control system tautly run from New York headquarters. From what was once described as a kind of holding

company in which at one point, managers were literally in-
structed to ignore New York directives and "just send earnings
back home" ITT became a tightly centralized organization.

The degree of centralization varies, of course, depending upon
the particular industry, but advanced industrial operations like
automobile and computer production which scan the planet for
the cheapest sources of raw materials and labor are highly centralized. Renault makes various components in Rumania, Spain,
Argentina which are all assembled in the same car in a number
of plants around the world. This means that decisions about how
much is to be made and when, where, and at what price it is to
be shipped must be made in the central headquarters. It also
means that each country where Renault has a components factory
is dependent upon decisions of the Paris headquarters and has
little leverage of its own. (Rumania could, of course, nationalize
the plant that makes all the gearboxes for Renault's "Estafette"
model, but the gearboxes would sit in Bucharest, since they are
useless for any other purpose.)

Stephen Hymer describes how the requirements of the global
corporation are accelerating the trends toward "centers of dominance," which McKenzie noted almost fifty years ago. "A few key
cities—New York, London, and Paris," he observes, "are already
on their way to becoming the kind of global cities where top decisions are made and great amounts of capital can be raised." Other
cities, such as Montreal, Toronto, Buenos Aires, and Singapore,
are "at the middle level of the pyramid of power," while at the
bottom of the pyramid are the operations centers (Akron, Gary,
San Juan, Monterrey) which make things in strict accordance
with plans developed in the global cities.

The science of centralization is based largely on the sophisticated control of communications. Hymer sees the global corporations as a pyramid. "At the bottom of the pyramid," he points out,
"communications are broken horizontally so there is no direct
interaction between operations centers—what communication
there is must pass through the higher power centers." IBM has
demonstrated a sophisticated computer system under which
global corporations will be able to monitor on a 24-hour-a-day
basis various aspects of the corporation's global activities: sales,

purchases, cash flow, credit lines, inventories, etc. Information flows to headquarters and then is relayed in what the demonstrator called "controlled access" to executives around the world. The higher the manager's rank, the more of the big picture he is allowed to see. (IBM officials explain in demonstrating the system that it upsets managers of subsidiaries to see the global tote board. They do better if they get just what they need for their own operation.)

It is now fashionable in business schools to preach decentralization of decision making. Executives are supposed to perform better if they have a greater range for creative thinking. Indeed, public relations vice-presidents like to talk about global companies as a collection of coordinate operations across the globe with each taking a heavy share of responsibility for the success of the whole. The fact is that only certain kinds of decisions are ever decentralized. In general, moves are being made to decentralize operations within plants at the same time that the global control of individual plants by the world headquarters is being centralized.

Lee Bickmore, until recently chairman of Nabisco, gave us one personal example of how far the reach of headquarters extends in a global corporation. In 1959, when he was senior vice-president, he went to Europe to ponder how Nabisco could best crash the new Common Market. He personally visited one grocery store after another, filling his attaché case with cookies, candy, and crackers. In his hotel room, Bickmore spread the goodies on the bed and, after a day or two of careful munching, decided on the best strategy for capturing the European palate.

In some companies, it is true, local management is permitted fairly wide discretion in handling local personnel and marketing matters. But the reality was well put by the chairman of Ronson's British subsidiary: "The Manager of a Subsidiary must accept that he enjoys a subordinate status, and that a Subsidiary company is an organ of the Parent Company, and that policy is basically formulated and handed down by the Parent Company." "You control a company if you control its capital expenditure, its products, and in great detail its operating budgets," a former British senior executive of Ford's subsidiary at Dagenham, England, complained to *The Sunday Times* shortly after he and

more than twenty other top executives quit. "All these are controlled by Americans over here, and ultimately by Detroit. The
amount of paper flowing to Detroit and back is unbelievable."

In their study *The Strategy of Multinational Enterprise,* based
on a six-year examination of the internal structure of global corporations, Michael Z. Brooke and H. Lee Remmers conclude
that despite "the current ideology of management which speaks
in terms of personal responsibility and participation," the logic
of the planetary enterprise will make each operation increasingly
dependent upon the world headquarters.

> . . . a decentralizing ideology masks a centralizing reality. The
> factors which create this situation include an integration of
> multinational operations, an increasing speed of technological
> change, and the rapid development of global techniques, strate-
> gies and information collection.

All of this raises what indeed is shaping up as the supreme political issue of our time: *i.e.,* whether it is really "rational" to attempt
to organize the planet through centralizing technologies into ever-
larger pyramidal structures. That is the case the new globalists
will increasingly be called upon to make as they seek to transform
our warring planet into a global market.

3

Personal Identity and Corporate Image

1

People who exercise power generally have a better sense of it than people who study power. The builders of the global corporations understood the political implications of their operations long before foundations began to give professors grants to study them. Corporate executives, accustomed to successful negotiations with kings, generals, and sheiks, and aware that their company balance sheet makes the national budgets of many sovereign powers look like the statements of some of their own subsidiaries, do not need to be persuaded that the global corporation has become a major actor in world politics. While political-science textbooks and government planning papers have given little attention to the radical implications of the rise of the global corporations, the World Managers think and talk of themselves as a revolutionary class. As the world begins to comprehend the power of the global corporations, those who run them are increasingly concerned with explaining and justifying that power not only to the outside world but to themselves.

In this chapter we shall be looking first at the sort of men who rise to the top in global corporations and will touch briefly on their quest for personal identity. Then we shall examine their efforts to legitimize the global corporation as an institution in an increasingly skeptical world. There is a subtle connection between the quest for personal identity and institutional legitimacy. As in any major institution, including churches, armies, and govern-mental bureaucracies, the career planning of those who make it to the top influences the character, image, and style of the global

45

corporation. At the same time, the organizational needs of the corporation are met by a selection process which propels a certain social character into the executive suite and relegates others to the outer offices.

Max Weber pointed out many years ago that for every new elite aspiring to political power, the principal problem is legitimacy. The more an aspiring elite questions conventional wisdom or challenges older elites, the more crucial the issue of legitimacy becomes. Whoever seeks political power must convince large numbers of people that his authority is not only inevitable but reasonable, and in the ultimate interest of those who are called upon to submit to it. The key to exercising political power is to articulate common goals for masses of people and to secure general agreement for the ruler's choice of means in achieving those goals. A political ideology is an instrument for achieving such a consensus on ends and means. Even the most repressive dictator cannot rule successfully by force alone. Official fantasies were as important an instrument of Hitler's dictatorial rule as the concentration camp. Millions of Germans who never had any reason to fear the midnight knock of the Gestapo were enthralled by the thought of being part of the Thousand Year Reich. Stalin knew how to elicit mass devotion from the same generation he sacrificed to the industrialization of Russia. In each case, seekers of power were able to articulate and to mass-produce a myth that caught the imagination of millions.

One important function of political ideology is to explain why one human being has a right to rule over another. In older civilizations kings ruled by divine right. To oppose the King was to shake one's fist at Heaven. Cortés was able to subdue Montezuma's empire with a handful of men partly because the Aztecs confused the barely literate soldier of fortune with one of their most sacred gods. As civilization evolved, blood and tradition became the most important symbols of legitimacy. A man had a right to rule because his father had ruled. In the interests of the continued stability and harmony of the state, the fiction was promoted that putting a crown on one's head, even when empty, endowed the wearer with wisdom, a sense of justice, and all other attributes of the good ruler. In other societies, such as Tibet, a sacred tradition developed whereby certain designated officials would choose the new Grand Lama when the old one died.

In the modern democratic state, the act of voting serves the same function. It provides a ritual for selecting a ruler whom the governed will normally accept. Voters will usually put up with an incompetent or unpopular man for his term of office in the interest of preserving the electoral system itself. In the twentieth century, rulers have based their appeal for legitimacy less and less on birth and tradition and more on skill and performance. Mussolini seized power, but he made the trains run on time. Hitler destroyed liberty in Germany, but he built the autobahns. The Brazilian generals tore up the constitution, but they produced an "economic miracle." The selection of rulers in Communist countries is undemocratic, but their legitimacy is based on their claim to represent the masses and their record in ending illiteracy and starvation and in raising the standard of living.

In marketing an ideology to justify their world management role, the men who run the global corporations make the same basic claim: superior management skills. But because corporations are not officially recognized as governments, the ideology of the World Managers clashes with some important established notions. That there is a distinction between the private economic sphere and the public political sphere is an important piece of conventional wisdom. Private profit seekers can fish in the one but not the other. Indeed, so the prevailing myth goes, the state can intervene in the private sphere to regulate, subsidize, or punish, but it is scandalous when an oil company or ITT acts like a government and makes public policy. The reason for applying different rules to governments and corporations is that the former, at least in a democratic society, are supposedly responsible to the electorate and the latter are not. To defend themselves against their enemies, foreign and domestic, the global corporations are seeking to establish one overriding point: they can create an integrated world in which everybody gains, but only if "obsolete" governments leave them alone.

The World Managers are aware that their own enthusiasm for the Global Shopping Center is not universally shared. In 1971, a group of top corporate executives, including the presidents of 38 leading global companies, meeting in Jamaica under the auspices of Business International, heard Atherton Bean, former chairman of International Multifoods, make a grim prediction that has already come true:

The MNF's [multinational firms] will get more attention year by year as they grow in world importance. The flak will get thicker. If we don't justify our existences before those who can affect and perhaps control our destinies, then we shall at least get pieces shot out of us, if we don't get shot down altogether.

2

Ideology also serves a private function which is as important as the public function. Tawney points out that each new phase of economic development "is the creation, not of strata long in possession of wealth and power, but of classes which rise from humble origins to build a new structure on obscure foundations . . ." The pioneers of the modern economic order, he argues, were "parvenus, who elbowed their way to success in the teeth of the established aristocracy of land and commerce. The tonic that braced them for the conflict was a new conception of religion which taught them to regard the pursuit of wealth as, not merely an advantage, but a duty." Calvinism welded the new capitalists into a disciplined force, "heightened its energies, and cast a halo of sanctification round its convenient vices." Surrounded by this ideological halo, what had once been merely a means of becoming rich became, in Martin Luther's term, a "calling." Tawney further points out that a "calling" is not something to which one is born, but is a "strenuous and exacting enterprise to be chosen by himself and to be pursued with a sense of religious responsibility."

The World Managers are the spiritual heirs of the entrepreneurs described so brilliantly by Weber and Tawney. They share many of the same assumptions about work, duty, and acquisition as the ultimate purposes of life. For all their celebration of tomorrow's technology, the speeches that the managers of global corporations make to one another often echo the copybook maxims of Benjamin Franklin. But the managers, aware that the "spirit of capitalism," as Weber calls it, can no longer be presented as religious truth, are groping for new ideas to rationalize the revolutionary historical role which they believe they are destined to play. The emerging ideology of the Global Shopping Center is the "tonic" for building an international consciousness among the new global managerial elite, and the World Managers feel the need to develop and spread it. "Practice is ahead of theory," Pfizer's President John J. Powers noted a few years ago. But while a general theory of the global corporation as a political institution is still lacking, there is no shortage of theorists. Indeed, for a fee of $40,000 a company can send its executives to participate in think-tank seminars such as the Hudson Institute's series on the future corporate environment 1975–1985. Not only do such seminars offer a tantalizing look at the future; they also help build a class consciousness—that is, a shared sense of goals and means for achieving those goals, a common awareness of problems and opportunities, and a strategic consensus for confounding their increasingly vocal enemies.

The managers of the global corporations share some of the specific characteristics Tawney noted in the earlier capitalist revolution of the sixteenth and seventeenth centuries. First of all, they are, to use Tawney's term, parvenus. To be sure, there are some like David Rockefeller, whose prospects for becoming chairman of the family bank, the Chase Manhattan, were always reasonably good, however he may have performed in his first job as assistant manager in the foreign department. Robert Sarnoff also inherited the management of a world enterprise, the Radio Corporation of America. Brooks McCormick, president of International Harvester, is the great-grandson of William Deering, who founded one harvester company, and of William S. McCormick, who started another. But most of the top managers of the global corporations come from humbler origins. In comparison with the generation that has constituted the "Eastern banking establishment," the Wall Street law firms, the brokerage houses, and the world of national security, the World Managers are not noticeably patrician, Eastern, or Ivy League.

Ironically, a number of the new globalists spring from the seedbed of American isolationism, the Middle West. Frank Cary, the chairman of IBM, was born in Idaho. Carl Gerstacker, the chairman of Dow, in Cleveland. John J. Powers, the man who, as the company public affairs division puts it, turned Pfizer "from a small specialty chemical house to a highly diversified worldwide organization," was a Chicago boy. So is Rawleigh Warner, Jr., chairman of Mobil Oil.

The World Managers are the embodiment of the new meritocracy which Thorstein Veblen predicted more than fifty years ago would end up running the country. The road to advancement for most of these men was not family wealth or connections but the development of certain skills. In only a few cases can they take credit for entrepreneurial miracles of the sort that were commonplace in the era of the Carnegies, Rockefellers, and Fricks. Lee Bickmore made a giant out of the National Biscuit Company. ITT was already a giant when Harold Geneen took over in 1959, but he made it into a colossus. Most managers, however, have had a less dramatic impact on their companies. They have presided over a process of steady growth and diversification. They have been empire managers rather than empire builders.

Most executives of the top U.S.-based multinational corporations have risen through the ranks over many years. The top three executives of Dow Chemical all began with the company immediately after receiving degrees in chemistry. The favorite avenues of advancement, depending upon the type of firm, are finance, accounting, engineering, and marketing. The chairman of Procter & Gamble started as a soap salesman and climbed the corporate ladder through the advertising department. Jacques Maisonrouge, an engineer by training, has spent his entire career with IBM, as has Frank Cary, the chairman, who began as a company salesman in Los Angeles. The chairman and chief executive officer of Chrysler is a certified public accountant who used to do the company books for an outside accounting firm. Exxon's president, Clifton C. Garvin, started as a process engineer at the company's Baton Rouge refinery. Soap and food companies tend to promote their market men to the top positions. The chairmen of Xerox, Minneapolis Honeywell, Singer, and Du Pont are lawyers.

The men who have risen to the top of the global corporations have arrived there because they have excelled in certain highly profitable organizational skills. Many of them have single-mindedly devoted their whole lives to the practice of these skills. In the tradition of America's first millionaire, Stephen Girard, who liked to say that "when death comes for me he will find me busy," the managers worship hard work.

Psychoanalyst Michael Maccoby conducted depth interviews with sixteen corporation presidents and vice-presidents in high-technology industries and found "very little inner conflict" in the group. In contrast to the stereotyped tormented middle-level executive in the clinical literature and TV morality plays, the men who have made their way to the executive suites are, Maccoby says, of a social character that fits corporate purposes. They adjust well, it seems, to the life of a hardworking potentate. Maccoby also interviewed and tested a much larger group of middle managers and concludes that those who do not make it to the top often show signs of being either too humanistic to exercise power with sufficient ruthlessness or too sadistic to exercise it with finesse. Middle-level engineers and scientists on Rorschach tests tend to see the corporation as a consuming monster to which they must make personal sacrifices entirely for careerist reasons. For those who are prepared to hop from opportunity to opportunity the corporation is a kind of graduate school. Top managers, on the other hand, according to Maccoby, exhibit as a dominant characteristic a strong corporate loyalty which, oddly enough, often stems from a sense of personal insignificance. Maccoby finds that a surprising number of men who have risen to the top of America's leading corporations see themselves as having little personal worth. (Several corporate chieftains who are the terror of their subordinates identify themselves as worms and mice on Rorschach tests). Such men believe that their extraordinary success is owed entirely to the corporation which has nurtured them and elevated them. Although the few original builders of great corporations whom he interviewed did not conform to this pattern, the typical attitude of the second-generation professional manager is that he owes his life to the corporation. Indeed, his study suggests that a profound feeling of dependence upon the corporation may be a psychological prerequisite to becoming a top manager. In high-technology industries the principal attitude that seems to distinguish middle-level executives from their bosses is their attitude toward the corporation. Middle-level managers in high-technology industry are primarily concerned with finding professionally rewarding work and will go almost anywhere to find it. They have little interest in the larger social significance of the company that employs them. The top managers, on the other hand, apparently need to believe that the institution which has given them a life can also save the world. Maccoby finds that the executive "justifies his own search for success, comfort, and interesting work in terms of the eventual benefit to mankind of increased productivity and economic growth."

In a parallel study, a Mexican psychoanalyst, Ignacio Millán,

after conducting 52 interviews of at least five hours' duration with
top managers of Mexican subsidiaries of global corporations,
concludes that the celebration of the Global Shopping Center in
many cases serves to protect Mexican executives from deep
psychological conflicts about their role in society. These conflicts
emerge rather strongly in dreams. One high executive, for example, "faithfully believes in the development of Mexico" and
thinks his company is helping to achieve it, but he dreams of
"slum huts" and "children naked and with big bellies." Under
questioning, he admits that he is "afraid of poverty and poor
people." Another dreams of a city covered by a glass dome with
crowds of poor people scratching and pushing to get in. Still
another dreams of being sexually humiliated by his American
boss and trying unsuccessfully to kill him. He is powerless because he is tied up in telephone wires. Dr. Millán suggests that
these dreams constitute social criticism which is repressed from
consciousness through the ideology of peace and plenty which
these managers faithfully accept and promote. The organization
men of the 70's, irrespective of nationality, propelled to the top
by traditional entrepreneurial thirst for money and power, it now
seems, feel a psychological need for a political religion.

The career of Harold S. Geneen, the former accountant who
rules ITT, although by no means typical, is perhaps the most
striking example of the meshing of individual character and corporate purpose. Geneen works 16 hours a day. "I must get rid of
you and start getting some work done," he will say to an interviewer at 6 in the evening. He increased company sales from $1
billion a year to $7.3 billion in 10 years by turning what was
essentially an electronics company into a global service bazaar
(ITT parks cars, manages mutual funds, operates hotels, sells life
insurance, trains secretaries, publishes books, dresses hair, etc.),
and he sees his work as a calling. "You work for money or am-
bition to begin with—but not for long. After that you work for
pride. . . . Nobody keeps me here at night. I'm not a nut. Perhaps
a hundred years from now the fact that a company grew a little
will seem like a paltry monument. But what else am I going to
do?" So concerned is Geneen at the prospect of idleness that he
stockpiles hobbies. His leisure minutes are divided among several
interests: a $100,000 yacht, a darkroom, golf, banjo, piano,
accordion. He even tried surfing in his late fifties. He is always on

the lookout for new hobby acquisitions. "If I have enough of them stored up," he says, "I'll always have something to do."

There is a popular legal fiction that company executives are servants of the stockholders. In formal organizational terms, this is, of course, true. And indeed, company executives who fail to deliver satisfactory annual increments of growth and profits may find themselves deposed. Corporate public relations departments like to point out that the corporation is a more democratic institution than the Congress, since corporate presidents and chairmen of the board are much easier to get rid of than Southern Senators. However, as long as top executives are seen as winners, they can bask in a world of privilege and power matched in our day only by the President of the United States and a few sheiks and commissars. Harold Geneen was paid $812,494 in 1971, which was two and one-half times as much as the next-highest-paid ITT official. He has an apartment off Fifth Avenue, a winter house at Key Biscayne not far from the Nixons', and a summer home on Cape Cod. He logs 100,000 miles a year flying in his private Boeing 707, which is about the size of the President's *Air Force One*.

In the company his word is law. About fifty very senior executives quit or were fired in this first decade. "Management must manage," he says, and his style is inquisitorial. His technique is to run executive conferences at various points around the world which start at 10 A.M. and sometimes finish at 3 the next morning. His "tight, buttoned-up control system," as one McKinsey consultant describes it, intimidates subordinates, and only the most ambitious and eager will put up with it. But Geneen keeps setting impossible goals (he demanded that his European managers increase sales by 100 percent in five years) and ruthlessly "cross-checking" his top executives far more in the style of a czar than in that of a chairman. "I don't want some proud guy to get into his own Vietnam and then suddenly hand me his resignation," Geneen says in explaining his refusal to give his lieutenants freer rein. "Hell, his resignation can't bring back the ten million dollars he'd lose."

Styles differ greatly from one corporation to another. By and large, the older global corporations, such as those in petroleum, make little pretense at democracy. Companies with a high proportion of professional engineers and scientists, such as IBM, affect a more egalitarian style. It is not uncommon for the president and chairman at Dow or CPC International to eat in the cafeteria with middle-level employees. (The emphasis in the General Electric dining room is on Spartan lunches with the calories listed. The CPC company restaurant includes, wherever possible, a credit on the menu to some company product—i.e., a poached egg on a Thomas's English Muffin.)

While ITT is uniquely a one-man show, the top managers of other global corporations also know how to act like potentates. Private corporate jets, although of more modest proportions than Geneen's, are now standard equipment for the principal managers of global corporations. When the chairman of Texaco made an inspection trip to Belgium, a high company official was assigned to test the Royal Suite of a leading hotel in advance of the chairman's visit, since a burned-out shaving light on an earlier trip had caused some company heads to roll. A part of the chairman's duties was to exchange gifts with the Belgian royal family. According to a leading business advisor to Texaco, the European vice-presidents were so fearful of the chairman's kingly wrath that they personally supervised the cleaning of the rest rooms in any Texaco stations he might spy on his way from the airport and insisted that the signs on all Texaco stations visible from the chairman's train get a quick new coat of paint. On more than one occasion, while waiting in the outer office to interview a corporate president, we noticed vice-presidents nervously girding themselves for an audience with the king. Saadia Schorr, the head of strategic planning for General Electric's international group, says the modern corporation is a "virtual dictatorship." A corporate executive, he points out, spends twelve hours a day in a democracy (most of them asleep) and twelve hours a day in a "totally autocratic society."

Despite his futuristic rhetoric, the World Manager is at heart an eighteenth-century man. Like that of the Encyclopedists, his religion is rationalism. One of the lasting benefits of international business, says Jacques Maisonrouge, is that it "has introduced rationality into international and human relations" and has reduced "the emotional and haphazard elements of life." Reason can triumph only by stamping out myth and superstition. The most dangerous myths of modern man, as the World Managers see it, are what Maisonrouge calls "national prejudices and fears."

The modern counterpart of the eighteenth-century cry *"Ecrasez l'infame!"* is Peter Drucker's slogan ". . . we need to defang the nationalist monster." As the Catholic Church was for Diderot the symbol of obscurantism and resistance to rational change, so for Maisonrouge the enemy is "irrational nationalism."

It is not the nation-state itself that is irrational, Maisonrouge maintains, but the "basically nineteenth-century viewpoint" which still dominates the nation-state. In the name of an outmoded myth, governments are interfering with the free flow of capital and technology. In a world that cries out for global integration and management, governments are behaving irrationally because they are tied to territories, and in trying to protect those territories they pursue such uneconomic goals as pride, prestige, and power for its own sake. Like the Mercantilists, the World Managers believe in "world peace through world trade," as the IBM World Trade Corporation slogan puts it. Politicians have nearly ruined the world with their patriotic wars, their antiquated borders, and their silly national pride, but businessmen can save it. Maisonrouge likes to compare the "fragmented political world in its ancient quarrels and rivalries" with international business at work "building new complex economic structures linking and crisscrossing national economies."

The global corporation and the world economy it is working to build are the modern embodiment of Adam Smith's invisible hand. The most reliable instruments of social progress are not the great decisions of politicians isolated from the real world in palaces and bureaucracies but the thousands of little decisions made each day by makers, buyers, and sellers of fuel, autos, computers, drugs, and packaged food, all based on nothing more "political" then healthy human acquisitiveness. "It is in reality the profit motive," says Carl A. Gerstacker, chairman of Dow Chemical, "that makes industry responsive to social needs." The new globalists firmly believe that the magic of the market, provided it is helped and not hindered by politicians, is the best, fairest, and freest regulator of human affairs. Subsidies, aggressive diplomatic representation in support of the overseas operations of U.S.-based global corporations, and government insurance programs are balm for the invisible hand, but Gerstacker complains that when the U.S. Government tries to interfere politically with the "normal process" of the market—as, for example, with capital-export controls—"it doesn't work." The United States, he told us, "should do as little as possible as a government . . . Dow is a growing boy. It needs freedom to find its way."

The global corporation is the ideal instrument for integrating the planet, the World Managers contend, because it is the only human organization that has managed to free itself from the bonds of nationalism. "The expansion of our consciousness to the global level," argues A. W. Clausen, president of Bank America, "offers mankind perhaps the last real chance to build a world order that is less coercive than that offered by the nation-state." The essence of the new corporate ideology and the new corporate strategy is not internationalism but antinationalism. We can look forward, Clausen says, to "an international corporation that has shed all national identity." Along with other spokesmen for global corporations, such as George Ball, he sees the "ultimate solution" to be the "supranational corporation which will not owe its charter to any nation-state and which will be equally resident—and equally nonresident—in any country in which it operates." Indeed there are many areas, he believes, where the corporation "could be trusted to fulfill the general interest without the sanction of a specific chartering government."

Dow's chairman, Carl Gerstacker, created a certain stir when he predicted the rise of the "neutral, anational corporation" with its headquarters on an island "owned by no one." Although he was apparently persuaded to delete the reference in the final printed version of the speech, he insisted when we visited him that he was deadly serious. In fact, a group had offered him the Minerva atoll near the Fijis in the Pacific. (He declined, he said, because he thought this particular group had too conservative a vision. "They're just fed up with government.") But other global giants are actively seeking to create an anational image and an antinational consciousness in a variety of other ways. The names "American" and "U.S." are quietly disappearing from some of the nation's oldest and most prestigious firms. American Metal Climax is now "Amax." American Brake Shoe is now "Abex." U.S. Rubber is "Uniroyal." SKF, the formerly Swedish ball-bearing company, holds its board meetings in various parts of its world empire, and the official company language is now English.

All of this is designed not only to blur images but to change loyalties. To function successfully on a global scale, a company must not appear to be an extension of any nation-state. It is now a commonplace in corporate speeches that management must not put the welfare of any country in which it does business above that of any other, including the United States. The "lack of parent-government influence," says Clausen, "would simplify the conduct of international business because there would be no extra-territoriality problem." In other words, corporations that are not identified with foreign powers are much less likely to be targets of political retaliation. Why make a point of your Americanism when local politicians all over the world are making political capital out of ritualistic attacks on the American colossus? Why fly Old Glory over your Paris or Frankfurt headquarters when students are demonstrating in the streets against the Vietnam War? Being "a good corporate citizen of each country in which we operate," which is official corporate code for the anational corporation, is a particularly sensible strategy when the U.S. Government's ability to defend the overseas operations of U.S.-based corporations with military power is shrinking. The day when the United States would overtly go to war to rescue a particular U.S. corporation appears to be over. Unlike those simpler days of U.S. imperialism, when the United Fruit Company's reputation for being able to call in the Marines or the CIA to its Central American banana fiefdom was a principal company asset, it is now better strategy to allay fears on that score, since the Marines at least are not likely to come.

The cultivation of distance between the anational corporation and the U.S. Government reflects the growing realization of corporate leaders that the character of U.S. hegemony is changing. As we shall explore further in the next chapter, there is a growing sense in corporate boardrooms that as a result of dramatic transformations in world politics and the world economy, the U.S. Government is no longer able to promote and protect corporate interests with traditional military strategies. More important, there is also a growing realization that the government in Washington may not perceive its interests to be the same as those of the global corporations. It is in this context that the worldwide attack on nationalism now being mounted in the public relations department of every global corporation takes on its real significance.

On January 6, 1971, 64 top executives of global corporations,

including 38 presidents and chairmen of the board, met in
Jamaica under the auspices of Business International "to consider
the subject of corporate response to anti-foreign nationalism."
The confidential discussion paper prepared for this "Chief Executive Officers Roundtable" gives a revealing picture of how the
World Managers see the problem of nationalism and what they
propose to do about it. "International corporations," the paper begins, "are losing a battle crucial to their profitability, to their
growth, and conceivably to their survival. They are losing it to
important segments of society that, since childhood, have been
surrounded by notions that a foreigner is to be viewed with suspicion and distrust, that a frontier is sacred, that sovereignty is to
be deified and protected with one's life." Nationalism, Business
International warns, is not merely a problem for global corporations in underdeveloped countries: ". . . the truth is that some of
the most serious problems for them are created by the governments of the parent companies."

The problems of "irrational nationalism," as global executives
see it, include any local official, law, or tradition that inhibits the
free flow of finance capital, technology, and goods on a global
scale. A crucial aspect of "irrational nationalism" is "differences
in psychological and cultural attitudes" that complicate the task
of homogenizing the earth into an integrated unit. While the most
obvious and expensive nationalist challenges occur when local
politicians discover that they have the power to nationalize the
oil within their frontiers or even to take over foreign-owned factories and mines, cultural nationalism is also a serious problem
because it threatens the concept of the Global Shopping Center.
"It is a sad fact of life," Bank America's President A. W. Clausen
laments, "that there is no such thing as a uniform global market."
National, cultural, and racial differences create "marketing problems." Thus, he points out, Helene Curtis had to color its
shampoo black to sell it in Thailand. There is no market for de-
odorants in some Asian countries because "there is no problem
of body odor." Nestlé has to brew over 40 varieties of instant
coffee "to satisfy different national tastes." National linguistic
peculiarities also frustrate worldwide advertising plans. General
Motors' "Body by Fisher," *Business Week* reports, emerges as
"Corpse by Fisher" in Japanese. The reason there are "nationalistic obstacles" in the path of the global corporation, the Chief

Executives Roundtable concluded, is that "the international corporation threatens the nation-state's very existence":

> Those who guide the nation-states are fearful that if the world economy is made more efficient and national borders are not allowed to impede the most efficient use of land, capital, labor, ideas, then the nation-state will have no reason to exist.

As the corporate executives themselves see it, "the nation-state has succeeded in attracting from organized religion the basic religious impulses of man." If the global corporation is to survive it must, in effect, establish its own religion. "The task of international business is facing its central response to nationalism—educating people that what it is doing is in the interest of every human being, that what it is doing will eliminate hunger and increase the goods and services available to everybody . . ."

A strategy for dealing with nationalism has evolved over the last few years. In the late 1960's corporate statesmen and professors were predicting the early demise of the nation-state. More recently, however, managers of global corporations have become more cautious and more diplomatic in discussing the future of the international system. The conclusions of the Chief Executives Roundtable in Jamaica, which reflect a consensus of several dozen of America's top global corporate executives, develop this more subtle approach:

> The nationstate is not withering away. Instead it will grow in terms of its role in organizing and improving the social standing and entire environment of its people . . . By and large, multinational corporations and nationstates have many parallel interests. When tension does occur, accommodation should be accomplished on a case-by-case basis.

Thus the frontal attack on the nation-state has been replaced by a subtler campaign against borders, cultural differences, protectionism, and "the fears of those people that attack the international corporation [which are] deeply imbedded in their psyches." As part of the campaign, global corporate executives have vowed to take a more active political role in suggesting a constructive role for nation-states in developing the Global Shopping Center. (Global corporations, the Chief Executives concluded in Jamaica, "should help developing countries to establish their national identity.") The global corporation must also make a "huge" effort "to educate people who would prefer not to be educated and who so deeply feel that the nation-state is necessary for their happiness."

3

The global corporation's appeal for a loyalty that transcends the nation-state rests on two fundamental claims. The first is that the planetary enterprise is the key to peace. By doing what comes naturally in the pursuit of profit, the global corporation brings harmony to the world. The international corporation must have peace, the Chief Executives Roundtable concluded. "It cannot itself be primarily engaged in armaments, for if it were, its own government would not allow it to be international. International corporations are primarily engaged in making peaceful goods for a peaceful society."

As the political scientist Jonathan Galloway has shown in his analysis of the military production of global corporations, many of the largest ones do have substantial weapons contracts. In comparison with their total output, however, the military side of their operations is small. While it is also true that many of the biggest global giants, such as ITT and IBM, grew to their present proportions with substantial help from the Pentagon, their primary customers are not American generals but civilians around the world. Businessmen have always been impatient with loyalties that cost money.

During the Cold War, firms like ITT patriotically provided executives, such as Robert Vogeler in Hungary, to engage in espionage for the U.S. Government. (Even now businessmen perform delicate information-gathering missions for the State Department or the CIA.) In 1938, ITT, through a German subsidiary, bought 28 percent of the stock of the Focke-Wulf company, which produced bombers to attack Allied shipping all during World War II. Thirty years later, the company received $26 million in compensation from the American government for damage done ITT's German plants by American bombers. Colonel Sosthenes Behn, the founder of the company, and other high ITT executives met with German officials in Spain and Switzerland to discuss the future of the company. Like several other U.S.-based companies, ITT had cordial relations with

Goering and Hitler before the war. ITT's communication services in Europe provided direct support for the Nazi war machine all through the conflict; but by the end of the war the company was also a major U.S. military contractor and company executives were working closely with Allied intelligence agents. As Anthony Sampson puts it in his study of the wartime activities of ITT, "the only power [Behn] consistently served was the supranational power of ITT."

At the same time, the managers of global corporations have been the first to proclaim the futility of a Cold War that inhibits free trade of "strategic" goods or closes off the great potential markets and labor pools of what once was known as the Sino-Soviet Bloc. Howard D. Harder, chairman of CPC International, who was among more than 100 leading industrialists to visit the Soviet Union in December 1971 on a trip planned by Business International and the U.S. Department of Commerce, thinks that trade with the U.S.S.R. might reach $2 billion by 1975. (It was scarcely $2 million in 1971.) "That would be great; I'm all for it." CPC, which has been making its Knorr soups in Ljubljana, Yugoslavia, thinks that the Soviets might like to have the soup formula too, as well as "our know-how to build the plant." Farm-machinery firms in particular see the opening of the Soviet market as a major breakthrough. U.S. chemical plants are being built in the Soviet Union, and the Chase Manhattan Bank has opened offices in Moscow and Peking. Even before President Nixon had arrived in Peking, soft-drink manufacturers were speculating in print about what it would mean to sell China's 800 million "just one Coke a week." Bank America's A. W. Clausen is interested in "helping prevent wars and other serious upheavals that cut off its resources, interrupt its communications, and kill its employees and customers."

Social and political conflict can be reduced to managerial problems and solved through technology. "International corporations," says Business International, "possess a high proportion of the technology, the managerial talent and private capital required for the solution of the economic and social problems of this planet. They can tackle development of the resources of the sea, economic development of poor countries, new housing everywhere, the protection of the human environment, the training of people for skilled managerial and technical work, and the creation of jobs for underprivileged people." In other words, everything that governments are supposed to do—and cannot.

The World Managers consistently use the development of the U.S. economy as their model for the world economy. "The world today is very similar to the American continent 100 years ago," the Chief Executives Roundtable discussion paper notes. "The world today and America then were on their way to becoming a single market." What if 100 years ago Nevadans had had the power to limit foreign investment or to demand that Nevadans own 51 percent of all foreign operations? "Luckily for Nevadans, the local government never had such power." Nations must relinquish these "arbitrary" and "irrational" restrictions on foreign penetration if we are to achieve what Maisonrouge calls "the global structure of excellence" based on the American Model.

In the process of managing the world as an integrated system, the World Managers believe that they are making the world, in Maisonrouge's words, "smaller and more homogeneous." The global corporation is a "great leveler" because it transfers technology, goods, and skilled people from the "privileged" parts of the globe to the "underprivileged." The carriers of the new globalism are executives and employees of global corporations who have developed a loyalty to their companies and to their professions which is far more important to them than their loyalty to their country. "Working far from their home base," Maisonrouge observes, "executives at a multinational-company headquarters soon find themselves exploring the global dimension, instead of thinking only in narrower national terms. And once that happens, they have become 'detribalized,' international career men." Maisonrouge himself is the most famous example of an executive whose personal fortunes are tied to a company rather than a country.

Global profit maximization demands the building of an anational consciousness, and global companies have discovered many ways to develop such a consciousness. Some make heavy use of international symbolism. The flags of eight countries fly over the Caterpillar Tractor world headquarters in Peoria, Illinois, each representing a division of the Caterpillar world empire. The Dow cafeteria in Midland, Michigan, offers typical dishes from each of the countries in which Dow operates. But managers understand that internationalist window dressing alone will not balance a strong American image. People tend to be more impressed by who runs the corporation than by what food it serves or what flag it flies. While a few top executives of U.S.-based multinationals are non-American—Peter McColough of Xerox and J. K. Jamieson of Exxon were born in Canada, and Ian McGregor of Amax was born in Scotland—in most firms, according to a Business International survey, "all key managerial jobs in the parent company are filled with nationals of the parent company country, and key staff of most foreign operations are also nationals of the parent company country." David Rockefeller and other global executives are calling for a change in these practices. The Chief Executives Roundtable, agreeing in principle that "any company that is seeking to maximize worldwide sales and profits should be moving toward a policy in which nationality has nothing to do with the staffing of the top management levels of a company," nonetheless sees as "overriding factors" the need for "competent local management and sound economic considerations"—which is corporatese for moving slowly.

Business International suggests that "the presence of well chosen local nationals on the board of an overseas subsidiary can augment other measures that many companies take automatically to deemphasize their national origin and assume local coloration." Anaconda for more than twenty years employed as its vice-president for Chilean operations a former Chilean Senator and Ambassador to the United States. ITT has had a former Prime Minister of Belgium and former U.N. Secretary-General on its European board. Chase Manhattan and Chemical Bank–New York Trust Company secure the services of such prominent citizens through "special worldwide advisory boards." But statistically, there are few invitations extended to non-Americans to join the parent company's board in New York or Chicago.

The internationalization of ownership is an obvious strategy for de-Americanizing U.S.-based global corporations, but it has yet to happen. Control is still squarely in American hands. "Nearly all multinational corporations would prefer 100 percent ownership of most foreign operations," the Chief Executives Roundtable concluded, "to facilitate optimum rationalization and management of global operations." Some company executives talk about dealing with local partners in terms of "taking in lodgers." The largest firms, such as IBM (and until recently Gen-

eral Motors), insist upon 100-percent ownership of all subsidiaries. Global corporations much prefer to give the appearance of
international ownership by selling small blocks of stock to widely
dispersed foreign holders. Thus no outside shareholder has enough
to challenge the controlling interest exercised by management
through its interlocks with a few large institutional shareholders.
Some companies are selling shares in local subsidiaries—a tactic
which, Business International points out, "lends the subsidiary the
aura of a truly local company" but which also involves "disclosure
requirements" and "constant scrutiny of the press and security
analysts." Global managers much prefer to sell the stock of the
parent locally. "Investors from every country where the company
does business should become Pepsico stockholders," says Pepsico
president Donald Kendall, "so that they would have a vested
interest, not alone in the company of which they own a part, but
in the operation of a free global enterprise system and a free
global market economy." Those who buy Pepsico stock get "a
piece of the action on a worldwide basis."

The Kendall strategy has a number of advantages for the corporation. It spreads the myth of international ownership while
control remains vested in the major stockholders. The Peruvian or
Filipino shareholder is not likely to show up at the annual meeting or make any other trouble. If a substantial portion of his personal wealth is in the shares of global giants, his interest will be
in the worldwide profit picture and not in the company's activities
in his own country. Thus the global corporation hopes to use its
stock to combat "anti-foreign nationalism" among the propertied
classes in every country in which it proposes to operate.

4

Harry Heltzer, chairman of 3M (which has outgrown its provincial name, Minnesota Mining and Manufacturing Company),
believes that the managers of global corporations are "the real
radicals" who alone can design solutions to the great problems of
mankind. Lee L. Morgan, executive vice-president, Caterpillar
Tractor Company, thinks the global corporation has hit upon
"the win-win situation." When U.S. firms invest abroad, "everybody benefits." Poor countries get needed technology, finance
capital, taxes, managerial expertise, and increased exports. U.S.

citizens get more jobs, improved balance of payments, and all the other benefits of an integrated, peaceful world. Carl Gerstacker says profits can be made in fighting pollution. Maisonrouge says there is money to be made in hiring and advancing women and in satisfying the longings of youth around the world for interesting and challenging work. A. W. Clausen of Bank America believes that there are profits in rebuilding and developing Southeast Asia. "I think we must turn vigorously to the private sector to close the income gap between the developed and the less-developed nations." CPC International believes that it can help solve the world's hunger problem by continuing to develop high-protein foods at relatively low cost. "The top executives of most of the multinationals, says José de Cubas, senior vice-president of Westinghouse, "are talking a language which is quite revolutionary and which would have been inconceivable ten years ago —quality of life, environment, social responsibility, services, leisure, enrichment, participation, job satisfaction." There is a "convergence of objectives" between the global corporation and "Latin American politicians, sociologists, and forward-looking businessmen."

This standard rhetoric of the multinationals, which can be summed up in the two words "everybody benefits," accounts for some of the ideological power of the new globalism. In their quest for legitimacy the World Managers are seeking to put together a new consensus that will incorporate every progressive movement and satisfy the deepest human longings. Globalism is an appealing ideology in a world torn apart by fratricidal wars. "World peace through world trade" is an attractive slogan on a planet that spends $200 billion a year on armaments to "protect" a world population most of whom earn less than $100 a year. It is a comforting thought that there are profits to be made in cleaning the air and sea and improving the overall quality of life, and more comforting still that these profits will eventually make *everyone* richer and happier.

These space-age utopians are in a position to take advantage of the most fashionable ideas of the twentieth century. This is an age of planning, and the new globalists are the only ones with the pretension, skill, and resources to plan on a global scale. This is the age of technology, and they control most of it. This is the age of meritocracy, and the power of the World Managers comes not only from what they own but, they argue, even more from what they know.

Moreover, fate has provided the new globalists with a convenient set of enemies. The failures and inadequacies of the nation-state are obvious. Even the most powerful nation cannot defend its territory from nuclear attack, maintain an old-fashioned empire, solve its most pressing internal problems—unemployment, inflation, urban decay—or stem the decline in social services. "Quality of life" became a cliché in the United States just when everyone noted its absence. When Southern Senators begin patriotic speeches with an apologetic "I may be old-fashioned, but . . . ," the American flag is shredded to make bell-bottom trousers, and the frantic response of the faithful is to put AMERICA—LOVE IT OR LEAVE IT slogans on their bumpers, it is evident that conventional patriotism has lost its magic. The Watergate scandals have reinforced a growing loss of faith among Americans in the very process of politics.

This loss of faith transcends ideologies. Socialism too has lost ground as a world religion as the "socialist camp" split into warring factions and the harsh realities of the Soviet state mocked the socialist dream. Corporate managers believe that despite the establishment of independent socialist regimes in North Vietnam, North Korea, China, Tanzania, Yugoslavia, and Cuba and the increasing role of the state in all advanced capitalist economies, communism as an ideology is running out of steam. The countries of Eastern Europe, including the Soviet Union, appear more and more to share the capitalist goals of economic growth and consumer abundance. Hungary and Rumania have reintroduced certain capitalist principles such as a modified profit system and interplant competition, and Hungary now has state-owned multinational corporations with plants in Western Europe. The Soviet Union appears to be becoming more technocratic and managerial, and less interested in making a revolution anywhere—including Russia. China too is eager to acquire technology from global corporations, but by licensing, not equity investment. It has learned from the Japanese how to acquire foreign technology without losing control of the advanced industrial sectors, as many underdeveloped countries have done. Indeed, technology consultant Jack Baranson points out, the Chinese now show more sophistication in negotiating license arrangements than the Japanese and are careful to obtain not only manufacturing know-how but basic design and engineering knowledge as well. But while China is welcoming corporations that bring needed technology and has already begun to allow foreign corporations to use its huge labor pool to manufacture exports, it still looks unlikely that Coke or Pepsi will ever reopen the door to the fabled Chinese market and reach those "800 million customers."

Despite the abatement of the Cold War, the disappointments of state socialism, and the eagerness of old ideological antagonists to embrace their technology, global corporations have yet to achieve the legitimacy they are seeking. Indeed, the growth of suspicion and hostility toward large business enterprises has matched the growth of their power. Global executives sometimes talk about their skyscraper offices as if they were besieged citadels. The global corporation, the Chief Executives concluded in Jamaica, is "highly misunderstood all over the world."

This ideological crisis of the global corporation is a reflection of the crisis of capitalism itself. The development of international production and the world market was an attempt to revitalize an economic system which in the 1930's appeared headed for catastrophe. Because the first law of oligopoly capitalism is growth, great firms by the 1930's had already outgrown national markets. Nationalist trade rivalries hampered the growth of the wider market and contributed to the breakdown that resulted in World War II. At the end of the war, great areas of the globe—Russia, China, Eastern Europe—passed under various forms of state socialism which dramatically limited the potential world capitalist market. The phenomenally successful American response was to build a Free World based on the dollar and backed by the atomic bomb. Within the Free World, economic integration and the free movement of goods and capital were encouraged to keep the door open to American goods and American capital. The result was a series of economic miracles that lifted the United States to a trillion-dollar economy and brought devastated Japan, Germany, and Western Europe to new heights of prosperity. Once the political infrastructure had been laid—the alchemy of Bretton Woods (which turned the dollar into gold), the massive capital infusions into Western Europe under the Marshall Plan, the European Common Market—the stage was set for global corporations to usher in a new era that not only would ensure the survival of the system but would lead to the world capitalist revolution—the Global Shopping Center.

In the 1960's, the ground rules of the revolution changed radically. The United States, it turned out, lacked the power to eliminate socialist enclaves within the global market, even in such a weak and obscure place as South Vietnam, and the 20-year attempt to do so had disastrous consequences for the American economy. At the same time, all hopes were abandoned of overturning the socialist revolutions in Russia and China through military pressure. These shattered hopes were replaced by new hopes of integrating the workers and peasants of Russia and China into the new global economy.

All of this has meant that the advancement of the world capitalist revolution now depends more on the initiative of corporations and less on governments. The increasingly political pretensions of the global corporation are thus unavoidable, but they inevitably mean more public exposure, and exposure carries with it the risk of increased hostility. A 1972 Harris poll suggests why this should be so. Since 1966 Harris has been asking the American public whether corporations should give "special leadership" in such political areas as "controlling air and water pollution," "wiping out poverty," "controlling crime," and "reducing the threat of war." Between 1966 and 1972 there was a dramatic increase in public expectation of business's capacity for social engineering but a dramatic decline in the public evaluation of business performance. Most Americans do not think business has "helped solve" any of these problems.

If, as the World Managers insist, it is proper to talk about the development of the Global Shopping Center as a revolution, then it is a revolution that has given birth to some powerful counterrevolutionary ideas. The first is what Robert Heilbroner calls "the radically challenging knowledge" that "economic success does not guarantee social harmony," nor, as Barbara Ward points out, does it guarantee ecological harmony. To put it another way, the American Model that Jacques Maisonrouge talks about looks less and less appealing as the trillion-dollar economy is beset by unemployment, inflation, crime, pollution, racial violence, terrorism, lack of meaningful work, and the psychological miseries of affluence—alienation, rootlessness, boredom—all of which are retailed in Sunday supplements around the world. Creeping doubts about the American Model flash in and out of consciousness even among the very people who are working hardest to replicate it. Not long ago we were given a businessman's tour of São Paulo by a prominent Brazilian industrialist who proudly showed us the sprawling shopping centers, superhighways, high-rise apartments that were springing up all over the city. When we asked him whether there was much crime, he responded quickly, "We're not that civilized yet."

The legitimacy problem of the World Managers has also been compounded by certain ideological contradictions which they themselves have unwittingly helped to generate. They are worried about what they call "the decline of the work ethic"—the fact that U.S. labor, in their view, "wants something for nothing." Akio Morita, president of Sony, believes Japan's phenomenal economic challenge to the United States is due to the "laziness" of the U.S. worker. Willis Armstrong, Assistant Secretary of State for Economic Affairs, told us that the "slippage" in the work ethic is making it hard for the United States to compete. Corporate executives are also worried whether the younger generation is willing to make the personal sacrifices to the corporation that its parents made. Yet, as Robert Boguslaw has pointed out, the leaders of high-technology industry have "implicitly turned Max Weber's ethic on its head":

> Hard work is simply a temporarily unautomated task. It is a necessary evil until we get a piece of gear, or a computer large enough, or a program checked out well enough to do the job economically. Until then, you working stiffs can hang around— but, for the long run, we don't either want you or need you.

Similarly, advertising campaigns celebrating lives of leisure, ease, and consumption have done nothing to strengthen the work ethic.

Moreover, there are contradictions between the traditional capitalist celebration of the individual and the development of the corporate "team" now so important to business success; between the celebration of "people's capitalism" and the reality that the controlling shares are managed by corporations, banks, insurance companies, pension funds, foundations, and a few family empires like the Rockefellers, Du Ponts, and Mellons; between the celebration of competition and the phenomenal rise of mergers, market sharing, and oligopolistic concentration; between glittering promises of social engineering and disappointing performance; between a "rugged individualism" which scorns government because, as David Rockefeller once put it, its efficiency can't be tested and the call for "partnership" and even rescue for the Lockheeds and Penn Centrals.

Still and all, the modern corporation has shown itself to be remarkably adaptable. While preparing to launch what the Chief Executives Roundtable called a campaign "to counteract the tons of propaganda and academic reports that are being widely circulated against private enterprise," global corporations are increasingly delighted to do business with commissars. Thus the end of the Cold War, the rapprochement with Russia and China, and the fading of the moral stigma attached to socialism creates something of a political problem for the global corporations. It was much easier to attack socialist and collectivist notions in the United States when those who argued for them could be dismissed as friends of the Kremlin, but today that designation fits David Rockefeller. But although the World Managers continue their opposition to the *expansion* of socialism and where possible, as we shall see in the next chapter, develop strategies to prevent it, they are quite prepared for a limited coexistence with socialism once it is firmly *established*.

There are, however, three ideological movements, each of which has arisen in part in reaction to the global corporation, which the global managers see as mortal enemies with whom no compromise is possible. The first is the gathering movement which challenges the objective of unlimited, unplanned economic growth and demands new qualitative criteria for distinguishing social development from antisocial growth. This group includes advocates of a "zero-growth economy" who question the ever-increasing accumulation of goods, or wonder whether "efficiency" defined in terms of quantitative output is an adequate social criterion of human development. They are making a much more fundamental attack on the underpinnings of the Global Shopping Center than anything in traditional socialist literature. Unlimited expansion of output is the fundamental law of oligopoly capitalism and the very raison d'être of the global corporation.

The second and related attack is the anticonsumption movement which focuses on the problem of global poverty. Dr. Ul-Haq, senior economic adviser to the president of the World Bank, questions the feasibility and equity of Western-style development for poor countries and suggests that they would do better with a "bicycle economy" rather than the American Model. Other anti-consumptionists question whether the flood of goods associated with advanced industrial societies is necessary or desirable for advancing human happiness, and they demand an economic policy that makes a distinction between life-enhancing and life-destroying consumption. The Consumption Ethic is now far more important to the success of the Global Shopping Center than the Work Ethic. As long as people in Singapore like to work, it doesn't matter if people in Massachusetts don't, but the global system will fall apart if both stop expanding their consumption. "Who needs it?" may indeed be the most revolutionary slogan of the past three hundred years.

The third attack comes from what might be called the anti-hierarchy movement—a loose assembly, transcending traditional class lines, of people who resist the rush toward global centralization on a variety of political, moral, scientific, or aesthetic grounds. The worldwide attack on pyramidal authority structures of all kinds, from the Catholic Church to the university, creates a menacing climate for the global corporation, for, as we have seen, the World Managers rest their claims on the centralized, rationalized, and hierarchic structure of the planetary corporation. In Parts II and III of this book we shall be examining the substance of these three attacks.

4

Corporate Diplomacy and National Loyalty

1

There is nothing new about merchants exercising political power. The most celebrated example is the East India Company, which in its day conquered a subcontinent, ruled over 250 million people, raised and supported the largest standing army in the world, deployed 43 warships, and employed its own bishops. Until Lord Canning proclaimed that the Crown was "tak[ing] upon ourselves the government of the territories of India heretofore administered in trust for us by the Honourable East India Company," the most illustrious of Britain's proconsuls—Clive, Hastings, Raffles, Cornwallis—had been operating an empire as a business enterprise. Indeed, the earlier British trading companies such as the Company of Merchants Adventurers (1505), the Russia Company (1553), and the Levant Company (1581) preceded the modern nation-state system. The ancestors of the World Managers were traders looking for spices and merchants out to corner the wool or cloth market, and they were deep in politics.

The earliest English overseas trade organization, the Company of the Merchants of the Staple, was organized in the early fourteenth century as a way of replenishing the royal treasury. As time went on, the Crown began to share more and more economic and political power with enterprising merchants, who no longer had to be ordered to venture forth to buy and sell in exotic places. For the Crown the burst of international corporate activity in the sixteenth century was an instrument for regulating trade and, later, for the development of new markets. Kings and companies prospered together. Companies were granted trade monopolies and many of the privileges of government, and in return they gathered an empire for the Crown. (The Virginia Company and the Plymouth Company developed the New World; three years after Russia Company traders set up shop in Moscow, Queen Elizabeth and Ivan the Terrible exchanged ambassadors; the East India Company pacified a subcontinent.) In short, the first international corporations played a crucial role in laying the foundation for the modern industrial empires, and in the process they became for a time governments themselves.

As Sigmund Timberg points out, "England, Holland, and the other great trading powers of the seventeenth and eighteenth century were delegating *political* power to their foreign merchants, when they permitted those merchants to engage—collectively and under the corporate aegis—in foreign trade." In Henry Maitland's phrase, these were "the companies that became colonies, the companies that made war." Timberg points out how international cartels are described in legal opinions as "private regulation," and counsel in drafting cartel agreements uses words like "neutral territory" and "spoils." Such a consistent use of political terms, he notes, "is more than a mere metaphor: it is a recognition of an underlying reality."

Karl Polanyi, the great economic historian, argues that the rise of the "market mentality" in the laissez-faire climate of the Industrial Revolution fundamentally altered the relationship of public and private government because it radically changed the very purposes of all government. The market economy created a "new type of society" under which "the market mechanism became determinative for the life of the body social." No wonder, he notes, that "the emergent human aggregation was an 'economic' society to a degree never even approximated." In a society that measures itself by the criteria of profits and product and believes in social regulation based on the fear of hunger and the love of gain, the line between public and private will always be blurred, for the functions of state and corporation overlap. The behavior of both is determined primarily by economic goals. As Polanyi points out, in the premarket mentality the motive of gain existed but it was "specific to merchants, as was valor to the knight, piety to the priest and pride to the craftsman. The notion of making the motive of gain universal never entered the heads of our ancestors." Once economics became the substance of politics, power passed to the largest economic organizations—i.e., those corporations able to use economies of scale with maximum effect.

The rise of the modern corporation has been paralleled by an extraordinary rise in the activities and pretensions of the modern nation-state. The contemporary state has had to share traditional kingly prerogatives with private corporations, but at the same time government has arrogated to itself managerial prerogatives unknown in all previous human history: the right to manage the economy through control of interest rates, money supply, foreign trade, taxes, quotas, and tariffs; the right to allocate resources within the society (as in the United States by means of a $90-billion military budget); the right to set limits on prices and wages; the right to choose which private corporations are to be subsidized or even rescued. Under the banner of national security, the modern state also demands the right to control where its citizens may travel, with whom they may trade, and what kinds of business arrangements they may make beyond its shores. At no time have states wielded anything comparable to the military might of the nuclear giants, and accordingly, states have never been bolder in proclaiming their legal right to bomb, invade, overfly, or blockade other nations at times of their own choosing. Neither the nation-state nor the corporation has preempted managerial powers exercised by the other. (An exception, perhaps, is that the Pentagon, not the East India Company or GM, runs the foreign military operations.) Instead, "private" companies and "public" governments, sharing many of the same managerial goals, such as growth and stability, have expanded their power together.

This chapter will discuss the relationship of global companies and the world's most powerful nation-state, the United States of America. The clash between the world corporation and the territorial state has recently aroused the interest of political scientists, who recognize that the emergence of the transnational corporation makes traditional academic descriptions of the international state system obsolete, and of national politicians everywhere, who understand that the concentration of economic power in private hands enormously complicates the task of running a "sovereign" state. But most of the discussion has concerned the conflict between the global corporation and those countries where the global corporation operates, the so-called "host countries." Operations in such countries, particularly when they are weak and under-developed, raise issues about economic penetration and political domination. Once a poor country accepts the global corporation as an instrument of development, it has already chosen a particular path of development with certain predictable consequences. These we shall take up in Part II. In Part III we shall be looking in specific ways at the impact of global corporations on the territory, society, and people of the United States. But here we are prin-cipally concerned with the relationship of U.S.-based global cor-porations to the U.S. Government. To what extent do they de-termine that mysterious concept, the "national interest"? To what extent are their ideas about how the world should be run likely to conflict with or even prevail over those of American politicians?

It is familiar folklore accepted by Marxists and capitalists alike that the interests of the U.S.-based global corporations and the interests of the U.S. Government are substantially identical. For the Marxist, the government is the instrument of the dominant economic power in the society. Since the state is the "executive committee of the ruling class," to use Marx's famous phrase, it is inconceivable that the interests of the corporations could clash with the interests of the state. At the same time, it is accepted capitalist dogma that what is good for corporations is good for the United States and vice versa. The richer and more powerful global corporations become, the more these riches and power re-dound to the benefit of the United States. When Servan-Schreiber warned of the "American Challenge," he couched his argument in political rather than economic terms. What really excited him was not the fact that a group of companies were becoming too power-ful but that they were *American* companies representing the power of the *United States*. Not so long ago, Bernard Baruch talked of the "essential oneness" of the U.S. Government's stra-tegic interests and the financial interests of U.S. corporations. More recently, however, it has become commonplace to talk about the coming clash between huge corporations and sovereign states. As we have seen, the World Managers themselves for more than five years have been carrying on an ideological attack on the very idea of national sovereignty, even to the point of predicting the death of the nation-state.

The relationship of U.S.-based global corporations and the

U.S. Government is a subtle and changing one. U.S. global corporations are not simple extensions or instruments of the U.S.
Government. Nor is the State Department the obedient servant of
every powerful American corporate interest. One reason for the
complexity of the relationship is that neither "the nation-state"
nor "the corporation" is a monolithic entity. Within the national
government there are differences in outlook and approach among
the Treasury Department, the Commerce Department, and the
Defense Department about what constitutes "the national interest" in particular cases and what role global corporations
should play in overall U.S. strategy.

It is equally clear that not all global corporations have the
same interests vis-à-vis the U.S. Government or follow the same
strategy. Whether a company is already well established overseas
or is about to embark on a big foreign investment program,
whether it is in mining or manufacturing, whether it operates in
"safe" developed countries or "unsafe" underdeveloped countries
are all factors that will determine its political outlook. Moreover,
a company may have one relationship with the U.S. Government
in the latter's role as chief architect of the world monetary system,
another in its role as the world's greatest military power, and still
another in its role as manager of the U.S. economy. Thus for the
global corporation, the U.S. Government is both a nuisance and a
necessity. For the government, the corporation is a source of national power and a frustrater of national policy.

The growth of the corporation, in Stephen Hymer's words,
"from the workshop to the factory to the national corporation to
the multi-division corporation" is a story of the continuing triumph of organization over territorial limitations. At each stage
the corporation has progressively liberated itself from territorial
ties until, as one high State Department official has put it, the
global giants now see the world as their oyster. While corporations can transcend territory, nation-states, even powerful ones,
are much less flexible. Their principal constituencies are land-
locked. Corporations whose primary loyalty is to their worldwide
balance sheet can move about the world looking for bargains in
finance, natural resources, and labor. But housewives trying to
balance the family food budget, workers looking for a job, or
local industrialists tied to the domestic market are not so mobile.
The raison d'être of a nation-state is the defense and development

of a specific territory. States are measured by how much territory they control and by what happens within the territory they administer. National loyalty is built on the sharing of space. Patriotism is the worship of a piece of earth, a mystical celebration of a common heritage based on cotenancy. Money and goods travel; most people do not.

2

Both Adam Smith and Karl Marx believed that a crucial characteristic of capital was that it was international. For Smith it was a matter of common sense that capital should be freed from national political barriers. For Marx the progressive expansion of the market through the internationalization of capital was a historical necessity for capitalism. The World Managers are the most active promoters of this Marxist prediction: the nation-state, which in the nineteenth century marked an advance over previous political organizations, is inadequate to the challenge of the global market. George Ball once predicted before the Canadian House of Commons that the logic of economics would lead inevitably to the integration of the United States and Canada. Parochial territorial loyalties give way to economic rationality.

That the interests and loyalties of capitalists transcend national territory was noted by Thomas Jefferson: "Merchants have no country of their own. Wherever they may be they have no ties with the soil. All they are interested in is the source of their profits." President Eisenhower made essentially the same point in 1960 in Rio de Janeiro when he declared that "capital is a curious thing with perhaps no nationality. It flows where it is served best." International companies have traditionally taken a relaxed view of patriotism. The great oil and chemical companies that had cartel arrangements with German firms at the outbreak of the Second World War were actively opposed to fighting Hitler. Adolph Berle describes the difficulties the State Department had on the eve of the war in getting U.S. companies to stop cooperating with the Germans in Latin America. During the Cold War, companies have been ingenious in their efforts to circumvent State Department and Pentagon restrictions on the sale of "strategic" goods to the Soviet Union and China. In 1973, the Philippine subsidiary of Exxon refused to sell oil to the U.S. Navy at Subic Bay because its overriding interest was to help enforce the worldwide Arab boycott of the United States. American bankers, believing that capital is both international and nonideological, have been doing business with the Russian and Bulgarian national banks for many years. Telling us about his bank's new loan to Bulgaria, Daniel Davidson, head of the Morgan Guaranty Bank in London, chuckled, "For all we know, they may be buying uranium with it."

Some sense of how little corporations can afford local loyalties is revealed by the history of corporate expansion in the United States. The earliest companies, the textile mills, were local in a political sense. They built and managed company towns, and the business and surrounding community grew together. But local loyalties were soon transcended as companies began to outgrow local and regional markets. Companies were quite prepared to sacrifice local communities to the building of the national market. The ghost towns of Massachusetts and Appalachia, once centers of local industry, were abandoned by corporations as they moved south and west looking for cheaper labor. A city like Gary, Indiana, became a service area for national corporations like U.S. Steel, which polluted its air and water for years without any sense of responsibility to the inhabitants. (U.S. Steel executives, with the exception of one minor vice-president, do not make their home in Gary.) Because large companies have an inherent drive toward ever-expanding growth, they simply cannot afford to tie themselves to any territory. That is the meaning of being "footloose," a word World Managers like to use to describe their operations.

The relationship of big corporations operating overseas with the U.S. Government has steadily evolved over the years. The latest stage in the relationship is due to the dramatic decline of the United States as the preeminent global power. A new era in world politics has arrived in which prudence dictates more catholicity in the choice of one's friends and more caution in the use of force. During the 25 years in which the United States was the most powerful nation on earth, the tighter and more notorious were the links between Washington, Wall Street, and Detroit, the better it was for U.S. companies. When the CIA removed Mohammed Mossadeq, an obstreperous Iranian premier who "irrationally" tried to interfere with Gulf's and Standard Oil's prospects for taking over his country's oil, or when the same agency rescued

Guatemalan banana land for United Fruit from a popularly elected "subversive" nationalist, these were U.S. patriotic initiatives applauded by businessmen. Capital and ideological purity were preserved together. The readier the Pentagon and CIA were to bring down or raise up governments in underdeveloped countries, the better the investment climate for U.S. corporations. U.S. military power was used to establish the ground rules within which American business could operate. The U.S. Government acted as consultant for rightist coups in Bolivia, Brazil, Chile, Greece, and Indonesia, and their generals opened their countries to U.S. investment on the most favorable terms. Wherever the flag has been planted around the world, in some 500 major military and naval bases and in the command posts of over a dozen military interventions, U.S. corporations have moved in. The construction of a worldwide military empire has been good business. Subsidized by public funds, U.S. companies have built roads, harbors, airports, hotels, and banks around the globe. The military budget is perhaps the best example of the compatibility of patriotism and profits. During the Cold War the Department of Defense has had $40 billion to $50 billion a year to distribute to U.S. corporations through procurement contracts. With $6 billion a year to spend on research, much of which went to finance development costs of civilian products like the Boeing 707, the Pentagon has been a major subsidizer of some of the largest U.S. corporations. When electronics and aircraft companies used to take full-page advertisements in newspapers and magazines to warn of the Soviet menace, they were, as they saw it, responding to a patriotic duty and a business opportunity simultaneously.

But the world scene has shifted. The United States is still the most powerful nation, but it can no longer run the world through either its economic power or its military might. The dollar is no longer as good as gold. The power of the State Department, CIA, and Pentagon to make and break governments is not quite what it was. America's 10-year agony in Vietnam demonstrated that the economic and political costs of pacifying a third-rate military power were more than any nation can afford. The Atomic Age version of the nineteenth-century empire is obsolete.

As early as 1966 American business leaders began to see that the costs of maintaining American supremacy by the Kennedy-Johnson military strategy were prohibitive. The massive overseas

military expenditures helped cause the serious balance-of-payments deficit and contributed substantially to inflation at home.
U.S. goods were becoming increasingly uncompetitive, and the
result by 1971 was the first trade deficit in more than two generations. The number one nation was becoming economically weaker
through its military policies. At the same time, the extraordinary
technological lead which the United States enjoyed at the end of
World War II was rapidly shrinking. The United States was losing
ground to Japan, Germany, and other industrialized countries in
the competition for the consumer market. The military budget,
which helped provide the U.S. technology lead with its extraordinary competitive advantages for U.S. firms in the first postwar
generation, no longer played the same role in the second generation because the whole nature of international competition had
changed. As the world appeared less and less subject to American
control, corporations found it prudent to advertise their Americanism less. Broken windows and bomb threats from militant
groups opposed to the U.S. intervention in Indochina helped
convince some American companies in Europe that they should
get rid of their American labels.

At the same time, a few corporate executives tried to use their
influence to persuade the Administration to back away from those
foreign and military policies which were damaging their own
interests. The chairman of Bank America, Louis Lundborg, spoke
out publicly against the economically counterproductive military
policy in Southeast Asia. Many more expressed their displeasure
with "obsolete Cold War policies" in private. In March 1968,
the advice of business leaders played a crucial role in persuading
Lyndon Johnson to deescalate the war.

The bilateral aid program which had been used to subsidize
U.S. corporations abroad was no longer politically acceptable
in the United States in its traditional form. Between 1950 and
1970, about 4 percent of all U.S. exports were financed by AID
(Agency for International Development) and its predecessors. The
"tie-in" arrangements which forced poor countries to buy U.S.
products with their foreign money was extremely profitable for
U.S. companies. In 1967, for example, a Senate investigating
committee found that public-health grants to certain Latin American countries were being used to buy drugs from Pfizer, Merck,
and other U.S. drug companies at substantial markups over their

U.S. prices. There is increased use of the Export-Import Bank to finance exports of global corporations. Through its voting power in international aid and financing organizations such as the World Bank, the U.S. Government still seeks to use public money to subsidize American global business, despite increasing resistance from Congress to foreign-assistance "boondoggles" and "give-aways."

Today the World Managers like to talk of themselves as "peace-mongers." It is a title "we can wear with pride," says Harry Heltzer, chairman of 3M. The resurgence of the gospel of the businessman's peace, a tradition dating back to Henry Ford and Andrew Carnegie, is a direct consequence of changes in world politics which the Vietnam War helped to dramatize. "Gunboat diplomacy does not work today," says Carl Gerstacker, who as an America Firster was against going to war with Hitler in the years before Pearl Harbor. A number of global-corporation executives with whom we have talked express similar points of view. The U.S. military establishment is too expensively and too visibly deployed. It is an economic drain and is becoming increasingly ir-relevant or even "counterproductive" in smoothing the path of U.S. corporations abroad. John Gallagher, chief executive of Sears' international operations and vice chairman of the Council of the Americas (an association of more than 200 corporations which account for over 90 percent of all U.S. corporate invest-ment in Latin America), told the Council at its December 1971 meeting that "as far as the protection of U.S. private investment in Latin America goes, we in the business community are literally on our own. . . . If we are on our own, as I think we are, then we must also act on our own."

3

What does it mean to be literally "on your own"? Somewhat less than what it sounds like. True, the prospects for rescue by U.S. military or paramilitary operations are not what they once were, because the tactics of the U.S. Government for protecting Amer-ican business interests abroad have changed. How they have changed is best illustrated by the U.S. role in the overthrow of the Allende government in Chile. When in 1970 John Mc-Cone, a director of ITT and former head of the CIA, offered his successor a $1-million contribution to help finance a quick covert campaign by the Agency to prevent the Marxist candidate from taking office, the offer was politely refused. On September 15, the State Department instructed Ambassador Edward Korry "to do all possible short of a Dominican type action" to prevent Allende's inauguration. But gunboat diplomacy was ruled out.

So too was ITT's timetable for spreading "economic chaos." Jack D. Neal, an ITT employee with 35 years' experience in the State Department, had prepared an 18-point program designed to produce a coup d'état. His methods included concerted economic pressure through the cutoff of credit and aid and the support of domestic antagonists of the regime. In time all his methods were employed, but not his schedule. What he recommended to be done in a matter of weeks was carried out over a period of three years. "Why should the U.S. try to be so pious and sanctimonious in September and October of 1970," Neal complains in a memorandum to his boss, Vice-President W. R. Merriam, "when over the past few years it has been pouring the taxpayers' money into Chile admittedly to defeat Marxism. [According to a former U.S. Ambassador to Chile, the CIA and other agencies spent $20 million to defeat Allende in 1964.] Why can't the fight be continued now that the battle is in the homestretch and the enemy is more clearly identifiable?"

The answer was that both the U.S. Government and the rest of the business community in Chile believed that ITT's plan for fighting Allende wouldn't work. On October 9, 1970, Merriam reported to John McCone:

> Practically no progress has been made in trying to get American business to cooperate in some way so as to bring on economic chaos. GM and Ford, for example, say that they have too much inventory on hand in Chile to take any chances and that they keep hoping that everything will work out all right. . . . According to my source [CIA contact] we must continue to keep the pressure on business.

Within a year the Nixon Administration's "game plan" for economic warfare against Chile began to take shape. In August 1971, responsibility for the formulation of U.S. foreign policy in Latin America had shifted substantially to the Treasury Department, then under the direction of John Connally. Originally a relatively low priority, Chile became a major concern after the nationalization of Anaconda's and Kennecott's copper mines. In October 1971, Secretary of State William Rogers told a closed meeting of executives from ITT, Ford, Anaconda, Purina, the First National City Bank, and Bank America, among others, that "the Nixon Administration is a business Administration. Its mission is to protect American business." The "new ball game with new rules," as John Petty, Assistant Secretary of the Treasury, had termed it, included cutting off Ex-Im Bank credits on which vital imports from the United States depended; pressuring multilateral institutions such as the World Bank and the Inter-American Development Bank (in which the United States has the dominant voice) to disapprove further loans to Chile; encouraging private banks to cut off credit (the line of short-term bank credit shrank from $220 million to $35 million in the first year of the Allende government); and terminating the aid program with the exception of military aid (which jumped from $800,000 in the last pre-Allende year to more than $12 million in two years).

None of these activities was particularly visible. Most Americans were unaware of any of them. But together they added up to a concerted campaign to bring about the downfall of a government whose internal policies conflicted sharply with the economic interests of U.S. corporations. The corporations themselves, despite their initial reticence to join with ITT (whose buccaneer methods a number of corporate managers we interviewed go out of their way to disparage), joined the campaign by refusing to sell spare parts for trucks and machinery even for cash and, in the case of Kennecott, as we shall see, conducting a worldwide legal battle to keep Chile's expropriated copper off the market.

What the Chilean case suggests is that the U.S. Government is still prepared to use its power to crush a government that in its view treats U.S. corporations improperly—there was no other "national security" issue in the Chile case—but that it will no longer take public responsibility for doing so. As CIA director William Colby stated, according to *The Washington Post*, during closed-door hearings on October 11, 1973, "the presumption under which we conduct this type of operation is that it is a covert operation and that the United States hand is not to show."

But despite the U.S. Government pressure on Chile, U.S. corporations are more "on our own" than in the past. Increasingly,

State Department officials are coming to the view expressed by Secretary of State Dean Rusk in 1962: "I don't believe that the U.S. can afford to stake its interests in other countries on a particular investment in a particular situation." There is a newly sophisticated view in the State Department that the government cannot defend the interests of some corporations in underdeveloped countries without jeopardizing larger U.S. interests there, including the interests of other corporations. Thus, some global-corporation executives operating in Latin America have complained that U.S. ambassadors there are "unhelpful" or "lacking in understanding." John Gallagher, head of Sears operations in Latin America, thinks the U.S. Ambassador in Colombia had a naive attitude toward that country's economic policy. The Ambassador seemed to approve local laws establishing taxes on the use of brand names, encouraging cooperatives, and regulating consumer-credit rates, none of which is good for Sears. The Ambassador, he told us, "has no understanding of our situation, especially when he tries to push us into joint ventures with local capital. It's none of their business." Charles Goodsell reports a similar reaction from a global-corporation board chairman operating in Peru who believes that the State Department is spreading a "welfare state" philosophy in Latin America by championing "radical forces." The Nixon Administration, sensitive to this sort of criticism, has passed the word to the Foreign Service to be more aggressively pro-U.S.-business in representing the United States abroad. All diplomats receive the following departmental directive: "Henceforth all officers will be evaluated on the basis of their concern for U.S. Business."

But in its aggressive new campaign to promote U.S. business interests abroad, the U.S. Government is acting more in the role of sales representative than as a political negotiator. The Commerce Department's Office of Export Development, headed by a former Sperry Rand official, David H. Baker, is developing consortia to bid on major foreign governmental projects such as the multibillion-dollar Sete Quedas hydroelectric project in Brazil. The office helped put together a $35-million air-control project in Colombia, and the U.S. Ambassador in Colombia, Leonard J. Saccio, helped 10 leading companies, including GM, Northrop, and Raytheon, to get the contract. *Business Week* describes the extraordinary efforts of former Republican National Committee treasurer J. William Middendorf II in what he calls the "death battle" to cut America's deficit through increased exports:

Middendorf's commercial attachés have bombarded Dutch business prospects with direct mail solicitations and follow-up visits. They have flooded Dutch banks and airline offices with brochures that are designed to induce visiting U.S. businessmen —whether on vacation or business—into considering the Netherlands as a potential market. "We've got 22 guys concentrating on trade," says Middendorf proudly, "and every section of the embassy has a role to play."

Thus in a sense the traditional roles of government and business overseas are becoming reversed. Diplomats are becoming salesmen and salesmen are becoming diplomats. Theodore H. Moran of the Brookings Institution has analyzed Kennecott's diplomatic strategy to prevent nationalization. Kennecott developed the following plan: It built a formidable "network of transnational alliances," to use Moran's term, in the hope no government would dare to expropriate its mines. It took out a large loan from the Ex-Im Bank and raised $45 million in additional capital "by selling long-term copper contracts with European and Asian customers to a consortium of European banks . . . and to a consortium of Japanese institutions." It sought imposition of legal obligations directly on the Chilean state and made maximum use of AID guarantees of the U.S. Government. "The aim of these arrangements," Robert Haldeman, executive vice-president of Kennecott's Chilean operations, told Moran, "is to ensure that nobody expropriates Kennecott without upsetting relations to customers, creditors, and governments on three continents." Moran notes that "Anaconda, Asarco, Freeport Sulphur, and Roan Selection have followed the lines laid down by Kennecott in negotiating for new concessions in Latin America, South Asia, and Africa." When the Chilean Congress, despite all these company efforts, unanimously decided to nationalize the mines, Kennecott sued in France, Sweden, Germany, and Italy to block all payments to Chile for nationalized copper sold in those countries. "Kennecott officials are determined to keep the heat on Chile," *Time* reported. "The Manhattan offices of General Counsel Pierce McCreary, who is directing the campaign, has the air of a war room."

The Council of the Americas is also deeply involved in corporate diplomacy. It regularly sponsors what its *Report* calls "high level delegations" of global-corporation managers to Argentina, Venezuela, Mexico, and especially Peru and Colombia, two members of the Andean Common Market. In Argentina, for example, the purpose of the company executives' visit was "to assist the entire private sector of the country in trying to make the proposed law to regulate foreign investment an effective instrument for Argentina's development." In Colombia, Council of the Americas representatives tried to get the government to suspend the toughest provision of the Andean Code, as John Gallagher reports, by making it clear to them "that we would retaliate by cutting off all new investment." In one instance, however, the Colombian Minister of Development denounced the Council's demands as *"terrorismo económico."* Henry R. Geylin, vice-president of the Council, reporting on "the diplomatic role of the multinational corporation," describes "corporation diplomacy" as a "very exciting new phenomenon into which we are going to have to put increasing efforts."

In late 1972, David Rockefeller reported to the Council on his own diplomatic efforts, a grand tour of Latin America which included a nationally broadcast decoration ceremony in the office of the President of Colombia with three former Presidents looking on. "The President was saying things I thought it difficult for any Latin American president to say about a name so identified with capitalism." Observing that "often the more democratic the country, the more hostile it is to foreign investment," the chairman of the Chase Manhattan Bank was pleased to note that this was not the case in Colombia, which he apparently considers a democracy. Different corporations have different foreign policies depending upon their interests. Sears, for example, has a much less sanguine view of Colombia than Mr. Rockefeller's bank, for the obvious reason, as a Sears vice-president pointed out to us, that banks have little to fear from a movement toward a state economy, since they can lend money to the government, but a consumer bazaar like Sears makes money only where private enterprise thrives.

Sometimes being "on our own" means that global corporations actually set U.S. foreign policy toward the particular country where they operate. This used to be obvious in the case of company-owned countries such as United Fruit's Honduras and Firestone's Liberia. They were private preserves. ("We must produce a disembowelment of the incipient economy of the country in order to increase and help our aims. We have to prolong its tragic, tormented, and revolutionary life; the wind must blow only on our sails and the water must only wet our keel," a United Fruit manager wrote a company lawyer about Honduras in 1920.) In 1931 the company employed armed bands to intimidate striking workers. Company planes were used to kidnap some of the strike leaders and fly them to El Salvador, and company thugs would chop up competitors' bananas with machetes as they lay on railroad platforms. In 1920, Firestone lent the bankrupt Liberian government money, in return for which the government agreed to accept an American financial adviser, to give the company control· over the only bank and the raising of any further foreign debt, and to let the company own all the most important distributorships of U.S. and European consumer goods.

To talk of an official U.S. policy toward such countries diverging in any way from United Fruit or Firestone policy was, of course, absurd. But now even these two countries are somewhat less in the thrall of a single company. United Fruit—now United Brands—has sold off some of its plantations in Central America to concentrate on marketing other people's bananas under the brand name "Chiquita," a more profitable and less politically sensitive way of doing business. Liberia has paid off its loans.

On occasion, U.S. companies also play a crucial role in setting the *operative* U.S. foreign policy, which in some cases diverges from the *official* foreign policy enunciated by the State Department. Officially, the United States during the Kennedy-Johnson years was cool toward the racist, minority government of South Africa. U.S. representatives at the U.N. joined in voting for resolutions condemning *apartheid*. Rhetorically, at least, the United States stands not for "stability" in southern Africa but for democratic change. Yet GM, Ford, and Chrysler, with major investments in South Africa, are powerful forces for legitimizing the regime and reinforcing the economy and government. (Company arguments that they are a liberalizing force are not convincing. Foreign investment and internal repression have risen sharply together in the last fifteen years.) It is also worth noting that the

Financial Gazette, a journal of the ruling party in South Africa, declared in June 1966 that "in times of emergency or war" GM plants "would be turned over rapidly to the production of weapons and other strategic requirements for defense of Southern Africa."

Often company policy eventually succeeds in shaping State Department policy. The Nixon Administration changed the policy of its predecessors in 1970 when the National Security Council adopted a secret policy paper, NSSM 39, which, according to a leak printed in *The New York Times*, calls for "deliberately expanded contacts and communication with the white governments of Southern Africa." While some of the argument for this change of policy was strategic (access to the Indian Ocean), the principal reason was to bring foreign policy into line with a reality that major U.S. companies had created long ago: South Africa under its present hospitable investment climate has a useful role to play in the new world economy.

Litton Industries' adventure in Greece is another illustration of the independent role companies can play in setting foreign policy. On April 21, 1967, a group of right-wing colonels seized power in Athens. Twenty-four days later, Litton signed a contract with the junta which gave it virtual carte blanche over the development of resources, social and economic in nature, that are directly related to economic growth. ("The first major U.S. industrial corporation to enter the nation-building business," *Air Force and Space Digest* exulted.) At a time when the U.S. Government was "at best coldly suspicious," to use the words of a former Litton manager in Greece, William W. McGrew, Litton's private diplomacy played a crucial role in the survival of the junta. Here is McGrew's own account in the *Columbia Journal of Business*:

> It is hardly possible to exaggerate the weight which Greek politics attaches to the actual or imagined attitude of the major Western powers, particularly the United States. In those first weeks of insecurity and apprehension, when most countries were slow to extend diplomatic recognition to the new regime, the Junta seized on the pending Litton offer as a means of demonstrating tangible support from a highly-regarded U.S. company —one, furthermore, with close contacts in the U.S. military hierarchy, and in good standing with the White House.

With more than a trace of bitterness, McGrew describes Litton's approach to nation building:

Shortly after the contract was signed, public relations men from the Beverly Hills headquarters had staged banquets in the provincial towns where they regaled local worthies with descriptions of the miracles to be wrought by Litton. Highly-paid consultants were brought to Greece for a quick tour of the boondocks. When they departed, they sometimes left a report behind, sometimes not. The regional offices sported two-story-high Litton neon signs. . . . The Greek junta probably got about what it bargained for, a political crutch to lean on during the early months of its rule until it could consolidate its power and establish normal relations with the rest of the world. The only loser in the whole deal, in fact, was the Greek taxpayer.

4

The goal of corporate diplomacy is nothing less than the replacement of national loyalty with corporate loyalty. If they are to succeed in integrating the planet, loyalty to the global enterprise must take precedence over all other political loyalties. Wherever possible, business diplomats will try to persuade governments, local businessmen, or anyone who will listen that there is no conflict between corporate goals and national goals. Governments that perceive such conflicts have succumbed to "irrational nationalism."

The global corporation is bidding for the loyalties of several different constituencies. To its workers in many lands it offers membership in a labor aristocracy which may mean (but not always) a few pennies more a day than the going wage. To local businessmen it offers participation as local managers, stockholders, and suppliers in a global enterprise with dimensions far beyond anything a limited national economy can promise. To governments it offers a familiar path to economic growth. But its most powerful appeal for loyalty is to the general public, and its message is simple and insistent: consumption is the key to happiness and the global corporation has the products that make life worth living. "Consumer democracy is more important than political democracy," the Council of the Americas suggests as a good slogan for its corporate members. The campaign to make one's primary identification with a product or style of life rather than with a political community is crucial to the evolvement of the corporate vision of a "world without borders." When America's leading biscuit maker projects an electronic message to the world showing nothing more than a box of Ritz Crackers floating across the TV screen, he is talking about a new kind of flag.

To command worldwide loyalties it is necessary to transcend national identifications. Corporations are more acceptable in foreign countries the less they are seen as extensions of their home governments. A corporation that is wholly owned by Americans and managed in New York can by selecting its name and local personnel with care pass either as a local corporation or as a vague world entity without identification with U.S. foreign policy. When a local subsidiary of a U.S.-based company is "Mexican-ized," calls itself Kimberly-Clark de México, or (like Celanese) drops "of America" from its name, it is perceived as less foreign and hence less threatening. (The head of CPC International's subsidiary in Mexico, Productos de Maiz, is happy to note that most visitors to the supermarket believe his company is Mexican.) More importantly, elements in the country eager to integrate themselves into an international economy can better protect their flanks from the "irrational nationalists" among their own coun-trymen. What might be regarded as "selling out" the country when an American company is involved can be made to look like "joint investment" when the American flag is kept in the back-ground.

Indeed, the ambassadors from IBM, Chase, and Sears are now trying to co-opt the nationalist impulse for their own purposes. Global companies actively try to promote themselves as spokes-men for the national economy. In Brazil, U.S. businessmen, as the Council of the Americas puts it, "organize national business-men" through the creation of the Businessmen's Council Brazil-U.S., which has become "the chief spokesman of the entire private sector, domestic and foreign, in Brazil." In Central America, Council representative Orlando Bertolone explains, we "inte-grated the foreign business communities into the national ones, lowered their silhouettes, and gave the foreign investor point of view a much better chance to be heard by the government, because it is now supported by the authority of national business."

To make their case that corporate loyalty is also patriotic, global corporations are performing a variety of political services for countries where they operate. The Council of the Americas, which calls itself "probably Latin America's best constituency in the U.S.," provides "hospitality and contacts" for government officials and businessmen from Latin America. It has, for example, carried on intensive lobbying activities in behalf of Colombian coffee planters. At the same time, the World Managers are more and more talking about the social responsibility of global corporations, particularly in underdeveloped countries. "Business must become involved in the large issue of the management of change," says Harvey Schwartz, vice-president of the Rockefeller-owned International Basic Economy Corporation operating in Latin America. Some global executives, John Gallagher of Sears, for example, think that global companies should make a "civic contribution" of about 2 percent of net profits that could go to projects particularly attractive to students, the military, and other important interest groups that might prove hostile to foreign investment. Another idea, Gallagher suggests, is to be more aggressive in helping the host country develop its own foreign markets. Thus Sears, which takes about $1 million in profits out of Brazil every year, ought to feel some obligation to help Brazil earn $1 million in foreign exchange by selling its goods somewhere in the Global Shopping Center. But one high Ford Motor Company executive, on the other hand, told us that he is dubious about companies' taking over the foreign-aid functions that are being rapidly cut back by the U.S. Government. "Our people would probably say 'screw them.'" U.S. aid programs, he noted, have only won enemies. Why would a corporation be more fortunate? (Executives are aware that many companies which declared war on poverty in the United States with full-page newspaper ads and a litany of good intentions have discovered that aid programs involved exceedingly difficult political problems and are as likely to elicit rage as gratitude from the "disadvantaged." For this reason some firms are quietly abandoning their social programs.)

But there are other ways of building corporate loyalty. In Chapter 3 we described the efforts of global corporations to build career ladders that can take enterprising and loyal managers close to the top of the pyramid. These career prospects are particularly attractive for executives from poor countries. Thus Brazilians,

Belgians, and Mexicans who serve the company's interests well in their own countries can look forward to a subordinate position in the executive suite in one of the global cities that oversee the corporation's entire world business—London, Paris, or even New York. When top executives see their careers tied to the global fortunes of their company rather than to the national economy, they become remarkably tolerant of outside economic penetration and even foreign political domination of their country. They see themselves as members of an international class, closer in what they eat, wear, read, and think to company people in other countries than to their fellow countrymen outside the company gates, most of whom are likely to be poor, barely literate, and hungry. In short, members of this new mobile elite are encouraged to consider themselves primarily as corporate citizens first. Dr. Max Gloor, director of Nestlé Alimentana S.A., says its executives must develop what he calls "special Nestlé citizenship."

Global corporations imitate nation-states in their efforts to develop company allegiance and corporate citizenship. IBM is experimenting with moving workers from one country to another to build international, company-oriented attitudes. The Cornell political scientist Andrew Hacker explores some of these efforts:

> Eastman Kodak's medical plans, IBM's country clubs, Richfield Oil's model homes, du Pont's psychiatrists, Reynolds Tobacco's chaplains, and even RCA's neckties with the corporate insignia—all are symptomatic of the effort to establish a feeling of community within the corporation. The middle-class employee no longer has an alternative community in which he can find a sense of belonging. The national government is too large and unwieldly to provide this satisfaction; and local governments are too ineffectual to cater to such deep-seated needs. Government provides various welfare services at various levels, but they are far from being programs that will meet the social and psychological needs of the middle class. Thus there has emerged the equivalent of a new kind of citizenship. It is not the same as our traditional view of citizenship. . . .

5

Despite a spate of premature obituaries, the nation-state is not "just about through as an economic unit," as Charles Kindleberger once put it. One important reason nationalism will not soon disappear is that global corporations need the nation-state. What they need is a different kind of nation-state. Almost everyone, except perhaps for the pure anarchist, has a vision of a perfect state which will liberate him and restrain his enemies. The World Managers are no exception. Great principles like free trade, anti-Communism, even sound money, are quickly discarded when they appear to get in the way of tomorrow's profits. The World Managers have an evolving vision of what constitutes the good state in the era of the Global Shopping Center. As we shall see in Chapter 5, although not yet a coherent vision, the World Managers' model of the Twenty-first Century State fulfills certain specific functions: it is a protector of the free movement of capital and goods; a regulator and educator of the labor market; a balancer of the private economy; a consensus builder able at least to ameliorate correctable injustices through transfer payments—i.e., social security, unemployment insurance, etc.—and a pacifier prepared to deal with the social effects of uncorrectable injustices, with force; a custodian of the national environment ready to maintain all aspects of social infrastructure essential to a good business climate—clean air, drinkable water, good roads, adequate schools, hospitals, communications, waste disposal, and above all, a reasonably contented population.

Traditionally, the greatest dependence of corporations on the state has been in the area of security. Above all, global corporations need stability—what some corporate planners like to call a "surprise-free world." That is, of course, not exactly a modest requirement, and the World Managers know that reality is less accommodating. But the task of anticipating and controlling the future is crucial. It is possible to put up with less-than-satisfactory political ground rules if you can count on some continuity, but it is not possible to do the kind of efficient planning that is the raison d'être of the global corporation when the rules are subject to precipitous change. Thus the World Managers are prepared to do business with "revolutionary" governments when they are firmly in the saddle. (Indeed, as one corporate strategist told us, socialism, far from being "the end of the world," is a "big help" because it ensures "stability" in large areas of the world. Planners in more than one U.S.-based company are eyeing the docile

labor force of Eastern Europe and even China.) But where it is
still possible to prevent leftist revolutionary governments from
coming to power or to help topple them when they do, corporate
managers take a less tolerant view of socialism. However aesthetically offensive U.S. executives sometimes find the local military
junta, their presence, on strictly business grounds, for repressive
rightist governments over socialist experimenters is clear. The
process of revolution is destabilizing. Property is endangered,
sales go down. At the very least, the "rules of the game," as U.S.
officials sometimes term local investment laws, are likely to
change. Consumption patterns are altered. Occasionally, there
is even a change in the value system on which private profits
depend. The terrorism that often accompanies revolution constitutes a continuing security problem. Official terrorism, such as
government torture in Brazil, does not ordinarily constitute a
security problem for corporations, for pacification programs,
however vicious, promote stability unless they are bungled. (The
typical corporate reaction to the suspension of civil liberties in
the Philippines in 1972 was voiced by Frank Zingaro, vice-president of Caltex: "Martial law has significantly improved the business climate. . . .")

But despite its extraordinary command of financial and technical resources, the global corporation has less military potential
than its eighteenth- and nineteenth-century predecessors. The reason has to do with the radical changes in the military environment
of the last generation. With the rise of the modern industrial
state, military power has become increasingly centralized in national governments. In the United States the trend is evident in
the efforts of the Justice Department to exert growing control
over local police. The modern industrial state is also less dependent upon private business for making war than the eigh-
teenth- or nineteenth-century state because it is in a state of
permanent mobilization. In 1902, J. A. Hobson in his book
Imperialism took it for granted that no "great war could be
undertaken by any European State . . . if the house of Rothschild
and its connexions set their face against it." No corporation or
group of corporations exercises that kind of veto power on the
White House and the Pentagon—which, indeed, pursued the
Vietnam War long after some of the country's corporate elite
wanted it ended. In 1940, Franklin Roosevelt was heavily de-

pendent upon the large corporations to provide the mobilization base needed for the war, and they exacted important concessions for becoming the arsenal of democracy. But after thirty years of a permanent war economy, in the military area corporations are rather more dependent upon the government than the other way around.

It is true, of course, that the state can no longer provide a high level of security either. As we have pointed out, territory, any territory, is indefensible in the nuclear age. Moreover, despite the massive sums spent on internal security, research on violence control, and an ever-tougher judicial system, the nation-state does not seem to be able to provide much security even within its own borders. "Monkey-wrench politics," the power of the powerless to make their presence felt, is on the rise everywhere. Airplane hijackings, office bombings, and street muggings are now so common in the United States that they are a factor in corporate decisions to move out of large cities (Carl Gerstacker notes that Dow's location in the small town of Midland, Michigan, which used to be considered a drawback in attracting executives, is now a selling point.) Corporations expect little help from the state in their major overseas security problem—terrorism and kidnapping. (Terrorism is so routine in the United States as well as Latin America, Sears' John Gallagher told us, that nobody bothers to report attacks on corporate property to the home office anymore. The Council of the Americas recently considered taking out large insurance policies on the lives of executives of client companies, but decided that that would probably encourage kidnapping. *Business Week* advises executives in danger areas, "you might even consider wearing disguises, which some executives are doing. False mustaches and beards are often used. At the least, vary the times and routes you travel to and from your work, or your golf or tennis club.")

What, then, is the security role which the United States is expected to play in the Global Shopping Center? What the World Managers want from the American state is a low military profile and a much more aggressive foreign economic policy. "It is time the United States developed an economic foreign policy instead of a political foreign policy," says Fred Borch, former head of General Electric. The basic contours of the Nixon foreign policy are precisely in accord with the global corporations' own political strategy. The best way to ensure that the Soviet Union and China do not disturb the vision of a Global Shopping Center is to include them in it. Some corporate executives talk of building a "belt of capitalism" which will tie the U.S.S.R. and China into an integrated global system. They count on increasing Soviet dependence on foreign technology and spare parts to moderate any remaining revolutionary zeal. "I think getting General Electric into China and the Soviet Union," a GE long-range strategist told us, "is the biggest thing we can do for world peace." Competition among nations will be waged with economic weapons instead of missiles, U-2's and proxy wars. In short, the corporate managers hope to usher in the era of peaceful coexistence advocated so long ago by Henry Wallace and Nikita Khrushchev.

When the executives call themselves "peacemongers," they are being perfectly sincere. It is in their interest that the game of nations be transformed from a military duel which no one can win and which threatens all their dreams. A world in which military power is paramount will be dominated by national governments, which for the foreseeable future will continue to have an effective monopoly on such power. But if economic power is dominant, corporations with control over an ever-increasing share of the world's production system, money markets, and communications resources will gain increasing political leadership. The more economic issues overshadow military security, the more the global corporation is likely to take power away from the nation-state. But of course, reality is less neat than college-course catalogs. Political and economic issues are inextricably intertwined.

Take the energy crisis, for example. In a time of scarcity, the U.S.-based energy companies gain in power because the U.S. Government is heavily dependent upon them not only to deliver oil, but also to provide the information in their exclusive possession needed to develop a national energy policy. (In February 1973, Richard Helms, former head of the CIA, told the Senate Foreign Relations Committee that the Agency had difficulty estimating petroleum reserves because U.S. oil companies were secretive and would not share such information with anybody.) The producing states, though they may raise the price, are still dependent upon the companies to market their oil. At some point, however, the presence of the U.S. Sixth Fleet in the Mediterranean becomes a relevant consideration in setting the price of crude. The same crisis that dramatized the vulnerability of the U.S. Government with respect to foreign oil supplies also dramatized the still greater vulnerability of Europe and Japan. Ironically, the crisis restored value to the dollar and some lost prestige to the United States.

The principal lesson of Vietnam, as global corporate managers see it, is that a military policy which leads to economic weakness needs updating. Thus a growing number of corporate leaders appear to favor cutting back U.S. overseas garrisons as a partial solution to the balance-of-payments crisis. Although some older corporate executives with personal experience as national-security managers harbor a sentimental and seemingly unshakable attachment to the NATO military policies of the Truman Administration, more and more are questioning the dollar value of maintaining a full-scale army in Europe. They also support the Nixon Administration's abandonment of many of the familiar ground rules of the Cold War because many of them realized long before the White House did that the United States can no longer afford them.

Nixon's map of the world, which bears little resemblance to the one that John Kennedy and Lyndon Johnson once used, is quite consistent with recent corporate thinking on how to achieve world stability. The J. Edgar Hoover view of the Soviet Union has been rejected. The Kremlin is made up not of international conspirators, but of pragmatic managers far more interested in securing their borders, developing their own consumer economy, and controlling their own population than in making revolutions in other countries. There is also a new, more relaxed view of how to handle underdeveloped societies. Guerrilla leaders are no longer seen in the simplistic terms of the Kennedy-Johnson era, when they were thought to be puppets on a long string from Moscow. (In the Truman Administration, it will be recalled, Mao was believed to be Stalin's agent.) The 2 billion people who live in Asia, Africa, and Latin America are not, Che Guevara and Lyndon Johnson notwithstanding, about to rise up and take America's wealth. They are hungry, divided, and vulnerable, and all the more so because the U.S.–Soviet détente makes it harder for small countries to play one giant off against another. Most Asian, African, and Latin American governments are in the hands of military dictatorships, rightist regimes, or technocratic modernizers, all eager for U.S. military aid, loans, and private capital, despite their growing insistence upon better terms. Many of the "unstable," "romantic" revolutionary leaders who used to upset Walt Rostow so much—Sukarno, Nasser, Nkrumah—are gone, replaced by men more willing to cooperate with the corporations.

Ideological purity and national pride, which were at the heart of the old Cold War strategies, are now seen in corporate boardrooms as carrying too high a price tag. "National differences should not be allowed to keep the people from doing whatever it is in their mutual interest to do," says Henry Ford II. "This is the basic philosophy behind the multinational corporations and the world will be better when this same philosophy gains wider acceptance in other aspects of human behavior." By mid-1973, U.S. and West European companies had entered into more than 1,200 cooperative agreements with state agencies of what in chillier days were known around Washington as "Bloc governments." Some take the form of "co-production," in which the Polish (or Hungarian or Soviet) government supplies the plant and the U.S. company supplies the equipment and know-how for the manufacture of goods destined primarily for the East European market. Singer, for example, operates a plant in Radom, Poland, to produce sewing machines under the Singer name for sale in the countries of Comecon (the Soviet version of the Common Market). The German-based global firm Siemens is producing X-ray machines in Hungary and buying telephone equipment from Bulgarian state-owned plants. East–West cooperative agreements take a wide variety of forms such as licensing, joint R&D programs, etc., all designed to accommodate the socialist doctrine of state ownership and the capitalist doctrine of private enrichment. Once it became obvious to top corporate managers that nothing short of a suicidal war would dislodge the Communist rulers in Moscow and Peking, it followed that peacemongering was good business.

But the most avid advocates of East–West trade are quite aware of the distinction between peacemongering and pacifism. They believe that U.S. military power still has a crucial role to play in promoting world stability, but they believe that this power must be exercised differently—more subtly and less expensively. As in a well-run town where the police are always there but not too much in evidence, the Global Shopping Center is kept at peace by a powerful, unobtrusive, and, where possible, multinational constabulary. Since Asian soldiers, according to Pentagon statistics, cost only one-fifteenth of what is spent on their American counterparts, and neither they nor their parents vote in U.S. elections, the use of "indigenous troops" around the world to keep order makes both fiscal and political sense. The Nixon Administration budget reflects this understanding. Vietnamization is now a worldwide policy. Local troops are hired with American tax dollars to carry out the police function once performed by U.S. soldiers.

Fighting wars by remote control is an essential component of the Nixon Doctrine. As Major General Ellis W. Williamson has put it, "We are trying to fight the enemy with our bullets instead of the bodies of our young men—firepower, not manpower." Thus highly sophisticated counterinsurgency equipment—magnetic detectors, surveillance radar, and seismic detectors—are furnished to "friendly" governments which increasingly are expected to do their own policing. (Corporations are using similar devices to solve some of their own security problems. The Wackenhut Corporation, for example, is offering its corporate clients an "electronic bloodhound.") The Nixon Doctrine, which has instituted a volunteer army to replace the draft, demands a new kind of soldier—professional, technologically trained, and unobtrusive. It emphasizes the discreet offshore presence of the Navy and the "quick fix" bombing operation which ensures that most of the corpses will be of a politically acceptable color. The disappearance of G.I. throngs from underdeveloped countries helps U.S.-based global corporations project their anational image. (It does little good for corporations to soft-pedal their own Americanism by such commonly recommended strategies as avoiding the local Hilton Hotel if there is a big military base around.) Official U.S. policy of buying the local military with prestigious equipment neatly dovetails with the corporation's own strategy of making local businessmen and politicians into good global citizens. Thus both business and diplomacy are conducted as joint ventures.

The vision of the Global Shopping Center is antigeopolitical. It transcends spheres of influence and elaborate power balancing. Yet it is by no means clear that this vision will prevail. The energy crisis, only the first and most visible of a series of resource crises that have begun to plague the industrialized world, portends a return to classic geopolitics in which industry will depend upon the military power of the state to ensure the uninterrupted supply of its lifeblood. After all, the entrepreneurs who ran the East India Company preferred to get along without the military power of the state, but in the end they had to engineer imperial wars to rescue them from political conflict that was beyond their power to master. In the Cold War years there was nothing much concrete to fight about; how close the world came to being reduced to radioactive rubble in the Cuban missile crisis we will never know, but that dubious battle was over such unmarketable commodities as honor and manhood.

If the Cold War was largely symbolic, the conflict shaping up today between the industrialized world and the Arab states, on the one hand, and among the industrialized states, on the other, is not. It is over a particular viscous substance on which nations have come to depend. In purely economic terms, as we shall see, the advantages all lie with the oil-producing states. Thus the temptation to introduce military power to shift that balance will obviously increase as the Arabs continue to demonstrate their bargaining power. The deterioration of petroleum diplomacy makes petroleum warfare more plausible. The U.S. Navy traditionally justifies its expanding budget before Congress by pointing out America's increasing dependence on foreign raw materials and the importance of "keeping the sea lanes open." Discussions of desert warfare in military journals are becoming almost as fashionable as handbooks of jungle warfare were ten years ago. (In 1972 a major military exercise took place in the Mojave Desert of California.) The oil-producing states take the threat of military action in the Middle East sufficiently seriously to discuss publicly plans for sabotage of the oil fields. (Militarily, the oil-rich lands of the Middle East are vulnerable, since their populations are sparse, but whether an occupation of the area would accomplish the objective of securing the oil for the United States is questionable.) The more the military dimension assumes importance in the global competition for resources, the stronger the power of the nation-state.

How do the military themselves regard the global corporations? Soldiers, whose raison d'être is the defense of territory, might be expected to be less than enthusiastic about the slogan "Down with Borders." Predictions of the early demise of the nation-state would, one might think, make generals and admirals nervous, since no other likely employers appear on the horizon. Nonetheless, the National War College Strategic Research Group has done a study which concludes that "the phenomenon of growing multinational enterprise, preponderately American, can play a major role in improving our overall political, military, and economic strength. . . ." The author of the study, Air Force Lieutenant Colonel Richard A. Bowen, thinks that there are certain strategic problems raised by global corporations, such as "the possibility of yielding weapons-oriented technology to the enemy and fear of diminishing industrial self-sufficiency." (Richard Helms, former CIA director, told us these were major security problems of the 1970's.) Nevertheless, the National War College study concludes that the global corporation is a tremendous force for building "the economic strength of the Free World." The National War College study proposes an "indirect" national-security strategy which sees the ultimate protection of the people and territory of the United States being achieved through the "proliferation of the American system of values and way of life":

> If we wish our values and life styles to prevail, we are obliged to compete with other culture and power centers. Multinational enterprise offers a tremendous lever to this end. Its growing arsenal of foreign-based business operations is working for us around the clock. Its osmotic action transmits and transfuses not only American methods of business operation, banking and marketing techniques; but our legal systems and concepts, our political philosophies, our ways of communicating and ideas of mobility, and a measure of the humanities and arts peculiar to our civilization.

The National War College study sees global corporations as national assets which "in periods of crisis and armed conflict" would be "committed in conjunction with other elements of national and allied power . . . to weaken the enemy by denying it resources and disrupting its external commercial and industrial assets and operations." This is, of course, a much more traditional way in Washington of looking at U.S. corporations abroad—as extensions of the national security establishment, rather than as ex-

pressions of the American zeitgeist—and it is precisely this outlook which makes countries that play host to global corporations
so apprehensive. During the Cold War, intelligence agencies have
regularly used U.S. foreign business operations as an intelligence
cover. Indeed, the CIA has a special office that does nothing but
maintain contact with corporations overseas. This office is responsible for the placing of agents on corporation payrolls, frequently
without the knowledge of top management. Continental Airlines'
operation of Air America in Laos and Flying Tigers operations
in the Pacific are two examples of business–government collaboration in the field of military intelligence.

In the last few years there have been many instances of the
U.S. Government's using global corporations to advance national
policy. Jack N. Behrman, who used to be Assistant Secretary of
Commerce, contends that global-corporation executives "will generally comply with mere requests of high government officials,
even when not backed up by statute, to prevent affiliates (even
minority owned) from undertaking transactions not consistent
with U.S. policy." Edith Penrose in her study of the international
oil industry says the United States has used the oil companies "to
bring economic pressure to achieve political ends" and gives as
one example Caltex's refusal to supply lubricating oil to a British
ship in a Japanese port "because the ship was on a time charter
to the Russians and was carrying Cuban sugar to Siberia." As
global companies expand their business with the Communist
world and as more and more of their assets become hostages to
host countries, such economic-warfare activities of global corporations are likely to decline. The World Managers have lobbied
hard to persuade the United States to change its strategies so that
the competing loyalties of the corporation will not be put to the
test. Conflict between the U.S. Government and global corporations over the sale of strategic goods may soon be only a Cold
War memory. But if the U.S. Government should revert to its
earlier economic-warfare policies, it is doubtful that it would get
anything like the compliance it received from the companies when
anti-Communism was still part of the business creed.

6

But if companies will not always do the government's bidding,
they are increasingly insistent that it do theirs. Government sup-

port for private business abroad, while perhaps not so close or aggressive as the Japanese Government's worldwide campaign in behalf of Japanese corporations, is an increasingly important factor in the expansion of U.S.-based global firms. It was strong official pressure from Washington that persuaded the Japanese to come to a "gentlemen's agreement" to "voluntarily" restrict steel exports to the United States at a time when the domestic steel industry was in serious trouble. Similarly, it took White House intervention to force the Japanese to accept a joint Texas Instrument–Sony 50–50 venture in Japan. The weaker the country that dares to stand in the path of a U.S.-based global corporation, the more likely the country is to hear from the Treasury Department or the White House and the more effective such pressure is likely to be. Michael Tanzer has recounted how the U.S. Government in 1965–1966 put pressure on the Indian Government to allow more scope for U.S. private enterprise in the fertilizer industry.

Not only is the might of the U.S. Government used to help U.S.-based global companies to get into foreign markets that are not always so happy to receive them; it is also used to protect American assets abroad once they are acquired. Under the Hickenlooper Amendment, passed in the Eisenhower Administration, the President is forbidden to send foreign aid to any country that nationalizes U.S. private property without paying what its owners or the State Department consider adequate compensation. (The provision was invoked against Ceylon in 1962 for nationalizing 63 gas stations belonging to Esso and Caltex.) More recently, global corporations have been attacking the Hickenlooper Amendment for being "too rigid" and "unusable." However, a Congressional mandate against giving loans to any country that nationalizes U.S. property was passed. All this suggests that when global-corporation executives, such as Philippe W. Newton of TRW (formerly Thompson Ramo Woolrich, a leading defense contractor), warn of "clash over matters of national interest, sovereignty, and policies" between nation-states and corporations, they must have something in mind other than the relationship of General Motors and the Nixon Administration. President Nixon once told Congress that he considers the global corporations an "instrument" for achieving "world prosperity" and proposed legislation that would substantially protect the interests of the established giants.

Yet in practical, specific ways, the growing power of a few global corporations is eroding traditional prerogatives of the most powerful nation-state. In Part III we shall be showing how corporate strategies interfere with the government's ability to manage the U.S. economy for stability—in particular, how they complicate the maintenance of full employment and an expanding tax base, the control of inflation and pollution, and the limitation of economic concentration and oligopoly. The conflict between the managers of global corporations and the managers of the U.S. Government is certain to grow as more and more crucial decisions about what the United States is going to look like in the twenty-first century pass into the private hands of business enterprises which proclaim themselves to be supranational and post-American.

5

The Great Crusade for Understanding

1

In February 1973, about 150 top executives of global corporations gathered at the Mayflower Hotel in Washington to talk about their image and what to do about it. The meeting was a part of what President Philippe W. Newton of TRW calls the "tremendous counter-effort by the business community" to turn back the growing attack on the Global Shopping Center. William R. Pollert, vice-president for international economic affairs of the National Association of Manufacturers, outlined for the assembled executives a "grass-roots" campaign for a "coordinated attack" on the enemies of the global corporation, chief among whom are the Congressional and labor supporters of the Hartke-Burke bill. The National Association of Manufacturers, he revealed, has set up a computerized system for getting company views to the right people at the right time. A computerized mailing list of 14,000 plants of the biggest 100 U.S.-based global corporations (soon to be expanded to the biggest 500), divided according to Congressional districts, has been prepared in the NAM headquarters. When an issue such as Hartke-Burke or the Clean Air Bill comes up, automatic contact is made with executives of companies with plants in the districts of those Congressmen who are "on the fence" or "need something." This "Legislative Coordinator List," Pollert reported, has already "generated" 1,800 letters on Hartke-Burke and deserves credit for the defeat of a bill that would have forbidden the use of federal funds to purchase goods manufactured with foreign labor.

The NAM strategy calls for increasing use of local plant man-

agers as propagandists in the local community because, as Pollert observed, local people will believe them before they believe
the NAM. "We at the NAM," he assured the executives, have
"great quotes for you to use," but each corporation must "cus-
tomize" the material for its own special audiences. In particular,
Pollert stressed, "we need to get something out for the ladies."
Workers can be reached by pamphlets without the NAM label
"so you can sneak them in." Widows, pensioners, and college en-
dowment administrators should be given the benefit of a recent
NAM study which "shows" that if the Hartke-Burke bill should
pass, the stock prices of 83 corporations would immediately plum-
met by $10 billion. On college campuses it is peace that "really
sells today." (A speech by Harry Heltzer, chief executive of 3M,
calling businessmen "the real radicals" and "peacemongers" was
distributed in a packet of materials prepared by this company
which all were invited to use.) "So we have a job of communicating to do," Heltzer concludes. "We must address ourselves to
the anti-business sentiment that exists in our society. In so doing
we should reach employees, school teachers, law makers, jour-
nalists, college professors, our own children—anyone who will
listen and support our cause in the voting booth.

The well-financed "crusade for understanding" employs three
time-honored public relations techniques. The first is to package
an irresistible vision. Thus public relations departments are portraying the Global Corporation in such terms that only devotees
of unemployment, depressions, and wars could be against it. The
World Managers' vision of One World inspired by the business
gospel of peace and plenty is being systematically promoted in
corporate speeches, industry studies, and planted cartoons and
editorials. (The NAM now distributes cartoons and editorials on
issues affecting global corporations to every newspaper in the
country.) Multinational corporations, Harry Heltzer says, are a
"powerful force for peace" because "their allegiance is not to any
nation, tongue, race, or creed, but to one of the finer aspirations
of mankind that the people of the world may be united in common economic purpose." Those who oppose the free movement
of capital, goods, and technology, he likes to say, exhibit a "Stop
the world, I want to get off" attitude. "Customized" versions of
the same sentiments (with most of the same words) can be found

in literally scores of speeches, editorials, and company statements by Mr. Heltzer's colleagues.

The second technique involves the merchandising of fear. The NAM booklet on "tax manipulation" is aimed at convincing American workers that the removal of tax incentives favoring foreign investment in the Internal Revenue Code, which organized labor is demanding, would "jeopardize your income, the welfare of your family, and America's economic status. . . . It's tax suicide." The World Managers like to characterize the issues surrounding global corporations as protectionism vs. free trade. (A standard theme is that as in the 1930's, protectionism will precipitate another Great Depression.) The attacks on the global corporations raise what Harry Heltzer calls "a hard cash issue" which "threatens the pay . . . and dividends" of employees and stockholders. (Caterpillar Tractor distributes a booklet called "Multinational Corporations and Your Paycheck.") In an era when political appeals based on fear appear to be more successful than campaigns based on unredeemable promises, the global corporations in mounting their counterattack are focusing public attention less on the Heavenly City and more on the Hell that will materialize if their plans are disrupted: trade wars, unemployment, depressions, stock-market crashes, nationalist rivalry, and armed conflict.

The third technique is also borrowed from politics. It is seldom necessary to make a devastating case against an idea if you can suggest that its principal protagonist has a hidden agenda. James Roche, former head of GM, for example, told *Newsweek* he indeed sees a conspiracy "on the part of some people" to bring about ". . . changes so radical that they would all but destroy free enterprise as we know it." The Chief Executives Roundtable in 1971 noted as one of its conclusions that the U.N. Economic Commission for Latin America (ECLA), "under the orientation given to it by its first head, Raúl Prebisch, has churned out nationalists." The executives fixed their gaze on other subversive figures. "The Latin American objective of economic independence," they noted, is also "fueled and encouraged by several US professors" who are "responsible for the creation of new impediments to the multinational corporation," such as "the fade-out formula," a proposal by such respected economists as Paul

Rosenstein-Rodan of MIT and Albert O. Hirschman of Harvard for gradual divestment of foreign investment in underdeveloped countries in favor of local ownership. "Tons of propaganda and academic reports" are being circulated "against private enterprise and foreign investment" by such professors which must "be counteracted." Donald Kendall, president of Pepsico (formerly Pepsi-Cola), sees something sinister in the recent flurry of attacks on advertising. Since advertising is becoming "more responsible"— he points out that not even the Coca-Cola Company, which a generation ago could claim that Coke was good for headaches, would today indulge in such huckstering—the attack on Madison Avenue is a disguised assault on "our whole system."

The "tremendous counter-effort of the business community" is a response to gathering public skepticism about what business spokesmen now regularly call "the social responsibility of corporations." In 1946 businessmen ranked second only to religious leaders in public-opinion polls as "the group that was doing the most for the country." A generation later Americans had learned a good deal more about pollution, the marketing of watered hot dogs and empty breakfast cereals, fictitious warranties, usurious "service charges," brutal employment practices, corporate support of South Africa, and other image-tarnishing activities. Ralph Nader had disturbed the American love affair with the automobile by demonstrating that the family car was a dangerous mistress. Dow Chemical Company, hounded on a hundred campuses, dropped its napalm contract. Corporations such as Gulf Oil, General Motors, and Polaroid were subject to public pressure and boycotts, largely abortive, for their activities in southern Africa. By and large, the companies have beaten back efforts such as Project GM to force major corporations to change profitable policies for social—i.e., noneconomic—reasons. Henry Ford, for example, takes a tough line on such matters. Pressed for a comment on the efforts of the Episcopal Church to get GM to leave South Africa, he replied, apparently without benefit of public relations counsel, that he didn't think "it's any of their goddam business . . . how South Africans run themselves." While fully 30 percent of all corporate annual reports in 1970 included discussions of what the companies were doing for humanity, and men like Du Pont's President C. B. McCoy think that business should argue with its critics less and confide in them more, America's leading corporate executives who make up the Business Council appear to prefer the hard sell. Thus they applauded warmly when Commerce Secretary Maurice Stans at their annual get-together in Hot Springs, Virginia, proclaimed: "Business is more than 99.44 percent pure. That is the percentage of transactions that bring full satisfaction to the buyer."

The gathering movement from consumer and church groups seeking to make business socially responsible was not originally aimed at global corporations as such. Its target was big business, the 500 largest U.S. companies, which in 1968 had 64 percent of all industrial sales and 74 percent of all profits in the most mammoth economy in the history of the world. These are, in fact, the global companies. Thus corporate public relations departments now realize that the most recent publicity on issues peculiar to operations abroad—export of jobs, interference in foreign policy, currency manipulation—are going to provide new ammunition to anticorporate groups. Noting that "the image of industry continues to deteriorate," Hale Nelson, vice-president for public relations of the Illinois Bell Telephone Company, told the Foundation for Public Relations Research in 1972 that business is in a "new game" that is being "played for keeps—and its name is Survival."

Ordinary citizens are not the only target of the Great Crusade. The global corporations are dramatically increasing their lobbying activities in Washington. A 1972 *Business Week* survey reveals that in response to anticorporate criticism and consumer and pollution legislation, the big companies are seeking to exert their influence in Washington as never before. According to the estimates of Professor Jimmy D. Johnson of American University, about 80 percent of the largest 1,000 companies have a "Director of Washington Services," as Kennecott calls its lobbyist, or else employ law firms, public relations agencies, and full-time "consultants" to do the same thing. (A full-time lobbyist's office can cost as much as $200,000 a year.)

The most celebrated activities of lobbyists concern the spreading of money. ITT, which does not hesitate to go to the top when it wants something, let the Nixon Administration know that there was $400,000 for the campaign if the Administration would be sensible about its antitrust policies toward the company. Taking no chances, Harold Geneen also intervened personally, as

Business Week reports, with "at least three Cabinet members, at least as many key White House aides, and a platoon of influential Congressmen and Senators" to complain about the "serious consequences" an antitrust prosecution could have.

The World Managers are becoming much less defensive about their lobbying activities. Harold Geneen told the Senate subcommittee on multinational corporations looking into ITT's activities in Chile that all citizens, including corporation presidents, have a Constitutional right to petition the government—including the CIA—for a redress of grievances. More and more top executives are themselves engaging in lobbying. General Motors Chairman Richard C. Gerstenberg, for example, is frequently in Washington testifying before Congress and, as *Business Week* delicately phrases it, testing the "political weather." Lee A. Iacocca, president of Ford, seemed genuinely hurt by the unflattering press he received when he arrived in the capital to lobby (unsuccessfully) against the Clean Air Bill.

2

What is the object of all these high-powered efforts at persuasion? What do World Managers want from the public and from the government? Most lobbying and propaganda campaigns are on issues that directly affect the companies' balance sheets. Soap companies do not want antiphosphate laws. (President Nixon's aide Bryce Harlow, later Procter & Gamble's vice-president for government relations, Ralph Nader charges, was responsible for getting the Nixon Administration to change its official attitude on phosphates almost overnight.) Steel companies want restrictions on imports. Automobile companies want to postpone compliance with federal antipollution standards. All global corporations want to kill the Hartke-Burke bill, although, as we shall see, some would favor a different sort of protectionist legislation.

Beyond these specific fights, the World Managers have larger, but vaguer, visions of the kind of world they would like to see. Much of what they call their "educational effort" is devoted to these visions. Calling themselves radicals, they see the need for a series of reformations to make possible the peaceful transition to a global economy: a reformation in public attitudes, a reformation in national political structures, and a reformation of the ground rules under which global business is conducted.

We have already talked about the kind of public attitudes the global corporations would like to encourage—more corporate loyalty, more product loyalty, and less national loyalty. In short, they want to build a faith that the corporation is the principal engine of progress and peace. It is standard rhetoric that the existing political structures are obsolete, but the alternative political vision is rather murky. Like most reformers, they know better what they are against than what they are for. Nonetheless, by reading enough speeches, testimony, and interviews it is possible to catch a fleeting glimpse of the new America that the World Managers would like to see.

When the United States is fully integrated into the Global Shopping Center, the Federal Government will limit its interventions into society to those tasks which are beyond the capacity of businessmen. Confident that the automatic processes of the market, provided these are regularly oiled with the latest managerial techniques, can solve most of the problems of the poor countries as well as the rich ones, the World Managers nevertheless see an expanding role for government. James P. McFarland, chairman of General Mills, talking about "The Corporation in 1990" at a White House Conference in 1972, echoed an increasingly familiar theme among businessmen: a call for "a genuine government–business partnership." In 1990, "government and business and labor—and in fact all elements of society—should be sitting down to plan the future, to establish national priorities and to agree upon objectives and strategy." The managerial task, says McFarland, is "the development of a national climate that will allow the orderly transition to a corporate structure able to meet tomorrow's challenge."

Since the corporation is the primary engine of development, the primary function of government is to enable the corporation to fulfill its promise. In the corporate vision of 1990, government no longer plays its traditional role under the Constitution. It is no longer the expression of national consensus—which, indeed, is worked out by means of a government–corporation–labor partnership.

The real job of government is to perform certain services

essential to the development of a good business climate. Most important is the management of the economy. It is the function of government to stabilize the economy—to stimulate or to cool the economy as needed whenever the natural regulating mechanisms of the market fail to work (which seems to be much of the time). The Federal Government, always in partnership with business, should control interest rates and other credit policy. When necessary, it should impose price controls and wage controls. All of us "will be asked to give up some of the prerogatives we have taken for granted," says McFarland. Government will continue to act as a pump primer of capital into the economy, through either the military budget or social programs. (At present the Department of Defense finances over one-half of all research-and-development costs in the U.S., including 90 percent of that done in the aviation and space industries.)

The second essential service is to develop the needed infrastructure for a global economy. In addition to the usual infrastructure expenses such as highways, harbors, communications networks, and shipping are environmental expenses. A constant theme in World Managers' speeches is that the government should pick up the cost not only of decontaminating the nation's already polluted air, rivers, and lakes but also of converting the industrial process so that the rate of new pollution will be slowed. Similarly, the cost of safety measures for consumers and workers should be subsidized with public money.

Government has a third function to play in smoothing the extraordinary transformation that global corporations are bringing about in the U.S. economy. Since economic logic argues for the relocation of U.S. production overseas, it is the task of government to subsidize, retrain, or move workers who are displaced in the process. Similarly, government should not try to protect inefficient noncompetitive industries such as shoes or textiles which cannot survive in a world without borders, but should rather assist them to become more competitive, or help reallocate their resources into new industries.

The nation-state has a crucial role in bringing about the world without borders. Only governments can abolish restrictions on the movement of goods and capital and make use of economic weapons such as quotas, tariffs, and taxes to ensure favorable treatment of U.S.-based global corporations in other countries.

Thus it is the increasingly complex task of government to pursue an aggressive (and often contradictory) foreign economic policy making use of both liberalization and protectionism. Only a centralized government in which the president enjoys great discretion to employ one or the other policy can play such a delicate balancing role. Thus an important part of the new managerial vision of the new America is a stronger centralized Executive and a relatively weaker Congress.

Finally, the task of government is to be an educator and promoter of values and certain forms of institutional change. McFarland foresees a "dramatically different" employer–employee relationship in 1990: more social pressure on corporations to expand services and benefits to employees along the paternalistic model of Japanese industry—day-care centers, corporate sabbaticals, etc. But all this must take place within the context of the private-profit system. Government must expand its priestly function as guardian of the ideology of the private-enterprise system. "The kind of structure we will have in 1990," McFarland concludes, "depends in good measure upon our ability between now and then to redefine capitalism in a manner which is understood and believed."

3

A clearer picture of the sort of political reformation global corporations have in mind can be gleaned from a recent piece of contract futurology on making Paris a "global city," prepared for a French Government planning agency by Howard V. Perlmutter and Hasan Ozbekhan of the Wharton School of Finance Worldwide Institutions Program. Professor Perlmutter, a consultant to a number of global corporations, was presumably being paid for his knowledge of the needs and preferences of the global corporations. Thus while his "Scenario A," which describes the "necessary infrastructures if Paris is to fulfill its vocation as a World Center," undoubtedly represents more advanced thinking than is typically done in corporate boardrooms, it is indicative of a direction which many executives themselves find congenial. He begins by pointing out that ". . . those cities that understand what infrastructures are needed . . . as the Global Industrial System (GIS) evolves . . . will become the 'global cities' of the 1980's." To become a global city, Paris must undergo a process of "denationalization" and "become less French." This requires a "psycho-cultural (or attitudinal) change of image . . . with respect to the traditional impression of 'xenophobia' that the French seem to exude." As this cannot be done directly, it is felt that it might be achieved by greater exposure of the population to other cultures, other languages, other ways of doing things and ways of being right. Perlmutter, a professor of social architecture, advocates "the globalization of cultural events," such as supranational rock festivals, as an antidote to "overly national and sometimes nationalistic" culture.

The most radical recommendation is that Paris cease to be the capital of France. Continuing its present role would make the city too "ethnocentric" to be a Global City. Orléans is to be the new "administrative capital of the French space." The "highest levels of the French government remain in Paris" (i.e., external and fiscal functions), but the administrative structure is moved elsewhere. Thus "the structure, outlook, and influence of the French government is *global* rather than purely French" and involves "responsibilities which clearly transcend the traditional French space."

In the Global City no one is a foreigner. Non-French executives of global corporations living in Paris should be able to vote for a Council of Paris and even be elected to membership. The Global City would, of course, have all the necessary infrastructure— deluxe hotels, conference centers, a telecommunications network much better than Paris' present notorious telephone system, a University of the World, and a "financial center." The reformed Paris would feature two types of living arrangements for global executives. One would be located in the heart of the city to cater to those executives "concerned with culture, entertainment, urban vitality," while the other would be for the more "family-oriented." It would be in a country setting featuring good air, trees, silence, good schools, and "stress-reducing facilities for culture-shock cases." Paris, the authors conclude, can become a "vital locus of planetized consciousness."

A prime target in the campaign to reform political institutions is the university. In the United States, under the stimulus of the Vietnam War some campuses became centers of radical questioning of some of the basic assumptions of America's business-oriented culture. Here too were centers of anticorporate demonstrations and propaganda, dramatic testimony in the era of growing government-business partnership that the university is the last remaining respectable institution with a degree of independence. Indeed, the original campus revolt of the 1960's, the Berkeley Free Speech Movement, was in important measure a reaction to Clark Kerr's vision of the "multiversity," which the students saw as a servant university for a totally integrated corporate society. It is precisely this tradition of independence in the academy that now worries some executives, for they see the university as the institution spawning, protecting, and advancing the countercorporate culture. (It was hardly reassuring when Harvard University under pressure voted its GM stock on the South Africa question in accordance with the recommendations of Ralph Nader rather than those of James Roche.)

As Thorstein Veblen demonstrated many years ago, universities that depend upon private capital for their survival are dependent upon capitalists. True, there are examples of a few conservative philanthropists showering money on academic centers that employ radicals and critics. Some businessmen have deeply believed the American ideology of free speech and free inquiry. But in moments of crisis, business liberalism tends to become shaky. During the "Red scare" of the 1920's and the Cold War of the 1950's, moneygivers, business alumni, and trustees, as might be expected, exerted their influence in such a way as to make the university conform to the prevailing mood and mores of the country.

The worldwide student revolution that reached its peak in 1968 with spontaneous, unrelated, but remarkably similar protests in the United States, France, Germany, and Mexico was a source of great anxiety for the World Managers. Since the crucial factors in the success of the Global Factory and the Global Shopping Center are technology and managerial skill, and universities are the traditional suppliers of both, the politicization of the university is a potentially serious threat to their global vision.

In some underdeveloped countries, particularly in parts of Latin America, the university has been the center of the two ideologies that most complicate the life of global corporations there: nationalism and socialism. Universities have a certain tradition of independence from and antagonism to the local government, and vocal expressions of hostility to all forms of "*yanqui* imperialism" are standard. In Mexico, for example, foreign companies are worried that university disorders, which represent virtually the only organized political dissent in the country, might spark a wider revolutionary response. (The government, it is generally believed, blocked the extension of Mexico City's superb subway to the university for fear that the students would attempt to paralyze the system.)

Thus foreign companies are openly counterattacking against politicized universities and politically unpalatable professors. In February 1970, for example, the new British university at Warwick, whose vice-chancellor, J. B. Butterworth, boasted "that he would create a university tailored to the needs of an industrial society," received a confidential report from the director of legal affairs of the Rootes Organization, Chrysler's British subsidiary, on the political activities of a visiting American professor named Montgomery. In Mexico the rector of the University of Querétaro, Hugo Gutiérrez, was summarily dismissed in 1965 two months after an exchange with the local manager of Coca-Cola and head of the chamber of commerce, who wanted a certain professor dispatched on a prolonged research trip because he had "funny ideas." The rector, an ex-actor, replied that he was concerned about the "funny ideas" of the Coca-Cola public relations department, but no one saw the humor, and the governor of the state fired him. (The rector had also encouraged a university study entitled "Who Owns Querétaro?" which did nothing to enhance his popularity with local politicians, U.S. corporations, or the Catholic Church.)

But most corporate influence on universities is exerted in more civilized ways. Hugh Stephenson of the London *Times* has given an interesting description of the University of Warwick, which has a Barclay's Bank Chair of Management Information Systems, a Volkswagen Chair of German, and a British Leyland Motors–endowed Chair of Industrial Relations. The university has done research on metal fatigue of direct interest to Massey-Ferguson, on tire fatigue of interest to Dunlop, and on vehicle instrumentation of interest to Chrysler. (The chief executive of British Chrysler is on the university's governing board.) The University Council in 1968 hired a firm of industrial consultants to make the university more efficient. (One of the recommendations was that since university democracy was "an amorphous and time-wasting system" the university would have to "come to terms with the age-old conflict between democratic principles and effective government. . . .")

Admittedly, the University of Warwick is not a typical university. But in many countries where they have operations the World Managers are seeking to exert influence on more traditional centers of learning. In Querétaro University, for example, according to Hugo Gutiérrez, Purina, Singer, Kellogg, Carnation and other companies each contributed less than $5,000 a year in the mid-1960's, for which they had a crucial voice in university policy. Elsewhere in Mexico, private universities, such as the University of the Americas and Anahuac University, have received important gifts from U.S. companies. Chase Manhattan donated the Anahuac Law School. Eastman Kodak has given a laboratory to the same institution. The advantages to the global corporations are rather clear. Not only do they buy a certain amount of local goodwill and show "social responsibility," but they also help ensure the development of nonideological, technically oriented centers of learning where research of interest to the companies can be done and an apolitical, value-free, nonactivist, achievement-oriented student body can be trained.

The model for such universities is now being developed by a variety of corporate planners and consultants. Howard Perlmutter, for example, is designing a University of the World, which, he says, is an "essential" component of the Global Shopping Center. It would develop a global outlook and would provide a uniform worldwide curriculum for the children of the World Managers. (This sort of service appears essential for the growing army of footloose executives. The manager of Nestlé's U.S. operations, a Swiss citizen, recently returned to Switzerland to take over as a world director of the company only to discover that his son could not get into a Swiss university because none would give him credit for his work in a New York high school.) In Professor Perlmutter's scenario on how to make the French capital a "global city," he proposes establishing there "a truly nonnational learning center . . . whose main purpose would be research, learning and teaching in how to develop global resources—industrial, commercial, agricultural, social, and cultural."

The University of the World is to be supranational, technical, and practical. "The U of W becomes an active partner in, and an

innovative contributor to, the work of the 'real' world," Professors
Perlmutter and Ozbekhan advise their Parisian clients. Students,
for example, will have "on the job" training in such important
academic pursuits as police work. The following is a complete
list of proposed departments for the University of the World:

HEALTH	ENVIRONMENTAL ECONOMICS
POPULATION CONTROL	WASTE DISPOSAL
EDUCATION	COMMERCE-INDUSTRY
CRIMINOLOGY	AGRICULTURE
LAW ENFORCEMENT	MINING
FIRE PROTECTION	LOCAL AND STATE GOVERNMENT
ECOLOGY	ADMINISTRATION

The political implications of a world curriculum that could be
disseminated by television in every country are obvious. The
power, authority, and prestige of national universities would be
undercut. Who would not rather stay at home by the TV and get
an MIT diploma, an elite passport to the outside world, than
study his own national traditions and local problems at, say, the
University of Nairobi? The global-university curriculum would
be geared to the needs of the "real world"—i.e., the emerging
Global Shopping Center. Criticism of the underlying values and
assumptions of the society would be muted. Doubt, searching for
alternative visions, and other inefficient intellectual activities
would be discouraged. (Perlmutter and Ozbekhan see the "ideological turmoil" of the present Paris educational system as creating "a real diffusion as to the intellectual direction of instruc-
tion.") A long-range strategist for a major U.S.-based electronics
company is advising the Brazilian Minister of Education on how
to make the University of São Paulo "less liberal in an emotional
sense" and "more responsive to the needs of industry." (He received a call from the Minister during our interview.) In short,
the worldwide educational reformation envisaged by the World
Managers is designed to integrate and rationalize the global production of commercially useful knowledge.

4

The heart of the legitimacy problem for the global corporation
is the clash between global corporate loyalty and national law.

Wherever global corporations encounter image crises, some local law or custom has usually been violated, at least in spirit, whether it be tax laws, currency-control laws, or some important tradition; e.g., the State Department, not ITT, is supposed to set foreign policy. It is evident that governments are losing control over important international transactions and that nominally private organizations are gaining control over such transactions. The ancient political question By What Right? keeps plaguing the global corporations as they become more assertive in acting like states. Their justification for their power, as we have seen, is efficiency; "We can deliver" is their political slogan.

But the World Managers know that neither slogans nor "education campaigns" are enough to legitimize the exercise of political power. Authority must be sanctified by law. Thus men like George Ball have been talking for many years about international chartering of global corporations by some world organization. (While some World Managers have speculated about the United Nations' playing such a role, and the thought of being regulated by an U Thant or some other mild international civil servant with a modest budget has certain attractions, most global corporations are not enthusiastic about the United Nations as the source of international corporate authority because of the large representation of underdeveloped countries which are "lacking in business experience." They would rather have organizations dominated by industrial countries, such as the Organization for Economic Co-operation and Development, do the regulating.) Jacques Maison-rouge wants an international governmental counterpart to the global corporation, a tripartite entity made up of labor, government, and company representation, which would set the new ground rules under which the companies would operate. The International Chamber of Commerce has proposed the adoption of international guidelines for regulation of the behavior of corporations and governments, and the Atlantic Institute, among others, sees a possible solution to the legitimacy problem in a "code of good behavior" to which all World Managers would faithfully subscribe.

David Rockefeller believes that the reformation must include the global corporations themselves. Stock ownership must become more truly multinational. Profit-sharing schemes and other incentives to give a "stake" in global enterprises to foreign workers should be expanded. Corporate executives should do more self-examination to determine whether they are really being as "socially responsible" as they should be. Corporations should take steps to "remove the air of mystery which sometimes surrounds them," advises the Atlantic Institute. Other executives have put it more bluntly. Corporations have a reputation for secretiveness which does nothing to build public confidence. (The reputation is understandable, since corporations spend millions of dollars in legal fees each year to keep what they regard as their business—i.e., how much money they are really making—from the prying eyes of labor unions, consumer groups, minority shareholders, and the Internal Revenue Service.)

The World Managers who are orchestrating the Great Crusade bear little resemblance in style to the entrepreneur of fifty years ago. Gone is the "Public Be Damned" arrogance of the Vanderbilts and the other robber barons. In its place is a liberal vision of a world corporate society promising peace and abundance. Behind the advertising and public relations compaigns is genuine ideological fervor—and creeping doubts. The World Managers, at least the ones with whom we have talked, believe that they have as good an answer to the problems of mankind as anyone. At the same time, they sense that convincing the world of this is a staggering task. Yet every failure of government, from torture in Brazil to Soviet anti-Semitism to the Watergate scandal, strengthens their conviction that they have a historic mandate to create a postpolitical world order.

The remainder of this book is an evaluation of the World Managers' global vision, based not on their motives but on their record of performance in rich countries and poor. It is on that emerging record that their quest for legitimacy depends.

PART

If the world were a global village of 100 people, 70 of them would be unable to read, and only one would have a college education. Over 50 would be suffering from malnutrition, and over 80 would live in what we call substandard housing.

If the world were a global village of 100 residents 6 of them would be Americans. These 6 would have half the village's entire income; and the other 94 would exist on the other half.

How would the wealthy 6 live "in peace" with their neighbors? Surely they would be driven to arm themselves against the other 94 . . . perhaps even to spend, as we do, more per person on military defense than the total per person income of the others.

—*Fellowship* magazine (of the Fellowship
of Reconciliation), February 1974

6

The Global Corporations and the
Underdeveloped World

1

"The only difference between the philosophical seers of literature and the pragmatic prophets of industry," E. M. de Windt, chairman of the Eaton Corporation, noted a few years ago, "is that men like Ford and Sloan can—and did—make things happen." The 1970's, he argued, is the decade of decision when businessmen must make their global vision prevail. "The World Company, owned, managed, and operated without regard to the physical, political, and philosophical boundaries of nationalism," the world's leading locksmith declared, "can well become a reality in this century . . . if we make things happen, if we look at the entire world as a market, and as a factory site, if we count customers before we count populations . . . if we structure world business to satisfy the needs and demands of the world's people, then business can, and will, become the moving force for world progress, and free enterprise will bring healthier, happier, and more productive lives to people everywhere. . . . By the end of this decade of decisions . . . business could have a bright global look."

The ultimate test of the World Managers' global vision of peace and abundance is the underdeveloped world. "By any quantitative measure the post–World War II era has been the most sucessful in international economic history," proclaims the 1973 International Economic Report of President Nixon. But not for the poor, who, as World Bank President Robert McNamara puts it, "remain entrapped in conditions of deprivation which fall below any rational definition of human decency." Two hundred million persons in India attempt subsistence on incomes that average less than $40 a year. Two-thirds of the people of the underdeveloped world—1.3 billion—are farmers, but some 900 million of them earn less than $100 a year. "We are talking about hundreds of millions of desperately poor people throughout the whole of the developing world," McNamara concludes. "We are talking about 40 percent of entire populations. Development is simply not reaching them in any decisive degree."

For the World Managers the underdeveloped world is the supreme management problem. To promote a global vision which bypasses those parts of the planet in which most of its population lives, where the problems of survival are the starkest, and where political explosions are everyday occurrences is beyond the capacity of even the most accomplished masters of oversell. A Global Shopping Center in which 40 to 50 percent of the potential customers are living at the edge of starvation without electricity, plumbing, drinkable water, medical care, schools, or jobs is not a marketable vision. In their bid for managerial power on a global scale, the men who run the global corporations must demonstrate that they have answers to the problems of world poverty.

As the development crisis outlined by McNamara and others becomes more obvious, the World Managers' claims that they have such answers are being increasingly questioned. A by-product of the development crisis is a crisis of confidence in the capacity of the global corporation to manage the world economy in the interests of those who are neither its stockholders nor its employees. The problem of world poverty now looks less susceptible to "businesslike solutions" than the experts of the 1960's led one to believe. As the head of the American Chamber of Commerce of Mexico put it recently, there is a "growing antipathy" toward big business from those who are yet to be convinced of its "contribution" to development. (In Mexico, as in the United States, the response is an "education campaign.")

The increasing use of "monkey-wrench politics" has further helped erode confidence in the capacity of global businessmen to manage politically explosive terrain. Thus the vulnerability of the corporate giant is suddenly dramatized when Firestone and Fiat executives are kidnapped in Argentina, and every top manager in politically unstable areas of the world must worry about his personal safety. (King Feisal of Saudi Arabia recently expressed his concern that by concluding an oil contract with a U.S.-based global firm he was risking raids on his territory from Palestinian guerrillas.) Thus the claim that the world company "will bring healthier, happier, and more productive lives to people everywhere" is becoming increasingly important in establishing its legitimacy, but it is becoming more of a challenge to establish such a claim.

But the underdeveloped world is more of a managerial challenge than a mere political marketing problem. The resources of the poor nations, including the raw materials on and under their territory, cheap labor represented by their teeming populations, and the potential customers represented by their expanding middle classes are, as we shall see, increasingly crucial to the plans of the global corporation. Incredible as it may seem, the poor countries have been an indispensable source of finance capital for the worldwide expansion of global corporations. How this system of welfare in reverse works will be a major concern of this chapter and the next.

Perhaps the best way to grasp the importance of poor countries to the economy of the United States and to the growth of global corporations is to assemble in one place some statistics that managers of corporate expansion and managers of the U.S. Government both need to know. What the corporate manager wants to know about underdeveloped countries is this:

What vital raw materials do they have and how dependent is he on them?

What kind of labor force do they possess, and for what wages will they work?

How many customers are there (now and in the future) with money to buy his goods?

The government manager is of course interested in many of the same questions, but from a different perspective. The country which corporate presidents eye as a cheap source of, say, tungsten, needed to make a particular product, the Pentagon regards for that very reason as a vital link in the national security system and the Commerce Department sees as indispensable to the maintenance of the U.S. economy. When corporate executives view particular countries as sources of profits and finance-capital, politicians see them as contributors to the U.S. balance of payments.

Present and Projected Importance of the Underdeveloped World to the U.S. Economy and Its Global Corporations *

I. INCREASING U.S. DEPENDENCE ON IMPORTS OF STRATEGIC MATERIALS

	% Imported from All Foreign Sources				% Imported from Underdeveloped Countries
	1950	1970	1985	2000	1971
Bauxite	64	85	96	98	95
Chromium	n.a.	100	100	100	25
Copper	31	17	34	56	44
Iron	8	30	55	67	32
Lead	39	31	61	67	32
Manganese	88	95	100	100	57
Nickel	94	90	88	89	71
Potassium	13	42	47	61	n.a.
Sulfur	2	15	28	52	31
Tin	77	98	100	100	94
Tungsten	37	50	87	97	37
Vanadium	24	21	32	58	40
Zinc	38	59	73	84	21

II. COMPETITION WITH OTHER ADVANCED NATIONS FOR THE NATURAL RESOURCES OF THE UNDERDEVELOPED WORLD

% of Total (1971) World Output of Strategic Materials

Strategic Material	Produced by Underdeveloped Nations	Consumed by All Advanced Nations	U.S.A.
Antimony	54.1	59.8	19.5
Bauxite	55.6	75.5	24.6
Copper	41.0	75.23	24.8
Fluorspar	46.4	80.7	26.3
Graphite	67.3	69.4	22.6
Lead	26.3	72.8	23.5
Manganese	41.5	33.7	11.0
Tin	80.5	83.8	28.5

*Sources and Definitions: See notes for pages 126–28.

III. INCREASING DEPENDENCY ON IMPORTED ENERGY SOURCES
U.S.A./OTHER ADVANCED INDUSTRIAL NATIONS
(as a percentage of total domestic consumption)

	1960	1965	1970	1971
Total Energy				
U.S.A.	6.2	10.55	8.4	10.2
West Germany	7.9	44.5	58.9	60.6
Japan	46.6	74.9	94.5	98.5
Oil				
U.S.A.	16.3	21.5	21.5	24.0
West Germany	83.8	90.4	94.4	94.7
Japan	100.0	98.2	100.0	100.0
Natural Gas				
U.S.A.	1.2	2.79	3.5	3.8
West Germany	0.0	29.3	22.7	29.3
Japan	0.0	0.0	32.3	34.5
Coal and other solid fuels				
U.S.A.	0.0	0.0	0.0	0.0
West Germany	6.5	7.6	8.8	7.7
Japan	13.3	26.5	56.3	58.7

IV. DIFFERENTIAL HOURLY WAGE RATES* IN SELECTED INDUSTRIES
UNDERDEVELOPED NATIONS VS. U.S.A.

	Average Hourly Rate (in dollars)	
	Underdeveloped Nations	U.S.A.
Consumer electronic products		
Hong Kong	0.27	3.13
Mexico	0.53	2.31
Taiwan	0.14	2.56
Office-machine Parts		
Hong Kong	0.30	2.92
Taiwan	0.38	3.67
Mexico	0.48	2.97
Semiconductors		
Korea	0.33	3.32
Singapore	0.29	3.36
Jamaica	0.30	2.23
Wearing Apparel		
Mexico	0.53	2.29
British Honduras	0.28	2.11
Costa Rica	0.34	2.28
Honduras	0.45	2.27
Trinidad	0.40	2.49

*Hourly wage rates for a given country and the U.S.A. are for comparable task and skill levels.

V. ESTIMATED UNEMPLOYMENT LEVELS IN
SELECTED LATIN AMERICAN AND ASIAN NATIONS*
(in percentages)

	1970
Argentina	19.0
Chile	13.0
Columbia	20.0
Korea	17.0
Pakistan	20.0
Panama	28.0
Philippines	27.0 (1969)
Puerto Rico	28.0
Venezuela	25.0

*These figures are from the Yearbook of Labor Statistics of the International Labour Office, Geneva.

VI. INCREASE IN MANUFACTURED EXPORTS
FROM UNDERDEVELOPED COUNTRIES

	Value, Millions of U.S. $			*Annual Growth Rate*
	1960	*1965*	*1971*	*1960–1971*
Brazil	23	109	424	30%
Hong Kong	434	788	2936	18%
Mexico	61	156	484	21%
Portugal	171	355	1172	19%
South Korea	5	107	873	60%
Spain	224	380	1771	21%
Taiwan	59	228	1588	35%

Neither the mineral wealth of the poor nations nor the energy crisis in the rich nations by itself explains the dynamics of corporate expansion into the underdeveloped world. It has long been an article of Marxist faith that the development of capitalism would take such form and that expansionism was an institutional *necessity* for the system. The notion that the survival of modern capitalism requires the absorption of the underdeveloped world into the global industrial system as "hewers of wood and drawers of water" has, understandably, never been a popular theory on Wall Street or in Detroit. Lenin's thesis that capitalism could grow only by exploiting weaker people always seemed unkind, and besides, his economic explanations for such a pattern were less than convincing.

But non-Marxist economists have in the past few years come up with their own theory to explain the rhythm of corporate expansionism. The need for a theory that would explain how, why, and, especially, when competitive forces would force corporations into new markets or require new ways of handling old markets had been obvious for many years. Orthodox theories were too static to explain the dynamic developments that were taking place in the rise of the global corporation. The basis of the new theory was developed in the 1940's by economists such as Harvard's Edward Mason who discovered that the growing power of the oligopolistic firms to ride over competitors and the Anti-Trust Division alike demanded a much more dynamic model of corporate behavior than Alfred Marshall's classic but static "representative firm." Students of the new science of marketing research in business schools then began to seek a theoretical explanation of how oligopolies achieve market power, deal with competition, maintain or increase their share of the market, and achieve essential economies of scale through bigness. A major explanation that emerged was the theory of the Product Life Cycle.

It is important to understand how global corporations take advantage of basic investments already made in research, packaging, communications, and marketing know-how to expand operations into new geographical areas at substantial savings. Such economies of scale are crucial to the strategy of corporate global growth. Thus, the quest for global profit maximization is pushing the world's largest corporations ever more into Asia, Africa, and Latin America for reasons that go well beyond the familiar ones —the need to jump over tariff walls to retain and augment former export markets, and the drive for essential raw materials. We can illustrate how the Product Life Cycle Theory helps to explain the expansion of global corporations into the underdeveloped countries by recounting (in simplified form) the story of the U.S. television industry.

In 1948 one hundred percent of all television sets were manufactured in the United States. By the time the first sets were marketed after the war, the industry had already invested millions in research and development. Most of these costs were not related to the invention as such but to postinvention costs for adapting the invention to mass production and a mass market. (It should be recalled that television sets had already been developed by the end of the 1920's. Indeed RCA ran an ad in *The New York Times* in September 1929 predicting that TV sets would be in American homes later that fall.) A major portion of postinvention costs go into "exploring" the market and, as many economists have shown, into increasing the market. In this first phase of the Product Life Cycle profits are relatively low because such costs are high and peak demand for an unfamiliar product has yet to be created.

By the mid-1950's the first phase in the biography of the television industry was drawing to a close. TV had become a necessity of life. As mass-production and mass-marketing techniques were perfected, costs dropped progressively. Profits were high. In short, this was the brief happy childhood of the industry pioneers. But already clouds were gathering. As some of the pioneers' crucial patents began to expire and their marketing techniques became known, less adventurous entrepreneurs started engaging in the sincerest but most unwelcome form of flattery: they entered the TV business by imitating the pioneers' technology at a fraction of their original cost. Because they could acquire the essential technology by simply purchasing a television set instead of a research laboratory, they quickly cut into the pioneers' exclusive hold on the market. The pioneers' oligopoly profits declined, and those of the cost-cutting latecomers correspondingly rose. In the executive suite in Radio City it was clear that something had to be done.

Just as the closing of the continental frontier forced American politicians in the 1890's to look abroad, so the impending saturation of the continental TV market forced the pioneer producers to think about new markets in transcontinental terms. Phase Two, the adolescence of the industry, which began in the middle 1950's, was marked by the development of an export market, principally in Europe. The pioneers were able to get a jump on the latecomers because they could take the production, marketing, and managerial knowledge they had developed for the U.S. market and apply it rapidly to Europe at little additional cost. In so doing they converted the race for profits into a world oligopoly competition and were able to restore their competitive edge over the latecomers by increasing their share of the global market even as their share of the U.S. market was declining. This competitive edge gave the pioneers relatively higher profits to invest in further advertising and market manipulation, which are the crucial investments for staying on top. For a few years the latecomers would be effectively barred from these new markets, because they would lack the specific knowledge and contacts needed to sell TV sets to Frenchmen, Germans, and Italians.

But here again the advantages of the pioneers were to be short-lived. The onset of middle age, Phase Three, occurred when the latecomers began imitating what the pioneers had been doing in Phase Two and started exporting to Europe. Once again they were able to copy the pioneers' methods at a fraction of their costs and thus cut into the pioneers' share of the market profits. Moreover, European countries, having recovered from World War II, were recapturing part of the export market with their own production. So the pioneers decided to build plants abroad to produce the TV's for the local markets at a cost that the latecomers, still in the export phase, could not meet. In this "import substitution" phase costs were reduced, not only because of savings in transportation expense but, more important, because the European (and later Latin American and Asian) governments treated foreign companies who produced on their soil much more favorably than they treated exporters. Because these governments wished to save scarce foreign exchange and to encourage their own domestic production, they used tariffs to limit imports. Thus "getting in under the tariff wall" was a good way for the pioneers to reduce costs and restore their high rate of profit. Once again the pioneers could achieve economies of scale by simply adapting knowledge already paid for in the home market to the dramatically expanding foreign market. For any individual company, as scores of business-school studies point out, it was not a matter of choice to locate productive facilities abroad. No pioneer company that wished to preserve its lead in market share and hence in profits could afford to abandon that market to the latecomers.

It was in Phase Three of the Product Life Cycle that the TV pioneers became truly global corporations. Their investment overseas accelerated at a dramatic rate, and overseas profits became crucial to the worldwide profit picture. At the same time, the conflicts associated with the expansion process became sharper. U.S. companies were buying up local competitors and exercising increasing power over the local economies. Thus they were a cause of concern to local governments, particularly in Europe.

Some companies began using their overseas factories in preference to their high-cost U.S. plants to export to other foreign
countries. The closing of U.S. plants formerly used for such
exports began to bring strong reaction from U.S. labor unions.
But despite these problems, the pioneers had recaptured a larger
share of the world market and hence profits were higher.

Phase Four, the mature years of the industry, opened in the
mid-1960's when a new generation of latecomers challenged the
pioneers' hold on the market. This time many of the challengers
were foreigners, and the focus of the challenge was the U.S.
market itself. The expansion of the Japanese electronic industry
into the U.S. market was a recapitulation of the earlier phases of
the product cycle that had worked so advantageously for U.S.
firms. The Japanese had duplicated U.S. technology at a fraction
of the U.S. firms' original cost, not by stealing it, as a few unsporting American businessmen like to charge, but by buying it
years ago under licensing arrangements from the same U.S. firms
they are now challenging. Almost all of Japan's acquisition of
new technology has been through the medium of licensing rather
than foreign investment. Companies that sold technology to the
Japanese in the 1950's for a quick profit had cause to regret the
decision in the 1970's. Japan had certain unique advantages. It
had a relatively low consumption level, and hence low wages, and
a high rate of productivity, thanks to the licensing of U.S. know-
how. Thus Japanese factories at substantially lower labor costs
could equal or surpass U.S. factories in productivity and quality.
As a result, the great Japanese firms, backed by favorable policies
of their government, were able to undersell U.S. firms in their
own home market. Sony, Toyota, Nikon, and Mitsubishi became
household words in the United States.

The response of the pioneers was to try to recapture the home
market by cutting production costs. Their strategy was to create
in the lowest-wage areas of the world, such as Hong Kong,
Taiwan, Singapore, and the U.S.-Mexican border area, what the
Brazilian economist Celso Furtado calls "export platforms" from
which cheaply produced TV sets (and cameras, computers, calculators, stereos, watches, etc.) could be shipped to the United
States at competitive prices. Thus it is in Phase Four of the
Product Life Cycle, what might be called the golden years of the
pioneer companies, that the underdeveloped world assumes a

critical role in the Global Factory. Because of the nature of global oligopolistic competition during a period of relatively free trade, no mature industry can afford not to expand its production facilities into the poor nations of Asia, Africa, and Latin America.

The driving force behind global oligopoly competition is the necessity to grow in order to maintain or increase market shares. This explains the interest of global corporations in poor countries, but it does not explain why these countries are in fact so poor.

2

How is it that the nations of the underdeveloped world, so fortunately endowed with raw materials, a huge labor force, and great potential markets, as we have seen, are in fact so poor? The rich have developed a number of comfortable explanations for this curious phenomenon. Most of them are deeply rooted in racism. Two generations ago it was commonly accepted that the planet contained a large number of "backward" nations or "minor races" ("lesser breeds without the law," in Kipling's phrase) which could never compete with the dynamic white Western world. In these nations for the most part lived the brown, black, and yellow people who make up roughly two-thirds of the world's population. But history is not congenial to such theories. The cradles of civilization—China, Egypt, the Mayan and Inca empires in Latin America, and the kingdoms of North Africa—were flowering at a time when the remote ancestors of the managers of the Western world were roaming Europe in barbarian armies. Many parts of what we call the underdeveloped world were once the richest and most culturally alive areas of the globe.

The symptoms of underdevelopment are easy enough to identify. All underdeveloped countries share in lesser or greater measure certain characteristics. A modern Gulliver might describe the typical underdeveloped country this way: "What a curious contradiction of rags and riches. One out of every ten thousand persons lives in a palace with high walls and gardens and a Cadillac in the driveway. A few blocks away hundreds are sleeping in the streets, which they share with beggars, chewing-gum hawkers, prostitutes, and shoeshine boys. Around the corner tens of thousands are jammed in huts without electricity or plumbing. Outside the city most of the population scratches out a bare subsistence on small plots, many owned by the few who lived behind the high walls. Even where the soil is rich and the climate agreeable most people go to sleep hungry. The stock market is booming, but babies die and children with distended bellies and spindly legs are everywhere. There are luxurious restaurants and stinking open sewers. The capital boasts late-model computers and receives jumbo jets every day, but more than half of the people cannot read. Government offices are major employers of those who can, but the creaky bureaucracy is a joke except to the long line of suppliants who come seeking medical help or a job. (For suppliants with money for a bribe the lines shorten miraculously.)

"Nationalist slogans are prominent, but the basic industries are in the hands of foreigners. The houses behind the walls are filled with imported cameras, TV's, tape recorders, and fine furniture from the United States or Europe, but the major family investment is likely to be a Swiss bank account. There appear to be three groups in the country distinguishable by what they consume. A tiny group live on a scale that would make a Rockefeller squirm. A second group, still relatively small in number, live much like the affluent middle class in the United States—the same cars, the same Scotch, the same household appliances. The vast majority eat picturesque native foods like black beans, rice, and lentil soup—in small quantities. The first two groups are strong believers in individual development for themselves and their family, but they see no solution for the growing plight of the third group. So they fear them, and their walls grow higher. For the third group disease, filth, and sudden death are constant companions, but there is an air of resignation about them. Life has always been full of pain and uncertainty and it always will be. The only development they see is the same journey from cradle to an early grave that their fathers and their grandfathers took."

There is a certain fatalism surrounding the standard terminology of economics. It is often said that poor countries are poor because they are deficient in what economists call capital stock: that is, they lack the tangible (and expensive) infrastructures that enable modern developed societies to function and to create more wealth—roads, communications systems, schools, machines, and factories. But capital stock, unlike mushrooms, does not grow wild. Its appearance at a particular time and place is the result of specific human decisions about investment taken in the past. When a primitive society begins to produce more than it consumes, it ceases to be what economists call a "static" society and begins the process of "growth."

The essential ingredient in this process is knowledge. It is the introduction of new ways of organizing work—i.e., a hoe instead of one's bare hands, a tractor instead of a hoe—that increases human productivity and generates savings that can be used to promote further increases in productivity in the future. Economists like to call these savings "finance capital," when they are actually invested for the purpose of maintaining and creating more wealth. The essential characteristic of finance capital is that it is made up of intrinsically worthless pieces of paper such as bank notes, stock certificates, and bankbooks which represent the surplus generated by wealth-producing activities of the past. Whether it will in fact produce further wealth for a country, or more important, whether it will create wealth-producing structures—i.e., factories—depends upon what those who control that finance capital decide to do with it. If a country is poor in wealth-producing structures (capital stock), it is because whoever controlled wealth in that country decided to invest their finance capital in something else or somewhere else.

The finance capital generated by the natural wealth of many countries of the underdeveloped world was not used to develop local factories, schools, and other structures for generating more wealth but was siphoned off to the developed world—first as plunder, then in the more respectable form of dividends, royalties, and technical fees—where it was used to finance the amenities of London and Paris and, more important, the industrial expansion of affluent societies. Most of the capital left in the poor countries was in the control of a small local elite closely tied to foreign capitalists who knew how to consume it in lavish living and where to invest it abroad for a good return.

Thus, because the power over the national wealth was largely in the hands of foreigners, the finance capital generated by past wealth-producing activities was not used to maintain, much less to expand, the local economy. The result was a process of wealth depletion which has resulted inevitably in lower consumption for the local population. The net outflow of finance capital from the underdeveloped societies weakened their capacity to develop the knowledge to produce wealth, and this further decreased their bargaining power.

A country can have rivers of gold and thousands of potential workers ready to mine it and yet be on the brink of starvation if it lacks the know-how to exploit its natural riches. Knowledge, as we are using it, means more than just the ability to make, use, repair, and improve machines. A crucial sort of knowledge that is particularly in short supply in underdeveloped countries is techniques of social organization. In advanced countries, systems of rewards and punishments work efficiently to motivate the population to produce more wealth. Perhaps the most decisive factor in the relative bargaining power of an advanced nation over that of an underdeveloped society is a difference in philosophical outlook. When we talk about the knowledge superiority of the West, we mean not only its superior technology to create machines, but also the technology to create and communicate a set of values that puts the creation of wealth at its center. The capacity of the advanced nations to spread to the "backward nations" the ideological foundations of modern capitalism—man's mission to conquer nature, the work ethic, the whip of economic necessity, the invisible hand—and to make the elites of poor countries disciples in the science of enrichment gave the industrial nations enormous bargaining power.

No aspect of the technological superiority of the developed world is more important than its mastery of the techniques of ideological marketing. In the last hundred years the superiority of the advanced nations in industrial and marketing technology has become crucial in preserving the dependent role of the underdeveloped world. Military technology still plays a role, to be sure, but the survival of the poor nations of Asia, Africa, and Latin America now depends upon how and on what terms they can relate to the world industrial system. The advanced nations continue to set those terms, not because they possess superior power in natural resources and labor—we have seen that the opposite is true—but because today, as compared with 500 years ago, they are far ahead of the rest of the world in wealth-creating knowledge.

The industrialized nations, as the studies of Raúl Prebisch, Hans Singer, and others have shown, have used their technological and marketing superiority to obtain terms of trade which, not surprisingly, favor them at the expense of their weaker trading partners in the underdeveloped world. Thus over the past twenty-five years, until the 1970's, because of the falling relative price of certain essential raw materials, the countries of the underdeveloped world have had to exchange an ever-increasing amount of such raw materials to get the finished goods and technological expertise they need. This steady worsening of the terms of trade between the rich countries and the poor is an important reason why the "gap" between them has continued to grow.

To understand the persistence of underdevelopment, it is necessary to focus on the historical process by which the institutions for creating wealth have evolved. Countries rich in the raw materials of wealth lack the internal political and economic structures to obtain the other essential ingredients of wealth or to convert their resources into a well-functioning economy and social order. A prime characteristic of every underdeveloped society is the massive failure of the essential systems that solve or manage the major social problems in developed societies. Thus the systems for providing pure water or sanitation do not work well or may not even exist. Schools, for diffusing the essential knowledge needed to create wealth, are absent. The system for raising and distributing food is inadequate. Competent structures for providing employment do not exist. The government typically lacks the power to collect adequate taxes and to invest adequate finance capital in those systems that will solve some of these other major problems.

Indeed, the lack of bargaining power of underdeveloped countries is due to three major institutional weaknesses. The first, as we have noted, is antiquated governmental structures. Laws are inadequate for collecting taxes, controlling foreign business, or preventing the drain of finance capital. Typically, the laws were drafted in an earlier and simpler day before masters of the new occult sciences, the accountants and the tax lawyers, had arrived on the scene. Many were written by the colonial civil service or by foreign corporations themselves, only too happy to provide technical assistance to the governmental agency in charge of regulating their activities. The laws on foreign investment in Liberia, to give just one example of such international legal aid, were drafted by the U.S. Government.

But, as we shall explore further in Chapter 8, the trend in the underdeveloped world is toward tougher laws, particularly in the area of transfer of technology and patents. However, a law is only as effective as its administration. The lack of competent, trained, and independent administrators is as crucial an aspect of the institutional weakness as the lack of effective laws. A global corporation is able to pay an annual retainer to a Wall Street law firm to represent its worldwide interests which is perhaps five times the entire budget of the government agencies in poor countries that are supposed to regulate it. An executive of a global firm in Buenos Aires told us that the company has on retainer a number of "bureaucratic spies" to inform it in advance of crucial procurement decisions of the Argentine state companies. Bribes, flattery, and job offers aside, the typical civil servant in an underdeveloped country is usually no match for the corporate negotiator. A casual comparison of the efficient German regulatory bureaucracy with the chaotic formalism of a typical Latin American counterpart gives some clue as to why corporations can wrest greater concessions (and greater profits) in a Colombia or a Pakistan or a Mexico than they can in Germany. Some measure of the desperation of governments of the underdeveloped world is their curious tendency to seek the professional advice of those U.S. business consulting firms which advise the very corporations they are seeking to control. The official in charge of scrutinizing transfer of technology contracts in a Latin American country which has enacted a tough law told us he has the money and trained personnel to examine about 400 out of 9,000 pending cases.

A second source of institutional weakness in underdeveloped countries is the lack of a strong labor movement. With the possible exception of Argentina and Honduras, there is no labor movement in all of Latin America's private manufacturing sector capable of effective bargaining with global corporations. In Singapore the government advertises the lack of a strong union and offers a five-year strike holiday to attract transnational business. In Part III we shall be exploring the problems of a yet-to-be-created transnational labor movement in bargaining with transnational capital. But in most of the poor countries of the world there is no bargaining at all.

A third source of institutional weakness that explains why the global corporation is able to exert such strong power in underdeveloped countries is the lack of competition from local business. It would seem that native entrepreneurs, who must compete with the global giants under disadvantageous terms for supplies, capital, and customers, would like to see them effectively controlled. And many do. The Guatemala Chamber of Commerce has so far waged a successful all-out campaign to keep Sears out of Guatemala, claiming that a Sears invasion would put 3,000 to 4,000 Guatemalan shopkeepers out of business. In Colombia, the president of the national banking association has publicly denounced and called for laws prohibiting the near monopoly by global banks of the profitable banking business. Yet as a recent study of the attitudes of Argentine businessmen suggests, many local entrepreneurs up to now have been tolerant, even enthusiastic, about the penetration of their economy by global corporations. The reason, of course, is that they have decided to join them rather than fight them.

Some local businessmen find that by cooperating with global firms they can do very well. (Many global corporations, for varying reasons, are trying to make maximum use of local suppliers.) But equally important for local businessmen, the arrival of a global company may mean an early opportunity to sell the family business at a good price. (Once foreign giants become established in the local market, the alternative may well be a forced sale at an adverse price, or bankruptcy.) Just as in an earlier age in the United States, family enterprises either went public in order to raise sufficient finance capital to maintain their competitiveness against larger national corporations, or sold out to them, or were finally put out of business by them. Now many local capitalists owning national businesses in the underdeveloped countries are faced with identical alternatives. Available statistics indicate that the usual outcome is that the family business is sold off. Of the 717 new manufacturing subsidiaries established in Latin America by the top 187 U.S.-based global corporations, 331, or 46 percent, were established by the buying out of existing local firms. The figure would have been higher, *Business Latin America* observes, except for the "scarcity of local firms" remaining in particular industries. Because of their superior power, global corporations, as we shall explore more fully in Chapter 7, are able to use local finance capital and their technological advantage to absorb local industry. It is a process which some local businessmen may deplore but which they have yet to find a way to stop.

3

Most underdeveloped countries have already made the decision to emulate the economies of the developed countries through a similar process of industrialization, and therefore dependency on outside technology, finance capital, and marketing techniques, especially the diffusion of the ideology of the consuming society, is built into their model of development. Once U.S. and European consumption values become the primary goals of economic growth for a nation, it has no choice but to sacrifice the buildup of its own technological capacity, a long and difficult process, for the possibility of the quick boom that foreign investment can bring. But there is an obvious price. The nation's technology becomes subject to foreign control. In India, Turkey, the United Arab Republic, Pakistan, and Trinidad, to take some examples from a 1964 United Nations study, more than 89 percent of all outstanding patents were owned by foreigners. Nothing has happened since to suggest that this trend is slacking. Indeed, for over 20 years there has been a cumulative increase in this crucial form of foreign control. Studies prepared by the government of Eduardo Frei in Chile show a precipitous increase (65 percent to 95 percent) in the percentage of Chilean patents owned by foreigners between 1937 and 1967. In Colombia 10 percent of all patent holders in drug, synthetic fiber, and chemical industries own 60 percent of all patents, and these 10 percent are foreign-based global corporations. (It should not be forgotten that the global corporation derives much of its power in the United States by dominating the patents in its field. According to a recent study by Sherer, the top 30 industrials in the United States own 40.7 percent of the patents in their respective industries.) Concentrated control of technology is a classic device for eliminating effective competition and thereby establishing oligopolistic control of the marketplace. The result is, of course, high profits, which can then be used to further consolidate the firm's dominant position by massive investments in advertising.

The same cumulative rhythm is felt in the case of finance capital, the second basic element of global corporate power. Subsidiaries of global companies are able to borrow from local banks and financial institutions on better terms than local businesses. They are preferred customers because their credit is backed by the worldwide financial resources of the parent company. When savings are in short supply, as is typical in underdeveloped countries, it is simply good business to lend to Ford or Pfizer rather than to the local laundry or sugar mill. During Argentina's 1971 credit squeeze when the availability of credit in the domestic economy was reduced 20 percent, local firms were forced to cut their borrowings by 42 percent, but global firms in Argentina actually *increased* their borrowings by 20 percent over the prior period. More and more scarce savings are already under the control of a branch of some global bank such as the Bank of America, Chase Manhattan, or the First National City Bank of New York. In Bolivia, for example, such banks control close to 50 percent of the country's private deposits. Clearly, the local branch of a global bank will prefer lending to a subsidiary of a global firm rather than to local grocers and farmers, and for the same obvious reasons locally owned banks have developed an international outlook in their lending policies.

But there are other reasons too. Banks and the corporations, as we shall see, are not entirely separate entities. Because of interlocking interests in ownership and management and complementary goals, global corporations and global banks do not deal with each other as strangers. Even if a branch bank were tempted to lend scarce local capital to a local firm in preference to a subsidiary of a global company, it would think twice before doing so in order to protect its long-term relationship with the parent company. The relationship between local subsidiaries of U.S.-based global companies and local branches of New York and Boston banks is touchingly close. In Argentina, an executive of a U.S.-based heavy-machine company told us, the First National City Bank, which makes about 80 percent of its loans to U.S. companies, charges a preferred rate to local subsidiaries of its worldwide customers, who in some cases are actually charged a negative interest rate. (This is the result of charging an astronomical-sounding 30 percent interest in an economy with an inflation rate of 60 percent.)

The companies are only too glad to help the banks in return. For example, the global clients of the First National Bank of Boston are asked to send the bank detailed monthly reports on their plans for the coming quarter and once a year a five-year projection of their expansion plans. By putting all such information together, the Boston bank can acquire the best economic intelli-

gence in the country—often much better than the information in
the hands of the Argentine government. The interest of global
banks and global corporations with overlapping ownership and
management is obviously to help each other, and, as Miguel Wionczek and others have shown, global banks and global companies have expanded together according to similar patterns and
at a roughly similar rate. What is good for global corporations is
usually good for global banks, and vice versa.

The power of the global banks over the economies of underdeveloped countries is due primarily, of course, to the scarcity of
finance capital. As we shall see in Chapter 7, the foreign firms
repatriate a substantial proportion of their earnings, and in addition, local wealth holders, worried about the stability of the economy, have a tendency to channel their money outside the country.
A complication from the standpoint of poor countries is what
economists call the "foreign exchange bottleneck." Because of
the dependence of the local economy upon foreign technology,
there is a great need for foreign exchange, which, typically, is in
even shorter supply than savings.

U.S. banks can exert considerable power over underdeveloped
countries that are poor in foreign exchange because they control
the faucets from which dollars flow. Thus five U.S. banks, Chase
Manhattan, Chemical, First National City, Manufacturers Hanover, and Morgan Guaranty, completely cut off short-term credit
to Chile after Allende came to power. Before the change of government in 1970, U.S. suppliers and banks supplied 78.4 percent
of all Chile's short-term credit needs—typically 90-day loans to
finance essential imports from the United States. (About 30 percent of Chile's foreign-exchange requirements are for food.) By
1972, in the midst of Chile's desperate foreign-exchange crisis,
loans from all U.S. banks totaled only $35 million (down from
$220 million in previous years). Whether one accepts the banks'
argument that their decision to cut credit was based only on conservative banking views of the Chilean economy or the Allende
government's charge that the banks were conspiring with the
U.S. Government to implement at least a portion of ITT's famous
plan to squeeze it out of office, the episode gives a rare glimpse
of the enormous power foreign banks exert over weak economies.

The third source of power of the global corporations in underdeveloped countries is their control over communications—i.e.,

their extraordinary competitive edge in using the technology of market manipulation to shape the tastes, goals, and values of the workers, suppliers, government officials, and, of course, customers on whom their own economic success in that society depends. The global corporation must not only sell concepts along with its crackers: it must continually sell and resell itself.

The technology of the marketplace is concentrated in the advertising agencies. The rise of the global corporation and the global bank has been accompanied by the globalization of the Madison Avenue firm. In 1954 the top 30 U.S. advertising agencies derived a little over 5 percent of their total billings from overseas campaigns. In 1972 the world billings of these same firms had increased almost sevenfold, and one-third of the $7 billion in total world billings came from outside the United States. (By 1971, J. Walter Thompson was earning 52 percent of its profits outside the United States and McCann-Erickson 61 percent.) The big U.S. firms enjoy a decisive competitive advantage over local advertising firms by exploiting economies of scale. Like the TV manufacturers whose story we recounted above, they can extend tried-and-true techniques developed and paid for in the U.S. market into the foreign market at little extra cost. (The advertising campaign has a product life cycle too.) The local firms without a history of investment in new techniques must start from scratch, and in poor countries the high investment needed to make "presentations" to potential clients is not easy to find. For this reason the two largest U.S. advertising agencies, J. Walter Thompson and McCann-Erickson, have steadily increased their share of the Latin American market which they have dominated for many years. (In 1957 they had 52 percent of the total billings in Latin America. By 1970 it was 56 percent.) In the four countries of Latin America where most of the investment of U.S.-based global corporations is concentrated, Mexico, Brazil, Argentina and Venezuela, 54 percent of the major advertising agencies in 1970 were U.S.-owned or -affiliated, up from 43 percent in 1968.

Because most local firms lack the modern technology for overcoming customer resistance and customer indifference, they are dependent upon the U.S. giants. As Geraldo Alonson, head of the Brazilian firm Norton and president of the Brazilian Association of Advertising Agencies, puts it, ". . . it is important to Norton to establish an international connection with an American agency. It's not reasonable for us to expect to keep our position in Brazil without knowledge from the United States . . ." True, a few of the largest Brazilian firms are growing at a faster rate than the U.S. firms, in large part because they have reached a critical size which makes it possible for them to afford specialists in "creativity" from J. Walter Thompson and other U.S. firms. (A "creative director" in Brazil can earn $50,000 and a top copywriter $35,000, compared with the average salary for an industrial engineer of $17,600. But if the alumni from J. Walter Thompson bring with them the knowledge needed to sell cigarettes, the generous salaries are a bargain.)

Advertising is playing a crucial role in Brazil's "economic miracle." Ogilvy & Mather, a U.S. advertising giant, recently took over Standard Propaganda agency and in partnership with a Japanese agency now represents Toyota and Matsushita in Brazil. The booming Brazilian consumer market is based on the copying of U.S. techniques as rapidly as possible. Credit cards and television are key ingredients in the miracle. Michael Heath, marketing services manager for Brazil's biggest cigarette manufacturer (70 percent U.S.-British owned), has set his sights on enticing 6 to 7 million additional smokers over the next generation by using TV advertising techniques recently banished from the U.S. airwaves.

The most effective single medium for spreading an advertising message is TV and radio, especially in countries with high rates of illiteracy. U.S. networks play a dominant role in underdeveloped countries, particularly in Latin America. The Columbia Broadcasting System, for example, distributes its programs to 100 countries. Its news-film service, according to its 1968 annual report, is now received by satellite "in 95 percent of the free world's households." The leading U.S. TV shows, such as *I Love Lucy, Gomer Pyle, Hogan's Heroes, Mary Tyler Moore,* and *Perry Mason,* are distributed throughout the continent. *Hawaii Five-0* was dubbed into six languages and sold in 47 countries. *Bonanza* is seen in 60 countries, with an estimated weekly audience of 350 million. In 1970 and 1971 both CBS and NBC sold more than a half billion dollars' worth of "cultural emissions" overseas. In 1968 ABC International had controlling interest in 16 foreign companies that operated 67 TV stations in 27 countries around the world. (In Latin America ABC affiliates reach roughly 80 million spectators.)

As Frank Shakespeare, former CBS executive and later USIA head, notes:

> The technology which is the essence of the communications revolution was created in this country. In the use of that technology for the dissemination of ideas and information and entertainment, we were the world's leaders. We dominated motion pictures and television for years; we still do. "Madison Avenue" has become a worldwide cliché for referring to the technique of marketing and that's the dissemination of ideas.

In the TV field particularly, U.S.-based global firms dominate underdeveloped countries because they can offer old programs at a fraction of the cost a local producer would have to pay to create a new program. Thus it is hardly surprising from the standpoint of economics that 40 percent of the TV programs in Peru, 50 percent of the programs in Bolivia, and 85 percent of the programs in Costa Rica are packaged by foreign corporations. If a series suffers a quick demise in the United States, its owners can still recover production costs in Latin America by peddling it along with a high-ratings series, since all series are sold in "packages." But foreign dependency in the mass media is a sensitive subject in some countries, and a number of them have laws prohibiting full or even partial ownership of TV stations. When Brazil passed such a law, Time-Life neatly circumvented it by signing a technical-assistance contract with two Brazilian networks with tie-in clauses that required them to take a certain number of Time-Life–produced programs. Such technical-assistance contracts and "affiliation agreements" obligating local stations to take old U.S. TV programs is standard practice for the three big U.S. networks.

Another sort of tie-in arrangement also favors the penetration of local TV and radio by the U.S.-based global communications giants. Latin American affiliates' business agreements with ABC Worldvision surrender to ABC the power to choose both programs and sponsors for their peak hours. As *Television* magazine pointed out in October 1966, "ABC can sell Batman to an advertiser and then place Batman along with designated commercials in any . . . country where the advertiser wants it to appear."

Global corporations are, of course, the most lavish advertisers. In Peru, for example, Channel 5, which earned 63 percent of all TV advertising revenue in the country in 1969, derived more than 11 percent of its total income from just two global companies, Procter & Gamble and Colgate Palmolive. (Procter & Gamble spends more on advertising than on its global payroll.) Thus the competitive advantage of the foreign networks is based not only on superior knowledge—i.e., programming and marketing techniques—but on superior global contacts.

TV is, of course, the most powerful communications medium for the global advertiser. But global companies exert great power in underdeveloped countries by virtue of their control of other communications media. CBS, for example, in 1970 sold 100 million records abroad. Its subsidiary W. B. Saunders Company, the world's largest publisher of medical, mathematics, physics, and scientific textbooks, concentrated on the Latin American market in those fields. United Press International (part of the Hearst worldwide publishing empire) and the Associated Press together accounted in 1970 for 72 percent of the news coverage in the 14 principal papers of Latin America. Global corporations dominate the advertising in such papers. In the first six months of 1969, Sears and IBEC accounted for 40 percent of all advertising revenue in *El Correo,* one of Lima's leading papers. *Reader's Digest* is published in 101 countries (9 different editions in Spanish alone) with a total non-U.S. circulation of 11.5 million. (In Mexico alone, with a potential readership about one-fifth that of the United States, 400,000 copies of *Selecciones del Reader's Digest* are sold each month.) Nor do U.S.-based companies ignore the vast audience unable to cope with the sophistication of the *Digest. Superman, Batman,* and *Terry and the Pirates* are the favorite reading of millions, translated into Spanish and Portuguese, courtesy of such global communicators as Warner Brothers.

Thus the three essential structures of power in underdeveloped societies are typically in the hands of global corporations: the control of technology, the control of finance capital, and the control of marketing and the dissemination of ideas. The process of emulation which we noted was the response of Western Europe and Japan to foreign expansion by U.S. global companies does not ordinarily occur in underdeveloped countries because their basic institutions, including domestic business enterprises, are too weak to make such a challenge. The result in most underdeveloped countries is the pervasive penetration of the global corporation throughout every key sector in the economy. In pre-Allende Chile, for example, 51 percent of the largest 160 firms were effectively controlled by global corporations. In each of the seven key industries of the economy, one to three foreign firms controlled at least 51 percent of the production. Of the top 22 global corporations operating in the country, 19 either operated free of all competition or shared the market with other oligopolists. The pattern is duplicated again and again in poor countries across the globe. Of the total sales of the 50 largest companies in Argentina, more than 50 percent are transacted by global corporations. Over the last decades, global companies have been increasing their hold on weak economies at an exponential rate. Thus in 1962 Mexico's rubber, electrical machinery, and transportation industries were already 100-percent foreign-owned. But by 1970 the metal industry was 68-percent foreign-owned (up from 42 percent in 1962) and the tobacco industry was 100 percent in foreign hands (up from 17 percent in 1962). In Brazil the pattern is even more pervasive. Already by 1966 global corporations accounted for some 64 percent of the total net profits in the five major dynamic sectors of the Brazilian economy (rubber, motor vehicles, machinery, household appliances, and mining). But by 1971 that share was up to 70 percent. By 1961 global companies owned 100 percent of automobile and tire production and 59 percent of machinery and approximately 50 percent of electrical-appliance manufacturing. Ten years later, foreign ownership in the latter two industries increased to 67 percent and 68 percent respectively. Fifty-five global firms received 66 percent of the net profits of the 100 largest private enterprises in Brazil in 1971, and the 45 largest local companies received 34 percent.

The colossal power of the global corporation to shape the societies of the underdeveloped world is not a matter for debate. The evidence comes largely from the corporations' own annual reports. But the burning political issue concerns the use of that power. Is the global corporation in the business of exploitation or development? It is to that question that we now turn.

7

Engines of Development?

1

The closest thing to a universal goal in the contemporary world is development, the twentieth-century embellishment of the myth of progress. Modern-day religion, philosophy, and psychiatry are absorbed with the challenge of individual development, the struggle of human beings to realize their full potential. For poor countries the word means escape from backwardness and foreign domination. For rich societies the word symbolizes heightened possibilities, the achievement of the affluent society, then its transcendence, a process culminating in a postindustrial world from which scarcity has been banished. The 1960's were hailed as the "Decade of Development," and the Cold War, which reached its peak during those years, was fought in the name of development. The issue was whether the "Free World model" or the "Communist model" would prevail. Rich, poor, capitalist or Communist, everyone is for development.

Much of the popularity of the term can be attributed to the fact that it can mean anything one chooses. In U.S. economic reports and state papers during the 1960's, development had a particular meaning. A developing society was one in which per capita income and gross national product were increasing. If a poor country in which each person was earning an average of $80 a year should pursue policies that would increase per capita income to, say, $100 within three years, that country was developing, indeed, at a spectacular rate. Similarly, if the sum total of goods and services exchanged within the society—i.e., the gross national product—should increase, that too was a test of develop-

148

ment. By these criteria a few countries around the world developed rather dramatically during the 1960's. Mexico, for example, went from a per capita income of $488 in 1960 to $717 a year in 1972. Brazil boasted an annual growth in GNP of more than 9 percent a year. According to the prevailing theories of the 1960's, societies that showed such economic growth were at the "takeoff" stage in development. Their increasing levels of economic activity would generate the savings needed to buy their tickets of admission to the twentieth century—roads, schools, hospitals, etc. —and an industrial capacity that would make their children comfortable.

By the end of the Decade of Development, however, despite dramatic economic growth in a few poor countries, it had become abundantly clear that the gap between rich and poor throughout the world was widening. A succession of studies by the U.N. and other international agencies established the statistics of global poverty: For 40 percent to 60 percent of the world's population the Decade of Development brought rising unemployment, decreases in purchasing power, and thus lower consumption. In a World Bank survey of income-distribution patterns in poor countries around the world, Irma Adelman and Cynthia Taft Morris found that the development track of the 1960's shows a "striking" increase in incomes, in both absolute and relative terms, for the richest 5 percent while the share of the poorest 40 percent shrinks. While according to such gross economic indicators as GNP the countries are developing, millions in the bottom 40 percent of the population actually have less food, worse clothing, and poorer housing than their parents had. As Brazil's President Emilio Médici once put it, "Brazil is doing well but the people are not."

Particularly in those countries which experienced "economic miracles," the pattern was increasing affluence for a slowly expanding but small minority and increasing misery for a rapidly swelling majority. Concentration of income in Mexico, for example, has increased significantly during the "Mexican miracle." In the early 1950's, the richest 20 percent of the population had ten times the income of the poorest 20 percent. By the mid-1960's the rich had increased their share to seventeen times what the bottom 20 percent received. A 1969 United Nations study reports that in the Mexico City area the richest 20 percent of the popula-

tion lived on 62.5 percent of the area's income while the poorest
20 percent attempted survival on 1.3 percent of the income. During the Decade of Development, according to U.S. Government
estimates, the share in the "Brazilian miracle" for the 40 million
people at the bottom dropped from 10.6 percent to 8.1 percent.
The richest 5 percent have increased their share of the national
income from 27.8 percent to 36.8 percent (A 1970 U.N. study
estimates that the share of the richest 5 percent is one-half of the
national income.) In September 1972, Robert McNamara, president of the World Bank, reported on what the continuation of
prevailing development policies, with their modest annual growth
rates and their income-concentration effects, would mean by the
end of the century. "Projected to the end of the century—only a
generation away—that means the people of the developed countries will be enjoying per capita incomes, in 1972 prices, of over
$8000 a year, while those masses of the poor (who by that time
will total over two and one-quarter billion) will on average receive less than $200 per capita, and some 800 million of these
will receive less than $100."

Most of the world lives in countries with a per capita income
of less than $200, and it is these countries which have shown an
increase in per capita income of no more than 1.7 percent a year.
But even in the Brazils and Mexicos, as we have seen, income concentration has meant that the benefits of the miracles do not flow
to the poor. It is an elementary but often forgotten bit of statistical truth that every million dollars Mr. Rockefeller receives increases the per capita income of every Mississippi tenant farmer.
Increases in national income, Mr. McNamara points out, "will
not benefit the poor unless they reach the poor."

When the global corporations proclaim themselves engines of
development, we can judge their claims only if we know what
development track they are on. A mechanical definition of development based on growth rates is obscene in a world in which most
people go to sleep hungry. A development model like Brazil's, in
which the stock market booms and two-thirds of the population is
condemned to an early death by poverty, hunger, and disease, is
a caricature of progress. If a development model is to have any
real meaning in a world in which most people are struggling just
to stay alive, it must, as the development theorist Dudley Seers
has pointed out, provide solutions to the most critical, interrelated

social problems of the late twentieth century: poverty, unemployment, and inequality. (A development strategy that does not cope with these problems must assume either escalating mass misery on a scale that cannot even be imagined or the mysterious disappearance of the world's poor.) The evidence of the 1960's is now in. It is an unhappy fact that the development track pursued by the global corporations in those years contributed more to the exacerbation of world poverty, world unemployment, and world inequality than to their solution.

In the light of the conventional development wisdom of the 1960's, these appear to be irresponsible charges. After all, global corporations do spread goods, capital, and technology around the globe. They do contribute to a rise in overall economic activity. They do employ hundreds of thousands of workers around the world, often paying more than the prevailing wage. Most poor countries appear to be so eager to entice global corporations to their territory, so eager in fact to create a good "investment climate" for them, that they are generous with tax concessions and other advantages. If corporations were really spreading poverty, unemployment, and inequality, why would they be welcomed?

The negative impact of the global corporation in the deterioration of living standards, employment rates, and economic justice around the world has occurred despite the fact that many corporate officials would like it to be otherwise and believe that it can be. The unfortunate role of the global corporation in maintaining and increasing poverty around the world is due primarily to the dismal reality that global corporations and poor countries have different, indeed conflicting, interests, priorities, and needs. This is a reality that many officials of underdeveloped countries, lacking alternative development strategies, prefer not to face.

The primary interest of the global corporation is worldwide profit maximization. As we shall see, it is often advantageous for the global balance sheet to divert income from poor countries. As anxious to be "good corporate citizens" as they are, the World Managers are the first to proclaim their primary allegiance to the shareholders. Global corporations, as they themselves like to say, are neither charities nor welfare organizations, although some devote modest resources to good works. (The Ford Motor Company, for example, is building schools in Mexico, asking only that the name FORD appear prominently over the door.) The claims of the global corporation rest instead on a theory of the marketplace which says in effect that by enriching themselves they enrich the whole world. In this chapter we shall examine the evidence that shows why it has not been so.

2

The central strategy of the global corporation is the creation of a global economic environment that will ensure stability, expansion, and high profits for the planetary enterprise. The implementation of that strategy depends upon the control of the three basic components of corporate power: finance capital, technology, and marketplace ideology. The record of the past dozen years suggests clearly that the global corporation has used these components of power, as one might expect, to promote its growth and profitability. But it is these very strategies which have had an adverse effect on distribution of income and on employment levels in underdeveloped countries around the world.

Let us look first at the financial policies of global corporations in poor countries. Perhaps the strongest argument in favor of the global corporations' claim to be engines of development is that they are a source of needed capital for backward countries. Particularly at a time when government aid programs are drying up, the foreign corporation, it is argued, is a crucial source of the finance capital that poor countries need to supplement local savings and to obtain foreign exchange. (Capital accumulation is of course a prerequisite for economic growth. If it cannot be raised abroad, so the argument goes, then it must be squeezed out of the hides of workers. In short, foreign private capital is the best available instrument for avoiding the Stalinist model of industrialization through forced labor.)

The claim that global corporations are major suppliers of foreign capital to poor countries turns out to be more metaphor than reality. The practice of global corporations in Latin America, as Fernando Fajnzylber has shown in his exhaustive study for the United Nations, has been largely to use scarce local capital for their local operations rather than to bring capital from either the United States or Europe. Individual investors and banks in poor countries for understandable business reasons normally prefer to lend money to Sears, Roebuck or General Motors than to some local entrepreneur without the worldwide credit resources of the planetary giants. Thus during the years 1957–1965, as Fajnzylber shows, U.S.-based global corporations financed 83 percent of their Latin American investment locally, either from reinvested earnings or from local Latin American savings. Only about 17 percent of U.S. investment during the period, therefore, represented a transfer of capital from rich countries to poor. A variety of studies, including those of the Argentine economist Aldo Ferrer and the Chilean government under the Frei regime, confirm the same trend: from 1960 to 1970 about 78 percent of the manufacturing operations of U.S.-based global corporations in Latin America were financed out of local capital. What these figures show is that global corporations are not in fact major suppliers of finance capital to poor countries.

True, in the manufacturing sector 38 percent of the financial resources being used by U.S. global-corporation subsidiaries in Latin America comes from reinvested earnings, which accountants classify as foreign capital. But this classification misses the real economic meaning of what has happened. These reinvested earnings were to a great extent generated by local resources. While they can be thought of as additions to local savings, they may well not be available for the urgent development needs of the country, since they are controlled by the global corporations and used for their purposes. A primary purpose is to take such earnings out of the country as fast as possible. Between 1960 and 1968, according to Fajnzylber's U.N. study, U.S.-based global corporations reported taking on the average 79 percent of their net profits out of Latin America. It makes good business sense to try for a quick return on a modest investment in countries which, like the Latin American republics, are considered relatively unstable. In contrast, the same corporations operating in the developed economies of Western Europe are much readier to leave their profits in the country. But of course the poor countries are precisely the ones that most need to keep the earnings for their development. This is but one example where sound business judgment and the needs of poor countries conflict.

Between 1965 and 1968, 52 percent of all profits of U.S. subsidiaries operating in Latin America in manufacturing—the most dynamic sector of the hemisphere's economy—were repatriated to the United States. This means that for every dollar of net profit earned by a global-corporation subsidiary, 52 cents left the country, even though 78 percent of the investment funds used to generate that dollar of profit came from local sources. If we look at the mining, petroleum, and smelting industries, the capital outflow resulting from the operations of global corporations is even worse. Each dollar of net profit is based on an investment that was 83 percent financed from local savings; yet only 21 percent of the profit remains in the local economy.

These aggregate statistics are confirmed by reports of individual companies. A retired executive of one of the three largest multinational banks recalls for us that in the late 1950's and early 1960's his bank always tried to use about 95 percent local savings sources for its local loans and no more than 5 percent of its dollar holdings. A vice-president of another U.S.-based global bank told us how profitable it is for his bank to lend what is substantially Latin American capital to U.S.-based global companies. "I should not really tell you this," he confided, "but while we earn around 13 to 14 percent on our U.S. operations, we can easily count on a 33-percent rate of return on our business conducted in Latin America."

However, these profitable practices, far from representing an import of capital, actually decrease the availability of local capital for locally owned industry. (Global corporations preempt financing because, as 1970 Chilean Government studies show, they can borrow about twice as much on their inventories and capital assets as can locally owned industries.) At the same time, scarce financing is retailed to the general public in the form of consumer debt at exorbitant interest. (In Colombia a prominent economist has estimated that the actual interest rate charged by Sears, including hidden charges, is in excess of 30 percent a year.)

The adverse financial impact of the global corporation in Latin America has to do not only with the source of its investment but with its character. A principal argument for foreign investment is that it supplies new capital through which the superior management skills of global corporations can be channeled into new productive facilities. (The World Managers sometimes argue that they can use local capital much more efficiently for the development of the country than can local entrepreneurs.) But again the record suggests otherwise. A study by the Harvard Business School of the 187 largest U.S.-based global corporations which account for some 70 percent of all U.S. investment in Latin

America shows that in the years 1958–1967 U.S. firms used a substantial part of their investment to buy up local firms. (About 46 percent of all manufacturing operations established in the period were takeovers of existing domestic industry.) Again, it is sound business judgment to buy an already operating plant rather than take the risk of building a new one, but changing ownership does not increase productive facilities needed for development.

What was called the American Challenge in Europe a few years ago is a fait accompli in Latin America. Local industry, particularly the most dynamic sectors, is more and more in the hands of American-based global corporations. To those who criticize the takeover of local industry in poor countries the World Managers have two answers. The first is that the global corporations make a greater contribution to development than local entrepreneurs. The companies are more efficient, can marshal more resources, and develop more advanced technology. Some even argue that they are "better citizens" of the countries where they operate than local businessmen. They have more scruples about paying bribes. If they repatriate earnings to stockholders in the United States, is that not better than repatriating them to a numbered bank account in Switzerland, a practice of some local businessmen who like to use nationalistic rhetoric to fight foreign takeovers but who have no interest in the nation except as a source of personal profit? Whatever truth there may be to all of this, it hardly justifies foreign takeover of industry in poor countries. There are more alternatives open to developing countries than domination by foreign firms or exploitation by native entrepreneurs.

The second reply of the World Managers to the charge of "economic imperialism" heard in Latin America and other underdeveloped regions might be termed the "it's a tough world" argument. Where, they ask, are poor countries going to get the capital and the technology to develop if not from global companies? Yes, they acknowledge, it might be better for the countries if they owned their own industry, knew how to run it, and had their own money to develop it, but they don't. They can't expect us just to give the money and technology. The stockholders wouldn't permit it. Therefore the social benefits from our investment, marginal as they may be in some cases, constitute the only development poor countries can realistically expect.

However, the "you can't get the money without us" argument turns out to be an exaggeration. Life is hard for poor countries, but not that hard. The fact is that the companies, as we have seen, bring in relatively little of their own money. The capital that global companies raise locally could also be available to local firms or to the government for development projects. Peter Gabriel, dean of the Boston University Business School, estimates that even reasonably tough tax policies in Latin America would produce considerable capital for significant development advances. Then too, other sources of outside capital exist. In 1972 Brazil floated a bond issue of $140 million, which was more than the capital contribution sent from the United States to all U.S. global-corporation manufacturing subsidiaries in all of Latin America during that year. Japan's phenomenal postwar development, it must be remembered, was based largely on the exclusion of foreign investment. Noting the experience of the Communist countries in obtaining foreign capital and technology without turning over their basic industries to foreigners, poor countries are taking a harder look at the traditional arguments of the foreign investor. (What this is likely to mean for both the poor countries and the global corporations is the subject of the next chapter.)

Another standard argument in chamber-of-commerce speeches around the world is that global corporations help solve the balance-of-payments problems of poor countries. One characteristic shared by poor countries is a lack of foreign exchange. The reason, of course, is that the more undeveloped a country is the less likely it is to make things that foreigners want. The only way to get dollars or pounds or marks needed to buy capital goods or consumer luxuries from the United States, Britain, or Germany is to make, mine, or grow something that these countries need or want. During the last decade the underdeveloped countries' share of world exports has declined precipitously. This has been due to the dramatic increase in trading among the developed countries (most of it stimulated by global corporations) and to the loss of markets and decline in price for certain agricultural products, such as hemp, for which synthetic substitutes have been found. In Latin America during the Decade of Development the value of exports declined as the price of imports rose. Compounding the balance-of-payments problem was a steep rise in foreign debt. By the mid-1960's service on foreign debt exceeded the value of new loans, and by the end of the 1960's Latin America's external debt had doubled.

The World Managers argue that it is precisely these unhappy facts of life which make the contribution of the global corporations so important. But again the figures are unsettling. There is no doubt that U.S.-based global corporations account for a significant portion of Latin America's total trade. In 1968 U.S.-based companies were responsible for 40 percent of all manufacturing exports from the region and more than one-third of the region's imports from the United States. More than half of all U.S. exports take the form of exports from U.S. parents to their subsidiaries overseas. This means, of course, that the claim of the global corporations that they have a crucial impact on the balance-of-payments situation of Latin America is absolutely correct.

The issue is the nature of the impact. Whether exports benefit a poor economy depends critically on the price. It does not help the foreign-exchange problem of a poor country to export goods at a bargain. When global companies buy from and sell to their own subsidiaries, they establish prices that often have little connection to the market price. Indeed, when the corporate headquarters is acting as both buyer and seller, the very concept of the market has lost its significance. The literature on how to run global corporations is filled with advice on how to set prices on intracompany transfers to maximize the global profits of the parent corporation. Such "transfer prices," as they are called, deviate from the market price for good business reasons. For example, if an automobile manufacturer with operations in many countries wishes to export from a manufacturing subsidiary it owns in one country to a distributing company it owns in another country, it is often advantageous for tax reasons to direct the exporting subsidiary to undervalue its exports. One common reason for this is that the taxes in the manufacturing country may be higher than the taxes in the importing country. Thus the artificial price charged on the export minimizes total taxes for the world corporation and increases its global profits, but the result in the manufacturing country is that it loses foreign exchange (not to mention tax revenues) it would have received had there been an arm's-length transaction between independent buyers and sellers. Another technique even more attractive to the world headquarters is to ship underpriced exports or overpriced imports to a tax-free port such as the Bahamas (known in the business literature as a tax haven) and then reexport the goods at their normal market value or even an inflated price to another subsidiary in the country where they are to be sold. This modern version of the 18th-century "triangular trade," in which cotton, rum, and slaves shuttling between the Caribbean and New England created an American upper class, offers the same sort of profitable flexibility for the global corporation. In an econometric study prepared as part of the research for this book it was found that 75 percent of U.S.-based global corporations in Latin America which are engaged in export conduct all such transactions with other subsidiaries of the same parent, under circumstances in which price can be controlled because the company is trading with itself. The study also shows that despite their claim to expand exports for poor countries, global companies in Latin America were outperformed by local companies in exports outside Latin America, and within Latin America (with the exception of Argentina, Brazil and Mexico) did no better than local firms. U.S. global companies, the econometric analysis reveals, consistently underprice their exports, charging on the average 40 percent less than prices charged by local firms.

At the same time, where it is to their overall advantage global corporations wildly overvalue their imports. Constantine Vaitsos has completed a detailed study of import overpricing in Colombia. By comparing prices charged by a large number of subsidiaries of global companies in the pharmaceutical, rubber, chemical, and electronics industries with world market prices, he found the following average overpricing: in the pharmaceutical firms 155 percent, in the rubber industry 40 percent, and in the electronics industry a range from 16 percent to 60 percent. When he compared the import price of certain popular drugs produced by U.S.-based global companies with the price charged in the United States, he found that the Colombian prices for the tranquilizers Valium and Librium were, respectively, 82 and 65 times higher than the established international market price. The price charged for the antibiotic tetracycline was almost ten times the U.S. price.

These special prices for poor countries, which are not limited to the drug industry, are of course passed on to local consumers—in a country with a per capita income of $300 a year. Transistors go for eleven times their U.S. price in Colombia, Vaitsos reports. A certain TV amplifier is sold for two and one-half times its U.S. equivalent. In Chile, according to Andean Common Market studies, overpricing ranges from 30 percent to more than 700 percent. According to the studies of Pedroleón Díaz, overpricing in Peru ranges from 50 percent to 300 percent and in Ecuador from 75 percent to 200 percent. U.N. studies reveal the same practices in other parts of the world, including Iran, the Philippines, and Pakistan.

In addition to the standard practice of overpricing imports are cruder practices which divert foreign exchange and tax revenues from poor countries. In Colombia, one of the leading government economists told us, foreign firms not infrequently collect the 15 percent subsidy the government pays on all exports on the basis of empty crates shipped to Panama. The head of a subsidiary of a European-based global corporation showed us boxes of pharmaceuticals that had just passed local customs in a Latin American country which contained 30 percent of their declared contents although the subsidiary had paid for full crates (at a price, incidentally, twenty-five times the world market price). Vaitsos estimates that overpricing in the drug industry alone in 1968 cost Colombia $20 million in losses of foreign exchange and $10 million in tax revenues.

There are several other advantages to the company in addition to tax avoidance in manipulating import and export prices. Minimizing local profits is often an essential public relations strategy. Moreover, in countries which impose a percentage limitation on the repatriation of profits, overpricing imports and underpricing exports are good ways to repatriate more profits than the local government allows. All of this makes good business sense, but its impact on the economy of poor countries is cruel. It means exorbitant consumer prices for such necessities as lifesaving drugs and a loss of tax revenues and foreign exchange. It is one more example of the basic conflict in outlook, interest, and goals between the global corporation and countries trying to solve the problems of poverty, unemployment, and inequality. As Harry G. Johnson, professor of economics at the London School and the University of Chicago, puts it, the purpose of the global corporation "is not to transform the economy by exploiting its potentialities—especially its human potentialities—for development, but to exploit the existing situation to its own profit by utilization of the knowledge it already possesses, at minimum cost of adaptation and adjustment to itself."

The various profit-maximizing strategies of the global corporations give us a glimpse of the true profits earned by the companies in poor countries. Thanks to the magic of modern accounting, these bear little relation to the figures that the companies report either to the local government or to the U.S. Treasury. To get a true picture of the annual return on investment that a U.S.-based global corporation derives from its subsidiary in, say, a Latin American country, it is necessary to include in the calculation overpricing of imports and underpricing of exports as well as reported profits, royalties, and fees repatriated to the global headquarters. This total can then be divided into the declared net worth of the subsidiary. Vaitsos performed this exercise for fifteen wholly owned drug subsidiaries of U.S.- and European-based global corporations. He found the effective annual rate of return ranged from a low of 38.1 percent to a high of 962.1 percent with an average of 79.1 percent. Yet that year these firms' average declared profits submitted to the Colombian tax authorities was 6.7 percent. In the rubber industry the effective profit rate on the average was 43 percent; the declared profit rate, 16 percent. Vaitsos' investigations are corroborated by other studies which conclude that during the Decade of Development the *minimum* rate of return of U.S.-based manufacturing corporations in Latin America could not have been much below 40 percent. But even these estimates understate the actual profits being generated. For example, neither the work of Vaitsos nor that summarized by the Rand Corporation could take account of the underpricing of exports or the fact that the subsidiary's declared net worth is usually considerably overvalued. Another and equally revealing approach has been taken by economists at the University of Lund, Sweden. In an analysis of 64 mining operations of U.S. companies in Peru between 1967 and 1969, they found that while the companies reported to the local government total profits of 60 million dollars, the declarations to the U.S. government on the identical operations showed profits of 102 million dollars. In 1966 the Peruvian Parliament established an investigatory commission to study the double accounting methods of the U.S.–controlled

Southern Peru Copper Corporation. For the years 1960–1965, the investigation found that Southern Peru had reported net profits to the Peruvian government of 69 million dollars, whereas to the U.S. Securities and Exchange Commission the corporation had filed net profits of some 135 million dollars.

These are some of the reasons which led Princeton economist Shane Hunt in the Rand Report to conclude that the "calculation of country-specific profit rates . . . presents a statistical challenge that the U.S. Department of Commerce has failed to meet, at least up to the present." A Colombian economist, Dario Abad, has pointed out the meaninglessness of officially declared profits by noting that between 1960 and 1968 the average *reported* rate of return for global corporations in all manufacturing sectors of the country was 6.4 percent. He found it "difficult to accept" that these global corporations would continue to enter Colombia at this rate of reported profitability while national firms were showing higher returns and the interest rate in financial markets was running between 16 and 20 percent. Abad's remarks are reflected in those of an assistant to the president of a large U.S.-based global corporation operating in Latin America who told us it was "no problem" to maintain real rates of return from 50 percent to 400 percent a year. "Calculations in general use in Latin America," Sol Linowitz points out, "estimate an average of $235 million annually in new direct investment during the past decade (omitting reinvested earnings) against $1 billion per year [reported] profit repatriation." These statistics, he notes sadly, are "accepted at face value by many Latins" despite the fact that they "overlook other benefits in export earnings and import savings" from these investments. An analysis of the widespread practice of transfer pricing, however, makes it clear that these "benefits" are accruing elsewhere than in the poor countries and thus make the capital outflow from Latin America even worse than these statistics suggest. The Guatemalan economist Gert Rosenthal, calculating the "financial contribution" of global corporations to the Central American Common Market countries, has found that while net capital inflows increased in the years 1960–1971 by 344 percent, outflows rose 982 percent.

High profit rates, on rare occasions when they are admitted by global corporations, are defended as justifiable compensation for the heavy risks of operating in countries where coups, kidnappings, and earthquakes are everyday occurrences. These risks seem manageable, however. In the last ten years, with the exception of Cuba and Allende Chile, no U.S. manufacturing subsidiary has been nationalized by a Latin American government. Global companies have on the whole tended to benefit from military coups such as those that Brazil and Bolivia have experienced in recent years. In any event, one can afford a string of disasters if he is able to recover anywhere from 47 cents to $4 a year on every dollar he invests. To be sure, in a profit system it is unsporting to begrudge investors high profits. But the system has yet to evolve to the point at which everybody profits. One man's profit usually means another man's loss. The profits of the global corporations derived from poor countries, it must be said, are made at the expense of the people of those countries. The proposition that developed and undeveloped countries will get rich together through the expansion of global corporations is, at best, exactly half true.

3

The second important contribution to development that global corporations claim is the transfer of technology. According to the conventional development wisdom of the past generation, U.S., European, and Japanese corporations can help close the gap between rich and poor by sharing their advanced technology with underdeveloped countries so as to help them increase their productivity, on which rapid economic growth depends. There is no doubt that the import of foreign technology has had a major impact on poor countries. But, as in the case of foreign capital which we have discussed, the import of foreign technology has not had the positive effects hoped for and claimed. Once again the reason is that the suppliers of the technology, the global corporations, and the recipients of the technology have conflicting interests, and the bargaining power has been on the side of the corporations.

Technology is the key to economic power in the modern world. Global corporations, as we have seen, are for the most part oligopolies. Their enviable position usually rests on some piece of exclusive technology which they are not anxious to make available to actual or potential competitors. At the same time, if they are to operate globally they are forced to spread their technology. Their strategy is to maintain maximum control in the process.

Why is technological dependence an obstacle to development? A crucial resource of any society is its capacity to develop the right kind of technology for its own needs. The very purpose of a patent system is to encourage the inventiveness of one's own citizens. When technology is controlled from abroad, it ordinarily means that funds for research and development go to the foreign firm to develop its technology still further—technology that is designed for worldwide profit maximization, not the development needs of poor countries. A critical shortage in poor countries is scientifically trained brainpower. In all of Latin America there are about 250,000 scientists (less than .5 percent of the labor force), as compared with 3 million in the United States. When technology is controlled by foreign corporations, it is advantageous, even necessary, for the few scientists to work for the corporations, often outside their country, rather than for the technological development of their own society. This is the meaning of the celebrated "brain drain." Why would not a scientist rather work in a superbly equipped company laboratory somewhere in the "advanced" world than struggle without funds to invent something in his own country?

The conditions under which global corporations transfer technology to poor countries create problems for them. A study of 409 "transfer of technology" contracts between global corporations and their subsidiaries in Ecuador, Bolivia, Peru, Chile, and Colombia shows that almost 80 percent of them totally prohibited the use of the transferred technology for producing exports. U.N. studies in India, Pakistan, the Philippines, Mexico, and Iran indicate the same widespread use of what the U.N. calls "restrictive business practices." In a few cases the contracts are more liberal. The local firm is permitted to export to neighboring markets too small to be of interest to the global giants, or to distant markets that are beyond its reach. The interest of the global corporation in restricting competition is obvious, but the adverse effect on poor countries seeking to earn scarce foreign exchange by exporting manufactured goods is equally obvious.

Technological dependence on foreign corporations enormously enhances the power they can wield in poor countries—power which, as everywhere, is abused when it is not checked. As José Epstein of the InterAmerican Development Bank points out, "one of the most important failures of Latin American–based mineral and oil producers was the lack of development of domestic research capability which would allow them to discontinue their overwhelming dependence upon outside research." Many problems associated with nationalization efforts in Mexico and Chile, to take two examples, have arisen because these countries lacked their own technological capability. Both China and Japan have understood the extraordinary importance of technological independence to economic development. For China the point was brought home rather graphically in 1960 when Khrushchev precipitately withdrew the Soviet technicians on whom the country was then so heavily dependent. The Japanese made their extraordinary strides in the postwar era by zealously developing their own technology and keeping it out of the hands of foreigners or by licensing it from foreign firms.

The World Managers like to disparage such criticism as expressions of irrational nationalism or wasteful pride. However, the attempt to prevent foreign control of technology is in fact quite rational. Because poor countries lack bargaining power, the technology that global corporations transfer is often obsolete and overpriced. As Epstein puts it, poor countries are likely to get "processes which elsewhere are being abandoned or on the verge of being abandoned." This phenomenon is easy enough to verify in the case of consumer goods. Refrigerators and washing machines of the 1950's are standard items in Bangkok or Accra department stores. Distributing the last generation's technology to poor countries is a good way to prolong its profitable life.

At the same time, global corporations consistently overcharge for the technology they transfer to subsidiaries in poor countries. Detailed investigations in Colombia, Mexico, and elsewhere have revealed overpricing of technology in every case. In one instance, a global corporation was selling machinery to its own subsidiary at a price 30 percent higher than it was charging for the identical item to an independent Colombian firm. In another, a subsidiary of a global paper company applied for a government permit to import used machinery which it claimed had a value of over $1 million. The government agency then solicited international competitive bids for new models of the same machinery and found that the going price for new models was 50 percent *less* than what the company was charging its subsidiary for used models. (Obsolete machinery thus transferred usually had a 0 value on the parent books, since it had already been fully depreciated for tax purposes in the home country.) Managers of global-corporation subsidiaries operating in Latin America whom we have interviewed admit that overvaluing of technology is "standard practice." One reason for overvaluation, of course, is to produce politically attractive financial statements. It is an easy way to make one's investment look bigger and one's profits look smaller. But this practice helps to explain some of the mystery of why poor countries are not "closing the gap."

A more fundamental criticism of the global corporation's role in technology transfer is that its own interests impel it to transfer precisely the sort of technology poor countries need least. Thus in many cases the imported technology is too expensive and too complicated. Having been developed for the needs of industrialized societies, it does not solve and may indeed aggravate the problems of poor countries. Yet, the governments of poor countries desire such technology as a badge of prestige and progress, and the corporations are happy to cultivate new markets for what they already produce. René Dumont, the renowned agronomist, points out that what most of the world needs is not gas-devouring four-wheel tractors which are expensive to buy, operate, and repair, but better hoes and ox plows. While Ford, British Leyland, and Honda have all developed relatively inexpensive ($500–$700) "minitractors," the major effort of the global corporations is to push their standard models. With few exceptions, the global corporations have not been inventive about tailoring technology to the needs of the underdeveloped world.

A principal reason, of course, is that executives of global corporations define these needs in terms of U.S. and European criteria—a heavy emphasis on individual consumption, private cars, individual refrigerators, expensive medical technology. The Chilean economist Jorge de Ahumada argues that every dollar spent in Latin America on doctors and hospitals costs a hundred lives—by which he means that if the dollar had been spent on providing safe drinking water a hundred lives could have been saved. Ivan Illich argues that every car which Brazil puts on the road denies fifty people good transportation by bus. However arbitrary these figures may be, the basic point is sound. Global companies transfer technology which they have developed at considerable cost and which they have successfully marketed in the already industrialized world. For the most part it is technology for enhancing private consumption, not for solving social problems. There are much greater possibilities of quick return if the company attempts to create a market for such private-consumption technology in the nonindustrialized world than if it takes the risk of experimenting with new technologies specifically designed for development needs. Moreover, the record of the large U.S. corporation in innovating cheap nutritious food, low-cost housing, mass transport, pollution-control devices, or other problem-solving technologies in the United States is less than impressive.

The one characteristic of global corporate technology with the most devastating consequences for poor countries is that it destroys jobs. Typically, poor countries abound in human resources. It is predicted that the labor force outside the Communist countries will increase by 170 million in this decade. Yet the sort of technology that global corporations export to poor countries is capital-intensive and laborsaving, because that is what they have developed in the United States as a response to high labor costs. Instead of making efficient use of the manpower of the underdeveloped world, however, such transferred technology tends to convert their human resources, which are their biggest assets, into social liabilities. As the Decade of Development began in 1960, the United Nations estimated that 27 percent of the labor force of the Third World was unemployed. By the end of the 1960's this figure had risen to 30 percent. Erik Thorbecke has estimated for the International Development Bank that 43 percent of the Peruvian labor force is "not needed in the production of that nation's national product." Unemployment in Colombia is about 36 percent. In 1960, the last year for which comparative figures are available, unemployment ranged from 22 percent in Argentina, Brazil, and Mexico to 42 percent in the poorer countries of Central America and the Caribbean. James P. Grant of the Overseas Development Council has calculated that the number of people fully unemployed approximately tripled in number between 1950 and 1965.

Unemployment figures are among the slipperiest of statistics. Supposedly, they are based on counting of people, but the unemployed are frequently invisible to census takers and government officials. Particularly in underdeveloped countries, such figures should be taken as gross indicators rather than precise measurements of an extremely serious and rapidly deteriorating world problem. It is always safe to assume that the problem is worse than the statistics suggest. There are many bits of definitional sleight of hand which governments employ to put their unemployment problem in the best light. Are seasonal workers who have a job a few days a year "employed"? Do the ubiquitous flower venders who hawk their wilted wares at traffic lights in Mexico City for a few pesos a day have "jobs"? Do the unemployment statistics include the man who volunteers to park your car in a parking lot (which does not employ him) in the hope of getting a peso tip? Latin America, and Asia and Africa too, abound in such people whom economists call "marginal" or "underemployed." The problem is rapidly becoming worse. Today more than 5 million people live in shantytowns and slums at the edge of the great cities of Latin America. By the end of this decade, because of the rapid migration to urban areas (including millions who can no longer sustain themselves on the land), U.N. studies indicate that the populations of Mexico City, Rio, and São Paulo will almost double. The "marginal population" is increasing at the rate of 15 percent a year.

The World Managers claim too that they hold the key to the unemployment problem. There is no doubt that global corporations employ an impressive number of people around the world. In many areas it is hard to conceive of what global-corporation employees would do if the company had not built a factory in that particular place. But the statistics, inadequate as they are, demonstrate dramatically that the global corporation has not begun to solve the global employment problem and has in fact been making it worse. The expansion of the global corporation has contributed to the expansion of world unemployment. Despite a dramatic increase in the importance of the manufacturing sector to the Latin American economy (25 percent of the total GNP in 1970, up from 11 percent in 1925), it employs a slightly smaller percentage of the total work force than it did 50 years ago. This is not to say that the global corporations are alone responsible for the growth in unemployment, but rather that their development track offers no solution to the problem and, indeed, is aggravating it. It is possible to document the job-destroying impact of global-corporation technology. Even the construction industry, once an important source of employment for poor countries at a stage of rapid industrialization, will no longer absorb as many new workers as formerly because cranes, bulldozers, and other laborsaving machinery are being substituted for labor. (In Singapore, however, because of special economic circumstances of that island economy and a vigorous public-housing program, the construction industry now absorbs a significantly higher percentage of the labor force than it did before the influx of the global corporations.) The mechanization of agriculture has had particularly negative impacts on the unemployment problem in Latin America. The trend toward large, mechanized farms controlled by agribusiness, according to a report of the Inter-American Committee on Agricultural Development, has dramatically increased crop yields, but it has not absorbed labor. Huge farms produce an average of 400 times what small farms can produce, but they employ only 15 times as many workers. Thus the trend is toward the use of less and less labor for each unit of output.

According to the development theory of the global corporations, increase in a country's growth rate is all that is needed to keep the unemployment rate at an "acceptable" level. However, as Raúl Prebisch has shown in his 1970 report to the Inter-American Development Bank, Latin America as a whole would have to grow at a yearly rate of 6 percent—an extremely difficult pace to maintain—just to keep up to the 1960 unemployment levels, which can hardly be considered "acceptable." Thus, on the basis of the experiences of the 1950–1970 period, it is now clear that economic growth alone will not solve the employment problem.

The economy can boom through an industrialization process which actually employs an ever-smaller percentage of the labor force. The technology transferred by the global drug firms, for example, is so laborsaving that no more than 3.4 percent of total costs represents labor. In the Venezuelan oil industry, Norman Girvan has calculated, the labor force was reduced by 33 percent between 1950 and 1966, and in the Dutch Antilles by 70 percent; in the petrochemicals industry, according to Charles Levinson, there have been "dramatic falls in unit labor costs." (In petrochemicals, Levinson maintains, the labor component is now under 10 percent of total cost.) The rapidly expanding use of capital-intensive technology has an adverse effect on income distribution. The returns on privately owned resources go to the owners of those resources—either to foreign companies and their foreign shareholders, or to a tiny group of domestic investors who already receive more than 40 percent of the country's income. Income concentration and unemployment feed on each other. "Raising the incomes of the poor in LDC's [less-developed countries]," James Grant points out, "should generate more jobs than an equivalent rise in the incomes of the wealthy, since the luxury goods bought by the well-off tend to be relatively capital-intensive in nature in developing countries, whereas the goods a poorer person normally purchases require more labor to produce." At the same time, income distribution is not likely to be improved significantly without an increase in employment possibilities for the bottom 40 percent of the population.

As the technology of global corporations operating in poor countries has become more sophisticated, the investment needed to employ a single worker, particularly in the chemical, machinery, paper, rubber, and food industries, where global corporations have concentrated their operations, has tripled. Dudley Seers, commissioned by the International Labor Organization to study high-technology industry in Colombia, found that whereas it took 45,000 pesos to employ one worker in 1957, by 1966 it took 100,000 1957 pesos. A more recent study, by one of the authors, of 257 manufacturing firms throughout Latin-America shows that global corporations use less than one-half the number of employees per $10,000 of sales that local firms do. From 1925 to 1970 the percentage of the Latin American work force employed in the manufacturing sector actually decreased. A *Wall Street Journal* report on Brazil gives some idea of what these figures mean in human terms:

> Far from helping such workers [60-cents-a-day cane harvesters] Brazil's modernization actually victimizes thousands. When a salt company bought new equipment, efficiency soared —but 7000 people lost their jobs. In Ponce de Carvalhos, many suffer indirectly from the mechanization of sugar plantations in far-off parts of Brazil. This has made the local plantations uneconomic . . . A 60 year old woman who had worked 20 years

on one plantation says she and 1000 other workers were told to "harvest your crop, plant grass for cattle, and get out." She now earns $6.50 a month washing clothes. A 41 year old man who worked 18 years at the Mary-of-Mercy sugar mill now peddles bread by the roadside for 54 cents a day.

Economists now agree that the "job crisis" is a consequence of what James Grant calls the "artificial cheapening of the price of capital and the artificial increase in the price of labor." Poor countries have encouraged "urban-oriented factories and large scale, mechanized farming as the fastest route to modernization at a time when the latest machines use less and less labor." Poor countries subsidize foreign capital by inflating interest rates, by making generous tax concessions, legal and illegal, and because of their inability to control transfer prices. At the same time, the modest improvements in minimum-wage laws, fringe benefits, and union bargaining power mean higher labor costs for global corporations, which often pay more than the traditional sectors of the economy. Thus global companies have every incentive to buy more machines and to employ fewer workers.

Some advisers to global corporations are beginning to issue warnings about the global employment crisis. The stability necessary to build the Global Shopping Center is threatened. Grant points out that Cuba had a 16-percent unemployment rate when Castro made his revolution—others have put it at more than 25 percent—and that leftist governments in Peru, Chile, and Sri Lanka (formerly Ceylon) are in part at least a reaction to severe unemployment. He believes that global corporations can and must shift to more labor-intensive technology in poor countries and points to the experience of Singapore, Hong Kong, Taiwan, and Korea during the last decade. These countries, he notes, "had very high rates of increase in their work forces in the 1960's, yet achieved rapid growth, drastically reduced unemployment, and at the same time, improved income distribution and dramatically reduced birth rates." But there were particular circumstances in these countries that make it unlikely that their experiences can be repeated. Taiwan and Korea received massive doses of U.S. Government aid under unique political circumstances. Taiwan, particularly, in the agricultural sector had as early as the 1950's carried out certain income-distribution reforms which have yet to be applied in Latin America, Africa, or most of the other Asian countries. In the 1960's there was little sign in most underdeveloped countries of a willingness to transfer income from the rich to the poor through land reform, taxes, or social security.

The People's Republic of China has helped to solve what used to be a mammoth unemployment problem before the Revolution through various forms of "reverse engineering" designed to convert capital-intensive technology into more labor-intensive technology. In Japan and Korea such operations as weaving and rubber and plywood production are much more labor-intensive than equivalent processes in the United States. The Japanese are now producing in Chinese communes 30,000 out of the 100,000 trucks they manufacture each year. Jacks, monkey wrenches, and tool kits are other items now being made in China for Japanese firms.

How far the global corporations are prepared to go in "reverse engineering" is open to question. Jack Baranson, former World Bank economist and now consultant on investment problems to global corporations, finds that the "predominant view" of U.S.-based multinational corporations on assisting developing countries to solve their own special technology problems is "largely negative." Most companies, he concludes, believe their past performance "in the admittedly limited adaptations of products and techniques to local conditions [has] been 'adequate.' " A very small number of firms, he says, recognize the need to develop "new transfer modes."

Remarkable experiments in training illiterate workers to perform skilled assembly-line operations in a matter of months have been conducted in Asia. Some Japanese-, U.S.-, and European-based global corporations are eager to learn from the Chinese their techniques for increasing productivity of unskilled labor. It is likely that global corporations will make increasing efforts to adapt their technologies of production to take maximum advantage of the cheap-labor market. Increasingly, they are likely to follow both labor-dispensing strategies (increased use of automation) and wage-reduction strategies (increased use of low-wage workers). Depending upon their product, firms will emphasize one or the other. Thus, for example, the petrochemicals industry is becoming increasingly laborsaving, while the electronics industry has been more and more relocating its operations to take advantage of cheap labor. But all global corporations will pursue some mix of both. The issue is how much these two strategies conflict with each other. Can a global corporation maximize its profits if it must develop specially tailored technologies for countries in differing stages of development?

Jack Baranson has analyzed with respect to the transfer of technology the basic clash between the financial goals of corporations and the development goals of poor countries. Employing the bottom 40 percent of the population or even absorbing the millions who swell the ranks of the unemployed each year is not an obvious way to make a quick return on one's investment. It is in the corporation's interest to develop a market among those who already have money rather than to support processes of income distribution that may create some wider market in the distant future. Managers who serve under the tyranny of the annual balance sheet cannot afford long-term visions. Developing countries are increasingly eager to gain control over technology to increase their bargaining power and self-reliance. Companies, as we have seen, are interested in maintaining tight control of proprietary rights, frustrating possible competition from local entrepreneurs, and maintaining what Baranson calls "managerial control and flexibility in allocating corporate resources on a global basis." During the 1960's these conflicts were resolved overwhelmingly in favor of the corporations, with disastrous effects on employment and income distribution. In the 1970's, as we shall explore in Chapter 8, the conflicts remain, but the power relation and, hence, corporate strategies are changing.

4

The third great source of power of global corporations in poor countries is the control over ideology—the values that determine how people live. In Chapter 6 we described how the global corporations are in a position to determine most of what people in poor countries see on the television or movie screen, hear on the radio, or read in magazines. The role which the Ministry of Propaganda plays in shaping values, tastes, and attitudes in what the U.S. Government likes to call "closed societies" global corporations are playing in many parts of the "free world." Through TV, movie-house commercials, comic books, and magazine ads, foreign corporations unquestionably exert more continuing influence on the minds of the bottom half of the Mexican people, to take one example, than either the Mexican Government or the Mexican educational system. A small fraction of the Mexican population goes to school beyond the third grade. The officially admitted illiteracy rate is more than 27 percent. Contact with school is for the vast majority of the population fleeting, but exposure to TV and the transistor radio is lifelong. As Lee Bickmore explained to us in describing his marketing plans for Ritz Crackers, one does not need to be able to read to get the Ritz message. His point was illustrated a few months later when we encountered an illiterate shoeless peasant in a poor Mexican village riding a burro laden with boxes of Ritz Crackers.

Nor can government propaganda match the power of advertising. On some of the main thoroughfares of Mexico City, government slogans exhorting the population to cleanliness compete for attention with huge billboards advertising beer, cosmetics, smart clothes, and other symbols of the good life. These billboards, prepared with the latest techniques of modern advertising, offer Technicolor fantasies of luxury, love, and power that no message from the Department of Health, however uplifting, is likely to disturb.

Throughout the underdeveloped world global corporations are thus successfully marketing the same dreams they have been selling in the industrialized world. Stimulating consumption in low-income countries and accommodating local tastes to globally distributed products is crucial to the development of an ever-expanding Global Shopping Center. The World Managers argue that they are cultivating tastes and educating for progress. Marketing the pleasures of becoming a "man of distinction" who knows and drinks good whiskey, of exercising power on the highway at the wheel of a new "Fury," or escaping to the South Seas via Pan Am offers the people of poor countries the prospect of "the good life" to which they can aspire. Telling poor people about products they have the money to buy right now, such as Coca-Cola and ITT's Twinkies (via its wholly owned subsidiary Wonder Bread), opens up new horizons. How, the World Managers argue, can the transfer of the consumption ideology, which had so much to do with the expansion of the U.S. economy, be bad for poor countries?

Whether the transfer of the marketplace ideology by global corporations is good or bad for development depends once again on what is meant by development. If the priority of development policy is to alleviate the most crushing problem of the under-developed world—mass poverty resulting from unemployment and inequality—then we must conclude that the transfer of the ideology of the global corporations to poor countries has had several disastrous impacts. First, despite Jacques Maisonrouge's claim that the global corporation is a great leveler and a great equalizer, corporate strategy actually reinforces the sharp class cleavages that exist in all poor countries. The principal targets of most global corporations are the enclaves of affluence within destitute societies. Peter Drucker, the father of the Global Shopping Center, points out that within the "vast mass of poverty that is India" there is "a sizeable modern economy, comprising 10 percent or more of the Indian population, or 50,000,000 people." Nabisco executives estimate that their potential customers in Brazil, a market they are just entering with a major advertising campaign, are no more than 20 million out of a total population of 105 million. Obviously, expensive capital goods such as automobiles, luxuries such as fine watches and cameras, and costly services, such as a plane ride to New York, are available to only a tiny fraction of the population in underdeveloped countries, although in absolute numbers it represents a sizeable market. These items are frequently imports and exhaust scarce foreign exchange. The mobile minority, encouraged by advertising to adopt the eating, wearing, and traveling habits of the American upper middle class, live imported lives.

Development, as Robert Heilbroner has pointed out, requires much more than encouraging economic growth within a given social structure: "It is rather the *modernization* of that structure, a process . . . that requires remaking of society in its most intimate as well as its most public attributes." Structural and institutional changes in the government, the educational system, the health system, the income-distribution system, and in the setting of economic priorities are obvious prerequisites to any serious attack on the problems of poverty, unemployment, and inequality. Yet for the elite in poor countries, membership in the international consumption community has a cooling effect on reformist zeal. In Latin America the university radical who by his late twenties is obediently sipping beer in front of his color TV in a comfortable house in the suburbs is a stereotype. Those who rent their comforts through installment debt, no matter what revolutionary impulses may lie dormant within them, do not like to think about, much less do anything about, social change.

What effect does the export of dreams have on those who cannot afford to indulge them? Not so long ago Thomas J. Watson, Jr., chairman of IBM, worried that if "we flaunt our wealth in those people's faces, we shall drive them either to despair or frenzy or revolution like none the world has ever seen. . . ." In the 1950's everyone in the development business worried about "the revolution of rising expectations." According to the prevailing theory, when Peruvian peasants or African bushmen caught their first glimpse of "tomorrow's kitchen" in a Hollywood movie or imported TV program or watched the rich basking in the sun in airline ads on billboards, their expectations, their drive for self-improvement, but also their envy would increase. If the expectations consistently outpaced the improvement in their living standard, there would be political upheavals all over the underdeveloped world.

Quantitative evidence of the impact of advertising on the bottom 40 to 60 percent of the population in the underdeveloped world is meager. This is not the population that the advertising agencies are ordinarily paid by clients to canvass. There has been little research, and most of it is impressionistic. But what there is suggests that the "communications explosion" to which the World Managers often allude has not had the revolutionary impact that some feared in the 1950's, but rather the opposite. Evangelina García, a specialist in "social communication" at the Central University of Venezuela and a consultant to McCann-Erickson, J. Walter Thompson, and other U.S.-based global advertising firms, says that the "most revealing and continually reconfirmed" finding of her studies on advertising is that the *marginales* (those who are barely hanging on) have "lost their perception of class differences." They think that there are, to be sure, rich and poor, she explained, "but that all have access to the same consumer goods" they hear about on the transistor or see on the TV. It is a matter of luck whether they have the money to buy them, and luck can change. Johnson's Wax conducted a survey of *marginales* and found that a common reaction in hovels with dirt floors was "I don't have a floor to wax, but I can buy the wax if I want to." Thus the byproduct of advertising campaigns is to give families without the bare necessities of life a spurious feeling of being middle-class.

Professor García was struck in her investigations with the power of the advertising message. Jingles and slogans repeated every few minutes on radios and TV's, especially in homes without other communications links to the outside world, become what she calls "mental clichés." When a slum family is asked what shampoo it buys, the common response is to quote back in precise words the company's own current slogan: "Because I want beautiful hair," "because Johnson and Johnson makes the very best . . ." etc., etc. Because the Venezuelan market is small, companies are constantly diversifying the products to reach the same people. Four years ago Ajax powder was the key to dishwashing happiness. Now the era of liquid soap has arrived.

An important impact of imported advertising campaigns, Professor García points out, is that "the values in the U.S. are reproduced in Venezuela, in relation to sex, love, prestige, race, etc." Today in Venezuela, she notes, "the housewife measures her happiness by whether she has a refrigerator . . . before a woman's happiness was to have children, depend on her husband, even to have goods but not to show them." Advertising, she concludes, creates a psychological dependence. One's sense of self-esteem is determined by what one buys. In effect, they are saying, "My security—my emotional security—depends upon what I consume." Advertising is popular among the very poor in Latin America. While a few intellectuals and nationalist politicians worry about the effects of scientific huckstering, most people appear to accept the rationale which the advertising agencies give for their activities. The advertiser is like a friend who tells you about all the wonderful things in the world that you didn't even know existed.

Marketplace ideology has a political impact on the poor in this century not unlike that of the state Church in past centuries. But whereas the Church may have pacified the wretched of the earth by promising them a heaven in a future life, the worldwide advertising agencies are selling solace through consumption for the here and now. Through both its program content and its advertising messages, TV has a socializing influence on poor countries (as, of course, it has in the United States). Studies of the impact of TV in Peru suggest that the poor embrace the TV culture because it offers new fantasies that permit escape from the rigid class structure of their country. It is hopeless for them to aspire to middle-class status in their own society, but vicarious identification with the clean-cut operatives in *Mission Impossible* costs nothing. (In the process, as William Shramm points out, traditional values such as religion, politeness, and relaxation are tossed aside in favor of the imported values of the U.S.-produced TV programs—the thrill of success, the thrill of violence, and the thrill of consumption.) The psychologist Muzafer Sherif noted many years ago in analyzing U.S. television that the mass media "by selecting and stressing certain themes at the expense of others, have the effect of creating and perpetuating ego-involvements which will not endanger the status quo. The values stressed are typically those which make no contribution to the process of social changes."

Global marketeers are not persuaded that there is anything wrong with spreading the thrill of consumption in poor countries. "The factory girl or the salesgirl in Lima or Bombay (or the Harlem ghetto)," says Peter Drucker, "wants a lipstick . . . There is no purchase that gives her as much true value for a few cents." The fact that she is in all probability malnourished and without a decent place to live does not mean that she is spending foolishly. Albert Stridsberg, an "international advertising specialist" writing in *Advertising Age*, says that we must rid ourselves of "the conventional range of ideas about what will minister to the poor man's physical needs. The psychological significance of his spending his money on a transistor radio may be more important than the physical benefit generated by spending the same money for basic foodstuffs." It is an interesting theory, especially when applied to a country like Peru where, it is estimated, a substantial number of all babies born begin life with serious, and possibly irreparable, brain damage due to malnutrition.

Creating and satisfying wants such as lipsticks and transistor radios while the basic necessities of life recede ever further perpetuates and compounds mass misery in poor countries. (In certain Peruvian villages a pathetic item is a piece of stone painted to look like a transistor radio. Peasants too poor to buy a real one carry it for status.) Global corporations have the enormous power to determine what does or does not give "psychological satisfaction." It is disingenuous to talk about the "dictates of the consumer" when the consumer is so thoroughly subject to the dictation of the modern technology of manipulation.

What are the long-range social effects of advertising on people who earn less than $200 a year? The peasant scratching out an existence on a tiny plot, the urban slum dweller subsisting on odd jobs and garbage scavenging, and the army of low-wage domestics, harvesters, and factory hands receive most of what they learn of the outside world through the images and slogans of advertising. One message that comes through clearly is that happiness, achievement, and being white have something to do with one another. In *mestizo* countries such as Mexico and Venezuela where most of the population still bear strong traces of their Indian origin, billboards depicting the good life for sale invariably feature blond, blue-eyed American-looking men and women. One effect of such "white is beautiful" advertising is to reinforce feelings of inferiority which are the essence of a politically immobilizing colonial mentality.

A crucial organizational strategy for those societies which have made real steps toward solving the problems of mass misery, unemployment, and inequality has been to mobilize the population by encouraging their sense of identity, as individuals and as members of a national community. A succession of visitors to China, Cuba, Tanzania and North Vietnam have been struck by the genuine enthusiasm of the people to participate in what they are repeatedly told are great social experiments. In these countries the population is continually being asked to believe that they are "new people" who by virtue of their own abilities and energies are able to transform their societies in ways unknown in human history. Backed by the power of the state, the primary appeal is to personal and national pride. Yet in societies where the advertising agency is the Ministry of Propaganda, the opposite appeal is made. The effect is to encourage the disparagement of local culture and the dependence on foreign culture. The psychiatrist Michael Maccoby tells the story of visiting a potter in a rural Mexican village who made magnificent painted plates of the sort that command high prices in New York. To honor his visitor, he served him lunch on plastic plates from Woolworth's. The subtle message of the global advertiser in poor countries is "Neither you nor what you create are worth very much. We will sell you a civilization."

Evidence has been accumulating in the last few years that the diet of the bottom 40 to 60 percent of the world's population is actually getting worse. Alan Berg in his Brookings Institution study of world nutrition problems notes that whereas production of beef in Central America increased dramatically during the 1960's, the per capita consumption of meat in those countries either increased marginally or declined. In Costa Rica, to take the most extreme case, meat production increased 92 percent from the early 1960's to 1970 but per capita consumption went down 26 percent. The reason, Berg notes, is that the meat is "ending up not in Latin American stomachs but in franchised restaurant hamburgers in the United States . . ." There has been a per capita decline of production and consumption of milk in India. Since eggs cost anywhere from 40 to 70 cents a dozen in poor countries, they are prohibitive as a source of protein. (In 1969 the average American consumed 314 eggs; the average Indian 8.) The decline of real purchasing power of the world's poor and the flight of the "marginal" forces to the city means that more people are eating worse than ever before. (In India, Berg reports, a family must have an income of $4 to $5 a month before it can afford an adequate diet. But more than 60 percent of the population fall well below this line.)

The deadly effects of the world hunger problem are obvious. In Brazil, children under five constitute less than one-fifth of the population but account for four-fifths of all deaths. According to Berg's study, malnutrition is the primary or contributing cause of death in 57 percent of all deaths in Latin America of one- to four-year-olds. The high infant mortality rate has a great deal to do with the high birth rate characteristic of poor countries (and of poor families in rich countries). People produce more babies in hopes that some at least will survive. Berg estimates that about a billion persons in the world today suffer the effects of malnutrition. More than 300 million children suffer "grossly retarded physical growth" due to not getting enough to eat. According to the nutrition expert Myron Winick, "the evidence is becoming more and more weighty that malnutrition in infancy permanently affects the minds of the children who have been affected." Even less severe malnutrition causes the dullness and apathy that well-fed foreign observers often choose to call laziness. In India, Berg estimates, the lack of vitamin A is the cause of blindness for more than a million people. The cost of caring for a blind population of one million over their lifetime at $25 per year is more than $1 billion.

Ultimately, the claim of global corporations to be engines of development must be judged in terms of the world hunger crisis. Food to sustain life and strength is the most basic human requirement. Severe malnutrition is both a consequence of poverty and a cause. Energy, mental alertness, and creativity are all directly related to food intake. "I think it could be plausibly argued," George Orwell once wrote, "that changes in diet are more important than changes of dynasty or even of religion." Striking changes in diet and food distribution have occurred around the world in our time, and global corporations have played an important role in these changes.

The hunger problem, nutrition experts are now beginning to understand, responds to no simple technical solution. (The highly publicized "green revolution" which dramatically increased crop yields by means of new hybrids, fertilizers, and tractors has actually aggravated income maldistribution and malnutrition in many areas of the world because it eliminated "marginal" farmers who could not afford the new technology.) Increase of food production does not mean more food for the poor. Students of the world hunger problem, like Mexico's Joaquín Cravioto, now recognize that the achievement of good nutrition needs to be treated as an ecological problem—i.e., malnutrition is a consequence of a subtle interplay of social, economic, and dietary imbalances. It turns out to be impossible to improve diet without also doing something about income distribution, employment, and sanitation. Thus some of the conventional development wisdom of the 1960's is being slowly revised in the light of new findings. For example, it used to be assumed that mothers in Latin America gave their babies low-protein gruel instead of milk because they did not know any better. The obvious solution was a house-to-house "drink more milk" campaign. Yet, Dr. Cravioto points out, it turns out that the Indian women in rural Mexico had a better sense of what to do to ensure their children's survival than the well-meaning doctors who were advising them. The reason why they were reluctant to give their babies milk was that many of them died from diarrhea. Proteins such as milk, eggs, and meat are excellent breeding grounds for bacteria, while protein-poor substances such as gruel are not good homes for germs. Thus, Cravioto concludes, the price of survival for the *marginales* in a society unable or unwilling to improve sanitation is malnutrition.

While it is important to understand these ecological relationships which contribute to the malnutrition problem, the basic cause of hunger is still what it has always been: eating too little. And the usual reason people eat too little is that they have too little money. The absolute decline in consumption for millions in the bottom 40 to 60 percent of the world's population is a direct consequence of increased concentration of income. The diet of the middle class is dramatically improving in many parts of the world. The new generation of Japanese is several inches taller and several pounds heavier than the last. But for the bottom, subsistence is getting harder.

María Souza is a 30-year-old mother of five children (two others died) who lives without hot water, sewage, or electricity in a mud hut in northeast Brazil. In 1972 she was interviewed by *The Wall Street Journal*: " 'Times are worse now,' says the gaunt, underfed Mrs. Souza. 'Now we get only two eggs a week. We buy no more oranges, no more bananas.' " Brazilian Government statistics show that the Northeast is growing at an even faster rate than the phenomenal national growth rate, which has averaged 9.8 percent between 1968 and 1972. However, a U.S. State Department report on the region concludes, "Real income of employed and partially employed workers for the lower two-thirds of the labor force has not increased in the past five years and probably has decreased." *The Wall Street Journal* notes that "Factories lured to the area by government tax incentives and other factors now employ about 900,000 workers. But nearly two-thirds of these workers earn less than the $30 a month that the government figures it costs to subsist in the cities. And on the farms fully 80 percent of all families earn less than $50 a year." Infant mortality is eight times the U.S. rate and, according to Nelson Chaves, a nutrition expert working in the area, "fully 20 percent of the children in the region's coastal belt suffer from malnutrition so severe that it has damaged their brains for life . . . Moreover, millions in the area of all ages fall prey to debilitating

diseases that sap their energy and lead to an early death." The
Journal survey reports on one of these millions, Manuel José, 37,
now too weak from hunger and disease to work in the cane fields
(where he might make as much as 60 cents a day). He walks
"the 15-mile round trip to Recife three days a week to beg to
support his pregnant wife and three children . . . His other
five children have already died."

The global corporations, it must be said, have compounded
the world hunger problem in three ways. First, they have contributed to the concentration of income and the elimination of
jobs. Second, through its increasing control of arable land in poor
countries, agribusiness is complicating the problem of food distribution. It is good business to grow high-profit crops for export
rather than to raise corn, wheat, and rice to support a local population without money to pay for it. In Colombia, for example, a
hectare devoted to the raising of carnations brings a million
pesos a year, while wheat or corn brings only 12,500 pesos. As
a result, Colombia, like most other poor countries in Latin America, must use scarce foreign exchange to import basic foodstuffs.
The development track of the global corporations features increased production of luxury items such as strawberries and
asparagus for the international suburban market. But the money
does not flow to the hungry majority, and those who used to
subsist on local fruits and vegetables now more and more find
them priced beyond their reach. Mexico, the agricultural expert
Rodolfo Stavenhagen warns, is about to face a critical food
shortage because agribusiness, which controls an ever-increasing
share of production, uses dollars instead of proteins and calories
as the test of what to grow, and what food is grown is increasingly
exported.

Finally, the companies' control of ideology through advertising
has helped to change the dietary habits of the poor in unfortunate
ways. Beginning in 1966, the major global food companies had
begun research on low-cost protein foods, baby cereals, soft
drinks, imitation milk, candies, snacks, soups, and noodles, and
by 1968 a dozen such products were on the market. Berg questioned a number of food and pharmaceutical companies seeking
to introduce such products in India and found that "corporate
image was the most important general factor influencing their
decision to become involved." While there was also a "strong

thread of social responsibility" on the part of some executives, the fact that image is a prime motive means, he points out, that "corporate contributions to national nutrition are likely to be token." The companies interviewed admitted that their new products were aimed at middle and upper income levels. One executive of a British-based global firm notes, "It is a sad fact that most nutritional food products marketed by commercial firms are aimed at the segment of society least in need of them." Another points out that even if the company obtained the ingredients for nothing, the cost of packaging them alone would make them "too expensive for the multitude who need them most."

"The food industry in developing countries has been a disaster . . . a minus influence," says Derrick B. Jelliffe, a leading nutrition expert. Companies are using advertising to take what Berg calls "blatant advantage of nutrition consciousness." J. K. Roy's studies in West Bengal show that poor families under the influence of advertising are buying patent baby foods "at exorbitant rates" although they could buy local cow's milk at much lower cost. They had been persuaded (falsely) that the packaged food had "extraordinary food value." In the Caribbean, Berg reports, nurses are employed by companies to get the names of new mothers at the hospital and then to "race to the women's homes to give free samples and related advertising."

In his studies of changing dietary habits in rural Mexican villages, Joaquín Cravioto finds that the two products which peasants want and buy the moment they come into contact with the advertising message are white bread and soft drinks. Bread becomes a substitute for tortillas. Depending upon how enriched it is, there may be some gain in protein and vitamins, but a loss in calcium. But the most important impact of this shift in eating habits in poor villages is that it takes a much greater share of the virtually nonexistent family food budget. Coca-Cola, nutritionally speaking, is a way of consuming imported sugar at a high price. People like the taste, but its popularity, as Albert Stridsberg points out, is due to the advertising campaigns of the global giants. "It has long been known that in the poorest regions of Mexico," he notes with satisfaction, "where soft drinks play a functional role in the diet, it is the international brands—Coke and Pepsi—not local off-brands, which dominate. Likewise, a Palestinian refugee urchin, shining shoes in Beirut, saves his

piastres for a real Coca-Cola, at twice the price of a local cola."
The result is what the nutrition expert Jelliffe calls "commerciogenic malnutrition." It is not uncommon in Mexico, doctors who
work in rural villages report, for a family to sell the few eggs
and chickens it raises to buy Coke for the father while the children waste away for lack of protein.

The companies say they are not to blame if primitive people
want to indulge their taste at the expense of their children and
their own health. Whenever they try to sell food as being "good
for you," executives claim, no one buys. But the reality is that
companies are investing heavily in campaigns to sell nutritionally
marginal food to economically marginal people. In Latin America, to take only one example of what Berg calls "antinutrition
education" campaigns of the food companies, a cornstarch ad
features a robust baby in order to give the false impression that
this classic stomach filler of the poor is actually good for one.
The villages and tribes of the world, Albert Stridsberg proclaims
in *Advertising Age*, "are eager to become 'consumers.' " The
problem, he says, "is to find products which can be priced within
their financial reach and still pay for branded advertising support and return a reasonable profit." Company campaigns have
succeeded in increasing consumption of white bread, confections,
and soft drinks among the poorest people in the world by convincing them that status, convenience, and a sweet taste are more
important than nutrition.

Global companies have used their great levers of power—finance capital, technology, organizational skills, and mass communications—to create a Global Shopping Center in which the hungry of the world are invited to buy expensive snacks and a Global
Factory in which there are fewer and fewer jobs. The World
Manager's vision of One World turns out in fact to be two
distinct worlds—one featuring rising affluence for a small
transnational middle class, and the other escalating misery for
the great bulk of the human family. The dictates of profit and
the dictates of survival are in clear conflict. In the next chapter
we shall consider whether they can be reconciled.

8

The Power of the Poor:
Changing Prospects for a Postcolonial World

1

How one looks at the problem of world poverty has a great deal to do with the view from one's window. In talking with top managers of global corporations in oak-paneled offices and private dining rooms high above Central Park or nestled in a suburban New Jersey wood, we were struck by their invincible faith in their power for good. To be sure, poverty, unemployment, illiteracy, and disease are not their favorite subjects. But development is a favorite subject, and the belief that they are running an engine of development is standard. On the fifty-sixth floor of a Manhattan skyscraper, the level of self-protective ignorance about what the company may be doing in Colombia or Mexico is high. The president is familiar with what he is producing in poor countries and is well briefed on his company's visible activities. ("Our subsidiary in São Paulo created two hundred jobs last year.") But the negative effect on local economies of the firm's accounting practices—underpricing exports, overpricing imports, overvaluation of technology—escapes him, not only because he finds such matters complicated, but also because he operates under a psychological need *not* to know. (Since it is only recently that the governments themselves began to acquire the technical capability to analyze transfer pricing, it is not altogether surprising that headquarters of global firms do not spend much time analyzing the adverse effects of their standard business practices on poor countries several thousand miles away.)

Managers of subsidiaries, on the other hand, whose office-

185

window view usually takes in at least a glimpse of the human meaning of underdevelopment—the bustling shoppers below share the sidewalk with a straggling army of shoeshine boys, beggars, and abandoned children—have a somewhat better understanding of what they are doing. "Oh, I know we overprice our imports," one executive told us, "but it's the only way we can get all our profits out of the country, given repatriation restrictions. Besides, our headquarters needs the liquidity for expansion in other countries." Living in a poor country, the subsidiary manager understands that the interest of the company in *worldwide* profit maximization may require minimization of profits in his country, and that while the company will benefit from the "efficient" allocation of profits, the country will not. When we had the opportunity to discuss at length the findings of the last chapter with respect to the impact of global corporations on capital formation, transfer of technology, and employment, we found a high level of awareness of these problems. A number of local managers expressed frustration with the home office's insistence that they engage in what one termed "extralegal practices." But there was always a ready rationalization. "If we don't engage in these practices, our competitors will, and where does that leave us two, three, or five years down the road?"

For the local manager who peers across the gulf that separates corporate image from corporate reality, the tension between what is good for the company and what is good for the country represents a moral dilemma. Of the many corporate executives interviewed in the preparation of this book, only eight were heads of subsidiaries in poor countries. But all of these expressed in some degree a certain moral distaste for some of the practices in which they were engaged.

One manager told us it was "common practice" to erect "dummy factories" in Mexico filled with nothing but a few pieces of barely working machinery. The purpose of these industrial Potemkin villages is to meet provisions of Mexican law which require that many products be manufactured inside Mexico so as to cut down on foreign-exchange-draining imports. Enterprising firms circumvent the law, bringing finished products across the border by the simple expedient of putting the local customs officials on a retainer. (In one case the final retail price of the goods, which was many times the price in the United States, was justified by the unusually high "start-up costs" of the dummy factory.)

A director of another global subsidiary told us how his company and other global subsidiaries in the same industry had gone into a joint venture in bribery, pooling resources to raise a $300,-000 payoff for a cabinet minister to forestall an inconvenient change in the country's foreign-investment law. One executive, commenting on transfer pricing, noted, "I've talked to headquarters people about taking profits out this way, but they argue right back that they will not and cannot change these things." Another suggested, "As long as there are loopholes in the laws or the bureaucracy, competitive pressures will make us take advantage of them." A German executive working for a global corporation in Latin America noted, "It is true for most people that things are getting worse and we are not helping matters." After conducting an extensive investigation of the price-fixing arrangement of U.S.-based global drug firms, Senator Russell Long has noted:

> For more than a dozen years, American drug manufacturers have been involved in a worldwide cartel to fix the price of "wonder drugs"—broad-spectrum antibiotics—at identical, grossly inflated and unconscionably high prices. . . . If we look at the evidence from Venezuela—where prices were not always identical despite the conspirators' efforts to make them so—the facts, I believe, will startle everyone . . . We know that whenever the local boys get caught in a price-fixing conspiracy, the important fellows at the top of the company always say, "We never knew anything about it. We told them never to do anything like that." . . . But here the top fellows in the New York offices were directly involved. If the matter could not be solved locally, the big guns were called in . . . Remember, their costs were about a cent and a half a pill as against a price of 51 cents to the consumer . . . Rather than engage in price competition, the conspirators have embarked on an extensive campaign to destroy their competitors . . . Without essential drugs, people die. Yet those who need them most—poor people 65 years and older—are those who can afford them least. These are the real victims, the persons from whom Pfizer, Cyanamid, Bristol, Squibb, and Upjohn have been wringing the fat expense accounts, the com-

pany cars, the six figure salaries, and the profit margins unheard
of elsewhere in American industry.

There is a common feeling among the executives living in Latin
America that the relationship between the firms and poor countries is highly unstable. "I don't believe that things can go on
like this," one bank official ventured. "Either they are going to
get wise and learn to control us or socialism or something is
going to bust out here." More and more global executives living
in poor countries, aware of the failure of the conventional development model of the 1960's to solve problems of mass poverty,
unemployment, or explosive social inequalities, are convinced
that the revolution of rising frustrations, to use the economist
Paul Rosenstein-Rodan's term, is going to force far-reaching
changes in the rules of the once-profitable game of making money
in poor countries.

Complaints about the obstreperousness of once-docile governments are now standard in corporate boardrooms. Fear of nationalization is a conventional element of corporate planning.
For good reason. In the last four years, according to a State
Department study, 34 countries in Latin America, Asia, and
Africa have resorted to a variety of measures designed to take
over or to force out U.S.-controlled operations in their territory
with a value of some $1.2 billion. The major nationalizations
have occurred in the petroleum industry—in Peru, Libya, Venezuela, among other countries. Most of the other takeovers have
been in strategic metals or in key social services such as transportation, communications, and banking. Nationalizations of industrial manufacturing during this period have been extremely rare.
(It should also be noted that the military governments in Bolivia
and Chile have returned properties nationalized by their predecessors.)

Global corporations find it convenient for public relations purposes to exaggerate the dangers of nationalization. But the growth
area in foreign investment is manufacturing and services, where
host governments have less interest in nationalizing foreign-
owned facilities and have only recently begun attempts to increase
their bargaining power with respect to global firms in other ways.
Indeed, a 1974 State Department study notes that since 1971 ex-

propriations and nationalizations have declined sharply, as under-developed countries have increasingly resorted to "other methods" such as regulation and disclosure requirements to increase bargaining power and control over global corporations. These efforts to control the operations of foreign corporations on their soil have greater potential, in our view, for fundamentally altering the power relations between global corporations and poor countries than the occasional seizure of oil fields and refineries.

The organization of the petroleum-exporting countries into OPEC, which in effect is a countercartel of once-poor countries blessed with oil to offset the long-established cartel arrangements of the oil companies, is the most dramatic example of the new bargaining power of underdeveloped countries. Until comparatively recently such issues as overpricing of imports, underpricing of exports, and overvaluation of technology were of interest only to the rich and the law and accounting firms they employ. A few years ago, no bit of information seemed more esoteric than the price of a barrel of oil in the Gulf of Aden. But in 1973 it became obvious that the real income of the average American (and average German and Japanese too) is directly affected by how these issues are resolved. To put it simply, the extraordinary profits which global companies by virtue of their superior power have been able to make in poor countries have represented a kind of subsidy for the American consumer. When the "profit faucet" from poor countries, as one manager termed it, is flowing at full force, it is possible for a company to show only modest worldwide profits which hide the extraordinary rates of return from poor countries (40 to 80 percent) that make it possible to keep consumer prices in the United States relatively low. But when the oil-producing countries, for example, begin closing the faucet by demanding and getting a higher price for crude and the companies wish to maintain their profit levels, visits to the local gas station in the United States must become more expensive. In 1960 a middle-class family earning $15,000 a year spent some 10 percent on petroleum and petroleum-related products. Today it must either spend more than 10 percent or else change its standard of living so as to consume less. As we shall see, oil is only the most obvious example of how changing power relations in faraway countries are changing life-styles in suburban America.

2

The elite in poor countries, whatever their ideology or their politics, are under mounting pressure to change the rules of the game in their dealings with global corporations, for they are coming to see that their own political survival may depend upon it. The inability of local governments in poor countries to use more of the finance capital generated by global corporations on their territory for local sanitation facilities, improved agricultural technology, internal communications, housing, education, and medical services has dramatized the fundamental flaw in the development model of the World Managers. As Brookings Institution economist Fred Bergsten puts it, "Most developing countries . . . have now learned that growth alone cannot guarantee the fundamental and politically central objectives of economic policy—full employment, relatively stable prices, equitable income distribution, and ultimately an enhanced quality of life." When too large a share of the earnings on foreign investment flows out of the country, the resulting economic crises—unemployment, stagnation, inadequate services, and income inequality —become political challenges for the leadership. In 1900, Paul Rosenstein-Rodan points out, people in poor countries had a per capita income about one-half that of people in rich countries. By 1970 the per capita income in poor countries was about one-twentieth of that in rich countries, measured in 1900 dollars (or one-fortieth in 1970 dollars). Most people in the world put up with very great inequalities, but when these inequalities appear to be increasing without prospect of being reversed and when they mean famine, epidemic, and certain death for millions of people, they cease to be merely aesthetic problems and acquire the status of political crises.

We are accustomed to thinking of left-wing governments, such as those of Cuba or Chile under Allende, as antagonists of global corporations. But we are now beginning to see some of the most right-wing regimes embarking on a nationalistic course designed to keep more of the profits earned by global corporations inside the country and available for its most urgent development needs. Brazil, a country that has produced a special sort of "economic miracle" by converting itself into a welcome mat for foreign corporations, provides an excellent illustration of the changes in the wind. (In an era when world leaders like Nixon and Brezhnev are shedding inconvenient ideologies without apology, one must expect some surprises from the lesser figures.) As much as the Brazilian generals may like foreign corporations and however much income they may personally derive from their presence, their jobs depend upon keeping 105 million people reasonably pacified. As a 1973 *New York Times* survey points out, that task is becoming harder:

> But the ticking of social and economic "time bombs" in Brazil appears to be growing louder and louder . . . One of the time bombs is education. As literacy spreads and the over-all education level rises, so will expectations and a desire for political freedom of expression . . . Brazil's racial problem may also become explosive as the gap between the status of dark and light skin widens. The boom has yet to improve the lot of the darker Brazilian, who is often absent from "the table of plenty." Of more immediate concern . . . is censorship . . . a potent time bomb because censorship is the strongest refuge of the corrupt and the incompetent.

In May 1973, the Brazilian Minister of Agriculture resigned and made an unusually candid public statement that provides a glimpse of the nationalistic feelings seething just below the surface in what has been considered the best investment climate in Latin America:

> Unfortunately, the governmental measures . . . have favored the industrial and commercial export sectors, which are increasingly foreign controlled, and thus everyday have made the results of the country's prosperity less and less Brazilian . . . The search for productive efficiency, although certainly necessary, has also smashed the interest of medium-sized rural producers, small and medium sized industrialists and businessmen. These are Brazilians.

From the point of view of a group of ambitious generals who have found the palace more congenial to their temperament than the parade ground, putting the squeeze on global corporations is sound political strategy. The alternatives are extraordinarily limited. In Brazil, as *The New York Times* summarizes it, "the regime clings to power by using systematic and brutal repressive methods against all opposition." But while the generals, quite obviously, have neither moral nor aesthetic problems with passing an electric current through the genitals of troublemakers, there are diminishing returns to torture. There comes a point at which large numbers of people can no longer be terrorized into accepting the certainty of misery. For regimes like those of Brazil, Iran, Greece or for relatively more benign one-party oligarchies such as Mexico, Kenya, or Peronist Argentina, the radical redistribution of income along the lines of Cuba or Tanzania is not an acceptable solution to the problem of escalating hopelessness. But there is another alternative. If more of the actual profits generated by global corporations within the country could be kept within the country, it would be possible to make some needed public investment in schools, tractors, houses, etc., and even raise incomes somewhat for the poor without disturbing the standard of living of the rich. In short, a bigger pie for Brazil can increase public contentment even if the way the pie is cut remains substantially unchanged.

There are several indications that the Brazilian generals are embarked on just such a policy. The 1971 Patent Law is the toughest and most sophisticated piece of legislation in the hemisphere for controlling the transfer of technology. (For more than ten years Brazil has led the fight in the United Nations against the stranglehold that the patent system poses for the technological development of poor countries.) A 1972 measure bars further entry into the Brazilian economy of foreign commercial banks, encourages the merger and strengthening of Brazilian banks, and limits foreigners to a 30-percent interest in investment banks— all designed, in the words of Finance Minister Delfim Netto, "to give a larger operational scope to the Brazilian economy." The following year Brazil passed a law creating huge trading corporations along the Japanese model which will help to ensure that Brazil does not overpay for imports or underprice its exports. Other measures that force global corporations to conduct more of their research-and-development activities inside Brazil, encourage competitive bidding and diversification of financing sources and trading partners, and limit the repatriation of profits all form part of an emerging pattern of economic self-protection which will change bargaining relations between the global companies and the generals. As Peter Gabriel, dean of the Boston University College of Business Administration and former management consultant in Latin America, summarized these developments,

"A prediction that Brazil will continue to favor the foreign investor once he has fulfilled his promise (i.e., brought his technology and know-how), even while all countries around her are successfully wresting ever more favorable terms from him, has to be founded on faith rather than historical precedent or current example."

To buy social peace by taxing a well-heeled foreign guest, especially one that has been engaged for years in resource-draining sharp practices, is an irresistible strategy for nationalist regimes of all sorts. The growing image problem of the global corporation makes the strategy all the easier. Corporate managers see danger signals from countries as diverse as Indonesia, Mexico, Colombia, Venezuela, and Saudi Arabia which suggest that the world company is now regarded by politicians in poor countries not only as a convenient whipping boy but also as a useful, if reluctant, partner in reform.

The big question is whether poor countries have the power to make such a strategy work. Much of the evidence examined in the last two chapters would suggest that they do not. If one focuses on the evidence of the 1950's and the late 1960's, as we did there, the picture that emerges is one of effective corporate control of all the principal levers of power in poor countries— banks, communications, technology, popular culture, and the loyalty of the upper classes. But the situation is changing. A series of developments in the world economy and in world politics now make it far more feasible than it has been in the past for poor countries to develop strategies that cut into the power of global corporations.

As we have seen, the key element in determining the relative bargaining power of foreign corporations and political leaders in poor countries is knowledge. The historic advantages of the companies have all been derived in one way or another from their possession of information, skills, and techniques unavailable to primitive governments. But a combination of mounting pressures is producing a global redistribution of knowledge which is working to the benefit of poor countries. There are three crucial types of knowledge which determine the balance of power in any bargaining relationship.

The first is the information on which each party bases its assessment of how much the other needs what he has to offer. To the extent to which they understand the dependence of the companies on the resources and cheap labor within their territory, the bargaining power of poor countries increases. Not so long ago the most striking characteristic of the governments and corporations of the great industrial powers was their near-omnipotence. In the era of U.S. political hegemony and seemingly unlimited affluence, there were no obvious limitations on the power of the industrial giants to take what they wanted from the poor countries on their own terms—or to exclude them from the twentieth century. Today the most spectacular characteristic of the great powers is their vulnerability. It has only recently been widely perceived that despite their still extraordinary hold on the world's wealth, the three great industrial powers—the United States, the U.S.S.R., and Japan—are beginning to look, each in its own way, more like pitiful, helpless giants. Japan is almost totally devoid of natural resources to run its industrial machine. It is dependent upon importing more than 98.5 percent of all energy sources it uses. The Soviet Union cannot raise sufficient food to support its population or to supply it with the consumer trappings now deemed essential for the success of its peculiar brand of socialism.

These developments mean that, increasingly, the rich countries will need the poor countries as much as, if not more than, the poor countries will need them. This is a new stage in world power relationships. In the age of imperialism the exploitation of the colonies was a convenience for the great European powers, but Marxist critics always had a difficult time demonstrating that it was a necessity. In the present era, marked as it is by increasingly intense competition among the industrial giants for scarce resources, "export platforms" (low-cost labor enclaves from which to export to the industrialized world), and new markets, the underdeveloped world takes on something closely akin to the crucial importance in global industrial planning that Lenin prematurely proposed for it in 1913. One indication of this is the dramatic increase in manufactured goods that the industrialized nations are now importing from underdeveloped nations. The increasing awareness within the poor countries of the vulnerabilities of the rich means some increase in bargaining power for the underdeveloped world. The change in power relationships is assisted by the growing realization that the giants can no longer help themselves through military power to what they need with the same abandon that characterized the pre-Vietnam world.

Another crucial bit of information that is changing power relationships to the advantage of poor countries is the increasing awareness that the industrial world is no longer a bloc. In the Cold War years poor countries tried, often successfully, to play the United States and Russia off against each other, exchanging political allegiance for foreign aid. But the strategy had limitations because in the end both the United States and the U.S.S.R. lost interest in buying political support with economic-development funds. (Military aid for maintaining a friendly or innocuous government in power is another matter and still plays an important role in the strategy of both countries.) But the competition for resources and profits among the United States, Japan, and Western Europe is infinitely more exploitable by sophisticated political leaders in poor countries. As John C. Lobb, former ITT executive and later U.S. director of Nippon Electric Co., Ltd., puts it, "The major trading nations are today engaged in world-wide economic warfare. The chief adversaries are the United States, Germany and Japan . . . it cannot fail to have far-reaching impact on economic theories, institutions, and business . . ."

One important impact is that poor countries with scarce raw materials or cheap labor to sell now have a choice of customers. The United States, Germany, and Japan are becoming ever more serious competitors for access to the raw materials and labor of underdeveloped countries because they are becoming ever more alike. The convergence of the industrialized nations constitutes a new opportunity for poor countries. When in 1955 the average American earned roughly six times what the average Japanese earned and four times what the average German was earning, the United States was virtually unchallenged in its consumption of world resources.

But by 1972 the per capita income in the United States was less than three times that of Japan and only slightly higher than that of Germany, and the gap continues to narrow. In these years there has been a corresponding jump in the energy consumption (a basic indicator of overall consumption) of the other industrial powers, with the result that there is now keen competition among them for the fuel on which to run their increasingly similar productive systems. (It is important to note that the Germans and

Japanese now feel some of the same pressures to move their production out of the home countries into poorer countries. For example, a recent report of the Nomura Research Institute, Japan's largest, concludes that "worsening pollution," the need for "inexpensive electricity," and the "constant rise in labor costs" in Japan "have made it more advantageous to shift to overseas production or to set up export bases abroad than to produce in Japan and then export.")

The industrial nations are attempting to get together to neutralize efforts of poor countries to take advantage of national rivalries. U.S.-based global firms are resorting to joint ventures with Japanese companies in Latin America, on the theory that regulated market and resource sharing is better than unregulated competition. Under the same theory, General Electric is now a minority shareholder in a Japanese electronics plant in New Jersey. Nevertheless, there is a perceptible shift in the balance of power between developed and underdeveloped countries. As global companies increase their share of the total trade of the advanced nations, the dependence of the rich on the poor will grow. The process is accelerated as more poor countries convert themselves into "export platforms." In 1960 there were only four underdeveloped countries that were significant exporters of manufactured goods. By 1968, according to the studies of Hollis Chenery of the World Bank, there were thirty. Beginning with low-skilled industries such as textiles, these countries had by the mid-1960's moved on to electronics, chemicals, steel, calculators, and computers. Chenery and Helen Hughes conclude that labor productivity in underdeveloped countries "is frequently higher for individual industries and even for the industrial sector as a whole than it is in developed countries." Escalating energy demands throughout the industrialized world, the intensifying competition for profits by employing cheap labor in tropical islands, African jungles, and the Chinese countryside, and the frantic search for out-of-the-way places to locate contaminating factories are all translatable into increased bargaining power for the Third World. Countries like Brazil and Indonesia, while traditionally members of the U.S. political orbit since their military coups of the mid-1960's, are, nevertheless, seeking to diversify their customers. Thus Brazil has been encouraging and receiving substantial German and Japanese investment. (According to recent projections, Japan will be the number-one foreign investor by 1978.) Iran, though designated a deputy peacekeeper for the eastern Mediterranean under the Nixon Doctrine, is nonetheless negotiating with China for the sale of oil, thus preserving a degree of economic independence from the United States which can be used to exact better terms.

There is another sort of knowledge filtering widely throughout the underdeveloped world. It is technical information about the behavior of corporations, specifically what terms they have agreed to in other countries and what techniques have been successfully applied to them in other parts of the world. Intelligence, both political and technical, is a key factor in any bargaining relationship. When one party to a negotiation knows more about his adversary than the adversary knows about him, he is likely to come off the winner. It is still true that by and large global companies know more about the pressures on the politicians with whom they deal in poor countries than the politicians know about them, but the knowledge gap is narrowing. At the same time poor countries are testing and improving certain techniques for controlling the behavior of global firms on their territory. News about how these work travels swiftly. When a country concludes a successful negotiation with a company or makes a successful effort to police harmful company practices, such victories have a demonstration effect in countries with similar problems, even those halfway around the world. The diffusion of knowledge of this third type now demands our more detailed attention.

3

The most dramatic aspect of the new strategy for dealing with global companies is the creation of sellers' cartels to offset the power of the buyers' cartels that have traditionally dominated the world resource markets. For most of the century poor countries were disorganized and easily manipulated by the handful of companies that controlled the major industries. (Petroleum was in the hands of the "seven sisters." As recently as the late 1960's seven global corporations with interlocking directorates controlled 83 percent of the copper production outside the socialist countries.) Because of such concentration in the hands of a few owners and managers and the divisions and rivalries in the formerly colonial world, it was easy for the global corporations to play poor countries off against one another and thereby keep the price of raw materials down. But overcoming traditional tribal, religious, and political differences in the interest of economic survival is now seen as a necessity among politicians in many poor countries. It is becoming obvious that collective bargaining over the exploitation of natural resources is the key to containing the power of the global corporations in this sector.

The first successful use of collective bargaining against the companies was OPEC, the Organization of Petroleum Exporting Countries. The coordination of what are principally Arab oil-rich nations has driven the price of a barrel of Middle East oil from $1.50 in 1970 to $9.50 in 1973. (This is of course reflected in an increase of approximately 25 cents a gallon in the filling-station price.) More significant than the nationalizations themselves are the new relationships now being established between oil companies and host governments once nationalization takes place. These are designed to keep technical knowledge flowing to the producing countries under much more advantageous terms. Service contracts, management agreements, turn-key operations, co-production and marketing agreements are examples of some of these relationships which we shall explore more fully below.

What the OPEC experience shows is that underdeveloped countries lucky enough to sit on large oil reserves now understand enough of the realities of the world market and world politics to keep for themselves much more of the money to be made from their oil. As the producing nations see it, the new prices are a form of reparation for years of wanton exploitation by the oil companies. But the oil companies, because of their oligopoly power, can adjust to the new state of affairs by passing the increased costs to the consumer.

The Saudi Arabians are negotiating for the purchase of significant interests in the marketing of petroleum products, including ownership of gas stations in the United States. Because of the worldwide energy shortage, the hold on the world marketing system of the global oil companies, which for many years was the chief obstacle to successful nationalization, has now been broken. When the Iraqi Government nationalized all its oil in 1972, the Soviet Union simply curtailed its shipments of oil to Eastern Europe and directed the countries in its economic orbit to order their oil from Iraq.

Although the power of the oil-producing countries is unique, there are now moves under way in other strategic raw-material sectors of the world economy for similar concerted action by underdeveloped countries. Thus, the four countries that control more than 80 percent of the exportable supply of copper in the world, Zambia, Chile, Peru, and Zaïre, have begun to organize along OPEC lines. Four underdeveloped countries control close to 95 percent of the world's tin supply. Four poor nations control approximately 50 percent of the supply of natural rubber and 50 percent of all the bauxite in the world, an indispensable component under current technology for making aluminum. (In late 1973, Secretary of the Interior Rogers Morton called the efforts of Jamaica and the other bauxite producers to get together a "minerals crisis" and spoke of the necessity to "wave the flag.") Only a few poor countries dominate the regional markets for timber, which Brookings Institution economist C. Fred Bergsten terms "the closest present approximation of a truly vanishing resource."

Poor countries are now even beginning to develop some solidarity across product lines. Thus copper-producing and aluminum-producing countries are seeking to coordinate their strategy so as to prevent the companies from substituting one metal for another. Similarly, coffee producers and tea producers are considering how to strengthen their combined hand in dealing with the corporations. Although the overwhelming advantages of submerging their differences and of presenting a common front in economic negotiations is becoming increasingly apparent to poor countries, individualistic nationalism is still strong. The U.S. National Commission on Materials Policy concluded in June 1973 that no "economic and political basis" exists for an effective cartel of raw-materials producers in any commodity except petroleum.

Although the most dramatic transformation in bargaining power relationships is occurring over vital raw materials, the most significant changes in the long run will probably take place with respect to the manufacturing sector. A crucial disadvantage of host governments in dealing with giant corporate guests is lack of knowledge of their internal operations. Governments are now beginning to pool their information in an effort to redress this balance. The Andean Pact countries and Mexico have joined forces to develop a central data collection unit which puts together information from all these market countries. The development of regional bureaucracies may well make it harder for foreign companies to corrupt national bureaucracies since Economics Ministry officials in one country will know that officials from other countries will be intensively studying what they do. Moreover, just as the increasing awareness that the resource-rich countries have more alternatives in exploiting those resources than the companies have in finding substitute sources has led to an increase in their bargaining power, so the news that one country has successfully controlled some aspect of corporate behavior spreads and encourages other poor countries to try the same techniques.

In the Cold War much was made of the "domino theory," the notion that a successful revolution in one country would embolden guerrilla leaders in other countries to try one too. It was always an absurdly oversimplified notion for the reason that revolutions cannot be turned on and off like faucets. They grow out of unique historical and political circumstances which can be neither mass-produced nor exported. But the techniques for monitoring and controlling the behavior of companies are much more easily exportable than the techniques for making revolutions. There is a domino effect operating when a government discovers that its neighbor has successfully imposed a control on a corporation and offers the information as to how to do it. Trying to exact the same terms as the first country is in the interests of the second country and can produce much in the way of increased revenues and foreign exchange for development. Thus many of the laws regulating foreign investment, repatriation of profits, foreign participation in key industries, and the transfer of technology developed by the Andean Common Market were quickly adopted by Argentina and Peru as national legislation and are now being considered by the Caribbean Free Trade Association. There is also an exchange of information between the Andean Common Market and the East African Common Market. It is small wonder, therefore, that the companies resisted so long and so fiercely the initial attempts by poor countries to regulate their activities.

Thus global corporations today find that they must accept less than what they would like in order to continue to do business in many parts of the world. Preferring the control and higher profits that come with total ownership, the companies are being compelled more and more to settle for management contracts under which they agree to furnish knowledge in return for access to raw materials and cheap labor. The eagerly sought commercial relations with the Soviet Union and other socialist countries which global companies have seen as a major growth area have, ironically, created problems for them in the underdeveloped countries. By 1973, it will be recalled, there were about 1,200 cooperative arrangements between Western capitalist companies and socialist states, not including such highly publicized operations as Fiat's, Pepsi-Cola's and Occidental's in the Soviet Union itself. In all of them the production is state-owned, at least in large part. As Samuel Pisar, one of the first lawyers to write a manual on how to make capitalist profits under socialism, explains, "You can't have dividends or profit participations. What you can have is a royalty payment for patents or know-how, engineering fees, management fees, interest, selling commissions." For the Soviet market itself an enterprising Western capitalist can form a "transideological corporation" which, as long as it is incorporated outside the U.S.S.R., can be owned on a 50–50 basis by a Soviet state company and a free-enterprising global corporation.

The ease and eagerness with which the pillars of the capitalist economy accommodate themselves to the rules of the game in socialist countries is not lost on the poor countries of the underdeveloped world. As Peter Gabriel notes, politicians in the underdeveloped world can hold up these precedents from Eastern Europe when they deal with the global companies. "If you went into Hungary with a management contract and no equity ownership, why can't you come here on the same basis?" Increasingly, as the companies feel the competitive pressures to make greater use of the poor countries, they will be at a loss for an answer. The "herd-instinct," as Gabriel calls it, that causes one global corporation to imitate another further strengthens the hand of the governments. There are strong competitive pressures to enter into management contracts and service agreements when there is no apparent alternative access to increasingly crucial areas of the world. Whereas only ten years ago countries were outdoing one another in making extravagant concessions to attract foreign companies, they are now learning from one another that it is far more advantageous to control the companies rather than turn the country over to them.

There are a number of techniques available to poor countries for establishing somewhat greater control over global corporations. One is to demand competitive bids. As long ago as 1968 Colombia abandoned the traditional policy in Latin America of allowing free entry to all comers and announced that only one auto maker would be admitted. Renault, which had the smallest share of the Latin American market at the time, offered the best terms. In Chile after Allende made moves toward nationalizing Ford, Fiat and British Leyland competed for the privilege of entering into a joint venture with the Marxist-oriented government to take over Ford's Chilean operations. (The fact that corporations cannot afford ideological solidarity in such circumstances is an advantage of no small import to weak governments.)

The new flexibility that permits poor countries to demand competitive bidding is a consequence of the sharpening economic competition among the rich countries, which more and more have similar resource needs. Until the late 1950's or early 1960's (depending upon the region), U.S.-based global companies dominated foreign investment almost everywhere. But between 1965 and 1971 the growth rate of German and Japanese foreign investment was approximately triple the U.S. rate. In many cases the Japanese have been able to offer better terms than the Americans. (The Minister of Fuels of a Latin American country told us that Japanese, German, and East European companies were bidding for mineral concessions which fifteen years ago would have gone as a matter of course to a U.S. corporation. The Japanese, he explained, offered much the best terms.) Indeed, it frequently happens that the Japanese, who are significantly increasing their investment in Brazil among other places in Latin America, are able to outbid the Americans. The Rand consultant Jack Baranson suggests it is because the Japanese are less impatient than Americans. They are readier to settle for a smaller profit this year or next in the hopes of establishing a more stable long-term relationship. In Peru the Japanese agreed to a time limit on their investment, worker participation in management decisions, and government control of their pricing and marketing practices. This is but one example of a certain generosity in dealing with the host governments which American managers with an eye on this year's balance sheet cannot bring themselves to show. (The fact that Brazil was never part of the Japanese Empire is an advantage, too.)

Underdeveloped countries have learned not only to diversify their sources of foreign investment, but to diversify their trading partners as well. Schooled in dollar diplomacy, they are eager to avoid the historic dependence of raw-materials producers on a single market. (The allocation of the U.S. market among various countries by means of the sugar quota is perhaps the best example of the attempt to preserve a buyer's market through trade restrictions and to use a crop that is a mainstay of several poor countries in the Caribbean as an instrument of political control.) In May 1973, thirty African countries ratified an accord to "concert and organize" their international trade plans.

As poor countries assume an ever-greater role in the world production process, they will seek maximum flexibility in dealing with global manufacturing corporations. Efforts have already begun to diversify sources of technology. Recently Brazil with the help of the World Bank conducted competitive bidding for $188.6 million worth of steel-making machinery. Non-U.S. global companies won $186.6 million of these contracts. Mexico and India are pursuing the same policies with regard to technology. World Bank experts predict that international competitive bidding will become "a new rallying cry" of poor countries in the 1970's. Underdeveloped countries are also finding new alternatives to meet their need for outside capital, such as selling long-term bonds, an option which ten years ago was unavailable. As the Andean Pact economist Constantine Vaitsos has observed, ". . . from March 1970 to March 1973 only one part of Brazil's placement of bonds in the foreign capital markets amounted to about $140 million, which was higher than the total funds (direct and indirect investments, both private and governmental) which came from the U.S. in 1968 and were used by U.S. subsidiaries in the whole of the manufacturing sector of Latin America." In 1971 Argentina started (under a right-wing military dictatorship) a "buy Argentinian" program, which the Peronist regime has continued. In both the economic and political spheres, countries like Argentina and even Mexico are seeking a new independence. Argentina is actively courting Japanese and German global companies as a counterbalance to U.S. firms and in 1973 recognized Cuba, North Korea, and East Germany. The President of Mexico, Luís

Echeverría, has sought to advertise his independence by making a highly publicized world tour that included Japan, China, and the Soviet Union.

The bargaining power of some poor countries is beginning to improve because they now see that, irrespective of domestic political differences, they share what might be termed common class interests vis-à-vis the rich nations. The end of U.S. hegemony and the rise of other rich nations to rival American economic power; the softening of the ideological cleavage between the "Communist" and "non-Communist" worlds, which makes it no longer necessary for poor countries "to stand up and be counted," as John Foster Dulles used to demand; and, in Peter Gabriel's words, "the growing solidarity among the LDC's [less-developed countries] and the dependence of the industrialized countries on both the supplies and the markets of the Third World" now hold out the prospect of a new world economy.

As the fall of Dienbienphu symbolized the end of an era in political relations between the strong and the weak, so Egypt's successful seizure of the Suez Canal heralded a new stage in economic relations. That event almost twenty years ago elicited a strong united reaction from the industrial nations of the West, including an invasion of Egypt. When in 1973 Panama challenged the United States in the United Nations over the American-controlled canal running through its territory and succeeded in having the Security Council conduct an unprecedented session on Panamanian soil which culminated in a resolution criticizing U.S. policy, not one capitalist power rose to America's defense. Indeed, the demonstrations of solidarity were on the other side. Egypt sent Panama what amounted to an owner's manual for canals.

4

That there is mounting pressure on politicians in poor countries to exact more economic concessions from global corporations is clear. That there are increasing opportunities to do this because of fundamental structural changes in the world political economy is also clear. What is less clear is the extent to which governments of poor countries will be able to marshal the skills and to recruit the incorruptible personnel to take advantage of their potential bargaining power.

One indication of the new pressures on governments in poor countries is the rash of kidnappings of corporate executives, particularly in Argentina. Ford paid $1 million to a terrorist organization to stop further attempts to kidnap Luis V. Giovanelli, an executive in Buenos Aires. Eastman Kodak paid a ransom of $1.5 million to get back one of its executives. In the last five years the guerrilla organization has collected more than $15 million in ransoms from more than 60 foreign and Argentine businessmen. In some cases the sums were paid as protection money after oral or written threats, without any overt act of the guerrillas. While a few firms have begun to take out kidnap insurance with Lloyd's of London, others have told us that their long-term strategy is to replace foreign executives with Argentines, who, presumably, will not make such good targets from a political standpoint.

One stated purpose of the terrorist campaign is to focus attention on the social contribution of the foreign corporations. (In the Ford kidnapping, the guerrillas insisted that the company donate its million-dollar ransom in the form of contributions to 22 provincial hospitals.) The effect of terrorism has been to push the Argentine Government into a more nationalistic stance, as evidenced by tough new laws on controlling pricing behavior, limiting access to local credit, and excluding foreign corporations from certain key areas of the economy. In other countries, such as Mexico, mounting peasant unrest, student disorders, and other signs of social instability are forcing the governments into a more militant public position with respect to global corporations. As we have seen, there are strong economic pressures in addition to these political ones that make it essential for politicians in poor countries to exact more money from the corporations.

But translating necessities into realities is another matter. No matter how favorable the terms of a negotiation with a global company may be, victory at the bargaining table is meaningless unless the terms can be enforced. There is a tradition in underdeveloped countries, as we have seen, of passing tough laws with infinite loopholes. One Latin American Economics Minister who had worked for several years for a U.S. bank told us that "whenever we introduced new or modified banking regulations, the multinationals usually found a way of circumventing them within six or eight weeks." The difficulty of policing internal company transactions is extraordinary, as the experience of the Internal Revenue Service in the United States make clear. Section 482 of the U.S. Internal Revenue Code requires that when a company sells to itself, the goods must be valued at an "arm's length," or independent-market-value, price. But IRS officials admit that because of the immense number of such transactions, they are less than confident that they are effectively enforcing this important revenue-protecting provision. The Internal Revenue Service, despite the political purposes to which it has been recently put, employs the best tax collectors in the world. If it cannot enforce legislation against transfer pricing, relatively unsophisticated bureaucracies in Latin America face an even harder task. It is for such reasons that the global companies themselves tend to discount the impact of the new laws controlling foreign investment. In an early-1973 internal memorandum, the staff economist of a large global bank gives his "preliminary feeling" that Mexico's new law on regulating foreign investment and controlling the transfer of technology "will *not* have a drastic impact on foreign investment in Mexico." Such laws, he points out, "are more visible to the public than a mere change in practice and thus help to fill the quotient of nationalism necessary in public policy." This attempt to "mollify, to some extent, the nationalist-reformist part of the domestic political spectrum," the memorandum points out, is similar to what is happening in Australia and Canada.

U.S. businessmen in Mexico are naturally not pleased by the new restrictions on their operations. (The U.S. Ambassador, Robert McBride, gave an angry speech charging that the Echeverría government was "changing the rules of the game"—to which the public response from the government, amid much applause, was "Gentlemen, you have gotten the point.") As the bank memorandum quoted above notes, "up to now, U.S. companies have had virtually complete freedom to do what they pleased in Mexico, as compared to the restrictions that are imposed upon them in the United States." But behind the tough speeches of the Mexican Government are more equivocal private conversations designed to soothe the feelings of foreign businessmen.

The seeming contradictions between public and private statements and between law and practice reflect a real ambivalence.

Governments in Mexico and other poor countries are determined to squeeze the global corporations for some of the excessive profits which they have been earning at the country's expense, but they do not want to drive them out altogether, as their development model is heavily dependent upon them. Moreover, the power of the consumer ethic must not be underestimated. It is an effective political weapon in the hands of the corporation. The middle-class women banging their empty pots in the streets of Santiago in 1971 served notice on Allende that a government unable to deliver the goods desired by those with money to spend was in trouble. For most poor countries the global corporation is the only source of such goods.

Thus, politicians in poor countries labor under certain handicaps in exploiting their improved bargaining power. When a new law is passed, there is a period of waiting during which the government tests the corporation to see what it will put up with and the company tests the government to see how corrupt and inefficient it is in translating the letter of the law into effective policy.

But with all the problems of enforcement, the existence of new laws does change the bargaining climate. The Andean Common Market is developing its own system of information and analysis of the flow and effects of foreign investment in South America. The careful work of Latin American economists on the real profit rates and the effects of transfer pricing has weakened the companies' credibility and hence their bargaining power. (The bank memorandum notes that Department of Commerce statistics on the profit rate of U.S. manufacturing subsidiaries in Mexico during the period 1966–1970 was 10 percent, but a Mexican analyst working with the companies' annual reports showed 22 percent, without even taking into account possible understatement due to transfer pricing.)

As a pioneering student of bargaining power, Miguel Wionczek, has noted, host governments have been almost totally dependent on U.S. Department of Commerce statistics. Only ten years ago, a recent Rand Corporation report points out, the U.S. Embassy was the "only source available to the Peruvian government regarding the extent of foreign investment in Peru." Now the Andean Common Market facilities for gathering information and analyzing investment effects are changing the distribution of knowledge and the bargaining relationships that depend so crucially on that knowledge. The conference of nonaligned nations meeting in Algiers in the summer of 1973 established a center for the study of the 500 leading global corporations to exchange information among poor countries to improve their bargaining power. Combining resources, the nations are able to afford information-gathering facilities which no individual nation could maintain. Harmonizing their policies and procedures, the Andean Pact nations are able to reduce the opportunities for the companies to play one country off against another and to avoid the pitfalls of past efforts at economic integration, such as the Central American Common Market, which accelerated the rate of takeover by U.S.-based corporations. By eliminating tariffs separating, say, Colombia and Peru, the Andean Pact nations have created one of the world's largest potential markets, one that a growing global company cannot afford to ignore. It is one thing for a firm to decide that the investment climate is too unsatisfactory in Chile to permit further investment. It is quite another matter to give up a market embracing millions of potential customers, especially when the Japanese and German competition is sure to be there.

Although global corporations, wherever possible, are continuing their pressure on poor countries to moderate legislation to control companies, the World Managers now know that they must expect lower profits from the underdeveloped world. How significant even a single assertion of local-government power can be for a corporation is indicated by the experience in Colombia. In 36 months the Colombian Comité de Regalias saved $24 million in excessive royalty payments by reviewing 395 contracts. If spot checking in one area only can produce such savings for the country, it is clear that the extralegal and nonreported profits have been a crucial element of global corporate operations. (Vaitsos' studies in Colombia, it will be recalled, concluded that 82 percent of effective profits came from overpricing of imports. Similar studies by the Andean Common Market in Peru put the figure at 50 percent.) Despite occasional cries of extortion and well-publicized predictions of doom, the managers of global corporations know that they can and must do business with poor countries under the new terms that are developing.

The changes in bargaining power outlined in this chapter make it likely that the poor nations will be able to keep significantly more of their productive output than in the past from both the sale of raw materials and the sale of labor. But unfortunately, there is less reason to be optimistic that the new riches flowing into poor countries will be equitably distributed in such a way as to make a dent in mass poverty. Some redistribution of income will no doubt occur. Per capita calorie consumption at the bottom of the society in Saudi Arabia has already improved. The middle class will be enlarged, as it has been in Taiwan. But the bottom 60 percent of the world's population will be relatively untouched by the new wealth of once-poor nations. Indeed, the improved bargaining power of the Arab nations has undoubtedly worsened the lot of the average Indian, who feels the inflationary effects of the increased price of oil.

In the face of the efforts of the poor countries to organize themselves for collective bargaining with the rich, the industrial giants are making moves toward counterorganization. Symptomatic of this effort is the attempt by David Rockefeller to organize "leading citizens" of the United States, Japan, and Western Europe into a Trilateral Commission designed to minimize the friction and competition that divide the giants and make them more vulnerable to the organizing efforts of the poor. In 1974, U.S. Secretary of State Henry Kissinger proposed Project Interdependence, an official rich man's club for developing a common strategy for dealing with the presumptuous poor.

Part of the evolving strategy, it now appears, is to evoke the shade of Admiral Mahan and nineteenth-century geopolitical rhetoric about the "lifeblood" of our civilization being in foreign hands. General Creighton Abrams talks of "a multidimensional threat" in which "many vital resources" will be "used as strategic weapons against us"—a situation requiring a "low violence" military force for "leverage in negotiations with friends as well as foes." However, the access of the United States to such strategic materials as copper, bauxite, and manganese appears relatively secure. (The United States, the largest copper producer in the world, now imports only 8 percent of its annual consumption. Australia, Alcoa's chairman says, could supply "free world" bauxite needs for a hundred years.) There is little doubt that officials in charge of U.S. resource policies on occasion use alarmist language which exaggerates the real changes in bargaining power that are taking place in an obvious effort to build counterpressure in support of the present world resource-distribution system so advantageous to the rich nations. However, Bureau of Mines projections indicate that by the end of the century the United States will be completely dependent on foreign supplies for such resources as aluminum, manganese, tin, cobalt, and tungsten, and more than 50-percent dependent for a number of others, including copper. Moreover, in Japan, Germany and other developed countries, which already are 50- to 100-percent dependent on foreign supplies, the degree of alarm is much more acute and much more justified.

Thus, the struggle over the riches of the earth has just begun. There are many imponderables. The faster Europe and Japan develop an industrial machine to rival that of the United States, the greater the pressure on the world resource supply and the greater the chance of serious splits among the rich nations. On the other hand, if the industrial nations are able to exploit the ocean bed on terms of their choosing, the bargaining power of particular resource-producing nations will diminish. A strong nationalist reaction in developed countries about "being pushed around by these people," public suggestions for the use of America's "food power," a not-so-veiled threat to withhold grain from hungry nations to extract acceptable terms on resources, and the threat of violence, low or otherwise, can all affect the outcome of the resource struggle. One thing is clear: as poor countries demand higher prices for their raw materials and their labor, global corporations will pass these increases on to the consumer unless they are prevented by law from doing so. Whether there is enough statesmanship and true international spirit in the rich countries to recognize that changes in bargaining power and resource pricing (including human labor) are long overdue in the interests of global justice and global stability will determine the character of world politics in the coming generation.

PART

9

The LatinAmericanization of the United States

1

At a particularly tense moment in the Watergate crisis, the veteran White House correspondent of *Time* magazine archly referred to the United States as a banana republic. Indeed, the constitutional crises provoked when the President is investigated to determine whether he is committing high crimes in office or the Vice-President is forced to resign for pettier crimes committed in a lesser office are more reminiscent of Latin America than what has generally been thought to be the world's most stable political system. Such parallels can be overdone. The hysterical political metaphor is not a substitute for analysis. The United States is not "becoming" another Brazil any more than it is "becoming" another Nazi Germany or Soviet Union, despite dire predictions from the left and the right. Nevertheless, it is now possible to discern certain structural changes in the United States which are causing the world's richest nation to take on some of the aspects of an underdeveloped country. Some of these changes are directly related to the rise of the global corporation.

To understand the impact of the global corporation on the majority of the people of the United States, which is the subject of the remainder of this book, we need to recall the principal elements of the global transformation we have been describing thus far. In the first place, the rise of the global corporation represents the globalization of oligopoly capitalism. In perhaps simpler terms, the new corporate structure is the culmination of a process of concentration and internationalization that has put the world economy under the substantial control of a few hundred business

213

enterprises which do not compete with one another according to the traditional rules of the classic market.

Second, the interest of these enterprises is *global* profit maximization, which may, as we have seen in our study of underdeveloped countries, require profit *minimization* in certain countries under certain circumstances. This is but one example of how the interests of global corporations and countries in which they conduct their operations may conflict. As we shall see in the chapters that follow, conflicts also exist between U.S.-based global corporations and their home country.

Third, the poor nations of Asia, Latin America, and, soon, Africa, long the hewers of wood and drawers of water for the international economy, are increasingly becoming the principal sites of new production. This dramatic shift from north to south, which could not have been predicted even ten years ago, is changing employment patterns and living standards in the United States.

Finally, this global economic process is producing a new concentration of political power in what are, in legal and political terms, private hands. In short, the managers of the global corporations are neither elected by the people nor subject to popular scrutiny or even popular pressure, despite the fact that in the course of their daily business they make decisions with more impact on the lives of ordinary people than most generals and politicians. The principal source of their power is their control of knowledge of three specific kinds: the technology of production and organization—i.e., how to make, package, and transport; the technology of obtaining and managing finance capital—i.e., how to create their own private global economy insulated from the vicissitudes of national economies by means of shifting profits and avoiding taxes; the technology of marketing—i.e., how to create and satisfy a demand for their goods by diffusing a consumption ideology through the control of advertising, mass media, and popular culture.

In this chapter and those that follow we shall be looking specifically at the effects on the United States of the reorganization of the world economy into a Global Shopping Center and a Global Factory. We shall be looking particularly at three sorts of changes in American society which we believe are intimately associated with the new role of the global corporation in the U.S.

economy. These changes have the effect of changing the pattern of production, the distribution of income, and the balance of power within American society to increase its resemblance to an underdeveloped country.

As we shall explore in the next chapter, the gap between rich and poor in the United States, as in underdeveloped countries, is widening. Dramatic changes in personal economic circumstances are occurring. Our large prosperous middle class, long considered the foundation of American stability, is increasingly squeezed by shrinking employment opportunities, high taxes, and inflationary prices. The members of many a $15,000-a-year family are merely honorary members of the middle class. The unemployed or absurdly underemployed university graduate, a familiar figure in India and Mexico, is no longer a rarity in the United States. While increasing numbers have pushed their way into the middle class during the last decade, membership involves a much more precarious existence than the purveyors of the American Dream promised.

The decline in jobs and the rise in prices have hit those below the middle class much harder. The welfare population largely comprises unskilled workers for whom jobs do not exist. In the center of every large city hundreds of thousands of Americans are living without decent food, light, plumbing—and without dignity or hope. As in Brazil, the first to feel the squeeze of a tightening economy are minority groups. In the United States the unemployment rate among blacks is two to three times the rate among whites. But even the moderately well-to-do face reductions in key aspects of their standard of living. There are meatless days even in Winnetka. The price and scarcity of gasoline have begun to restrict the use of the automobile as entertainment. The shortage of heating fuel and electric power means colder houses in winter and hotter houses in summer than many Americans are used to. Compared with what most of the world endures, these indicators of a decline in the standard of living are perhaps barely worth talking about. But in the context of American expectations of something bigger and better every year, they are significant indeed.

What do these changes have to do with the rise of the global corporation? As we shall show in succeeding chapters, a great deal. The argument can be summarized briefly. In the interest of maximum global profits, the managers of the world corporation are creating, often unconsciously, a global system in which the long-term role assigned to the United States is completely changing what it produces and consequently what its people do. Production of the traditional industrial goods that have been the mainstay of the U.S. economy is being transferred from $4-an-hour factories in New England to 30-cents-an-hour factories in the "export platforms" of Hong Kong and Taiwan. Increasingly, as the cars, TV's, computers, cameras, clothes, and furniture are being produced abroad, the United States is becoming a service economy and a producer of plans, programs, and ideas for others to execute. The effect is to eliminate traditional jobs on the assembly line and thereby to reduce the blue collar work force and to replace these jobs with others (probably a smaller number) requiring quite different skills. Because people are not fungible, the man who assembles radios cannot easily become a computer programmer or a packaged-food salesman, to name two recent growth occupations. Unemployment and reduced income result.

As in underdeveloped countries, such as Brazil, for example, the effects of unemployment are not equally distributed over the entire population. They are concentrated in certain regions. The counterpart to Brazil's Northeast, a crisis region of a developing economy, is Appalachia, an area that the energy industry has exploited but not developed. Certain formerly industrial communities of New England, the Midwest, and the Pacific Coast now face the same fate.

The change in employment patterns—the decline in labor-intensive production and the corresponding rise of skilled service jobs—has led to a redistribution of wealth and income which, once again, is more in the tradition of the underdeveloped world than in that of the Affluent Society. As we shall show in Chapter 10, a careful look at income statistics reveals that the average employee, as opposed to top executives, is earning a *decreasing* share of the national income. John Kenneth Galbraith has called our attention to the commonplace but still curious phenomenon that pleasant work is generally much better paid than unpleasant work. But the global corporation is eliminating unpleasant jobs on American soil either by automating them or by exporting them. All of this means that, contrary to the American Dream, there is a trend in the United States toward greater inequality.

The patterns of distribution of income and wealth are nowhere near so stark as in underdeveloped countries, but some of the same processes we have just examined with respect to Latin America are at work here.

The United States trading pattern is beginning to resemble that of underdeveloped countries as the number one nation becomes increasingly dependent on the export of agricultural products and timber to maintain its balance of payments and increasingly dependent on imports of finished goods to maintain its standard of living. To earn the foreign exchange to buy the energy and certain raw materials on which Americans are increasingly dependent, and the TV's, cameras, and other basic consumer goods which, more and more, are produced abroad, the United States must export increasing amounts of grain, lumber, and other agricultural products. (Unlike poor countries, however, the U.S. also exports "software"—i.e., technical knowledge.) In recent years this trading pattern has resulted in food shortages and skyrocketing food prices at home, a phenomenon long familiar in poor countries but a new one in the United States.

2

This chapter begins our inquiry into the connections between corporate growth and the adverse social changes in the United States to which we have just alluded. We shall be focusing on the role of global corporations and banks in this process. Although all but a few of the top 500 industrial firms in the U.S. and almost all the top banks qualify as centrally planned global enterprises, important segments of the economy are still in the hands of primarily national firms. Although small business is not global in either outlook or operation, much of it is dependent on global firms for survival. Certain giant firms which concentrate on domestic services, such as constructing office buildings and operating the telephone system, do not plan or act like global corporations. Government too is an important actor in the economy. We will not be concerned with the activity of these primarily national sectors of the U.S. economy, because it is the global corporation which is the most rapidly growing sector and the most dynamic agent of change.

Probably the most dramatic illustration of the planning power of global corporations and what it can mean for ordinary American citizens is provided by the energy industry. The international petroleum giants have been the pioneer global corporations. They were the first to develop global planning, to locate a high percentage of their assets abroad, and to perfect the art of transfer pricing and the science of tax avoidance.

About 6 percent of the world's population lives in the United States, but these 200 million people consume over 30 percent of the world's energy output. (During much of the last generation before the Japanese and Europeans began to be big oil consumers, the percentage was higher.) Until recently, Americans burned fuel at a bargain rate. But between 1970 and 1973, even before the Arab boycott and the official proclamation of the Energy Crisis, the price for crude rose 72 percent. In some cases the price of natural gas has risen 200 percent since 1970. James E. Akins, formerly the State Department's chief petroleum expert, predicts that "world consumption within the next twelve years is now expected to exceed total world consumption of oil throughout history up to the present time."

Although consumption in the United States has been cut back by government programs, blackouts, brownouts, service-station shutdowns, winter school closings, and rationing, demand, both U.S. and worldwide, far outpaces the *available* supply. This situation is a direct consequence of some of the structural changes in the world economy to which we have alluded. The decisions about production, pricing, research and development, and distribution in the energy field have been substantially in the hands of the global energy companies, the "seven sisters"—British Petroleum, Gulf, Mobil, Shell, Texaco, Exxon, and Chevron (Standard Oil of California). (Purely domestic energy companies account for approximately one-third of annual U.S. energy consumption.) For many years Exxon and other global energy companies have been earning substantially higher profits abroad than in the United States. Because 300 billion barrels of the proved 500-billion-barrel world oil reserves are in the Arab countries of the Middle East, the companies have been concentrating their development activities there. Because of their oligopolistic control over the world energy market, they have held the commanding power to decide how much oil is produced, where it shall go, the price to be charged, and where, through transfer pricing techniques, to declare their profits.

The power of the global energy companies in the U.S. economy is based on a combination of special privileges: uniquely favorable oil concessions in foreign countries backed by the power of the U.S. Government in the name of "national security" (in 1948 Aramco's concession area in the Middle East was larger than the combined areas of Texas and California); special tax advantages unavailable to any other industry (a 22-percent—until recently, 27.5-percent—depletion allowance plus a secret "national security" tax concession making royalty payments to foreign governments eligible as a credit against U.S. taxes); near-monopoly control of oil reserves, transportation, refining and marketing facilities. In 1949, according to the Federal Trade Commission, the "seven sisters" controlled 65 percent of the estimated crude reserves in the world, 88 percent of crude production outside the United States and the U.S.S.R., 77 percent of the refining capacity outside the United States and the U.S.S.R., two-thirds of the tanker fleet, and all major pipelines outside the United States and the U.S.S.R. (It need hardly be added that the same companies dominated production, refining, marketing, and distribution within the United States.) Despite recent nationalizations and the rise of a few European and Japanese companies, 8 global companies, 5 of them U.S.-based, still control 48 percent of world production and a degree of vertical integration and market sharing permitted no other industry. Immunity from antitrust prosecution has been justified on "national security" grounds. (One documented piece of evidence of conspiracy in the industry is found in a Swedish parliamentary committee report that the local subsidiaries of Shell, Texaco, Gulf, and Jersey Standard arranged weekly meetings to "fix uniform rebates, commissions, bonuses, discounts, and other selling terms.")

Because the petroleum companies have had near-monopoly power over production and distribution, they have, for much of the last generation, been able to set world market prices at will. This explains, in part, their extraordinary profits. Oil companies such as Exxon like to advertise that their profit rates are lower than those in many other industries. This is true if one looks at the consolidated balance sheet of the energy companies in which oil, coal, uranium, and other less immediately profitable energy operations are lumped together. But if one looks just at the oil business, the return has been immense. Between 1948 and 1960, the net income of the oil companies derived from the Middle East alone was over $14 billion. While profit rates have been declining in the U.S. and Venezuelan operations, the annual rate of return on fixed assets invested in the Middle East rose from 61 percent in the 1948–1949 period to 72 percent a decade later. This is due to the fact that costs are much lower in the Middle East. (A Chase Manhattan Bank study of the early 1960's computed the cost of producing a barrel of Middle East oil at 16 cents, as compared with $1.73 a barrel for U.S. oil.) The companies have been able to use their enormous profits from foreign operations to finance their expansion into the energy fields which they hope to dominate in the next generation—shale, coal gasification, nuclear power, etc. When Standard Oil (New Jersey) changed its name to Exxon at a cost of some $100 million, it announced thereby not only that it had outgrown New Jersey but that it had transcended the oil industry itself.

Global oligopolies develop ever greater and more concentrated power through various forms of "cross-subsidization." John Blair, former counsel to the Senate Anti-Trust Committee, defines this term as "the actual use by a conglomerate of monopoly profits earned in another industry to subsidize sales at a loss or at an abnormally low profit." Throughout the American economy the giants are using their dominant position in one sector of the economy to acquire a commanding position in another. For example, a successful seller of soft drinks can use its oligopoly profits to subsidize a foray into related industries like the potato-chip business or unrelated industries like the trucking business. Because it can afford to outadvertise smaller established companies, it ends up with a large share of their market. Nowhere is this process of cross-subsidization clearer than in the world of oil and related products. The big companies can use their enormous Middle East profits to consolidate their hold on the distribution system in the United States or to forestall competitors from exploiting alternative energy sources. Thus the same people, essentially the managers and directors of the "seven sisters," end up controlling the pace of exploitation, distribution, and price of petroleum and future energy sources to replace it such as coal, natural gas, and uranium.

Because the energy industry pioneered the globalization of American business, it is one of the best and most instructive examples of the planning power of global corporations—and how this power can be misused. The oil companies are largely responsible for what the former State Department petroleum expert James Akins calls "spectacularly wrong" projections about supply and demand. These estimates of their own domestic well capacity were accepted uncritically by government petroleum planners and they were "almost always exaggerated." (Domestic oil production is down about 8 percent since 1970, and this trend is likely to continue. The addition of approximately 2 million barrels a day by 1980 from Alaska's North Slope is likely to be more than offset by the rapid dwindling of the Texas and Oklahoma oil fields.) At the same time, the decline in natural-gas production and its effect on the demand for oil were largely ignored in the government. In 1970, President Nixon's Task Force on Oil Imports, dominated by representatives of the industry, predicted no significant rise in the price of crude and projected a demand in the United States in 1980 of 18.5 million barrels a day, of which no more than 5 million would need to be imported. By 1973 the United States was already importing well over 6 million barrels, and some revised projections for 1980 are as high as 24 million barrels a day. (Akins estimates that about 35 percent of projected U.S. consumption in 1980 must come from the Eastern Hemisphere.)

Because the information about oil reserves, real costs of drilling and distribution, and their own long-range strategies is in the exclusive hands of the companies, it is impossible to know the extent to which the celebrated Energy Crisis that began in 1973 is real or manipulated. There is considerable evidence, as committees of Congress began to discover in 1974, that available supplies are far more ample than the long lines at gas stations and "crisis messages" from the White House would suggest. Indeed, fuel stocks in the U.S. were at an all-time high in 1974. The critical issues have concerned pricing and timing. It has been in the interest of the companies to orchestrate the worldwide flow of oil in such a way as to maximize profits. In times and places of surplus, it has been company strategy to keep petroleum products off the market. Moreover, during the 1974 energy crisis, when the U.S. domestic price of crude was controlled below that of Europe and Japan, oil companies maximized global profits by maintaining their previous level of imports and increasing the supply to

Europe and Japan. This, in part, explains why Japanese and European consumers did not experience the same serious shortages as did motorists and homeowners in the United States. (Company advertisements that appeared in major newspapers in 1974 claiming that the tankers lining up off the American coast could not unload their cargo for technical reasons understated industry resources and resourcefulness.)

An "energy crisis" which pushes up the price of oil, drives smaller, independent producers out of business, and ensures historic industry profits is something less than a disaster from the companies' viewpoint, however much it may disrupt, inconvenience, or impoverish other citizens. (If it can be presented to the public as a natural disaster compounded by "Arab greed" rather than a massive planning error—real or deliberate—the companies can qualify for relief in the form of additional government subsidies or immunity from environmental controls.) Some knowledgeable students of the petroleum industry such as former Occidental executive Christopher Rand and MIT professor Morris Adelman offer impressive evidence that there is no shortage of fossil fuels in the ground and that indeed, in Rand's words, "the inventories of the world's available fuel have been increasing rather than diminishing, even when measured against the annual rise in the rate of the world's consumption." The suddenness with which lines at gas stations appeared and disappeared, the puzzling display of sudden anger and sudden friendship from the Arab boycotters, and the quick jump in gas prices and oil-company profits all within a few short winter months in 1974 aroused widespread public suspicion that the Energy Crisis was stage-managed. Certainly the profit statements of the "seven sisters" suggest that this was a marketable crisis. When it miraculously lifted, the public was grateful for the opportunity to buy 60-cent gasoline, and a number of troublesome independent operators in the petroleum industry had been eliminated. The extent to which the crisis was the result of conspiracy may not be known until historians are given access to the oil companies' equivalent of the Pentagon Papers.

There is little doubt that the oil companies made serious planning errors. When oil-company executives are subjected to the sort of scathing public questioning by Senate committees that once was reserved for suspected subversive screenwriters, and whispers of nationalization are heard in the corridors of Congress, it is evident that management has been careless with the company image. But up to now the energy giants have been able to profit from their planning errors by pushing their results onto the public.

In the late 1950's, the oil companies finally went too far in taking advantage of their superior bargaining power with the producing countries. Accustomed to renting pliable sheiks along with their oil reserves, they assumed that they could continue indefinitely the cheap and easy access to Arab oil supplies that had financed their mammoth growth. In 1958 and 1959, the major companies reduced their posted prices and tax payments to oil-producing nations and thereby stimulated the creation of OPEC—at first a weak protective society, but now grown into an effective sellers' cartel to offset the cartel power of the companies. (According to conservative estimates, between 1973 and 1985 Kuwait, Saudi Arabia, and the smaller sheikdoms of the Persian Gulf are in a position to earn $227 billion in oil revenues.)

The worldwide energy crisis is not a problem of absolute shortages of energy sources. It is a political crisis over who shall control these resources; who shall decide where, when, and how they are to be distributed; and who shall share in the enormous revenues. The United States is rich in coal and shale. Solar energy, nuclear fusion, wind, and even the recycling of wastes are all possible alternative sources of energy to run the world industrial machine. There may not be an energy crisis in fifteen or twenty years. Rand attributes the lack of refinery capacity in the United States to the fact that "the major American oil companies have neglected to build refineries in the past few years because there has not been as yet enough profit in the enterprise." But, for the present, the problem remains: how are the factories, houses, offices, and cars of the world, with their ever-increasing demand, to be fueled during these transition years until such alternatives are developed? Energy sources that can be exploited only with nonexistent technology or at prohibitive cost, no matter how abundant they may be, are irrelevant to this transitional crisis. Having absorbed well their lessons at the Harvard Business School and the London School of Economics, the new oil technocrats of the Middle East have elected to limit the exploitation of their reserves to delay their exhaustion and to maximize their profits. Their optimum schedule for producing oil is not the same as the schedule of consumption in the industrialized world. It is correct to argue, as Professor Adelman and other petroleum experts do, that there is no worldwide shortage of recoverable oil in the ground, but it is an academic point if those who control the reserves will not permit them to be exploited fast enough to meet rising demand.

While the U.S.-based oil companies now issue standard warnings about the Energy Crisis, they are engaged, in the words of David Freeman, head of the Energy Policy Study, in a "massive exercise in picking the pocket of the American consumer to the tune of billions a year." Not only do energy companies pass on the cost increases of crude to the consumer, but, as Professor Adelman has calculated, they "increase their margins and return on investment" as a result of price increases. In Britain, for example, a recent tax increase of 28 cents a barrel was matched by a price rise of 42 cents a barrel. Because the energy giants are classic oligopolies (in 1969, 8 companies controlled 81.8 percent of all production in OPEC countries), they need not worry about price competition and hence can afford to take a relaxed view of price increases. As long as they can pass such increases on to American motorists and homeowners, they have no great incentive to drive a hard bargain with the Arab countries—particularly when the Arabs are in a position to restrict the supply. Thus Professor Adelman charges the global oil companies with being mere tax collectors for the sheiks, and Senator Henry Jackson calls for government intervention in the negotiating process because the companies "cannot be credible bargainers with OPEC." Confidential papers of the Arabian-American Oil Company subpoenaed by the Senate Subcommittee on Multinational Corporations show that the company welcomed price increases because "their profits increased in proportion to the price rise."

Given world petroleum needs and the distribution of supply, the bargaining power of the Arab states can only increase. The Shell Oil Company now estimates that by 1985 total U.S. import requirements will rise to 15 million barrels a day, of which 78 percent will have to come from Arab countries. At the same time, the company predicts that world consumption will double. Since other industrial countries such as Japan are even more dependent on Middle East oil supplies than the United States and since the Arab countries wish to exhaust their reserves at a slower rate than the companies would like, oil shortages and skyrocketing prices which are then likely to be charged will by that year cost the United States an estimated $70 billion a year in the loss of foreign-exchange reserves. To try to keep the U.S. balance of payments in equilibrium, the United States must export increasing amounts of agricultural products. As the 1972 Soviet wheat deal made clear to customers at the supermarket, huge shipments of grain exported abroad reduce the short-run supply in the United States and drive up the price of bread and meat. Thus while the energy companies are able to adjust to the new realities of international oil politics by translating scarcity into profits, the U.S. consumer (and his counterpart in other countries as well) is paying the price in many ways.

As the bargaining power of those in control of energy resources increases, the United States will be faced with a series of uncomfortable choices. One would be a sharp decline in the use of energy in the United States. Homes at 65 degrees, autoless Sundays, and a ban on nonessential electric appliances might be just the beginning. Furthermore, emergency power to ration and allocate scarce resources would further strengthen and centralize the power of the Executive in Washington. (More optimistically, it could also lead to some basic rethinking about the wisdom of maintaining economic growth on ever-increasing consumption and waste of finite natural resources, but as yet there is no sign of this.)

By 1980, Chase Manhattan Bank experts project, the foreign-exchange reserves of Arab countries from their oil revenues will be in excess of $400 billion. (In 1970 their foreign-exchange reserves were about $5 billion; four years later they had jumped tenfold.) These huge dollar reserves pose a serious problem for the world monetary system. A dollar represents a claim on goods and services. The world is fast approaching the point at which the claims outstanding may well exceed the goods, services, and investment opportunities of interest to the oil-producing nations. Additional dollars will then become as unappealing a medium of exchange for their precious oil as Indian rupees. The Arab sheiks can spend only a fraction of their bulging dollar reserves on Cadillacs and Mediterranean cruises, and their sparsely populated countries even under the most ambitious development schemes could not absorb more than a small fraction. The Arab states are attempting to buy into retail, refining, and marketing operations in the U.S. petroleum industry through joint ventures with U.S.-based companies. Saudi Arabia is becoming a major holder of real estate on the West Coast and by early 1974 had already acquired two California banks. But none of these acquisitions makes much of a dent in the dollar stockpiles of the Middle East. The unanswered question now plaguing the world's bankers is whether the international monetary system can find any way to recycle the extraordinary foreign-exchange holdings of the oil-producing states. In the next few years they will continue to be absorbed in Eurodollar deposits and U.S. Treasury bills, but, as a senior Chase Manhattan Bank executive predicts, within a few years "there will be severe difficulties" unless there are "structural changes" in institutional markets. Thus the glut of dollars no less than the scarcity of oil threatens the stability of the international structures for the creation and maintenance of wealth.

The Energy Crisis is perhaps the most dramatic illustration of these growing vulnerabilities that make the United States look more like an underdeveloped country, but it is only a part of a larger problem. Increasingly, poor countries of the underdeveloped world are coming to understand that their very survival depends upon their taking control over their natural resources and using their increased bargaining power to end what has amounted to a subsidization of the rich nations. (To the argument that the favorable oil concessions of two and three generations ago merely represented what the traffic could bear, their reply is that the traffic pattern is now beginning to change and that, increasingly, they will resist being drained on other people's terms.) This shift in viewpoint, as we saw in the last chapter, is present in the manufacturing industries as well. As the leading U.S. producers of drugs, electronics, packaged food, chemicals, automobiles, and engines become more dependent upon "export platforms" in poor countries, the politicians and generals in charge of those countries may be expected to exact a large share of the profits of global corporations to preserve their own political position. If the governments of underdeveloped countries can succeed in keeping more finance capital in the country, thereby restricting its use for financing of worldwide expansion, they will profoundly affect the way global corporations do business.

Some indication of how important the extraordinary profits available to global corporations in weak and underdeveloped societies have been for their worldwide operation was given us by a top manager of a large U.S.-based manufacturing corporation operating in Latin America. He told us that it was standard practice for his firm, and he believed for many others, to finance expansion in the United States and Western Europe from the excess earnings generated in Latin America. When the "profit faucet," as he termed it, is turned off because local politicians have learned how to police transfer pricing and technology transfers, the expansion programs are threatened, especially when outside capital is scarce and expensive. We have noted in Part II how extensive the practice of transfer pricing is and what huge disguised profits this practice can generate.

Their greatest achievement, the global corporations claim, has been to sustain an unprecedented standard of living in the major industrial countries in which their headquarters are based. That is the great source of their power and the basis for their extraordinary claims on the future. But how important to the maintenance of that standard of living has been the power to exact extraordinarily favorable terms and conditions from poor countries? What will happen to the industrial societies when those terms and conditions change? We have no idea how much our prosperity depends upon the cheap and easy access to raw materials and labor in weak and dependent societies. We do know that our dependence on imported raw materials and foreign labor will increase significantly in the next few years and that changes in bargaining power will force the affluent society to reexamine patterns of consumption that have come to be accepted as laws of nature. It is then that the three-way conflict between the global corporation, American consumers, and poor countries is likely to become more acute. How it is to be resolved will determine how much peace or justice we can expect in the twenty-first century.

3

We must now ask ourselves a troublesome question. If we are right in the assessment that the policy decisions of U.S.-based global corporations in many areas, such as in the energy field, are causing the United States to begin to resemble underdeveloped societies in important respects, how is it that these decisions are allowed to be made? How is it that global corporations continue to exercise the key planning function in American society— in energy policy, transportation policy, and employment policy, to give three examples—when those decisions are producing plainly irrational results for the majority of Americans?

The answer in the United States, as in the poor countries we considered in Part II, can be found only by examination of the distribution of power in American society. An understanding of the process by which the power to make crucial economic decisions for a society becomes concentrated in a few hands and the cumulative effects of that concentration is the intellectual key to understanding how and why such decisions are made. Major social analysts such as Max Weber, Thorstein Veblen, and Joseph Schumpeter have amplified and explained the obvious relationship between economic power and political decisions and in particular why concentrated power produces decisions to the advantage of the few and to the disadvantage of the many. So undebatable is the relationship between concentrated economic power and narrow self-serving political decisions that it represents a meeting ground for Karl Marx and Adam Smith. The prophet of socialism believed that the state under capitalism was the executive committee of an exploitative ruling class. But Adam Smith, the prophet of capitalism, also worried about the social effects of concentrated economic power. Capitalists are forever trying "to widen the market and narrow the competition," and the latter is always against the public interest. "By raising their profits above what they naturally would be [capitalists] levy for their own benefit an absurd tax upon the rest of their fellow citizens."

In the remainder of this chapter we shall be examining why the process of globalization itself has been accompanied by a steep rise in the rate of concentration. In short, there are intrinsic requirements of global oligopoly capitalism that lead to ever-increasing concentration of power and wealth. The problem is not that certain individuals who have risen to preeminent ownership or managerial positions in global corporations are greedy or lacking in public concern. After all, greed is the oil of capitalism. Greed, or to put it in less Biblical terms, acquisitiveness, is supposedly the motivation that makes the system work. The drive for ever-greater accumulation is integral to that system and does not depend upon personal idiosyncrasies. Under traditional capitalist theory, private greed was supposed to lead to public good because of the character of the market. Competition would restrain the selfishness of each to the benefit of all.

However, certain structural changes in world capitalism that we have considered and others that we are about to consider now make it increasingly difficult to reconcile entrepreneurial acquisitiveness with the public interest—if we define public interest to include the health, safety, welfare, and comfort of at least 60 percent of the population. The global corporation, essentially because it does most of its trading with itself, has delivered the coup de grâce to the market. True, the power accumulated by giant oligopolies by the late 1950's to control supplies, set prices, and create demand had made an anachronism of the classic concept of the market even before Big Business became global. But globalization completed the process. At the minimum, almost half of the transactions involving U.S.-based global firms are those in which the buyer and the seller are essentially the same —i.e., intracorporate sales, loans, and other transfers. In such situations the notion of a fair market price is lost. When parties to a transaction are not dealing at arm's length, there are no external criteria for judging the public consequences. The negation of the market means that global profit maximization becomes the guiding star in every transaction and that corporate managers have far more freedom than classic entrepreneurs to arrange profit-maximizing strategies at the expense of the public interest.

Thus by ushering in a postmarket economy and transforming the nature of competition, the rise of globally oriented companies has removed constraints that formerly restricted the size, power, and audacity of the firm. The concentration of power necessarily involves the decline of countervailing power. When a firm buys its former competitors, it is removing checks on its power. Similarly, as we shall show, when a corporation develops the mobility to move its plants out of the United States, it has already gone far to defang its less mobile union adversaries. The rise of the global corporation over the U.S. economy has thus occurred simultaneously with the accelerating concentration of power in the hands of the 500 biggest U.S. corporations. Virtually all of these corporations are global—in the location of their assets, the source of their profits, and their production and marketing outlook. Each is dependent to a significant degree on its foreign operations.

Just as they did in the underdeveloped world, during the course of the last generation the top 500 corporations have dramatically increased their position of dominance in the American economy. In 1955, 44.5 percent of all Americans working in manufacturing and mining worked for the top 500 corporations; by 1970, the figure had risen to 72 percent. In the same period, the top 500 increased their share of all manufacturing and mining assets in the country from 40 to 70 percent. There is an accelerando to the concentration process as one nears the pinnacle. In 1970, the top 9 corporations in the industrial and mining sectors accounted for some 15 percent of total assets and sales in the country. Furthermore, during 1955–1959 the largest 200 industrial corporations increased their share of total industrial assets each year by an average of 1 percent. Ten years later, this average rate of concentration had doubled: they were taking over an additional 2 percent of total assets each year.

The rhythm of accelerated concentration is sustained by the perpetual process of merger. Between 1953 and 1968, there were over 14,000 mergers of manufacturing corporations in the United States, in which the acquiring corporations obtained $66 billion in new assets. The top 100 corporations accounted for only 333 of these mergers, but in the process they acquired $23 billion in new assets, or roughly 35 percent of all merged assets acquired during the period. In the late 1960's, the merger of industrial giants accelerated at an exponential rate. Almost 60 percent of the $23 billion of new assets were acquired in the four most recent years studied (1965–1968). (In 1965, for example, 1,496 domestic firms disappeared through merger, the highest number in the history of the United States up to that time.) Although comprehensive data for the following years are not available, many indications point to a continuation of the same trend of accelerating concentration. Despite antitrust laws written with a ferocity to intimidate the uninitiated, prosecutions are few and courts are lenient. (Of all the mergers between 1950 and 1967, only 199 were challenged. Almost half of these, it might be added, were small firms of less than $100 million in sales. The government won 90 of these challenges, and in only 48 out of 14,000 mergers during the period were the companies required to divest themselves of anything.)

If we turn to the service sector, the pattern of cumulative increases in concentration is equally striking. The term "service sector" includes lawyers, dishwashers, travel agents, and masseurs, but when we are focusing on the services that earn most of the money in the United States (as opposed to those that employ the most people) we mean banks, insurance companies, other financial institutions, and the communications and transport industries—in short, the social infrastructure of the country.

In looking at poor countries in Part II, we noted that the control of ideology by global corporations through the mass media was as important a source of their power as their control of finance and technology. It was the interaction of the three that enabled powerful corporate interests, mostly foreign-based, to make major planning decisions which adversely affected the problems of mass poverty, unemployment, and inequality. The same mutually supporting use of these three elements of corporate power can be seen in the United States, and with some of the same effects.

Any discussion of the power of the mass media in the United States must of course begin with television and radio. The typical American spends three and a half hours a day watching TV and two and one-half hours listening to the radio. The industry estimates that about 87 percent of the population is exposed to television each week and 90 percent to radio. Because the network's franchises, its most valuable property, cost next to nothing (a few million dollars in legal fees to obtain or protect its right to broadcast over the fifteen stations it is allowed to own and the 200-odd affiliate stations), profits are enormous. The networks have used these profits to finance their expansion into many unrelated areas. CBS owns Steinway Piano; Holt, Rinehart & Winston publishers; and, formerly, the New York Yankees. RCA, NBC's parent, owns Random House, Hertz car rentals, and Cushman & Wakefield real estate. While the electronic media are not the sole source of information beyond the village, as in countries with large illiterate populations, they are, as the editors of *Look* and *Life* discovered, increasingly replacing magazines, as well as books and newspapers, as the primary source of news and entertainment. About 96 percent of the entertainment to which 87 percent of the population is exposed each week is produced by the three networks. About 75 percent of the country looks to the three networks as its primary source of news.

The principal purpose of this mass diffusion of news and entertainment is to sell products. Each year, it is estimated, the average viewer sees 40,000 commercials. In 1968, advertisers spent over $3 billion on television. (Total advertising revenues in all media have jumped since 1945 from $3 billion to $20 billion. About 30 percent of the advertising business is handled by the ten largest agencies, which nearly doubled in size during the 1960's.)

Advertising is also the mainstay of the newspaper business. (The average newspaper devotes 60 percent of its space to ads.) The marketing function of newspapers is more important to those who finance them than the communication function. For this reason, size of the market rather than quality of the content is the crucial determinant of whether a newspaper shall live or die. The bigger a newspaper's readership, the more advertising revenue it can command. In rational economic terms most cities cannot "support" more than one newspaper. Thus, less than 15 percent of the 1,500-odd cities in the United States with a daily newspaper have more than one and at least half the nation's daily papers are owned by newspaper chains. Seventy-five percent of all newspaper news is supplied by the two major wire services, Associated Press and United Press International.

The same groups (the banks and financial institutions) that are the major sources of noncorporate finance capital also have significant interests in the communications media. The process by which large corporations use their predominant power to gain increasing control within one sector of the economy and then to use that power to gain control over other sectors—i.e., cross-subsidization—goes far to explain the rapidity with which the global corporations accumulate ever-increasing power and undermine sources of countervailing power.

4

No one understands this process better than bankers. Nine of the top 10 companies in the United States in terms of assets are global banks. Of 13,000 banks in the United States, the top 4— the Bank of America, Chase Manhattan, the First National City Bank, and Manufacturers Hanover Trust—had in 1970 over 16 percent of all bank assets. The top 50 had 48 percent. More important, the top 4 had increased their rate of concentration dramatically. From 1965 to 1970 they were increasing their share of total bank assets at roughly twice their expansion rate during the previous ten years. As in the control of technology and mass media, the concentration of power has proceeded in the finance sector at an exponential rate.

That the rich get richer is well established as folk wisdom ("Nothing succeeds like success") and Biblical truth ("To him who hath shall it be given"). There is nothing especially mysterious about why large banks grow faster than small banks. What is striking about the growth of banks is not so much that a few financial giants have come to dominate the money industry as that they also dominate other sectors of the economy as well. The largest banks exercise significant influence in a number of the country's leading manufacturing and mining companies, the transportation industry, the media, and public utilities.

Banks have certain advantages over other corporations in their ability to use cross-subsidization. The most mobile of business enterprises, they can change the focus of their activities from country to country as financial conditions change. Thus the top U.S. banks which invaded London during the Eurodollar boom of the 1960's are now retrenching somewhat in the City and expanding their activities elsewhere. Similarly, they are more flexible in dealing with regimes of all political hues. As the world economy becomes more integrated, even the most militant Communists, who also need hard currency, cannot afford to offend the international bankers.

The process by which banks have expanded their control of the nonbanking sectors of the U.S. economy has involved three major strategies. The first is the use of their enormous holdings of industrial stocks which they either own or manage for customers in trust accounts. In 1971 banks owned $577 billion in corporate securities in their own portfolios and had control of an additional $336 billion in trust funds. Together these assets in the hands of banks amount to almost $1 trillion. Trust funds are portfolios of securities given to banks to manage, usually for widows, children, estates, pension funds, or charitable institutions. In 1971, in addition to the banks' own holdings, bank trust departments held 22 percent of all the outstanding voting shares of all publicly held U.S. corporations. For more than 80 percent of these shares the bank had "sole investment responsibility"—which meant that it could buy and sell the shares at will and vote the stock at shareholder meetings.

Thanks to the continuing investigative work of Congressman Wright Patman's Subcommittee on Banking and Currency and Senator Lee Metcalf's Subcommittee on Budgeting, Management and Expenditures, we know a good deal about how banks have translated that trillion dollars into what one subcommittee calls "enormous potential power for good or evil." Economists generally agree, and managements are acutely aware, that a shareholder in control of 5 percent of a publicly held corporation cannot be safely ignored. According to the Patman Subcommittee, there is "considerable evidence" that corporations seek to establish "close contact" with such shareholders, who are almost invariably large institutional investors. Corporate management regularly consults them on "any major corporate decision, such as a proposed merger, a new stock issue proposal or any pending decision which may seriously affect the company's operations." Corporate managers listen to the bankers' answers, since they have the power to sell off large blocks of stock and cause a decline in its value, thereby hurting the reputation of management and, perhaps more importantly, the value of its stock options. Moreover, when a bank or insurance company controls 5 percent of a company's stock, it can exert crucial voting power in the event of a proxy battle. (It is much easier to enlist the support of a 5-percent shareholder than to recruit 5,000 small investors.) Institutional investors dominate annual shareholders' meetings on the relatively rare occasions when fundamental issues of corporate policy are put up for a vote.

The top 49 banks have a 5-percent or greater share in 147 of the top 500 industrials. They have a 5-percent or greater interest in 17 of the top 50 transportation companies, 29 of the top 50 life insurance companies and 5 of the top public utilities. Some specific examples provide a more vivid picture of the power of America's largest global banks.

By examining interlocking directorates and stock ownership of the leading U.S. banks, the economist Peter Dooley has identified fifteen major financial groups in the United States. A group is a collection of nominally separate corporations which pool their resources to enhance their combined power. By far the most powerful is the Rockefeller-Morgan group, the coordinated financial operations of the descendants, beneficiaries, and employees of John D. Rockefeller and J. P. Morgan. As early as 1904, John Moody, the founder of *Moody's Industrials*, still the leading directory to the labyrinth of high finance, concluded that it was impossible to talk of the Rockefellers and Morgans as separate economic actors, so intertwined were their various activities.

Taking another look at the Rockefeller-Morgan empire in the mid-1960's, Peter Dooley concludes that "it is not possible to separate these groups." The power base of the Rockefeller-Morgan group is the control of six of the country's largest banks: the Chase Manhattan Bank, the Rockefeller family depository, of which David Rockefeller is chairman; the First National City Bank; Manufacturers Hanover Trust; the Chemical Bank of New York; the Morgan Guaranty Trust; and Bankers Trust. In the mid-1960's, according to Patman Subcommittee research, these banks dramatically increased their holdings of one another's stock and consolidated the interlocks among their boards. Together four large interlocking New York banks, according to a 1973 Senate Government Operations Committee report, hold 21.9 percent of United Airlines, 24.7 percent of American Airlines, and 13.8 percent of Western Airlines. The Chase Manhattan Bank alone holds substantially more than 5 percent of United, American, Northwestern, and Western. Chase (with two other Rockefeller-Morgan banks) has voting rights to 23.1 percent of the stock of CBS, to 24.6 percent of ABC, and to 6.7 percent of NBC. In addition to the principal airlines and the three major networks, the Rockefeller-Morgan group has effective control of key sectors of the mining industry. (It is scarcely necessary to mention the Exxon Corporation, until recently Standard Oil, the largest energy corporation in the world and the source and constant nourisher of the Rockefeller family fortune.) In 1967, Chase had a 5.5-percent interest in Reynolds, and Morgan had a 17.5-percent interest in Kennecott (which in turn owns Peabody Coal, the world's largest coal company) and a 15.5-percent interest in American Smelting and Refining.

No committee of Congress or anyone else has been able to show exactly how large banks use their power in the communications and transportation industries and how their huge holdings may affect the public interest. We have some ideas on this, which we shall take up in the next section. Whether banks have too much power over other parts of the economy is controversial. Whether Congress should have the information to determine whether this is so is not. Public authorities do not have the regular access to the information on the interaction of crucial institutions necessary to understand the present U.S. economy and how it works.

Banks have reinforced their concentration of ownership and control by means of a second strategy, the liberal use of the interlocking directorate. The Patman Subcommittee found that the top 49 commercial banks had 5 percent or more stock control *plus* interlocking directorates with 5,270 companies. Dooley's 1966 study "The Interlocking Directorate" in the *American Economic Review* concludes that "most of the larger corporations have been interlocked with other large corporations for many decades." What are interlocking directorates and why are they important? An interlock occurs when a corporation elects an executive or director of another corporation to be on its board of directors. There are many possible motives behind the practice. Sometimes it is to get expert business advice from a proved success in another field; sometimes to embellish an annual report with an eminent name. Still another possibility is to suppress competition by inviting representatives of competing firms to share in coordinated planning for the industry. (This practice is prohibited by the Clayton Act of 1914, but Dooley's study shows that "nearly one in every eight interlocks involves companies which are competitors.") There are special reasons why corporations like to invite bankers to sit on their boards and why bankers like to accept. "By electing a banker to the board of directors," Dooley notes, "a company may expect to have more ready access to bank funds while the banker can watch over the operation of the company and reduce the risk of lending to a distressed borrower." On the other hand, banks like to elect company officers to their boards to "attract large deposits" and "reliable customers" for large loans. Adolph Berle, perhaps the most influential analyst of the American corporation, describes how interlocking directorates enhance the power of banks:

> As trustees, these banks are large stockholders. As suppliers of credit, they have the influence of lenders. With interlocking directorates, they potentially can influence the decision-making function of the operating corporate managers.

In 1914, Louis Brandeis branded the practice of interlocking directorates "the root of many evils" because of the "fundamental law that no man can serve two masters." In the early years of the century populist sentiment was running high, and even Woodrow Wilson was condemning the bankers for their "monopoly" of money. Running for office against banks in Texas a generation ago was the equivalent of running against King George in the Irish wards of Chicago. Today most populist attacks against bigness, banks, and interlocking directorates have a faintly quixotic air since the U.S. economy has been hurtling for so many years in the opposite direction.

The third and most important strategy of banks for extending their influence over the nonbanking sectors of the economy has been the use of cross-subsidization. Just as oil companies could use their economic power to enter the coal business or the nuclear-energy field or a newspaper chain could use its oligopoly profits to buy TV stations, so the largest banks have in the last ten years systematically used their power over the banking sector to enter, and eventually to dominate, unrelated fields such as insurance and equipment leasing. It had been an article of faith in the New Deal days that the speculation of banks in the stock market was a prime cause of the Great Crash. Accordingly, until the mid-1960's banks were effectively prohibited by law not only from dabbling in the stock market but from venturing into virtually all other new financial pastures. Essentially, they were supposed to confine their business to gathering in deposits and lending out money.

The Bank Holding Act of 1956 was designed to reaffirm control of banks, but it contained a rather obvious loophole that permitted nonbanking corporations to own both banks and non-related industries. Though ostensibly intended for the small-town rural banker who might want to own the local hardware store along with the family bank, the one-bank holding company has been used to establish the banking conglomerate in which a single corporation controls travel services, insurance, commercial paper, consumer credit, credit cards, leasing of industrial equipment, data processing, and certain types of mutual funds. No single lawyer's invention has contributed more to the concentration of wealth in America; banks can use cross-subsidization to drive independent entrepreneurs out of all these businesses.

The First National City Bank, which took the lead in creating a one-bank holding company, Citicorp, and the other banking giants that followed expanded their activities in this direction— not only because of their own passion for growth but also because their foreign competitors were thinking and acting the same way. In the mid-60's similar developments in the banking industry were taking place in France, Britain, and Germany, where legislation was already more permissive than in the United States. Thus, as in the industrial field, the intensification of world-wide oligopolistic competition forced further concentration in the U.S. economy.

The one-bank holding company permits banks to transcend legal and financial restrictions that pertain to banks and to cross geographical borders otherwise barred to them. The size of the banking giants permits them to achieve certain economies of scale which in effect pay for their expansion. Thus, for example, banks went into the data-processing business with virtually no initial investment because they had unused time in their own computers. In 1969 new legislation was passed—supposedly to close the loopholes that had permitted banks to escape much intended regulation; but as it finally emerged from the Congress, the new law almost perfectly suited the interests of the large commercial banks. While it helped to prevent the takeover of banks by non-banking conglomerates, it ratified the right of banks to expand into other "closely related" financial activities. Thus, Americans hold over 56 million BankAmericards, owned by Bank of America, or Master Charge cards, owned by Inter-Bank, a consortium of the Rockefeller-Morgan–controlled New York banks. For the banks the card is a way of selling 18-percent loans without taking up a bank officer's time. Leasing arrangements are now responsible for what is probably the most rapid and significant growth in the power of banks over nonbanking activities. Banks are consolidating their hold over the aviation industry by financing both the seller and the buyer of the same equipment, the aircraft manufacturers and the airlines. Between 1971 and 1974 about $15 billion in sales have been financed through such arrangements. The leasing of equipment is thus one more device for accelerating the diversified growth of banks. "Tomorrow Citicorp will be bigger and in more places," the company promises.

5

That the same institutions which have become global banks have also extended their power into almost every strategic sector of the U.S. economy is clear. What that extension of power means is a matter of debate. Indeed, the proper role of bankers in our society has been a matter of controversy even before Andrew Jackson's clash with Nicholas Biddle over the chartering of the National Bank shook the foundations of the young republic. Despite the advertising campaign to convince anyone with a steady income that "you have a friend at Chase," most people do not think so. The popular image of the banker—a rather stuffy man who arrives at the office late and from time to time forecloses on mortgages—was established in turn-of-the-century melodramas and, despite millions spent in institutional advertising, is not yet wholly refurbished. Commercial banks, Wright Patman notes, having "crept into every crevice of the American economy," are in a position to make too many crucial decisions affecting the rest of us. Some Marxist critics are strongly impelled to show that banks dominate the industrial economy because this thesis represents the fulfillment of Hilferding's and Lenin's prophecies about the evolution of capitalism. The conflict of interest between industrialists and bankers is seen as part of a "fatal contradiction" which will lead to the collapse of capitalism.

Our view is different. Banks play two different roles—one in the regulated and another in the nonregulated sector of the economy—with different public consequences. In the nonregulated, dynamic sectors such as the drug, computer, and communications industries and the fast-growing industrial conglomerates like ITT and Gulf & Western, banks played a crucial role in supporting company management by facilitating its acquisition campaign. This is Wright Patman's summary of what happened:

One of the favorite pastimes of concentrated financial power is promoting concentration in nonfinancial industries. There is substantial evidence that the major commercial banks have been actively fueling the corporate merger movement. A 1971 congressional report, for example, found that major banks financed acquisitions, furnished key financial personnel to conglomerates, and were even willing to clean out stock from their trust departments to aid in takeover bids. Thus Gulf and Western, one of the most aggressive conglomerates of the 1950's and 1960's (92 acquisitions involving almost a billion dollars in eleven years), expanded hand in glove with Chase Manhattan. Friendly representatives of Chase made funds available and provided advice and services that assisted Gulf and Western in its acquisitions. In return, in addition to the customary business charges for Gulf and Western's accounts and loans, Chase secured banking business generated by the newly developing conglomerate that formerly had gone to other banks, and was recipient of advance inside information on proposed future acquisition.

Indeed, the accelerating increase in the power of banks is a direct result of the feverish pace of global corporate expansion. Banks have grown in large measure in the last ten years because the dynamic industries have high cash-flow requirements. Following their clients overseas, the largest banks have formed consortia to cap their control over the Eurodollar market. Although large industrial firms such as IBM and GM have traditionally financed most of their expansion from internal capital, they are increasingly resorting to outside financing, particularly for their foreign operations (over 30 percent of their capital requirements in the United States and 50 percent of their capital requirements overseas are met through outside financing). But despite the fact that banks hold large blocks of the stock of such corporations and have representatives on their boards, there is no evidence that the banks have "taken over" these dynamic corporations. (It must be said at the outset, of course, that there is little evidence of anything concerning the internal relationships of banks and corporations because not only are the deliberations secret but much of the financial data to prove or disprove the thesis that banks dominate industry is also beyond the examination of the Executive, Congress, or the public.) That role of outside financing for U.S.-based global corporations, however, has now become most crucial as the need for additional capital to keep pace with Japanese and European competitors becomes more acute. German and Japanese banks directly control major industries in their countries. Oligopolistic competition may well encourage similar developments in the United States.

Thus in the nonregulated growth industries, principally the global giants we have been considering up to now, the question whether banks use their financial power and stockholdings to dictate to the management of such firms scarcely arises because their interests are the same. The bank is as interested as the corporation's own management in promoting corporate policies that will produce growth so that its holdings will appreciate and its loans will be repaid. Edward S. Herman, professor of finance at the Wharton School, puts it this way:

> What impresses me most in examining intercorporate relationships is not centralized control, banker or otherwise, but the network of personal and business affiliations and contacts and the mutually supportive character of so much of the business system. . . . One can deduce that activities carried out by substantial business firms, no matter how odious, will not be subject to open criticism by important businessmen who are part of the corporate-banking network. If [Dow, GE, Honeywell, North American Rockwell and other major Vietnam war suppliers] were to produce gas chambers under contract with the Pentagon, their decisions would be accepted in silence by the community of leading business firms.

The issue, it seems to us, is not whether the interests of bankers and the interests of corporate management are in conflict but whether bankers are in a position to use their concentrated financial power against the public interest.

When we turn to the regulated sector of the U.S. economy, however, a different picture emerges. It is in the regulated industries that the banks' "enormous potential power for good or evil" is crucial. These industries—power companies, airlines, radio and television, railroads, telephone companies—represent essential services of the society, the social infrastructure on which all other economic growth depends. The one characteristic of these companies is that they are all heavily subsidized by government. Though all are technically private firms, and are privately owned, the government will not allow any of them to stop performing its essential services. They cannot be permitted to go out of business however great their financial losses.

The power of banks over the transportation sector and how that power is used has recently been illustrated by the Penn Central debacle. The Patman Subcommittee notes that "a number of financial institutions played a major and perhaps dominant role in the management of the Penn Central and its predecessors." The chairman of the world's largest privately owned railroad at the time it went into bankruptcy was Stuart T. Saunders, a director of the Chase Manhattan Bank and of the large Philadelphia commercial bank First Pennsylvania Banking and Trust Company. Chase and its closely interlocked ally Morgan Guaranty were major creditors of the railroad. The chief financial officer of the railroad was David C. Bevan, president of a large Philadelphia bank. Beginning in 1963 at the behest of these and other bankers who dominated the railroad's board, Penn Central began a major diversification program, principally into real estate, with the heavy use of commercial bank loans. At a time when service was declining and rolling stock needed replacement, the Patman Subcommittee notes, the real estate operations "were competing with the Railroad for the same limited sources of credit at a time when the Railroad was having trouble obtaining needed financing." In short, Penn Central's finance capital was used to cross-subsidize the real estate expansion. The "disastrous expansion program," according to the Subcommittee, produced a net cash drain of $175 million. The same bankers in charge of Penn Central had also pushed heavily for a merger with the New York Central two years before the final collapse. "Thus, we see," the Subcommittee report notes, "that those most anxious to see the merger consummated were people in the financial aspects of the transaction, and who knew or cared little or nothing about running a railroad. Ultimately, the financial experts' judgment proved to be disastrous."

It is characteristic of regulated industries that they incur much greater debt than other firms dare incur. The reason they are such good customers for banks is that they are stable. Their growth rates are steady and predictable, their stocks have high yields, and they cannot be permitted to go out of business. It is the near-certain prospect of government rescue that makes no-risk social-infrastructure investment attractive for banks. Unlike the situation in the private sector, where fairly large corporations can disappear, even bankruptcy does not mean the end of a railroad, airline, or major military contractor or a default on its loans. If necessary, the Federal Government will keep it in operation and eventually satisfy its creditors.

This arrangement, which would make Adam Smith wince, might be termed bankers' socialism. A good illustration of how it works is seen in the case of the 1971 Lockheed loan. In 1969, Lockheed, then the number one defense contractor, borrowed $400 million from a consortium of 24 banks. In 1970, while working on the L-1011 Airbus, the company ran into such serious financial difficulty that bankruptcy seemed imminent. Six representatives of the major banks that had lent the $400 million met in March of that year with Deputy Secretary of Defense David Packard to negotiate their rescue. The result was a $250-million loan guarantee, which the Nixon Administration proposed and the Congress narrowly passed in August 1971, by which the U.S. taxpayer relieved the rescuing banks of all risk. The case illustrates the hold that huge corporations—particularly those in transportation, utilities, and the defense industry—have on the rest of the society. Despite its inefficiency and mismanagement, Lockheed was subsidized by the U.S. taxpayer because of its very size. Too much was at stake to permit Lockheed to fail— 24,000 jobs, $2.5 billion in outstanding contracts, $240 million advanced by airlines. (The collapse of Lockheed, the banks argued in support of the rescue operation, would lead to the collapse of TWA.) A number of the same banks that had lent so much money to Lockheed (Chase, Morgan Guaranty, Bank of America, Wells Fargo, Bankers Trust) had also lent money to the major airlines threatened by a Lockheed bankruptcy.

If we turn our attention to the public utilities, we see the same combination of huge external debt owed to banks and the heavy representation of bankers on the board of directors that we saw in the Penn Central case. Consolidated Edison of New York, the power company that services the New York City area, operates under a board of directors made up of individuals who are also directors of some of the country's largest banks and insurance companies: Manufacturers Hanover, Metropolitan Life, First National City, Chemical Bank. Indeed, not only is Con Ed dominated by men with important bank connections, but the great majority of such connections are with institutions included within the Rockefeller-Morgan network. Six of the ten largest shareholders are commercial banks. (Indeed, according to Senator Lee Metcalf's investigations, Chase Manhattan is among the top ten holders of 42 utilities, Morgan Guaranty Trust is among the top ten of 41 utilities, Manufacturers Hanover Trust is among the top ten of 31 utilities.)

Utilities are exceedingly good customers for banks. More than 50 percent of the total capitalization of Con Ed of New York is in long-term debt financing. Because it is a regulated monopoly, it need fear no competition. Its customers have nowhere else to turn to run their electric kitchens or their office-building elevators and air conditioners. Bronx Borough President Robert Abrams calls this enviable position "a cost-plus relationship with society." Utilities, he charges, need not cut costs to maintain profits. They need merely raise prices to the customers. Between 1964 and 1969, Con Ed reduced the amount spent on plant additions nearly 10 percent at a time when expansion of service was clearly needed, but increased its payments to the holders of its long-term debt by about 9 percent a year. (By 1969 the power company was paying 93 percent of its annual income to banks and other holders of its stocks and bonds.) No one can prove a direct relationship between this sort of financial management and the persistent power failures that plague the city of New York, but the New York State Public Service Commission blames Con Ed's faulty equipment for the massive 1973 power failure in Queens. There is strong evidence here, as in the Penn Central case, that putting bankers in charge of public utilities is no way to run either a power company or a railroad.

A whirlwind tour of who owns America, such as we have just completed, is essential to an understanding of the preeminent power of the global corporations over American society. Moreover, as we noted in our discussion of Latin America, one cannot understand global corporations without comprehending their interconnections with global banks. There is also an intimate and necessary connection between growth and concentration. In a world dominated by oligopolistic competition, the quest for the one leads inevitably to the other. The result is that managerial control of the technology, the finance capital, and the instruments for developing and disseminating ideology vest in a few hundred individuals. The principal decision makers in the 200 top industrial corporations and the 20 largest banks, which control such a huge proportion of the nation's wealth and its capacity to produce wealth, number fewer than a thousand persons. These individuals are the planners for our society.

Since the days of Thorstein Veblen analysts of the American corporation have theorized about what it means that salaried executives have taken over the day-to-day management of the great business enterprises from the owners. Veblen dreamed of the socially minded engineer who, free of the temptation to accumulate a personal fortune, would run the corporation in accordance with the public interest. Berle and Means's classic analysis of the separation of ownership and management laid the foundation for Galbraith's concept of the technostructure—essentially propertyless sellers of skill whose vision of the corporation was broader than the traditional entrepreneurial vision. If in fact the interests of the technostructure and the interests of owners were different, such diversity in outlook between them would, it was argued, provide a crude system of checks and balances. It did not really matter that the Rockefeller family owned the largest energy company, the largest banks, the largest insurance companies, etc., because the managers of these enterprises were not necessarily responsive to their will. Thus the answer to the Wright Patmans was that it was hard to translate huge holdings into political power because the owners did not make the crucial decisions.

  Although the theory is somewhat more elegant than our simplification suggests, it has never been supported by much empirical evidence. The simple fact that managers are easier to get rid of than owners should cause a certain skepticism about the vaunted managerial takeover. Recent studies confirm our skepticism about the supposed conflict in interest and outlook between the very rich and the aspiring rich. In brief, the distinction between owners and managers is disappearing as top management in the major corporations acquires substantial blocks of stock through options, bonuses, and special opportunities. Professor Wilber Lewellen's study for the National Bureau of Economic Research *The Own-ership Income of Management* indicates that in recent years top managers are steadily earning substantially more of their income from ownership of their own corporations than from salary. By the early 1960's the leading members of the technostructure were earning more than 50 percent of their total income from their stockholdings in their own corporations. Our own studies updat-ing these findings, discussed in the next chapter, confirm the trend through 1972.

It is now common for corporate managers of major corpora-tions to have holdings of several million dollars. The gulf between these respectable fortunes and the superfortunes of the major stockholders is great, to be sure, but the manager who depends on his shares in his own corporation for the major share of his own income has precisely the same personal interest in maximiz-ing corporate growth as the $100-million shareholder.

6

Ever-greater concentration of economic power through a pro-cess of cross-subsidization across industrial sectors and geograph-ical frontiers is now a crucial dynamic of the world political econ-omy. The acceleration of this process by which a small number of large economic units employ their advantages to acquire ever-greater market shares appears inescapable as long as corporate executives and government managers continue to think as they now do. One reason why concentration is proceeding at an ex-ponential rate is the rapid erosion of sources of national power that might have been expected to restrain this expansionary process.

We must now ask the same crucial political question about the United States we posed in connection with Latin America: why is there so little countervailing power to resist the corporate take-over? If our analysis is correct that global banks are increasingly coming to dominate the vital social services of the society—trans-port, utilities, etc.—and are using their enormous influence to pro-mote good financial return often at the expense of good public service, why has this been allowed to happen? If global corpo-rations, having assumed the principal planning power in our so-ciety, are unable to deal satisfactorily with our major social prob-

lems—inflation, unemployment, the energy crisis, pollution—
why do they continue to exercise such power?

The answer is structural weakness in major institutions of our
national life, which might have been expected to balance off the
power of the global corporations. As a result, the United States is
looking more and more like an underdeveloped country. As in
Latin America, the obvious candidates to oppose the power of the
corporations—labor unions, small businessmen, and, especially,
the government—are completely inadequate. Why should this
be so?

Of these three candidates, we shall have little to say here about
the first two. The decline of the power of labor in the face of the
globalization of business is so important a matter that it deserves
a separate chapter. The decline of small business and regional
business is a vital part of the structural transformation in the
American economy, but it is a relatively simple matter to explain.
During the nineteenth century and the early years of the twentieth century, interests of Southern farmers, New England mill-
owners, and New York bankers often conflicted, and these regional and sectional differences served to fractionate and hence
to check the power of business as a whole. By the mid–twentieth
century, however, the United States had been fully integrated
into a national market and these historic conflicts among entrepreneurs had largely disappeared. The same techniques now being used to develop the global market—modern transportation,
accounting, marketing, etc.—were successfully employed to create the integrated U.S. market, and in the process local pockets
of resistance to the march of the great corporations were eliminated. The decline of competition and the disappearance of
thousands of small firms with competing interests have consolidated the political power of business.

But why does government lack the power to control global
corporations? In Latin America, as we saw, government bureaucracy is weak, corrupt, and inefficient, but the Nixon scandals
notwithstanding, that is hardly a fair description of the U.S. Government. Inefficiency abounds and corruption exists, but the
government is not weak. Indeed, over the past generation, the
Federal state apparatus has claimed and exercised ever-greater
power. The centralization of authority over the economy in the

Executive Branch and, finally, in the President's office has made this the era of Big Government. Yet Big Government is unable to control Big Business.

The easy explanation is that politicians who achieve high office and the public administrators they appoint have little desire to control the expansion and exercise of corporate power. The dominant ideology in mid-century America is the celebration of growth and bigness. No government dedicated to steady, spectacular economic growth as the prime tool for maintaining social peace can afford to take a tough line with big corporations. For those who have come to power in America in the last thirty years, the notion that there were any fundamental conflicts between corporate interests and the public interest simply did not arise. The power of the United States rested so clearly on the power of the great corporations.

Therefore, it has seemed quite reasonable to the last five administrations to staff those parts of the Federal Government that regulate the economy with men on loan from the great corporations and banks. The Federal Government is in a position to exercise little countervailing power against big corporations in large measure because of government–business interlocks in the most strategic areas of the economy. The interlocking process begins with the campaign contribution. The stark truth is that no one can be elected President of the United States under our present system without massive financial contributions from big business. This has been a fact for almost one hundred years, but its true significance was dramatized in the Nixon Administration. So anxious were the managers of such corporations as Gulf Oil, Braniff Airways, Phillips Petroleum, Ashland Oil, American Airlines, Minnesota Mining and Manufacturing, Goodyear Tire and Rubber, and Carnation to contribute to the President's already overflowing campaign chest that they broke the law (for which they received suspended jail sentences and small fines). It is clear from the behavior of ITT, milk producers, and banks that corporations regard campaign contributions as investments, not charity. They are buying shares in an Administration which they have reason to expect will be responsive to their interests. Here is a list of some of the major corporate contributors to the Nixon 1972 campaign:

Robert Allen	Gulf Resources & Chemical	
	Corp.	$ 100,000
	American Airlines	75,000
Elmer Bobst	Warner-Lambert Phar-	
	maceutical Co.	100,000
Nathan Cummings	Consolidated Foods Corp.; board chairman, Assoc. Products Inc. (manufacturing and wholesale food)	44,356
Frederick L. Ehrman	Lehman Corp. (investment banking)	63,578
Harvey, Leonard & Raymond Firestone	Firestone Tire & Rubber Co.	212,153
Max M. Fisher	Chairman, Fisher–New Center Co., co-chairman, Finance Committee	125,000
Henry Ford II & Family	Ford Motor Company	99,775
J. Paul Getty	Getty Oil	75,000
Howard Hughes		150,000
	National Airlines	50,000
	Standard Oil Co. of California	50,000
	Phillips Petroleum Co.	100,000
Roger Milliken	Deering Milliken Inc. (textiles)	84,000
John A. Mulcahy	President, Quickley Co. (steel subsidiary of Pfizer, Inc., pharmaceuticals)	573,559
W. Clement Stone	Combined Insurance Co. of America	2,000,000
Arthur K. Watson	Former board chairman, IBM World Trade	300,000
Claude C. Wild	Gulf Oil Corp.	100,000

Sources: See Notes for this page.

(Some of Mr. Nixon's ambassadorial appointees from large corporations apparently felt a touching sense of obligation to the man who made it possible for them to be addressed for life as "your Excellency." The ambassadors to Ireland, France, Britain,

Jamaica, Switzerland, Trinidad, and the Netherlands together invested slightly over $1 million in the 1972 campaign.)

From the start, regulatory agencies have been dominated by the industries they were supposed to regulate. When the first regulatory agency, the Interstate Commerce Commission, was being debated in 1884, Charles Adams, director and later president of the Union Pacific Railroad, characterized with refreshing candor what is still the predominant attitude of industry toward Federal regulation. Writing to a Massachusetts Congressman who had asked his help in defeating a "radical" regulatory measure, he observed:

> What is desired, if I understand it . . . is something having a good sound, which will impress the popular mind with the idea that a great deal is being done, when, in reality, very little is intended to be done.

As the historian Gabriel Kolko has shown, the railroads were proponents of moderate regulatory legislation as an alternative to the tougher measures the antirailroad forces in the country were pushing. The ICC was staffed from the beginning with a high proportion of railroad lawyers and others sympathetic to the industry. The ICC is still dominated by proindustry commissioners. Whether one accepts Kolko's view that regulatory agencies have always been captives of the industries they are supposed to regulate or the more conventional view that they begin as crusaders and gradually ossify, the effect is the same. In the words of former Federal Communications Commissioner Nicholas Johnson, the regulatory agency is now "a leaning tower of Jell-o."

An impressive qualification for becoming an FCC commissioner is to own a television station, just as it is helpful to have worked for the gas industry if you want to serve on the Federal Power Commission. The plausible argument for taking businessmen on loan to be regulators of their own industry is that they are the ones with the experience to do the job. But the theory that it takes one to catch one is contradicted by consistent practice. The business journal *Forbes* notes that "it is hard to see how the troubled natural gas industry could have a regulator more to its tastes than the new chairman of the Federal Power Commission" (John N. Nassikas, a Manchester, New Hampshire, utilities lawyer). Other recent FPC commissioners include Rush Moody,

Jr., a Texas lawyer representing Pennzoil, an oil conglomerate; and Carl E. Bagge, a Boise lawyer who also represented Pennzoil. In 1972 the Federal Power Commission granted the natural-gas industry huge price increases and, in the words of former FPC Chairman Lee White, "abandoned the consumer."

Bankers are even better represented in government than utilities lawyers. Peter Flanigan, Special Assistant to President Nixon for International Economic Affairs, was vice-president of Dillon Read, the investment house, before his public service, as was C. Douglas Dillon before serving as Under Secretary of State and Secretary of the Treasury in the Eisenhower, Kennedy, and Johnson Administrations. David Kennedy, Nixon's first Secretary of the Treasury, was (and is once more) chairman of Continental Illinois National Bank. Charles E. Walker, who resigned as Under Secretary of the Treasury in 1972, had been chief lobbyist for the American Bankers Association. Chase Manhattan, the Rockefeller family bank, has been particularly generous in lending its officers for service in strategic government posts, particularly in international economic regulation. Some of the more prominent Chase alumni include Paul A. Volcker, Under Secretary of the Treasury for Monetary Affairs; John R. Letty, Assistant Secretary of the Treasury (international affairs); and Charles Fiero, Director of the Office of Foreign Direct Investments in the Commerce Department. Members of the board of directors of Chase Manhattan have been equally public-minded. John McCloy (longtime chairman and counsel) and Eugene Black ran the World Bank from 1947 to 1962 before passing it on to George Woods of the First Boston Corporation. (Other Chase directors include John Connor, Secretary of Commerce in the Johnson Administration; William Hewlett of Hewlett-Packard, member of various Presidential advisory boards and a partner of David Packard, Nixon's first Deputy Secretary of Defense; and Gilbert Fitzhugh, Chairman, President's Blue Ribbon Defense Panel.)

"The value of your stock will rise," Wright Patman pointed out to David Kennedy during the Secretary of the Treasury's testimony in favor of the one-bank holding company. (Kennedy still had major stockholdings in Continental Illinois National Bank and Trust Company, of which he had been chairman and to which he would soon return.) Bankers in government have been protective of their own interests, as have businessmen on loan from utilities and defense contractors. To a greater or lesser degree this has always been true since the United States became an industrial nation. The government–business interlock goes a long way to explain why the world's most powerful government is ineffective in checking the expanding power of business. To a significant degree, Big Business and Big Government represent identical interests.

Although the blurring of private and public interests is an old story, a new dimension must now be added. Even if the U.S. Government were run by a thousand Wright Patmans it would still lack the power to control effectively the activities of global corporations. Any government, however strong its motivation to keep the power of business in check, lacks the tools to manage a national economy in such a way as to balance off competing interests and hence ensure long-term stability as long as global corporations are so powerful. The reason for this, as we shall explain more fully in the next chapter, is that our public legal and political institutions have not kept pace with the extraordinary changes in the private productive system. We still have a tax system, a monetary policy, an employment policy, and a trade policy that are barely adequate for controlling national firms at a time when big business has gone global. There has thus developed a structural lag between the public and private sectors of our social system. The very machinery of government, whoever operates it, is currently inadequate to cope with the globalization of Big Business. As we shall see, the government planners do not have enough knowledge about the activities of global corporations to make the crucial planning decisions for the society. Thus the managers of the corporations have become the principal planners for the society by default.

It has been a persistent theme of this book that knowledge is the critical component of power. In Latin America, as we saw, global companies are able to build their power and, at an accelerating rate, to neutralize government control because their near monopoly of the technologies of production, finance, and marketing permits them to elude government's relatively feeble efforts to regulate them. The same power that enables corporations in Latin America to conceal their ownership, plans, and intracorporate dealings and hence frustrate government control over them operates also in the United States. It is one key structural reason, in our view, why the world's richest society is looking more and more like an underdeveloped country.

Existing disclosure requirements are hopelessly inadequate to permit government to exercise power over global corporations. In March 1972, to give one example, Senator Lee Metcalf attempted to obtain from the Securities and Exchange Commission a list of the largest shareholders of what are probably the two most strategic companies in the American economy, GM and Exxon, and was told that the Commission did not have that information. When the Senator wrote the companies directly, he was told that the information was "privileged and confidential." The U.S. Government now has no way of knowing how and by whom the largest corporations in the country are controlled.

But the business-government interlock has been so strong that controlling the misuse of corporate power has been something less than an obsession. The dominant role of Big Business in both political parties, the financial holdings of certain key members of Congress, the ownership of the mass media, the industry-government shuttle in the regulatory agencies, and, most important, the ideology prevailing throughout the society of salvation through profits and growth all help to explain why the government of the world's mightiest nation musters so little power to protect the interests of its people.

10

The Global Corporation and the Public Interest:
The Managerial Dilemma of the Nation-State

1

The most striking symptom of the LatinAmericanization of the United States is the multiple management crisis that now confronts the world's most developed nation. Observers from Latin America such as Yale Professor Carlos F. Díaz-Alejandro have reminded us that by the late 1960's the United States was experiencing "inflationary recession . . . campus disorders . . . frequent power shortages, creaky and bankrupt railroads, erratic mails"—all familiar landscape in underdeveloped countries, but disquieting to behold in the world's leading exporter of managerial know-how.

As the United States prepared to enter the mid-1970's, "stagflation"—higher prices coupled with a downturn in employment—long a curse of underdeveloped economies, had settled into the U.S. economy. Keynesian theory could not explain it, and the Treasury could not adequately control it. Exxon and its friendly competitors, having acted as the nation's sole planners in energy matters, stopped talking about tigers for our tanks and started extolling the health advantages of cold houses. The multiple transportation crisis which hit the Northeast rail system, the major aircraft producers, and the trucking industry compounded the problems. Cutbacks in fuel meant cutbacks in production, which in turn meant cutbacks in jobs. There was also a scarcity of foodstuffs, animal feed, and other raw products characterized by a Federal Reserve Board economist as "unprecedented—the first time in western history in a peacetime situation . . ."

Each crisis intersects with others. Together they constitute an unprecedented managerial problem for the U.S. Government. In addition, what Otto Eckstein, former member of the Council of Economic Advisers, calls "instability at the center of national power," otherwise known as the Watergate Effect, has brought to the U.S. economy for the first time some of the political uncertainties traditionally associated with underdeveloped countries.

Our thesis in this chapter is that there is a connection between the mounting instability in the United States (and other advanced capitalist states) and the structural changes in the world political economy that we have been tracing. A global transformation has been taking place in the private productive system which has not been reflected in government. The driving force behind the globalization of industry is a managerial revolution that has made it possible to centralize industrial planning on a global scale. As the Senate Finance Committee report on U.S. global firms puts it:

> The coordination of MNC [multinational corporations] operations requires planning and systemization of control of a high order. In the largest and most sophisticated MNC's, planning and subsequent monitoring of plan fulfillment have reached a scope and a level of detail that, ironically, resemble more than superficially the national planning procedures of Communist countries.

But the managerial revolution in private industry has not been duplicated in government. The public sector had its managerial revolution under the banner of Keynesianism almost forty years ago. That revolution established a new body of official truth: artful government regulation of the economy is necessary to keep unemployment down (at whatever level considered acceptable), to prevent inflationary price rises, and to stimulate economic growth. The breakthroughs in the art of planning in this generation have been in private industry rather than public administration. The private techniques for avoiding regulation are more highly developed than the techniques for enforcing it.

The essential strategy of the managerial revolution in industry is, as we have seen, cross-subsidization—i.e., the use of power and resources developed in one "profit center" to start or to expand another. The cross-subsidization strategy is used within the United States by electronics firms to conquer the bread market or by banks to become buyers and leasers of aircraft. When the system becomes global, the parent company can shift profits through transfer pricing, "profit-loan swaps" and other accounting miracles on a worldwide scale, cross-subsidizing its various operations with the profits of others. (Smaller, national firms are unable to do this.) Centralized planning for a centralized system of profit maximization leads inevitably to economic concentration, because only by expanding or at least maintaining its share of the market can an oligopolistic firm hope to compete successfully with the other giants. Where a small number of such firms pursue similar strategies for growth by extending their control more and more into new industries, new products, and new geographic regions, the result is what Robert Averitt has termed a "dual economy." (This characterization was once reserved for underdeveloped countries.) The "center" economy, comprising a few hundred firms, controls over 60 percent of the productive and financial resources of the country and employs the bulk of organized labor. The "periphery" economy is made up of thousands of smaller firms dependent on the giants for their survival, and whose workers do not normally belong to unions. Averitt has verified empirically what Galbraith and others have noted about the unequal division in the U.S. economy between a few unsinkable giants and thousands of vulnerable smaller entrepreneurs.

Large corporations plan centrally and act globally, and nation-states do not. It is this difference that puts government at a disadvantage in trying to keep up with and control the activities of global corporations. As individual business units become more powerful and more mobile, as their balance sheets become less and less accurate reflections of real economic activity, government finds itself handicapped, administratively and politically, in regulating the economy with traditional Keynesian methods. The ease with which global corporations can conceal or distort information vital for the management of the economy is creating the same sort of administrative nightmare for the advanced industrial state that underdeveloped countries have lived with for years.

In this chapter we shall explore how the information gap in such areas as tax, banking, and trade arises and how this gap frustrates important government policies. Not only are the global companies able to escape national regulation through centralized worldwide planning and mobility, but since they are the largest firms, they have the greatest political muscle. Their political power stems from their ability to sprinkle more cash at campaign time, when the regulators are running for office, and to supply from their own ranks a generous number of commissioners and assistant secretaries to the regulatory process regardless of which party is in power. But most important, when the giants, unlike the local mill or drugstore, threaten to pull up stakes or collapse if the government deals with them too harshly, their threats are effective political weapons.

The dramatic spread of global corporations overseas in the mid-1960's has compounded the management problems of the White House, the Treasury, and the Federal Reserve. Keynesian-based fiscal and monetary policies once reasonably effective when the U.S. economy was less concentrated and was only minimally dependent upon commercial and financial transactions taking place beyond its borders are increasingly inadequate to manage the North American division of the global economy. It is sometimes argued that the dependence of the United States on the world economy is exaggerated. After all, exports and imports account for only a little more than 10 percent of the U.S. gross national product. But the mystical use of the gross national product is no more revealing here than in the area of military expenditures, where for many years it was official cant that the Pentagon budget was not "excessive"as long as it did not exceed 10 percent of GNP.

Exports and imports can hover around 10 percent and still have the most profound impact on more than two-thirds of the American population. The reason is perhaps best illustrated by the story economist Milton Friedman tells in which he compares the managers of the public sector to the circus clown who instead of bringing the stool to the piano breaks his back pushing the piano to the stool. The parable makes the point that governments distort their own domestic economies in order to solve their balance-of-payments problems. In recent years the United States has tried, with some success, to solve its balance-of-payments difficulties by pushing agricultural exports. (Hence the famous Soviet wheat deal of 1972.) The effect, of course, was to drive up the price of bread and meat at the supermarket and thus to cut the purchasing power of Americans.

The interdependence of the U.S. economy with other parts of the world economy is not a new phenomenon. The continuing effort among nations to export inflation to one another is a familiar game in international finance. However, the speedup of the globalization process around 1966 has made the American economy dependent upon economic activity outside the United States to an unprecedented degree. U.S. corporations became increasingly dependent upon overseas "export platforms" for producing consumer goods for the American market. The dramatic rise in consumption in other advanced industrial countries was creating global demand in excess of finite supplies of natural resources. An ever greater percentage of transactions of U.S. global corporations was being integrated into a global intracorporate system replacing the traditional concept of an independent market. Overnight transfers of huge cash reserves from one country to another by global banks and corporations and the use of unregulated, international money markets were making it extremely difficult for the United States and other advanced nations to control their domestic money supply. At a turning point sometime between 1965 and 1968 the interrelated process of concentration and globalization was accelerating fast enough to change the behavior of our domestic economy. In this chapter we shall explore the nature of this structural transformation.

The accelerating globalization of the U.S.-based corporations and their increasing dependence on their foreign operations is confirmed by a Department of Commerce study of 298 U.S.-based companies that account for some 66 percent of all U.S. foreign sales. In 1966, foreign sales as a percentage of U.S. domestic sales were 30 percent; four years later the figure was up to 37 percent. Between 1966 and 1970, foreign assets of overseas subsidiaries measured as a percentage of the parents' domestic assets went from 29 percent to 32. But the importance of foreign operations to U.S.-based global corporations can be more clearly shown by comparing the after-tax income of foreign subsidiaries and the after-tax income of the U.S. parents. In 1966, foreign income was 24 percent of domestic income. But in 1970, a recession year in the U.S. and a boom year overseas, foreign income jumped to 44 percent of domestic income. As long as business cycles were out of phase, as in 1970, the great advantage of the global corporation over its strictly national competitors was, in the words of the Senate Finance Committee Report, "that it could insulate itself, by geographical diversification, from the vicissitudes of recession in any one country or region. It is well known that some of the largest American corporations were able to show acceptable results on their *consolidated* income statements for 1970 only because of the buoyancy of profits in their operations abroad." A Business International study of 125 U.S. global firms responsible for 40 percent of U.S. investment in manufacturing operations overseas illustrates how the dependence of these companies on their global activities accelerated in the mid-1960's. Between 1960 and 1966 the fixed overseas investment of these countries rose from 21 to only 25 percent of their fixed investment in the U.S. In the next four years it shot up to 41 percent. These were the years when America's biggest bankers also became confirmed globalists. In 1965, 20 U.S. banks had a total of 211 foreign locations. Seven years later, one could seek out a friend overseas at the Chase or First National City Bank (and a few others) in any of their 627 offices across the planet. More importantly, foreign deposits as a percentage of domestically held dollars for the nine New York banks which control more than 50 percent of all offshore dollars rose precipitously in the mid-60's. In 1965, foreign dollar deposits at their overseas branches were less than 30 percent of their domestic holdings, but by 1972 this figure had more than doubled to 66 percent.

While the dependence of specific U.S. corporations and banks on their overseas activities is much discussed, the overall dependence of the U.S. economy as a whole on these activities is less well understood and little analyzed. What does it mean to the average American wage earner and consumer that the biggest economic units of the country are now so dependent on their foreign operations? What structural changes have taken place in the U.S. economy as a result of the globalization process? What effect do these changes have on the government's ability to manage the economy? Let us look at some of the impacts of the great corporate exodus of the 1960's.

More than 20 percent of all corporate profits is derived from abroad. As we have seen, for many of America's major firms their foreign profits mean the difference between running in the black and running in the red. Moreover, the actual magnitude of foreign-derived earnings should also include profits derived on

exports and imports and take into account the possibility of substantial disguised or unreported profits obtained, as we showed in
Part II, by transfer price manipulations.

The dramatically increased dependence on foreign investment
and the changed character of that investment have had profound
employment effects in the United States. Before 1966, as Leontieff had shown, U.S. exports had a relatively higher labor component than did U.S. imports. A given increase in exports would
result in a healthy increase in U.S. jobs, while additional imports
would have a minimal effect on employment. But increasingly
after the early 1960's such predictions no longer worked. The
reason, we strongly suspect, was the rise of the "export platform."
Between 1966 and 1970, there was a rise of 63 percent in exports
produced in U.S. factories of global corporations (with a lower
labor component) and a spectacular 92-percent rise in exports
from their foreign subsidiaries (more labor-intensive). According
to the Department of Commerce study, the 298 U.S.-based global
firms had a 5.3-percent annual growth rate in employment overseas during these years, compared with a growth rate in domestic
employment of only 2.7 percent. By the end of 1970, more than
25 percent of all their workers were outside the territory of the
United States. (At the same time, the capacity of the U.S. manufacturing sector as a whole to provide jobs for Americans was
declining at a rate six times that of the 1950's.) When more than
a quarter of worker and managerial energies of the leading
industrial firms are outside the country, it is questionable whether
the Federal Government will be able to develop an effective employment policy.

There are other equally dramatic indicators of structural
changes in the U.S. economy associated with the rise of the global
corporation. In 1961, the sales of all U.S. companies manufacturing abroad represented only 7 percent of total U.S. sales. In
1965, the proportion of foreign to domestic sales crept up to
8.5 percent—but in the late 1960's, the picture changed abruptly.
By 1970, foreign sales were almost 13 percent of total sales of all
U.S. manufacturing corporations. In the quest for foreign profits
(which, as we have seen, now exceed 20 percent of corporate
profits in the United States), the U.S. global giants were making
more and more of their new investment overseas. In 1957, U.S.
companies were investing about 9 cents for new plant and equip-

ment overseas for every dollar similarly invested at home. Again in the mid-1960's there was an abrupt upward shift, so that by 1971 they were placing 25 cents abroad for every dollar of new investment for plant and equipment in the domestic economy.

When so many different indicators register changes in the same period, it strongly suggests that something important has happened. In this chapter we shall explore the significance of these changes for the average American citizen who looks to his government to provide a reasonably stable economic environment in which to live and work. More specifically, we shall be asking what it means when the economic environment created by America's largest firms is increasingly beyond the control of the U.S. Government.

2

If knowledge is power, ignorance is impotence. In Part II, we traced many difficulties of the governments of underdeveloped countries to the simple fact that foreign firms knew more about them than they did about their gigantic guests. But since the mid-1960's in particular, the late-model governmental machinery in Washington has also lagged far behind the new economic realities of the private sector. In large part, government is losing the relatively little power it has had to regulate with reasonable effectiveness because it does not know what it is regulating. What once were laws in such areas as tax, banking, securities, and controls are now looked upon in the sophisticated corporate world as little more than shoals to be avoided by careful steering. The U.S. Government is a little like the orchestra conductor who discovers midway through the symphony that the principal players have left.

There is, in short, an institutional lag between the public and private sectors, and it is this lag which is helping to bring about a structural transformation in American capitalism. There is, of course, nothing new about structural transformations in American capitalism. In the past such transformations have elicited reforms. Thus the rise of the trusts brought the regulations of the Progressive era and the Great Depression brought the New Deal. (Whether reforms of sufficient magnitude and imaginativeness can be devised to deal with the present transformation is a matter we shall take up in the final chapter.)

A good illustration of institutional lag is to be found in the latest episode in the continuing contest between banks and regulators of banks. Since Woodrow Wilson's New Freedom and the organization of the Federal Reserve System, the provisions of the Glass-Steagall Act and other banking laws have been designed to protect U.S. borrowers from unsound banks. But it is possible for global banks to avoid many of these provisions by lending to U.S.-based global corporations from the estimated $100-billion Eurodollar pool. The Federal Reserve Board does not know how many Eurodollars there are, who holds them, or when or how they might enter the U.S. economy. It lacks an adequate administrative staff even to raise such questions.

Just as the Fed is handicapped in making monetary policy because the operations of the Eurodollar market are beyond its knowledge and control, so too the SEC is crippled in making a determination about the financial reliability of the operations of U.S. corporations outside the United States. For example, a New Jersey bank recently created a Cayman Islands corporation which purchased a Costa Rican ferryboat company. An idyllic investment for U.S. citizens, to be sure, evoking pictures of paddleboats and mountain lakes—but the SEC has no Costa Rican division.

As we shall explore in some detail, the Internal Revenue Service is also easily confounded by the skilled use of exotica and complexity in intracorporate dealings. A company such as Sears, Roebuck can make worldwide investments by means of its own offshore bank. The interest payment is a cost item rather than a profit item, as a dividend would be. Hence the company can take a deduction for what otherwise would be taxable income. (In earlier days global corporations used offshore insurance-holding companies for the same purpose, but as the Internal Revenue Service picked up the scent, the insurance operations went out of fashion and the banks began to appear.)

The globalization of U.S. corporations not only has made it difficult for government to keep up with their multifarious activities but also has contributed to a lag in perception among public administrators. Regulatory agencies lack not only the budgets and staff to police corporations adequately, but, perhaps more important, lack the time and perspective to understand the real nature of their own problems. There is a general failure to grasp the fact that the changes which are occurring in the world economy are truly systemic. Hence, inadequate analysis and patchwork policies. A symptom of this difficulty is the weekly crisis. One week there is an energy crisis. Two weeks later, someone discovers an employment crisis. When government planning and newspaper headlines are in perfect phase, it means that fashion has become a substitute for analysis.

The institutional lag that cripples governments in their efforts to prevent global corporations from circumventing the spirit of tax, securities, and banking laws is due in no small measure to the technological breakthroughs of the accounting industry. The space-age alchemists have discovered the incantations that turn banks into nonbanks, dividends into interest, and profits into losses. Research and development in tax avoidance conducted in programs of international business at institutions of higher learning such as New York University and Columbia University is at least five years ahead of government research on loophole closing. The desultory pursuit of tax avoidance is not due to an absence of personal zeal among Washington bureaucrats but to a lack of funds to take on the alchemists and a lack of knowledge as to what their clients are doing.

Skilled obfuscation is now an essential accounting tool. The challenge is to create a tidy world for investors, regulatory agencies, and tax collectors to scrutinize, which may have little or no resemblance to what an old-fashioned bookkeeper might have called the real world. Indeed, it is often desirable to create a different world for each. Corporations give their stockholders one picture of how well they are prospering and the Internal Revenue Service another. (In 1966, for example, the oil industry showed profits of $3 billion on its own books, but reported $1.5 billion to the IRS.) As Congressman Charles Vanik observes, ". . . for their stockholders they wear their wedding clothes; for the tax man, they wear rags."

When in the 1960's investors decided that growth potential rather than dividends was what made a stock worth buying, the alchemists were able to supply instant earnings by switching depreciation schedules, inventory calculations, and the timing and characterization of foreign remittances. Thus the Senate Finance Committee notes: "In many cases, profits, interest, and cash remittances of other types from affiliates to parents were stepped up well past 'normal' rates in order to dress up the parents' annual reports at year-end in 1970."

"I wish to hell the stock market didn't want to see the earnings go up all the time," the frustrated chairman of a hotel chain is quoted as saying in Adam Smith's *Supermoney*. "Every year is not always bigger than last year, and we have to bend things around a lot to get them to come out right." But retailing reality can be dangerous. "Then the stock would go down, and we'd be at a disadvantage vis-à-vis our competitors in hiring executives, making new hotel deals, and so on." Leonard Spacek, former chairman of Arthur Andersen & Company, thinks that the magic words "generally accepted accounting principles" on corporate financial statements are a "fiction." (Accounting principles are "generally accepted" by corporate clients when they produce the right results.) "My profession appears to regard a set of financial statements as a roulette wheel to the public investor," Spacek observes sadly. David Norr of the American Institute of Certified Public Accountants agrees. "Accounting today permits a shaping of results to attain a desired end. Accounting as a mirror of activity is dead."

Accountants are hired miracle workers. If there were not a market for financial alchemy in the corporate world, accountants would still be trying to mirror economic history instead of rewriting it. The head of a major drug company has a maxim that captures the new attitudes of the executive suite: "One good accountant is worth a thousand salesmen." This is a neat way of turning the morality of Benjamin Franklin on its head. Because of the upside-down morality that pervades the battle for profits (a Wall Street analyst and a Senate investigator independently came up with the phrase in our interviews), honesty is an expensive policy. Warren Avis, the rent-a-car entrepreneur, who finally stopped trying harder, states flatly that in today's business world "it is unprofitable to be honest."

The rise of the accountant to his present eminence also symbolizes the transition from the Steel Age to the Paper Age. The contemporary corporation is obsessed more with paper representations than with real things. The appearance of growth and the appearance of profits in handsomely presented annual reports has not infrequently been achieved at considerable waste of intrinsically valuable commodities. Indeed, in the rush to make paper profits, corporations, as we shall examine in Chapter 12, have extravagantly sacrificed such scarce resources as timber and petroleum.

The realization that the world's *long-term* supply of critical materials for the support of human life and modern industry is limited may be the single most revolutionary idea in economics since Adam Smith. Neither Marx nor Keynes doubted the infinite availability of the earth's resources to feed economic growth. Fortunately, there are indications that the worship of stock certificates is declining in the wake of the Energy Crisis and related commodity shortages. For example, a seat on the Chicago Mercantile Exchange which in the early 1960's sold for $3,000, in contrast to $500,000 for a seat on the New York Stock Exchange, now sells for $115,000. At present writing, you can pick up a seat on Wall Street for $92,000.

Occasionally corporations have outsmarted themselves with their elaborate internal economics. In their study of the money management of global firms, Professors Robbins and Stobaugh cite the case of an oil company that forgot why it had arranged its transfer pricing in a particularly bizarre way and ended up believing in its own fictitious losses. "Such," they marvel, "is the power of self-delusion." Some business consultants with whom we have talked confirm this experience. (It is also evident that costing procedures in the hermetic intracorporate world encourage the consumption of resources with abandon. In the years when oil companies paid what they wanted for world resources, Arab sheiks did not yet go to Harvard Law School, and oil was cheap, global corporations thought nothing of spending thousands of gallons of gasoline to fly components around the world to take advantage of some tax or tariff saving.) But it is relatively rare that the company confuses its own long-term interests because its accountant has done his job too well. Usually, the victims of institutionalized obfuscation are the government and the public.

Corporate executives are keenly aware that these problems exist, but, predictably, they identify them with industries other than their own. (The psychoanalytical research of Michael Maccoby gives a good illustration of corporate loyalty at work at the subconscious level. When he asked engineers if there were not some piece of morally reprehensible technology which they might refuse to work on, chemists drew the line at electric chairs and electronics engineers recoiled at the thought of gas chambers.) Whether it is true, as executives maintain, that most businesses report fairly, it still leaves these questions: Which ones don't? What is the extent of their distorted reporting? What import does the obfuscation have on the economy? What does it mean that the managers of the public sector do not know the magnitude of the distortion in our national statistics that are supposed to instruct them in what to do for our economic health?

For those charged with managing the U.S. economy, both the domestic concentration of power and the globalization of the United States' largest corporations have created an information gap of two different sorts. One concerns missing information. We noted in the last chapter that government regulatory agencies are unable to acquire the names of the largest stockholders of the largest corporations, banks, and utilities—i.e., in behalf of which interests the biggest blocks of shares in the country are being voted. The power of the energy companies has allowed them to regard vital information about oil reserves as "proprietary," to be disclosed to government only on their own terms and at their own pace. (The State of California has sued Exxon to get such information.) It has been impossible to assess the impact of the Eurodollar market and the use of "export platforms" on the U.S. economy with the precision necessary to make monetary and fiscal policy because the crucial data are in the hands of the companies and not the government.

More important than missing information is distorted information. U.S. trade statistics, for example, are an aggregate of *reported* values of export and import transactions of U.S. corporations. In 1970, U.S.-based global companies accounted for some 70 percent of total U.S. exports and 42 percent of all imports. The Senate Finance Committee concludes that a minimum of 27 percent of all exports consisted of intracompany transactions. Further, from the committee study it will be clear that an additional 43 percent of all exports have also escaped the market because of the possibility that the buyer and seller are controlled by the same people, but available public information is inadequate to confirm the point. Our estimate, derived from the 1972 Business International study, convinces us that at least 50 percent of all U.S. exports are bypassing the market. The Business International study of 125 U.S.-based global corporations which account for more than 16 percent of total U.S. manufacturing sales, 26 percent of all U.S. nonagricultural exports, and over 70 percent of all recent foreign direct investment outflows shows that by 1970, 57 percent of their total exports were made to their own overseas affiliates. (On the basis of this study, we believe 50 percent is a conservative estimate, because it leaves out agricultural exports, and these are largely intracompany transactions.) As a recent Rand Corporation study concluded, because of the widespread use of transfer pricing and the importance of intracorporate transactions in the U.S. economy, Department of Commerce balance-of-payments statistics on foreign trade and foreign-earned income are "totally unreliable."

In 1968 a study group of the Conference Board, a group sponsored by major corporations, foresaw that "political and financial competition for the possession and control of [information] would increase dramatically as a consequence of the technological explosion in data gathering. Information as distinct from property or energy," its report concluded, "will be an indicator of social wealth and power." So too, politics "will increasingly become the management of information." The significant decline in cost in processing a unit of information, *New York Times* financial analyst Leonard Silk points out, will mean an "increase in both numbers and size of national and multinational corporations." Thus access to information is becoming ever more crucial to the management of both the large corporation and the modern industrial state. How the information war between business and government turns out will determine their relative power positions. As we shall now see, the managerial crisis of the U.S. Government is rooted in a crisis of knowledge and understanding.

3

The Keynesian model of the modern capitalist economy is based on a set of assumptions about the vitality of the competitive market as a social institution. The theory on which governmental policy-making is based assumes that the market fulfills certain crucial public functions that in other systems such as socialism or state capitalism are fulfilled by governmental institutions. These functions include allocation and distribution of resources, the

268   GLOBAL REACH

setting of social priorities, and the development of needed goods and services. In this section we shall look at some of these classic functions of the market and consider how the intersecting and cumulative effect of mounting concentration and globalization of the U.S. economy has negated the market as a social institution in significant ways.

When buyers and sellers in arm's-length market transactions set prices, these prices are reliable signals for both consumers and government administrators. The buyer can assume he is getting fair value because no one else seems to be able to make the same product any cheaper. Consumers as a class can assume that the producer will compensate society for the social contribution to his product—that is, he is expected to pay the social costs of production, in most cases by contributing his fair share of taxes. Thus some fraction of the price a buyer pays for, say, chemicals goes, according to theory, to compensate society for the atmospheric filth engendered by the production of the chemicals, either in the form of private investment in antipollution devices or in the form of taxes to support a government antipollution program. Keynesian-based theory and policy-making have yet to confront one of their most important implicit assumptions: that buyers and sellers will be able to arrange their private affairs in such a way as to pay via government such public costs of production.

It also assumes that government administrators can rely on prices as signals for allocating resources in the society. If petroleum is cheap and the oil companies are vigorously seeking to sell more and more, there must be an ample supply. Despite certain "imperfections" of the market, such as oligopoly concentration, short-run prices are sufficiently responsive to the laws of supply and demand so that they can be influenced by government economic policies. Thus where demand is constant relative to an increase in supply, the result should be falling prices, and conversely, where supply is constant relative to a decrease in demand, again the same result follows. The Keynesian manager had certain tools for increasing supply and decreasing demand in the economy, and these constituted his principal weapons against inflation. His tool kit also included devices for stimulating the economy to produce growth and full employment during periods of recession or depression.

Until the 1960's and the onset of the "stagflation" phenomenon, the Keynesian tools worked rather well for a substantial proportion of the American population. Despite minor recessions, the U.S. economy was stable. Until the mid-1960's, real income climbed for all but those at the bottom of the society. The economy grew. The stock market boomed.

But then something happened. By the mid-1960's, the economy was responding less and less to Keynesian policies in the predicted way. When the Federal Government offered tax credits and other incentives to increase investment and hence employment and the supply of goods, output did not increase at the anticipated rate. Similarly, when the Federal Reserve Board raised interest rates or tried to curtail the money supply, which, theoretically, would cut demand and reduce the inflation rate, the anticipated did not happen. The reason was that market "imperfections," instead of being occasional and correctable, as the theory assumed, were becoming stubborn and systemic. The market no longer fulfilled the modified role as social regulator it still played in the Keynesian system, because its effects had been negated by two crucial economic developments, each having cumulative effects and each reinforcing the other. We refer, of course, to the concentration and globalization of the key industries and financial institutions of the U.S. economy.

Concentration is an age-old problem of capitalism. Since the days of Berle and Means it has been clear that the higher the degree of concentration the greater the market failure. Oligopolists can frustrate government attempts to create more jobs by stimulating demand, because instead of producing more as the government hopes, they can keep their output constant and take advantage of the increase in demand to raise their prices. On the other hand, when the managers of the economy wish to reduce inflationary pressures through tight money policies, oligopolists can ignore these policies too by passing on to the consumer the increased costs of raising capital. There is mounting evidence that this is exactly how the oligopolies that dominate industry and banking are behaving. In 1970, the top four firms in motor vehicles accounted for 91 percent of all output, the top four in tires 72 percent, in cigarettes 84 percent, in detergents 70 percent, and on and on. The consumer pays the modern oligopoly firms what economists call an "administered price" because he has no place else to go for the products that have come to be regarded as necessities of modern civilization. As we saw in the last chapter, the same degree of concentration exists in the banking industry. The foreign activities of U.S. banks, which are becoming much more important (foreign deposits of the biggest banks are now some two-thirds of their domestic deposits), are increasingly concentrated. Almost all foreign deposits, according to Andrew Brimmer of the Federal Reserve Board, are in the hands of 20 multinational banks. Indeed, just 4 banks—Chase, First National City, Manufacturers Hanover, and Chemical, all members of the Rockefeller-Morgan group—have about 38 percent of all foreign deposits.

The concentrated power of a few hundred industrial and banking giants has undercut the effectiveness of the principal tools of Keynesian monetary and fiscal policy. The British economist Thomas Balogh puts it this way:

> The so-called Keynesian "synthesis" which for a time swept the academic board, was soon accomplished by Keynes's liberal disciples. With but marginal modifications that neo-classical theory of social harmony and income distribution was reconnected to the newly erected macro-economic edifice, in which the automatism of the market economy, with its assurance of full employment and optimal resource allocation, was simply replaced by the twin *deus ex machina* of the Treasury and the Central Bank.
>
> At the precise time when markets were being increasingly dominated by national and international oligopoly power, theoretical orthodoxy ensured that the very problem to which this would give rise would be ignored or dismissed.

Take monetary policy. The Keynesian model assumed that demand could be effectively controlled through adjustment of the interest rate. If the rate is raised corporations will reduce their borrowings, the economy will cool, and the inflation rate will fall. But the pattern of oligopolistic competition for ever-greater shares of the market and its accompanying grow-or-die ideology now mean that corporations will continue to borrow regardless of the cost of credit simply because of their power to "pass on" their cost increases to consumers who have no alternative. That this willingness to increase borrowing with little concern for the interest rate is a relatively new phenomenon can be seen by a comparison of the ratio of short-term indebtedness to cash in the 1950's with the situation in the current period. In the early 1950's, corporations on the average had $8 of cash for every $10 in short-term debt. In the 1969–1973 period, corporations had so extended their debt that they held only $2 in cash for every $10 of current liabilities. Thus even in a period of rapidly rising interest rates, corporations' current borrowings were permanently accelerating much faster than their increase in current cash holdings. Interest-rate policy appeared to have substantially less effect on the rate of credit expansion than in the past because corporations continue heavy borrowing even when the Fed is pursuing a deflationary credit policy. Similarly, when the managers of the economy wish to stimulate expansion of the GNP, they must expand credit at an ever-faster rate, and this course has inflationary effects.

The very process of credit restriction feeds concentration, not only for industrial corporations, as we have seen, but for the banks themselves. When money is tight and there is intense competition for funds to lend, big banks, as one might expect, obtain such funds when small banks cannot. (The big banks, of course, have a ready set of prime borrowers—principally the large global corporations.) Thus in 1973, according to the Federal Reserve, 9 New York City banks, 6 of which belong to the Rockefeller-Morgan group, accounted for more than 26 percent of all commercial and industrial lending by banks in the United States. (There are 220 banks, according to the Fed, which do virtually all the large corporate lending in the country.) About half of all the money lent by these New York superbanks goes to global corporations—with the result, as George Budzeika of the New York Federal Reserve Bank has noted, that about 90 percent of the entire indebtedness in the U.S. petroleum and natural-gas industry, two-thirds in the machinery and metal products industry, and three-fourths in the chemical and rubber industries is held by these same 9 New York banks. "On the whole," Budzeika concludes, "New York City bank behavior in the past two decades has shown that it is very difficult to control large banks whenever demand for credit is heavy. The growth and profits of these banks—their very viability—depend upon their ability to satisfy the credit demands of their customers. These banks, therefore, are strongly motivated to find loopholes in control measures and to press credit expansion to a greater extent than may be deemed advisable by monetary authorities."

It is the big banks, the very ones whose lending policies are most important to control in the interests of managing the economy, that of course have the resources to escape control. For medium and small banks, Budzeika points out, "lack of information and skills prevents them from adjusting quickly to changing levels of monetary restriction." The ability of large banks to insulate themselves through international dealings and other techniques from the intended effects of tight credit policies means, Budzeika contends, that "the only way to restrain [them] efficiently is to reduce the overall liquidity of the banking system." But that is a drastic remedy with serious side effects. Because large banks can evade mild credit restrictions, serious efforts to cool the economy by means of monetary policy must be so Draconian as to create even higher unemployment and idle factories. But too high a rate of unemployment is politically unacceptable. Therefore only moderate monetary policies are pursued, and since these affect only smaller firms, they further contribute to the very concentration at the heart of the problem—a classic "vicious circle" of the sort that has plagued the governments of poor countries for years. Indeed, in the era of concentration, the management of the U.S. economy has come to resemble the management of a difficult medical case. A drug to alleviate one set of symptoms exacerbates another. Thus the dilemma for the Keynesian managers: give a placebo that does nothing but encourage further increases in concentration or administer a strong drug and risk having the patient go into shock.

Fiscal policy is the other Keynesian managerial remedy. It is administered in two forms, government expenditures and taxes. The Federal Government is the biggest spender in the country. In theory, governmental profligacy is supposed to have a healthy stimulating effect on the economy by increasing aggregate demand. Indeed, "pump priming" via Federal spending has been considered essential to the rapid expansion of the economy. But the spending has been of a special sort, and it has had special effects.

In the last generation, almost 80 percent of total Federal revenues has gone to purchase "national security": the military and space budgets, atomic energy, veterans' payments, interest on old war debts, etc. Since the sellers of "national security" turn out to be the leading electronics, energy, transportation, and metals industries—all oligopolies—the effect of government spending is to accelerate the process of concentration that has made the United States a dual economy. The benefits of government spending go overwhelmingly to the "center" industries, and the result is a playing out of what Stephen Hymer calls the "law of uneven development." Pentagon checks do not go to Appalachia or other depressed areas where wages are low and jobs are scarce. As a general rule, they go, as Professor Barry Bluestone has testified before the Joint Economic Committee, to the industries with the highest profits, the highest wages, and the least unemployment. Thus the result is "excess demand" in the very sectors of the economy that can most easily pass on increased costs to the consumer (ultimately the taxpayer) and inadequate demand in the rest of the economy: another vicious circle in which the uneven impacts of economic policy produce unintended effects and further intensify the process of dualism in the U.S. economy.

The principal tool of Keynesian fiscal policy is the tax law. It is implicitly assumed that managers of the economy are relatively free to raise or lower taxes at will and that if the rates are progressive, changes in the tax law will have a reasonably equal impact on people all across the society, rich and poor alike. In the Keynesian state, concerned politicians are expected to make modest reallocations of income by using the taxes of the rich for welfare payments to the poor. They are not, however, expected to use the tax laws to shift the burden of running the government from the rich to the middle class. If that happens, something is wrong.

There is abundant evidence that this is precisely what has happened. Corporate income as a percentage of total income earned in the United States has remained relatively constant in the last five years. But the corporations in these same years have been paying a significantly reduced share of total taxes. In the year 1958, the annual corporate tax contribution (not including social security contributions) was 25.2 percent of Federal revenues. By 1973 it had declined to less than 15 percent. In these years Federal expenditures have not gone down. Instead, the slack in corporate tax revenues has been picked up by individual tax-payers. Income is being reallocated by the tax system in such a way as to subsidize corporations at the expense of other taxpayers.

Congressman Charles Vanik has documented the extent of corporate welfarism under our tax laws. His conclusion is that the largest and most powerful corporations pay less than their weaker competitors. In 1969 the top 100 giants paid at the rate of 26.9 percent, but all corporations below the top 100 paid at the average rate of 44 percent. "Out of 17 oil companies studied," Vanik reported to the Joint Economic Committee in 1972, "10 paid less than 10% in 1969 and 7 paid less than 10% in 1970. The timber industry giants pay effective rates of between 10–20 percent on large pretax incomes." Although other large industries also have enviable tax rates (U.S. Steel paid an effective rate of 2.1 percent on a quarter billion dollars in income in 1969), the most impressive tax subsidies have been reserved for the oil and timber industries.

These two cases illustrate the use of fiscal policy to achieve social goals other than collecting revenue, and they also illustrate how such policy has failed. The well-publicized tax subsidies to the petroleum industry include the percentage depletion allowance, fast write-offs for "intangible" drilling and development costs, and the Foreign Tax Credit. The Treasury reported to the Congress in 1969 that percentage depletion is a "relatively inefficient method of encouraging exploration," since over 40 percent of it is paid for foreign production. Thus the admirable social goal of encouraging self-sufficiency in petroleum is defeated because the company policy of global profit maximization dictates otherwise.

When the timber industry's capital-gains tax subsidy was passed in 1943, President Roosevelt vetoed it, calling it a tax bill "for the greedy, not the needy." The bill was designed, of course, to encourage investment in reforestation, but Vanik points out that there are over 52 million acres of private forest land in need of reforestation. The timber companies, it appears, have not been spending their considerable tax savings (in 1965 more than $140 million from the special capital-gains subsidy alone) on planting more trees.

The oil shortage and the paper scarcity symbolize the dimensions of the managerial crisis. The last generation of the U.S.

economy has been marked by a galloping dependence upon fossil fuels and paper packaging. Industry planning has been devoted to removing any inhibitions we may have against the extravagant depletion of our natural resources. In 1960, for example, when the annual growth rate in sales of the petroleum industry fell to a mere 2.5 percent, the industry launched what Charles J. Guzzo, senior vice-president of Gulf, called the "greatest sales attack of all time" to increase demand. Through the industry lobby, the American Petroleum Institute, the oil companies pushed their Travel Development Program under the slogan "Take to the Road for Fun." (Simultaneously, power mowers and weekend powerboats suddenly became middle-class necessities.) "If we can get people to drive only two more miles a day," R. W. Weston of the Ethyl Corporation brightened, "the industry will sell three billion more gallons of gasoline a year. . . ." Makers of motor oil began "beating the drums for frequent oil changes" and, as *Business Week* reported, began pressing for three-day holidays and the suppression of "scary" accident statistics.

Thirteen years later, gasoline is in short supply and the critical shortage reverberates through the whole economy. What happened? The market failed to do its job of resource allocation because of an inherent failure. Under the tyranny of the annual balance sheet (and even the quarterly statement), corporations have little incentive to plan for future resource scarcity, especially since they could anticipate profiting from such scarcity. Since the oil companies have been responsible to no one but their shareholders, they have had little reason to do otherwise. Here is one case where the concentration of private economic power through the control of corporation and political influence has negated the social function of the market as resource allocator.

If we return to the matter of taxes, we shall see another. Were the invisible hand attached to a rational brain, it would arrange our affairs differently. We would not see corporate taxes going down during the same period in which corporate pollution of the environment is going up. Yet, as we saw, the corporate share of the tax burden is being reduced as the social impacts of corporations are sharply increased. Taxes are supposed to pay the social costs of production according to conventional wisdom, but the negation of the market through concentration, transfer pricing, and other accounting miracles means that governments are in-

creasingly powerless to recover the social costs of production
(pollution being one example; dislocation of workers, another)
through taxes. We do not know what pollution is costing us as a
society. The position of the corporations, as we shall show, is that
the Treasury, a euphemism for taxpayers in general, should bear
the principal costs of pollution control through direct subsidies
to corporations. But that, of course, is a way of saying that private
profits should be made at the expense of continuing public deficits
and sacrifices by small taxpayers.

It is evident that fiscal policy, like monetary policy, is being
frustrated by the negation of the market. The tax incentives to
the timber and oil industries did not produce the desired social
results because the companies were under no compulsion to use
their tax savings for exploration or reforestation and their planning for short-term global profits indicated better uses for money.
The failures of tax policy illustrate a political inhibition on the
use of Keynesian policies that Keynes foresaw at other points in
his theory but not here. In his *General Theory*, Keynes recognized that once labor is sufficiently organized, governments no
longer can assume flexibility in wages. They can always permit
wages to rise, of course, but encouraging wages to fall in the face
of union opposition is usually not a politically viable alternative.
But the same holds true for corporate taxes. Large corporations
have too much political power to permit mere politicians to take
away tax privileges, no matter how badly the plums interspersed
through the Internal Revenue Code may have failed in their
social-engineering functions. The depletion allowance remained
not because of its irresistible logic but because of the hitherto
irresistible power of the major oil companies.

Tax privilege and concentration feed on each other. The provisions of the Internal Revenue Code on corporate reorganization have encouraged the concentration of business by making
mergers attractive from the tax standpoint. Similarly, the hand-
somest gifts in the government's catalogue, the Internal Revenue
Code, are reserved for the largest corporations, who alone have
the resources to hire people with the patience to read it. As a
1972 Library of Congress study reveals, 57 percent of the benefits of the Investment Tax Credit in 1965 went to the 260 largest
corporations. Fifty-five percent of the benefits under the Accelerated Depreciation Range, according to Senator Alan Bible, goes

to the 103 largest corporations. As we shall now see, the biggest corporations are also the ones best able to take advantage of the considerable inducements under the tax law to invest abroad.

4

Private planners had outdistanced public planners long before American business had its global growth spurt of the late 1960's. But the globalization process has further undermined the government's efforts to use fiscal and monetary policy to manage the economy. The central planners in the world headquarters of global corporations, having transcended the territory of the United States, are now able to frustrate standard Keynesian remedies in the ordinary course of their business.

The widespread use of transfer pricing so central to the cross-subsidization strategies of the global corporation is designed, as we have seen, to create what amounts to a private economy. Prices are set according to the requirements of global profit maximization; they are thus insulated to varying degrees from real market pressures. "Prices in an economic sense," one former Treasury official told us, "do not exist. The price charged is strictly a matter of relative power." Just as concentration effectively negates the operation of the domestic market in important respects, so too transfer pricing distorts the interaction of the international market and the domestic market. When large percentages of total exports are underpriced and imports are overpriced because the central planners in headquarters wish to shift income out of the United States, the prices, of course, represent misleading signals. Another possibility is to transfer income into the United States by over-pricing exports and underpricing imports. These transactions can be disguised through the use of offshore subsidiaries located in "tax havens." Because of such price manipulations the government planner does not know to what extent imports and exports represent the true value of the goods involved or to what extent the export and import accounts are being used to facilitate intracorporate financial flows.

It is almost impossible for government to control financial flows in the implementation of balance-of-payments and other policies when it does not know the extent of such disguised transactions. Moreover, when prices are set for the purpose of shifting money rather than of reflecting the market value of goods, there

can be a net drain for the society as a whole even as the corporation is maximizing its own global profits. (We saw how this
operated in underdeveloped countries.) When U.S. firms undervalue exports, the American economy must give up more resources than it gets back in foreign exchange; this means aggrava-
tion of the balance-of-payments problem. From our interviews
with government officials and corporate executives, from the
standard advice found in textbooks on corporate finance, and
from the studies noted earlier, it is clear that the practice of
charging transfer prices which deviate from market value is
becoming increasingly widespread.

Occasionally the government will indict a company for the
fraudulent use of transfer pricing. Recently Litton Industries was
indicted for undervaluing imports from its Mexican assembly
plants to avoid some $216,000 in customs duties. (Another U.S.
company with similar "satellite" operations in Mexico made a
$3-million settlement to escape prosecution for falsified invoices.)
According to a memorandum of the Senate Investigations Subcommittee, grain companies manipulate transfer prices to obtain
big subsidies. (". . . the export subsidy program cost American
taxpayers $333 million in agricultural subsidies in connection
with the Russian grain deal.") The memo, which was made public
by Jack Anderson, details how it worked:

> . . . we have information that one company (Cargill) sold wheat
> to its wholly-owned South American affiliate (Tradex-Panama).
> The company collected the subsidy when it showed proof of
> shipment to its affiliate.
>
> The affiliate then sold the wheat to another affiliate in Geneva
> which thereupon made a final sale for $2.20 (a bushel) or 10
> cents above the American price. . . . As far as we can tell, the
> wheat never left the ship on which it was originally loaded, and
> all transfers were mere paper transfers.
>
> This practice was repeated numerous times . . .

The moment at which corporate planning and government
planning most directly collide is tax time. True, global corporations have, with the help of accounting virtuosos, developed the
technology of finance into a high art which serves many nontax
corporate purposes. It is sometimes useful to export components
to a subsidiary in a free-trade area at a price low enough so that

the subsidiary can contribute over 50 percent of the value and thus qualify for tariff relief. Sometimes transfer pricing is used to establish loss leaders in new markets. If World Inc. cross-subsidizes its foreign subsidiary World Inc.–Belgium by exporting at an artificially low price, the subsidiary can undersell local competition. The competitors uncharitably term such activities "dumping," and where possible they try to get their own governments to do something about it.

In their study of the financial technology of global corporations Robbins and Stobaugh list many of the devices by which a global corporation can shift funds from one part of its operation to another: interest on intracorporate loans, fees for know-how, dividends, royalties. The freedom to accelerate or to defer such payments can make an enormous difference to the worldwide profit picture. The profitability of the enterprise would have been impaired, Robbins and Stobaugh conclude on the basis of computer simulation studies of intracorporate flows of a hypothetical global corporation, "if it had been deprived of any of the tools in its financial kit." It is easier to repatriate capital and reduce the firm's U.S. taxes if it is called debt instead of equity. (This particular piece of alchemy explains why foreign subsidiaries make greater use of debt financing.) The judicious allocation of expenses among subsidiaries also serves a variety of corporate purposes.

These decisions as well as the basic policies on transfer pricing are made at corporate headquarters. As the treasurer of a global firm interviewed by Robbins and Stobaugh puts it, "Even where we have sophisticated local management, both long-term and short-term financing is determined in San Francisco and not just left to the discretion of local management. . . . I don't say that our companies don't have any leeway. They are part of our team and we like to use their brains just like they were sitting right here. . . . But someone along the line has to say 'this is what we do,' and that's San Francisco."

But a principal use of central planning in the global enterprise is tax minimization. Here the use of accountants to stage-manage multiple layers of reality is particularly effective in keeping the tax collector confused. Some firms, according to one tax consultant to global corporations we talked with, employ five different sets of books in their foreign subsidiaries. Set One is to keep track of costs of production; Set Two is for the local tax collector; Set Three is for the Internal Revenue Service; Set Four is for world-wide accounting purposes; Set Five for currency transactions. Because of their ability to take advantage of certain provisions of the Internal Revenue Code, especially those which permit deferral of tax on foreign earnings and a credit for foreign taxes, a U.S.-based global company is likely to keep a greater share of a dollar earned abroad than a dollar earned in the United States. Oil companies, it will be recalled, significantly lowered their U.S. taxes by calling royalty payments to Arab governments for petroleum concessions "taxes." (By contrast, income taxes paid to states are allowed as mere deductions against income, not credits against taxes.) Between 1954 and 1970, the reduction of U.S. tax revenues through the process of the foreign tax credit jumped 660 percent. Although some form of tax credit to alleviate the burden of double taxation seems fair, the tax credit in its present form results in an annual loss of revenues of over $4 billion. One reason is that large corporations are free under present law to mix income from high-tax countries and low-tax countries in such a way as to achieve minimum overall tax liability. Although there is now a ceiling to the foreign tax credit to prevent such "pooling" arrangements, the global corporation can avoid the effects of the ceiling through transfer pricing. (The ceiling rises with the level of foreign-source income. Thus the corporation can always increase or reduce by selling to a foreign subsidiary at a bargain or buying from it at a premium.)

But the problem posed by the tax credit transcends the technical. In 1970, before-tax corporate profits on U.S. direct investment abroad were more than 20 percent of the total profits of American corporations. As former Treasury expert Stanford G. Ross points out, the tax-credit and other provisions of U.S. law are biased in favor of foreign investment. But as investment abroad goes up, revenues from corporations for the U.S. Treasury go down. Professor Peggy Musgrave estimates that if foreign taxes were treated no more favorably than state taxes, and un-distributed earnings abroad (which often escape tax permanently) were taxed no differently from undistributed earnings in the United States, the tax burden for all other taxpayers would be reduced by $3.4 billion.

The Internal Revenue Code is strongly biased in favor of for-

eign investment. This violation of the principle of neutrality—
i.e., treating all taxpayers alike insofar as is possible—is justified,
as in the timber and oil subsidies, to accomplish a nontax objective, in this case to stimulate foreign investment. But like the
other cases, the use of fiscal policy for nonfiscal purposes has
backfired. Not only does the Treasury lose billions in revenue, but
the tax incentives to invest abroad contribute to the process of
concentration, which, as we have seen, complicates the managerial tasks of the Federal Government in many other areas. In
1966, 80 percent of taxable income from foreign sources was
earned by 430 corporations all with assets of a quarter-billion
dollars or more. Only large global corporations able to purchase
skills in the technology of finance which have the mobility to
shift and allocate income internationally can work their way
through the labyrinthine provisions of the Internal Revenue Code
to maximum advantage. Here again the large global corporation
achieves economies of scale by adapting financial-management
skills developed in one part of the world for use in another,
thereby eventually absorbing its smaller nationally based competitors who lack such economies. This cumulative process of
ever-greater concentration is inherent in the very nature of oligopoly competition. Thus globalization and concentration go
hand in hand.

Tax havens are theoretically available for everybody. According to the *Economist Intelligence Unit,* they meet a "basic need."
They exist "to enable individuals to increase or dispose of wealth
which they have won as they see fit and not at the whim of their
rulers." But global corporations, having little patience for the
whim of all rulers, are their best customers. A tax haven such
as Grand Cayman Island advertises its "complete freedom from
all forms of taxation." Once described as "the island which time
forgot," this Caribbean paradise now boasts 95 banks and more
telex cables per capita than any other spot on earth. The New
Hebrides, a relative newcomer to the tax-haven industry, advertises its "beauty, colourful history, balmy tropical breezes . . . a
unique Anglo-French government, eight banks, seven accounting firms and (of course) freedom from taxation . . ." The global
corporation has a wide choice of locations for its offshore headquarters—the Bahamas, Bermuda, the Cayman Islands, Panama,
among others. (*Grundy's Tax Havens,* a bible for tax avoiders,

evaluates the various candidates in terms of communications, political stability, freedom of currency movements, etc.)

A tax haven is in reality an accounting drama. The company books reflect a commendably high level of activity being transferred to tropical islands eager for "development." But a visit to the stage set is apt to be disappointing. In 1971 the Fidelity Bank of Philadelphia, one of the country's largest, made loans of $120 million from its Nassau branch, but the branch consisted of one desk, a closet, a file cabinet, and a telephone.

No one knows the sums diverted each year to tax havens by U.S.-based global operations. The Syntex Corporation, for example, which makes about 50 percent of all the birth-control pills sold in the United States, has a $7.5-million plant in the Bahamas which generates tax-free income. As the *Economist Intelligence Unit* notes, the corporation drastically reduces its U.S. income by "writing off a large slice of its U.S. profits against research; the fruits of this research can then be used internationally, for instance, in a free port—to earn profits free of U.S. tax." Thus tax havens are important vehicles for both domestic and global cross-subsidization.

The Treasury has long been aware of the popularity of tax havens and such other accountants' paradises as "safe harbors" and "escape hatches," and since 1921 it has had legislative tools to control their use for tax avoidance. In the 1960's the Internal Revenue Service developed new legislation and a new set of regulations for Section 482 of the Revenue Code which gives the Treasury power to combat tax-avoiding transfer pricing by stepping in and recalculating prices so as to "clearly reflect income." Section 861b gives the Treasury similar powers to reallocate expenses between the U.S. parent and the foreign subsidiary which, as we have seen, is often located in a tax haven. But there are enormous problems in administering these provisions. Stanford G. Ross, who played a key role in foreign tax reform in the Kennedy Administration, believes the reform legislation of the 1960's was not effective because of the complexity of international transfer pricing and financing operations. The key problem has been the government's lack of information on costs and profit margins in a global system, and the lack of enough knowledgeable enforcement officials in the Treasury. (As we saw in underdeveloped countries, the combined budgets of the legal and accounting departments of the major firms are many times the administrative budget of the policing agencies.) Another rather recent alumnus of the Internal Revenue Service who helped develop the new regulations for Section 482 told us that the Service did not substantially add to its enforcement staff once the complex regulations were on the books.

The 1962 reform legislation was supposed to subject "tainted" tax-haven profits to U.S. tax, but as tax analyst Philip Stern has noted, "something must be amiss, for now—a little more than a decade after the enactment of the 1962 law—tax havens, rather than being on the wane, are on the increase. Corporate tax lawyers receive a steady stream of enticing literature glorifying the tax climate of some new island or territory . . . Clearly, American corporations must be succeeding in 'untainting' a significant amount of tax haven profits." Stern cites some of the enormously complex special concessions such as the DISC (Domestic International Sales Corporation). For the avowed purpose of stimulating exports, this 1971 legislation creates a mini–tax haven in the United States for corporations adept enough to take advantage of its provisions. (Some tax lawyers, Stern reports, joke that DISC has turned the United States into a "mini–Banana Republic"—another portent of the LatinAmericanization of the world's richest industrial nation.)

Thus the interrelated processes of concentration and globalization are shrinking the U.S. tax base and helping to compound an already serious financial crisis. Just as the agility of the mobile corporation to operate beyond the effective regulation of all governments makes it possible to frustrate fiscal policy, so also in monetary policy. We saw earlier in the chapter how the sheer bigness of a few banks and a few hundred of the corporate customers allowed them to undermine the effectiveness of the Federal Reserve's credit policies. Now we shall look at the way in which the globalization of the money market frustrates governmental efforts to regulate the nation-state's domestic money supply.

Between them global corporations and global banks now dominate the international flow of money. The Keynesian vision of how to control international money transactions assumed a market in which national banks and national corporations transacted their business within the context of national boundaries. International transfers of capital, although affected by conditions in

GLOBAL REACH

different countries, were supposed to be carried out by independent borrowers and lenders. At the same time it was assumed that most financial transfers would be accomplished through banking institutions rather than intracorporate flows. Public-sector institutions could, it was believed, control all of this sufficiently to protect the soundness of the national currency because the government would have, to use economists' jargon, "perfect information" about what the private institutions were doing with their money—i.e., governments would be able to respond quickly enough to the behavior of banks and corporations to make effective changes in monetary policy.

These assumptions no longer hold. Two stories of the abortive efforts of two governments to gain control over their own money supply will illustrate the point. Between 1964 and 1968, U.S. corporations built up large deposits in their branch operations in Europe. (These offshore deposits are known as Eurodollars. Most are in Europe, but the term applies equally to Deutsche marks or indeed any accumulation of a readily convertible currency anywhere but in the country of its origin.) The very buildup of Eurodollars was in part a reaction to the Johnson Administration's efforts to deal with the balance-of-payments problem by limiting direct foreign investment. In 1968, the managers of the Federal Reserve became concerned about the "overheating" of the U.S. economy as a consequence of the Vietnam War and adopted certain measures for cooling it. One was to lower the interest rate that could be charged on certificates of deposit. Typically, certificates of deposit are sold in denominations of $100,000 or more and hence are vehicles for corporate rather than individual savings. The Fed's hope and expectation was that the money would be attracted into Treasury bills, which, unlike bank deposits, are not lent out for business expansion. Since the money sits in the Treasury, making Treasury bills an attractive investment is a standard way to reduce the supply of money in circulation. But in 1968 and 1969, things did not happen according to plan. Instead, when the certificates of deposit were cashed, the funds went to the Eurodollar market because of the higher interest rates offered there. From there they were returned to the United States via the intrabank borrowings of the New York parents from their own foreign branch offices in the Eurodollar areas. The inflow of these borrowed funds, in turn, permitted a relative increase in the loans of the New York banks: precisely the result the Fed was trying to avoid. Moreover, unlike U.S. deposits, the Eurodollar funds were, until late in 1969, entirely unpoliced. In that year the Federal Reserve imposed what is known as a fractional reserve requirement on borrowed Eurodollar deposits—for every thousand dollars of deposits the bank must maintain a certain proportion as reserves. Since previously there was no fractional reserve requirement with respect to Eurodollar funds, banks were much freer to lend these than their U.S. deposits. The result was a greater expansion of credit in the U.S. economy than would have been the case if these deposits had been channeled into Treasury bills.

In the late 1960's, Germany too was worried about inflation. One measure the government used was to revalue the mark, an action which, by reducing export demand—German goods became more expensive abroad—would, it was hoped, diminish inflationary pressures in the economy. Other measures included attempts to reduce its domestic money supply and to raise short-term interest rates to dampen domestic investment. But the higher interest rates attracted the short-term liquid assets of global corporations and banks, and dollars began to flow into Germany in great numbers. Under the fixed exchange rate system that existed at the time, the Central Bank had to take in more dollars than before to maintain the par value of the mark. Forced to buy up dollars in exchange for marks, the Central Bank was actually adding to its domestic money supply, thereby further feeding inflation. Thus the globalization of the money market in effect meant that the German government could no longer control its own money supply.

These experiences illustrate the loss of a crucial aspect of national sovereignty, the control of the domestic money supply. A 1973 study of the UN explains how "multinational corporations may affect the stability of currencies." Noting that their "recorded transactions do not usually reveal the whole story," the study, buttressed by others, strongly suggests that global corporations are making massive use of unrecorded transactions for shifting liquid assets in anticipation of devaluation. It is these untraceable movements of short-term capital that are causing many of the problems. In the first nine months of 1971 more than $11 billion in unaccountable funds left the U.S. (Capital flows otherwise unaccountable are listed in the balance of payments as "errors and omissions," a term which serves as an accounting waste-basket, much like "miscellaneous" in the family budget.) In the first quarter of 1973 there was a mysterious outflow of about $4.2 billion reflected in the U.S. "errors and omissions." At the same time, Germany experienced a mysterious inflow—about 7 billion DM in "errors and omissions." (In the same quarter there were recorded capital outflows from the U.S. primarily through cor-porations and banks amounting to $3.8 billion and a correspond-ing inflow to Germany of 6 billion DM.)

Not all short-term movements can be attributed to global cor-porations. But such corporations control between $160 billion and $268 billion in liquid assets. This is anywhere from one and a half to two times the total world reserves in the hands of gov-ernments. A movement of from 1 percent to 3 percent of these funds is, in the words of the Senate Finance Committee Report, "quite sufficient to produce a first-class international financial crisis." Compared with national firms, global corporations, the Senate Committee noted, have a much greater impact on the international monetary system because of their dominance of world trade, their globally coordinated financial management, and the greater speed with which they can act. The issue does not primarily concern the motives that keep the World Managers and their bankers so busy. They deny being predators on the international money market. Their mysterious transnational money movements, they say, are merely defensive. However easily the money movements of global corporations can be ex-plained as prudent planning, rather than speculation, the fact remains that for their own purposes a handful of men can for the first time quickly and effectively undercut the ability of central banks to defend their currencies.

The Eurodollar market, now a prime instrument for the money movement of global corporations and banks, has become a cen-tral banker's nightmare. This "huge creation of private interna-tional liquidity," as Harvard's Professor H. S. Houthakker has termed it, is the instrument that permits the rapid shifting of funds. In his view the Eurodollar market "almost certainly contributes powerfully to the inflationary pressures that no nation has suc-ceeded in keeping under control." Because the Eurodollar market is relatively unpoliced and regularly violates the first principle of conservative banking—never borrow short to lend long—it is courting a liquidity crisis of a scale not equalled since the Great Depression. Sudden withdrawals by major depositors, which now include the oil-producing nations as well as the global corporations, or significant defaults in a world business decline could cause a global panic.

Thus, the integration of the world economy, not withstanding all its benefits, has further undermined the use of monetary policy for controlling inflation. "We have learned," the editors of *Fortune* noted as 1974 began, "that the more a country becomes part of the world-wide market, the more it loses control over events." To maintain stability in the domestic economy and equilibrium in the nation's balance of payments *vis à vis* the rest of the world simultaneously is becoming progressively harder.

In December 1971, in response to a worsening trade deficit, the U.S. devalued the dollar 11 percent. According to traditional theory this should have stimulated lagging U.S. exports because U.S. goods would become more attractive for foreign consumers. The balance of trade would be further helped by the corresponding rise in the price of imports in the U.S. since, presumably, demand would fall. But things did not work out according to plan. The real volume of exports, except for agricultural goods, did not rise perceptibly. Foreign-based global corporations exporting to the U.S. and the overseas subsidiaries of U.S. global firms, fearing the loss of their share of the American market, did not raise prices to the extent anticipated. As oligopolists, they could afford to trim their profit margin of the moment to assure long-term stability of their market shares. Thus the power of global oligopolies to set prices irrespective of market forces frustrated the intended effect of the devaluation because of their command of so much of world trade.

Moreover, for the first time since the early post-World War II days the business cycles of the major industrial countries have converged and are now in phase. Unlike the 1960's, when downturns in the U.S. economy coincided with upturns in most other foreign economies, the American, European, and Japanese economies are now slowing down and speeding up at roughly the same time.

It is reasonable to assume that the new phasing of business cycles has a great deal to do with the speed at which the world

political economy is being integrated through the globalization
of its largest corporations. Owing to revolutionary developments
in international management and communications, an event in
one part of the world has an immediate impact in other parts.
Global corporations and banks act as instant transmitters. Then
too, because production changes are dictated centrally by the
global headquarters but are carried out in many different countries, changes in productive output are, increasingly, occurring
simultaneously across the planet. This new stage in global interdependence is shortening what economists call the "foreign trade
lag" (the time it takes to transmit supply and demand changes
between different economies). The convergence of business cycles
is a major factor complicating the task of maintaining stability
in each national economy.

In the past when the U.S. economy was in a slump and the
Europeans and Japanese had upturns in their economies, the
effect was positive, since strong markets abroad for U.S. goods
at a time when domestic demand was slackening helped restore
balance to the U.S. economy. Similarly, when the U.S. economy
was booming and the other industrial nations were on a downturn, the effect was a healthy one. Foreign nations would reduce
their own demand for American products and increase their
exports to the U.S., thus adding to the supply of goods in the U.S.
and decreasing inflationary pressures. But today, when all industrial nations experience upturns and downturns together,
world trade no longer functions with such positive consequences.
Thus global interdependence has transformed the world political
economy in such a way as to turn formerly stabilizing effects into
destabilizing effects.

In 1972 just after the U.S. devalued the dollar for the first time,
Europe, Japan, and the U.S. were all beginning to recover from
a downturn in the economy. This meant that Japanese and European consumers, instead of being at the height of their "boom,"
as in the 1950's and 1960's, did not have the relatively larger
quantities of spendable income to buy significant amounts of U.S.
imports. Because trade results from the first 1972 devaluation
were so disappointing, the managers of the U.S. economy concluded that a stronger dose was needed. They were driven to what
proved to be an experiment in overkill, because more modest
measures had been frustrated by the ability of global oligopolies

to insulate their prices from the effects of devaluation. (The managers had also failed to take account of the convergence in business cycles.) In February 1973 the dollar was devalued another 6 percent. This time all the industrial countries were in the boom phase of their business cycles. Demand was high in Europe and Japan not only for U.S. agricultural products but for copper and other raw materials which previously had been too expensive for the international market. By September the U.S. had a trade surplus of $873 million. The dollar again was strong.

But the rapid improvement in the U.S. balance of trade was accomplished at a heavy cost to the American consumer. The cut in the price of U.S. goods abroad and the rising demand there resulted in massive exports from the United States. The relatively decreased domestic supply of goods in a time of rising consumer affluence resulted in a dramatic price rise in the U.S. This time foreign and U.S.-based global corporations were not reticent about raising their American prices since they saw that the U.S. economy was heading toward an inflation rate once reserved only for underdeveloped countries. (By the end of October 1973, import prices in the U.S. were up some 17 percent over the previous year.) Since more and more basic U.S. consumer items—shoes, tires, cameras, electronic appliances, etc.—are manufactured in export platforms abroad, the rise in the cost of imports had a big inflationary effect.

The response of the Nixon Administration was once again to impose direct price and wage controls. But again, the controls exacerbated the problem. Since prices of goods sold by U.S. companies abroad were not subject to control, more and more scarce commodities were diverted to the foreign market. For example, the fertilizer industry shipped so much of their supply overseas that food production in the U.S. was threatened. The government was forced to remove domestic price controls for the industry, and within a few days the price of fertilizer in the U.S. jumped almost 40 percent. In short, the domestic effects of policies for promoting equilibrium in the foreign sector of the economy have been both unpredictable and destabilizing. "We have come into a very unusual period," former Secretary of the Treasury George Shultz notes, "where we more or less cast loose from beliefs that we once held to be unarguable. We have cast off from a large number of these old moorings and we have not yet found new ones." Here is another managerial dilemma for the United States. The global transformation of the world economy can continue to be spearheaded by U.S.-based global corporations (barring a complete change of the world monetary system) only if the dollar remains strong. Confidence in the dollar requires some minimum level of stability in the U.S. balance of payments accounts. Yet the very policies employed to maintain equilibrium in the nation's external transactions appear to lead inevitably to internal instability, specifically, unemployment and inflation. Once again, old remedies aggravate new diseases.

5

We now consider what the concentration and globalization of the U.S. economy mean for the average American citizen. Our focus is the personal economic security of those Americans with a family income of $24,000 or less—about 95 percent of the population. What has the new world economy of the global corporation meant for this group in terms of income and jobs?

America's favorite stabilizing myth is the "income revolution." It is reasonably well established that during the New Deal and World War II there was a redistribution of income along more egalitarian lines. In the 1950's, this trend continued to be documented in studies and celebrated in *Fortune* editorials. As recently as 1961, Paul Samuelson was writing, "The American income pyramid is becoming less unequal." But by the late 1960's, the picture clouded. "If we stick to the figures," Census Bureau economist H. P. Miller reported in 1967, "the answers are clear and unambiguous and contrary to widely held beliefs. The statistics show no appreciable change in income shares for nearly 20 years." That the "income revolution" has ground to a halt and that indeed there is something of an "income counter-revolution" is borne out by a series of other recent studies. T. Paul Schultz of the University of Chicago in a 1971 Rand report concludes that income inequality "has apparently increased substantially." He suggests that after decades of confidence in "the egalitarian redistributive influence of the U.S. economy" a reappraisal "of our progress toward equalizing economic opportunities may be warranted." A 1972 study by Peter Henle of the Library of Congress, published by the Labor Department, reveals "a slow but persistent trend toward inequality" for the period 1958–1970.

(In 1960, the richest 20 percent of American families took home 43 percent of total family income. By 1969, they had increased their share to 45 percent, with the extra 2 percent all going to the top half of the richest families.) Henle's data, which are confirmed by other studies, strongly suggest that the recent gains of the top 20 percent came not from the bottom of the society—i.e., the poorest 20 percent—but from lower-middle-class wage and salary earners—i.e., the next 40 percent.

Not everyone who has examined the complex but politically explosive subject of income distribution agrees that the trend is unfavorable. Sanford Rose of *Fortune,* writing in late 1972, is convinced that "we seem to be making progress toward greater equality." His principal argument is that a greater proportion of the national income is going to "wages and salary" and a correspondingly smaller proportion is going to "profits." His point, to put it simply, is that "workers" are gaining at the expense of "capitalists," and hence income must be being redistributed along more equitable lines.

The problem with Rose's analysis, which did not have the benefit of Peter Henle's findings published the same month, is that the dichotomy between wage earners and profit receivers is misleading. By Rose's use of aggregate wage and salary statistics, Raymond Firestone, Harold Geneen, Henry Ford, and Richard Gerstenberg are all transformed into "workers" earning a "wage." It is necessary therefore to inquire what is happening *within* the wage-and-salary sector, lest we celebrate the victory of the "income revolution" prematurely. What we find when we do make such an inquiry offers no grounds for optimism. Peter Henle has found in his study of wages and salaries for all male workers (including Henry Ford) for the period 1958–1970 that the lowest-paid 20 percent of all workers suffered a decline in their share of about 10 percent (from 5.1 percent to 4.6 percent of total wages and salaries) while the top 20 percent increased their share from 38.2 percent to 40.6 percent. This is, of course, a significant increase in inequality, and the trend is continuing. In 1972, during the period of wage and price controls imposed under Nixon's New Economic Policy, the average production-line worker received a 7-percent increase in his weekly salary over the previous year, while senior management (chief executive officers) received increases of almost 15 percent. (In dollar terms, the low-

income "workers" took home on the average an extra $8.87 a
week, while the high-income "workers" averaged an additional
$107 in their weekly paychecks.) The tables below give a clearer
picture of the growing inequality in the wage-and-salary sector.

The deterioration of income distribution appears to have gathered momentum in the same years during which the twin processes of concentration and globalization in the U.S. economy
also became evident. Such a showing of mere coincidence in
time, of course, falls short of demonstrating a causal connection.
But there is, we believe, strong independent evidence for suspect-
ing that the behavior of global corporations has materially contributed to the worsening pattern of income distribution in the
United States in recent years.

In a capitalist society, a crucial source of income is the ownership of productive wealth. Those who must live by their labor
alone, whether an assembly-line worker or a basketball star, are
necessarily limited in what they can earn. There are only twenty-

TABLE I

THE MANAGERIAL OWNERS: WHAT THEY EARN AND
WHERE IT COMES FROM
(*in current dollars*)

For the Year	1960	1963	1969	197:
Total Average *After*-Tax Income of the Chief Executive Officer	244,140	221,036	333,493	379,!
As a Manager of the Corporation	116,445	107,596	148,966	178,:
As an Owner of the Corporation	127,695	113,440	184,527	201,!
Ownership Income as a Percentage of Total Income	52.3%	51.32%	55.33%	53.0
Average Market Value of the Chief Executive's Stockholdings in his Corporation	1,685,288	2,664,557	4,017,262	5,148,
Total Average *After*-Tax Income of the Top 5 Executives	154,066	154,203	200,390	228,
As Managers of the Corporation	83,727	84,357	111,785	132,
As Owners of the Corporation	70,339	69,946	89,145	96,
Ownership Income as a Percentage of Total Income	45.66%	45.29%	44.37%	42.0

Sources and Definitions: See notes for pages 292–93.

TABLE II

"THE FACTS ABOUT INCOME INEQUALITY": THE GROWING GAPS, IN REAL AND CURRENT INCOME BETWEEN SELECTED WORKERS AND MAJOR CORPORATION EXECUTIVES; SELECTED YEARS, 1960–1972

(in dollars)

		1960	1963	1969	1972	% Increases in Gaps 1960–1972
Gaps Between Total Incomes of Chief Executive Officers and those of						
Personnel Directors	Real	239,420	212,288	295,224	292,487	22.16%
	Current	232,660	208,672	316,948	359,000	54.30%
Production Workers in Manufacture	Real	247,355	220,532	304,731	303,067	22.52%
	Current	239,790	216,284	327,487	373,163	55.62%
Janitors, Porters, Cleaners	Real	249,024	222,425	306,640	305,025	22.49%
	Current	241,289	218,032	330,127	376,282	55.95%
Gaps Between Average Total Incomes of Top 5 Executives and Those of						
Personnel Directors	Real	146,373	144,051	171,941	169,629	15.89%
	Current	142,586	141,839	184,385	207,511	45.53%
Production Workers in Manufacture	Real	154,308	152,295	181,448	180,209	16.79%
	Current	149,716	149,451	194,924	221,674	48.06%
Janitors, Porters, Cleaners	Real	155,977	154,188	183,357	182,167	16.79%
	Current	151,215	151,199	197,564	224,793	48.66%

Sources and Definitions: See notes for pages 292–93.

four hours to the day and only so many years of strength and energy. The important source of accelerating income for the very rich is wealth in the form of stocks, bonds, and other interests in the productive system. The concentration of productive wealth is more pronounced than the concentration of income, although there is a serious lack of information as to identity of the real owners of the largest blocks of stocks, bonds, and trust holdings in America. In 1953 the richest 1 percent of all adults owned 92 percent of all trust holdings. The latest figures show no change. Twenty years ago 2 percent of all adults owned 90 percent of all corporate bonds and virtually 100 percent of all state and municipal bonds, and again there is little evidence of change.

The interaction of corporate concentration and productive-wealth concentration explains to a significant degree why income distribution is worsening in the United States. Because the industrial giants such as GE and ITT have absorbed thousands of smaller firms in the last generation, a share of stock in these corporations represented in 1970 a much larger share of America's productive wealth than it did in 1950. A significant share of the stock of the largest global corporations is going to their own top managers. Table I above shows the average total income of the chief executive officers and the average total income of the top five highest officers in a representative sampling of 44 of the nation's global corporations. What these figures demonstrate is that in the upper reaches of America's corporations there is no "technostructure" made up of managers with interests distinct from those of the owners. Increasingly, the managers are the owners, deriving an increasing proportion of their income not from their managerial skills but from the stock they own in their own corporations. A glance at the annual earnings of our sample of 220 men in charge of some of America's largest corporations (there are no women) shows them to be at the very top of the income pyramid. (So wide is the income gap in this country that in 1970 you could join the richest 20 percent with a family income of only $14,000.)

We have argued that the concentration in the manufacturing, transportation, communication, banking, and other dominant service industries has led to further concentration of income-producing wealth and hence further concentration of income. We now turn to the impact of globalization on income distribution. Have the decisions of America's major corporations in the 1960's to make a quantum leap in foreign investment had an impact on what the average American can expect to earn?

The whole subject of the employment impact of global corporations—whether they increase or reduce employment possibilities for American workers—is a matter of intense political debate. The global corporation cannot afford the image of job destroyer which organized labor is attempting to pin on it. Thus, this issue is one that the global corporation must either win or defuse if it is to gain the legitimacy it seeks. For this reason, the public charges and countercharges of unions and companies on overall employment impacts, though each side is armed with studies, must be understood as a form of political advertising. The battle of the studies is a matter to which we shall return. Here we shall suspend judgment as to the overall employment impact and note the changing employment picture in certain key industries. The unfavorable changes coincide with changes in the investment behavior of the companies dominating such industries and in our view can be substantially explained thereby.

The first big wave of foreign investment, as we have seen, affected such industries as shoes, textiles, electronics assembly, and leather. U.S. factories began to close down; there remain thirteen shoe factories in Lynn, Massachusetts, which fifty years ago had almost one hundred. Basic goods formerly produced in the United States for both export and the U.S. market in the very industries that once were major employers of unskilled, semiskilled, and irregularly employed workers are now produced abroad. Both Henle's and Schultz's studies confirm the fact that unskilled, part-time, and semiskilled workers suffered a greater decline in their share of national income than skilled workers during the first wave of foreign investment (1958–1967). But, as we noted in Part II, by the late 1960's underdeveloped countries were demanding that local factories be more than simple assembly operations and that the skill level and number of jobs in the factories of Singapore, Taiwan, and South Korea be increased. Congressman Joseph M. Gaydos describes how the American worker has lost his once exclusive hold on the skilled-labor market:

The unschooled girls of Taiwan can do just as well assembling complex TV components as the high school graduates of New

Jersey. The untrained workers of African or Asian nations can be taught to produce complex products ranging from tiny transistors to giant turbines, as readily as the skilled workers of Pennsylvania or the West Coast. And the depressed inhabitants of the most squalid slums of the Far East can be taught to make specialty steel products just as well as the experienced workers of Pittsburgh.

Both the increasingly stringent requirements of the underdeveloped countries and the savings to be achieved by the use of overseas skilled labor have led to the second wave of foreign investment of the late 1960's and early 1970's. More capital-intensive operations employing high-skilled workers were moved abroad during this period, with the result, as the Henle and Schultz data show, that the share of national income going to *skilled* workers in the United States began to drop perceptibly during the same years.

Not only did the transfer of investment from local factories to overseas factories affect those who were thrown out of work; it exerted a downward pressure on wages generally. The threat to move, whether or not actually voiced in labor negotiations, had a sobering effect on labor militancy. The reason for the decline in the bargaining power of labor is a matter of detailed examination in Chapter 11. But the effect of that loss in bargaining power is reflected in labor's increasing inability to achieve its "fair return." (Labor receives a "fair return" when the wage of an additional worker equals his contribution to the firm's total output. Put differently, it is this wage rate which maximizes the efficiency of the economy and at the same time maintains equilibrium in the supply of and demand for jobs.) MIT economist Lester Thurow has found, in comparing labor's actual return with the ideal "fair return" for the period 1929–1965, that labor never achieved its "fair return," while capital always exceeded it. But until 1960, labor was improving its position and the gap was narrowing. Since 1960, however, labor's share has remained constant, about 33 percent less than its "fair return," while capital's actual return has increased steadily over its "fair return." (In 1960, according to Professor Thurow, the actual return was 51 percent higher than "fair return"; five years later it was 62 percent higher.) Under modern capitalism, the bargaining power of unions is important for maintaining relative equilibrium between capital and labor. Concentration and globalization have weakened labor's bargaining power, and the result, not surprisingly, is that middle-income and low-income workers are sharing less in the new prosperity.

There is another reason in addition to job displacement and the weakening of unions why this should be so. Over the last few years an ever-greater proportion of new investment dollars of the largest U.S. firms has been invested abroad. By 1972, as we have noted, 25 cents out of every dollar was going into overseas plants and equipment. The upsurge in foreign investment has thus had certain ironic effects. It is true that since the mid-1960's the foreign investment activities of U.S.-based global corporations have produced a significant positive impact on the U.S. net balance of payments, due to the fact that the amount of capital flowing back to the United States in the form of reported profits, interest, royalties, and technical fees on past foreign investment is exceeding the amount currently invested abroad. (In 1961, net capital inflows were $1.2 billion; by 1967, $1.4 billion; by 1973 they had reached $6.2 billion.) The impact of U.S.-based global corporations on the trade side of the balance-of-payments account is less clear. If the result of foreign investment is to reduce production for export and increase imports, the effect is, of course, negative. If, on the other hand, the process indirectly stimulates more production of goods in the United States (parts, service, new products, etc.), then it is positive. As we shall see shortly, this is an area in which the answers depend upon the specificity of the questions. Thus the U.S. Tariff Commission study for the years 1966–1970 offers a range of estimates of the overall positive trade impact (from a low of $242 million to a high of $3.85 billion) and notes that the effects vary enormously from industry to industry (a positive impact of $1.4 billion in one to a negative impact of $1.9 billion in another).

Thus while the foreign investment activities of U.S.-based global corporations have indeed brought cheer to balance-of-payments watchers in the United States, the cheer, as Professor Robert Gilpin points out, has not spread very far into our society. He sees a connection between foreign investment and loss of job and income opportunities for workers—particularly the lower ranks of white and black blue-collar workers. The creation of capital stock abroad does not create jobs nor raise wages for American workers as would a corresponding investment in the United States. (Whether the long-term impact is to create more jobs in the United States than would otherwise exist is, of course, a matter of hot debate. But no one argues that moving a factory from Akron to Taiwan will have anything but an immediate unfavorable impact on workers in Akron.) The return on foreign investment which generates interest, dividends, and fees but not blue-collar wages for American recipients is thus a benefit to capital but not to labor. Gilpin pinpoints these important effects of foreign investment in his report to the U.S. Senate Committee on Labor and Public Welfare:

> The effect of foreign investment is to decrease the capital stock with which Americans work; this decreases the productivity of American labor and real wages below what they would have been if the foreign investment had not taken place. By one estimate, the annual rate reduction in labor's income is around $6 billion. This is obviously a rough estimate but it serves to indicate that the export of capital benefits the owners of capital and management more than labor as a whole.

A crucial determinant of income distribution is, of course, the job market. If employment possibilities are increasing, so also will wages—not only because there are more jobs for more people to fill but also because employers in a time of labor scarcity must pay more. Thus the income-distribution and employment questions are inextricably linked. The great statistical battle of the 1970's between the AFL-CIO and the principal lobby for the global corporation, the Emergency Committee for American Trade (later reinforced by the Department of Commerce and the Harvard Business School), is fought in a spirit of awesome scientific exactitude. The AFL-CIO brought forth from its computer a mass of figures which showed that U.S.-based global corporations were responsible for a net loss of 500,000 jobs between 1966 and 1969. ECAT's study of 74 global corporations performed on more congenial computers showed "a major positive contribution" to the growth of employment in the United States: to be precise, an additional 300,000 jobs. A more recent Harvard Business School study by Professor Robert Stobaugh comes to an even more euphoric conclusion. ". . . the aggregate effects of U.S. foreign direct investment on U.S. employment" are so substantial and positive that they are responsible for saving or creating "a total of perhaps 600,000 jobs." This study was immediately retailed to the public in large ads in major newspapers and magazines.

Obviously, these extraordinary discrepancies reflect not sloppy mathematics but sharply differing perceptions of reality. It is, of course, primarily the differing assumptions under which numbers are fed the computer that produce the widely disparate results. But beyond this, some numbers are likely to give better insight than other numbers. Global corporations provide sketchy employment data; information about the behavior of individual firms is frequently held back on grounds that it might give aid and comfort to the competitors. Thus the U.S. Tariff Commission study of global corporations complains that "comprehensive data to support the analysis required" in looking at employment impacts "were not available in a suitable form." Employment statistics tend to be aggregate statistics for an entire industry rather than for individual firms. The bias in favor of aggregate analysis rather than microeconomic examination of data with respect to specific firms, communities, and regions is reinforced by current fashion in the economics profession. Keynesian economists are specialists in macroeconomics, with the result that microeconomics—the examination of effects by industry, sector and region —has been neglected. "Since World War II," Soma S. Golden writes in *The New York Times,* "the superstars in economics have been the men who knew how to manage the aggregates, how to pull the levers of fiscal and monetary policy. . . . But that developing skill no longer seems to be enough."

The use of aggregate figures can have a mystifying effect. For example, the ECAT study states that the representative sample of 74 global corporations "increased their domestic employment (exclusive of employment gains through acquisition) more rapidly than the average manufacturing firm." Their rate of new job creation was about *75 percent greater* than that of all other manufacturing firms. (Their average rate of employment growth was 2 percent compared with a national average for the manufacturing sector of 1.4 percent.) But these figures were derived from an aggregation of employment statistics over a ten-year period. If you look at the 1960–1965 period and the 1965–1970 period separately, a different sense of reality emerges. (The justification for separating these two periods is our earlier conclusion that the pace of globalization dramatically increased in the second half of the decade and that the character of foreign investment changed in significant ways.) What appears from this process of disaggregation is the strong suspicion that the ability of global corporations to create new jobs is dramatically declining. In the first half of the decade the sample firms were creating new jobs at a rate 67 percent higher than the national average, but by the second half the job-creation rate was only 4.9 percent higher than the national average. (It should not be forgotten that these are among the largest firms in the country, with the advantages of oligopolies; that they expanded significantly inside the United States during the 1960's and, consequently, should be assumed to be the nation's largest employers.) Yet, in the latter half of the 1960's, when the rate of job creation in the entire manufacturing sector registered an 8.3-percent decline compared to its 1960–1965 value, *the decline for global corporations was 40 percent.* Thus there is considerable doubt whether as a long-term trend the U.S. global corporation is going to continue having a positive impact on domestic employment.

The Harvard Business School estimate that the global corporation has saved or created 600,000 jobs in the United States is arrived at in the following way: There are, according to Raymond Vernon, 250,000 jobs in the headquarters of parent companies (mostly staff). "If there were no foreign direct investment," the Harvard study concludes, the jobs of an additional 250,000 production workers and 100,000 supporting workers "would be lost." To be sure, the study cautions, "no one at this stage should claim that such estimates are accurate or that this many workers would be unemployed." But the basic question dominating the study, "What would have happened if the foreign investment had not been made?," together with a predetermined answer, constitutes the basic assumption behind the study—an assumption that is crucial to the results. "If the investment were assumed not to be made," the authors of the Harvard study note, "the alternative use of funds by the company for such purposes as investing in the production of other goods or paying dividends was not considered. We assumed that if a worker lost his job, then he was unemployed regardless of what happened to him."

The use of such "this is how it would be if history were different" techniques is unsatisfactory for confronting the real world. The results cannot be verified, because history does not oblige with instant replay. Figmental logic, as the historian Fritz Redlich calls it, can be used to lead one in any direction. The proof of this is that the AFL-CIO studies come to totally different conclusions because their "might have been" assumptions are different. Thus the favorable studies of the companies assume that if a worker now employed by a global corporation were not working for the corporation he would be unemployed. The labor studies assume, on the other hand, that he is infinitely employable in the United States if only the corporations will keep their capital in the country. Both assumptions are too simple, and the result is that as to short-term employment effects, the battle of the studies is inconclusive.

There is a certain fatalism in all these studies. The company computers all operate on the assumption that foreign investment is "defensive"—i.e., that if the company did not locate a factory in a cheap labor market abroad, a Japanese or European firm would take over the market and the displaced American worker would be unemployable. (Union computers, on the other hand, act as if comparatively high labor costs in the United States make little difference in the competition with foreign corporations.) But even assuming that all foreign investment is "defensive," there are ways to protect a market position other than building a factory in Taiwan. Companies could have put more money into research and development in the United States to replace the diminishing stock of basic innovative ideas on which future production depends. Such an investment policy would have had a greater domestic multiplier effect than foreign investment. We could also ask what would have happened to the U.S. employment picture if U.S. firms had not been so ready to sell off their comparative advantage to their competitors by licensing technology to them for quick profits.

As to overall impacts on employment over the last few years, whether negative or positive, it is impossible to make a definitive judgment. As to impacts over the long run, the trends are unfavorable. As long as we talk about employment in the aggregate, there is little more to add. But if we look at the sectoral and regional effects of foreign investment, the dislocation global corporations cause by closing factories in the United States and opening them somewhere else is obvious. On computer tapes, jobs may be interchangeable. In the real world, they are not. A total of 250,000 new jobs gained in corporate headquarters does not, in any political or human sense, offset 250,000 old jobs lost on the production line. When Lynn, Massachusetts, becomes a ghost of its former self, its jobless citizens find little satisfaction in reading about the new headquarters building on Park Avenue and all the secretaries it will employ. The changing composition of the work force and its changing geographical location brought about by the globalization of U.S. industry are affecting the lives of millions of Americans in serious and largely unfortunate ways.

The structural transformation of the world economy through the globalization of Big Business is undermining the power of the nation-state to maintain economic and political stability within its territory. Old remedies do not work, and new ones are yet to be found. Loss of control over money, increasing concentration of income and wealth, failure to maintain employment, and mounting debt are symptoms of the permanent managerial crisis that now afflicts advanced industrial societies as well as poor countries. Inflation, in the words of Arthur Burns, "threatens the very foundation of our society." Territorially based government lacks the imagination and the power to develop a political response to the dynamic global economic forces which, more and more, are shaping our lives.

11

The Obsolescence of American Labor

1

In building their Global Factory, the World Managers have revolutionized the nature of work across the planet. By internationalizing production, they have developed the global payroll. In 1971, the world's 27 major electrical and electronics companies employed 3,940,833 persons, and the 12 world leaders of the automobile industry had a worldwide work force of 2,401,223. The largest U.S.-based global firms, such as Ford, ITT, Chrysler, Kodak, and Procter & Gamble, employ more than one-third of their work force outside the United States. As of 1966, U.S.-based global corporations employed overseas 3,324,321 non-Americans, approximately 30 percent of their total payrolls. The figure is unquestionably much higher today. What does it mean that a 14-year-old girl assembling transistors in a Hong Kong factory, a German waiter in a hotel, a typing instructor in Mexico, and a senior accountant commuting from Westport all work for the same company?

The World Managers like to say that such corporate families make for international harmony. The globalization of work means more jobs and better jobs for everybody. "The division of labor is one of the tried and true economic principles," Nelson Rockefeller lectured President Nixon in his Report on Latin America, "which will be as valid in 1976 as it was in 1776." If illiterate Hong Kong children do what they do best (working on assembly lines fourteen hours a day for 30 cents an hour) and Westport accountants make their unique contribution, everybody benefits. It is less than astonishing that this theory has elicited

303

some strong negative reactions from organized labor. Nothing is better calculated to weaken the bargaining power of labor than management's prerogative to divide and shift tasks at will on a global scale.

In this chapter we shall be exploring the impact on the American worker of current patterns of corporate decision making about what work is to be done, where it shall be done, and who is to do it. We shall also be examining labor's response.

Organized labor in the United States was slow to perceive what was happening to it until a significant share of the nation's TV, camera, electronics, and automobile production had been shifted out of the United States. The awareness level increased dramatically, however, after 1966 when global corporations sharply accelerated their production overseas for export to the U.S. market. By the 1970's George Meany, quoting what he calls a "conservative" Congressional estimate, was pointing out that 20 percent of all cars, 40 percent of all glassware, 60 percent of all sewing machines and calculators, 100 percent of cassettes and radios, and "large proportions of U.S. production of shirts, work clothes, shoes and knitgoods" had already been displaced by imports, a substantial portion of which were coming from American-owned foreign factories. Today labor statesmen are vocal in denouncing the "runaway shop," yet they are understandably confused as to what to do about it. In the last chapter we recounted the battle of statistics currently being waged by global corporations and organized labor. The corporations, it will be recalled, argue that the internationalization of production actually creates jobs in the United States despite the rising rate of U.S. plant closings. Labor, on the other hand, claims that in the electronics industry alone over a recent three-year period more than 5,000 jobs a month were lost to foreign subsidiaries of U.S. global companies. The battle, as we argued in the last chapter, cannot be resolved unless certain assumptions are made much more explicit than either side has yet been willing to make them.

But even if industry's cheery projections about job creation in the United States should, despite contrary evidence, turn out to be true, they provide small comfort for the thousands of American workers who have been put out of work by the transfer of production overseas or for the communities that have been badly hurt by plant closings. The AFL-CIO has testified that between

1966 and 1971, the U.S. Division of the Global Factory lost 900,000 jobs. Some of these job losses may in fact have been attributable to the decline in defense contracts in recent years, particularly in the aerospace and electronics industries. But there are innumerable examples throughout the United States of production transfers throwing thousands of Americans out of work. Here are a few: Westinghouse closed its Edison, New Jersey, TV plant and moved production to Canada and Japan. Emerson Radio closed down its Jersey City plant and transferred production to Admiral's operation in Taiwan. General Instruments transferred its TV-tuner production from New England plants to Portuguese and Taiwanese factories (laying off between 3,000 and 4,000 workers, according to AFL-CIO Research Director Nat Goldfinger). Motorola discontinued its U.S. picture-tube plant and sold its machinery to a General Telephone & Electronics subsidiary in Hong Kong. Warwick Electronics has left Arkansas and Illinois for Mexico. Zenith Radio, according to its chairman, Joseph S. Wright, has laid off more than 7,000 workers because of its transfer of production to Taiwan. Singer and Burroughs have discontinued production of desk calculators in the United States and now make them in Japan for the U.S. market. The Hartford plant of the Royal Typewriter Company (owned by Litton Industries) was closed and production moved to England, with a loss of more than 1,300 U.S. jobs. American food-processing companies now export frozen Mexican strawberries in great quantities to the United States, forcing the Louisiana strawberry industry to shift nearly half the acreage planted in strawberries to other uses. Bulova has transferred production to a new plant near Pago Pago, American Samoa, where 60 Samoans assemble some 210,000 watch movements flown in from Switzerland for eventual shipment to the U.S. market. (The 21,000-mile airlift for these watches is more than offset by tariff savings. There is no duty on watches imported from a U.S. territory. Moreover, American Samoa offers a ten-year tax holiday for new plants.) Says Bulova's President Harry B. Henshel, "We are able to beat foreign competition because we are the foreign competition."

The list is endless. An AFL-CIO spokesman has testified that the transfer of production overseas is making the United States "a nation of hamburger stands . . . a country stripped of industrial capacity and meaningful work . . . a service economy . . . a nation of citizens busily buying and selling cheeseburgers and root beer floats." George Meany argues that GE has licensed to Japanese firms more than 84 major items, including a Carrier System microwave device, late-development radars, machine guns, gunsights, gyrocompass systems, and boilers for nuclear reactors. Despite the fact that most of these items were developed with the U.S. taxpayer's money courtesy of the Department of Defense, no U.S. workers will benefit from their production. The export of high technology to licensees abroad means short-run higher profits for the companies—but, Andrew Biemiller, director of legislation for the AFL-CIO, argues, the United States is thereby losing its technological edge. By selling the Thor-Delta launch rocket to Japan, the McDonnell-Douglas company is helping the Japanese to become independent of U.S.-produced rockets. "This one-time sale, which of course benefits the U.S. balance of payments this one time, will adversely affect the U.S. balance of payments for years to come," he maintains. Northrop is licensing production of F-5E fighter planes in Taiwan, and Lockheed is now assembling the Safeguard antimissile system in Hong Kong with the help of 700 natives who earn $2 a day. The effect, says Biemiller, is to cut U.S. workers out of the international weapons trade. (The companies respond that without such coproduction arrangements they could not compete with British, French, and Russian arms pushers and wouldn't sell any airplanes or rockets at all.)

In Part II we argued that given existing patterns of oligopolistic competition, the "runaway shop" which becomes the "export platform" in an underdeveloped country is now a necessity of life for the U.S.-based corporation. The profitability and growth of the firm require it to make the same use of cheap labor its European and Japanese competitors make. Because wages have been rising rapidly in Japan, the Crown Company, a Japanese firm, is moving its television production facilities to Seoul, South Korea, where wages are one-fifth of the Japanese rate. Kasuga Seiki can make cassettes in Hong Kong, paying its workers $65 a month instead of $350 in Japan. European firms like Grundig and Bayer are moving to Iceland for similar reasons. Of course, cheap labor is only one reason why global corporations shift production out of their home country. Avoiding taxes, circumventing tariffs, and steering clear of stringent antipollution controls are all reasons why global corporations build factories abroad. Certainly such firms as Volvo and Michelin are not investing in the United States because of cheap labor. (It is worth noting, however, that Michelin is putting its plant in South Carolina, a relatively low-wage region with strong antiunion legislation.)

The World Managers, sensitive to such criticism as UAW President Leonard Woodcock's charge that the companies don't care that they are causing unemployment in the United States, like to minimize their interest in coolie labor. (Woodcock is fond of quoting Thomas Jefferson's observation about merchants without a country: "The mere spot they stand on does not constitute so strong an attachment as that from which they draw their gain.") Their sudden interest in Taiwan, global managers argue, has nothing to do with either their treasure or their heart being there. They want merely to be better able to make use of supply markets. It is not usually considered good taste to talk about 14-cents-an-hour help, but occasionally an entrepreneur breaks loose from the public relations department and gives an honest answer. "In South Korea, Taiwan, and Indonesia," says Henry Ford II, "we see promising markets and we see an attractive supply of cheap labor." William Sheskey told the House Ways and Means Committee how he purchased a modern U.S. shoe factory, shut it down, and shipped the lasts, dies, patterns, management, and much of the leather to Europe:

> I am making the same shoes under the same brand name, selling them to the same customers with the same management, with the same equipment, for one reason. The labor where I am now making the shoes is 50 cents an hour as compared to the $3 I was paying. Here is a perfect example of where I took everything American except the labor and that is exactly why I bought it.

Relocating production in Mexico, Taiwan, Brazil, or the Philippines is an even more irresistible way to cut costs. In the office-machinery field, a company must pay its U.S. workers about ten times what it pays its Taiwanese and Korean workers and about six times what it pays its Mexican workers. In the last few years more than 50,000 jobs have been created along the

Mexican border, and exports from the area back to the United States have climbed from $7 million in 1966 to $350 million in 1972. During the latter year, imports from Taiwan to the U.S. market amounted to $1.3 billion. No amount of statistical magic can obscure the commonsense conclusion that servicing the U.S. market from Taiwanese and Mexican factories rather than U.S. factories deprives American workers in the affected industries of their jobs.

2

However, the continuing exodus to the export platforms of the underdeveloped world is creating problems for the American labor movement in addition to structural unemployment. Corporate organization on a global scale is a highly effective weapon for undercutting the power of organized labor everywhere. Capital, technology, and marketplace ideology, the bases of corporate power, are mobile; workers, by and large, are not. The ability of corporations to open and close plants rapidly and to shift their investment from one country to another erodes the basis of organized labor's bargaining leverage, the strike. While it may be true to argue, as IBM's Arthur Watson does, that when a plant is closed in the United States and opened in Korea "we have not lost jobs; one can trade jobs internationally," the trading process does not benefit the worker who has lost his job and cannot afford to sit home until the uncertain day when his town feels the beneficial effects of industrial expansion overseas. Even when World Managers defend their labor policies, they unwittingly attest to their great bargaining edge over organized labor.

The power of corporations to neutralize the strike weapon is not merely theoretical. It is used. Perhaps the most celebrated example is the strike at Ford's British operation in 1970. After a summit conference with the Prime Minister, Henry Ford II delivered a stiff note to the British people. "We have got hundreds of millions of pounds invested in Great Britain and we can't recommend any new capital investment in a country constantly dogged with labor problems. There is nothing wrong with Ford of Britain but with the country." Shortly thereafter he shifted back to Ohio a proposed £30-million operation for building Pinto engines. The following year he pointedly announced that

Ford's major new plant would be put in Spain, a country that offered "social peace."

Management finds that its power to close an entire operation in a community and to transfer everything but the workers out of the country produces a marvelously obliging labor force. The threat, real or imagined, of retaliatory plant closings has caused unions in both Europe and the United States to moderate their demands and in a number of cases to give "no-strike" pledges. There have been enough cases in which global corporations have used their superior mobility to defeat unions to make the threat credible. Dunlop Pirelli, to give one example, closed its Milan-area plant and moved it across the Swiss border, where it proceeded to rehire Italian workers as low-wage migrant labor. (The savings in pensions and accumulated seniority rights accomplished by this thrifty maneuver were, one would hope, passed on to the purchasers of rubber tires around the world, but there is no evidence of this.)

There are also less drastic alternatives available to management which further weaken labor's bargaining power. One is the layoff. A Burroughs subsidiary making computers in France suddenly laid off one-third of its workers on orders from its headquarters in New York. (The case is a good illustration of how the interests of subsidiaries are subordinated to the corporation's global strategy, for the plant in question was operating at near capacity and was making good profits. Evidently some company consideration having nothing to do with the French operation itself dictated the layoff.) Neither the French Government nor the outraged local manager could do a thing about it. A global corporation can also protect itself from a strike by establishing what is called "multiple sourcing"—i.e., different plants in different countries producing the same component. It is a strategy by which the corporation can make itself independent of the labor force in any one plant. Chrysler, British Leyland, Goodyear, Michelin, and Volkswagen are among the many firms which use this technique for managing their labor problems. When Ford in Britain was faced with a strike at the plant that was its sole supplier for a crucial component, the company reclaimed the die used in the manufacture from the struck plant and had it flown within five days to a German plant. As *The Times* observed

in 1970, "In some cases Ford has beaten strikes by 'pulling' tools
and dies in time to start alternative production before employees
in the original firm have stopped work." Unions are attempting
to organize a campaign to counteract plant juggling as a strike-
breaking strategy and are beginning to achieve some successes.

The confrontation of capital and labor, a battle scarcely more
than 100 years old, has now moved to the global stage. Because
it is easier to write a check than to move a worker and his family,
the owners and managers of capital, as we have seen, enjoy
certain advantages over labor. Paul Ramadier's studies confirm
that strikes in global companies are on the average of shorter
duration than strikes in domestic firms in Europe. He attributes
this fact to the superior bargaining power of the global companies. (IBM's Jacques Maisonrouge, on the other hand, prefers
to explain the fact that his French workers stayed at their jobs
during the massive strikes of 1968 as evidence of their international outlook.)

A number of lesser advantages also inure to the global corporation because of its very structure. Because lines of authority
are kept deliberately murky in many global enterprises, the local
union does not know with whom it should deal. Many union
leaders in Europe complain of "buck-passing" in negotiations.
They are unable to get a decision out of the local manager and
are never sure what issues he has the authority to settle. Labor
unions up to this point lack anything comparable to the sophisticated communications system of the corporations. Thus they have
difficulty finding out what the corporation may have paid in other
countries or whether there are precedents for the concessions they
are demanding. Corporations surmount differences in language,
customs, and outlook by spending money for translators, language
schools, and cram courses on local culture which unions do not
have. The airborne executive corps can develop a properly states-
manlike international consciousness as its members dart in and
out of the capitals of the world, but for the union organizer in
Liège or Milan, without anything equivalent to the global intelligence system of the corporation, the mysteries of the outside
world continue to loom large. These mysteries represent a management asset.

The most crucial mysteries concern the company's books. The
complexity of intracorporate balance sheets, further obfuscated

by the miracles of modern accounting, makes it exceedingly difficult for unions to find out how much money the employer is
making or, indeed, if he is really losing money, as he frequently
claims. Transfer pricing and other mysterious intracorporate
transactions, hidden behind the veil of consolidated balance
sheets, are formidable obstacles for union negotiators trying to
get an accurate picture of what the local subsidiary of the global
company can and should be paying in wages. (Of course, companies seek to maximize or minimize income depending upon
whether they are talking to shareholders, tax collectors, or workers. In ITT's frenetic growth campaign, the company bookkeeper
has on occasion employed rather unusual accounting methods to
demonstrate "record earnings." In 1968, ITT's consolidated balance sheet showed $56 million in "miscellaneous and nonoperat-
ing income," of which, a diligent analyst discovered, $11 million
was attributable to its having sold off properties and investments
in Europe.)

A global company often bargains with several unions representing different parts of its conglomerate empire. Because of the
way unions are typically organized, what impact they have is
limited to that phase of the global operation in which the labor
dispute is taking place. They have little leverage to affect other
aspects of the global operation, although, as we shall see, they are
trying to develop that leverage. Most unions are nationalistic and
cannot afford to risk jobs to support workers in other countries.

Moreover, unions lack a tightly organized structure for dealing
with the global corporate hierarchy. Thus they not only are at a
disadvantage because they know less about the company than the
company knows about them but also lack the common purpose
that unites the worldwide operation of a global corporation—i.e.,
global profit maximization. In Europe the ideological splits of the
Cold War that divided Communist and non-Communist unions
still persist, though they are growing weaker. Moreover, there
are sharp differences between "pragmatic" labor leaders looking
for a bigger paycheck and more job security and "ideological"
union functionaries who, in Charles Levinson's words, want not
merely a bigger piece of the pie but a voice in baking it. In
general, European unions are more radical than U.S. unions in
demands for a share in management decisions about the workplace, but they are less well organized and, with few exceptions,

appear to have even less comprehension of the nature of the challenge which the global corporation poses to workers. Moreover, legislation hampers organizing efforts in many parts of the world. Like the United States, both Germany and Holland have laws against sympathy strikes and secondary boycotts. Countries such as Greece, Ireland, Singapore, Malaysia, and Indonesia advertise their repressive labor legislation.

Nonetheless, the exploitation of wage differentials in different parts of the world by the global corporations is causing unions to dust off the classic phrase "international worker solidarity" and to try to make it relevant to "bread and butter" bargaining. But even as U.S. union leaders begin to realize that the army, 34,000 strong, of 30-cents-an-hour child laborers in Hong Kong is not only a sin to be deplored at the annual convention but a real and growing economic threat to American workers, they are confused about what to demand. Should the wages in Hong Kong and Detroit be the same? Not even powerful unions in Europe are making demands for parity with U.S. workers. Despite the logic in paying the same wage for the same work for the same company irrespective of race, creed, color, or national origin, the practical union organizer is reluctant to ask for it. Given the risk that the company may decide to pull out altogether, he is happy if he can get a few more francs or marks a day. The only case of an American union's successfully negotiating international wage parity is the United Auto Workers contract covering Canadian automobile workers. But this was a special case because of a long history of governmental and union efforts to harmonize labor policy. International solidarity has yet to extend to Brazil or Singapore, where, of course, there are no local unions. However, the boldness with which such governments are competing with one another in offering their docile labor force to global corporations is posing a challenge to the American union movement which it knows it can no longer ignore.

3

In examining the response of U.S. unions to the growth of the global firm, it is essential to understand what has happened to the American labor movement. To begin with, only 23 percent of the work force in the United States is organized, a fact which the nation's chief organizer, George Meany, who apparently is uninterested in representing a widely diverse labor force, accepts with equanimity: "Why should we worry about organizing groups of people who do not appear to want to be organized?" Since World War II the labor agitator has been replaced by the labor statesman who hopes for more from White House dinners than from the picket line. Big Labor, represented by the Executive Council of the AFL-CIO, has worked hard over the last generation to integrate the unions into American life in return for a junior partnership with Big Business in shaping the national consensus.

The more integrated into national life a union movement becomes, Len De Caux observes, the less international it is likely to be. During the Cold War years, U.S. unions devoted considerable attention to foreign affairs (about a quarter of the AFL-CIO budget is spent out of the country), but these efforts involved taming foreign unions rather than assisting them to become an effective balancing force against large corporations. Working closely with the CIA through such operations as the American Institute of Free Labor Development, the U.S. labor movement helped check the power of Communist unions in Europe and helped build docile unions in Latin America. More than 70 global companies were happy to contribute to the budget of the AIFLD, for George Meany's organizing efforts in Latin America were the best possible insurance against the emergence of a radical homegrown union movement. It should be noted that Meany's motives were anti-Communism rather than a desire to help Big Business expand into the underdeveloped world free of local labor agitation. (The depth and persistence of his feelings are attested to by his attacks on President Nixon for being soft on Communism.) But the effect of the campaign was to create for the American labor movement exactly the wrong type of bureaucratic reputation and image for uniting the workers of the world to protect themselves against the global corporation.

Then too, some of the biggest global corporations have been impervious to union organization. IBM, Sears, and a number of other giants have a long history of successful resistance to organization from outside. An important part of the reason for this is that global oligopolies can pay higher wages than smaller domestic firms by passing on the costs to the consumer who has nowhere else to turn for his computers, toaster, or tractor. (The good oligopolist, it will be recalled, rarely stoops to price competition.) John Kenneth Galbraith argues that since "any conflict with labor [in the United States] can be resolved at the expense of third parties" there is "a greatly diminished tension" between workers and management in the giant companies, and until recently this has been true. In many parts of the world the employees of global companies constitute a labor aristocracy, with higher wages and more fringe benefits than are available elsewhere in the society, but the total number of these employees appears to be shrinking. Anaconda's and Kennecott's employees in Chile are a good example. Because they were used to highly preferential treatment, they presented a formidable problem to the Allende government in its efforts to bring greater equality into the Chilean economy. British subsidiaries of U.S.-based food, detergent, and pharmaceutical companies generally pay higher wages than local firms in the same industry. On the other hand, Herman Rebhan, director of international affairs for the United Auto Workers, argues that the global corporation's reputation for generosity is exaggerated and claims that "Philco [owned by Ford] pays less than domestic industries do in some underdeveloped countries." In general, however, companies like IBM that wish to exclude an outside union must pay more than the local going rate.

Despite the disadvantages of disorganization which hamper organized labor's response to the global corporation both in Europe and in the United States, some notable successes have already been scored. Most of these have occurred in Europe. When AKSO, N.V., announced plans to close three plants in the Netherlands, Belgium, and Germany, unions in those countries coordinated strikes which forced the company to abandon its plans. Dutch workers actually occupied the AKSO plant at Breda. The unions were also able to get the EEC Industries Commission to intervene against this proposed massive capital transfer. When Caterpillar refused to recognize an affiliate of the British Amalgamated Engineering Union in West Scotland, British union members went out on strike and forced the company to concede. A local in a German affiliate of Hoechst Chemicals successfully intervened to force the reinstatement of a union organizer in the firm's Turkish plant. During the 1970 strike at Ford's Dagenham plant, French and German workers refused a company request to work overtime, to make up for the production decline in England, as a gesture of solidarity with the British workers. The UAW successfully put pressure on Ford when Ford Venezuela fired a union activist. British unions have interceded with British Leyland in behalf of Chilean employees. There have been sympathy strikes by international affiliates in connection with labor disputes in such places as the Fiji Islands, India, Spain, Malta, and Senegal against such companies as British Petroleum, Michelin, Firestone, and Goodyear.

The stories of union success at international bargaining can be matched with a long list of failures. Affiliates of the International Federation of Chemical General Workers' Unions were unsuccessful in dissuading Michelin Tire from displacing a European plant with a new $100-million Canadian operation. When Dunlop Pirelli fired some of its Italian workers, the union's attempt to organize a worldwide strike netted exactly 60 strikers. In a survey of workers in Chrysler's Canadian plant, 53 percent of them said they would be willing to go on strike in support of American workers, with whom they have explicit mutual economic interests, but only 10 percent would take such a step for British workers and only 9 percent for Mexican workers. (However, 62 percent said they would be glad to give moral support to their Mexican brothers.)

Given the difficulties in transnational, transcultural labor organizing, only limited progress has been made in recent years. In Europe the secretariats of the International Metalworkers Federal, the International Federation of Chemical General Workers' Unions, and the International Union of Food and Allied Workers' Associations have led the drive for international bargaining with global companies. One key figure is Charles Levinson, secretary-general of the chemical workers' federation (ICF). They have succeeded in getting such imperious giants as Dunlop Pirelli, Nestlé's, and Philips to start talking with international-union officials. The broad media coverage of the worker occupation of the AKSO plant "set the cause of international unionism ahead two years," says Levinson. A few months later, Levinson's union forced Michelin, which in all its 83 years had never bargained with strikers, to negotiate with 130 workers at its Clermont-Ferrand plant. By organizing a World Michelin Council embracing 80 percent of Michelin's unionized employees in 12 countries,

Levinson was able to dissuade German and Italian workers from working Sundays to make up for the production halt at the French plant. British, Dutch, and German Ford workers have agreed not to work overtime where it could adversely affect a strike in any of the three countries. British and Dutch workers for Shell have made similar agreements. "We are getting local unions around Europe to back each other up," says Levinson, who claims support from 75 affiliated unions in 60 countries with a total membership of 4.5 million. "The time when the multi-nationals can deal arbitrarily with us is over," he says. But the optimism is excessive, for the international labor organization has little power.

The international secretariats are aware that they operate under a serious handicap. They are labor bureaucrats without a base in the factories themselves. And union officials who do have such a base are much readier to sacrifice the vision of international worker solidarity for a better contract at their own plant. For this reason, international-union officials are encouraging meetings between shop stewards of such global companies as Philips and Ford, but the lack of money for travel, translators, and facilities makes regular meetings at the grass-roots level difficult. Levinson is seeking to demonstrate to the union locals that international organization can provide indispensable services for their own bargaining efforts. The IMF and the ICF are computerizing information on the metal and chemical industries to supply locals with crucial information about pay scales and conditions of work in other parts of the employers' worldwide operations. Shell workers in the United States, striking for a voice in establishing health and safety conditions in the plant, can cite for American management what concessions Shell has made in the area in other parts of the world. Similarly, in Latin America unions can cite conditions in U.S. and European plants to bolster their argument in disputes on assembly-line speed or work breaks.

Although European unions are beginning to develop international strategies for combating the "runaway shop" and the "divide and rule" tactics of the global corporation, the idea of international labor councils in fact originated with the United Auto Workers. As early as 1956, Walter Reuther, who with his brother Victor was considerably ahead of the rest of the U.S. labor movement in appreciating the challenge of the global corporation, proposed the establishment of international auto councils representing Ford and General Motors employees in various parts of the world. The purpose was to raise standards in poorer countries and to move toward parity in working conditions. Six years later the first worldwide conference of auto workers was held in Frankfurt, and the first world auto council was established at Long Beach, California, in 1966. Unlike the AFL-CIO, which has relied on protectionist legislation as the primary weapon to halt the runaway shop, the UAW has tried to remove management's chief incentive for shifting production abroad by agitating for an end to coolie wages. The UAW has worked closely with the international-union secretariats in Geneva. (Levinson used to work for the auto union.) It has helped to reorganize the Japanese auto unions after a Communist-organized strike in the late 1950's was totally crushed by the Japanese auto companies. Although the small Japanese car has cut heavily into the U.S. market, the UAW has preferred to improve wages and working conditions in Japan rather than restrict Japanese cars in the United States. "We never looked upon Japanese workers as our enemies," says Herman Rebhan, head of the union's International Affairs Division. The union also trains labor leaders in Venezuela and in other parts of Latin America. The Americanization of business practices around the world has made the experience of the U.S. labor movement increasingly relevant to other labor movements and may in fact be leading to the Americanization of global labor relations. In Britain, for example, new legislation is bringing industrial relations more in line with U.S. practice. (Even union officials admit privately that Henry Ford had a point in his famous denunciation in 1970 of the British brand of labor chaos.)

The UAW is developing a new set of tactics for dealing with global corporations. One important objective is common worldwide contract-termination dates. A single termination date was achieved almost by accident in the United States when contracts in various companies expired one by one while the workers continued on their jobs without any contract. The union found that the common contract date greatly enhanced its bargaining position and is seeking to extend this advantage on a world scale. The UAW's preferred strike tactic is to close down only one or two plants rather than take on the entire industry. Herman Rebhan of the UAW points out that the tighter the integration of the production process, the more vulnerable a company becomes to worker intervention. For example, there are two key plants in Europe that supply all the transmissions for Ford's and GM's operations on the continent. A strike in these plants would bring production to a rapid halt.

Worldwide bargaining is the most important tactic for trying to overcome the structural advantages of the world corporation. It enables unions to internationalize demands, introducing ideas for improvement in working conditions in one country that have been successfully tried in another. But the companies are in a stronger position to centralize their worldwide bargaining efforts than the unions. General Motors' Detroit headquarters maintains a tight centralized control over bargaining anywhere in the world. All labor agreements, whatever the country, says Irving Bluestone, head of the UAW's General Motors Division, must be approved in Detroit before they go into effect. Ford, on the other hand, is more decentralized, although executives from Detroit regularly advise Canadian management on how to negotiate with the union. Moreover, in response to the growing cooperation among unions across national lines, a group of nine major global corporations, including Singer, Michelin, and General Electric, now pool information on international unions for use in developing negotiating strategies and are also coordinating their lobbying activities. (Recently 16 major global firms with major facilities or headquarters in New Jersey met with the New Jersey Congressional delegation to urge defeat of the Hartke-Burke bill.)

The argument for closing the gap between Ford workers in the Philippines and Ford workers in Detroit sounds radical at first, but, UAW officials point out, a policy of moving toward equal pay for equal work is eminently fair given the facts that the cost of the company's capital investment is the same in rich countries and poor and that the price at which the product is sold is approximately the same whether sold in a poor country or exported back to the United States. But humanization of working conditions, if achieved, although it would undoubtedly slow the exodus of plants from the United States, would not necessarily solve the problem of the runaway shop. Global companies do have other reasons besides low wages for going abroad. A docile labor force hamstrung by local antiunion legislation in Singapore is preferable to a discontented labor force in Lordstown even if you have to pay them approximately the same. In addition, tax holidays, avoidance of antipollution costs and local tariffs, and increasing the firm's share of the local market are also important reasons for moving production out of the United States which the UAW proposals for equalizing working conditions would not affect. Moreover, a world divided between an international labor aristocracy integrated into the global corporate economy and an unorganized army of the poor scratching for survival outside the factory gates is something less than an adequate alternative global vision.

4

Because of its relatively weak bargaining position vis-à-vis global corporations, the U.S. labor movement is demanding legislation to redress the balance. The AFL-CIO takes a tough protectionist line which it has sought to dramatize by its sponsorship of the Hartke-Burke bill, a tougher piece of legislation than is likely ever to be enacted. Corporate opponents of the bill like to emphasize the mandatory quota on imports it would impose, a measure that would turn the clock back to before 1934, when the United States first embarked on a program of progressive liberalization in trade. In the intervening years, free trade has become part of the holy writ of the American consensus, and thus in their crusade for understanding the corporations have little difficulty in portraying Meany as an antediluvian standing in the path of progress. (The fact that the UAW attacks the measure as protectionist too helps their case.)

But the heart of the law is its tax provisions, and these are harder to attack with lofty arguments about how free-trading corporations stop depressions and wars. In the last chapter we described how well global corporations fare under the current tax law. Tax incentives provided for U.S. corporations operating overseas amount to a $4-billion subsidy. *U.S. Oil Week* notes that, in 1972, 19 major oil companies paid a combined Federal tax of $685 million on combined income of $11.4 billion—an effective tax rate of 5.99 percent. "The larger the company the smaller the tax percentage," the magazine once observed, "because larger firms are involved abroad where royalties [paid to host governments] can sometimes be treated as federal income taxes" which qualify for the U.S. tax credit. Hartke-Burke would remove the foreign-tax credit and the tax-deferred provisions of present law and thus bring the tax burden of foreign-operating corporations more in line with that of the average citizen and smaller national firms who have no choice but to stay at home. For the corporations it is a very expensive reform, but one that is hard to oppose effectively in a country so concerned with high taxes and unequal taxes that the term "taxpayer revolt" is becoming a political cliché. (On the need to eliminate the tax incentives that encourage investment abroad at the expense of U.S. jobs, the UAW is fully in accord.)

The third major provision of Hartke-Burke is a grant of Presidential power to prohibit the export of capital and technology, presumably to prevent American firms from setting up China or Brazil as an archcompetitor in the next generation as they helped to set Japan up in the last and to spur technological innovation at home. The UAW also wants a licensing requirement for capital and technology exports:

> Licenses should be issued only when the investment can be shown to be in the interests of the people of the United States. The licenses should require the corporations to conform to a code of good behavior in relation to the foreign workers whom they employ and to guarantee full protection against loss of wages or fringe benefits to any of their American workers whose jobs or incomes might be adversely affected by the investment.

In addition, the UAW wants a special tax on "excessive profits" and criminal sanctions against corporations that "engage in speculation against the dollar." (The Nixon Administration's bill, by contrast, would end tax deferral on profits left abroad only for any *new* global corporate investment in tax havens used for substantial export to the United States, and then only if the President does not find the continuation of such privileges to be "in the public interest.")

Perhaps the most eagerly sought provisions concern adjustment assistance to workers who have lost jobs because their employers have disappeared to Italy or to Taiwan. Pointing out that since 1959, the year that marked the big push toward globalization of U.S. business, the U.S. unemployment rate has been running two and a half times that of its major trading partners (except Canada), Leonard Woodcock, president of the UAW, says that those who are put out of work by this process must be re-trained and relocated at government expense.

There is also a precedent for adjustment assistance in the United States in the legislation creating Amtrak, the new pas-senger-railroad system. Any worker laid off or downgraded as a result of changeovers in the railroad system is assured of full wages and fringe benefits for up to six years. Moreover, if he is transferred somewhere else, the government pays his moving expenses and compensates him for any loss he may incur in the forced selling of his home or the cancellation of his lease. Such provisions are no more than what most large corporations provide for their executives when they are transferred. Finally, he is en-titled to a retraining program at government expense. The only way the United States can eliminate its inefficient industries with-out victimizing workers, the UAW argues, is to establish similar benefits to help all affected employees to adjust to the new divi-sion of labor now taking place across the world.

Present legislation for adjustment assistance, Woodcock points out, is hopelessly inadequate. It took twenty months for 300 Chrysler workers laid off in 1971 to receive any help under exist-ing law. Under the Nixon Administration–proposed trade bill, Woodcock charges, "the majority of workers in manufacturing—those earning less than the average wage—would suffer cuts of nearly one-fourth in the benefits presently available to them if they should be displaced by imports. . . ." The global corpora-tions, on the other hand, tend to have liberal views on adjustment assistance. They recognize that the pockets of unemployment which they leave behind represent a serious political problem for them, one they are happy to solve with the taxpayer's money. Thus the U.S. Chamber of Commerce proposal for worker bene-fits is far more generous than the Administration proposals and is remarkably close to what the unions are demanding. A large minority in the Chamber, however, who represent domestic in-dustry, have tried to block the initiative.

The split within the Chamber is a concrete example of a wider division taking place in the United States between global corpo-rations and such national territorially based industries as textiles and glass. These latter industries, which claim they cannot sur-vive without legal curbs on imports from foreign competition, obviously prefer a solution that requires their competitor to pay a tariff rather than one that pays off displaced workers with tax dollars. Increasingly, this split is going to be mirrored in the union movement itself as the differing short-term interests of workers in the national and international sectors of the U.S. economy become more apparent.

The global companies have several lines of defense against the unions' demands to change the rules of the game through legislation. The battle of statistics to prove that overseas production creates jobs in the United States continues. On another front in the same battle, the companies argue that their imports into the United States are of marginal importance. (In 1970, according to the Senate Finance Committee, U.S.-owned foreign factories exported only $4.7 billion worth of goods to the U.S. market, or about 30 percent of total U.S. imports.) Then too, the companies like to argue that their foreign operations are a boon to the American consumer. There they are on weak ground, as the following price list for Westinghouse products made in the Far East suggests:

	Price in Japan	Price at U.S. Port	Suggested Retail Price in U.S.
Portable Radio (#RF43W07)	$17.88	$21.35	$ 59.95
AM-FM Tuner Amplifier (RCF9100)	31.74	38.80	159.95
Tape Recorder (TSC8020)	70.65	90.00	219.95

Source: See Notes for this page.

The theory that cheaply produced imports "discipline" prices in the United States can perhaps be sold to those U.S. consumers who manage to get along without radios, shoes, or cars. Nat Goldfinger of the AFL-CIO notes that between 1960 and 1970, a decade in which the U.S. shoe industry substantially moved abroad, prices of shoes in the United States rose 46 percent— nearly a third faster than the Consumer Price Index as a whole. (Such agribusiness firms as Del Monte and Heinz transferred a significant portion of their vegetable and fruit production from the United States to Mexico. They achieved considerable cost savings, but supermarket shoppers are well aware that prices have continued to rise. As we have noted before, the global oligopolies feel no compulsion to compete on prices or to pass on the extraordinary production saving achieved in Hong Kong to consumers in Dubuque or San Diego.)

The most powerful argument the global corporations can marshal against legislation to curb their power is that the attempt comes too late. American society is already so dependent on their activities that it cannot afford to curb them because the consequence would be economic chaos. The standard warnings—or threats, as labor calls them—of the global corporations are all too credible. If the U.S. Congress decided to undermine the present highly favorable world investment climate with some of labor's suggested reforms, business confidence would be shaken and the economy might well suffer. A depressed stock market, a drying up of new investment, and a substantial increase in unemployment are all possible consequences of a successful campaign to curb the global corporations. By spearheading such a campaign, the U.S. labor movement makes itself a candidate for national scapegoat. Labor's dilemma, the choice between doing nothing and watching jobs disappear, on the one hand, and risking an economic tailspin by fighting the giants, on the other, is symptomatic of a larger crisis.

5

The fundamental crisis of the American labor movement is a crisis of human obsolescence. In the global reorganization of production, the American worker has less and less of a role because the American standard of living requires wages which have priced him out of the world labor market and also in part because of automation. Both are contributing significantly to increasing structural unemployment. Even though labor is still a critical component in production, and competition in cutting wage costs is in many industries the key factor in the drive for higher profits, there is less work for human beings to do in the production process than in the past, at least as modern capitalist society defines work. Since production is an activity more efficiently carried out by a few than by many, the byproduct of efficiency and increased productivity is the superfluous man whose only social function is to consume.

Worker alienation is now a fashionable subject in the United States, and for good reason. In December 1972, the Department of Health, Education and Welfare published a report entitled "Work in America" which concluded that nearly half of American workers are dissatisfied with their jobs. Harold L. Sheppard and Neil Q. Herrick have concluded on the basis of an in-depth study of 400 male union workers that one-third of them hated their work and could not be persuaded to like it by the conventional rewards of factory life such as more money, shorter hours, or longer vacations. "Turnover rates are climbing," they point out. "Absenteeism has increased as much as 100 per cent in the past ten years in the automobile industry. Workers talk back to their bosses. They no longer accept the authoritarian way of doing things." In Lordstown, Ohio, 8,000 young auto workers walked out of GM's modern plant, where Vegas are produced on the fastest-moving assembly line in the world, not for money, but for a voice in shaping the workplace.

The decline in the work ethic is a favorite theme of the World Managers, who believe that if everyone in America worked as hard as they do the country could win the productivity battle with the Japanese and conquer unemployment too. But the decline in the work ethic is a direct consequence of changes in the nature of the task. "My dad always had pride in his work," steelworker Fidencio Moreno explained to a *Newsweek* interviewer. "When he'd come home, us kids would run up to him and say, 'How'd it go?' My dad always had pride in his work. He'd talk about all the things the customers would say and do. Me, I go home, they don't understand a damn thing. All I do is dump a little coal into an oven. Why would my wife or my kids be interested in that?" American workers are restless, the HEW report concludes, because of "dull, repetitive, seemingly meaningless tasks, offering little challenge or autonomy."

Worker alienation is a phenomenon that has invited a variety of explanations which differ according to the analysts' economic interest and political bias. George B. Morris, Jr., General Motors vice-president in charge of industrial relations, thinks there isn't much of a problem. "There's a lot of writing being done on this subject of 'alienation' by people who don't know what they are talking about." The conventional businessman's view is that if workers worked harder and complained less, they would be happier. But there are a growing number of top executives who, like GE Senior Vice-President Walter Dance, see "a potential prob-

lem of vast significance to all industrial companies . . ." Alienation, he told a GE stockholders' meeting, "involves a gut feeling
on their part that industrial society has left them with the dull,
hard, dirty jobs—and doesn't care." Union officials, aware that
the humanization of work opens up issues of industrial relations
far tougher and deeper than the traditional trade-union demands
on which labor bureaucrats have built their power, are skittish
about the subject. (After all, the reorganization of the workplace
might lead uncomfortably close to the reorganization of unions.
According to a recent poll, about the same proportion of workers
who are dissatisfied with their jobs are also dissatisfied with the
union leadership.) A few union spokesmen have preferred to
blame the lack of dignity and respect workers feel on the job on
academics who write about it rather than on the workplace itself.
But increasingly, despite what some union officials call the "elitist
nonsense" that pours forth from universities on the subject, more
and more of them are recognizing that "blue-collar blues" is a
real problem. Leonard Woodcock, once a skeptic, was so impressed by Volvo's experiments in job redesign that the UAW is
now actively pursuing its own experiments along these lines.

"Jobs haven't changed. People's expectations have," says
Professor Fred Foulkes of the Harvard Business School. Eighty
percent of the work force has now completed high school. The
worker has more leisure and more "discretionary income" than
the typical worker of 1940, who had an eighth-grade education.
Hence the revolution in rising expectations on the assembly line.
True as all this may be, jobs have changed. For one thing, the
United States has become a service economy. Shortly after the
turn of the century, the sociologist Daniel Bell notes, only three
in every ten workers were employed in service industries. By
1968, six out of ten were in the service sector; and by 1980, he
estimates, it will be close to seven out of ten. Employment in
manufacturing, mining, and agriculture will continue to fall.
(Between 1947 and 1968, almost half the agricultural workers
in the country left the farm.) The greatest growth industry in
the United States in the last generation has been government.
One out of every six Americans now works for some governmental bureaucracy. Within ten years, Bell calculates, no more
than 22 percent of the total labor force will be at work producing
goods in factories. (The Rand mathematician Richard Bellmann

GLOBAL REACH

goes so far as to predict that by the year 2000 only 2 percent of the labor force will be needed to produce all the goods Americans can use or sell.) The work force in the service economy is thus predominantly a white-collar force. In 1900, only 15 percent of American male workers wore a white collar on the job; in 1970, about 42 percent of the male labor force could be classified as having white-collar jobs.

Two questions arise. What role has the global corporation played in bringing about these enormous changes in the American labor force? What do these enormous changes have to do with worker discontent? The first question is much easier to answer than the second. The rationalization of production for profit by automation, whether on the farm or in the factory, has led to the growing obsolescence of the American worker. The globalization process has dramatically accelerated this predictable trend of advanced capitalist societies.

Daniel Bell has given a good description of what has happened in the industrial world of the global corporation:

> Skills are broken down into simpler components, and the artisan of the past is replaced by two new figures: the engineer, who is responsible for the layout and flow of work, and the semi-skilled worker, the human cog between machines—until the technical ingenuity of the engineer creates a new machine that replaces him as well. It is a world of coordination in which men, materials, and markets are dovetailed for the production and distribution of goods—a world of scheduling and programming, in which the components of goods are brought together at the right time and in the right proportions so as to speed the flow of goods. It is a world of organization—of hierarchy and bureaucracy—in which men are treated as "things" because one can more easily coordinate things than men. Thus a necessary distinction is introduced between the role and the person, and this is formalized on the organization chart of the enterprise. Organizations deal with the requirements of roles, not persons. The criterion of *techne* is efficiency, and the mode of life is modeled on economics: how does one extract the greatest amount of energy from a given unit of embedded nature (coal, oil, gas, water power) with the best machine at what comparative price?

Centralization of decision making, division of labor, and a management emphasis on the global balance sheet rather than product quality are the prime characteristics that distinguish the workplace in the Global Factory from the workshop of the early industrial era. For anyone tempted to romanticize those good old days, a dose of Charles Dickens, Theodore Dreiser, Upton Sinclair, or Friedrich Engels is a necessity. (Entrepreneurs were by no means always obsessed with giving good value, a point dramatized in Sinclair's *The Jungle*, but in earlier days, firms were forced to compete by selling quality.) Life was hard for workers in the era of long hours, low pay, and dirty work. But a large percentage of the work force in 1900 either grew things themselves or fashioned things by hand with the aid of relatively simple tools. For many there was at least a possibility of a personal identification with product that no longer exists, although the worker had less personal freedom, as measured by both free time and discretionary income. He had responsibility for whole operations in the manufacturing process. Because the task was not broken up into small components, as in the modern assembly process, a worker could feel that he spent his day creating something. Today the man who faces a high-speed assembly line consumes his day in intrinsically meaningless muscular twitches—for example, turning a screw or pulling heavy cases off a conveyor belt. He is a cog in a machine he never even gets to see. As John Johnson, an assembly-line worker in Chrysler's Lynch Road factory, puts it, "The jobs that you do degrade you. You don't feel like a man." The aluminum-and-glass warehouse on Park Avenue with its rows of steel desks and electric typewriters is the assembly line of the service economy. Clerks, secretaries, supervisors who spend their programmed days in exhausting routine are as alienated from the "service" they are supposed to be giving as the assembly-line worker is from the "production" to which he is making his tiny contribution.

In *The Hidden Injuries of Class*, Richard Sennett and Jonathan Cobb explore through a series of depth interviews the feelings of worthlessness that plague working people, feelings that have driven so many young workers to hard drugs. (In one Chrysler plant, a UAW official reports, 500 out of 4,000 workers are heroin addicts.) The feelings of injured dignity come not only from the meaninglessness of work but from the prevailing social climate which disparages manual labor and grants prestige only to marketable intellectual skills. The education for which their parents sacrificed, which was supposed to have brought freedom, has turned out to be the entrance requirement for a boring job. Feelings of inadequacy, Sennett and Cobb find, are reinforced by the daily routine of hierarchic organization with its insistent message from the top: "My time is more valuable than yours." The young worker internalizes the prevailing corporate myth that a person's worth is determined by his position in the hierarchy, and, while he may complain about "the system," in his heart he believes that his unfulfilled life is his own fault. If Daniel Bell and Alain Touraine are right in their predictions about a "post-industrial society" in which the growth of the economy is more and more dependent on the intellectual work of a few, feelings of meaninglessness are bound to increase. As Sennett and Cobb put it, ". . . to the extent that this linking of personal dignity and personal ability becomes *more* productive economically, estrangements from meaningful action are going to mark the tone of the culture ever more strongly." In short, the Global Factory, which represents the most rational and economically productive meritocracy in history, for that very reason offers the greatest affront to the human dignity of those on the bottom. To convert the superfluous, nonverbal worker of average intelligence into a pensioner by means of the guaranteed annual income or, as some have suggested, to award him an annual "consumer in residence" grant might keep him off the street, but it would solve none of these problems.

The managers of the global corporations, though they sometimes disparage them, are acutely aware of the human problems that increasingly affect the American work force. Another attraction for transferring U.S. production to underdeveloped countries is to escape the peculiar labor tensions of advanced industrial society. (Some firms are discovering, however, that they are merely replacing one set of tensions with another.) The World Managers are also casting an envious eye at the Japanese model of labor relations, which seems to encourage the Japanese national passion for work. In a sense, this model is a throwback to the paternalism of the company town. Corporate loyalty is built primarily through job security. Once hired, a worker knows that he will spend his life with the company. (There is, however, a class of temporary workers within large plants and in smaller sub-contractors who do not rate a lifetime job.) The worker sings the company song. He identifies himself publicly not by his profession but by his company. Workers and employers take company-paid trips together. Takeshi Hirano, president of one of Japan's biggest canning firms, attends at least ten employee weddings a month. Most firms have management–labor councils that discuss not only hours and wages but production rates, new machinery, and working conditions. The payoff, from management's view-point, is a strong team spirit. "We all have pride working here, knowing it is the most reputable supermarket in Japan," says Ni-roshe Naruse, a 29-year-old checker in Tokyo: a pledge of allegiance to stagger the mind of the executives of A&P. But in Japan too, worker alienation is increasing. The sort of labor unrest which the United States began to experience in the 1950's and Germany in the 1960's appears to be spreading to Japan in the 1970's.

However short-lived the paternalistic model of labor relations may turn out to be in Japan, U.S. executives are looking at it longingly. To win labor peace and even company loyalty from the workers, the introduction of day-care centers and recreational facilities into the plant is a small price to pay. Thomas Watson once wrote a company song for IBM, and other global companies, as we have seen, work hard building loyalty among the executive class. But the prospect of Harold Geneen doing morning setting-up exercises with his electricians or David Rockefeller picnicking regularly with his tellers, in the Japanese tradition, seems remote. The more likely strategy for obtaining labor peace in the United States is the judicious use of the threat of the runaway shop.

It is a sign of American labor's weak bargaining position that it is increasingly prepared to give up its principal weapon, the strike, to keep U.S. companies from moving out of the country. The National Maritime Union recently offered a no-strike pledge in an effort to keep at least some U.S.-owned shipping under the American flag. (It is now down to about 5 percent.) The United Steelworkers have adopted a no-strike pledge, in large part to encourage the steel industry not to leave the country. Another example of a new docility in American labor is the 1971 contract between the International Union of Electricians and GM's Frigidaire plant at Dayton, Ohio. After the company said that it was considering "relocating its plant outside the Dayton labor market," the union agreed to a two-year wage freeze and some wage reductions of up to $20 a week in return for GM's promise to rehire 850 workers and to stay in Dayton. The Shoe and Boot Workers Union sold a 1973 five-year contract with Stride-Rite shoes to the rank and file, even though it offered no wage or cost-of-living increase, by telling them it was necessary to keep the plant from moving out of the country. (GM likes to remind its Vega workers of the foreign competition by putting up signs in German and Japanese in its Lordstown plant.)

Increasingly, however, global companies are recognizing that the paternalistic model, even if it could be achieved, would not be enough to cure "blue-collar blues." There has also been a revival of interest in theories of "job enrichment" or the "humanization of work." Job enrichment is an industrial psychologist's term for making a job come closer to what Paul Goodman used to call "man's work." In the vernacular of the company's department of human behavior, it is a way of making jobs more "challenging," "rewarding," "fulfilling," or "self-actualizing." Professor David Sirota of the Wharton School lists five characteristics of job enrichment: greater responsibility; greater autonomy in carrying out responsibility; increased closure (doing the whole thing); more immediate feedback as to how well the worker has done; and more recognition for doing a job well. Stanley E. Seashore and J. Thad Barnowe, industrial psychologists, believe that since the blues (which they see as quite independent of collar color) "can be traced to features of the job and job setting that insult the ego . . . there are feasible, low-cost, low-risk ways to improve working conditions that matter most for workers." The AT&T experiments of the 1960's lend some support for their optimism. When telephone-company employees were permitted to write and sign their own letters answering customers' complaints or expressing sorrow about having to cut off their service instead of having the supervisor tell them what to write, their attitude toward their job brightened noticeably. But, as Sirota notes, most cases of worker discontent are not so easily handled. More recent experiments have had to go much further in giving workers responsibilities that were formerly restricted to supervisors and managers. The Gaines Dog Food plant in Topeka is

General Foods' effort to avoid the absenteeism and sabotage that plagued its Kankakee, Illinois, plant. A *Newsweek* report describes the plant this way:

> While it is highly automated, the plant is still burdened with a number of menial jobs with a sizable potential for boredom. So, to insure that both the rewarding and unrewarding jobs are shared equally, [management] devised a model workers' democracy. The employees are split into semiautonomous teams, ranging in size from six to seventeen, depending on the operation. Each team selects its own foreman and, at the start of each shift, determines how to meet production quotas, divides up job assignments and airs grievances. Moreover, each worker is trained to do practically any job in the plant, from filling bags on an assembly line to monitoring the complicated controls of machines that cook and mix the pet food.

The worker teams put pressure on slackers and malingerers and help solve one another's personal and family problems. Everybody, regardless of status, eats at the same cafeteria, and the plant manager plays Ping-Pong with workers at lunch. The payoff for the company in worker morale and in reduced absenteeism is impressive. Similar experiments are being carried out by Travelers Insurance, Corning Glass, and Motorola. (In Corning's Medford plant, worker teams setting their own production goals increased production by 20 percent.)

But "job enrichment" is neither a low-cost nor a low-risk panacea for the companies. As Sirota points out, the problem at Lordstown was principally one of old-fashioned speedup. It takes a lot of Ping-Pong to get workers to adjust to an assembly line in which a car comes flying past them for their quick attention every 36 seconds. But slowing down the production line means higher costs. Giving workers management functions also involves risks for the companies which are just beginning to appear. American workers and the American union movement, while more vociferous in demanding a bigger share of the pie than European workers, have been notably less interested in a voice in baking it. Workers' management and workers' control are traditional ideas in Europe because the French, German, and Italian unions have socialist roots. (The fact that many workers'-management schemes actually dilute company prerogatives very little is another matter.) Most U.S. unions continue to disavow interest in sharing management functions. They have also looked skeptically at "job enrichment" schemes as a company tactic for co-opting workers and reducing the power of the union. Recently, however, the UAW is cooperating in an experimental project in an auto-mirror plant in Bolivar, Tennessee.

Any experiment that fundamentally changes the decision-making process in the plant is as much a challenge to unions as it is to the companies, but it is a challenge that some of the more forward-looking unions may be prepared to accept. Once companies begin to see the explosive potential of real changes in the structure of the workplace, they may well lose their enthusiasm for "job enrichment." There is some evidence of this already. When the employees at Kaiser's failing plant in Fontana, California, took over essential management functions and turned the operation around, Kaiser executives were delighted. But when some of the workers began to reason that if they were acting like management they should be paid as management, the executives saw trouble. The price of ending worker alienation may be a generation unwilling to increase productivity for the benefit of a $200,000-a-year executive class and the portfolios of banks, insurance companies, and pension funds.

6

The obsolescence of American labor must be seen as a part of a world problem. In the Global Factory there is a steadily declining need for human hands. England, for example, has suffered a tremendous increase in unemployment among industrial workers since it became a nerve center for international banking. "The very strength of the cosmopolitan activities," the economist Robert Rowthorn observes, "has helped to undermine its strictly domestic economy." True, the distribution of labor around the world is uneven. There are areas, such as Taiwan, Brazil, and Korea, that have a shortage of skilled labor. (Taiwan has even begun to restrict certain kinds of foreign investment for this reason. T. W. Hu, its economic counselor in Washington, who takes an extraordinarily international view of these matters, is advising U.S. firms to bring more capital-intensive technology to the island, since the current labor shortage is driving wages for

young female employees at General Instruments from $25 a
month to $35 a month.)

In the 1960's, Western Europe's economic boom drew millions
of migrant workers from Italy, Turkey, and Yugoslavia. But
industrial Europe is now finished with its need for temporary help
and is anxious to get rid of them. If history is any guide, the employment boom which some areas of the underdeveloped world
are now enjoying may prove to be temporary, and they may
themselves not escape the automation of their own industries.
This despite the real efforts at "reverse engineering" now going
on in these areas to take advantage of the abundance of cheap
labor. Some hint of this possibility is provided by recent experience in the Mexican border area. When a group of plants just
over the Rio Grande which had been surveyed in 1967 were revisited two years later, it was discovered that about half of them
had already been closed down.

American labor has lost much of the "countervailing power" it
built up in the 1930's and 1940's because companies have
learned how to erode it by pitting their international mobility
against the unions' immobility. Nationalism and protectionism
are weak reeds on which to construct a strategy for a labor come-
back. Although there is an economic logic today uniting the
workers of the world that did not exist when Marx coined his
famous slogan, the prospects for global unions organized for
worldwide bargaining are not promising.

The global corporation confronts the unions with essentially
the same challenge it has posed to government—the structural
lag. Like regulatory agencies, the principal institutions for labor
bargaining were devised for a simpler day when the global spread
of big business was not even imagined. As a result of the transformation of the world economy, organized labor is losing power
in its struggle to protect the interests of workers. As we saw in
the last chapter, the mobility of capital and the immobility of
labor and government are adversely affecting income distribution
in the United States and causing serious structural unemployment. As a result, the economic security of the average American
is threatened.

12

The Ecology of Corporations and the Quality of Growth

1

The transcendent debate of the 70's concerns not socialism, but growth. Indeed, it is asserted by partisans on various sides of the debate that all the great social issues inherited from less apocalyptical times, such as justice, democracy, and freedom, can be resolved only through a sensible attitude toward the growth of human institutions. The practical problems of politics are thus problems of scale. Humanity must find an appropriate scale for its political and economic institutions, or it will eventually be crowded out of existence or drowned in its own waste. The debaters differ only on what is sensible—less growth or more growth.

The exponents of growth limitation are immoderate in their analyses, predictions, and rhetoric, and hence are much the more interesting. (In contrast, the growth advocates speak in the familiar tones of official complacency.) The celebrated Club of Rome study *Limits to Growth* states flatly, on the basis of computer calculations, that "the limits of growth on this planet will be reached sometime within the next hundred years." (The electronic oracle spits out a timetable of doom. Tungsten will be exhausted in 40 years, the demand for chromium will exceed the supply in 235 years, etc.) The only answer, says the computer, is a zero-growth economy. Developed countries must merely replace their depleted capital and human resources without accumulating more of either. Since a policy of "no growth" is unlikely to commend itself to poor countries which have been taught that

334

their survival depends upon growth, they are to be induced to cooperate by grants of $1,800 per head from the rich countries. The proposal is eminently attackable on grounds of social justice, practicability, and the methodology undergirding its analysis. But the alarmist message, if exaggerated, has the ring of truth. "Industrial man in the world today is like a bull in a china shop," states the manifesto of British environmental scientists, "A Blueprint for Survival." By continuing his age-old mission to conquer nature, he is "reducing it to rubble in the shortest possible time. Continued exponential growth of consumption materials and energy," the British scientists warn, is impossible. The deterioration of the quality of air and water throughout the industrializing world, the ecological imbalance caused by such milestones in the march of progress as inorganic fertilizers and insecticides, and the increasing threat to the life-support systems of the ecosphere are so well documented in hundreds of sober reports, and in many cases so easily sniffed and tasted, that they are no longer debatable. "A Blueprint for Survival," echoing *Limits to Growth*, calls for a "stable society."

The exponents of the "greater growth" economy like to ridicule the prophets of doom. Against the oracular arrogance and apocalyptical passion of the latter they have mobilized the power of positive thinking. Technology will rescue its inventors. President Nixon believes that "the inventive genius that created those problems in the first place" will solve them. David Rockefeller is confident that "we can afford the kind of environment we want once you and I and all of us have agreed to work harder at our jobs." Liberal and conservative economists alike denounce "zero growth" as a plan to preserve existing inequalities, to consign the poor countries to permanent underdevelopment, and to condemn future generations to rising unemployment. (Some add a caustic word to the effect that all this is to be courted merely to suit the aesthetic sensibilities of upper-middle-class intellectuals and nature lovers.) Since a significantly more equitable division of the world economic pie is patently improbable, the growth advocates argue, people at the bottom have no hope but to trust that bigger pies yield bigger crumbs. Societies, they point out, have no choice but to grow. In the lexicon of the modern corporation and the modern nation-state alike, the opposite of growth is death. The "stationary state" that John Stuart Mill pondered well over a hundred years ago, however aesthetically appealing, is simply not possible.

The positive thinkers seek to refute the prophets of doom by emphasizing society's capacity to correct its ecological excesses and to restore the proper balance between nature and modern industrial growth. They like to make the eminently plausible point that it is the quality of growth more than its rate that determines whether man and nature will remain at war. The raison d'être of the global corporation is planning for growth on a global scale. It is the institution with the most direct responsibility for producing malignant growth in modern society, and accordingly, under the present system, it is the one institution on which hopes for benign growth must rest.

In this chapter we shall be exploring the quality of growth generated by the global corporation, particularly its impact upon American society. We shall be trying to describe the specific quality of the special sort of growth produced by global firms and to understand something of the relationship between the structure of the firm and its products. Our attention will be focused on three quite different sorts of products. First, because the issue of growth is now so tangled with the pollution debate, we shall start with an examination of the waste products that escape from factories—i.e., the impact of corporate expansion on the environment. Specifically, what is there about the sort of goods global firms produce and the way they produce them that contaminates the environment? More important, does the structure of the firm permit the introduction of significantly less polluting technologies? Can technology rescue its inventors via the global corporation?

Second, after looking at these involuntary products of global corporations we shall focus on the products which they intend to turn out. What effect do the internal drives of the corporation for profits, growth, and security have on the quality of the goods they put on the market? In short, in determining the character of his productivity, how responsive is the global oligopolist to social needs in America, and how responsive can he be?

Finally, we shall be looking at the kind of human growth big corporations foster. In the last chapter we focused on the psychological and spiritual costs of division of labor for people who work on assembly lines or in robot jobs in offices. Here we shall be looking at the executive class of the global corporation. These men (and an occasional woman) are America's principal planners. What possibilities for personal growth does the corporation afford them? And what impact do career pressures within the firm have on the kind of social planning for America which this executive class is able to do?

2

The issues of growth—how much, how fast, what kind—are the crucial questions surrounding the future of the global corporation. We have discussed in this book a variety of instabilities and inequities associated with corporate growth. Theoretically, all are correctable, at least to some extent. But the ecological problems of growth pose a more fundamental challenge. If the social costs of infinite corporate growth—pollution, concentration of power, inequitable income distribution—are as high as they appear to be, our social system cannot support indefinitely so upsetting an institution. To talk about global corporations that do not grow or that voluntarily limit their growth is to talk about a fundamental transformation of that institution which defies both its own basic ideology and the laws of oligopolistic competition: the struggle for ever-increasing shares of the market; the use of cross-subsidization to expand new and bigger markets; and, the oligopolist's golden rule, "Do as the others do, but more so."

Thus limitless, exponential expansion has been a necessity for corporate survival. The strategies for maintaining the rate of expansion are familiar. The ever-increasing use of advertising stimulates ever-greater demand. The availability of consumer debt, which now stands at $170 billion and represents a $2,200 burden for the average family earning $11,000 a year, makes it possible to sell more goods than people have current income to buy. The restless search for novelty creates needs people did not know they had. The development of throwaway products—from Kleenex to Fords—ensures an infinitely renewable demand. The continuous speedup in transportation and communication means that more goods can reach more people ever more rapidly.

That corporations control technology and that air, water, noise, and visual pollution are a direct consequence of the way corporations have been using technology need no demonstration.

Smoke, heat, empty beer cans, chemical and nuclear wastes are
the byproducts of technological development, and technological
development is the principal dynamic of corporate growth. All
this is clear enough. What is less clear is why corporations grow
the way they do.

Technological determinism has acquired the status of a folk
cult shared, as Barry Commoner has pointed out, by technophiles
and technophobes alike. According to Simon Ramo, founder of
TRW, a successful high-technology firm, technology is an instrument for predicting the future and solving social problems. Because man "must now plan on sharing the earth with machines,"
he must "alter the rules of society, so that we and they can be
compatible." Those who fear the "technological takeover" also
endow technology with its own "laws" and its own "imperatives."
But such Frankensteinian metaphors obscure reality. What looks
like a "technological imperative" is in fact the result of a series
of human decisions. Men decide to make machines and they
decide how they shall be used. Most of the decisions are now
made in global corporations.

What is the relationship between corporate organization and
the kinds of decisions that produce malignant growth? A careful
examination of the quality of economic growth in the United
States over the last generation offers some answers. From 1946
to 1971, pollution levels in the United States rose anywhere from
200 to 2,000 percent, while total production rose only 126 percent. Barry Commoner has calculated that during this period the
output of certain crucial sectors of production grew at many
times that rate and that these sectors contributed crucially to the
energy drain and the rise in pollution. Some examples: nonreturnable soda bottles, up 52,000 percent; synthetic fibers, up
5,980 percent; mercury for chlorine production, up 3,930 percent; electric power, up 530 percent; electric housewares (can
openers, blenders, corn poppers, etc.), up 1,040 percent. At the
same time, he calculates, production of food, textiles, clothing,
household utilities, steel, copper, and other base metals grew at
about the same rate as the population (about 42 percent). The
essence of the extraordinary change in the U.S. economy since
World War II is that "new production technologies have displaced old ones." Synthetic detergents for soap, synthetic fibers
for natural fibers, aluminum, plastics, and concrete for steel and

lumber. "In general," Commoner concludes, "the growth of the U.S. economy since 1940 has had a surprisingly small effect" on basic human needs:

> That statistical fiction, the "average American," now consumes, each year, about as many calories, protein, and other foods (although somewhat less of vitamins); uses about the same amount of clothes and cleaners; occupies about the same amount of newly constructed housing; requires about as much freight; and drinks about the same amount of beer (twenty-six gallons per capita!) as he did in 1946. However, his food is now grown on less land with much more fertilizer and pesticides than before; his clothes are more likely to be made of synthetic fibers than of cotton or wool; he launders with synthetic detergents rather than soap; he lives and works in buildings that depend more heavily on aluminum, concrete, and plastic than on steel and lumber; the goods he uses are increasingly shipped by truck rather than rail; he drinks beer out of nonreturnable bottles or cans rather than out of returnable bottles or at the tavern bar. He is more likely to live and work in air-conditioned surroundings than before. He also drives about twice as far as he did in 1946, in a heavier car, on synthetic rather than natural rubber tires, using more gasoline per mile, containing more tetraethyl lead, fed into an engine of increased horsepower and compression ratio.

The harmful environmental effects of these technological changes are easily demonstrated. The technology of agribusiness, feedlots, inorganic fertilizers, and synthetic pesticides has upset the ecological balance in many ways. Synthetic nitrogen fertilizers make it possible to grow more crops on less land—but the farmer, as Commoner points out, "must use more nitrogen than the plant can take up. Much of the leftover nitrogen leaches from the soil and pollutes the rivers." Because the use of chemical fertilizers kills off nitrogen-fixing bacteria which are the source of natural nitrogen fertilizer, the buyer literally becomes "hooked" on the product because in using it he has "wiped out the competition." Similar harmful environmental effects and similar dependency follow from the use of synthetic pesticides.

Detergents, synthetic fabrics, and organic chemicals have had a powerful and negative impact on the environment. The "brightener" in detergents, a light-reflecting additive which makes clothes look whiter but does nothing to remove dirt, uses about three times the energy needed to produce oil for soap manufacture. In his *Introduction to the Chemical Process Industries,* an engineering textbook, R. M. Stephenson points out that there is "absolutely no reason why old-fashioned soap cannot be used for most household and commercial cleaning." But detergents have largely swept laundry soap from the supermarket shelf, with a resulting twentyfold increase in polluting phosphates in rivers, lakes, and seashores. Synthetic fibers too require more energy to produce than natural fibers, through a process that gives off intense heat and renders the fiber nonbiodegradable—i.e., it must be burned, thereby adding to air pollution, or it must be added to the nation's already staggering rubbish heap. The heavy, gas-gorging automobile requires a highly toxic tetraethyl lead additive to suppress engine knock which is a direct result of the extraordinary increase in engine power. As automobile engines have become more "efficient"—i.e., as their compression ratio has increased—the emission of smog-producing nitrogen oxide has also increased (about seven times during the years 1946–1970).

There are numerous other examples of the contaminating and energy-draining consequences of industrial progress. What emerges is a clear pattern of decisions made by the leading corporate controllers of technology that has led to the increase of pollution and the squandering of resources at a geometric rate. Why? It is obvious that corporate executives, who cannot escape breathing a little city air on the way to the office and also heat their homes with oil and gas, are not deliberately trying to foul the environment or exhaust the resources. The World Managers pride themselves on being consummate planners, and the implications of an escalating environmental crisis for future profits, to say nothing of executive comfort, is by now fairly obvious. Yet the polluting technologies grind on.

The principal reason why global corporations, agribusiness, soap companies, automobile manufacturers, and chemical producers have developed pollution-prone technologies is that it has been very much in their short-run interest to do so. Two notable characteristics of the new technologies have been increased output per unit of labor and increased profit rates (based on sales). In 1947, when the soap industry sold soap, the profit rate was 30 percent of sales. In 1967, when the industry was selling two boxes of detergent for every box of soap, the profit rate had risen to 42 percent. During the same period, the labor input has been cut by 25 percent for the industry. The Product Life Cycle, which we have seen amounts to a law of life for the oligopolistic firm, means that the corporation must constantly innovate to maintain or increase its market share for the purpose of keeping its profits high. (The profits on pure detergents, Commoner calculates, are about 52 percent.)

In the chemical industry the drive for profits has also led to a rapid rate of innovation and product replacement—and an unusually high profit rate. As J. Backman writes in *The Economics of the Chemical Industry*, "The maintenance of above average profit margins requires the continuous discovery of new products and specialties on which high profit margins may be earned while the former products in that category evolve into commodity chemicals with lower margins." Commoner calls this rapid rate of innovation in the chemical industry "an ecologist's nightmare," for the speed in moving new products to the market means "there is literally not enough time to work out its ecological effects." Similarly, the use of soil-depleting nitrogen fertilizers produces much quicker and higher profits than soil-restoring natural fertilizers. The profit on a high-powered, high-polluting $3,000 car, according to *Fortune* magazine, is twice as high as on a lower-powered $2,000 car. (Henry Ford II remarked not long ago that "minicars make miniprofits.") In most cases in which new environmentally destructive technologies have replaced less destructive technologies, there has been a significant increase in profitability.

Rising ecological damage is thus a direct consequence of the quest for ever-increasing profits. Expansion through innovation for quick return appears to involve heavy social costs (mostly environmental) that never show up in the company's annual statement. The costs of ruined land, depleted resources, filthy water, and foul air must eventually be paid by consumers, shareholders, employees, and their children. In many cases, this is a debt that cannot be paid with money.

The experience of the Soviet Union suggests that the crucial explanation of the pollution process has more to do with a country's value system than any other aspect of its social system. Despite the near-universal public ownership of the means of production, a primary planning goal, as in most other socialist countries, is increased individual consumption, a political priority which demands ever-increasing productivity without regard to social costs. The dead fish floating in Lake Baikal and the Dniester River make it clear that ostensibly socialist planned economies are also prepared to sacrifice the environment and upset the natural balance in order to accumulate more goods at lower economic cost. Productivity without regard to its ecological effects in order to satisfy "needs," whether they are programmed by a government planning agency or by a corporation's advertising department, is a recipe for environmental disaster. The little we know of the Soviet Union's machinery for evaluating and compensating for social costs in the industrial process suggests that it does not work very well. In the effort to catch up with the United States, the Soviets have emulated the polluting technologies of the capitalist countries. For any underdeveloped country there is an extraordinary temptation to do this to increase productivity and the short-run supply of scarce goods.

But the failure of alternative systems such as those of the Soviet Union and Yugoslavia to alter the quality of growth so as to reduce social costs should not obscure the fact that the ideology and structure of the global corporation effectively prevent it from even considering the social costs of growth in its competitive race to increase productivity. The prime examples of malignant economic growth are all the result of a failure to "think holistically," as René Dubos and other natural and social scientists have put it. The organization of technology in the modern corporation means that problems are broken down into components and solved one by one. The basis of corporate efficiency, as we have seen, is a highly advanced stage of division of labor. As Galbraith has put it, "Nearly all the consequences of technology, and much of the shape of modern industry, derive from this need to divide and subdivide tasks."

The disastrous ecological effects of modern technology are a direct result of their economic success. Pesticides, artificial fertilizers, new chemical processes, high-powered automobiles all do what they are supposed to do. They kill bugs, increase yields, step up manufacturing productivity, and offer speed and excitement to suburbanites. But each has unintended consequences which corporate engineers and managers are paid not to think about. The interest of the corporation is to ignore and, where necessary, to obscure such consequences. Taking account of the social costs of production, not to mention paying for them, means lower productivity and lower profits. Corporate employees, despite a certain amount of rhetoric to the contrary, are not paid to exercise "social responsibility." Those who are responsible for the productive process are encouraged to keep their nose to the assembly line and to leave the big picture to others.

Indeed, using productivity as their standard, companies find it easier to invest in a campaign to fight pollution controls than to invest in new technology for reducing pollution. Lobbying and public relations expenses can be defended in the corporate hierarchy as a legitimate cost of maintaining productivity, since if Congress does impose higher standards within a short period of time, productivity will fall. (More money will have to be spent to produce the same number of cars, and some of this expense, at least, will have to be absorbed by the companies instead of the customers.) To redesign technologies in which billions have already been invested to make them conform to ecological requirements means giving up the profits on already-paid-for plant and equipment and takes huge, often open-ended investments in research and development, without a promise of any increase in total profits. Safety, health, and environmental impact are not big sellers.

With respect to pollution control, there is a sharp and growing conflict between corporate managers and the public. The raison d'être of the corporation is growth principally through increased productivity. Ecological survival appears to require a qualitatively different sort of growth, probably at a lower rate, to be accomplished by technological innovations which, in the short run at least, will reduce the productivity of individual firms. The battle is already joined. David Rockefeller believes that "unrealistic pollution abatement costs on industry" will mean that the United States will price itself out of world markets and that jobs will suffer. ". . . it seems clear that we will be forced to step up our productivity through ever improved technology."

He has put his finger on a real social dilemma. In a world of oligopoly competition, no single nation dares impose significantly greater antipollution costs on its own corporations than the other

GLOBAL REACH

advanced industrial nations are prepared to impose. But the chairman of Chase Manhattan Bank appears to believe the answer to this most global of problems lies in "individual sacrifices in comfort and convenience." Father should walk to work. Mother should wash at night, when industrial uses of power are lightest. Son should trade his electric guitar for an acoustic model. Daughter should eschew insecticides and put up with a few bites at her picnic. But production should increase. The call to self-sacrifice would no doubt have pleased David Rockefeller's Baptist grandfather, who also believed in personal thrift and corporate extravagance. But the heart of the pollution problem is the technology for making and marketing goods, and that is firmly under the control of corporations with no incentive to pay the price to change the quality of growth. (It is perhaps worth noting that the electric guitars and washing machines of New York City, along with all other household uses, account for 25 percent of the city's annual electricity requirements. Round-the-clock lighting and air conditioning at the Chase Manhattan Bank and the other commercial buildings account for 44 percent of the energy drain.)

Many companies are spending more on advertising their concern or, as in the case of one major phosphate producer, in proclaiming the inevitability of pollution, than they spend on controlling their contaminating wastes. While it is not uncommon to read in an annual report that the company is spending anywhere from $10 million to $50 million on pollution control, it is seldom noted (as U.N. environmental expert John G. Welles points out) that such impressive sums usually represent about 1 to 2 percent of sales. The Dow Chemical Company has been one of the corporate leaders in developing global pollution-control guidelines and has made heavy investments in pollution-abatement procedures. Dow's chairman, Carl A. Gerstacker, believes that "we can save enough money [in pollution control] so that we can at least break even or get the job done—on balance—at no net cost." Many managers of other global corporations are skeptical of Dow's claims. John Welles interviewed about one hundred managers of global companies on pollution questions and summarizes their common dilemma: "Of course we should do more to clean up our pollutants, but how can we afford to when our competition at home and abroad won't?" Particularly for old plants, the cost of abating pollution is likely to be prohibitive. For "very high polluting plants such as nonferrous metals smelting and refining operations," Welles's research suggests, "pollution havens" in the underdeveloped world are going to provide an answer. (In Mexico City's English-language newspaper the State of Mexico advertises for polluters: "RELAX. WE'VE ALREADY PREPARED THE GROUND FOR YOU. If you are thinking of fleeing from the capital because the new laws for the prevention and control of environmental pollution affect your plant, you can count on us." The use of "pollution havens" is already well advanced. There are dozens of refineries along the 1,700-mile Caribbean coast. One petrochemical complex on the south coast of Puerto Rico belches smoke clouds as far as 90 miles away. The lovely island of St. Croix, according to the president of the Caribbean Conservation Association, "now gets oil spills two to three times a week.")

But neither "pollution havens," public relations campaigns, nor the relatively modest investments they can afford to make in pollution control will solve the problem for the global corporations. As one official of a waste-disposal firm told Welles, "The presidents of some of the largest firms in the world point with pride in their speeches about what they are doing to clean up the environment. What they don't know is that some of their plant superintendents are still dumping poison into the rivers or sending them out the stacks . . . at night." Particularly in the case of the older plants which are the worst polluters, balance-sheet-conscious executives are unwilling to spend the money to clean them up unless, as one of them told Welles, "we have a gun at our head in the form of a government regulation we know is about to be enforced. And then we may decide we should close down the plant."

The managers of the largest firms are expending considerable energy to make sure that the gun is never loaded. Laurance S. Rockefeller is chairman of a Citizens' Committee charged with advising the President on environmental matters from the public's point of view. The National Industrial Pollution Control Council, on which sit 63 chief executives of major firms, is, according to testimony of political scientist Henry Steck before the Senate Subcommittee on Intergovernmental Relations, "performing a kind of propaganda role for the industry." The use of industry spokesmen to make policy recommendations on pollution con-

trol, he suggests, is a little like putting the town madams on a
Vice Control Committee. There is no particular reason why a
president of Procter & Gamble, who heads the NIPCC's Detergents Subcouncil, should be especially alert to the dangers of
suds. The same invincible logic that puts weapons manufacturers
in the Pentagon and bankers in the Treasury is now making environmental caretakers of some of the nation's leading polluters.
Their expertise is undeniable, but their incentive to assess "industry's fair share" of the cost of environmental reform is open to
doubt. The fact that environmental policy is so clearly tailored
to the interests of the global corporations reflects a continued
national commitment to traditional forms of growth. Nothing
suggests the power of the corporations so clearly as their continuing ability to spend the social capital of the nation—its air,
water, and earth—for the accumulation of finance capital.

3

As we have noted, private productivity is both the test of
economic success for a corporation and the justification for its
assault on nature. Without the corporate passion for growth, so
the argument goes, we would not have the goods to satisfy human
needs. But it is clear that productivity, no less than growth, deserves a qualitative definition. As many have observed, needs are
assessed and met in contemporary America in eccentric ways.
Dogs are well fed, and an estimated 20 million people are hungry.
(Paul Ehrlich points out that official U.S. nutritional standards
for dog food are higher than those for many human foods, and
for this reason it is a staple for many poor families in America.)
The three soap companies who share the market offer the consumer a dazzling array of virtually indistinguishable products,
but there is a housing shortage, a lack of medical facilities, and
a reluctance to invest in nonpolluting technologies. Many theories
for these seemingly skewed priorities of production have been
offered. The explanation of the neoclassical economist, based on
the creed that the market is alive and well and the customer is
king, is unlikely to convince any but other true believers that
human beings really prefer lipsticks to breathable air, or that for
cars, drugs, televisions, or airplane rides there remains anything
that resembles a classical market.

John Kenneth Galbraith has developed a much more plausible

theory. The big corporation, by virtue of its size and power, can create and control the market. Large corporations, he points out, constitute a "planning system" in the U.S. economy. They determine what customers shall eat, drink, wear, and smoke and how their homes shall look and, within broad limits, what price they shall pay for what they buy. We now turn to the question of how this power is used. Specifically, what is the connection between the growth of the global corporation and the kind of products it puts on the market and their cost? Is the huge firm, as its proponents like to argue, able to offer the consumer better products at lower cost than smaller firms?

There is an immense and complicated economics literature about the relative efficiency and inefficiency of bigness. The proponents of bigness argue that the larger the firm the greater the economies of scale that can be achieved, the greater the ability to innovate, and hence the greater the output at the least cost. But there is considerable contrary evidence which can only be suggested here. In 1959, Professor Joe S. Bain studied optimal plant size in various industries and concluded that the efficiency to be achieved through concentration varied considerably from industry to industry. (The optimal plant size in the automotive industry was 20 percent of the market, but in cigarettes, meat packing, petroleum, soap, and rubber it was less than 5 percent. The actual concentration in all these industries is, as we have seen, considerably higher.)

In analyzing the question whether the sort of corporate growth that caused 4,550 firms to disappear in 1969 alone and has concentrated close to two-thirds of the nation's manufacturing assets in 200 companies is "efficient" or "inefficient," we need to look a little more closely at these favorite words of the economist's art. A system can work very efficiently for some people and not for others. The most usual meaning of corporate "efficiency" is that by virtue of good management, oligopolistic advantages, innovative breakthroughs, luck, or some combination of all of them, productivity is high and the shareholders are getting an uncommonly high return on their investment. John Kenneth Galbraith, in a spirit more of resignation than of enthusiasm, argued in *The New Industrial State* that since only the large organization with teams of specialists can successfully market "culturally exciting" inventions (the pop-up toaster was his prime example), they will end up with an ever-increasing share of the consumer's dollar and will achieve higher profits than smaller firms without similar advantages. Thus there is a "technological imperative" in favor of bigness.

It is true that a number of the top 200 firms, virtually all of which are global corporations, have made exceptionally high profits during the postwar boom years. But John M. Blair, former chief economist of the Senate Subcommittee on Antitrust and Monopoly, notes that in a study of 30 industries, increasing size was accompanied by rising profit rates in slightly less than a quarter of them. "In the other three-quarters the tendency was either in the opposite direction or there appeared to be no relationship whatever. Since a higher rate could be the result of either superior efficiency or greater monopoly power, the failure of the companies with presumably the greatest monopoly power to earn the highest rates suggests the possibility that they may be even less efficient than their smaller rivals."

Caspar W. Weinberger, Secretary of HEW in the Nixon cabinet, believes that the acquisition by the giants of "established, healthy firms, making good profits" is "a matter of concern not only for competition but for social and political institutions." Such concern is reinforced by the studies of Johan Bjorksten, who finds that in one out of every six mergers involving manufacturing firms the acquired firm went out of business. It is hard to argue that the disappearance of talent and productive facilities is a contribution to national efficiency even where it may simplify the life of the managers of the acquiring firm.

Promoters and managers of large corporations have an interest in accelerating size which the public does not necessarily share. Galbraith correctly points out that sheer size constitutes a "bureaucratic advantage" for what he calls the "technostructure"— i.e., the managers, marketeers, and technicians who run large corporations. Like an expanding army, a mushrooming technostructure guarantees plenty of room at the top. A force of 400,000 employees deployed around the world plausibly entitles the commander-in-chief of ITT to a salary one hundred times that of the privates on the assembly line. As disappointing as the returns to the shareholders have been in many conglomerates, the empire builders themselves have not done badly. (Indeed, the only way for the modern entrepreneur to amass a personal fortune in his

lifetime, short of inventing Xerox, is to put together a conglomerate.)

The bigger the corporation, the bigger the company airplane,
the higher the salary, and the more indistinguishable from owners
top managers become. Moreover, the more diversified the firm,
the more security it achieves, at least until it overreaches itself in
the manner of LTV and Litton. (In industrial empires, no less
than political empires, sweeping decisions made at a distance,
often with the aid of comforting but misleading analogies, do not
always produce the best results.) ITT, which grew from forty-
seventh to ninth place among U.S. corporations in ten years, puts
its eggs in many widely disparate baskets under the theory that
there will always be customers for Wonder Bread even if the
market for Distant Early Warning Systems should dry up. (A
merger is also an easy way to enter new markets at a stroke. For
example, American Tobacco Company, now American Brands,
through recent mergers, now has 29 percent of its sales in Beam
bourbon, Sunshine biscuits, Jergens lotion, and Master locks,
none of which must carry a label indicating that it is harmful
to health.)

To have all these large corporations under a single roof does
nothing to increase corporate efficiency. As Professor George J.
Stigler points out, "Why should GM be appreciably more efficient than say a once again independent Buick Motors?" The economist Walter Adams points out that "the unit of technological
efficiency is the plant, not the firm." Big factories can be more
efficient than little factories, but nothing suggests that having
many factories is more efficient than having one. The relentless
drive for new acquisitions is more for balance-sheet drama than
for product excellence. As the House Antitrust Subcommittee
found in its 1969–1970 hearings, conglomerates have been impelled to take over companies primarily for the cosmetic effect
on the books. (When ITT was defending its takeover of Hartford
Insurance before the Justice Department, it used the argument
that it would have a serious liquidity crisis with respect to its
foreign companies if it were not allowed to keep Hartford's big
cash deposits.) Through various feats of accounting that permit
pooling of profits, a company can use the profits of an acquired
company to show a dramatic rise in earnings per share. The result, at least until the investors catch on, is a rise in the value of

the stock greater than would be justified by the profits of either company alone.

What is the effect of bigness on product quality? Marshall McLuhan notes that in the large enterprise, management objectives "change faster than any management can." There is such a rapid turnover of products that commitment to quality and craftsmanship is a luxury. The attention of the financiers and marketeers who now dominate top management of global corporations is elsewhere.

In the world of the global oligopolies, products are shaped not to the requirements of public need but to the requirements of corporate growth. These are not the same. In 1966, the British Institute of Marketing changed its definition of marketing. "Assessing consumer needs" was scrapped in favor of a more revealing one: "Assessing and converting customer purchase power into effective demand for a specific product . . . so as to achieve the profit target or other objectives set by a company." Marketing is now recognized as the science of need creation.

The genius of the large corporation is not invention, but the development and marketing of individual inspiration. Numerous studies confirm the familiar folk myth. Fundamental scientific breakthroughs seldom happen in giant company laboratories. They take place in bedrooms, garages, and makeshift laboratories: for example, Moulton's bicycle, Carlson's Xerox, DeForest's vacuum tube, Wankel's rotary engine, Von Neumann's computer, etc. The dial telephone was invented by an undertaker and the ball-point pen by a sculptor. A French monk invented the principle of hermetically sealed refrigeration. Two concert pianists invented Kodachrome in their kitchens. Studies by Edwin Mansfield, Jacob Schmoockler, John Jewkes, David Sawes, and Richard Stillerman, among others, confirm that big companies have an indifferent record when it comes to basic inventions and that there is no consistent correlation between company size and research-and-development expenditures.

There are many reasons why global oligopolies are not efficient at producing scientific breakthroughs. There is the obvious point made by Arthur Koestler and others that scientific creativity, like artistic creativity, involves "large chunks of irrationality," and hence insight cannot be programmed or organized. Then too, despite the generosity of government in subsidizing company research in such areas as computers and jet aircraft, management does not like to spend research funds to follow scientific will-o'-the-wisps, which is what all truly novel ideas at some point appear to be. (Thomas J. Watson, Jr., tells the revealing story of how the disk memory unit, the heart of the random-access computer, was invented only because "a handful of men . . . broke the rules" by ignoring management's order to drop the project, which was getting too expensive.) Victor Papanek, dean of the School of Design of the California Institute of the Arts, notes that more than 90 percent of the annual spending by corporations and the government for research and development is devoted to last-stage designing of hardware for production, not product innovation. Much of the research, he says, is simply to by-pass other firms' patents.

Finally, large companies have a longing for stability and security, sometimes as strong as their desire for profits. For this reason, high-risk projects, especially those which threaten to dislodge existing technologies in which heavy investments have already been made, do not commend themselves to top corporate managers. There is no incentive to contribute to the rapid obsolescence of the technologies they are presently marketing. This fact of corporate life may explain why Chrysler, which by 1962 knew how to produce a nearly pollution-free gas-turbine engine, abandoned it in favor of bigger and more contaminating versions of the traditional high-compression engine. Global oligopolies invest substantial funds each year in technology suppression—the buying up of potentially threatening inventions to be stored, perhaps forever, in the company's files. (In 1970, General Motors, Ford, and Chrysler accepted a consent decree which in effect admitted that they had conspired for 17 years to keep antipollution devices off the market.)

Products of oligopolistic competitiors have become more and more alike, and once again the reason can be traced to the structure of the firm. Cars (in the same price range), toothpaste, packaged food, etc., are virtually indistinguishable from one another, irrespective of brand label. Reducing the number of essentially different products and marketing identical products under different brand names constitutes "efficiency" from the standpoint of the company because it thereby achieves economies of production, but the consumer is much less of a "sovereign" than he was when there were a greater number of firms producing essentially different products. (The casual connection between labels and product was dramatized for us on a recent visit to an applesauce factory. As the cans came rolling off the assembly line, a group of women grabbed them at random and arbitrarily pasted on one of six different labels representing supposedly competing product lines.)

The most profitable sort of innovation for a large corporation is what is known as product differentiation. This is a polite term for irrelevant or marginal changes in a product for the purpose of creating new markets without basic new production costs. In 1970, according to Theodore Levitt of the Harvard Business School, companies tried to introduce into the nation's supermarkets about 5,200 ostensibly "new" products. Typically, such innovations do not require heavy investment in new technology, but rather much more modest expenses for advertising, marketing, and promotion. Product changes are designed increasingly with the advertising department in mind. One of the crowning achievements of the product differentiator's art is the Life Saver, which has achieved its extraordinary sales by marketing a hole. The automobile manufacturer's annual marketing task is to convince anyone able to borrow $3,000 that he cannot live without the minor design changes that now render last year's model a symbol of all that is old and unworthy. The soap manufacturer's job is to convince the housewife that she needs a variety of specialized soaps for different household tasks. Even more important in the market-creation process than superficial or illusory product changes are changes in packaging. (The switch to nonreturnable bottles or to plastic jars was accompanied by campaigns emphasizing customer safety and convenience.) Such package redesign is also a good way to cut as much as 5 or 10 percent of unit production costs and, by means of such devices as the handy six-pack, to increase volume of sales.

Since highly concentrated industries compete not on price but on such marginal product differences, they account for most of the nation's advertising budget. Real differences in quality among essentially similar products of oligopolistic competitors, if they exist at all, are not obvious to consumers. Therefore, consumer loyalty must be attracted by various persuasive techniques. Sometimes the Madison Avenue copywriter will emphasize a supposedly unique feature such as Kent's "Micronite" filter, but most often he will seek to win customers away from his client's competitors by selling a mood that has nothing to do with the product. (The thrill of flying, the delights of the hunt, and the joys of a cool mountain stream have all been promoted in recent cigarette ads.) The modern ad writer sells happiness, envy, fear, and excitement, and along with them, some product. Increasingly, the largest corporations are advertising themselves, often barely mentioning what they sell. Promotion of the company is sufficient when there is little choice in product.

The consumer must, of course, pay the costs of his own seduction. Advertising expenses are duly passed on to him in the form of price increases. Since there is almost no alternative to the products marketed by oligopolists and they do not engage in price-cutting, he has no choice but to pay. The effect is, of course, inflationary. Harry Skornia, former president of the National Association of Educational Broadcasters, says that he knows of no case of price reductions after a successful advertising campaign despite the standard claim that advertising lowers consumer costs by increasing the market. The consumer is thus paying for marketing "services" he did not ask for and which do him no perceptible good—in effect, an industry-imposed tax. (The argument that advertising "informs" customers is becoming increasingly difficult to reconcile with the facts. The modern trend in advertising, in contrast to fifty years ago, is to say as little of substance about the product as possible.) In the soap industry, to take one of the biggest advertisers, *Advertising Age* has calculated that advertising costs represent about 10 percent of sales. Fortunately for the biggest companies, who are also the biggest advertisers, they are able to achieve certain economies of scale in marketing. Thus, for example, during the years 1954–1957 American Motors spent $57.90 in advertising costs for every car it sold, but General Motors spent only $26.60. These figures explain why the kind of productivity increases that the biggest companies can achieve through advertising serve the interest of management. Money made by lowering unit costs is always more welcome than money made on risky new investment.

But the consumer also pays in other ways. Spectacular marketing campaigns which sell the vicarious thrills of sex and danger or the tranquillity of a mountain stream divert attention from product quality. (Institutional advertisements celebrating company altruism have the same effect.) Company statements look better when costs are reduced by substitution of cheaper materials, package redesign, or, as is evident to longtime buyers of chocolate bars, giving the customer less. (Sometimes companies are carried away by this practice. Not long ago McDonald's, now rapidly becoming a global purveyor of hamburgers, was fined a modest $1,800 for shaving a quarter-ounce off its "quarter-pounder.") Nicholas Tomalin in an investigation for the London *Times* discovered that the British cigarette Players Medium has been shortened 4 percent since 1939. The company spends considerable funds at regular intervals to determine whether randomly selected test smokers will notice the fifth of a milimeter that has been sliced off their favorite cigarette.

The head of Britain's biggest brewery thinks "it doesn't matter whether you are making sugar, bolts and nuts or beer, the management skills are the same." Such attitudes are commonplace throughout the Global Factory. Increasingly, as we have seen, the leading executives of global corporations are money managers and marketing specialists with little direct interest, experience, or pride in their products. A passion for quality and craftsmanship increases costs and inhibits company growth. Accordingly, those who may still harbor such nineteenth-century attitudes do not rise to commanding positions in the global oligopolies. The productivity of the modern corporation is defined not by what it produces but by how much its earnings grow. As GE puts it: "Progress is our most important product."

4

Thus it is that the internal structure of the global corporation has shaped the kind of product it produces. It also shapes the character of the people who work for it—not only those on the assembly line, as we have seen, but also those in executive positions. A recent study of the American Management Association based on the response of 2,800 corporate executives concludes that job alienation "has not merely spread to, but may even thrive in, the managerial suites of American business." Eighty-three percent of the respondents, mostly lower and middle management, define personal success in terms other than business success. Approximately the same number believe that their definitions of success are changing. Some typical responses: "Success is to be who I am." "Some people still believe that money is success. I don't believe that anymore." About two-thirds of those questioned doubt that the organization they work for is interested in or even aware of their personal life aspirations, and an approximately equal number say they do not look to their work to satisfy those aspirations. Since the growth process of global corporations means that an ever-increasing proportion of the nation's executives, engineers, and managers are going to end up working for large organizations, the implications are serious. The study suggests that the quality of that corporate growth has a stunting effect on personal growth. The goals of corporations and the individual goals of those who work for them appear increasingly to be in conflict.

Canadian management consultant Barrington Nevitt thinks that the very pace of change and growth in the modern corporation "transforms the old executive into a die-hard" with "no human satisfaction." Out of touch with the organizational problems that brought him to the top, he is frustrated. Possibly so, but there is considerable evidence that men who have struggled to the top manage to adjust to the exercise of great power. (A recent study indicates that they live longer than their subordinates.) One hears little from the Geneens and the Rockefellers about being alienated from their work. On the other hand, the anxieties of middle-level executives are a favorite theme of modern American fiction. Kenn Rogers, author of *Managers: Personality and Performance*, quotes a typical confession:

> "What are my living circumstances? What do you want me to tell you, Doc? I wake up at three in the morning; I feel paunchy and tired. I look at my wife snoring next to me with two pounds of makeup smeared all over her face. Both my kids, God bless them, are inches taller than I am. Both tell me that I'm a square and a supporter of a hypocritic society. Big deal. I then think of the job, and I just know they're gonna make Harry executive vice-president and not me. My secretary will be consoling, always trying to stick her big tits into my face. Stupid broad. You can't get involved in the office. Weekends I play golf at the country club, have a couple of drinks, go home, eat, watch TV, play cards with the neighbors, hear a little gossip, go to bed, go

to work. Come next August I'll be thirty-seven. I often wonder, 'How is this different from what my old man and my mother used to do?' Except their way of life wasn't as expensive as mine. They were never as much in hock as I am."

Professor Rogers offers a primarily psychological explanation for what he calls the "mid-career crisis." People in their mid and late thirties are, he finds, subject to depressions. In some cases their success brings a sense of emptiness. ("We were much happier when we had to struggle," one of his subjects says.) Perhaps the aging process does have something to do with executive discontent. But it is possible to identify specific ways in which corporate organization contributes to the mid-career crisis. Jacques S. Gansler, a former vice-president of ITT, believes the heart of the problem is that more and more managers cannot accept the goals of their corporation. "As the educated middle manager gets more and more exposed and more and more involved, he begins to question the profit-only motives of his corporation, but he is confronted with an incredible conflict between what he hears from the top as to what he should do, and what he personally feels he should do." The publicity of the late 1960's about the shoddy products and shoddy practices of some of the nation's most powerful corporations has had its effect inside those organizations.

The global corporation, as we have seen, is intent upon transferring community and national loyalties to itself. But the whole-hearted allegiance of sensitive people is hard to hold when the corporate enterprise itself appears to be losing legitimacy. In the last few years such industrial pillars as Coca-Cola, Carnation, Standard Oil of California, and ITT's Wonder Bread have all been cited by the Federal Trade Commission for misleading advertising. Thirty million cars and trucks have been recalled since 1966 because of shoddy workmanship discovered too late. None of this is helpful to managerial morale. Some indication of the effects of the consumerist movement on potential corporate employees is offered by E. E. Weiss, vice-president of creative marketing at Doyle Dane Bernbach, Inc., who says that "advertising is viewed as almost the *last* [vocational] choice by the top 20 per cent of campus talent. . . ." No doubt advertising agencies will continue to be supplied with creativity from the nation's leading universities, but increasingly, it will be coming without enthusiasm and without illusions.

The extraordinary psychic and financial rewards of top management do not encourage moral doubts. For a tiny group with access to company jets and the right to be received at the White House, individual purposes and company purposes blend agreeably. (Crawford H. Greenwalt, former president of Du Pont, in his book *The Uncommon Man* compares individuals who make up a corporation to flowers in a garden, musicians in a symphony orchestra, and drops of water in a waterfall.) But for those who work for them, increasing doubts about the meaning and worth of many company activities are eroding corporate loyalty and causing inner conflicts. (The psychoanalyst Ignacio Millán in the course of depth interviews with Mexican managers of global corporations discovered that many of them revealed through dreams unconscious guilt about engaging in what appears to be the widespread practice in Mexico of falsifying company books to avoid taxes and to obscure profits. At the conscious level they took a certain pride in their skill at figure juggling, rationalizing it as a way of keeping money out of the hands of corrupt politicians.)

Nor does hierarchical structure of the global corporation help managerial morale. Routinization and compartmentalization of managerial function is the executive equivalent of the assembly line. It is the result, of course, of division of labor, the primary strategy for achieving corporate efficiency. Top management knows that molding managers to corporate needs (including shuttling them and their families about the country every few years) exacts a human toll. (Over 2.5 million people are moved each year in corporate transfers. A dreary joke at IBM is that the company initials really stand for "I've Been Moved.") The incidence of depression, drug addiction, and alcoholism among executive wives is understandably high. Robert Seidenberg, a Syracuse psychiatrist who has many such executive families as patients, says that moving "is a severe trauma probably as great as divorce. It's like uprooting a tree or a bush—you simply can't flourish transplanted five or six times."

Many top firms invest a certain amount of money and effort in trying to do something about these problems. Some are trying to cut down on executive transfers. "Organizational Development" and "Humanistic Management" are some of the names for

GLOBAL REACH

various techniques to improve executive performance by increasing "job satisfaction." "T-Groups and sensitivity training are used widely in large corporations." According to management specialist Warren D. Bennis, "half of the top executives of *Fortune*'s 500 have been sensitized." Some companies are trying to decentralize certain management functions to give middle-level employees more range for creativity. In technologically oriented firms especially, companies try to create the "democratic environment" that Bennis says is indispensable to scientific progress. But technologists at the middle-management level in high-technology industries, according to a three-year investigation by Michael Maccoby, though they find their work "technically interesting, creative, important to the company, and not exceedingly supervised," are "nagged by thoughts of being merely part of a huge machine" and do not think they have "much power to affect the policies of the company." A number thought that their work encouraged cooperation and fairness, but not compassion, generosity, or idealism. Over half of the engineers he interviewed said they would rather run a small company than reach a high level in a large one.

Partly to combat the growing anticorporate image, partly to counter executive alienation and improve employee morale, U.S.-based global corporations have been committing time, rhetoric, and some money to what is called "the social responsibility of business." Jules Cohn in *The Conscience of the Corporation* studied 247 large corporations and found that 201 of them had some form of urban social-affairs program. (All but 4, however, were set up after the ghetto explosions of 1965.) Corporations give away a little over $1 billion a year, which represents about 1 percent of their net profit before taxes. (The average individual in the United States donates approximately 2.5 percent of his income to charity.) The tax law allows deductions of up to 5 percent for a corporation, but the classic corporate argument is that the money belongs to the shareholders and they should give it away when (or if) it is distributed as dividends.

Corporate spokesmen, aware that the public is skeptical of corporate altruism, like to argue that good works are also good business. They talk about the market potential of social problem solving and the profits to be made in meeting social needs. But the Cohn study suggests otherwise. The experience to date (through 1970) is that meeting social responsibilities—i.e., minority employment, hiring and training the "disadvantaged," assistance to community economic development, black capitalism, and environmental improvement efforts—turns out to be more expensive and less profitable than the companies anticipated.

Jacques S. Gansler, former ITT vice-president, concludes in his paper "Social Responsibility and the Multinational Corporation Executive" that there has been a significant reduction in the interest and support by corporations in the social area over the last few years. Gansler's own experiences in ITT are revealing. After failing at Singer to interest the company in making even a small commitment to socially oriented research and development, he tried a different tack at the company "serving people and nations everywhere." He sought to introduce some social planning into the use of his division's charitable-contributions budget, but found that "the group officer responsible for public relations" had effective control of the money. He was spending it the way Cohn found most firms do—small subventions to non-controversial, image-enhancing community efforts such as the local Little League. ITT, Gansler notes, "is world famous for its business planning, but there were no plans in the social area." Concerned that the charitable budget remained at $11,000 while sales climbed from $30 million to $85 million, he was "repeatedly told that this was not an area in which I should do anything if I wanted to get anywhere within the corporation. Thus, I never even got to try my approach of using research and development money for socially useful projects, and I left ITT shortly thereafter."

5

The world's only global planners argue that huge organizations alone are capable of planning on a planetary scale to solve the colossal problems now confronting mankind. But the evidence is uncomfortably compelling that the kind of planning that hitherto has produced impressive corporate growth produces the wrong kind of social growth. The disparity between what modern man needs and what the modern corporation produces appears to be widening. Of course, needs are to a great extent subjectively determined. If people want to spend their money on a second or third car, a bigger TV screen, an electric wax-paper cutter, or a

prepackaged partridge, rather than on making their cities habit-
able or their air breathable, corporate statesmen argue, who is
to say these are not needs? The hunger in the Soviet Union for the
fruits of frivolous production suggests that the worldwide demand
for consumer goods cannot be wholly attributed to the Svengalis
of Madison Avenue. Consumption, always a favorite play activity
of the rich, is being democratized.

But there are, we believe, objective tests for evaluating whether
the social growth now being programmed by the corporate planners is good or bad. The fundamental criterion is survival. The
internal dynamic of the big corporation compels it, despite all its
hopes and claims, to be the principal agent of pollution in the
contemporary world. Whether one believes the more alarmist
projections or the less alarmist projections, there is a point at
which the earth's ecosystem will tolerate no more gases, sludge,
radioactive wastes, or excessive heat. The record to date of the
capacity of the global corporations constantly to increase their
output and to control pollution at the same time is anything but
encouraging. With few exceptions, the World Managers have yet
to demonstrate a level of concern in any way commensurate with
the problem. The tyranny of the annual balance sheet has forced
most of them to resort to deception, procrastination, and propaganda as a substitute for innovating pollution-free technology.

Nor is the global corporation able to plan balanced social
growth in the cities. The symbol of the unbalanced growth which
is the trademark of the great corporations is their great office
headquarters which rise out of the desolation that marks the inner
core of so many of America's major cities. The kind of social
growth programmed by the corporations is bringing choked highways, decaying neighborhoods, and barely functioning public
services to the metropolitan centers. Despite a certain amount of
good intentions and a great deal of public relations, the big companies have been unable to reconstruct the large areas of Detroit,
Washington, and other cities that were destroyed in the urban
riots of the late 1960's. It is not surprising. Reconstruction on a
vast scale is a governmental function which is not profitable. Subsidizing and rehabilitating poor people, an aspect of social planning that is absolutely necessary for social peace, is not a good
way to make money.

The internal pressures within the corporation do not favor

innovation for the solution of public problems for similar reasons. It is more profitable to develop more complex and more expensive technology than to design simple tools. Providing ever more sophisticated products for an affluent minority is highly profitable. Providing for the basic sanitation, nutrition, health, transportation, and communication needs of the majority within the present postmarket economy is not. It is possible, as designer Victor Papanek has demonstrated, to produce a vehicle for $150, a radio receiver for 9 cents, and a $9 one-channel TV set. There is a desperate need for such cheap, simple forms of technology, especially in underdeveloped countries, but this is not where the big profits are to be made. There is a compelling need to husband scarce energy resources and to innovate products and processes that make lesser energy demands. But the marketing departments of global corporations were, until the 1973 energy crisis caught them unprepared, pushing bigger engines, more energy-sapping gadgets, and resource-draining packaging. The global corporation, it must be said, has had a strong vested interest in waste.

Finally, because the global corporation derives its great economic advantages through centralization, information control, and hierarchical organization, it is inherently antidemocratic. The rapid concentration of planning power in the hands of fewer and fewer corporate managers (as smaller companies become absorbed) produces organizations in which professional growth and personal fulfillment are increasingly hard to achieve. Hierarchy creates psychological dissatisfaction because it deprives individuals of a crucial aspect of their personal identity, social participation and decision making. Division of labor interferes with the human need to create something with integrity and wholeness. An antidemocratic structure cannot plan democratic growth, either for the society or for its own employees.

The success of a social system ultimately depends upon the achievement of balance. It needs social balance, which avoids the dangerous concentration of wealth and power in a few hands. It needs ecological balance, which avoids the misuse of natural resources—above all, air and water. Finally, it needs psychological balance, which avoids the human costs of alienation—a process of enslavement that takes place, as Marx wrote, when the power man has given to things "sets itself against him as an alien and hostile force." We need a holistic perspective for evaluating the quality of growth. The impacts of the peculiar system of growth associated with the global corporation on social, ecological, and psychological balance must be examined together. The achievement of balance in one sphere at the sacrifice of another cannot produce a system that works in any lasting or human sense. The empirical evidence to date casts great doubt on the capacity of a global system dominated by global corporations to achieve such equilibrium.

13

The Transformation of Wealth and the Crisis of Understanding

1

The global corporation is the most powerful human organization yet devised for colonizing the future. By scanning the entire planet for opportunities, by shifting its resources from industry to industry and country to country, and by keeping its overriding goal simple—worldwide profit maximization—it has become an institution of unique power. The World Managers are the first to have developed a plausible model of the future that is global. They exploit the advantages of mobility while workers and governments are still tied to particular territories. For this reason, the corporate visionaries are far ahead of the rest of the world in making claims on the future. In making business decisions today they are creating a politics for the next generation.

We have shown that because of their size, mobility, and strategy, the global corporations are constantly accelerating their control over the world productive system and are helping to bring about a profound change in the way wealth is produced, distributed, and defended. There are a number of elements in this extraordinary transformation, but the global corporation is the most dynamic agent of change in a new stage in world capitalism.

In assessing the role the global corporation is playing and ought to play in this sweeping process, the issue is not whether the World Managers wish the global corporation to be a force for peace, stability, and development, but whether it can be. We would put the question this way: Given its drive to maximize world profits, the pressures of global oligopolistic competition, and its enormous bargaining power, can the global corporation modify its behavior in ways that will signficantly aid the bottom 60 percent of the world's population—in the rich nations as well as in the poor?

In answering this question we have looked at both short-run and long-run effects. In the short run, the challenge of the global corporation concerns stability; in the long run, development. There has never been a time since the Great Depression when there has been more economic uncertainty around the world. But the corporate prospect of a world without borders offers something more distressing than uncertainty. It is a vision without ultimate hope for a majority of mankind. Our criterion for determining whether a social force is progressive is whether it is likely to benefit the bottom 60 percent of the population. Present and projected strategies of global corporations offer little hope for the problems of mass starvation, mass unemployment, and gross inequality. Indeed, the global corporation aggravates all these problems, because the social system it is helping to create violates three fundamental human needs: social balance, ecological balance, and psychological balance. These imbalances have always been present in our modern social system; concentration of economic power, antisocial uses of that power, and alienation have been tendencies of advanced capitalism. But the process of globalization, interacting with and reinforcing the process of accelerating concentration, has brought us to a new stage.

The role of the global corporation in aggravating social imbalance is perhaps the most obvious. As owner, producer, and distributor of an ever greater share of the world's goods, the global corporation is an instrument for accelerating concentration of wealth. As a global distributor, it diverts resources from where they are most needed (poor countries and poor regions of rich countries) to where they are least needed (rich countries and rich regions).

Driven by the ideology of infinite growth, a religion rooted in the existential terrors of oligopolistic competition, global corporations act as if they must grow or die, and in the process they have made thrift into a liability and waste into a virtue. The rapid growth of the global corporate economy requires ever-increasing consumption of energy. The corporate vision depends upon converting ever-greater portions of the earth into throwaway societies: ever-greater quantities of unusable waste produced with each ton of increasingly scarce mineral resources; ever-greater consumption of nondisposable and nonreturnable packaging; ever-greater consumption of energy to produce a unit of energy; and ever more heat in our water and our air—in short, ever more ecological imbalance.

The processes that lead to psychological imbalance are more difficult to analyze than the processes of social or ecological imbalance. But the World Managers have based their strategy on the principles of global mobility, division of labor, and hierarchical organization—all of which may be efficient, in the short run, for producing profits but not for satisfying human beings. The very size of the global corporation invites hierarchy. The search for economic efficiency appears to require ever more division of labor and to challenge traditional loyalties to family, town, and nation. Another name for mobility is rootlessness. There is nothing to suggest that loyalty to a global balance sheet is more satisfying for an individual than loyalty to a piece of earth, and there is a good deal of evidence that being a "footloose" and airborne executive is not the best way to achieve psychological health— for either the managers themselves or their families. By marketing the myth that the pleasures of consumption can be the basis of community, the global corporation helps to destroy the possibilities of real community—the reaching out of one human being to another. The decline of political community and the rise of consuming communities are related. Each TV viewer sits in front of his own box isolated from his neighbor but symbolically related through simultaneous programmed activity and shared fantasy. How much the pervasive sense of meaninglessness in modern life can be attributed to the organizational strategies and values of the huge corporation we are only beginning to understand, but for the longer run the psychological crises associated with the emerging socioeconomic system are potentially the most serious of all, for they undermine the spirit needed to reform that system.

If we are right that the strategies of growth of the global corporation are incompatible with social, ecological, and psychological balance, why will such growth be permitted to continue? Is the earth—or indeed, the corporation itself—so lacking in self-correcting mechanisms that we are doomed to be diverted with upbeat balance sheets while we and our descendants wait for the air to give out? Stephen Hymer argues that high noon for the global corporation has already come and gone. The highly centralized hierarchical model of organization is simply too much at odds with the aspirations of too many of the 4 billion inhabitants of the planet for greater control over their own lives and greater political participation. (There is instability in every major hierarchical organization, including the Catholic Church, universities, the American and German armed forces, and authoritarian states like the Soviet Union.) Why should the global corporation be successful in establishing its political legitimacy to gather more and more public decisions into private hands at a time of worldwide political awakening?

Public anticorporate criticism is growing. Monkey-wrench politics also threatens the symmetry of the corporate global model (oil boycotts, kidnapping, extortion, bomb threats, trucker stall-ins). The worldwide resource scarcity jeopardizes global planning, which was based on the assumption that transportation costs could be kept low and that ships, trucks, and planes would always be available. Winging components and managers around the world to take advantage of differentials in labor costs, tax rates, and tariffs may no longer be the key to higher profits. If the Global Factory, with its worldwide division of labor, no longer represents the ultimate in economic efficiency, much of the rationale for the global corporation is gone. Is it possible that resource limitations are forcing an alternative model of a world economy in which *decentralization* is the hallmark? Perhaps the wave of the future is not the "Cosmocorp" but the backyard steel factory?

Whether global corporations will continue to increase their power will depend upon how successfully they can adapt to rapid change. They are more adaptable than government, because their goals are simpler, their bureaucracies are often more authoritarian, their planning cycle is shorter, and fewer conflicting interests need be heard. The dependence of advanced capitalist societies on privately controlled sources of power for maintaining employment, transferring money, and distributing technology and services is so great that government as a practical matter can no longer control them. The very advantages the global corporation enjoys over government—principally mobility and control of information—are creating a structural lag. Government is operating under a set of economic assumptions and legal theories which treat the corporation as if it were a private and national institution when it is in fact a social institution of global dimension. While the structural lag makes it possible for the corporation to accumulate more and more power, this lag renders increasingly ineffective the traditional tools of government for trying to achieve social stability. Thus in its continual quest for its own stability the global corporation is helping to create instability for society as a whole. As social, ecological, and psychological imbalances become more pronounced, the temptation increases to maintain the appearance of stability with repressive measures. For example, the gospel of growth requires a tolerant attitude toward inflation, but the management of inflation demands tough governmental controls. "There is little doubt," says Storey-Boekh Associates, bank-credit analysts not given to bleeding-heart rhetoric or to casual predictions of fascism, "that we could correct a lot of problems with a large dose of authoritarianism, at least for a while, but the chances of operating a successful inflationary economy like Brazil within the confines of democracy are just about nil."

The prospect, then, is not the death of the nation-state in a world without borders, but the transformation of the nation-state. The increasing impotence of the nation-state to solve its domestic affairs with traditional economic policies will probably drive it to seek survival by more direct and more violent means. The breakdown in the consensus among the industrialized nations on the international ground rules governing economic activity and the growing struggle over scarce resources signal a return to protectionism and economic nationalism. As oligopolistic competition among U.S., Japanese, and European firms intensifies, they will increasingly call upon their governments to back their efforts. The fading of the Cold War is making modern replays of World War I–type geopolitics more plausible. Despite their laudable vision of world peace through world trade, global corporations are more likely to act as instruments of competitive economic and geopolitical rivalry. In sum, if global corporations do not undergo profound changes in their goals and strategies, or are not effectively controlled, they will continue to act as disturbers of the peace on a global scale.

2

What, then, can be done? Some argue that the corporation itself is able to regulate its own behavior in response to the requirements of human survival so as to eliminate the negative aspects of the new world economy and to preserve the positive. If, for example, direct investment in poor countries turns out on balance to be negative, a corporation could transfer technology by means of service contracts to locally owned enterprises in preference to owning them itself. Such discussion usually breaks down because the participants have different evaluations of what is and what is not worth preserving. In any event, we are skeptical, regrettably, about the capacity or the willingness of the world enterprise to reform more than its image. Increasing numbers of corporate executives are, as individuals, concerned about the negative impacts of the global corporation, but they operate within a system of such fierce competition that they cannot translate their concern into corporate policy. The heart of the problem is excessive power, and the self-imposed limitation on power is not characteristic of human institutions. The issue, then, is what can be done to develop countervailing power in such a way as to achieve greater social, ecological, and psychological balance.

The dilemma is clear. The challenge posed by the global corporation is systemic, and the response must be systemic; but systems are not reformable at a stroke. Even revolutions proceed step by step. Both short-range reforms and long-range visions are essential to the process of developing a world order more acceptable than the one that appears to be emerging. But unless short-range reforms are examined in the light of long-range preferences, they are likely to be ineffective or even regressive. In addition, specific reforms must also be analyzed within a global framework. Political and economic interdependence is the hallmark of the new stage of global oligopoly ushered in by the world enterprise. Interdependence in some form is inescapable; isolationism and autarchy are not viable alternatives for most nations. But not all modes of interdependence are positive or necessary. Many produce negative side effects and accentuate the inequalities of the present system. Short-range proposals that do not confront the present global distribution of power and the development model merely reinforce those modes of interdependence which are at the heart of the problem.

The globalization of the world political economy and the developing managerial crises of the nation-state are creating the necessity, and perhaps the political foundations as well, for a process of planetary reorganization. But such a reorganization cannot be willed into being—even if there were enough people with enough power who could agree on what the new world should look like. The process of change unfolds in separate steps.

A particular step can be analyzed intelligently only if the longer-range goals and values underlying it are made explicit. What is the analysis of the problem that underlies this solution? Is it correct? What is the next likely step? Who wants this reform, and why? Inventing plausible-sounding proposals for dealing with the global corporation is not particularly difficult, but such proposals are not worth much attention unless they represent real political forces. We will now look at a series of specific reform measures for which some political support exists or appears to be imminent.

The energy crisis, the secret diplomacy of ITT, and the involvement of large corporations in the scandals of the Nixon Administration have intensified the long and often futile struggle for adequate corporate disclosure. If there is to be more effective government control of global corporations, there must be some fundamental reforms in the process by which information crucial for society is produced, used, and diffused. Power is corruptible, but power exercised in secret is inevitably so. To make a beginning on a campaign to encourage the social responsibility of global corporations, governments and citizens must know what these corporations own, what they are doing, and what they are planning. The books of global corporations—that is to say *all* sets—ought to be public documents. Sufficient information should be disclosed on a continuing basis to enable the Treasury to analyze the real nature of all intracorporate financial transactions. Corporations should be required to disclose to public authorities the extent and nature of their reserves of crucial materials. What mines, mineral reserves, and land does the corporation own, and where? How did it acquire them, and what did it pay? What arrangements have been made for foreign technology licensing, and under what terms? What taxes does the corporation pay to what countries? What tax concessions have been received, and from whom? Who are the real owners of the largest blocks of stock of global corporations and global banks? What investments does the corporation plan over the next five years, and where? What studies has the corporation done on local-employment impacts of such projected investment?

These are indispensable data for the development of any rational program for national or international regulation of global corporations—or even for a rational decision that none is needed. There are other important questions as well. We recognize that there are many technical problems involved in drafting legislation to elicit adequate disclosure. A joint committee of Congress should be appointed to make a full-scale study of existing disclosure requirements, to assess their inadequacies, and to prepare comprehensive legislation for compelling disclosure in crucial areas for all corporations over a certain size. Such a test would automatically include all corporations with sufficient foreign activities to have an important impact on the U.S. economy.

We have heard the argument in talks with global-corporation executives that however reasonable new disclosure requirements might be, their imposition by national legislation would put U.S. firms at a competitive disadvantage. Japanese and German firms, free of such restrictions, would take over America's markets. The argument bears scrutiny. The fact is that in some important areas, other industrial countries have more stringent disclosure requirements than the United States. In Japan, for example, corporations are required to give the tax collector and the shareholders the same profit figures. This eminently reasonable disclosure requirement, completely at odds with the ethic of the new alchemists, has not put Japanese firms into bankruptcy. A similar requirement here would not bankrupt IBM either. Moreover, there is historical evidence that where the United States takes the lead in regulating global corporations in areas that frustrate fiscal or monetary policy, other governments, having similar interests vis-à-vis their own global corporations, follow suit. When the United States adopted Subpart F of the Internal Revenue Code in 1962 to curb the use of tax havens, other industrial countries, including Great Britain and Germany, adopted similar legislation.

Nevertheless, the disparity in the type, severity, and enforcement of disclosure requirements is obviously a serious problem. No government is likely to put its own major industry at a serious competitive disadvantage even to regain its sovereignty. A most important task of foreign policy, therefore, is the harmonization of disclosure requirements among the major countries in which global corporations are based. An international convention for standardizing accounting definitions and practices is an example of an important legal reform which, if enforced, could effect a change in the way global corporations conduct their worldwide affairs.

As the managerial crisis deepens, governments will have stronger incentive to set new ground rules within which oligopolistic competition continues. It is clearly in the interest of all such governments not to permit the power balance between governments and corporations to shift further in ways that subvert national policies for the management of the home economy. Thus all governments, to varying degrees perhaps, have incentives to break the power of corporate secrecy. Whether there is sufficient statesmanship to see and to act upon this common interest is another matter. But no area of international cooperation is more important. The United Nations and its specialized agencies should encourage and support this harmonization process. It should play a role in publicizing and communicating the information that is disclosed. But if disclosure requirements are to have teeth, they must be enacted by national legislatures and enforced by national governments.

3

Corporate statesmen and business reformers talk little in public about the need for more disclosure. Instead, they talk about international regulation. The enemies of the global corporation, principally organized labor, also talk about regulation. Not surprisingly, they usually have diametrically opposite things in mind. From the viewpoint of the global corporation, the problem is not how to curb its power but rather how to get rid of obstacles that stand in the way of expanding it. True, some corporate executives have expressed concern that the great disparities in national law on such matters as taxes, securities regulations, antitrust, and balance-of-payments controls permit global corporations, in Charles Kindleberger's words, to slip "between the cracks of national jurisdictions." The inflation and sudden popping of Bernard Cornfeld's offshore investment bubble, Investors Overseas Service, offers an extreme example of how to wriggle between the cracks of law and constitute oneself a juridical nowhere man.

But more respectable firms, led by even more respectable law firms, play the same game whenever possible and, needless to add, more successfully.

But usually global corporations argue, as Kindleberger notes, that they are "cabined by . . . overlapping regulations" which inhibit their flexibility. The greatest source of strength for the global corporation is its ability to plan centrally for profit maximization on a world scale. The more regulations, such as investment restrictions, that inhibit global planning, the less the corporation can maximize its unique advantages. James W. McKee, president of CPC International, complains that satisfying "inconsistent demands of governments" creates problems for global corporations because they are subjected to "contradictory sets of policies and laws." He proposes simplified and harmonized patent procedures and common food and drug standards. "When we have similar policies and laws governing corporate behavior in all countries, the fear that multinational companies could operate as a law to themselves will disappear," he argues.

A variety of proposals have been put forward to accomplish this purpose. Several suggestions for an international "code of conduct" covering the rights and duties of states and global corporations have been made at a variety of international meetings. Jacques Maisonrouge of IBM proposes an "international counterpart to multinational companies," on the model of the General Agreement on Tariffs and Trade or the International Monetary Fund. Paul M. Goldberg and Charles Kindleberger propose a General Agreement for the International Corporation along the lines of GATT which would establish an agency to "act as ombudsman for corporations and countries seeking relief from oppressive policies." George Ball, on the other hand, calls for an "international companies law" or "world chartering" of the "Cosmocorp," administered by an international agency. Global corporations "should become quite literally citizens of the world"—i.e., "stateless." Such proposals are attempts to legitimize most of what global corporations are now doing by establishing minimal and largely unenforceable limits on their power to penetrate all national borders in the process of private global planning.

Regulation of global corporations by an international agency sounds plausible and progressive. Why not an international political body to act as counterpart and counterweight to the global corporation? The problem, of course, is that present international agencies or any new agency in the foreseeable future are too weak to regulate the corporate giants. To pretend otherwise is to settle for the patina of regulation instead of the substance. Indeed, from a corporate standpoint, the best way to escape regulation from such outmoded national agencies as the Internal Revenue Service and the Anti-Trust Division is to shift the burden to an international agency with broad unenforceable powers and a modest budget.

Paradoxically, the precondition for effective international regulation, in our view, is the restoration of certain powers to national governments and local communities to manage their own territory. Only a spurious and a dangerous internationalism can be built when nations are relieved of the vestments of sovereignty save the power to make war. Nations unable to diagnose and solve their internal problems lash out at one another—sometimes out of a need to divert domestic attention, sometimes out of pure frustration. In the United States, the preoccupation of the President with military affairs has grown as his ability to deal with the domestic sources of social discontent has declined. (It was far easier for Lyndon Johnson to send 500,000 troops to Vietnam than to send 50 voting registrars to Mississippi.)

"Sovereignty" is a word with an old-fashioned ring and a diminished reputation. And rightly so. To the modern ear it suggests selfishness, isolationism, and arbitrariness. In foreign affairs, governments invoke the concept of sovereignty to justify doing whatever they like to whomever for whatever reason suits their fancy. Ultimately, it is the appeal to sovereignty that justifies the crushing of students in Prague with tanks, the systematic bombardment of civilians in Laos and Cambodia, and a catalogue of other evils all committed in the name of national security. Nations use sovereignty to escape accountability. It is evident that if there is to be either peace or justice, nations must accept limitations on this sort of sovereignty.

But there is another sense in which the word is used—the exercise of publicly accountable power for the public benefit. When we say that the new international economy now being built by global corporations threatens the sovereignty of the nation-state, we mean that its principal domestic powers and functions—the power to raise revenue, maintain employment, provide adequate social services, encourage the equitable allocation of income and wealth, maintain sound currency, keep prices and wages in line: in short, the power to maintain a stable social equilibrium for the greater majority of its population—is being seriously undercut. Thus, even where there is a will to shift domestic priorities in the interest of social justice, the ability to develop new priorities is impaired.

The underlying reason for the socially disruptive effects of global corporations is that they are still treated as private organizations despite their increasingly public role. Public authorities are incapable of dealing with them because our laws are still based on the old myths of nineteenth-century free-market capitalism in which private entrepreneurs take private risks for private rewards. But that hardly describes the owners and managers of IBM or Exxon. The free market is largely a historical relic. It has been transformed by three systemic forces over the last 40 years: accelerating concentration of industry and banking, increasing intervention of government into the "private sector," and now the spectacular rise of the intracorporate (nonmarket) economy of the global oligopolies. Together these forces have speeded the decline of the market and further negated its classic social functions.

The U.S.-based global corporation has achieved a stage of advanced technology unparalleled in the world. (Only the state enterprises of the Soviet Union can come close to duplicating the space-technology feats of U.S. companies.) But the accumulation of technological skill in global corporations bears no resemblance to the storing of sides of beef in the old local butcher shop. These technological skills which are the basis of the corporations' power represent not private but social property. The technology was assembled with direct subsidies, tax write-offs, and other benefits traceable to the public treasury. The social capital of the nation —its air, water, and mineral treasure—has been expended in the process. Much of the foundation of the extraordinary wealth of global corporations, therefore, is social property in origin and character and ought to be treated as such.

So too, many of the risks of the global enterprise are social. Not only is the risk of financial loss spread to the taxpayers in cases such as the Lockheed loan guarantee, but the risks of bad company planning in the pollution or employment area, for example, now fall squarely on the average citizen, who must bear the brunt of corporate mistakes or pay the costs of correcting them. Because the managers of global corporations are making major social-planning decisions for the society and many of these decisions are filled with risks, the responsibility of these individuals to the public must be defined by law.

Global corporations must be regulated to restore sovereignty to government. Public authority must be shared at the supranational, national, state, local, and neighborhood levels; yet how this is to be done is by no means clear. The crucial point, however, is that the power of the corporation, a private organization with limited purposes and extremely limited accountability, must be circumscribed to permit broadly accountable, democratically selected, and socially committed public authorities to govern. For the productive system to be made socially responsible to the people of the United States, its activities must be regulated in such a way as to support national development objectives. For this to be possible, there must *be* clearly articulated national priorities, debated and adopted by democratic procedures. The United States needs a national development plan which sets out a vision of the society we are hoping to achieve and the policies for achieving it. Some basic goals should be a significant reduction in waste and pollution; full employment; control of inflation; major improvement in availability of public services—health, education, transportation, etc.; major investment in reconstruction of cities and towns; and decentralization of political authority. It is now clear that the nation cannot achieve these goals by allowing global corporations to continue as the principal planners for the society. Such crucial decisions for the society as a whole as how many cars are to be manufactured and how much energy is to be produced can no longer be left in private hands.

There are no ready-made solutions. Staffing GM or Exxon with an army of civil servants would not in itself change the goals and strategies of the corporation. To substitute the concentrated power of a public bureaucracy for a private one may permit the firm to moderate its goal of profit maximization, but it does not necessarily make it responsive to community needs. We need an urgent public debate on a variety of new forms of public ownership and control for our strategic industries and on how production priorities should be set. (In a time of resource scarcity and

worldwide famine, there are many things that should not be made
by anyone.) We already live in a mixed economy, and it is now
time to re-examine the mix.

Much has been made in the United States of consumer sovereignty. The productive system supposedly produces the goods in
the amounts people want. But we know enough of the actual
workings of the economy to realize that much of the time the
consumer-king is a figurehead. A development plan, however,
should aim at more than the restoration of consumer sovereignty.
It should strive toward more participation in the work place—
worker sovereignty—and more real participation in the political
process—citizen sovereignty. A national development plan, in our
view, ought to have three main approaches. First, such a plan
ought to encourage investment in the United States in such a way
as to meet the basic needs of the American people. There exist in
government offices various inventories of basic social needs—
housing, medical care, transportation systems. The national development policy should stimulate the buildup of the social capital
of the United States. At the same time, the subsidies which
encourage the accumulation of private wealth with public money
should be ended.

The bias in our laws favoring foreign investment should be
systematically removed. Tax laws should not be used to encourage
foreign investment. The elimination of tax deferral, permissive
use of the tax credit, havens, percentage depletion, and other
special privileges for particular industries is essential. If there are
to be any nonfiscal purposes to be served by the Internal Revenue
Code, they should be the encouragement of investment in the
United States for job creation, the development of alternative
technologies, and the extension of needed social services. Because
corporate taxpayers, especially large ones with foreign operations,
qualify for the many special concessions scattered through the
Internal Revenue Code, U.S. tax law is no longer progressive.

A major investment program should be undertaken in the
development of alternative technologies, particularly those which
are cheaper, more resource-saving, and simple. A rational development program for the people of the United States would
include a heavy investment in the public development of a variety
of technologies to make the American people "self-sufficient"—
independent not only of foreign governments but of a few oil

companies too. Another priority for such a development program would be investment in job-creating rather than job-displacing technology. As Keynes once put it, investment abroad "does not stimulate employment a scrap more than would an equal investment at home . . ." Professor Robert Gilpin, in his report for the Senate Committee on Labor and Public Welfare, "The Multinational Corporation and the National Interest," notes, "The national interest of the United States would be best served by an industrial strategy which emphasizes technological innovation rather than defensive foreign investment." It should, we believe, be a priority in a rational development program for the United States to stimulate possibilities for useful work in the United States. (There is no doubt that the definition of both "work" and "useful" will change in the next generation.) To encourage investment in job-creating technology in the United States, U.S. law should no longer subsidize corporate growth through foreign investment.

A second priority of a development plan for the United States would be to encourage a more equitable distribution of income and wealth, not only in the United States but worldwide. The Senate report just cited confirms our own findings: "The real issue is that foreign direct investment tends to shift the national distribution of income to the disadvantage of blue-collar workers." Corporations are increasingly dependent on their foreign profits and are using them to increase their size and power while productivity in the United States is declining and with it the opportunity for increased wages. The systemic connection between concentration and bigness, on the one hand, and maldistribution of income and political power, on the other, is so strongly supported by the evidence that an explicit policy to reverse these systemic trends is needed.

It should be the objective of the United States to decentralize the economy so as to curb oligopoly power. An essential preliminary step in the preparation of a comprehensive development plan therefore would be a systematic examination of those specific practices which lead to concentration and undercut the power of government to manage the economy. U.S. tax and banking laws are much too loose in permitting and encouraging cross-subsidization, especially in the banking industry. Evidence is already available, for example, to justify the elimination of the "one-bank holding company." Banks, in short, should be required to get out of nonbanking businesses. Interlocking directorates of banks and industrial corporations should be prohibited by law.

In the furtherance of an income-redistribution policy there is a strong argument for breaking up the most concentrated industries by law. The great global corporations cannot be broken up, however, except in the context of a larger development plan. There must be a clearly articulated employment and income policy which includes government responsibility to develop real employment possibilities, not make-work; otherwise global corporations may well be vindicated in their prediction that restriction of their power will bring massive economic dislocation and worldwide depression. In short, reorganization of major corporations, although badly needed, cannot be done without reorganization of the goals and priorities of the whole society.

A third objective of a national development program should be a reasonable level of self-sufficiency in raw materials and manufactured goods. The global strategy of the U.S.-based global corporation is to do more and more of its growing outside the United States. This process is causing the United States, like Great Britain, going into the twentieth century, to become, in Professor Gilpin's words, a "rentier society which lives off investment income." Not only is such a society dependent on others and hence vulnerable to political vicissitudes everywhere, but a nation of coupon clippers quickly loses the sources of inner strength when it lives off the productivity of others. When the U.S. economy is dependent upon foreign investment to maintain levels of employment, to keep the balance of payments in line, and to expand the wealth generated by American business, the result, as Gilpin puts it, is "neglect of domestic investment opportunities and social needs. Resources flow abroad to facilitate corporate growth rather than to improve America's cities, decrease her dependence upon foreign sources of energy, or seek out new commercial investment opportunities in this country. The result is to accelerate a shift in the global distribution of industrial and economic power away from the United States."

We are not so nationalistic as to deny the need for a redistribution of economic power in the world. On the contrary, in a world where 6 percent of the population consumes 30 to 60 percent of some of the most vital resources, such a redistribution is long overdue. We cannot support a waste economy here without threatening subsistence elsewhere in the world. But the global corporation, operating under its present ground rules, is not the instrument to bring about economic redistribution. While its particular global strategy does indeed break down national frontiers, it strengthens class divisions. The global enterprise may spread wealth geographically, but it concentrates it politically and socially. Thus in the fulfillment of its global vision both justice and stability are eluded.

The way to accomplish a worldwide redistribution of economic power is not to further concentrate it in the private hands of American companies but to adopt directly a rational policy to accomplish this purpose. Policies that would most help to shift economic power from rich to poor countries include the very proposals which global corporations spend the most money to oppose—preferential trade treatment, divestment of foreign ownership, encouragement of locally owned industry, and higher prices for raw materials. A rational policy for the redistribution of economic power in the world would include a program of capital grants by rich countries to poor countries without forcing them to adopt the "development" model of the global corporation.

To hedge in the private power of the corporation, public institutions must be strengthened at many different levels simultaneously. We have talked about the need for strengthening the national government to be able to manage the economy. But the immediate and noticeable negative impacts of the global corporation are felt in cities and towns where factories are located or goods are sold. The essential strategy of the global corporation makes it an antagonist of local interests everywhere.

The local community in the United States has the same ambivalent relationship to global corporations as do underdeveloped countries. There is always a price to absentee ownership. The company president in New York cannot be expected to concern himself with the traffic, housing, pollution, or fiscal problems of Schenectady or any other city where his plants may be located. This is no less true, as is now becoming more common, when the president of the parent company lives in Tokyo. Local communities in the United States face the same fundamental issues of public policy as do Latin American republics. How much foreign —i.e., nonlocal—investment do they wish to accept? On what terms? What does it mean to have the local economy controlled from outside?

Some local communities are likely to begin questioning the wisdom of turning over the dynamic sectors of their economies to large corporations and to recognize that such corporations can play a useful role only if the community itself knows where it wants to go. The first priority for a community, whether in Argentina, Kenya, or Ohio, is to set its own development priorities: How many jobs must be created? What kind of technology should it develop? What sorts of products should it make? What are its consumption needs? If the local community is to develop the power to protect the interests of the people, it should seek greater self-sufficiency and self-reliance. Until the community knows what it wants and what it can do on its own, it is not in a position to bargain effectively with global corporations.

Self-sufficiency does not mean isolationism. It may be that local communities in the United States can begin to establish direct commercial relationships with one another without the mediation of the global corporation. There is no reason why direct relationships with communities outside the United States could not also be established. But the community would control the modes of interdependence to a much greater extent, and the criteria for establishing relationships would be local public needs instead of a global profit maximization.

Local communities in the United States might well begin to make the same analysis of their situation as underdeveloped countries are doing. Foreign ownership and control destroys local initiative and precludes the development of local entrepreneurial talent. Where possible, towns, cities, and regions should seek loans and indirect portfolio investment from global corporations as an alternative to being taken over. It is worth recalling that the development of the United States in the nineteenth century and of Japan in the twentieth century were accomplished with substantial amounts of foreign capital, but it was mostly in the form of bonds and other types of indirect portfolio investment. The suppliers of capital from abroad did not end up owning or managing either nation. Local communities should consider whether they prefer, as some underdeveloped countries do, to buy technical services from global corporations rather than have them manage or own local industry or, indeed, whether the community itself should own and manage key industries, as is the case in some cities which operate public utilities and transportation systems. There is no particular reason why community-run golf courses and bus companies should be in the American tradition and community-run food stores, clothing factories, refineries, and other facilities for making cities and towns more self-reliant should be considered un-American. The reality that corporations providing essential public services, such as transportation, communications, and power, are social institutions should now be recognized, and, increasingly, they should be subject to community ownership and management. The principle of the TVA—regionally based, publicly controlled corporations—is now being proposed for the energy industry in Vermont and West Virginia, and a national program of public ownership has been proposed in Congress. The issue of deep government involvement in the American economy was settled long ago. The issue that remains is not "socialism versus capitalism," as it used to be put, but whether government intervention in an evolving, mixed economy is going to reinforce the present patterns of distribution of wealth in American society or change those patterns of distribution in the direction of greater equality and better social services for the majority.

Within the context of a national development program there are many practical steps that could help insure greater bargaining power for local communities in their dealings with global corporations. Corporations could be required to file a plan with local authorities covering the corporations' local operations.

The plan should include an estimate of its employment requirements by categories for the period and reports on what research it is undertaking to increase local employment opportunities, what expenditures it is making to improve job safety, and what plans it has to increase worker and community participation in basic management decisions affecting the community. Any local public authority should have access to all plans submitted by other local operations of the same company anywhere else in the world. (Such a provision might help accelerate the process of reducing inequalities of wages, working conditions, etc.—a frequent claim of global managers which experience to date does little to justify.) The corporation should be required to conduct studies at its own expense of the amounts and impacts of pollution it emits in the community. It should present a plan for pollution abatement, with costs and sources of funding. Finally, it should offer a demonstration of its financial impact on the community—i.e., whether it is taking out more in profits and disguised financial flows than it is putting in through taxes and payroll. In order that the community can determine whether the corporation is having a positive or negative impact on its own balance of payments, the city council should have access to *all* sets of the local subsidiary's books and such financial information from headquarters as is necessary for such a determination. Where a corporation has a dominant position in a community because it controls a large percentage of the local economy and is a principal employer and taxpayer, its mode of operation determines key political and social choices for the whole population. Its members should have the right from time to time to vote on whether the community is benefiting from the presence of the corporation. The renewable community franchise ratified by public referendum would give the public the chance to assess the costs and benefits of the local corporate activity and require the corporation to make the case that it is acting responsibly through public debate instead of periodic TV pronouncements.

But local reforms will not succeed unless they are integrated into national policy. Unless there is Federal legislation setting national standards for building up the countervailing power of local communities and labor, global corporations can always play one local community off against another. Local communities that waken to the need for their own development programs may not represent a "good investment climate," and as long as more apathetic and manageable communities exist, corporations would be likely to move there. For this reason there should be legal prohibitions on the power of global corporations to exploit their mobility. A corporation should not be allowed to move into a community, pollute it, drain it financially, build dependencies, and then disclaim responsibility for the problems it creates as it leaves. What those responsibilities are and how they are to be enforced must be established by law.

How can our institutions be stretched to cope with these fundamental politicoeconomic issues? There are a number of possible approaches. Scott Buchanan, Ralph Nader, and others have proposed that "public directors" be added to the board of directors of large public corporations, either appointed by management or elected by the shareholders. But the local community has an even stronger right to representation on the board than small share-holders. Unfortunately, the whole fight to make corporate boards more representative may be beside the point. A good many stud-ies suggest that outside directors on the boards of large corpora-tions play largely ceremonial roles, that indeed the whole board of directors is often window dressing. Proposals to expand the board of directors are in some ways less ambitious versions of the "codetermination" system now being tried in several European countries. In Germany, for example, one third of a Supervisory Board (Aufrichtsrat) is elected by employees, which elects a Managing Board (Vorstand) to handle day-to-day management decisions. This system has allowed for relatively ineffective repre-sentation of workers' interests. If the interests of the local com-munity and the corporation's own workers are to be represented through the board of directors, then corporate laws should be amended to specify the crucial corporate decisions that must be submitted to the board.

Marcus Raskin has suggested that the presidents of General Motors and other giant firms ought to run for their offices. Cer-tainly they exercise more political power over the daily lives of citizens than most elected officials. Whether it is possible to change our political system to recognize that fact in the context of a still nominally "free enterprise" economy is another matter. But there is surely no reason why the officials in charge of regu-lating Big Business ought not to submit themselves to the elec-torate. Candidates for membership on regulatory commissions should be elected, not appointed. Their constituency should be the public, not the industry they are regulating.

The rise of the global corporation is the culmination of the modern industrial era, the playing out of a certain system of val-ues. The prospect of the Global Shopping Center confronts the species with a series of fundamental choices about the purposes of human existence. Unless we are prepared to look at those ques-tions at the deepest level, our response to the accelerating human predicament will be trivial.

Our system of measurement reveals what we value most deeply. By what standard do we pace ourselves? By the quantity of goods produced and the number of times they are transferred from one hand to another? By the amount of energy we burn? By the amount of precious paper we accumulate? By the number of human operations that can be transferred to a reliable machine? By how well we conquer nature? These are the dominant standards of the industrial world.

But there are other standards. We could develop a holistic meaning for efficiency (now defined simply as the most output from the private sector at the least cost to it). We could impose qualitative standards for what we produce—i.e., What human functions does it serve? We could build in the human factor in the assessment of costs—i.e., What does it do to men, women, water, air, and our social system to produce these goods? We could start putting a negative value on wasted lives. We could ask, "Efficient for whom?" As long as the contemporary corporate definition of efficiency is accepted by society as a whole the global corporation will dominate our public life.

The designers of the Global Factory and the Global Shopping Center have assumed that concentrating crucial decisions in a few hands is the key to smooth management, the antidote to anarchy and chaos. The World Managers believe that they are sophisticated enough to maintain a highly centralized system with just enough decentralization and participation to satisfy people's psychological needs and political yearnings. But perhaps it is really necessary to choose: Centralization vs. decentralization. Private power vs. public participation. Global politico-economic empires vs. communities founded on face-to-face politics. A process of equitable distribution of access to goods and claims on the future, which are the indispensable bases of freedom and the power to exercise political choice, vs. an ever more sophisticated system of accelerating repression. The search for stability through mindless growth vs. a more modest model of stability.

This is an apocalyptical age, and prophecies of doom are commonplace. Yet when the prophets and counterprophets are still, there remain two inescapable imperatives for human survival: First, because we now know that the resources of the earth are finite and the biosphere is not infinitely forgiving, each generation must act as trustee for the next, or at some unpredictable but certain point there will be no next generation. Thus we are the first generation to have the awareness that man has the power to end history and the first that may have the destructive technology to end it ourselves.

Second, there can be no freedom in a world system rooted in social injustice. The structures and institutions of repression have become so global and interdependent that it is no longer possible, as it was in ancient Athens, to maintain the liberties of a few on the slavery of many. It is an insuperable task to achieve democracy in the United States within a world system in which the majority are doomed to hunger and hopelessness and pacified by official terror or official lies. (Watergate is only the most obvious example of the boomerang effect of pursuing antidemocratic policies abroad.) An American political economy that is less and less able to offer stability for the middle classes or hope for the poor can be governed only with the same heavy hand now so familiar in failed democracies around the world.

The political functions of the market—to replenish social capital, to achieve social balance, and to preserve and expand the possibilities of human freedom—have been negated by its own creatures, global corporations that operate beyond markets. The market as an effective political management and distribution system is almost gone, but the myth of the market still forestalls serious public planning, and the market mentality, to use Polanyi's term, is still a driving force for more mindless accumulation and waste.

We are all prisoners of old political labels. The new system needed for our collective survival does not exist. Increasingly, the most powerful argument voiced in defense of the global corporation is precisely this lack of alternatives. Compared with avaricious local business, it is said, global firms are better. They pay more in taxes, they employ more people, and they cheat less. Compared with dictatorial and corrupt governments, the World Managers are relatively enlightened and honest. Compared with selfish local interests clutching at privilege, global corporations are less parochial. Compared with the Stalinist police state, a world run by the global corporation promises more freedom and less terror. Those who hold increasing power over our lives defend it with the argument that there is nothing better.

But there are other ways to organize our resources and our lives that transcend the old labels and categories. Both a global vision and radical decentralization and diffusion of political power now appear to be requirements of a stable and just human order. The intellectual and political task of reconciling the two is staggering. But our institutions are our own creations.

The purpose of social organization ought to be human development—the building of structures that give individuals, acting in cooperation with others, the rights and powers of participation where they work and where they live. The democratization of institutions—toward increasing employee management in the factories, neighborhood government, direct participation of citizens in community reform, and publicly controlled utilities—is not efficient in terms of corporate profits, but it appears to be much more efficient than the Global Shopping Center for developing the potential of human beings and for saving scarce, exhaustible resources. Under the rationalized, centralized management system of the global corporation it is profitable to convert 21 pounds of inexpensive grain protein into 1 pound of expensive meat protein.

The search for a systemic alternative is intimately bound up with a change in the global value system. As Tawney and others have shown, the goal of infinite accumulation was not present in the Middle Ages. Greed is a special characteristic of our modern economic system, which depends upon it as a primary incentive of social organization. The market mentality which puts economic activity, irrespective of purpose, at the center of the universe is a product not of human instinct but of social organization. Competitive individualism, a system in which community develops from common consumption rather than shared feelings, is increasingly incompatible with survival of the species, but it too is socially conditioned, and hence new values can be learned to take its place. The values needed for survival, if one reflects on it, turn out to be the familiar democratic values preached by prophets and sages since the beginning of history—respect for human dignity, justice, frugality, honesty, moderation, and equality.

These values will not come to replace the contemporary outmoded values—competitive individualism, comfort, waste, infinite growth, and security through accumulation—because human beings suddenly learn altruism. They will come to be the dominant values of the coming century, if at all, only if enough people are awakened to their necessity for the survival of the species. The extraordinary transformation of the world political economy is creating new awareness that, just as people in rich countries share problems once thought to be the exclusive property of poor countries, so the dislocations inherent in this new stage of capitalism transcend traditional class lines. Small businessmen and labor unions feel some of the same effects from the mobility of global corporations, and consumers, taxpayers, and citizens concerned with ecological balance experience the same sense of impotence in the face of the expansion of corporate power. With this growing awareness comes the possibility of a new shared political consciousness for reconstruction. But the battle for survival is always a race against time. The critical question is whether we can adapt our institutions and ourselves to a rapidly changing environment—in time.

For this reason, the development of new knowledge becomes absolutely crucial. We have talked much in this book about knowledge as a principal dynamic of social change. The prospects for human survival depend upon what we can learn about our condition and how fast. Knowledge and values are inextricably bound up with each other, despite the current convention that they are not. No knowledge or institution for the development of knowledge is value-free. The contemporary emphasis on specialization reflects a self-defeating judgment that holistic analysis is neither possible nor desirable. The questions we put to our computers are steeped in parochial bias. If we are to survive as a species, we shall need to cultivate a profusion of alternative political assumptions. To free ourselves from the straitjacket of orthodoxy, usually a brilliant theoretical model of how the system functioned in the last generation, we need to encourage a variety of analyses that attempt to deal with social, ecological, and psychological reality together.

The road to alternative practical solutions leads by way of social experimentation. The United States could use its extraordinary surplus to finance a variety of experiments in public ownership and public planning, in the support of small-scale technology, in the development of strong neighborhoods. We do not have such an abundance of ideas that we can ignore what is to be learned from a wide range of social systems. We could confront head-on the dilemmas and disappointments of socialism as it has evolved in other countries. (For this reason, the efforts to suppress social experimentation abroad, as in Cuba or Allende's Chile, are not only cruel but shortsighted.) We could see whether with our unique wealth, our relatively stable history, and the benefits of hindsight we could not learn from the accomplishments and mistakes of others to build an American community in which we would also act as global citizens. In confronting a threatening future, the only advantage we have over the dodo is a dynamic consciousness to match a changing environment. That is the great gift that offers us our chance to shape our institutions to the realities of a new age.

Notes for Text and Tables

1 : The World Managers

Page 13

Willkie quotation by Maisonrouge comes from his speech "Growth of the Business World," Nov. 13, 1969. Maisonrouge is perhaps the most articulate and thoughtful of the new breed of global corporate managers and has publicly pondered the political implications of global corporations more than most. For this reason we have treated him as a typical spokesman of the new ideology and have quoted him extensively. Others could have been chosen who say the same things less well. Speeches of corporate executives quoted in the text are available from public relations departments of their corporations.

Quote from Peccei can be found in "Will Businessmen Unite the World?," Center for the Study of Democratic Institutions, Santa Barbara, Calif., *Occasional Paper,* April, 1971.

Ball statement is quoted in Jacques Maisonrouge, "After the American Challenge—The American Model," Nov. 5, 1969.

Page 14

Reference to a "global shopping center" is found in Peter Drucker, *The Age of Discontent,* London: Pan Books, Chapter 5.

Quotes from Maisonrouge are from "How International Business Can Further World Understanding," delivered Sept. 16, 1971.

Page 15

The comparisons between the GNPs of countries and corporations are found in Senate Finance Committee, *The Multinational Corporation and the World Economy* (1973), p. 8. It is interesting to note that the transactions between Ford subsidiaries in Germany and Belgium constitute 25 percent of Belgium's total foreign trade transactions.

Page 16

Gerstacker quotes can be found in "The Structure of the Corporation," prepared for the *White House Conference on the Industrial World Ahead,* Washington, Feb. 7–9, 1972.

Quote from Union Carbide spokesman is cited by Gyorgy Adam in *The New Hungarian Quarterly,* 1970, p. 203.

Kindleberger's quote is in his *American Business Abroad,* New Haven: Yale, 1969, pp. 179–82.

389

Page 17

Banking profit figures are taken from J. H. Allan, "Banks Are Rushing Abroad Pell-Mell," *The New York Times,* p. 56f., Jan. 27, 1974.

Department of Commerce statistics are found in "Special Survey of U.S. Multinational Companies, 1970," National Technical Information Service, U.S. Dept. of Commerce, Tables 1 and 3.

The reference to Stephenson can be found in his book *The Coming Clash,* London: Weidenfeld & Nicolson, 1972, p. 5.

Simmonds statistics are from "Multinational? Well, Not Quite," *World Business: Promises and Problems,* Courtney Brown, ed., New York: Macmillan, 1970, p. 49. Articles cited in this volume also appeared in the *Columbia Journal of World Business.*

Page 18

Maisonrouge quote can be found in "After the American Challenge," *op. cit.*

Spencer is quoted in *Newsweek,* Nov. 20, 1972.

Page 19

Ball quote is from his speech delivered May 5, 1967, to the New York Chamber of Commerce, New York, N.Y.

Powers quote can be found in his speech "The Multinational Company," September, 1967.

Maisonrouge is quoted from his address to the American Foreign Service Association, Washington, D.C., May 29, 1969.

Business International Report is entitled *Corporate Planning Today for Tomorrow's World Market,* July, 1967.

Maisonrouge reference can be found in "Growth of the Business World," Nov. 13, 1969.

Page 20

Ash quote is from the *Columbia Journal of World Business* Vol. 5, No. 2, March–April, 1970, p. 92.

Page 21

Ball is cited in Robert Heilbroner, "The Multinational Corporation and the Nation-State," *The New York Review of Books,* Feb. 11, 1971.

Page 22

Singer statistics are in "Global Companies: Too Big to Handle?," *Newsweek,* Nov. 20, 1972.

Statistics for General Instruments are in Louis Turner, *Multinational Companies of the Third World,* New York: Hill & Wang, 1973, Chapter 7.

Page 24

Rockefeller speech is entitled "The Future of the Multinational Corporation." May 1, 1972.

Maisonrouge quote is from "Growth of the Business World," *op. cit.*

2: From Globaloney to the Global Shopping Center

Page 26

Statistics offered by Perlmutter are taken from "Super-Giant Firms in the Future," *Wharton Quarterly,* Winter, 1968.

Statistics on corporate profits are from *International Investment Production,* U.S. Council, International Chamber of Commerce, New York, 1969, mimeo.

Page 28
Reference to the loan syndicate and bank consortium and to First National City Bank, is found in J. H. Allan, "Banks Are Rushing Abroad Pell-Mell," *The New York Times,* p. 56*f.*, Jan. 27, 1974.

Reference to Singer is taken from "Global Companies: Too Big to Handle?," *Newsweek,* Nov. 20, 1972, p. 96.

The quote from Meigs is from *Newsweek, op. cit.*

Page 29
Finance Committee excerpt is from "Implications of Multinational Firms for World Trade and Investment and for U.S. Trade and Labor," Hearings before the Committee on Finance, U.S. Senate, Feb. 1973.

A discussion of cash-management systems is found in Michael A. Brooke and H. Lee Remmers, *The Strategy of the Multinational Enterprise.* New York: Elsevier, 1970, p. 285.

LDC difficulties in generating local investment funds is found in Ronald Müller, "Poverty is the Product," *Foreign Policy,* Winter 1973/74.

Page 30
"heavenly city . . ." reference is from "Singapore: Global City," speech by S. Rajaratnom, Feb. 6, 1972.

Video-recorder discussion is in Louis Turner, *Multinational Companies of the Third World,* New York: Hill & Wang, 1973, pp. 178–79, quoting interview with Abe Morgenstern, IUE official.

Dichter quote is in "The World Customer," *Harvard Business Review,* Vol. 40, No. 4, July–August, 1962, p. 113.

Page 31
Bickmore is quoted in *Forbes,* Nov. 15, 1968.

Pages 32–34
Quotes can be found in David Finn, *The Corporate Oligarch,* New York: Simon & Schuster, 1969, p. 130. For a further examination of oligopolistic concentration in less-developed countries, see Chapter 7 below.

Page 35
Maisonrouge quote is from "International Marketing," delivered to The Conference Board, Oct. 21, 1971.

Page 36
Eells can be found in "Multinational Corporations: The Intelligence Function," *World Business: Promises and Problems,* Courtney Brown, ed., New York: Macmillan, 1970.

Reference to the Ford economic analyst can be found in Sanford Rose, "The Rewarding Strategies of Multinationalism," *Fortune,* Sept. 15, 1968, p. 101.

Page 37
Gerstacker quote is found in "The Structure of the Corporation," prepared for the White House Conference on the Industrial World Ahead, Washington, Feb. 7–9, 1972.

Reference to Hymer is in his "The Multinational Corporation and the Law of Uneven Development," in J. N. Bhagwati, ed., *Economics and World Order from the 1970's to the 1990's,* New York: Macmillan, 1972, pp. 113–41.

Page 38
McKenzie quote is from "Concept of Dominance and World Organization," in the *American Journal of Sociology,* July 1927.

Page 39
J.-J. Servan-Schreiber's work is from *The American Challenge,* New York: Atheneum, 1968, pp. 13–14. See also Rainer Hellman, *Amerika auf dem Europa Markt.* For a discussion of European counterattacks to the American Challenge, see Christopher Tugendhat, *The Multinationals,* New York: Random House, 1972, pp. 41–57.

Page 40
Speech by Fred Borch, "The Future of International Trade," was delivered Nov. 13, 1972.

Behrman is quoted in Richard Eells, *Global Corporations,* New York: Interbook, 1972, p. 25.

Page 41
The figures for GE's foreign expansion are from Turner, *op. cit.,* Chapter 7.

Voss and Thornbrough are found in Sanford Rose, *op. cit.,* p. 104.

Fortune quote is in issue of Sept. 15, 1968.

Page 42
On the degree of centralization, production decision-making at headquarters and the associated "worldwide sourcing" of resources see Gyorgy Adam, "Some Implications and Concomitants of Worldwide Sourcing," *ACTA Oeconomica,* Vol. 8 (2–3), 1972, pp. 309–23.

For a discussion of "plans developed in the global cities," see Robert Cohen, "The System of U.S. Cities in an Era of Global Business," Research Center for Economic Planning, New York, December 1973, unpublished paper, also to appear in Ph.D. dissertation, Columbia University, forthcoming.

The discussion of IBM's data-bank monitors is from a personal interview and demonstration.

Page 44
Quote is from Brooke and Remmers, *op. cit.,* p. 285.

3: Personal Identity and the Corporate Image

Page 46
For a discussion of Max Weber on legitimacy see Richard J. Barnet, "International Law and the Control of Violence," in Richard Falk, ed., *The Future of International Law,* Vol. III, Princeton, 1972.

The functional relationships between ideology and other forces of social change are analyzed in Ronald Müller's "The Social Sciences and Society," in Müller and Arnold, eds., *Power and the World Political Economy: A Social Science Focus* (forthcoming).

Page 47
Bean's remarks were delivered at the Business International Roundtable for Chief Executive Officers, Jamaica, Jan. 6–10, 1971.

Page 48
Tawney quote is found in Foreword to Max Weber, *The Protestant Ethic and the Spirit of Capitalism,* New York: Scribner's, 1958, pp. 1a–7.

Page 49
Quote from Powers is found in his "The Multinational Company," Nov. 21, 1967.
The discussion of the "eastern banking establishment" is from Richard J. Barnet, *The Economy of Death,* New York: Atheneum, 1969, and William Domhoff, *The Higher Circles,* New York: Random House, 1970, pp. 89–101.

Page 50
The colorful details of Geneen's life have been recounted in a series of articles: "Geneen's Moneymaking Machine Is Still Humming," *Fortune,* September 1972; "Harold Geneen Has No Time to Be Nice," *Life,* May 19, 1972; "Succession Plan at ITT," *Business Week,* April 1972; "Clubby World of ITT," *Time,* March 27, 1972. Also see Anthony Sampson, *The Sovereign State of ITT,* New York: Stein & Day, 1973, pp. 123–28, as well as the *Time* cover story of Sept. 8, 1967.
The reference to Maccoby's studies, and others that will follow, are from personal conversations during the preparation of his book *The Corporate Individual,* New York: Simon & Schuster, forthcoming.

Page 51
Millán is cited from "The Dreams of Mexican Executives," paper presented to the American Anthropological Association, Nov. 20, 1971.

Page 54
The quotes attributed to Schorr are taken from a personal interview, Dec. 13, 1972, conducted by Joseph Collins.

Page 55
Gerstacker is quoted from "The Structure of the Corporation," delivered at the White House Conference on the Industrial World Ahead, Feb. 7, 1972.

Page 56
Clausen is quoted from "The International Corporation: An Executive's View," *The Annals of the American Academy of Political and Social Science,* September 1972, p. 21.

Page 57
Clausen quote *op. cit.*

Pages 57–60
The discussion by top executives took place at the Roundtable for Chief Executive Officers organized by Business International, Jamaica, Jan. 6–10, 1971.

Page 61
Galloway is taken from his article "The Military-Industrial Linkages of U.S. Based Multinational Corporations," *International Studies Quarterly,* December 1972, pp. 491–510.

Page 61
Sampson's analysis of ITT's history and activities is found in his book *The Sovereign State of ITT,* New York: Stein & Day, 1973.

Harder's quote is in a CPC International Public Relations Department release.

Clausen quote *op. cit.*

Page 64
Kendall quote can be found in his "Corporate Ownership: The International Dimension," in *World Business: Promises & Problems,* Courtney Brown, ed., New York: Macmillan, 1962, p. 257f.

Heltzer reference is in a 3M Public Relations Department release.

Morgan is quoted from "The Win-Win Strategy," presented to the White House Conference on the Industrial World Ahead, Feb. 7, 1972.

Page 65
Clausen quote is from "Some Thoughts on Economic Initiatives for Lasting Peace," June 27, 1972.

De Cubas speech is available from Westinghouse.

Page 68
For an analysis of the impact of the Vietnam War on the American economy, see Thomas Riddell, "The U.S. Economy and the Impacts of Vietnam," Ph.D. dissertation, American University, Washington, D.C., 1974.

Harris poll was taken in February 1972.

Page 69
Armstrong's remarks are taken from a personal interview, Oct. 19, 1972, conducted by Joseph Collins.

Boguslaw quote is from his book *The New Utopians: A Study of System Design and Social Change,* Englewood Cliffs, New Jersey: Prentice Hall, Inc., 1965, p. 25.

Page 71
Reference to the "bicycle economy" comes from Mahbub ul Haq's article "Employment in the 1970's: A New Perspective," pp. 266–272 in C. K. Wilber, ed., *The Political Economy of Development and Underdevelopment,* New York: Random House, 1973.

4: Corporate Diplomacy and National Loyalty

Page 72
For a discussion of the East India Company, see Brian Gardner's *The East India Company,* New York: McCall Publishing Company, 1971.

Reference to the Company of the Merchants of the Staple is taken from Paul J. McNulty, "Predecessors of the Multinational Corporation," *Columbia Journal of World Business,* May–June, 1972.

Page 73
For further discussion of political power and the purposes of government see Sigmund Timberg, "The Corporation as a Technique of International Administration," 19 University of Chicago Law Review, 1952, pp. 742–43, and Karl Polanyi, "Our Obsolete Market Mentality," *Commentary,* Feb. 1947.

Page 76
Hymer from "The Multinational Corporation and the Law of Uneven Development," in J. N. Bhagwati, ed., *Economics and World Order from the 1970's to the 1990's,* New York: Macmillan, 1972.

Page 77
See Berle's *The 20th Century Capitalist Revolution,* New York: Harcourt Brace, 1954.

Pages 78–79
For a review of U.S. government intervention and corporate involvement in underdeveloped countries since World War II, see Richard J. Barnet, *Intervention and Revolution,* New York: Mentor, 1972.

Page 79
The reference to the decline of U.S. economic prestige can be found in Raymond Vernon, *Sovereignty at Bay,* New York: Basic Books, 1971. See also Chapter 10 below. The increasing competitiveness of other industrial countries is primarily a function of two factors. First, the successful reconstruction of Western Europe and Japan by the 1960's allowed them not only to be successful in the export markets, but also to begin the expansion of their own foreign equity investment. It was not until the late 1960's that these countries' wage rates began to rise relative to productivity, increasing even as they continued to enjoy the export advantages of relatively undervalued currencies. Second, the acceleration of the rate of technological diffusion contributed to their growing competitiveness. For a demonstration of the latter point in the petrochemicals industry, see Robert B. Stobaugh, "The Product Life Cycle, U.S. Exports and International Investment," unpublished D.B.A. thesis, Harvard Business School, June 1968, App. C. Also see Vernon's discussion, *op. cit.,* pp. 90–112.

Page 80
The reference to AID-financed exports is from Michael Hudson and Denis Goulet, *The Myth of Aid,* New York: IDOC, North America, 1971, p. 86.

The facts on health grants to Latin America are found in the *Congressional Record,* Feb. 10, 1966, pp. S2886–S2894 and Hearings Before the Subcommittee on Monopoly of the Select Committee on Small Business, U.S. Senate, Part 18, Aug. 6, 11, 17, 18, 1970.

Page 81
Gallagher is cited in Council of the Americas, *Report,* Vol. 7, No. 3, September 1971, pp. 10–11.

The discussion that follows regarding ITT and Chile is derived from ITT documents released by Jack Anderson and published by the Chilean Government.

Page 84
Goodsell is from his paper "Diplomatic Protection of U.S. Business in Peru," in Daniel A. Sharp, ed., *U.S. Foreign Policy and Peru,* Austin: University of Texas Press, 1972, pp. 267–68.

Pages 84–85
Quote citing the foreign service directive and also the reference to Middendorf are found in "World Trade: A U.S. Ambassador's New Business Role," *Business Week,* Dec. 16, 1972, p. 38.

Page 85
Quote referring to "the air of a war room" is found in *Forbes,* Dec. 1, 1972, p. 27.

Page 86
Reference to *"terrorismo económico"* was the response of Jorge Valencia Jaranillo to the contents of a letter sent to the President of Colombia in 1971

by representatives of the Council of the Americas (at that time called the Council for Latin America) in attempting to disarm that country's approval of the Andean Pact Decision 24. The letter is published in its entirety with an analysis thereof by Miguel S. Wionczek, "La Reacción Norteamericana ante el Tratado Común a los Capitales Extranjeros en el Grupo Andino," *Comercio Exterior*, May 1971, pp. 406–408.

Geylin is cited in Council of the Americas, *Report*, September 1971, pp. 4–5.

Rockefeller in a speech delivered before the Council of the Americas, Dec. 5, 1972.

Pages 86–87
The discussion of "company-owned countries" is from Louis Turner, *Multinational Companies of the Third World*, New York: Hill & Wang, 1973.

Pages 88–89
McGrew quote is from his article "Litton's Noble Experiment," in the *Columbia Journal of World Business*, Vol. VII, No. 1, January–February 1972, p. 65.

Pages 89–92
A further discussion regarding the public relations promotions of corporations in host countries can be found in Joseph Collins, "Global Corporations and United States Policy Toward Latin America," Jan. 8, 1973, mimeo, Institute for Policy Studies.

Page 92
Reference to Gloor comes from his "Policies and Practices at Nestlé Alimentana S.A.," delivered at the British Management Institute Conference, July 1966.

Hacker quote is from *The Corporation Takeover*, New York: Harper & Row, 1964, pp. 260f.

Kindleberger is quoted from "The International Corporation," *American Business Abroad*, New Haven: Yale, 1969, p. 207.

Page 94
Zingaro is quoted in *Business Week*, Nov. 4, 1972.

Page 95
Borch from speech "The Future of International Trade," Nov. 13, 1972.

Pages 96–102
For an examination of the Nixonian brand of warfare, see Michael Klare, *War Without End*, New York: Random House, 1972.

Page 102
For further discussion of government-company relations see Edith T. Penrose, *The Large International Firm in Developing Countries: The International Petroleum Industry*, Cambridge, Mass.: MIT Press, 1968, as cited in Robert O. Keohane and Van Doorn Ooms, "The Multinational Enterprise and World Political Economy," *International Organization* XXVI, No. 1, Winter 1972, p. 84.

Page 103
The studies of Michael Tanzer are found in his *The Political Economy of International Oil and the Underdeveloped Countries*, Boston: Beacon, 1969, pp. 243–56.

5: The Great Crusade for Understanding

Page 107
Roche is quoted in *Newsweek,* May 24, 1971, p. 77.

Page 109
Public-opinion poll on the business community is cited in Richard J. Barnet, *Roots of War,* New York: Atheneum, 1972, p. 141.

For a discussion of corporate social responsibility and public relations campaigns see "The American Corporation," *Newsweek,* May 24, 1971.

Page 115
See Veblen's *The Higher Learning in America: A Memorandum on the Conduct of Universities by Businessmen,* New York: Sagamore, 1957 (first published in 1918).

Page 116
Butterworth is quoted in Hugh Stephenson, *The Coming Clash,* London: Weidenfeld & Nicolson, 1972, pp. 62–63.

6: The Global Corporations and the Underdeveloped World

Page 123
De Windt is found in "Business Survival in the Seventies: Is the World Company the Answer?" delivered before the Mid-America World Trade Conference, Chicago, Feb. 25, 1971.

McNamara quote is from "Social Equity and Economic Growth: A Plan for Action," delivered to the Board of Governors, World Bank Group, Washington, D.C., Sept. 25, 1972.

Page 124
For a typical discussion of the "growing antipathy" toward big business, see Frank B. Loretta as quoted in *Times of Latin America,* April 4, 1973, p. 3.

Pages 126–28

Table I.
U.S. Department of the Interior, *First Annual Report of the Secretary of the Interior Under the Mining and Minerals Policy Act of 1970*: Appendices, March, 1972, as cited in *The United States and the Developing World: Agenda for Action,* Overseas Development Council, 1973, pp. 13–39. Copper and sulphur figures for 1971.

Table II.
Figures for advanced nations excluding socialist economies are computed from: *Mineral Industry Surveys,* U.S. Department of the Interior, Washington, D.C., 1973, pp. 4–18; *U.N. Statistical Yearbook, 1972,* New York, 1973, p. 541; *Mineral Yearbook,* Vol. III, U.S. Department of the Interior, Washington, D.C., 1971; *Metal Statistics 1973: The Purchasing Guide of the Metal Industries,* New York, 1973.

Estimates for all advanced nations' (excluding socialist economies) consumption of antimony, bauxite, fluorspar, graphite, and manganese are derived by the use of an adjustment coefficient. The adjustment coefficient assumes homogenous production functions between advanced nations. It was derived by averaging the ratios of all advanced nations' consumption to that of U.S. consumption in the four instances where data were available.

This coefficient (3.07) was then applied to the consumption figure giving the advanced-nation percentage consumption estimates.

Table III.

United Nations, *World Energy Supplies,* Department of Economic and Social Affairs, Statistical Papers, Series J, Nos. 6, 15, 16. Oil statistics are taken from *B.P. Statistical Review of the World Industry,* London: British Petroleum Corp., 1973, 1969, 1960. See also Joel Darmstadter, *et al., Energy in the World Economy,* Baltimore: Johns Hopkins University Press, 1971, for Resources for the Future, and U.S. Bureau of Mines, *An Energy Model for the United States,* Information Circular 8384, 1968, and other Bureau of Mines releases, as cited in *The United States and the Developing World, op. cit.,* p. 136.

Table IV.

United States Tariff Commission, *Economic Factors Affecting the Use of Items 807.00 and 806.30 of the Tariff Schedules of the United States,* Washington, D.C., 1970, as cited in G. K. Helleiner, "Manufactured Exports from Less-Developed Countries and the Multinational Firms," *Economic Journal,* March 1973, p. 21.

Table V.

Figures are official rates found in *Yearbook of Labour Statistics,* International Labor Office, Geneva, 1972, pp. 426–429, corrected by a conversion coefficient to determine the rates. Coefficient taken from International Labor Office, *op. cit.,* p. 90. A 1970 ILO case study of Colombia discovered that while the "official" unemployment rate as listed in the 1964 Census was 4.9 percent, the actual rate in the urban areas alone exceeded 20 percent of the labor force. Therefore, a conservative estimate indicates that the real rate is at least four times the official rate. It is also apparent from other available information that the disparity between the real and official rates extends far beyond Colombia. In India, for example, a worker who is "gainfully employed for one hour a day is officially listed as employed." Thus the need to correct the official rate by the coefficient determined by the Colombian study to give a *conservative* estimate of the dimensions of unemployment. Also see Paul Bairoch, *El desempleo urbano en los paises en desarrollo: presentación general del problema y elementos de solución,* Geneva: International Labor Organization, 1973.

Table VI.

Growth of "Export Platforms" from *International Economic Report of the President 1973,* Washington, D.C.: Government Printing Office, March 1973, p. 66.

Page 129
The first pioneering synthesis of the Product Life Cycle Theory can be found in Raymond Vernon, "International Investment and International Trade in the Product Life Cycle," *Quarterly Journal of Economics,* Vol. 80, 1966, pp. 190–207. An initial attempt to use the Product Life Cycle Theory for deriving welfare implications of global corporations is R. E. Caves, "International Corporations: The Industrial Economics of Foreign Investment," *Economica,* Vol. 38, February 1971, pp. 1–27. In our view, Caves's theoretical results, pointing toward an increase in world welfare through the expansion of global corporations, are erroneous because of his failure to assume the conglomerate (i.e., vertical and horizontal integration) structure of the typical international firm and the incorrect assumption of interindustry mobility of domestic labor. The latter is particularly incorrect in underdeveloped countries because of structural rigidities. On this see R. S. Eckaus, "The Factor Proportions Problem in Underdeveloped Areas," *American Economic Review,*

September 1955. A historical interpretation, utilizing the Product Life Cycle Theory, can be found in an excellent work by Mira Wilkins, *The Emergence of Multinational Enterprise: American Business Abroad from the Colonial Era to 1914*, Cambridge, Mass.: Harvard University Press, 1970. Many of the empirical demonstrations of the Product Life Cycle Theory have been admirably collected and presented by Louis T. Wells, Jr., ed., *The Product Life Cycle and International Trade*, Boston: Harvard Graduate School of Business Administration, Harvard University, 1972. For an interpretation somewhat similar to ours on the use of the Product Life Cycle as a theory of international expansion of more developed countries see Theodore H. Moran, "Foreign Expansion as an 'Institutional Necessity': The U.S. Corporate Capitalism: The Search for a 'Radical' Model," *World Politics*, Spring 1973. Many of the elements in the Product Life Cycle Theory cited above were derived from a relatively new field of economics called Theory of Industrial Organization. Among the leaders in this field is Edward S. Mason. A comprehensive representation of Mason's numerous works in industrial organization is *Economic Concentration and the Monopoly Problem*, Cambridge, Mass.: Harvard University Press, 1957. For the wide influence that Mason's work has had in various areas in economics and political economy see Jesse W. Markham and Gustav F. Papanek, eds., *Industrial Organization and Economic Development: In Honor of E. S. Mason*, Boston: Houghton Mifflin Company, 1970. Other pioneers in industrial organization are Joe S. Bain, *Industrial Organization*, New York: Wiley, 1968, and F. M. Scherer, *Industrial Market Structure and Economic Performance*, Chicago: Rand McNally, 1971.

Page 130

On types of postinvention costs see essays in Wells, Jr., ed., *op. cit.*

It is a historical consistency of industrialized societies that "latecomers" have accelerated growth compared with "pioneers," be they individual corporations or nation-states. The advantage to new entrants rests on the low-cost benefits derived from the accumulated advances in technology of others. This was a key aspect of Thorstein Veblen's political economy. *Cf* his *Imperial Germany and the Industrial Revolution*, New York: Macmillan, 1915. For an empirical verification of this point historically, see S. J. Patel, "Rates of Industrial Growth in the Last Century: 1860–1958," in B. E. Supple, ed., *The Experience of Economic Growth*, New York: Random House, 1963, and Alexander Gershenkron, *Economic Backwardness in Historical Perspective*, New York: Praeger, 1965.

Although many economists, both orthodox and Marxist, use the term monopoly profits (and/or rents) when referring to oligopolies, we shall use throughout this book the less ambiguous term of oligopoly profits in order to maintain consistency with the text discussion.

Page 132

On Japan's almost sole reliance on foreign acquisition of technology through licensing see T. Ozawa, "Imitation, Innovation, and Japanese Exports," in *The Open Economy: Essays on International Trade and Finance*, edited by Kenen and Laurence, New York: Columbia University Press, 1968; also the discussion in *The Multinational Corporation: Studies on U.S. Foreign Investment*, U.S. Department of Commerce, Bureau of International Commerce, Vol. 1, March 1972, p. 86.

An additional advantage enjoyed by Japanese and other global corporations from certain West European countries has been tax subsidization via export-rebate programs, which was one of the reasons for the enactment of the U.S. Government's Domestic International Sales Corporation (DISC) trade legislation. Some writers have maintained that part of the Japanese global corporations' sustained success in the U.S. market during the 1960's can be explained by the practice of alleged "persistent dumping." There is, however, little evidence of persistent dumping, although "sporadic dumping" is a common practice of many global corporations—for example, the U.S. chemical industry in Europe. See C. P. Kindleberger's excellent discussion in *International Economics*, 5th ed., Homewood, Illinois: R. D. Irwin, 1973, pp. 152–57. As is noted in the text below, selling temporarily at or below costs is a classic device by which global corporations enter new markets, particularly in underdeveloped countries, with the effect of eliminating small national firms which cannot absorb the losses that effective price competition would necessitate.

Further discussion of the need for U.S. global corporations' low-wage production areas, leading to Phase Four of the Product Life Cycle, is found in a Tariff Commission Report from which we quote: "Producers of television receivers state that without access to labor at costs comparable to those of foreign producers in the assembly functions, it would be virtually impossible for the U.S. industry to maintain a significant share of the U.S. market—a substantial part of which is already supplied by imports . . ." (p. 104). Concerning Tariff Provisions 806.30 and 807.00, which basically put tariffs only on the foreign value-added proportion of imports from U.S. global corporations' export platform operations in poor countries, the Commission notes that "the major producers of semiconductors for the mass U.S. market are also major users of item 806.30" (p. 97). "Increasingly intense competition in both the foreign and the domestic markets from foreign producers has been, according to U.S. producers, the compelling factor in their decision to conduct assembly operations offshore" (p. 99). *Economic Factors Affecting the Use of Items 807.00 and 806.30 of the Tariff Schedules of the United States*, Report to the President on Investigation No. 332-61 Under Section 332 of the Tariff Act of 1930, U.S. Tariff Commission Publication 339, Washington, D.C., September 1970.

Page 133

For a discussion of ideological rationalizations by the rich for the underdevelopment of the Third World, see Richard J. Barnet, *Intervention and Revolution*, New York: rev. Mentor ed., 1972, and *Roots of War: The Men and Institutions Behind U.S. Foreign Policy*, New York: Atheneum, 1972.

Page 135

On the lack of finance capital in underdeveloped countries, we are not saying that no finance capital was invested in them. However, many studies have shown that infrastructure investments—e.g., port and railroads—were designed primarily to facilitate the outflow of resources and did not contribute to the overall development of these countries. Michael Barratt Brown, *After Imperialism*, New York: Humanities Press, 1970, on India and Africa; Celso Furtado, *Economic Development of Latin America: A Survey From Colonial Times to the Cuban Revolution*, Cambridge University Press, 1970; and Gunnar Myrdal, *Rich Lands and Poor*, New York: Harper & Row, 1957.

For evidence on the finance-capital contribution of foreign trade and investment to the economic growth of Britain in the eighteenth and nineteenth centuries see Phyllis Deane and W. A. Cole, *British Economic Growth: 1688–1959*, Cambridge University Press, 1964, pp. 28–39. Various specific breakdowns of this evidence show quantitatively the much higher rate of return derived from trade and investment in the then less-developed versus more-developed countries. See Michael Barratt Brown, *op. cit.*; Eric Williams, *Capitalism and Slavery*, Chapel Hill: University of North Carolina Press, 1944; J. Nehru, *The Discovery of India*, New York: Doubleday and Company, 1956. For example, "By the 1790's, the value of English incomes derived from the trade (including slaves) with the West Indies was about four times larger than the income from trade with all the rest of the world." This and other sources are reviewed in an illuminating historical comparison of the human and social costs of development between Western capitalist countries and the Soviet Union in Charles K. Wilber, *The Soviet Model and Underdeveloped Countries,* Chapel Hill: University of North Carolina Press, 1969, Chapter VI.

For estimates of the widening relative and absolute gaps in consumption as between rich and poor nations, over time, see the calculations of Paul Rosenstein-Rodan presented in Chapter 8 below; also Irving B. Kravis, "A World of Unequal Incomes," in *Income Inequality,* by *The Annals* of the American Academy of Political and Social Science, September 1973.

In our view, it is beside the point whether the net outflow of finance capital from the developing countries resulted in an absolute decline in consumption or a relative decline vis-à-vis the more-developed countries. The key point is that this outflow hindered and/or prevented the accumulation of knowledge necessary to maintain bargaining power. We use the term knowledge to mean both information *and* the skills and techniques to use information accumulated over time (i.e., embodied knowledge). On the one hand, the concept "knowledge" refers to information or facts about real, empirical phenomena, and on the other, it refers to positive *and* normative training, education, and experiences which determine judgments, opinions, and ideas about how to interpret information and for what purposes to use such information.

Page 136
For further discussion of the problems concerning techniques of social organization, see David Apter, *The Politics of Modernization,* Chicago: University of Chicago Press, 1965; *Study of Modernization,* Englewood Cliffs: Prentice-Hall, 1968; Frederick Harbison and Charles A. Myers, eds., *Manpower and Education: Studies in Economic Development,* New York: McGraw-Hill, 1965. David C. McClelland states that a paramount reason for slow growth in underdeveloped countries is the lack of what he calls "N-Achievement," which leads to a lack of organizational aspirations for building the necessary institutions for the development process. We disagree with this interpretation and instead believe that it was primarily the process of wealth depletion and the consequent failure to develop wealth-creating knowledge which did not permit the evolution of modern techniques of social organization. See McClelland's *The Achieving Society,* Princeton: Van Nostrand, 1961, and *Motivating Economic Achievement,* New York: Free Press, 1969.

Page 137
For an excellent review of the theoretical analyses of terms of trade see Stephen D. Krasner, "Trade in Raw Materials: The Benefits of Capitalism," delivered at the International Studies Association Convention, New York, March 16, 1973. (Mimeo, Dept. of Government, Harvard University.) Technically, the studies of Prebisch and others identify the advanced countries' oligopoly power, which we call superior bargaining power, as a major cause of the deterioration in terms of trade. Hans W. Singer, "The Distribution of Gains Between Investing and Borrowing Countries," in American Economic Association, *Readings in International Economics,* Homewood, Ill.: R. D. Irwin, 1968; and Raul Prebisch, *Towards a Dynamic Development Policy for Latin America,* New York: United Nations, 1964. Direct econometric tests of the impact of foreign trade on underdeveloped countries' economic growth extending across 44 countries and for a time period of over 30 years has shown that these impacts are either inconsistent and/or negative for the majority of poor nations in this sample. See Ronald Müller, *The Relationship Between Foreign Trade and Economic Development: A Theoretical and Econometric Investigation,* Ph.D. dissertation, The American University, 1970.

An example of institutional weaknesses such as host economies' laws governing the operations of multinational corporations can be found in Norman Girvan, "Making the Rules of the Game: Country-Company Agreements in the Bauxite Industry," *Social and Economic Studies,* Institute of Social and Economic Research, University of the West Indies, Vol. 20, No. 4, December 1971, pp. 383–84, where "the company itself controls the information about prices, costs, reserves, alternative expansion paths, production conditions, and all the other factors which are needed to devise proper Government policies . . . for example, pricing and taxation formulae are specified in ways which make it difficult or impossible for Governments to change them in the light of new knowledge." Another example is the pharmaceutical companies that continue to sell internationally drugs which have been banned in the United States by the Food and Drug Administration. There have been a number of instances in which the use of these drugs by consumers (both citizens of the country of purchase as well as visitors and tourists) has resulted in death. For an account of this practice see the *Washington Post,* June 9, 1974, p. K1.

For a detailed statement of institutional weaknesses underlying the lack of bargaining power see Ronald Müller, "The Multinational Corporation and the Underdevelopment of the Third World," in Charles K. Wilber, ed., *The Political Economy of Development and Underdevelopment,* New York: Random House, 1973, pp. 124–51. A more condensed version of this article appears in *Foreign Policy,* Winter 1973/74, entitled "Poverty Is the Product."

The first notable mention of bargaining power in the literature on foreign investment appears in Charles Kindleberger's *American Business Abroad: Six Lectures on Direct Investment,* New Haven: Yale University Press, 1969. An early systematic attempt to use the bargaining-power framework to derive foreign-investment policies for underdeveloped countries is found in Ronald Müller's "The Political Economy of Direct Foreign Investment: A Policy Appraisal for Latin American Governments," prepared in 1969 for the Prebisch Commission, published by the Inter-American Development Bank, Special Studies Division, Washington, D.C., 1970. A pioneering step to use the bargaining-power analysis to gauge the impacts of global enterprises on host economies is Constantine Vaitsos' "Interaffiliate Charges by Transnational Corporations and Intercountry Income Distribution," Ph.D. dissertation, Harvard, 1972.

Page 138
For the unwillingness of U.S.-based global corporations in agribusiness to permit agricultural trade unions, and the resulting negative effects on health and pay for workers in the Philippine banana industry, see Bernard Widerman, "Banana Boom: Fruits for Only a Few," *Far Eastern Economic Review,* Jan. 21, 1974, pp. 52–53. This behavior is perhaps reminiscent of these same firms' policies in the United States. However, organized labor has evolved and with significant bargaining power vis-à-vis multinationals in the raw-material sector such as oil in Venezuela and copper in Chile. For discussion of Singapore labor legislation see Louis Turner, *Multinational Companies and the Third World,* New York: Hill & Wang, 1973, p. 187.

On related aspects of weak organized labor in less-developed nations see also the reference notes in Chapter 11, below.

Page 139
The reference to Sears in Guatemala comes from an interview with Gert Rosenthal, National Planning Office, Guatemala, May 7, 1973. See also his *The Role of Private Foreign Investment in the Development of the Central American Common Market,* Guatemala, March 1973, a study prepared under the auspices of the Adlai Stevenson Institute of International Affairs, Chicago, and the Permanent Secretariat of the CACM; revised manuscript in preparation for publication.

The reference to the Colombian national banking association is from an interview with a Colombian banking official in May 1973.

For economic reasons, because global firms are increasingly being forced to raise the proportion of "local value-added" in their operations, they may turn to the use of local suppliers as one means of meeting this requirement. This is a politically expedient way to counter arguments about their negative impacts on domestic enterprises. For examples of such arguments from Brazil, see Chapter 8 below.

The statistics are taken from J. W. Vaupel and J. P. Curhan, *The Making of Multinational Enterprise,* Boston: Harvard Business School, 1969. More detailed calculations of the Vaupel and Curhan statistics are found in Ronald Müller, "The Multinational Corporation and the Underdevelopment of the Third World," *op. cit.*

Business Latin America, Jan. 15, 1970.

Page 140
The United Nations study is "The Role of Patents in the Transfer of Technology to Developing Countries," New York, 1964, pp. 94–95, as cited in Constantine Vaitsos, "Patents Revisited: Their Function in Developing Countries," *Journal of Development Studies,* October 1972.

The patent statistics for Colombia are found in Vaitsos, *ibid.* For Argentina, see Jorge Katz, "Patents, The Paris Convention and Less Developed Countries," Discussion Paper No. 190, Yale Economic Growth Center, November 1973, pp. 15–19. Importantly, in all cases examined, less than 10 percent of all patents of global corporations registered in poor countries are ever utilized. For example, in Peru from 1960 to 1972, a total of 5,796 patents were registered—94.9 percent by foreigners, 5.1 percent by nationals. Of these patents, only 54 (0.9 percent) were ever utilized in production, and all of these 54 by U.S. subsidiaries. In the Colombian drug sector for the similar period, 2,534 patents were registered but only 10 ever utilized. See Azi Wolfenson, "Incidencia Económica de las Transferencias en el Modelo de Desarrollo del Peru Dentro del MARCO del Acuerdo de Desarrollo," (COFIDE), Peru, 1973, p. 15. Herein lies a crucial source of oligopoly and/or monopoly power of the global corporation. For once these patents are registered, neither national nor foreign competitors can enter the product market covered by the patent—even if it is not being exploited by the patent holder.

Scherer's study is found in *Hearings on Economic Concentration,* Part 3, pp. 1194–98, as cited in John M. Blair, *Economic Concentration: Structure, Behavior and Public Policy,* New York: Harcourt Brace Jovanovich, 1972, p. 205.

Page 141
The statistics on Argentina are from Aldo Ferrer, "El Capital Extranjero en la Economía Argentina," *Trimestre Económico,* No. 150, Abril–Junio 1971, and "Empresa Extranjera: Observaciones sobre la Experiencia Argentina," Seminar on Política de Inversiones Extranjeras y Transferencia de Tecnología en America Latina, organized by ILDIS/Flacso, Santiago, 1971.

The statistic for Bolivia is from Miguel Wionczek, *La Banca Extranjera en America Latina,* Novena Reunión de Técnicos de los Bancos Centrales del Continente Americano, Lima, 17–22 de noviembre de 1969. Of the 7 commercial banks constituting the Jamaican banking system: 5 are wholly owned subsidiaries of MNB's, 1 is 75 percent foreign-owned and the other is 49 percent U.S.-owned. Norman Girvan, *Foreign Capital and Economic Underdevelopment in Jamaica,* Institute of Social and Economic Research, University of the West Indies, Jamaica, 1971, p. 170. In certain countries, foreign banks are officially not permitted in commercial banking or must have a local part-

404   GLOBAL REACH

ner, but they still can operate and indeed exercise significant power in merchant and investment banking as well as in leasing, a new form of financing. For a discussion of leasing as a substitute for short- and medium-term financing see "Mexican Leasing Offers Way Out to Companies Caught in Credit Squeeze," *Business Latin America,* July 25, 1968, p. 238; "Adela Gives a Major Impetus to Spread of Leasing in Latin America," *Business Latin America,* April 9, 1970, p. 114; "Leasing Comes of Age in Latin America: FNCB's Strategy for Entering the Market," *Business Latin America,* Jan. 20, 1972, p. 24; "Peruinvest is Sophisticated Capital Source for Medium-term Loans of Working Capital," *Business Latin America,* May 4, 1967, p. 142; "New Types of Commercial Financing Provide Working Capital in Mexico," *Business Latin America,* June 8, 1967, p. 179.

For further discussion of global banks' lending preference, see Chapters 9 and 10 below.

Page 142
Miguel Wionczek, *op. cit.* For another detailed examination see Frank Mastrapasqua, "U.S. Bank Expansion via Foreign Branching: Monetary Policy Implications," *The Bulletin* (of the Institute of Finance, New York University) Nos. 87–88, January 1973: "While some banks have shown impressive earnings from foreign operations, the expanding role of U.S. firms into the international area has left the major American banks little choice but to develop foreign facilities. A bank which does not have adequate foreign operations might find itself in a precarious position when one of its corporate clients decides to take on a foreign project. Failure to accommodate the clients' financial needs abroad might lead to the loss of that customer's domestic business to a competitor who has satisfactory foreign facilities. The implications for domestic business alone may have provided the necessary impetus to go abroad." Also see Jeremy Main, "The First Real International Bankers," *Fortune,* December 1967.

These banks are all part of one group, the so-called Rockefeller-Morgan Group. See Chapter 9 below.

There are a number of articles concerned with the withholding of U.S. credit, both public and private, since the Unidad Popular came to power in Chile. See for example, *The Wall Street Journal,* Sept. 29, 1971, and Oct. 14, 1971, and Oct. 18, 1971; *The New York Times,* Oct. 7, 1971 and Oct. 14, 1971; also, the *Washington Post,* Oct. 15, 1971. For a further report, written after the overthrow of the Popular Unity Government, see the *Washington Post,* June 2, 1974. For a report of a loan of approximately $150 million offered by a number of private U.S. and Canadian commercial banks, see "Economic Briefs," *Latin America,* Nov. 16, 1973, p. 363.

Page 143
1972 world billing figures are from *Advertising Age,* Feb. 26, 1973, and Feb. 15, 1965.

1971 profit figures for J. Walter Thompson and McCann-Erickson are found in Armand Mattelart, *Agresión Desde el Espacio,* Buenos Aires, Siglo XXI, 1973.

J. Walter Thompson and McCann-Erickson statistics are from *Advertising Age,* March 31, 1969, and March 29, 1971, "Eleventh Annual Exclusive Survey of Agencies Operating Outside the U.S.," as cited in Alan Wells, *Picture Tube Imperialism: The Impact of U.S. Television on Latin America,* New York: Orbis Books, 1972, Table XVIII, p. 185.

For concentration figures of U.S. ad agencies in Mexico, Brazil, Argentina, and Venezuela see Mattelart, *op. cit.*

Page 144

Alonson quote and salary figures are in Ramona Bechtos, "Brazil's Marketing Scene Reflects Nation's Growth," *Advertising Age,* Feb. 12, 1973.

Reference to Ogilvy & Mather is found in Ramona Bechtos, "Brazil Agencies Big on Creativity: Many Executives Boast JWT Experience," *Advertising Age,* Feb. 26, 1973.

Reference to Heath is from Ramona Bechtos, "Key Consumer Goods Growing Fast in Brazil: Ad Budgets Keep Pace," *Advertising Age,* March 5, 1973.

CBS Annual Report, the distribution of U.S.-produced television shows, and the statistics for ABC International are found in *Directory of the Networks,* The Network Project, No. 2, February 1974, pp. 4, 6, 20, respectively.

The reference to "Bonanza" and "cultural emissions" is from Mattelart, *op. cit.*

Page 145

Shakespeare is quoted from *U.S. News and World Report,* May 1, 1972.

Statistics on U.S. programs are from Mattelart, *op. cit.*

Reference to Time-Life is from Mattelart, *op. cit.*

Quote referring to *Batman* is from R. Tyler, "Television Around the World," in *Television Magazine,* October 1966, p. 33, as cited in Alan Wells, *Picture Tube Imperialism: The Impact of U.S. Television on Latin America,* New York: Orbis Books, 1972, p. 122.

Page 146

The Channel 5 reference is from Mattelart, *op. cit.*

The reference to Procter & Gamble is found in Mattelart, *op. cit.* W. R. Cowles, vice-president of public relations at Procter & Gamble, refused to verify this during a telephone conversation with us on Jan. 17, 1974.

The reference to Saunders is from *Directory of the Networks,* The Network Project, No. 2, February 1974, p. 1.

The discussion of UPI, AP, *El Correo, Reader's Digest,* and the comic books is taken from Mattelart, *op. cit.*

Page 147

For a detailed analysis of this pattern of cumulative and systemic increases in concentration by MNC's in these countries, see Ronald Müller, "The Multinational Corporation and the Underdevelopment of the Third World," *op. cit.,* and the reference note to page 187 in the next chapter.

The figures for Chile are taken from Luis Pacheco, "La Inversión Extranjera y las Corporaciones Internacionales en el Desarrollo Industrial Chileno," in *Proceso a la Industrialización Chilena,* Santiago: Ediciones Nuevas Universidad, Universidad Católica de Chile, 1972, and Corporación de Fomento de la Producción (CORFO), *Las Inversiones Extranjeras en la Industria Chilena Período 1960–69.* Publicación 57 a/71. Febrero 1971. For an analysis of Mexico see Ricardo Cinta, "Burguesía Nacional y Desarrollo," in *El Perfil en 1980,* III, 1972, Mexico: Siglo XXI, pp. 165–209; and for Argentina see Aldo Ferrer, "El Capital . . ." and "Empresa Extranjera . . . ," *op. cit.*

Figures for Brazil for 1966 and 1971 are based on data published in *Visão,* Sept. 7, 1967, and Aug. 28, 1972, as are all individual industry figures for 1971. Industry data for 1961 are from Ruben Medina, *Desnacionalização —Crime Contra o Brasil?,* Rio de Janeiro: Editora Saga, 1970, p. 91, except for those on electrical appliances, which were estimated indirectly by us. Largest enterprises are defined by size of net profits earned. See also Fernando Fajnzylber, *Sistema Industrial e Exportacion de Manufacturas: Analisis de*

Experiencias Brasil, Rio de Janeiro: United Nations, ECLA, 1971. For a detailed analysis of U.S. global companies' holdings in Brazil, including impacts on labor, land, and legal institutions, see Marcos Arruda, "The Impact of Multinational Corporations on the Contemporary Brazilian Economy," unpublished monograph prepared for a graduate research tutorial, Dept. of Economics, The American University, Summer 1973 (5 chapters plus an extensive bibliography).

7: Engines of Development?

Page 149
Per capita income for Mexico can be found in *Economic and Social Progress in Latin America,* Annual Report, 1972, Washington, D.C.: Inter-American Development Bank. GNP statistic for Brazil can be found in United States Agency for International Development Economic Data Book 1973, Washington, D.C.: State Department, Office of Financial Management.

On accelerating income concentration in poor countries through the "take-off" phase of economic growth see Cynthia Taft Morris and Irma Adelman, "An Anatomy of Income Distribution Patterns in Developing Nations: A Summary of Findings," Economic Staff Paper No. 116, IBRD, September 1971. An excellent conceptual and analytical survey of the income problem is found in James E. Weaver and Charles K. Wilber, "The Role of Income Distribution in the Process of Economic Development," paper presented to the International Studies Conference, Washington, D.C., 1974. For international comparisons of income inequality, particularly as between rich and poor countries, see Irving B. Kravis, "A World of Unequal Incomes," in *Income Inequality* by *The Annals* of the American Academy of Political and Social Science, September 1973.

For evidence of the deterioration of the bottom 40 percent in Chile see Oswaldo Sunkel, "Subdesarrollo, Dependencia y Marginación: Proposiciones para un Enfoque Integrado," IDB/UN Seminar on Marginality in Latin America, Santiago, Nov. 23–27, 1970, p. 36.

Médici is quoted in *The New York Times,* Dec. 8, 1971.

For the comparison of the richest 20 percent with the poorest 20 percent of the Mexican population, see James P. Grant, "Multinational Corporations and the Developing Countries: The Emerging Job Crisis and Its Implications," Washington, D.C.: Overseas Development Council, January 1972, p. 6.

Page 150
The U.N. report is by the Economic Commission for Latin America (ECLA), *Economic Survey for Latin America,* New York: 1969.

The U.S. estimate is from H. P. Miller, unpublished study, U.S. Bureau of the Census, Washington, D.C., 1971; the Latin American estimate is from ECLA, *The Distribution of Income in Latin America* (E/CN-12/868), New York: United Nations, 1970. Both the U.N. and the U.S. studies show increasing income concentration, but the U.N. study shows a much greater rate of accelerating inequality. A detailed comparison of the two studies is given in Ronald Müller, "The Multinational Corporation and the Underdevelopment of the Third World," in Charles K. Wilber, ed., *The Political Economy of Development and Underdevelopment,* New York: Random House, 1973, pp. 124–51. A more condensed version of this article appears in *Foreign Policy,* Winter 1973/74, entitled "Poverty is the Product." It is important to note that for the 1950–70 period there is a rough but clear correlation in growing income concentration to increasing intensity of global corporations in those poor countries where they invest most heavily. Besides Mexico and Brazil, two other examples are the Philippines and Jamaica. In 1956, the poorest 40 percent of Philippine families received 12.6 percent of total family income, which decreased to 11.7 percent by 1971. The share of the lowest 60 percent remained constant at 25 percent. In 1971, the richest 10 percent of families received 37.1 percent. Philippine Government, Bureau of the Census (1971). In addition, for Jamaica in 1958, the poorest 60 percent earned 19 percent of total national income and the richest 10 percent earned 43 percent. Norman Girvan, *Foreign Capital and Economic Underdevelopment in Jamaica,* Institute of Social and Economic Research, University of the West Indies, Jamaica, 1971, p. 220.

Income-distribution data are notoriously inadequate. Solon L. Barraclough, a Cornell professor of economics, for example, estimates margins of error of 40 percent. However, the time-series data used in the test do give adequate *trend* changes in *redistribution* because the base and end periods in each study have been similarly compiled.

The McNamara quote is from his address to the Board of Governors, World Bank Group, Sept. 25, 1972, pp. 6*ff.*

Page 151
The reference to Seers is from his article, "The Meaning of Development," in Charles K. Wilber, ed., *The Political Economy of Development and Under-development, op. cit.,* pp. 6–14.

Pages 151–52
The underlying methodology and analytical framework for this and the prior chapter incorporate Gunnar Myrdal's theory of "Cumulative Causation," found in *Rich Lands and Poor,* New York: Harper and Row, 1957; Celso Furtado's analysis of the changing size *and* composition of aggregate demand over time in both poor and rich countries, *Economic Development of Latin America: A Survey from Colonial Times to the Cuban Revolution,* Cambridge: Cambridge University Press, 1970; and "The Concept of External Dependence in the Study of Underdevelopment," in Charles K. Wilber, ed., *The Political Economy of Development and Underdevelopment, op. cit.,* pp. 118–23, into a theory of expansion of the global *oligopoly-conglomerate* corporation. The latter draws on the oligopoly theories in the literature on industrial organization and product-life-cycle hypotheses cited in the prior chapter. These three elements are then integrated via the analytical concept of "cross-subsidization." The first systematic, empirical use of this concept was John Blair's empirical work on the cross-subsidization practices of oligopoly firms in his *Economic Concentration: Structure, Behavior and Public Policy,* New York: Harcourt Brace Jovanovich, 1972. The concept covers the oligopoly-conglomerate's use and accounting techniques of capital, mechanical and organizational technology, and marketing. We have explicitly extended Blair's focus on inter-industry cross-subsidization in a given country (his work is largely on the United States) to cover the well-documented use of transnational cross-subsidization between the subsidiaries of the parent's entire global network. Our methodology assumes that the behavioral criterion governing the parent's management of the global network's finance, technology, and marketing resources is the maximization of worldwide profits through the short-run maintenance of and/or increases in global market shares. Explanations of this methodology and examples of its use can be found in Ronald Müller, "Transfer of Technology and National Economic Development: A Systemic Analysis of the Multinational Corporation," in papers and proceedings of the June 1973 American Association for the Advancement of Science/CONICYD International Conference on Science and Man in the Americas (forthcoming); "The Systemic Analysis of Power in the Economics of Multinational Corporations," in papers and proceedings of the March 19, 1973, University of Texas/American Enterprise Institute Conference on U.S.-Latin American Interactions in

the 1970's (forthcoming); with Richard Morgenstern, "Multinational Corporations and Balance of Payments Impacts in LDC's: An Econometric Analysis
of Export Pricing Behavior," *KYKLOS*, April 1974. A more detailed version of
this article appears in *Trimestre Económico*, January/April 1974; "The Multinational Corporation and the Underdevelopment of the Third World," *op. cit.;*
and "The Developed and Underdeveloped: Power and the Potential for
Change," papers and proceedings of the August 1974 World Conference of
Sociology, Toronto (forthcoming).

Pages 152–53
Fajnzylber is from Fernando Fajnzylber, *Estrategia Industrial y Empresas
Internacionales: Posición relativa de America y Brasil*, Rio de Janeiro: United
Nations, CEPAL, November 1970, p. 65. The original source labels host
country as "local and third countries." Since the participation of third countries plays such a small and insignificant part, we have omitted the designation
to avoid misleading labels.

Other studies include Ferrer, "El Capital Extranjero . . ." and "Empresa
Extranjera . . . ," *op. cit.;* Corporación de Fomento de la Producción (CORFO),
Analisis de las Inversiones Extranjeras en Chile . . . Período 1954–1970, No.
20, Enero 1972; and *Comportamiento de las Principales Empresas Industriales
Extranjeras Acegidas al D.F.L. 258*, Publicación No. 9–A/70. División de
Planificación Industrial, Departamento de Diagnóstico y Política, Santiago,
1970; *Las Inversiones Extranjeras en la Industria Chilena Período 1960–69*,
Publicación 57 a/71. Febrero 1971. Also see Dario Abad, "Las inversiones
extranjeras—divergencia de intereses y posibilidades de una reconciliación de
intereses," in Albrecht von Gleich, ed., *Las inversiones extranjeras privadas
en Latin America*. Hamburg: Instituto de Estudios Iberoamericanos, 1971;
and ODEPLAN (Oficina de Planificación Nacional), *El Capital Privado
Extranjero en Chile en el Período 1964–1968 a Nivel Global y Sectorial*,
#R/PL/70-007, Santiago, agosto de 1970.

For example, Gert Rosenthal's data, *The Role of Private Foreign Investment
in the Development of the Central American Common Market*, Guatemala,
March 1973, a study prepared under the auspices of the Adlai Stevenson Institute of International Affairs, Chicago, and the Permanent Secretariat of the
CACM, revised manuscript in preparation for publication, on Central America
show that foreign firms in Guatemala's manufacturing sector absorbed yearly
from 28 percent to 38 percent of total annual local bank loans to that sector
in the period 1965–1969. In the public-utilities sector the annual figure ranged
from 75 percent to 100 percent. For all sectors the figure ranged from 11 percent to 15 percent. On the use of local savings, Rosenthal's detailed data and
analysis on MNC's in Central America concluded that "In short, the foreign
firm is financed, wholly or in part through internal [local] savings, and not
with additional external financing" (p. 235).

"38 percent of the financial resources . . ." is found in Fajnzylber, *op. cit.*

Fajnzylber, *ibid*. In manufacturing the figure was lower but increasing, going
from 42 percent to 52 percent in the period 1960–1964 and 1965–1968.

Statistics on repatriated profits, *ibid*. If we add to these figures the fact that
an estimated 46 percent of global corporations' investment funds in Latin
America went into the purchase of local businesses (see below), then the net
outflow of finance capital increases further. For a detailed analysis of this
outflow see Ronald Müller, "The Multinational Corporations and the Underdevelopment of the Third World," *op. cit.* For the Central American Common
Market Area, an indication of the foreign-exchange drain associated with
MNC's is seen by the fact that between 1960 and 1971, new capital inflows
increased by 344 percent while total *reported* remittances went up by 982 percent. See Rosenthal, *op. cit.*, Table 43.

Page 154

On the use of local savings we should emphasize that short-term local financing is as important as long-term financing, particularly since global corporations' borrowing power (relative to local firms') allows them continuously to roll over their short-term loans and, as P. P. Streeten and S. Lall found in Colombia, "in many cases . . . provide the bulk of local financing for foreign investors." These authors, in a U.N. study of 159 firms (12 solely local, 45 solely foreign, 64 majority-foreign-owned, and 38 with less than 50 percent foreign equity) in 6 countries (Kenya, India, Iran, Jamaica, Colombia, Malaysia), using one estimation technique found that for over 40 percent of the sample firms "it would be cheaper for the host economy to substitute its own capital for the existing foreign capital. Further, had they included royalty payments, it would even more "turn the result against foreign capital." In summary they note, "we may be justified in concluding that they [global corporations] do not offer any marked financial benefits to the host countries." United Nations, *The Flow of Financial Resources: Private Foreign Investment: Main Findings of a Study of Private Foreign Investment in Selected Developing Countries,* UNCTAD, TD/B/C.3/III, Geneva, July 3, 1973.

The discussion of decreasing availability of local capital for locally owned industry is from the CORFO studies, *op. cit.*

Estimate of Sears' interest charge is taken from an interview with Hector Melo, Institute of Economic Investigations, University of Colombia, Bogotá, April 30, 1973, conducted by Joseph Collins.

Page 155

Statistic on manufacturing operations is found in *Business Latin America,* Jan. 15, 1970. For the figures on the buying up of local businesses, see J. S. Vaupel and J. P. Curhan, *The Making of Multinational Enterprise,* Boston: Harvard Business School, 1969. The calculations from Vaupel and Curhan are given in Müller, "Poverty is the Product," *op. cit.*

For an example of multinational agribusiness corporations' absorption techniques see Bernard Wideman's "Banana Boom: Fruits for Only a Few," in *Far Eastern Economic Review,* Jan. 21, 1974, pp. 52–53.

Page 156

The reference to Brazil's bond issue is from Constantine Vaitsos, "The Changing Policies of Latin American Governments Toward Economic Development and Direct Foreign Investment," Junta del Acuerdo de Cartagena, mimeographed document, J/AJ/36/Rev. 1, April 26, 1973, p. 27, to appear in the papers and proceedings of the University of Texas/American Enterprise Institute Conference on U.S./Latin American Interactions in the 1970's. By 1971, total Third World use of foreign private capital markets reached approximately $3 billion, about equal to official bilateral lending and some two-thirds of foreign direct investment in that year. The Brookings Institution, *Reassessing North-South Economic Relations: A Tripartite Report from 13 Experts from the European Community, Japan, and North America,* Washington, D.C., 1972, pp. 19, 25.

Statistics for the declining share of underdeveloped countries in world exports are found in United Nations, *Handbook of International Trade and Development Statistics,* 1972, U.N. Publication Sales No. E/F 72.11 D.3., Table 4.1, p. 193. See also the references to p. 166 in the preceding chapter for explanations of this decline and United Nations Economic Commission for Latin America (ECLA), "The Expansion of International Enterprises and Their Influence on Development in Latin America," in Part Four of *Economic Survey of Latin America, 1970,* New York, 1972.

Page 157
For a discussion of Latin America's external debt see Raúl Prebisch, *Change and Transformation: Latin America's Great Task,* report submitted to the Inter-American Development Bank, Washington, D.C., July 1970.

Reference to manufacturing exports is found in Herbert K. May and J. A. Fernandez Arena, *Impact of Foreign Investment in Latin America,* Council for Latin America, January 1970. For the 1950–1970 period foreign firms in Latin America exported on the average less than 10 percent of their sales, and for microderived Latin America export figures, see Müller and Morgenstern, *KYKLOS, op. cit.;* and *Trimestre Económico, op. cit.* For aggregates on Latin America and Europe see R. David Belli, "Sales of Foreign Affiliates of U.S. Firms," in *Survey of Current Business,* L. No. 10, October 1970, U.S. Dept. of Commerce, Washington, D.C. In the eight-country Streeten and Lall U.N. Study, *op. cit.,* of 147 firms with up to 100 percent foreign participation, 133 exported 9 percent or less of their total sales during the late 1960's. The export situation as discussed in the prior and in the next chapters, however, has been changing since the start of the 1970's for certain "export platform" countries.

For technical literature on the use of intracompany transfer prices see Michael Z. Brooke and H. Lee Remmers, *The Strategy of Multinational Enterprises: Organization and Finance,* New York: American Elsevier Publishing Company, 1970, and Sidney M. Robbins and Robert B. Stobaugh, *Money in the Multinational Enterprise: A Study of Financial Policy,* New York: Basic Books, 1973.

Page 158
Data on foreign versus local export performance and underpricing of exports are from Müller and Morgenstern, *KYKLOS, op. cit.,* and *Trimestre Económico, op. cit.* For the use of these same overpricing techniques in the transfer of capital equipment, see below.

On the problems of transfer pricing as specified by Tel Aviv's University Professor of Business Administration, Yair Aharoni, ". . . in a cluster of corporations controlled by the same top management, earnings may be changed at will by changing the charges for goods and services within the cluster. Presumably, rational management will use the mechanism of transfer prices in a way that will minimize the total tax burden on the company, showing higher earnings in countries where the rate of taxation is lowest." "On the Definition of a Multinational Corporation," in A. Kapoor and Phillip D. Grub, eds., *The Multinational Enterprise in Transition,* Princeton: The Darwin Press, 1972, p. 11, while Harvard's Business Professor Robert Stobaugh has found that "There have been hundreds of allocations by the IRS in recent years, with such allocations typically resulting in greater profit reported by the U.S. parent and a correspondingly lesser profit reported by the subsidiary." Robert B. Stobaugh, *The International Transfer of Technology in the Establishment of the Petrochemical Industry in Developing Countries,* United Nations Institute for Training and Research (UNITAR), Unitar Report No. 12, New York, 1971.

Import overpricing in Colombia can be found in Constantine V. Vaitsos, "Interaffiliate Charges by Transnational Corporations and Intercountry Income Distribution," submitted in partial fulfillment of the requirements for the degree of Doctor of Philosophy at Harvard University, June 1972. The Colombian (Bogotá) daily newspaper *El Espectador,* Feb. 6, 1970, p. 1A, reporting on an official government investigation, stated that chlordiazepoxide (Librium), a drug used in the treatment of mental illness, was overpriced by 6500 percent. The weighted average percentage of import overpricing in Colombia for drug subsidiaries was 155 percent in 1968, and for the years 1966–

1970, it was 87 percent. Streeten and Lall, *op. cit.*, p. 12. For a fuller presentation of overpricing data see R. Müller, "The Multinational Corporation and the Underdevelopment of the Third World," *op. cit.*

Page 159
For Andean Pact studies see Pedroleón Díaz, *Analisis Comparativo de los Contratos de Licencia en el Grupo Andino*, Lima: octubre 1971, pp. 19–23, and Vaitsos, "Interaffiliate Charges . . . ," *op. cit.*, p. 52. In a Peruvian study on the year 1969 for 4 manufacturing industries, 55.8 percent of the total imports of capital equipment and production inputs of MNC subsidiaries were purchased from the parent system. Azi Wolfenson, "Incidencia Económica de las Transferencias en el Modelo de Desarrollo del Peru Dentro del MARCO del Acuerdo de Desarrollo," COFIDE, Peru, 1973, p. 13.

For findings on non-Latin underdeveloped countries see United Nations Conference on Trade and Development (UNCTAD), *Restrictive Business Practices*, TD/122/Supp. 1, Santiago de Chile, Jan. 7, 1972., pp. 9–11; For a review of Latin American findings, UNCTAD, *Transfer of Technology Policies Relating to Technology of the Countries of the Andean Pact: Their Foundations; A Study by the Junta del Acuerdo de Cartagena*, TD/107, Dec. 29, 1971.

Reference to export subsidies is taken from a personal interview with Gabriel Misas, Bogotá, April 1973, conducted by Joseph Collins.

Page 160
Effective annual rates of return on net worth of global corporations' subsidiaries in Latin America: Vaitsos, "Interaffiliate Charges . . . ," *op. cit.*; Rand Corporation, "Evaluating Direct Foreign Investment in Latin America" by Shane Hunt, in *Latin America in the 1970's*, R-1067-DOS, prepared for U.S. Department of State, Santa Monica, December 1972; and R. Nelson, T. P. Schultz, and R. Slighton, *Structural Change in a Developing Economy* (under contract with the Rand Corporation), Princeton University Press, 1971, pp. 80–83.

On the average, 82 percent of these effective profits were derived solely from overpricing of imports. Raymond Vernon among others has attempted to make the argument that the Vaitsos study is not representative, citing studies in Australia and New Zealand which found no systematic tendency for import transfer prices to be higher (see his *Sovereignty at Bay*, New York: Basic Books, 1971, p. 139), although there were great variations compared with world prices. The results in these *two developed countries* are to be expected for the very reason that they have developed taxation and other regulatory institutions which permit effective control. Obviously, however, these results cannot be used to refute those obtained in underdeveloped countries where neither legal nor regulatory mechanisms for control existed during the pre-1970 period. The Vernon argument also overlooks the fact that similar results to those of Vaitsos were found (as we noted in the text earlier) in almost all other poor countries studied. See R. Müller, "The Multinational Corporation and the Underdevelopment of the Third World," *op. cit.*, and the exchanges between Vernon and ourselves in *Foreign Policy*, Winter 1973/74 and Summer 1974 issues.

U.S. mining companies in Peru, University of Lund, Sweden, study is presented in Claes Brundenius, "The Anatomy of Imperialism: The Case of the Multinational Mining Corporation in Peru," *Journal of Peace Research*, Vol. 9, 1972, pp. 189–207.

The Peruvian Parliament investigation of Southern Peru Copper Corporation's profits is in C. Malpica, *Los Dueños del Peru*, Lima, 1967, pp. 174–81. See also Claes Brundenius, *op. cit.*, pp. 199–201.

Page 161

The Rand Report quoted from is Shane Hunt, Rand Corporation, *op. cit.,* p. 136. A detailed breakdown on nationalization statistics is given in the next chapter.

Dario Abad's comments are found in his "Las inversiones extranjeras— divergencia de intereses y posibilidades de una reconciliación de intereses," in Albrecht von Gleich, ed., *Las inversiones extranjeras privadas en Latin America,* Hamburg: Instituto de estudios Iberoamericanos, 1971.

Central American private capital flows on balance of payments is in Gert Rosenthal, *op. cit.* The results for Central America compared with those of the "less underdeveloped" countries of Latin America bear out a consistent finding running throughout our research: the poorer and less developed a country or region is, the less is its bargaining power and control, and therefore the greater the negative impacts of foreign equity investment. See Ronald Müller, "The Political Economy of Direct Foreign Investment: An Appraisal for Latin-American Policy Making," prepared summer 1969 for the Prebisch Group; published Washington, D.C.: Inter-American Development Bank, Special Studies Division, July 1970.

Page 163

Statistics on scientists in Latin America are from José Epstein, "Transfer of Technology from the Point of View of Recipient Countries," speech delivered to the Transfer of Technology Conference sponsored by the OECD, Istanbul, October 1971. For more comprehensive data on the lack of scientific resources in Latin America, see the series of studies (ScA/PS-1 to 8) on transfer of technology done for the Organization of American States, Regional Scientific and Technological Development Program, Washington, D.C., 1972—particularly the works of Jorge Katz, Miguel Wionczek, and the Science Policy Research Center of the University of Sussex.

"Restrictive business practices": for the Andean Group, 92 percent of domestically owned firms which licensed technology from global corporations were prohibited from engaging in exporting, and these findings are not unique to these countries. See also the UNCTAD reports, *Restrictive Business Practices* and *Transfer of Technology Policies . . . , op. cit.,* as well as United Nations, *Restrictions on Exports in Foreign Collaboration Agreements in India,* TD/B/389, Sales No. E-72, II, D.F., 1972. Also Constantine Vaitsos, "The Process of Commercialization of Technology in the Andean Pact," Department of Scientific Affairs, General Secretariat of the Organization of American States, Washington, D.C., 1971.

Page 164

Epstein, *op. cit.*

Page 165

See Ronald Müller, "The Multinational Corporation and the Underdevelopment of the Third World," *op. cit.;* Constantine Vaitsos, "The Process of Commercialization . . . ," *op. cit.;* Miguel Wionczek, "Nacionalismo Mexicano e Inversión Extranjera," *Comercio Exterior,* Dec. 7, 1967, pp. 980–85; and citations in Leopoldo Solis, "Mexican Economic Policy in the Post-War Period: The Views of Mexican Economists," *American Economic Review,* June 1971 (Part 2, Supplement) Vol. 16, No. 3. Interviews with members of a capital-goods study project of the United Nations Development Program (UNDP) team in Mexico also confirmed these findings on the overvaluation of technology transfers by global corporations, Mexico City, June 1973.

In addition to the overpricing examples given in the text see also Streeten and Lall, *op. cit.,* p. 14.

Reference to Dumont is found in Louis Turner, *Multinational Companies and the Third World,* New York: Hill & Wang, 1973, p. 152.

References to Ahumada and Illich are found in "Outwitting the More Developed Countries," *New York Review of Books,* December 1969.

Page 166
The U.N. estimate for 27 percent of the labor force is from United National Economic and Social Council, *Development Digest,* No. 4, 1969. The 30 percent estimate is based on the percentage of the unemployed plus the percentage (weighted) of "underemployed" (i.e., less than substantial full employment throughout one work year) of the labor force.

Thorbecke is quoted from *Employment and Output: A Methodology Applied to Peru and Guatemala,* Paris: Development Center, OECD, 1970, p. 4.

The unemployment figure for Colombia is taken from *Survey of the Alliance for Progress, Colombia—A Case History of U.S. Aid,* a study prepared at the request of the Subcommittee on American Public Affairs by the staff of the Committee on Foreign Relations, U.S. Senate, together with a report of the Comptroller General, Feb. 1, 1969, Government Printing Office, Washington, D.C., 1969, p. 146. For more recent works see William C. Thiesenhusen, "Latin America's Employment Problem," *Science,* CLXXI, March 5, 1971, pp. 868–74; International Labor Organization, prepared by Dudley Seers, *et al., Hacia el Pleno Empleo: Un Programa para Colombia,* Preparado por una Misión Internacional Organizada por la Oficina Internacional de Trabajo, Ginebra, 1970; and Erik Thorbecke, "Desempleo y Subempleo en la America Latina," IDB and U.N. Seminar on Marginality in Latin America, Santiago de Chile, Nov. 23–27, 1970.

The 22-percent and 42-percent figures are from Thorbecke, OECD, *op. cit.,* p. 4.

"Multinational Corporations and the Developing Countries: The Emerging Jobs Crisis and Its Implications," Washington, D.C.: Overseas Development Council, January, 1972. See also James Grant, "Equal Access and Participation vs. Trickle Down and Redistribution: The Welfare Issue for Low-Income Societies," paper presented to the One Asia Assembly 1973, New Delhi, Feb. 5–7, 1973.

Page 167
For statistics on employment in the manufacturing sector in Latin America see Inter-American Development Bank, *Socio-economic Progress in Latin America,* Washington, D.C., 1971, and Erik Thorbecke, "Desempleo y Subempleo en la America Latina," Inter-American Development Bank and U.N. Seminar on Marginality in Latin America, Santiago de Chile, Nov. 23–27, 1970.

Page 168
For documentation of the "job-destroying impact" of global corporations' investments see Ronald Müller, "The Multinational Corporation and the Underdevelopment of the Third World," *op. cit.* See also William C. Thiesenhusen, *op. cit.*

Another example of the limited ability of global corporate technology to create jobs can be seen by the fact that, of the final market price of semifabricated aluminum products derived from Jamaican bauxite production, only 5 percent goes to pay for labor costs. See Norman Girvan, "Making the Rules of the Game: Country-Company Agreements in the Bauxite Industry," *Social and Economic Studies,* Institute of Social and Economic Research, University of the West Indies, Vol. 20, No. 4, December 1971, p. 80. See also his "Multinational Corporations and Dependent-Underdevelopment in Mineral Export Economies," *op. cit.,* p. 516.

The reference to Singapore is taken from a personal interview with Paula Echeverria, city planner, Washington, D.C., with extensive experience in Latin America and who has also recently completed a private consulting study of Singapore.

Raúl Prebisch, *op. cit.*

For statistic on global drug firms, see Díaz, *op. cit.*

Girvan's statistics are found in "Multinational Corporations and Dependent-Underdevelopment in Mineral Export Economies," *op. cit.,* p. 515.

Levinson is from his *Capital, Inflation, and the Multinationals,* London: George Allen & Unwin Ltd., 1971. Net job increases can occur only when the rate of increase in the capital–labor ratio associated with foreign investment is offset by a sufficiently higher rate of new investment. For a more detailed treatment and coverage, see Ronald Müller, "The Multinational Corporation and the Underdevelopment of the Third World," *op. cit.*

Page 169
The relatively greater capital intensiveness of multinational corporations' technology has been further verified by J. Pickett, D. Forsythe and N. McBain, "The Choice of Technology, Economic Efficiency, and Employment in Developing Countries," Overseas Development Administration, February 1973, and R. Mason, "The Transfer of Technology and Factor Proportions Problem: The Philippines and Mexico," UNITAR Research Report No. 10, New York. In addition, William H. Courtney and Danny M. Leipziger, in a study of 1,494 subsidiaries of U.S. MNC's, found no significant difference in technology used in MDC's versus LDC's in 5 of 11 industries investigated. In the other 6 they found no systematic bias for more or less labor using technology in LDC's. "Multinational Corporations in LDC's: The Choice of Technology," preliminary draft, Bureau of Economic and Business Affairs, Oct. 12, 1973. This last finding is also confirmed in D. Cohen, "The Role of the Multinational Firm in the Exports of Manufactures from Developing Countries," Discussion Paper No. 177, Yale Economic Growth Center, May, 1973.

In stating that "Income concentration and unemployment feed on each other," we are assuming that, as is the case in most underdeveloped countries, there are no significant social-transfer programs—social security, progressive income taxes, for example.

Grant is quoted from "Multinational Corporations . . . ," *op. cit.,* p. 14.

Seers's study is found in *Hacia el Pleno Empleo, op. cit.* The figures are in constant 1958 pesos, corrected for inflation.

The study of 257 manufacturing firms in Latin America can be found in Müller and Morgenstern, *KYKLOS, op. cit.,* and *Trimestre Económico, op. cit.* See also Streeten and Lall, *op. cit.,* p. 17, whose 8-country study also confirms these employment impacts.

Quote from *The Wall Street Journal* is from a two-part series on April 14 and 21, 1972, p. 1.

Page 170
Grant, *op. cit.*

For the discussion of wage rates paid by foreign-owned vs. locally owned firms, see Carlos Díaz-Alejandro, "Colombian Imports and Import Controls in 1970/71: Some Quantifiable Factors," Discussion Paper No. 182, Yale Economic Growth Center, July 1973, which reports the finding that foreign-owned enterprises, holding firm size constant, paid higher wages than national firms. However, the relatively greater use of foreign exchange by MNC's showed significantly higher imports per employee and significantly higher "trade deficits" (exports minus imports) per worker.

On income distribution and employment impacts in Singapore, Hong Kong, etc., these were also the first Third World countries to experience "export platform" investments. See prior and next chapters.

Page 171

Information concerning Japanese auto production in China is taken from an interview with Jack Baranson, former chief economic consultant for the Rand Corporation, on multinational corporate expansion into the Far East, April 4, 1973. With the foreign exchange earnings generated by these manufacturing operations the Chinese are financing the importation of sorely needed technology. See Baranson, "Cars in the China Shop," *Insight,* Vol. III, No. 5, May, 1973; "Japan's Trade With China and Technology Transfer," Washington, D.C., June, 1973 (mimeo); see also "Business Outlook on the Chinese Automotive Market," in William Whitson, *Doing Business in China,* New York; Praeger, forthcoming.

Page 172

Quotes from Baranson are from "The Drive Toward Technological Self-Reliance in Developing Countries and MNC Attitudes in Latin America," paper presented to the University of Texas/American Enterprise Institute Conference on *U.S.-Latin American Economic Interactions in the 1970's,* Austin, Texas, March 21, 1973.

A pioneering effort on the part of a multinational corporation to adapt production techniques (capital/labor factor proportions) to the needs of developing nations is Cummins Engine's project in India as discussed in Jack Baranson's "The Cummins Diesel Experience," in *Manufacturing Problems in India,* Bombay: Popular Prakashan, 1970. There are isolated examples of other corporate moves in this direction. Ford is encouraging its tractor distributors in poor countries to give product assistance to local farmers, although it is not increasing the amount of labor used in tractor production. British Leyland Motors has also developed new product design but not increased the use of labor in its poor-country production sites. An example that does stand out is the experimental Utrecht pilot plant of Philips, which is trying to minimize the cost of raw-material and intermediate-component inputs as well as the level of skills in its Third World electrical factories. However, as Louis Turner has concluded, "this particular approach has not actually led to much job creation . . . but governments cannot expect many other companies to follow suit unless they are consistently cajoled." See Louis Turner, *op. cit.,* pp. 153, 163–65.

Page 173

Mexican rate of illiteracy is taken from Johnson Research Associates, *Area Handbook for Mexico,* prepared for The American University, Washington, D.C.: Government Printing Office, 1970, pp. vii, 166–67.

Page 174

Drucker quote is from *The Age of Discontinuity,* New York: Harper & Row, 1969, p. 107.

Quote from Heilbroner is found in Robert L. Heilbroner, "Counter-revolutionary America," *Commentary,* April 1967, p. 32. This essay was reprinted in an important volume, Neal D. Houghton's *Struggle Against History: U.S. Foreign Policy in an Age of Revolution,* New York: Washington Square Press, 1968.

Page 175

Watson quote is found in "Computers and Advertising in the 1970's," address delivered at the Thirty-fifth Annual Conference of the Advertising Association, Brighton, England, May 2, 1969, p. 99.

All data and other findings of Evangelina García are from a personal interview with her conducted by Joseph Collins at the Sociology Department, Central University of Venezuela, Caracas, May 5, 1973.

Page 177
William Shramm is quoted in Mary Strong, "TV in Peru," New York University Department of Anthropology, mimeo.

Peter Drucker is *op. cit.,* p. 119.

Albert Stridsberg is quoted from "New Marketing, Ad Message May Save Underdeveloped Nations," *Advertising Age,* Sept. 22, 1969, p. 64.

The transistor-radio observation was made near Puno, Peru, June 1972.

Page 179
Statistics for meat production, Berg quote, and reference to India are found in Alan Berg, *The Nutrition Factor: Its Role in National Development,* Washington, D.C.: The Brookings Institution, 1973, pp. 66, 65, 43, respectively.

Frances Moore Lappe, in stating that it has now become economically feasible "to concentrate the world's agricultural resources on feeding animals, not people" has noted that "the rich minority of the world feeds as much grain to animals as the whole rest of humanity eats directly; there is as much protein in oilseeds, that for the most part go to livestock, as there is in all the meat protein humanity consumes; and nearly half of all the fish caught in the world, containing protein as good as meat, is fed to livestock." "The World Food Problem," *Commonweal,* Feb. 8, 1974.

Page 180
Estimate of the impact of a lack of vitamin A is from Berg, *op. cit.,* p. 26.

References made to Joaquín Cravioto are from personal interviews with one of the authors in May 1973, Mexico City.

Page 181
The Wall Street Journal, op. cit.

Page 182
The discussion of agribusiness complicating food distribution and the Colombian statistic are from an interview with Gabriel Misas, staff member DANE (National Bureau of Statistics, Colombian Government), April 30, 1973. The Colombian Embassy in Washington, D.C., verified on Jan. 14, 1974, that this statistic was "more or less correct."

Reference from Stavenhagen is taken from personal interviews with Joseph Collins, January–February 1973.

Page 183
Reference to Jelliffe is found in "Commerciogenic Malnutrition?," *Nutrition Reviews,* Vol. 30, No. 9, September 1972.

Page 184
On reasonable profits, we can point out, for example, that in the 8-country U.N.-sponsored study of Streeten and Lall, *op. cit.,* their detailed quantitative analysis covered 159 firms of which 12—i.e., 8 percent—were purely locally owned. It is important to emphasize that their analysis was not able to take into account the effects of underpricing of exports, overpricing of imports, and overvaluation of net worth (through technology transfers), all of which have, as is shown above, a high statistical probability of occurrence. In light of this unavoidable but significant omission, their findings, we feel, more than confirm the general results of our own work. Given these missing elements, they nevertheless

found that "the main conclusion that we should note is that on a fairly reasonable set of assumptions *nearly 40 percent of the firms in the six countries taken together have negative effects on social income.* A slightly higher percentage have negative effects on the balance of payments in this version of the LM [Little-Mirrlees] model. This has serious implications, both from the viewpoint of general investment policy and from the narrower viewpoint of dealing with foreign investors," p. 21; italics theirs.

8: The Power of the Poor

Page 186

Referring to the discussion of "efficient" allocation of profits, the Harvard Multinational Research Group has found that after the global enterprise reaches medium size, detailed centralized supervision over all subsidiaries becomes increasingly difficult and is gradually replaced by the issuance of "guidelines" governing more important aspects like financing and marketing. Since the guidelines are determined by and on behalf of the parent's total system needs, the point remains that the global enterprise is largely a centrally controlled economic system. See U.S. Tariff Commission's findings on this matter. For Harvard findings, see Sidney M. Robbins and Robert B. Stobaugh, *Money in the Multinational Enterprise: A Study of Financial Policy,* New York: Basic Books, 1973, Chapters 1–3.

The necessity for *worldwide* profit maximization and the use of "extralegal practices" to insure a corporation's position "two, three, or five years down the road" is explained by the incremental finance capital that would be forgone by any one company if it ceased such practices, leading to an inability to maintain its rate of expansion and thus to maintain its worldwide market shares relative to other global companies which continued such practices.

In reference to local subsidiary managers: As in any large economic system which must rely on central planning, disputes occur particularly between "field" and "headquarters" staff. Ultimately, however, it is headquarters which makes the final decision and field staff which must execute it. It is the subsidiary managers of the underdeveloped nations, though, who are closest to and most conscious of the extralegality of some of the companies' policies. In the interviews here under discussion, they were most conscious of the countries' poverty and these policies' impact on poverty. It is the closeness to the scene and actual participation in the scene, contrasted to the headquarters staff's distance, which at least in part explains the moral disquietude expressed by the executives in this group of interviews.

Page 187

The German executive went on to say, "I've often wondered what would happen if some of us were hired by these governments, for we're the ones who really have the information on our techniques. We could probably save them more money in a year than our entire lifetime salaries." When asked why he did not implement such an idea, his response indicated reference to the instability of Latin American governments versus his and his family's personal income security and the fact that he was already "locked in" *(eingeschlossen)* to his career.

Long quote is from *Congressional Record—Senate,* Feb. 10, 1966, pp. 2886–94. The non-U.S. companies involved included Le Petit and Hoechst.

Page 188

U.S. State Department, *Disputes Involving U.S. Foreign Investment: July 1, 1971 Through July 1, 1973,* Bureau of Intelligence and Research, RECS-6,

Washington, D.C., Feb. 8, 1974. This is in contrast to the fact that global corporations in the manufacturing sector account for some 50 percent of total nonpetroleum foreign investments in the underdeveloped world. *Survey of Current Business,* Commerce Department, September 1973, p. 26.

Page 189

For oil-company profits on operations in the Middle East from 1948 to 1960 see Charles Issawi and Mohammed Yegane, *The Economics of Middle Eastern Oil,* New York: Praeger, 1962, pp. 180–91, and for later periods G. W. Stocking, *Middle East Oil,* Nashville; Vanderbilt University Press, 1970, pp. 400–405.

For data for calculating impact of increased petroleum prices on consumers in other advanced nations see V. N. Pregelj, "Monthly Family Expenditures for Energy in West Germany and Japan, 1962–1972," Library of Congress, Congress Research Service memo, Nov. 20, 1973. The pre-"energy crisis" estimate of 10 percent is taken from Report for American Petroleum Institute, *The Impact of Deregulation on Natural Gas Prices,* prepared by Foster Associates, Inc., Washington, D.C., August 1973. Post-"energy crisis" detailed estimates were not available at the time of this writing. However, for example, Steve Babson and Nancy Brigham estimate, on the basis of Commerce Department statistics, that of a 1972 family income of $10,000, some 5 percent was spent on energy for housing needs and 14 percent on transportation. *Why Do We Spend So Much Money?,* Boston: Popular Mechanics Press, 1973. By early 1974, various sources were attributing some 40 percent of the increases in the consumer and wholesale price indices of the United States to rising fuel prices alone. See *Business Week,* Feb. 23, 1974, and various O.E.C.D. press releases on member countries' statistics for the period January–April 1974.

Page 190

Bergsten is quoted from "The Threat from the Third World," *Foreign Policy,* #11, Summer 1973, p. 102, also reprinted in Richard N. Cooper, ed., *A Reordered World: Emerging International Economic Problems,* Washington, D.C.: Potomac Associates, 1973.

Rosenstein-Rodan is found in "The Haves and the Have-Nots Around the Year 2000," in J. N. Bhagwati, ed., *Economics and World Order,* New York: Macmillan, 1972, p. 29.

Page 191

The increasing pressure on multinationals in Brazil is coming from a variety of institutional sources including the bishops of the Roman Catholic Church, the World Council of Churches, the Order of Brazilian Lawyers, etc. See Brady Tyson, "Brazil: Nine Years of Military Tutelage," *Worldview,* monthly journal of the Council on Religion and International Affairs, New York, July 1973, pp. 29–34. For a review of church activities to pressure for change in the operations of global corporations in various parts of the world, see the July 1973 issue of the *Corporate Examiner,* Vol. 2, No. 7, published by the National Council of Churches, New York.

Quote is taken from "Brazil Creates Industrial Boom," in Western Hemisphere Survey, *The New York Times,* Jan. 28, 1973, pp. 56*f.*

Quote from the Brazilian Minister of Agriculture is taken from the transcript of resignation as published in *Journal do Brasil,* May 12, 1973. Translated from the Portuguese.

The New York Times quote, *op. cit.*

Page 192

The 1971 Brazilian patent legislation benefits from the "demonstration effects" of earlier Peruvian and Andean Common Market legislation. It has been characterized as one of the most sophisticated and strongest such laws in any capitalist nation. As described in Chapters 6 and 7 above, patent regulation is one of the most crucial areas of host-country control over global corporations. The new Brazilian law provides for an unprecedented change which requires that the owner of a patent (not the government) must prove effective utilization or forgo patent protection. See Aracama Zorrauuin, "Tendencias Actuales de la Propiedad Industrial en America Latina," *Revista del Colegio de Abogados,* 1972.

Delfim Netto is quoted from "Brazil Forming Bank-Led Groupings to Fortify Local Industry," *Business Latin America,* April 6, 1972, pp. 105–106.

On Brazil and Japanese model see *Survey of the Economic Development of Brazil: Comparative Study of Economic Development of Brazil and Japan,* prepared by the (Japanese) Overseas Technical Cooperation Agency for the Ministry of Foreign Affairs, Government of Japan, in agreement with Ministry of Planning and General Coordination, Government of Brazil, Tokyo, March 1973. This study completes three parts of the aforementioned agreement, including the analysis of similarities and differences, the usefulness of a Japanese model, and possible future economic problems of Brazil based on the past experiences of Japan. Under the agreement the second volume, as yet to appear, will cover "possible areas of economic cooperation between Brazil and Japan." Volume I is perhaps significant reading for anyone who cares to speculate on the future geopolitics of these two nations.

Page 193
Gabriel is quoted from "The Multinational Corporation in the World Economy: Problems and Prospects," draft of a paper presented for Conference on Industrial Relations and the Multinational Corporation, University of Chicago, May 1–2, 1973, pp. 20–21.

For a detailed statement of the theory and analytics of bargaining power, see Ronald Müller, "The Developed and the Underdeveloped: Power and the Potential for Change," papers and proceedings of the August 1974 World Conference of Sociology, Toronto (forthcoming), and *The Political Economy of Direct Foreign Investment: An Appraisal for Latin-American Policy Making,* Special Studies Division, Inter-American Development Bank, Washington, D.C., July, 1970. See also reference notes to preceding chapter.

See notes to Chapter 6 above. Our methodology underlying the assessment of bargaining power is derived from J. von Neumann's and O. Morgenstern's seminal work, *Theory of Games and Economic Behavior,* Princeton, N.J.: Princeton University Press, 1953; and the works of Professor Jiri Nehnevajsa, chairman, department of sociology, University of Pittsburgh, particularly his *Anticipations Theory* (unpublished manuscript); as well as F. Modigliani and K. Cohen's "The Significance and Uses of Ex Ante Data," Mary Jean Bowman, ed., *Expectations, Uncertainty, and Business Behavior,* New York: Social Science Research Council, 1958. For a general and recent survey of the variables affecting bargaining power in underdeveloped countries see Paul Streeten, "Government Policy Towards Foreign Manufacturing Investment," Section V of a report submitted to UNCTAD, United Nations, New York, 1973.

Page 194
Statistic for Japan is found in Table III, Chapter 6.

While the opportunity for LDC's to establish new bargaining relationships with MNC's is being enhanced by the changing relationships of dependency, much will depend "on the host government's own ability to act intelligently and firmly in a game played with a highly sophisticated rival." Paul Streeten, *op. cit.,* p. 27.

Page 195

Lobb quote is taken from "Japan, Inc.—The Total Conglomerate," *Columbia Journal of World Business,* March–April 1971, p. 39.

The figures for 1955 are approximate. The 1972 figures are nominal, not real, from U.S. State Department, "Economic Growth of OECD Countries, 1962–1972," news release, Bureau of Public Affairs, August 1973.

On the meaning of convergence, not only in per capita consumption but also in production technology, see Richard D. Cooper, *The Economics of Interdependence,* New York: McGraw-Hill, 1968. See also Ronald Müller, "The Developed and the Underdeveloped . . . ," *op. cit.*

Discussion regarding competition between industrial powers for energy consumption is found in Commission of the European Communities, *Energy and Europe,* Luxembourg, November 1972. For the striking correlation in per capita energy consumption as per capita income levels have converged, see Inter Technology Corporation, *The U.S. Energy Problem,* Vol. II, Appendices Part A, prepared for the National Science Foundation, ITC Report C-645, November 1971, pp. A-53–58.

Page 196

Quotes on Japan are taken from Nomura Research Institute, Investment Report 73G-1, June 25, 1973, Tokyo, pp. 1, 3, 7, 9, 10, 13.

For a detailed account of the rapid expansion of the export-platform area of Mexico see Donald W. Baerresen, *The Border Industrialization Program of Mexico,* Lexington, Mass.: Lexington Books, D. C. Heath and Company, 1971.

Hollis Chenery and Helen Hughes, "The International Division of Labor: The Case of Industry," paper presented to the European Conference of the International Society for Development, The Hague, October 24–27, 1971. The countries seem fairly well divided between Asia and the Subcontinent, Africa, and Latin America. The trend toward export-platform investment in underdeveloped countries by global corporations has been accelerated even more by the rapid increase in these countries' marginal productivity of labor. Both Chenery and Hughes and Gyorgy Adam cite an increasing incidence of higher labor productivity in export-platform operations than in advanced countries. See Adam, "Economic Life: International Corporations in the Early Seventies," *The New Hungarian Quarterly,* Vol. XIV, No. 49, Spring 1973, and "Some Implications and Concomitants of Worldwide Sourcing," *Acta Oeconomica,* Vol. 8 (2–3), pp. 309–23, 1972. The quantative dynamics of the move to export platforms are impressive. Whereas in 1962 slightly more than half (51 percent) of underdeveloped countries' manufactured exports went to advanced market economies, by 1970 the figure was up to 60 percent. For these years the average rate of increase of exports to the industrialized world was running at 13.6 percent per annum, but this hides the fact that the rate jumped to 21.3 percent during 1967–1969. Of the increase in developing countries' manufactured exports to developed market economies between 1962 and 1971, 80 percent was accounted for by the U.S., the United Kingdom, Japan, and West Germany—the top four foreign investors in the underdeveloped world. U.S. imports of manufactures from developing countries grew at an annual rate of 17.8 percent in the 1962–1971 period—sufficiently large to increase the U.S. share of developing countries' manufactured exports from 30.2 percent in 1962 to 42.1 percent in 1971 and accounting for 47.8 percent of their total increase during the period. Calculated from *Trade in Manufactures of Developing Countries Review,* various issues 1969–1972, United Nations, New York. Products covered are Standard International Trade Classifications (SITC) sections 5–8, excluding petroleum and unworked nonferrous metals.

Another indicator of the export-platform expansion comes from *The Competitiveness of U.S. Industry: Report to the President on Investigation No. 332-65,* U.S. Tariff Commission, Washington, D.C., April 1972: By 1969 South Korea, Taiwan, and Hong Kong, the first export platforms of American global corporations, were included among the top 13 exporting countries to the United States; their combined manufactured exports were exceeded by only 4 other countries—Canada, West Germany, Japan, and the United Kingdom. This contrasted with 1965, when 10 more developed countries ranked before them in this listing. By 1971 all underdeveloped countries' share of *total* U.S. imports was larger than that of any individual advanced nation.

Besides the product groups cited in the text, Louis Turner, *Multinational Companies and the Third World,* New York: Hill & Wang, 1973, Chapter 7, in summarizing the growing body of evidence on "export platforms," finds a wide range of industries from automobile engines, machine tools, aerospace, and cameras to plastics, toys, and wigs. "Capital intensive industries like oil and chemical refining seem to be holding out, but even here the development of new transportation technologies like pipelines are making these companies more 'footloose' and able to respond to the different incentives they are offered [i.e., tax minimization and the absence of costly environmental controls], even if labor costs are not particularly important to them," p. 181.

Probably the least publicly recognized "export-platform" operations are those of global agribusiness corporations like Del Monte and Heinz, although since 1968 their expansion rates are among the highest and the cost and tax savings among the greatest of all industries. See U.S. Senator James Abourezk's summary of studies and testimony in *Congressional Record—Senate,* No. 9, 1973, pp. S20227–34, and Jim Hightower, *Hard Tomatoes, Hard Times,* for the Agribusiness Accountability Project, Cambridge, Mass.: Schenkman, 1972, for food-growing and processing industries and impacts in the United States. See also Chapter 11 below. For an example of impacts on labor and consumer-goods prices in the local areas of these export-platform operations, see the Mexican strawberry discussion in the preceding chapter.

Raymond Vernon has noted in *Sovereignty At Bay: The Multinational Spread of U.S. Enterprises,* New York: Basic Books, Inc., 1971, pp. 107–108, that "By 1970 the product cycle model was beginning in some respects to be inadequate as a way of looking at the U.S.-controlled multinational enterprise." This refers to the fact that in recent years the first phase of the cycle, initial production in the domestic home market, has been bypassed and we have seen the introduction of final products, intermediate products, and/or component parts that were first being produced in low-wage areas. Although this may negate the simplicity of the model as a theory of the *firm,* it by no means weakens but rather strengthens the hypothesis we have derived from the model: to wit, the global corporations' international mobility of capital and knowledge increase the institutional necessity of these firms to expand into the Third World. See G. K. Helleiner, "Manufactured Exports from Less Developed Countries and Multinational Firms," *Economic Journal,* March 1973, pp. 42ff.

Page 197

The 1978 projection for Japan is from the Los Angeles *Times,* Feb. 13. 1973.

This necessitated expansion is verified in the statistics which show the changing geographical composition of foreign investment of the major home countries of global corporations. Japan, starting from a low base, is each year steadily increasing its amount of foreign investment; in 1972 it invested $2.5 billion, triple the amount of 1971, with the annual amount by 1980 estimated at $35 billion. Over 51 percent of this is currently located in underdeveloped countries, and the figure is projected to increase in the future. Japan's foreign investment *could slow down,* however, depending on its ability and decisions on how to use its foreign-exchange reserves in the face of recent oil-price hikes. See Nomura Research Institute, Investment Report 73G-1, June 25, 1973, p. 31. A similar phenomenon is under way in Germany. Despite predictions and statistical trends to the contrary, in the early 1960's U.S. global manufacturing enterprises increased the book value of their investments in Latin America by a greater rate than in Canada or in the European Community during the period 1967–1970. The same was true for Asia. David T. Devlin, "The International Investment Position of the United States: Development in 1970," Department of Commerce, Survey of Current Business, October 1971.

The 83 percent figure of "free world" copper production is from Claes Brundenius, "The Anatomy of the Multinational Mining Corporations in Peru," *Journal of Peace Research*, Vol. IX, 1972.

Page 198
Prices of Arabian light crude are published in *Platts Oilgram*.

The increase in the price of gasoline can be found in *Platts Oil Price Handbook*, New York: Platts Oilgram, 1974, 1973, 1972, 1971, 1970. See also *The New York Times*, May 19, 1974, Section F, and May 26, 1974, Section F.

OPEC nations in the Persian Gulf increased their revenues from $1 billion in 1957 to $3 billion in 1969. The Teheran Agreement of 1971 increased the revenues over and above those of a 1970 agreement. For the 1970–1975 time frame, this 1970 agreement already had resulted in an additional $8.5 billion over the $10 billion that would have been received under pre-1970 arrangements. Conservative estimates indicate that 1970's payments of $7 billion will increase to $55 billion by 1980. S. D. Krasner, "Trade in Raw Materials: The Benefits of Capitalism," paper presented at the International Studies Association Convention, New York, March 16, 1973, mimeo, Dept. of Government, Harvard University. pp. 23–24.

For the discussion of passing cost increases on to the consumer see Morris Adelman, *World Petroleum Markets*, Baltimore: Johns Hopkins University Press, 1972, and "Is the Oil Shortage Real?," *Foreign Policy*, Winter 1972/73. For a fuller treatment of the markup practices of oil companies see the next chapter.

Page 199
For a discussion of new moves in other strategic-raw-material sectors see Fred Bergsten, "The Threat from the Third World," *Foreign Policy*, Summer 1973, and his statement to the Subcommittee on Foreign Economic Policy, House Foreign Affairs Committee, "Hearings on Global Scarcities," May 15, 1974, outlining the growing movement to "O.P.E.C.-like" arrangements among poor-country producers of coffee, bauxite, bananas, tin, and cotton. For a detailed account of the techniques and results of increasing bargaining power see "The Bauxite Battle: U.S. Aluminum Firms in Jamaica Face New Demands Under 'Partnership' Plan," *The Wall Street Journal*, May 29, 1974.

There is no doubt that the momentum of increased bargaining power of these CIPEC countries (Intergovernmental Council of Copper Exporting Countries) has been diminished by the 1973 coup d'état in Chile. However, over time the pressures will increase on the Chilean generals to internalize a greater proportion of value-added from their copper industry for the reasons outlined in the text. This will be especially true after 1975, by which time Chilean dependence on external-sector debt renegotiations will have lessened substantially.

Brookings Institution colleagues Fred Bergsten and Theodore Moran, in seemingly different interpretations of the potential for increased bargaining power in resource-rich underdeveloped countries, end up, however, in a similar vein. Bergsten appears to accept de facto the ability of these countries to swing the terms of trade in their favor. He warns against "cannibalistic competition" on the part of the developed nations and advises a unified policy approach to consuming nations as the best possibility for offsetting the new power of the poor. Moran, though, argues that the poor countries which take over the control of the production stage of highly vertical-integrated commodities like copper and bauxite could quite possibly lose out because they do not control the distribution and final-sales stages of the industry. Thus his advice is for poor countries to go easy or they may well enter a new era of dependence and domination. Both conclude, therefore, that the poor countries would be advised to restrict their bargaining-power potential. In our opinion, this conclusion and its respective arguments are subject to criticism. Bergsten's warning on consuming nations' unity overlooks the increasing differences that must emerge and are emerging as between Europe, Japan, and the United States which trace themselves to respective differences in their dependency on foreign sectors and therefore in differences in their economic foreign policy. Moran's argument, based on differing demand needs and buyer-seller behavior over the business cycle in advanced nations and thus varying degrees of dependence on purchases from the Third World, overlooks the fact that this is inconsequential (as is shown in oil) where poor countries control a substantial amount of world exportable supplies (say 30 percent or more)—exactly the case in most strategic raw materials. See their respective articles in R. D. Cooper, ed., *A Reordered World: Emerging International Economic Problems*, Washington, D.C.: Potomac Associates, 1973. The literature on this topic is voluminous. A good bibliography is found in the various articles of the aforementioned work. See also Joseph Grunwald and Philip Musgrove, *Natural Resources in Latin American Development*, Baltimore: Johns Hopkins Press, 1970.

For a more detailed account of the central data-collection unit of Mexico and the Andean Pact and the resulting increase in their potential bargaining power see Shane Hunt, "Evaluating Direct Foreign Investment in Latin America," in *Latin America in the 1970's*, RAND Corporation, R-1067-DOS, December 1972; Miguel S. Wionczek, "Hacia el Establecimiento de un Trato Común para la Inversión Extranjera en el Mercado Común Andino," *Trimestre Económico*, April–June 1971; Constantine Vaitsos, "The Changing Policies of Latin American Governments Toward Economic Development and Direct Foreign Investments," Junta del Acuerdo de Cartagena, mimeographed document J/AJ/36/Rev. 1, April 26, 1973. See also United Nations, *Multinational Corporations in World Development*, Department of Economic and Social Affairs, New York, 1973, p. 86; Carlos Díaz-Alejandro, "Direct Foreign Investment in Latin America," in C. P. Kindleberger, ed., *The International Corporation: A Symposium*, Cambridge, Mass.: MIT Press, 1970; but note the change in his views in an essay written approximately two years later, "Latin America: Toward 2000 A.D.," in J. N. Bhagwati, ed., *Economics and World Order*, New York: Macmillan, 1972, pp. 250–53.

Page 200

An interesting example of how member countries use ANCOM Decision 24 for increasing bargaining power is the 1971 Ecuadorian decree which prohibited foreign banks from maintaining savings and time deposit accounts. The government justified the decree on the basis of defending "national banks and coordinating the necessary legislation for the execution of the Andean Pact" and because they have been "utilizing local savings to finance foreign investment." *Business Latin America*, March 18, 1971, p. 87.

The increase and diffusion in techniques of bargaining-power strategy is also being accelerated by specific education programs given to policy makers from underdeveloped countries. See "International Firms and Development

Strategy," 41st study seminar, Institute of Development Studies, University of Sussex, May 13–June 14, 1974.

Page 201

For a discussion of cooperative arrangements, see Gyorgy Adam, "The Big International Firms and the Socialist Countries," paper presented to the International Colloquium of the National Center for Scientific Research on *The Growth of the Large Multinational Corporation,* Rennes, France, September, 1972.

Pisar and Gabriel are quoted from Peter Gabriel, "The Multinational Corporation in the World Economy: Problems and Prospects," draft of a paper presented for Conference on Industrial Relations and the Multinational Corporation, University of Chicago, May 1–2, 1973, pp. 20–21, 22, and 28, respectively.

Certain of these East Europe operations are quite similar to the export-platform phenomenon in underdeveloped countries described above. That is, particularly European global corporations are using these socialist coproduction sites to either manufacture or assemble component parts for shipment to West Europe. In either case, as with LDC export platforms, they represent a transfer of production formerly conducted in the home country. See Gyorgy Adam, *op. cit.*

For a good example of global corporations' willingness to comply with restrictions in socialist countries which they historically have refused to do in underdeveloped countries see "Joint Venture Agreements in Eastern Europe: Guidelines for Drafting J. V. Agreements," Control Data Corporation, 1973.

Page 202

On global auto firms in Latin America, see Jack Baranson, *Automotive Industries in Developing Countries,* Baltimore: Johns Hopkins Press, 1969; Also Ronald Müller, 1970, *op. cit.*

On why global oligopolies can become increasingly vulnerable to bargaining-power pressure from poor countries *after* "latecomers" have joined "pioneer" entrants in a host economy see Frederick T. Knickerbocker, *Oligopolistic Reaction and Multinational Enterprise,* Boston: Basic Books, 1973, particularly some of the suggestions on increasing bargaining power taken from a report prepared in 1970 by Raymond Vernon for the Indonesian Government.

GM initially submitted a bid, then withdrew. Both Leyland and Fiat had lesser shares in the region than the U.S. firms, and both are much more dependent on *non*-home-country sales than their North American competitors.

The discussion of Japanese and German foreign-investment growth rates is taken from United Nations, *Multinational Corporations in World Development,* Dept. of Economic and Social Affairs, New York, 1973, p. 146, Table 10.

Baranson suggestion is from his "Japan's Trade with China and Technology Transfer," Washington, D.C., June 1973, mimeo, pp. 8–10.

Page 203

For a discussion of political control through trade restrictions see Richard J. Barnet, *Intervention and Revolution,* New York: revised Mentor edition, 1972.

The reference to the 30 African countries is from T. A. Johnson, "Africans Ratify Accord on Trade," *The New York Times,* May 28, 1973. For how African countries are learning quickly from Latin America and the Mid-East about the use and implementation of bargaining power, particularly in the mineral extractive sector, see Ruth Morgenthau, "Multinational Enterprises and African Politics," paper presented to the Yale Conference on the Multinational Corporation as an Instrument of Development, May 11, 1974.

Statistics on contracts and "a new rallying cry" are from N. M. McKitterick, ". . . and in Brazil, the U.S. Lag is Shown," *The New York Times*, May 27, 1973, Part III, p. 14.

Vaitsos is taken from "The Changing Policies of Latin American Governments Toward Economic Development and Direct Foreign Investments," Junta del Acuerdo de Cartagena, mimeographed document J/AJ/36/Rev. 1, April 26, 1973, p. 27.

On the courting of global companies from different home nations, Carlos F. Diaz-Alejandro adds a further reason why underdeveloped countries' bargaining power is on the rise owing to their playing off of oligopolies from 'different developed nations. He notes, "But my own guess is that the presence of a socialist camp which does not threaten militarily Western Europe and Japan tips the scale in favor of a scenario of at least oligopolistic rivalry among developed country interests, permanently at the verge of warfare." See Carlos Diaz-Alejandro, "North-South Relations: The Economic Component," Center Discussion Paper No. 200, Economic Growth Center, Yale University, April 1974.

For a comprehensive review through 1972 of the bargaining-power control measures being implemented by underdeveloped countries see Francisco Orrego Vicuña, "El Control de las Empresas Multinacionales," Sobretiro de *Foro Internacional*, Vol. XIV, n° 1, El Colegio de Mexico, 1973.

Page 204
Gabriel is quoted from his article "The Multinational Corporation in the World Economy: Problems and Prospects," draft of a paper presented for the Conference on Industrial Relations and the Multinational Corporation, University of Chicago, May 1–2, 1973, pp. 6–7.

An account of the dispute over the Panama Canal is in "Heat, Canal Recall Suez," *The Washington Post*, March 20, 1973. See also "World Vetoes the U.S.: This Round to Panama in Canal Dispute," Los Angeles *Times*, March 25, 1973.

Page 205
A discussion of the Argentine laws is in *The New York Times*, Aug. 3, 1973, p. 3.

That these political and economic pressures are by no means restricted to the poor countries is evidenced by the fact that more-developed countries such as Canada are enacting laws which, in the words of *Time*, are "designed not to keep out foreign capital but to make sure that it comes in on Canada's terms." With the emergence of the Watson Report, and later the Grey Report *(Foreign Direct Investment in Canada*, Ottawa, 1972) and other studies documenting the extent of U.S. multinationals' domination of the Canadian economy, political pressures have come not only from the Left parties, such as the New Democratic Party, but from liberals and conservatives as well urging the Canadian government to assert itself with foreign capital. The country's first Foreign Investment Review Act, passed in December 1973, will give the government "veto power" to check certain types of penetration and expansion of foreign multinationals in Canada and "force American companies into hard-nosed bargaining with the Canadian government." In the words of Alastair Gillespie, Minister of Industry, Trade and Commerce, "Now we're going to be more than a mere appendage of foreign corporate giants south of the border." *(Time*, Dec. 17, 1973, page 100.)

Page 206
For further discussion of Internal Revenue Code Section 482 see Chapter 10 below.

McBride is quoted from his speech before the Annual Meeting of the U.S.–Mexico Businessmen's Committee, Acapulco, Oct. 12, 1972.

For further references see Guy Meeker, "Made-out Joint Venture: Can· It Work for Latin America?," *Inter American Economic Affairs*, Spring 1971, pp. 25–42. For the results in a survey carried out by the Harvard Business School see Richard Lawrence's article in the *Journal of Commerce*, Nov. 15, 1971.

Page 207

Among the economists studying real profit rates and the effect of transfer pricing are Fernando Fajnzylber, Sergio Bitar, Ricardo French Davis, Constantine Vaitsos, Jorge Katz, and Miguel Wionczek, to name but a few. Most of them, like the new oil technocrats of the Arab countries, received their graduate training in the United States or England.

Wionczek discusses the dependence upon Department of Commerce statistical data in "Hacia el Establecimiento de un Trato Común para la Inversión Extranjera en el Mercado Común Andino," *Trimestre Económico*, April–June 1971.

Page 208

The Colombian results are taken from Constantine Vaitsos, "The Process of Commercialization of Technology in the Andean Pact," report #ScA/PS-13, Department of Scientific Affairs, Organization of American States, Washington, D.C., March 1972, pp. 23–24.

9: The Latin Americanization of the United States

Page 215

The data on unemployment rates are presented in U.S. Department of Commerce, Bureau of the Census, *The Social and Economic Status of Negroes in the United States*, Current Population Reports, Series P-23, No. 38, 1970, p. 48. Daniel R. Fusfield in *The Basic Economics of the Urban Racial Crisis*, New York: Holt, Rinehart and Winston, 1973, p. 48, states that in 1970 when the official unemployment rate was 4.9 percent, the average rate for blacks in central-city ghettos (inhabited for the most part by nonwhites) was 9.6 percent of those actively seeking work and 11 percent for those who would take work if the opportunity existed. In addition, R. E. Hall and R. A. Kasten in *Brookings Papers on Economic Activity*, February 1974, have found that blacks with matching socioeconomic status and educational achievement earn over 8 percent *less* than their white counterparts in identical occupations. They advise caution "in making optimistic interpretations of the very significant recent improvement in the relative earnings of blacks."

Some argue that but for large-scale injections of military spending the state of the U.S. economy today would not be significantly different from that of the 1930's, particularly with regard to unemployment. See Paul M. Sweezy, "Capitalism, For Worse" in Leonard Silk, *Capitalism, The Moving Target*, New York: Quadrangle, 1974; see also A. H. Raskin, "Six Percent Is Only the Tip of the Iceberg," "Review of the Week," *The New York Times*, June 25, 1972.

Page 216

For further discussion of the shift in production to low-wage areas in the underdeveloped world see the tables in Chapter 6, which show wage differentials in the United States and selected underdeveloped countries (mostly "export platforms").

For statistics on share of national income earned by executives versus average employees see the next chapter.

Reference to Galbraith is found in *Economics and the Public Purpose,* Boston: Houghton-Mifflin, 1973, pp. 264–66.

Page 218
That the United States consumes over 30 percent of the world's energy output is a well-known fact. See "U.S. Oil Nightmare Worldwide Shortage," *The Washington Post,* June 17, 1973, p. A14.

George Donkin, formerly of the Federal Power Commission (FPC), has calculated that the wellhead price of natural gas in certain producing areas of the country has risen, in some cases, as much as 200 percent. For this information, see George L. Donkin, Cornell Energy Industry Study, "The Competitive Effects of Interdependent Actions Among Buyers and Sellers in the Natural Gas Producing Industry," paper presented to the British Columbia Energy Conference, Vancouver, B.C., April 18, 1974.

In May 1973, the FPC authorized a 73-percent rise in the price that natural-gas producers charge buyers for gas at the wellhead. One of the three companies involved, Tenneco Oil (Texaco and Belco Petroleum were the other two), according to the FPC staff, would increase its return on equity investment to approximately 48 percent. The staff also estimated at the time that a 200 percent price increase at the wellhead, which is what some companies argued for, would have increased the rate of return on equity to 113 percent. This information is cited in Morton Mintz, "Tripled Natural Gas Prices Sought: FPC Approval Seen," *The Washington Post,* June 18, 1973, p. A1. Moreover, in some cases, the natural-gas producer and the pipeline purchasing the gas at the wellhead are subsidiaries of the same parent company. For example, in the words of Representative George E. Brown, Jr., "The producers are fond of arguing that this 45-cent price is the result of 'arms length bargaining' between the producers and pipeline companies and that this bargaining has established a 'competitive market price.' However, testimony at the Belco, Tenneco, Texaco hearing has disclosed that the producer in question, Tenneco Oil Company, and the pipeline company in question, Tennessee Gas Transmission Company, are both wholly-owned subsidiaries of a single parent corporation, Tenneco, Inc." See the testimony of Representative George E. Brown, Jr., before the Senate Commerce Committee, March 19, 1973.

Page 219
For an important analysis of the American bargaining position in the Middle Eastern oil-producing nations at the close of World War II see Joyce and Gabriel Kolko, *The Limits of Power: The World and U.S. Foreign Policy,* New York: Harper & Row, 1972, pp. 69–73 and 413–27.

The reference to Aramco is taken from its publication "Arabian Oil and World Oil Needs," 1948, p. 35.

Among other things, the oil-depletion allowance was a result of the oil industry's enormous political power, both in Washington and in various state capitals. The mandatory oil-import quotas which successfully restricted the supply of cheap foreign oil from 1959 to 1972, to cite but another example, according to *Business Week* (May 17, 1969), added $4 billion per year to the price of oil paid by American consumers. As *Business Week* candidly quoted the chairman of one "major" company, "whenever we got into trouble we always went to Sam [Rayburn] or Lyndon [Johnson] to get us out. We never prepared for the day when the liberals would be in charge of Congress" (Feb. 2, 1974, p. 58).

GLOBAL REACH

Federal Trade Commission (FTC), *The International Petroleum Cartel,* Washington, D.C., 1952. The FTC report can be found in *Governmental Intervention in the Market Mechanism,* AntiTrust and Monopoly Subcommittee of the Senate Judiciary Committee, Washington, D.C., 1969. The Information from the FTC Report well presented in *Middle East Oil and the Energy Crisis,* Part I (No. 20) by the Middle East Research and Information Project (MERIP), Washington, D.C., 1973, written by Joe Stork.

For statistics on control of world production see Fuad Rohani, *A History of OPEC,* New York: Praeger, 1971, p. 105. For an extended analysis of the U.S. oil situation to 1985 see Richard C. Barnett, "Domestic Energy Outlook," study prepared for Graduate Seminar in the Political Economics of International Trade, Department of Economics, American University, 1973.

For discussion of the various Swedish selling terms see *Governmental Intervention in the Market Mechanism,* Subcommittee on AntiTrust and Monopoly, Senate Committee on the Judiciary, Washington, D.C., 1969, pp. 570–72.

Page 220

Statistics for net income of the oil companies and the rate of return on fixed assets in the Middle East are from Charles Issawi and Mohanned Yeganeh, *The Economics of Middle East Oil,* New York: Praeger, 1962, pp. 121–22, and 110–13, respectively. See also, particularly re the Chase Bank study, George Stocking, *Middle East Oil,* Nashville, Tenn.: Vanderbilt University Press, 1970, on oil income. The relationship between Middle Eastern oil and the multinational companies is explained in detail by the Middle East Research and Information Project (MERIP), "Middle East Oil and the Energy Crisis," Parts I and II, Washington, D.C., 1973.

The advertising cost incurred by Exxon to change its name is from testimony presented by George Piercy, February 1, 1974, before the Senate Subcommittee on Multinational Corporations, Senate Committee on Foreign Relations.

Blair is quoted in *Economic Concentration,* New York: Harcourt Brace Jovanovich, 1972, p. 42.

The National Economic Research Association of Washington, D.C., found that all of the 25 largest petroleum companies were involved in the production of natural gas; 18 were involved in the production and/or amassing of reserves in uranium; 11 were involved in the production of coal; and 20 were involved in the exploration of oil shale. In addition, in 1970 petroleum companies accounted for 72 percent of all natural-gas production and reserves; 20 percent of coal production and 30 percent of coal reserves; 25 percent of uranium milling and 50 percent of uranium reserves. Small Business Committee, House of Representatives, Washington, D.C., 1971. When we examine the case of coal—the nation's most abundant energy resource—we can see how the oil companies which have amassed great reserves of coal can play one fuel off against another and thereby increase their bargaining power. When the energy crisis was approaching and coal was recognized as a possible substitute fuel, "the [coal] industry itself invested only $9 million in mining research between 1969 and 1973." However, now that the crunch has hit and something has to be done to increase coal output, the "U.S. Bureau of Mines now wants to spend $43 million in public revenues during the next fiscal year to increase mine production." *Business Week,* March 9, 1974. In other words, the taxpayers will spend more in the next year to increase output than the industry itself has spent in nearly five years. For additional information on the expansion of major oil firms into various other fuels see United Mine Workers Union, "Who Controls Your Future," *United Mine Workers Journal,* July 15–31, 1973. For details and analysis concerning the energy industry, competition, and antitrust matters see Stanley H. Ruttenberg and Associates,

The American Oil Industry: A Failure of Antitrust Policy, New York: Marine
Engineers Beneficial Association, December 1973.

Page 221

An excellent overview of the central issues involved in the study of the energy
industry can be found in Hearings before the Anti-Trust and Monopoly Subcommittee, Senate Judiciary Committee, June 26, 27, 28, 1973. Particularly
useful are the testimonies of John Wilson and David Schwartz of the Federal
Power Commission. There are numerous other sources of information on the
energy industry and the impact of its operations on the United States and
the underdeveloped world. For instance, see Jack Anderson, "Aramco Backed
Saudi Oil Price Rise," *The Washington Post,* Feb. 5, 1974; Robert Entman and
Clay Steinman, "The Sovereign State of Oil," *The Nation,* Jan. 26, 1974; Angus
McDonald, "Big Oil," Center for Science in the Public Interest, Washington,
D.C., 1974; Martin Lobel, "Where Do We Go from Here?" *Environmental
Action,* January 1974; William Farrell, "Blacks Fear Layoffs and Rising Costs
in Energy Crisis," *The New York Times,* Jan. 26, 1974; Vernon Jordan, "The
Energy Crisis: For Blacks a Disproportionate Burden," *The New York Times,*
Feb. 9, 1974; and Robert Engler, "Energy & Public Policy," *Social Policy,*
November–December, 1973 (the entire issue of this periodical is devoted to
the energy crisis). Engler's *The Politics of Oil* is still a widely recommended
volume for the background of the oil industry.

The statistics that follow are taken from James E. Akins, "The Oil Crisis:
This Time the Wolf Is Here," *Foreign Affairs,* Vol. 51, No. 3, April 1973,
p. 463. It will be noted that Akins' views are substantially different from those
of oil economist M. A. Adelman, who foresees a breakup of OPEC and a vast
surplus of oil. See M. A. Adelman, *The World Petroleum Market,* Baltimore:
Johns Hopkins Press, 1972, and "Is the Oil Shortage Real?," *Foreign Policy,*
Winter 1972–73.

The influence of the energy industry on the generation of demand for gasoline is discussed in the next chapter.

Page 222

According to a study by the Cost of Living Council, oil exports from the
United States in 1973 increased 284 percent over those of 1972. Although the
total amount of oil exported is relatively small—53.3 million barrels—its importance lies in its being symbolic of the global firm's drive to maximize global
earnings rather than to serve any one country. See the remarks of Representative Les Aspin, *Congressional Record,* Nov. 8, 1973, H 9779-80.

For the first quarter of 1974, according to *Business Week,* "soaring oil company profits [were] out in front [in this] better than expected" three-month
corporate performance. During this period in which consumers and small business were hard hit by the effects of the energy crisis, oil company earnings were
up by an average of 82 percent over the first quarter of 1973. *Business Week,*
May 11, 1974. As a whole, 1973 was also an exceptionally good year for major
oil-company profits, the top nine companies having an average rate of increase
of 45.2 percent (for the first nine months) over profits for the same period of
1972. All oil companies during the latter period posted an average increase of
30.3 percent. (1973 figures prepared by Public Interest Communications, San
Francisco, Calif.)

Page 222

For a discussion of the view of the energy crisis as being real or manipulated
and "Arab Greed," see Christopher Rand, "The Arabian Fantasy," *Harpers,*
January, 1974.

For discussion of the possible advantages enjoyed by the major oil companies as a result of the crisis see Leonard Moseley, *Power Play*, New York: Random House, 1973; Fuad Rohani, *A History of OPEC, op. cit.;* and Rand, *op. cit.*

An impressive discussion of energy supply, demand, and industry performance along with a noticeable display of public discontent was presented at "A Crisis in Power," The Citizen's Energy Conference, Feb. 15–18, 1974, Shoreham Hotel, Washington, D.C. Particularly informative are the presentations by Professor Barry Commoner, Scientists Institute for Public Information; Attorney Martin Lobel, counsel to Senator William Proxmire; David Schwartz, Federal Power Commission; Vic Reinimer, Senate Government Operations Committee Staff; Christopher Rand, former employee of Occidental Petroleum and Standard Oil of California; James Hightower, Agribusiness Accountability Project; Charles Hayes, International Vice President, Amalgamated Meatcutters Union; and Jeff Faux, Exploratory Project for Economic Alternatives.

On the founding of the Organization of Petroleum Exporting Countries, see Fuad Rohani, *op. cit.*

Page 223
For example, chief Saudi Arabian Oil Minister Ahmed Zaki Yamani was educated at Harvard. *The Wall Street Journal*, April 1, 1974.

Adelman, *Foreign Policy, op. cit.*

Page 224
S. David Freeman, "The Consumers Stake in the Energy Crisis," The Ford Foundation's Energy Policy Project, Washington), D.C. (mimeo), 1973, p. 5.

Adelman's calculations on margin increases and return on investment as well as the British case are found in his *The World Petroleum Market, op. cit.*

Statistic for control in OPEC countries by 8 companies is taken from Rohani, *op. cit.*, p. 105. In addition to the oligopolistic control of production in the OPEC, the Federal Trade Commission has recently documented the oligopolistic control which the eight largest companies have maintained over crude supplies, refining, and distribution in the United States. In short, according to the FTC, the 8 largest companies have acted as a "classical monopolist." See "Preliminary Federal Trade Commission Staff Report on Its Investigation of the Petroleum Industry," Washington, D.C., July 2, 1973. Subsequently the FTC staff issued another report advocating that the 8 divest themselves of "40 to 60 percent of all refineries and all pipelines." *The Wall Street Journal*, Feb. 25, 1974, p. 3.

See Adelman, *Foreign Policy, op. cit.; World Petroleum Market, op. cit.*

Jackson is quoted in *Time*, May 7, 1973, p. 47.

Documents from Aramco subpoenaed by the Subcommittee on Multinational Corporations, Senate Foreign Relations Committee, in March 1974. See also Jack Anderson's discussions on Aramco in "The Washington Merry-Go-Round," *The Washington Post*, Jan. 11, 14, and 28, 1974.

Estimated U.S. oil import requirements taken from Shell Oil Company, *National Energy Outlook*, March, 1973, p. 25.

Page 225
On American wheat exports to the U.S.S.R., see the Permanent Subcommittee on Investigations, Government Operations Committee, U.S. Senate, *Russian Grain Transactions*, hearings conducted July 20, 23, and 24, 1973.

For an analysis of the less-publicized (relative to the gasoline shortage) natural gas shortage in the United States see Andrew C. Gibas, "Natural Gas Shortage—Is It Real?," address delivered by the chairman of the Circle Pines (Minnesota) Utilities Commission, to representatives of gas utilities at a convention of the Minnesota Municipal Utilities Association, June 21, 1973 (Circle Pines, Minn.). For the structure of the natural gas industry, see the testimony of John W. Wilson, Federal Power Commission, before the Senate Anti-Trust and Monopoly Subcommittee of the Senate Judiciary Committee, *op. cit.*, June 27, 1973. The eight major integrated international oil companies, which were charged in late 1973 by the Federal Trade Commission with conspiring to monopolize the supply of petroleum in the United States, represent eight of the ten largest natural-gas producers in the United States.

In addition, see Tad Szulc, "What's Next in the Oil Crisis?," *Esquire*, May 1974, p. 178, for an interesting analysis of possible future developments in the U.S. energy situation.

The 1970 Arab foreign-exchange is from the World Bank, the 1980 estimate from the Chase Manhattan Bank; both are cited in Priscilla S. Meyer, "Arab Investors," *The Wall Street Journal*, March 5, 1974, pp. 1 and 26.

Page 228
Adam Smith quote is from *The Wealth of Nations*, New York: Modern Library edition, 1937, p. 256.

Page 229
The analysis and statistics underlying the "negation of the market," via the maximization of worldwide profits by global corporations, are presented in the next chapter. For a typical example of domestic U.S. transfer pricing as a market-negation mechanism see the Tenneco case in reference notes to p. 218 above.

Page 230
Statistics on the top 500 corporations are from "Fortune 500," published yearly in the May issue of *Fortune*. By 1974 the top 500 corporations' share of total employment had risen to 76 percent, while their shares in total sales and total profits of all industrial corporations had increased to 65 and 79 percent respectively. See "The Fortune 500," *Fortune*, May 1974.

From 1947 to 1968, according to former Assistant Attorney General in charge of anti-trust Richard W. McLaren, "the 200 largest corporations in manufacturing increased their share of that sector's total assets from 47 to 61 percent. McLaren quoted by Leonard Silk, *The New York Times*, May 27, 1972, p. 57.

The 1970 statistic for the top 9 corporations is found in *Forbes*, Nov. 15, 1971.

The statistics for the largest 200 industrial corporations that begin with the 1955–1959 period as well as those regarding corporate mergers can be found in *Investigation of Conglomerate Corporations*, Staff Report of the Antitrust Subcommittee, House of Representatives Committee on the Judiciary, June 1, 1971, pp. 41, 35, 40.

By 1972, the Federal Trade Commission and Securities and Exchange Commission reported (*FTC-SEC Quarterly Financial Report for Manufacturing Corporations*, 1st quarter, 1972) that 350 manufacturing corporations had 70 percent of the total assets of manufacturing companies. The most accurate measure of concentration, value-added (the value of shipments minus the cost of materials), reflects the same trend as the better-known measures used in the text: Between 1947 and 1966 the largest 50 U.S. corporations increased their share of total value-added in manufacturing from 17 percent to 25 percent; the largest 200, from 30 percent to 42 percent. In presenting these figures, John Blair notes, "There are no known sources of overstatement in these figures, but there are several sources of understatement." *Economic Concentration*, New York: Harcourt Brace, 1972, pp. 69–70.

432   GLOBAL REACH

Page 231
Statistics on mergers and prosecutions are found in Texts of Complaints, Federal Trade Commission and Department of Justice, mimeo, 1967. See also Betty Bock, "Mergers and Markets: An Economic Analysis of Developments in the Mid 1960's Under the Merger Act of 1950," *Studies in Business Economics*, No. 100, p. 94. See also Robert T. Averitt, *The Dual Economy*, New York: W. W. Norton, 1968.

Reference to the 1,496 firms absorbed and other merger statistics is from *Investigation . . . , op. cit.* The top 200 U.S. global corporations accounted for 40 percent of all mergers but acquired 50.5 percent of all merged assets. See also Harry H. Lynch, *Financial Performance on Conglomerates,* Boston: Harvard School of Business Administration, 1971, p. 36.

Another indicator of the accelerating absorption of national smaller firms by U.S. global corporations comes from a sample of 74 global firms conducted by the Emergency Committee on American Trade. For the years 1960 to 1970, 42 percent of the reported increase in employment of these firms was due solely to acquisitions of other companies; *The Role of the Multinational Corporation in the United States and World Economies,* Washington, D.C., 1973, Table 13. This report is further analyzed in the following chapter, Section 5.

Discussion of mass media through "75 percent of the country looks to the three networks as its primary source of news" is taken from Peter M. Sandman, David M. Rubin, and David B. Sachsman, *Media: An Introductory Analysis of American Mass Communications,* Englewood Cliffs, N.J.: Prentice-Hall, 1972. Profitability of the three major broadcasting companies is discussed and analyzed in *Directory of the Networks: The Network Project,* 105 Earl Hall, Columbia University, New York, February 1973, Part I, pp. 1–22. In addition, see *Broadcasting,* Apr. 17, 1967.

The estimate of 40,000 commercials is found in Howe Martyn, "A World Mission for Marketing," *Economic and Business Review,* Temple University, Fall 1970.

Page 232
The $3-billion expenditure on advertising is from Sandman *et al., op. cit.,* p. 131.

The $3 billion and $20 billion figures are found in Lee Loevinger, "Advertising Abuses and the Worst Cure," *Vital Speeches,* October 1972.

The 30-percent figure is found in Sandman *et al., op. cit.,* p. 137. However, the top 10 ad agencies' market share declined from 58 percent to 53 percent between 1960 and 1972, making advertising one of the few industries in which concentration lessened. *Advertising Age,* Feb. 15, 1965, and Feb. 26, 1973.

Reference to 60 percent of average newspaper space devoted to advertising is from "You and the Commercial," *CBS Reports,* TV interview with Dr. Erich Fromm, April 26, 1973.

Statistic on daily newspapers in U.S. cities is found in David Deitch, "The Political Economy of American Newspapers." *Perspectives,* No. 6, 1973, p. 4.

Reference to AP and UPI is found in A. Kent McDougall, ed., *The Press: A Critical Look from the Inside,* Princeton, N.J.: Dow Jones Books, 1966, pp. 106–108.

Page 233
Statistics on banks are from *Fortune,* Directory of Largest Non-industrial Corporations, published yearly. For increase (1955–1970) in 4 largest banks' share of total assets of all banks see the *Federal Reserve Bulletin,* September 1963, and Federal Reserve Bank data reprinted in *Statistical Abstract of the*

United States, 1971, p. 437. See the next chapter for large banks' concentration in commercial and industrial lending.

The 1971 figures of $577 billion, $336 billion, and $1 trillion are found in Representative Wright Patman, "Other People's Money," *The New Republic,* Feb. 17, 1973, p. 14, in data derived from the staff of the House Banking and Currency Committee, *op. cit.* See also Patman's remarks on this topic in *The Congressional Record,* June 21, 1972, p. H-5914.

At the time of the Patman study, the top ten banks (in terms of trust assets) were *Morgan Guaranty Trust, Chase Manhattan, Bankers Trust New York, First National City Bank,* United States Trust Co., Mellon National Bank and Trust Co., *Manufacturers Hanover Trust Co.,* Wilmington Trust Co., First National Bank of Chicago, Continental Illinois Bank. The banks in italics are all part of one coordinated group, the Rockefeller-Morgan Group (see text below).

Page 234
The 22 percent of outstanding voting shares is found in "Banks Trust Units Said to Go 'Go-Go,' Affect Stocks More," *The Wall Street Journal,* Jan. 11, 1973.

In a recent study covering a large sample of major U.S. banks, it was shown that in a significant number of cases on important proxy votes, banks obtain the right to vote their preferred stocks, which otherwise carry no voting privilege. David Kotz, "The Role of Financial Institutions in the Control of Large Non-Financial Corporations," Ph.D. dissertation, University of California at Berkeley, 1974.

Reference to 80 percent of these shares is found in *Commercial Banks and Their Trust Activities: Emerging Influence on the American Economy,* staff report for the Subcommittee on Domestic Finance, House of Representatives Committee on Banking and Currency, Washington, 1968, Vol. 1, p. 1.

". . . enormous potential power for good or evil" is quoted from *Commercial Banks and Their Trust Activities . . . , op. cit.,* p. 3.

Reference to corporations' seeking to establish "close contact" is from *ibid.,* pp. 25–27, and a personal interview with Subcommittee Counsel Benet D. Gellman, conducted by Michael Moffitt.

A classic example of the power wielded by large institutional investors, primarily global banks, was the 1969 affair between the Leasco Data Processing Equipment Corporation and the Chemical Bank of New York that came about when Leasco Chairman Saul Steinberg attempted to absorb the bank against the will of its chairman, William S. Renchard. At Renchard's behest, "the nation's big banks, rocked by the thought of one of their number being taken over, did cluster together to create what one banker calls 'a massive groundswell of opposition,'. . ." Besides pushing legislation in Washington and Albany to discourage the takeover of such financial institutions, "one thing that did happen was that Leasco's stock plunged from 140 to 106 in two weeks—driven down, many on Wall Street believe, as bank trust departments sold what Leasco shares they held. . . . In the end, says a Wall Street friend, 'Saul found out there really is a back room where the big boys sit and smoke their long cigars.' " And as Steinberg candidly admitted, "I always knew there was an establishment, I just used to think I was a part of it." *Business Week,* April 26, 1969.

With regard to the importance of corporate meetings the reader is referred to the *Wall Street Journal,* April 30, 1974, p. 4. The 1974 Annual Meeting of IBM was attended by 980 shareholders, which is roughly less than one-fifth of 1 percent of IBM's total 558,332 shareholders.

The data for the paragraph on the large holdings of the 49 largest banks surveyed by the Patman Committee can be found on p. 91 of *Commercial Banks and Their Trust Activities* . . . , *op. cit.*

Page 235

For Peter C. Dooley's essay, "Interlocking Directorate," see *The American Economic Review*, June 1969, pp. 314–23.

For a comprehensive analysis of the power of the Rockefeller financial group, see James C. Knowles, "The Rockefeller Financial Group," Warner Modular Publications, Module 343, 1973, pp. 1–59. Dooley and Knowles both cite Paul Sweezy's 1939 study of "Interest Groups in the American Economy," in the U.S. National Resources Committee, *The Structure of the American Economy*, Washington, D.C., 1939.

For the increasing closeness of the relationship between the Rockefeller-Morgan group banks in the 1960's see *Commercial Banks and Their Trust Activities, op. cit.*, Table IV-A.

Data on ownership of major airlines and networks are taken from *Disclosure of Corporate Ownership*, Report Prepared by the Subcommittees on Intergovernmental Relations and Budgeting, Management and Expenditures, Senate Government Operations Committee, Washington, D.C.: Government Printing Office, 1973, pp. 55–64.

For a recent discussion of Exxon, see *Business Week*, "The Middle East Squeeze on the Oil Giants," July 29, 1972, pp. 56–62. Although the identity of Exxon's largest stockholders is not public information (the company refused to divulge such information to Senator Lee Metcalf in March 1972), it is well known who the company's major stockholders are and who benefits most from the company's operations.

Reference to Reynolds, Morgan, and American Smelting and Refining is found in *Commercial Banks and Their Trust Activities* . . . , *op. cit.*, pp. 4, 697, 703.

Page 236

The Patman study is *op. cit.*

Dooley, *op. cit.*, p. 319.

Page 237

Dooley, *op. cit.*, pp. 317–18.

Berle, "Our Problem of Financial Power," *The Washington Post*, Aug. 11, 1968.

Brandeis is quoted by Dooley, *op. cit.*, p. 314.

Wilson is quoted in *Commercial Banks and Their Trust Activities* . . . , *op. cit.*, p. iv.

Page 238

See *The Growth of Unregistered Bank Holding Companies*, House of Representatives, Committee on Banking and Currency, 1969. See also Sanford Rose, "The Case for the One-Bank Holding Company," *Fortune*, May 15, 1969.

For the rapid growth of one-bank holding companies, see H. Erich Heineman, "Bank Holding Battles Are Only Begun," *The New York Times*, Jan. 10, 1971, and Frank Porter, "One Bank Holding Firms Hit," *The Washington Post*, Nov. 2, 1969.

On the activities of European banks which put competitive pressures on American banks to form one-bank holding companies see Frank M. Tamanga, "Commercial Banks in Transition: From the Sixties to the Seventies," in *Banking in a Changing World*, Lectures at the 24th International Banking Summer School, Italian Bankers' Association, Chianciano, Italy, May 1971, and "The

Role of U.S. Banks in the Changing Pattern of International Banking," Department of Economics Study Paper (mimeo), The American University, Washington, D.C., October 1973.

Concerning the existence of unused time (excess capacity) in banks' computer operations, this would indicate either inefficient investment policies or planned expansion into nonfinancial activities since appropriate-sized computers were available. Personal memo from Professor R. D. Morgenstern, Department of Economics, Queens College, City University of New York.

Discussion of the 1969 legislation is found in "One Bank Holding Company Bill Becomes Law," *Los Angeles Times*, Jan. 1, 1971.

For the origins of the section of the law concerned with the takeover of banks by nonbanking conglomerates and the Leasco Affair, see *Business Week*, April 26, 1969, *op. cit.*

Statistics and a discussion of credit cards are found in *The Wall Street Journal*, Dec. 22, 1969.

Page 239
Statistics on leasing arrangements are from David Rockefeller, "One Bank Holding Companies: A View From Inside," *The Wall Street Journal*, June 30. See also Robert L. Parrish, "Aircraft Leasing," *Airline Management and Marketing*, June 1970, p. 51. On leasing as an alternative to financing in the underdeveloped world see Chapter 6 above.

Citicorp quote, analysis of that bank, and the potential future of leasing in the consumer market are found in David Leinsdorf *et al.*, "Citibank: A Preliminary Report," Washington, D.C.: Nader Task Force on First National City Bank, 1971.

Patman is quoted from "Other People's Money," *op. cit.* As Patman candidly observed in *Business Week*, "They [commercial banks] have got too damn much power and that's all there is to it." July 24, 1971, p. 67.

For a Marxist interpretation of this question see, for example, Robert Fitch and Mary Oppenheimer, "Who Rules the Corporations?," *Socialist Revolution*, Vol. 1, Nos. 4, 5, 6, 1970. For a different Marxist view, see "Resurgence of Financial Control: Fact or Fancy?" by Paul M. Sweezy, *Monthly Review*, November 1971.

Page 240
Patman is quoted from "Other People's Money," *op. cit.*

A partial listing of the "more important" bank consortia can be found in the Senate Committee on Finance, *Implications of Multinational Firms for World Trade and Investment and for U.S. Trade and Labor*, Washington: Government Printing Office, February 1973. Of the 18 consortia listed by this source, 13 have American representation.

Contrary to theories of the firm in modern orthodox and Marxist economics, the large corporation's chief criterion covering expansion is maximization not of profits but of cash flow, the amount left over from gross income after all costs, including dividends, are paid off. It is roughly equal to depreciation allowances plus retained earnings. The maximization of cash flow is from management's view the optimal level of profits for pursuing maximum growth. A corporation can break even in terms of no losses or earnings and yet still maintain a high growth rate due to large depreciation allowances. Thus cash flow measured against net worth is the only consistent criterion for assessing the future expansion plans of a global corporation. The more capital-intensive an industry, the more important cash flow becomes. See M. Z. Brooke and H. L. Remmers, *The Strategy of the Multinational Enterprise: Organization and Finance*, New York: American Elsevier Publishing Co.,

1970, whose detailed examination makes it clear that control over cash flow (sometimes called cash budgeting) is control over investment and "represents control over the operations of a subsidiary and, as such, is almost always held at head office," p. 103. For a provocative analysis relating cash flow to macroeconomics to explain the growing problem of ineffective government stabilization policies, see Charles Levinson, *Capital, Inflation, and the Multinationals,* London: George Allen & Unwin Ltd., 1971, Chapter VII.

Page 241
Herman is quoted from "Do Bankers Control Corporations?," *Monthly Review,* June 1973, pp. 25–26.

Page 242
The collapse of the nation's largest railroad is thoroughly described and analyzed in the report of the Subcommittee on Domestic Finance, House of Representatives Committee on Banking and Currency, *The Penn Central Failure and the Role of Financial Institutions,* Washington, D.C.: Government Printing Office, 1972.

The affiliations of the Penn Central's directors with major financial institutions are detailed in *The Penn Central Failure . . . , ibid.,* p. 4 and Chart 2.

Detailed information on the Penn Central's major stockholders and creditors can be found on pp. 5–11, *ibid.*

The Penn Central's diversification program is described on pp. 23–148, *ibid.*

The remainder of the Penn Central information is found *ibid.,* pages 11 and 31.

Page 243
The Lockheed episode and its subsequent rescue by the Federal Government is described in *Business Week,* May 15, 1971, "The Case for Helping Lockheed," pp. 41–42, and *Fortune,* June 1971, p. 67. A list of "Lockheed Banks" can be found on p. 70. See also *Aviation Week and Space Technology,* March 16, 1970, pp. 22–23. See also *Aviation Week and Space Technology,* Aug. 9, 1971, p. 24, and the remarks of Sen. William Proxmire, *Congressional Record,* July 26, 1971, pp. S27140–52. The House of Representatives debate is also useful. See the *Congressional Record* of July 30, 1971, pp. H28340–99.

Page 244
Members of the board of directors of Consolidated Edison who are interlocked with the country's major financial institutions are Chairman Charles F. Luce, director of New York Life Insurance; Williams A. Renchard, director of Chemical Bank and New York Life; Richard S. Perkins, director of Citicorp and New York Life; Milton C. Mumford, director of Equitable Life; Frederick Eaton, director of Citicorp and New York Life; William Beinecke, director of Manufacturers Hanover Trust. These can be found in *Standard and Poor's Directory of Corporations,* 1973. Knowles, *op. cit.,* explains the relationship between the Rockefeller financial group and Consolidated Edison more fully.

Con Ed information on owners is from the Federal Power Commission which requires privately owned utilities and natural-gas pipelines to file lists of their ten largest securities holders. The commercial banks referred to are Chase Manhattan (three times), Bankers Trust, Manufacturers Hanover Trust, and Chemical Bank of New York.

Metcalf's remarks are from the *Congressional Record,* June 28, 1972, p. S10434.

Percentage of long-term debt equity can be found in *Moody's Public Utilities,* 1973. The Federal Power Commission has stated that this is not an isolated phenomenon among utilities. See the Federal Power Commission, *National Power Survey,* 1972, Part I, Section 1, p. 9.

Abrams is quoted in *The New York Times,* July 29, 1973.

Financial information on Consolidated Edison (and other utilities) can be found in *Moody's Public Utility Manual,* 1970, pp. 70–84.

For an interesting survey of the financial structures of major southern utilities, and the role of major financial institutions, see "Southern Power Companies"—A Special Supplement, *Southern Exposure,* Summer/Fall 1973, Institute for Southern Studies, Atlanta. The investigation into the financial structures of Southern utilities revealed that, at least as far as the major utilities are concerned, the predominant pattern of ownership and, presumably, control is not significantly different from the ownership of Consolidated Edison. For example, the Carolina Power & Light Company's largest shareholder is First National City Bank of New York, utilizing three different nominees, or "street names." Two other major Rockefeller–Morgan banks are among the top ten shareholders of the utility (Chase Manhattan and Manufacturers Hanover Trust Co.). The Carolina utility's second-largest shareholder is Wall Street's largest brokerage firm, Merrill Lynch, Pierce, Fenner & Smith. To cite but another example, the two largest shareholders of the Florida Power and Light Company, First National City Bank of New York and Chase Manhattan, hold over 10 percent of the stock in the utility. Thus, we can see that the power of the country's major commercial banks, particularly trust departments, has extended to a position of dominance in utilities throughout the country.

Reference to New York State Public Service Commission is found in *The New York Times,* July 29, 1973.

The strong evidence that emerges from an examination of the Penn Central, Con Ed, and other regulated and quasiregulated companies (e.g., Lockheed) in various areas of social infrastructure suggests the following pattern by which banks use these companies: Banks derive two forms of income streams from these operations. First, a high-income stream from interest on the loans extended to these firms which are needed for continued capitalization available only from external—i.e., bank—sources, not from retained earnings. Retained earnings are low because of the second type of income: namely, through their voting control the banks promote a high dividend-payout policy. High dividends accomplish both continued dependency of the firm on the bank for investment capital and increase in the value and investment leverage of its trust assets. The House report on the Penn Central failure provides the data for quantifying these two advantages. Importantly, should the dividend-payout rate be inadvertently or otherwise set too high and thereby lead to a liquidity crisis for the firm, the bank's risk is minimal, since local and/or federal government will intervene with some form of subsidization. As is noted in the text, government must intervene in such cases as Penn Central and Lockheed because the failure of such firms is disastrous to the region's or nation's economy. Thus the Penn Central failure forced the Fed to interject a massive amount of liquidity into the commercial-paper market in order to avoid a debt-liquidation crisis. For a highly readable and accurate portrayal of the Penn Central debacle and the near-miss money crisis, see Adam Smith, *Supermoney,* New York: Random House, 1972.

For an overview with analysis of the electric utility industry in the United States see Senator Lee Metcalf and Vic Reinemer, *Overcharge,* New York: McKay, 1967.

Page 245

Corporate concentration of power and an example of the type of influence it can have on social infrastructure planning have been documented by Bradford C. Snell in terms of public transportation. Snell has recorded the near-collusive efforts of General Motors, Goodyear Tire Company, and Standard Oil of New Jersey (Exxon) in "creating a public transport market for their complementary products of buses, tires, and petroleum." Typical of their activities in many cities across the nation was their successful effort to influence Los Angeles, in the 1930's, to give up its highly efficient low-cost and low-polluting electric tramway system and to substitute in its place the use of General Motors buses (GM controls 90 percent of the city bus market) with Goodyear tires and Standard petroleum products. Not only did this combined effort of the three companies succeed in creating a bus–tire–petroleum market where there had been none, but it also of course led to a city transportation system which over the years had to favor systematically roads and internal-combustion vehicles rather than other, more ecologically efficient systems. See Bradford C. Snell, *American Ground Transport: A Proposal for Restructuring the Automobile, Truck, Bus, and Rail Industries*, presented to Subcommittee on Antitrust and Monopoly of U.S. Senate Committee on the Judiciary, Feb. 26, 1974, G.P.O., Washington, D.C.

Veblen's views are actually different from both Galbraith's and Berle and Means's and, in our view, closer to the statistical reality. Owners' interests are close to those of the top management of a firm, the latter being the "Captains of Solvency" and interested in financial returns or, in the terminology of this book, in maximizing economies of scale through the use of finance capital. Owners and financial managers are then distinguished from production managers or "engineers," whose aims are to maximize efficiency through the capturing of economies of scale in the use of mechanical and organizational technology. The latter are Veblen's members of the technostructure. Galbraith, Berle, and Means, however, lump into their technostructure all management of the firm as contrasted to owners. Veblen's views are found in *The Theory of Business Enterprise*, New York: Scribner's, 1904. A detailed analysis of these points is in Jon Wisman, "The Role of Technology in Economic Thought," Ph.D. dissertation, The American University, Washington, D.C., 1974. Galbraith's ideas on the technostructure are in *The New Industrial State*, Boston: Houghton Mifflin, 1967; Berle and Means's in their *The Modern Corporation and Private Property*, rev. ed., New York: Harcourt Brace & World, 1967.

Page 246
Wilber Lewellen, *The Ownership Income of Management*, National Bureau of Economic Research, 1971.

An exhaustive documentation and analysis of the concentration phenomenon in all other advanced economies, with comparisons of economic and political impacts with those in the United States, can be found in Helmut Arndt, ed., *On Economic Concentration*, Vols. 1 & 2 (rev. ed.), West Berlin: Duncker & Humbolt, 1971. These volumes are essential reading for anyone interested in understanding the extent to which modern capitalism is transforming itself. Arndt is professor of economics and law at the Free University, Berlin.

On the integration of the American economy and the rise of organized business see Dudley Dillard, *Economic Development of the North Atlantic Community*, Englewood Cliffs, N.J.: Prentice-Hall, 1967, Chapters 19, 20–23, and 36.

Page 249
The secret list of leading Republican contributors was subpoenaed from the White House by Common Cause in June of 1973. The list was subsequently made public and was discussed in *The New Republic*, "Super Contributors," August 11, 1973, and *The Washington Post*, Sept. 29, 1973, p. A-1.

The "Oligopolist's Dilemma"—"If I don't do it others will"—comes out not only as regards the use of transfer-pricing techniques for overpricing imports and underpricing exports into and out of poor countries. It also surfaced in the "secret campaign contributions" to the Nixon Re-Election Committee. Gulf Oil's Vice President Claude C. Wild was quoted in *Newsweek,* Nov. 26, 1973, p. 34, as saying, about the fact that since other companies were making these secret gifts, "if his firm didn't, 'it might end up on a blacklist or bottom of the totem pole.' " The oligopolist's dilemma and transfer pricing to avoid the public's knowledge about corporate funds came together in what *Newsweek* characterized as "money-laundering through foreign subsidiaries and Swiss bank accounts . . . a lesson in corporate wheeling and dealing. Ashland [Oil, Inc.] drew its donation from a subsidiary in Gabon; American Airlines hid its contribution in phony invoices routed through Lebanon. Both firms laundered their money through Swiss banks before passing it on, in cash, to the President's Re-Election Committee." *Ibid.*

Page 250
Forbes, Nov. 1, 1969.

Adams is quoted in Gabriel Kolko, *Railroads and Regulation 1877–1916,* Princeton, N.J.: Princeton University Press, 1965, p. 37. For development of the essential themes presented in *Railroads and Regulation,* crucial to an understanding of the role of the Federal Government in the modern economy, see *The Triumph of Conservatism: A Re-Interpretation of American History 1900–1916,* Glencoe, Ill.: Free Press of Glencoe, 1963.

The first ICC was dominated by prorailroad commissioners. Thomas M. Cooley, who Chicago, Burlington & Quincy Railroad executive Charles E. Perkins said was the "sort of man he would trust to regulate the railroads," was the first chairman of the ICC. Augustus Schoonmaker, a railroad attorney and political associate of President Grover Cleveland, was a second commissioner. And Aldace F. Walker, who became chairman of the board of the Atchison, Topeka & Santa Fe Railroad, was the third. (The other two were "political appointments" of President Cleveland.) For the industry-oriented composition of the ICC, see individual backgrounds in *Who's Who in Government,* Chicago: Marquis Who's Who, 1972. See also Robert Fellmeth, *The Interstate Commerce Commission,* Report of the Nader Study Group on the Interstate Commerce Commission, New York: Grossman, 1970, especially Chapters 1, 2, and 5 and Appendix 4.

The conventional view regarding regulatory agencies is succinctly reviewed by John M. Blair, *Economic Concentration, op. cit.,* p. 663. See also *The Washington Post,* June 7, 1973, editorial page.

Johnson is quoted in Mark J. Green, ed., *Monopoly Makers,* New York: Grossman, 1973, p. 80. Inefficiency is also a factor in the regulatory agencies' inability to regulate activities of business. On this matter see James Landis, *Report on Regulatory Agencies to the President-Elect, 1960.*

With reference to the staffing of regulatory agencies, an example of "government–corporate interlocks" is appointments to the Federal Power Commission between 1969 and 1973 (testimony of Congressman George E. Brown, Jr., before the Anti-Trust and Monopoly Subcommittee of the Senate Judiciary Committee, June 26, 1973):

Rush Moody, Federal Power Commissioner, formerly a Texas oil-industry lawyer; an ex-Gooch lieutenant (Mr. Frank Allen) is now his chief assistant.

R. Gordon Gooch, former Federal Power Commission General Counsel, now with the Washington office of a major Houston law firm. A long history of representing Texas oil interests.

Charles Walker, a native Texan, formerly Under Secretary of the Treasury, now a principal oil-industry lobbyist. His brother was the first Federal Power Commissioner to advocate deregulation.

Stephen Wakefield, now Assistant Secretary of the Interior, formerly assistant to Federal Power Commission General Counsel Gooch and an associate in Gooch's Texas law firm.

Kenneth Lay, in 1973 Deputy Under Secretary of the Interior; formerly assistant to Federal Power Commissioner Walker, and an economist with the Exxon Corporation in Texas.

Page 251

For the backgrounds of the members of the Federal Power Commission, see the following volumes of the *Congressional Record:* Remarks by Senator Frank Moss, May 21, 1973, pp. S9448–49; testimony of Representative George E. Brown, reprinted in the *Record,* May 21, 1973, pp. S9459–60; remarks of Senator William Proxmire, June 11, 1973, pp. S10854–55; exchange between Senators Moss, Norris Cotton, and Theodore Stevens, June 13, 1973, p. S11096. Also, testimony of Representative George E. Brown before the Anti-trust and Monopoly Subcommittee of the Senate Judiciary Committee, June 27, 1973, *op. cit.* Information on FPC price increases can be found in *The Washington Post,* May 31, 1973, p. A1. In addition to the existing proindustry composition of the FPC, which, because it regulated the price charged for natural gas at the wellhead, will make crucial decisions regarding the cost of energy to American consumers for the next 20 years, President Nixon recently appointed Robert Morris, a San Francisco attorney for Standard Oil of California (on natural-gas matters), to the FPC. However, the Senate, led by liberals such as Warren Magnuson and Proxmire rejected the Morris nomination.

White is quoted in *The Washington Post,* June 18, page A8, 1973. A classic analysis of the ineffectiveness of regulation over public utilities compared with utilities not regulated can be found in George Stigler and Claire Friedland, "What Can Regulators Regulate?," *Journal of Law and Economics,* Vol. 5, October 1962, pp. 1–17.

For the period to the 1960's Stigler has found only a "very modest effect on preventing concentration via the Sherman Anti-Trust laws compared to other countries without regulation." See his "The Economic Effect of Anti-Trust Laws," *Journal of Law and Economics,* Vol. 11, Oct. 1966, pp. 225–59. University of Wisconsin Professor Willard F. Mueller, in "Current Policy Issues in Anti-Trust," paper presented to AFL-CIO, Labor Study Center's Conference on Corporate Power, May 1974, analyzes two further problems associated with antitrust legislation and enforcement: academic lag and thwarted efforts of government research. After citing studies of the literature on industrial conglomeration and noting the low priority it has been given by industrial-organization economists until the late 1960's Mueller states, "This is a serious indictment . . . it is an admission that most research tends to lag, much less anticipate, important organizational changes in our economy" (p. 19). Mueller finds the FTC no better in a critical analysis of a November 1972 staff report, *Conglomerate Merger Performance: An Empirical Analysis of Nine Corporations.* The study, according to Mueller, made inadequate use of the FTC's authority to obtain necessary data, pledged secrecy to the 9 firms involved concerning the characteristics of each individual firm, based its conclusion upon aggregated data obscuring the impact of varying firm size, and finally made no attempt to examine ". . . such central conglomerate hypotheses as reciprocity, cross-subsidization or mutual forebearance" (pp. 9–13).

Biographies of bankers are found in James D. Knowles, "The Rockefeller Financial Group," Warner Modular Publications, Module 343, 1973, pp. 42–44, and assorted newspapers and business journals.

Patman is quoted in "House Unit Backs Curbs on Banking," *The New York Times*, April 18, 1969.

Page 252
Almost predictably, the man chosen as the country's "energy czar" at the height of the oil crisis was drawn from the upper strata of the corporate hierarchy. William Simon, "energy czar" and Deputy Secretary of the Treasury, was a senior partner at the leading investment-banking firm of Salomon Brothers, and, according to *Fortune*, "his share of the profits sometimes exceeded $2 million a year." January 1974, p. 77.

On the relationships between economic concentration and political power, particularly in the American context, see Grant McConnell, *Private Power and American Democracy*, New York: Knopf, 1966; Reinhard Bendix, *Work and Authority in Industry: The Ideologies of Management in the Course of Industrialization*, New York: Harper & Row, 1956, Chapters 5 and 7; and Morton S. Baratz, *The American Business System in Transition*, New York: Crowell, 1970, particularly Chapter 6, "The Industrial Oligarchs and Social Policy." On the political consequences of economic concentration, Joseph Schumpeter in *Capitalism, Socialism and Democracy*, New York: Harper, 1947, pp. 140–41, concluded:

"Even if the giant concerns were all managed so perfectly as to call forth applause from the angels in heaven, *the political consequences of concentration would still be what they are*. The political structure of a nation is profoundly affected by the elimination of a host of small and medium-sized firms the owner-managers of which, together with their dependents, henchmen and connections, count quantitatively at the polls and have a hold on what we may term the foreman class that no management of a large unit can ever have; the very foundation of private property and free contracting wears away in a nation in which its most vital, most concrete, most meaningful types disappear from the moral horizon of the people."

The influence of special interest groups within the Federal government has been described by a number of Ralph Nader's group studies. Among them are *Who Runs Congress*, New York: Grossman, 1972. See also *The Interstate Commerce Commission, op. cit.*

Historically, not only the executive and legislative branches of government but the Supreme Court as well has been particularly responsive to the needs of business. For a historical overview of this phenomenon see Michael Parenti, *Democracy for the Few*, New York: St. Martin's Press, 1974, particularly Chapters 5, 8, 12–16. For an overview of this trend in Supreme Court decisions in recent years see "Tipping the Scales: High Court Favors Business More Often in Antitrust Cases," *The Wall Street Journal*, May 21, 1974.

Page 253
Metcalf's remarks are found in the *Congressional Record*, April 25, 1972, pp. E4242–46. See also p. S22141 in the *Record* of June 24, 1972; pp. S10432–43 in the *Record* of June 28; and August 16, 1972, pp. S13603–05.

"Privileged and confidential" information is quoted from the *Congressional Record*, April 25, 1972, pp. E4242–44. See also *Disclosure of Corporate Ownership, op. cit.*, Part I. Metcalf later attempted to learn the identity of the 30 largest shareholders of 18 large oil companies. Of the 18, only 4 (Arco, Mobil, Conoco, and Ashland) complied with Metcalf's request.

For evidence of the U.S. government's inability to obtain sufficient knowledge for formulating adequate policies to deal with the energy crisis see Julius Duscha, "Oil: The Data Shortage," *The Progressive*, February 1974, pp. 23–26.

10: The Global Corporation and the Public Interest

Page 254
"LatinAmericanization of the United States" is from Felipe Pazos, as cited in Carlos F. Díaz-Alejandro, "Latin America: Towards 2000 A.D.," in Jagdish Bhagwati, *Economics and the World Order: From the 1970's to the 1990's,* London: Macmillan, 1972, footnote, p. 249.

Federal Reserve Board economist on recent scarcities is quoted in Samuel I. Katz, "Imported Inflation and the Balance of Payments," *The Bulletin,* New York University Graduate School of Business Administration, Institute of Finance, No. 91–92, October 1973, p. 45.

Page 255
Otto Eckstein, "instability at the center of national power," quoted in *The New York Times,* Nov. 4, 1973.

Senate Finance Committee on the planning capabilities of multinational corporations is found in *Implications of the Multinational Firm for World Trade and Investment and for U.S. Trade and Labor,* Report to the Committee on Finance of the United States Senate and its Subcommittee on International Trade, Investigation No. 332–69, Government Printing Office, Washington, D.C., 1973, p. 159.

Page 256
The dualistic structure of the American economy is discussed in Robert T. Averitt, *The Dual Economy: The Dynamics of American Industrial Structure,* New York: Norton, 1968. See also John Kenneth Galbraith, *Economics and the Public Purpose,* Boston: Houghton Mifflin, 1973. For other literature on concentration and the ineffectiveness of antitrust measures see Chapter 9.

Pages 257–58
The exact timing of the turning point by which we identify the transformation to the U.S. political economy cannot, of course, be identified with a precise date. Precision identification of the turning-point date will have to await further hypothesis-testing in the future. However, our own findings indicate a date between 1965 and 1968. The identification of the transformation itself is based upon a multitude of indicators cited throughout this book, all pointing to basic structural changes in the *transaction processes* of the financial and industrial sectors of the United States and of other economies. The most basic of the structural changes is, of course, the globalization of the Western world's largest industrial and financial enterprises themselves.

In the financial sphere, indicators of the turning point are the start and then acceleration of the Eurodollar and Eurobond markets (1963–1965); the start and then acceleration of "off-shore safe-havens" of U.S. global banks and their "Edgebank" expansion overseas (1964–1966); the start of the unprecedented U.S. bank-merger movement (1965). In 1966 the following long-term trend values were broken: the log of the Dow Jones index breaks off from its long-term trend and starts a constant and relative decrease from earlier periods; the velocity of money starts a steady and persistent rise above its former long-term trend values; and the money supply (demand deposits plus time deposits) relative to GNP reaches and goes beyond its 1929 historic values. By 1968 with the start of the U.S. One Bank Holding Company Act and the U.S. government's voluntary and, later, mandatory balance of payment acts the period is described by financial expert Frank Tamagna as "convergence of United States multinational corporations and multinational banks into an integrated U.S. economy 'in exile.'" For further description and explanation of these indicators of transformation see Frank M. Tamagna, "The Role of U.S. Banks in the Changing Pattern of International Banking," Department of Economics Study

Paper, Washington, D.C.: The American University, November 1973; and "Commercial Banking in Transition: From the Sixties to the Seventies" in *Banking in a Changing World,* Lectures at the 24th International Banking Summer School, Italian Bankers' Association, Chianciano, Italy, May, 1971; also various articles by economic experts in Thomas G. Gies and Vincent T. Apilado, eds., *Banking Markets and Financial Institutions,* Homewood, Ill.: Irwin, 1971; "International Business Review: The Monetary Muddle," issue of *Saturday Review World,* Jan. 26, 1974, particularly articles by R. N. Cooper ("The System in Disarray") and Leonard Silk ("Out of the Woods Comes the Snake"). Also G. M. Meier, *Problems of World Monetary Order,* New York: Oxford University Press, 1974; Otmar Emminger, *Inflation and the International Monetary System,* Per Jacobsson Foundation, Basel, Switzerland, June 16, 1973; and Robert Lekachman, *Inflation: The Permanent Problem of Boom and Bust,* New York: Random House, 1973. For quantitative analyses of trend changes in monetary, credit, liquidity, and stock market indicators see various monthly issues in 1973 through first half of 1974 of R. Storey, ed., *The Bank Credit Analyst,* published by Storey, Boeckh & Associates, Montreal, Canada.

In the industrial sector the most crucial indicator of structural transformation, which first became significant around 1965, has been ever more rapid shifts in where *and* by whom goods are being produced, notably the use of "export platform" operations. By 1968 the export platform had begun a second phase, the creation of production facilities in underdeveloped countries which had not gone through the normal product life cycle, i.e., had never been utilized in the home domestic economy. See Chapters 6 and 8 above for a more detailed statement on export platform operations and indicators. Other indicators of the transformation turning point will be found below as measured by the rates of change (and their second differentials) in the foreign to domestic ratios of assets, sales, employment, investment, and profits in terms of global corporations themselves and in terms of the total U.S. corporate sector. Also, indicators focusing on the upsurge in concentration in both the industrial and financial sectors are given in this chapter and in Chapter 9. Finally, starting in the early 1970's, there has been a convergence in business cycles between advanced nations so that the highs and lows of the cycles are all largely in-phase.

Data (assets, sales, and profits) indicating the increasing importance of their foreign operations to U.S. global corporations and the U.S. economy from *Special Survey of U.S. Multinational Companies, 1970,* National Technical Information Service, U.S. Department of Commerce, November 1972, Tables 1 and 3. This survey is the data base for similar figures reported in the Senate Finance Committee, *op. cit.,* pp. 431–52. That this trend continues (through 1972) is indicated in "Offshore Bonanza: Foreign Ventures Fetch More Profits for Firms Located in United States," *The Wall Street Journal,* Nov. 1, 1973, p. 1: "On top of a profitable 1972 for foreign operations many U.S.-based companies expect 1973 to wind up even better. Some are looking for profit increases of 30 percent, 40 percent and 50 percent on their already lucrative foreign operations. In some cases, profits from abroad will offset lackluster domestic trends."

Page 259

The quote from the Senate Finance Committee is taken from Senate Finance Committee, *op. cit.,* p. 433 (italics ours).

For the turning-point indicator of foreign to domestic fixed investment see Business Internation Special Research Study, *The Effects of U.S. Corporate Foreign Investment: 1960–1970,* New York, 1972, p. 48. Similar results are also obtained when using the foreign to domestic ratios for gross investments and assets.

U.S. global banks' expansion of branch operation is found in Andrew Brimmer, "American International Banking Trend and Prospects," before the 51st Annual Meeting of the Bankers' Association for Foreign Trade, Boca Raton, Fla., April 2, 1973, Table 1.

Figures on foreign deposit holdings of the nine New York city banks are from Frank Mastrapasqua, "U.S. Bank Expansion Via Foreign Branching; Monetary Policy Implications," *The Bulletin* of the New York University Graduate School of Business Administration, Institute of Finance, Nos. 87 and 88, January 1973. For further data on foreign deposit holdings and concentration indicators in these holdings see notes to pp. 270 and 271 below.

Pages 259–60
On the Leontieff paradox, see W. Leontieff, "Domestic Production and Foreign Trade: The American Capital Position Reexamined," Proceedings of the American Philosophical Society, Vol. 97, 1953, pp. 332–49; and its most recent affirmation in R. E. Baldwin, "Determinants of the Commodity Structure of U.S. Trade," *American Economic Review,* Vol. 61, 1971, pp. 126–46. However, the latest data and calculations released by the U.S. Tariff Commission comparing the 1958/60 period with 1968 show a new trend emerging which is consonant with our argument of the increasingly significant role of U.S. global corporations' relatively labor-intensive manufactured imports from their export-platform operations in underdeveloped countries. In an examination of individual *traditional* exports and imports over this decade, there was a 10 percent decrease in capital intensity of imports relative to exports; but Leontieff's findings, although weaker, were still confirmed. In contrast, the opposite of the Leontieff paradox was found in an examination of *new* exports and imports that had entered into U.S. trade since 1960. Thus in 1968 the capital intensity of *new* imports has been considerably less (about 10 percent) than that of *new* exports. Also, *new* imports are substantially less capital-intense than *new* domestic production for shipment to the U.S. market, while there is identical capital intensity between *new* exports and *new* domestic shipments. When labor intensity was measured directly these findings were further confirmed: *new* imports were more labor-intense than both *new* exports and *new* domestic production, "pointing up once again the labor-intensive character of the upsurge in imports that the U.S. has experienced in recent years." U.S. Tariff Commission, *Competitiveness of U.S. Industries,* TC Publication 473, Washington, D.C., April 1972, pp. 147–50.

The role of U.S. global corporations in creating these "new" imports becomes clear when the growth of these firms' percentage of total U.S. manufactured imports is considered. Global corporations accounted for 23 percent in 1968, an estimated 37.6 percent by 1972, and a projected 50 percent by 1975 (estimated in "U.S. Multinationals—The Dimming of America," a report prepared for the AFL-CIO Maritime Trades Department Executive Board Meeting, Feb. 15–16, 1973). The trend toward a reversal of the Leontieff paradox due to the U.S. global corporations' transnationalization of production is an illustration of a little-known problem relating to types of innovation undertaken by modern industrial firms. The "export platform" (an innovation in financial and organizational technology but not mechanical technology) has been analyzed and described as a "process" innovation as opposed to a "production" innovation. See Frederick T. Knickerbocker, *Oligopolistic Reaction and Multinational Enterprise,* Boston: Basic Books, 1973. Although process and product innovation can both extend the life of oligopoly profits from a given production-product line, it is only the latter which can deal with real material problems such as new scarcities in resource supply or new forms of viral diseases. To the extent that process innovation can extend the oligopoly profit flow of a given product innovation, it allows firms to delay their R&D efforts in real production breakthroughs. Whether or not the globalization of domestic oligopolies through direct foreign investment (a process innovation) has acted as a disincentive mechanism in industries experiencing retarded rates of technological growth is still a question to be investigated. Such industries include metallurgy, electronics, chemicals, and pharmaceuticals.

Page 260

Data on increased exports of U.S. global corporations and their subsidiaries are from Senate Finance Committee, *op. cit.* pp. 305–306, 354.

Employment data on U.S. parents versus their affiliates is from Thomas Kraseman and Betty Barker, "Employment and Payroll Cost of U.S. Multinational Companies," *Survey of Current Business,* October 1973. Considering only those 223 global firms in the manufacturing sector, the 1966–70 employment growth, domestic versus foreign, presents an even more pessimistic picture, posting an annual increase in the United States of 1.9 percent, in foreign developed areas of 5.5 percent, and in the foreign underdeveloped areas of 8.3 percent. (For the manufacturing firms compared with the entire sample, there was a significantly higher increase in their foreign employment relative to domestic employment. Between 1966 and 1970, foreign employment as a percentage of their total employment in manufacturing went from 22.45 percent to 25.39 percent, whereas for all firms in the sample the increase was from 23.23 percent to 25.12 percent. For a more detailed statement on employment impacts see section 5 of this chapter.) These figures are not surprising when compared with average annual growth in payroll cost per *employee* for the same sample: in the United States 5.9 percent, in developed areas 6.5 percent, and in underdeveloped areas 4 percent. *Ibid.* For data on the U.S. manufacturing sector's labor-absorption capacity, see *Economic Report of the President, 1973,* Washington, D.C.: Government Printing Office, 1973, p. 226.

Data for the ratio of foreign to domestic manufacturing sales are drawn from U.S. Department of Commerce, *Survey of Current Business,* October 1970, and the *Economic Report of the President,* Washington, D.C.: Government Printing Office, 1973. The 1970 foreign sales figure was a "total universe" estimate by the Senate Finance Committee, *op. cit.,* pp. 430–33. The "take-off" in the trend value of this ratio occurs between 1964 and 1965 and increases continuously through 1970 (after correcting for differences in foreign and domestic business cycles).

More than 20 percent of all U.S. corporate profits are derived from abroad: taken from Peggy Musgrave, "Tax Preferences to Foreign Investment," Commerce of the United States, Joint Economic Committee, *The Economics of Federal Subsidy Programs, Part II—International Subsidies,* Washington, D.C., 1972. Her figure represents the total foreign gross (before tax) profits divided into total worldwide gross (before tax) profits of all U.S. corporations. Her numerator does not include repatriated royalties and fees and profits derived from export sales of U.S. corporations. Both these items are a return on invested resources of the United States and dependent upon foreign transactions. Adding the 1970 values of these two factors into Musgrave's numerator would raise the value of her ratio to 24.8 percent. The royalty and fees figure of $1.92 billion is taken from the Department of Commerce. Profits on exports were estimated at $2.56 billion by applying a before-tax return on sales of 7 percent to the FOB value of total U.S. general merchandise exports for 1970. The 7 percent return on export sales is conservative, since it is significantly below the average rates on domestic transactions in both manufacturing and agriculture. Profits on imports accruing to U.S. corporations cannot be reliably estimated because of the problem of double counting due to the fact that much of these imports are intermediate inputs. Nevertheless, making a conservative guess of profits accruing in the United States from import transactions at being roughly 3 percent of the

446

total value of merchandise imports, and adding this into the Musgrave numerator, gives a value for the ratio of some 26.2 percent. A more sensitive, but by necessity a more conservative, estimation of the dependency of total U.S. corporate profits on the foreign sector, including direct investment returns, is the following: total "balance of payment income" from U.S. foreign investment (as defined in Department of Commerce *Survey of Current Business,* September 1973, p. 34) plus estimated profits from export and import transactions, all divided into total U.S. before tax corporate profits (excluding inventory valuation adjustments). Since in 1970 the U.S. was in a recession while its major foreign markets were near the peak of their business cycles, this alternative measure was calculated for the year 1972. For that year the resulting figure is some 17 percent. There is little doubt in our mind, however, that these figures (on the extent to which profits accrued in the United States are now dependent on foreign transactions) are significantly underestimated. In Part II of this book we have given substantial evidence to the degree to which transfer pricing manipulations lead, in *host* countries, to the underreporting of foreign-derived income as recorded by the U.S. balance of payment statistics. Theoretically such unreported income from *host* countries shows up in the consolidated worldwide income statement of global corporations. Yet under present disclosure requirements it is impossible to determine just how much of such income is included in total U.S. domestic corporate profits. There is, however, little doubt that a substantial proportion is, in fact, included in U.S. corporate profits, and therefore our most conservative estimate of 17 percent should more than likely be on the order of 20 percent.

Pages 260–61
Data on the ratio of foreign expenditure for plant and equipment over domestic expenditure for plant and equipment, in manufacturing, are taken from U.S. Department of Commerce, *Survey of Current Business,* January 1970 and March 1973. The five-year average ratio of foreign to domestic new plant and equipment investment was 11.6 percent for 1957–1962 (with 1958 not available). For the five years ending 1972 this average was 20.7 percent.

Page 262
Discussion of the Eurocurrency's volume, creation, and intricacies is found in Fritz Machlup, "Euro-Dollar Creation: A Mystery Story," *Reprints in International Finance,* Princeton University, No. 16, December 1970, and Senate Finance Committee, *op. cit.,* pp. 455–517. See also Milton Friedman, "Monetary Trends in the United States and United Kingdom," *The American Economist,* Vol. XVI, Spring 1972, No. 1, pp. 4–17; "The Euro-dollar Market: Some First Principles," in Gies and Apilado, *op. cit.,* pp. 102–12; Fred Klopstock's statement before the Subcommittee on International Exchange and Payments of the Joint Economic Committee, June 22, 1971; and "Recent Institutional and Structural Changes in International Banking" (unpublished mimeo), Federal Reserve Bank of New York, Jan. 17, 1972. Part of the debate surrounding the Eurodollar market, and a topic touched upon later in this chapter, is to what extent Eurodollar transactions lead to creations and thus to increases in various countries' domestic money supply. Both Machlup and Friedman are of the view that Eurodollar transactions do lead to further monetary creation, while Klopstock is in a dissenting position. The lack of knowledge concerning Eurodollar creation is put as follows by Machlup: "If the present essay cannot reach definitive conclusions deciding all controversies on the subject, it will at least attempt to show why some such conclusions cannot be obtained on the basis of the empirical evidence available at present and why certain conceptual obscurities have led us into blind alleys" (*op. cit.,* p. 220). The $100 billion estimate for the Eurodollar market is from United Nations, *The Multinational Corporations in World Diplomacy,* New York, 1973, p. 12.

NOTES FOR TEXT AND TABLES

Page 263
The 1966 profits of the oil industry, book versus reported, are found in Charles Vanik, "Corporate Federal Tax Payments and Federal Subsidies to Corporations for 1972," *Congressional Record,* House of Representatives, Aug. 1, 1973.

Quote on deceptive corporate-earning reporting from the statement of Congressman Charles Vanik, "On 1971 Corporate Income Tax," in *Tax Subsidies and Tax Reform,* hearing before the Joint Economic Committee, Congress of the United States, 92nd Session, Government Printing Office, Washington, D.C., 1973, p. 17.

Pages 263–64
Quote from Senate Finance Committee, *op. cit.,* p. 431.

Page 264
Quotes on the earnings rush and accounting from Adam Smith, *Supermoney,* New York: Random House, 1972, pp. 197, 205, and 206 (explanatory parentheses ours).

Warren Avis is quoted from Tom Rider's show *Tomorrow,* NBC-TV, February 1974.

Page 265
On Keynes and Marx: More specifically although both assumed short-run resource scarcity neither took into account the very real possibility of long-run resource scarcity, i.e., unlimited economic growth was infinitely possible. Neither theory made allowance for constrained economic growth rates which could not be exceeded. For an interesting attempt to overcome this methodological bias in both orthodox and Marxist economics see Nicholas Georgescu-Roegen, *The Entropy Law and the Economic Process,* Cambridge, Mass.: Harvard University Press, 1971.

A cost comparison of a seat on the Chicago Mercantile Exchange and one on the New York Stock Exchange is found in Katz, *op. cit.,* p. 45.

Corporate losses due to elaborate internal accounting in "How the Multinationals Play the Money Game," interview with Sidney Robbins and Robert Stobaugh, *Fortune,* August 1973, p. 138.

Pages 265–66
Discussion of corporate loyalty and the subconscious is in Michael Maccoby, *The Corporate Individual,* New York: Simon and Schuster (forthcoming).

Pages 266–67
Data on the level of intercorporate transfers in U.S. import/export trade: Senate Finance Committee, *op. cit.,* pp. 271–81 and 305–21. Our own estimate is derived from Business International Special Survey, 1972, *op. cit.,* pp. 27–28. In this sample, the percentage of parents exports coming under the use of transfer pricing went from some 43 in 1960 to 54 in 1966 and reached 57 in 1970.

Page 267
The structural lag in the government's need for information and the negation of the market, in this case in regard to the foreign trade sector, are seen in the following remarks by Raymond Vernon: "It would not be unreasonable to assume that these units (global corporations) are parties on one side or another of nearly one-half the world trade, outside of agriculture." Noting that our present understanding of these corporations "is still incomplete, even rudimentary," he pinpoints an important lag in current disclosure requirements vs.

needs in the area of governmental balance of payments policy. "There are grounds for the view, for instance, that the 'export' of U.S. central office and technical services by U.S. parents to foreign subsidiaries may be understated in the official figures by as much as several billion dollars a year . . . as a practical matter official agencies may not be in a position to adjust reported data of this sort since the data so reported are in accord with current accounting practice." Raymond Vernon, "A Program of Research and Foreign Direct Investment," in C. F. Bergston, *The Future of the International Economic Order: An Agenda for Research,* New York: D. C. Heath, 1973, pp. 93 and 95.

The Commerce Department data are described as unreliable by Shane J. Hunt, "Evaluating Direct Foreign Investment in Latin America," in *Latin America in the 1970's,* a report prepared for the State Department by Rand (R-1067-DOS), 1972, p. 132. A critical attitude toward the Commerce Department statistics is also found in Thomas Horst, "The Impact of U.S. Investment Abroad on U.S. Foreign Trade," Brookings Institution, unpublished mimeo, January 1974.

The finding of the Conference Board Report on the competition for information and Leonard Silk's statement on information as a political issue are found in Leonard Silk, "Data Technology Impact," *The New York Times,* July 19, 1973, p. 47.

Page 269
On Keynesian tools and their ability to maintain stability and equilibrium of the economy we should note that this chapter is not an investigation into the causes of instability and disequilibrium so much as it is an outline of the reasons why current economic policy is inadequate to deal with the stabilization issue. In our opinion and as noted in the text, the causes of inflation are not singular. It has already been implied—and is to be further commented on—that inflationary pressures are due to an overly expanding and increasingly uncontrollable money supply (with related changes in the pattern of debt structure, financing, and liquidity) as well as real supply scarcities of both the "structural bottleneck" and aggregate types. The latter, of course, have been compounded by growing ecological constraints still largely ignored by both individual aspirations and governmental growth policies. Also ignored, as we shall outline below, have been certain structural changes in real world output which characterize the impacts of global corporations on changes in "foreign trade lags," in turn, bringing about a significant convergence in the business cycles of more developed nations starting in the early 1970's. As to unemployment, the other half of the stagflation problem, this will be taken up in section 5 of this chapter.

The impact of oligopoly price-behavior that is making Keynesian monetary and fiscal policy tools increasingly ineffective for stabilizing the economy has been found in recent econometric studies. A major quantitative factor analysis by Nancy S. Barrett, Geraldine Gerardi, and Thomas P. Hart *(Prices and Wages in U.S. Manufacturing: A Factor Analysis,* Lexington, Mass.: Heath, 1973) suggests that ". . . structural changes in the manufacturing sector since 1960 weakened the political efficacy of aggregate demand remedies for inflation" (p. 68). Barrett *et al.* attribute this growing inefficacy and at times "perverse" policy results to a higher level of variation in price vs. wage determination in the manufacturing sector. Barrett *et al.* show increasing all-manufacturing variation over the period tested but relatively constant results for a subsample in consumer durables. In the former, concentration was increasing over time, but in the consumer durable subsector tested, concentration was relatively stable. For all manufacturing industries Barrett *et al.* conclude that "the industry analysis of price behavior suggests that the Keynesian remedies for inflation potentially not only had a perverse impact on but also were not neutral with respect to relative prices of profits across manufacturing industries" (p. 97). These recent results are consonant with our own analysis, as are the findings of Otto Eckstein and David Wyss, "Industry Price Equations," *Conference on Econometrics of Price Determinations*, Washington, D.C., Oct. 30–31, 1973, and Otto Eckstein and Gary Fromm, "The Price Equation," *American Economic Review*, Vol. 58, December 1968, pp. 1159–83. A theoretical and empirical review of oligopoly-induced "profits inflation" is found in M. K. Evans, *Macroeconomic Activity: Theory, Forecasting, and Control*, New York: Harper & Row, 1969, Chapter 11, concluding that "it is our contention that much of postwar inflation can be explained only with reference to profits inflation." Even before WW II there was detailed quantitative confirmation of oligopoly "administered price" behavior, see R. L. Hall and C. J. Hitch, "Price Theory and Business Behavior," *Oxford Economic Papers*, May 1939, 2:pp. 12–45. A Marxist theoretical treatment of the distributive consequences of oligopoly pricing is Michael Kalecki, *Selected Essays on the Dynamics of the Capitalist Economy*, Cambridge University Press, 1971. For a good review on the problems of economic models used for determining stabilization policy, and supportive of a basic thesis of our own work, see Thomas Muench and Neil Wallace, "On Stabilization Policy: Goals and Models," *American Economic Review*, Vol. 64, May 1974, pp. 331–37. Muench and Wallace conclude that "useful stabilization policy might use nontraditional instruments and must be tied to a detailed analysis of the market structure" (p. 337).

Pages 269–70
1970 concentration data are from Department of Commerce, *Annual Survey of Manufacturers, 1970: Value of Shipment Concentration Ratios*, Washington, D.C.: Government Printing Office, 1972.

Page 270
Foreign deposits were equal to two-thirds of the domestic deposits for the 9 members of the New York Clearing House Association according to Frank Mastrapasqua, "U.S. Bank Expansion Via Foreign Branching: Monetary Policy Implications," *op. cit.*, p. 23. Twenty global banks accounted for virtually all foreign deposits, with 4 holding 38 percent, according to data presented by Andrew Brimmer, "Multinational Banks and the Management of Monetary Policy in the United States," to a Joint Session of the 58th Annual Meeting of the American Economic Association and the 31st Annual Meeting of the American Finance Association, Toronto, December 1972, Table III. A further indication of concentration in U.S. global banking is found in "Foreign Branches of U.S. Banks and U.S. Operations of Foreign Banks," staff paper of the Committee on Banking and Currency, U.S. House of Representatives, prepared under the direction of Jane D'Arista, p. 2: in 1971, 12 banks accounted for 85 percent of all foreign branches and held 83 percent of all foreign assets.

The quote on the effect of concentration on Keynesian theory and policies is by Lord Thomas Balogh with P. Balacs, "Facts and Fancy in International Economic Relations," *World Development*, March–April 1973, p. 83. A treatment similar to ours, on why power rather than the laws of supply and demand dictate in what manner and for whom the social functions (allocation and distribution) of markets will perform, can be found in a recent paper by Carlos Díaz-Alejandro, in which his analysis "view[s] markets as creatures of social and political systems, not as mechanisms arising spontaneously out of economic necessity. Which markets are allowed to operate and how, which are encouraged and which are repressed are political decisions, both nationally and internationally." This view of power versus the market also reflects our own; Díaz-Alejandro notes that "power, whether military or corporate, abhors an uncontrolled and truly competitive market." See Carlos F. Díaz-Alejandro, "North-South Relations: The Economic Component," *Discussion Paper No. 200*, Economic Growth Center, New Haven, Conn.: Yale University Press, April 1974. See also Helmut Arndt, *Markt und Macht* [*The Market and Power*],

Tubingen, West Germany: J. C. B. Mohr, 1973, particularly Chapter 7; John Kenneth Galbraith, "Power and the Useful Economist," *American Economic Review*, Vol. 63, March 1973, pp. 1–11; and Vernon L. Smith, "Economic Theory and Its Discontents," *American Economic Review*, Vol. 64, pp. 320–22, who suggests that a "new microtheory will, and should, deal with the economic foundations of organization and institution, and this will require us to have sophisticated treatment of the technology of *transacting*. . . . As long as market failure is defined in terms of failure to achieve costless Pareto-efficient allocations, every real world institution . . . is in danger of 'failure.' Fortunately for the economy, but unfortunately for academic economics, this formulation of the problem of Pareto efficiency is not the problem that real markets and other allocative institutions attempt to solve" (p. 321, italics ours).

Pages 270–71
The ratio of corporate cash to short-term debt is from the *Bank Credit Analyst, op. cit.,* various issues. With the upturn starting in 1965, there has also been a constant increase in the reliance of corporations on financing their investment projects via the use of externally derived funds. External sources of funds represented 21 percent of total sources in 1964, rose to 26 percent in 1965, and accelerated to an average 36 percent in 1970; from Sidney Homer *et al., Supply and Demand for Credit in 1970,* New York: Salomon Bros. & Hutzler, March 1970. Although consumer relative-to-business credit gets squeezed during periods of monetary restraint (see below), there has been a continuous rise in total consumer credit as measured against disposable personal income throughout the post-World War II years. This ratio, for the five years ending 1954, averaged some 11 percent; by the end of 1969 its five-year average was almost 19 percent; and it reached a record value of over 20 percent in 1973; from various issues *Federal Reserve Bulletin* and *Economic Report of the President: 1974.* The most significant indicator, however, of the need for providing ever greater amounts of credit in order to increase real output of the economy is seen by the ratio of the change in total bank credit to the change in real GNP (measured in 1958 dollars). Already for the period 1960–1965 it took an additional 68 cents of credit to produce an additional dollar of real GNP, up from an average value of 30 cents in the period 1949–1960. Then from the period 1966–1968 the value shot up to 1.32 and from 1970 through the end of 1973 averaged 1.84. Thus on all counts the pattern of the economy's debt structure since the mid-1960's has been showing an increasing deterioration in individual, corporate, and bank liquidity, echoing similarities of pre-1929 days. In addition, from 1958 through 1967 the velocity of money (measured as turnover of demand deposits at New York) increased by about 30 percent every three years. From 1967 to 1970, during which it broke its 1929–1930 value, the three-year increase was 36 percent, while from 1970 to 1973 the rise was 60 percent. (Figures on bank credit, real GNP, and velocity from *Bank Credit Analyst, op. cit.,* June 1974.) This mounting illiquidity of the U.S. financial system (including Western Europe's Eurodollar market) of course increases the probability of a major collapse via a debt liquidation crisis, the avoidance of which requires massive money injection by the Federal Government, as the Penn-Central crisis of 1970 and the Franklin Bank of New York rescue in May 1974 demonstrate. Such injections, however, further compound the problem of controlling inflation. See also the end of Section 4 of this chapter.

Pages 271–72
Concentration data in industrial and commercial lending are from the Federal Reserve, *Weekly Statistical Release,* October 24, 1973. Statements on monetary control and further concentration data are found in George Budzeika, "Lending to Business by New York City Banks," *The Bulletin,* New York Uni-

versity Graduate School of Business, Institute of Finance, Nos. 76–77, September 1971, pp. 18 and 60. The Fed's inability to effect an economic downturn through interest-rate policy is econometrically verified by the work of Nancy Barrett, *et al., op. cit.,* p. 24. The study finds that oligopolies pass on to the consumer the increased cost of capital, as they can the costs of other factors of production and thus do not have to reduce their borrowings.

Page 272

Not only do smaller businesses feel the effects of monetary restraint to a greater extent than do larger businesses, but in addition, former Federal Reserve Board Governor Andrew Brimmer has found, during such periods the business sector receives a rising share of bank credit while a shrinking share goes to households. Brimmer points out that a disproportionate share of this instability can be traced to the activities of roughly 20 multinational banks which are an integral part of the Eurodollar market and 60 other large U.S. banks which are dominant in their respective domestic regions. Andrew Brimmer, *op. cit.,* December 1972.

On percentage of total Federal revenues for national security see Richard Barnet, *The Economy of Death,* New York: Atheneum, 1969, p. 5. See also the estimates of Barry Bluestone in his Testimony to the Joint Economic Committee, U.S. Congress, Feb. 29, 1972.

Page 273

The matter of the global corporation and uneven development is examined by Stephen Hymer, "The Multinational Corporation and the Law of Uneven Development," in Jagdish Bhagwati, ed., *Economics and World Order: From the 1970's to the 1990's,* London: Macmillan, 1972, pp. 113–40. Barry Bluestone's Testimony is *op. cit.*

Although the decreasing share of corporate taxes in total government revenue can be explained by the 1962 and other changes in the tax law, it is important to realize that these major legal modifications to the tax code were made to facilitate the expansion of U.S. multinational corporations in overseas areas. There can be no doubt that multinational corporations have taken advantage of these changes, but the outcome and impact on the average U.S. taxpayer has been that she/he is now bearing a greater burden than ever for payment of taxes. Thus while the shares of profits in national income stay relatively constant, and while the share of salaries and wages stay relatively constant, the share of wage and salary earners' tax payments drastically increase. Both the decline in the contribution of the corporate income tax and the declining ratio of the corporate income tax over the individual income tax are shown in various issues of the *Economic Report of the President,* Washington, D.C.: Government Printing Office. The percentage contribution of the corporate income tax declined from an average of 22.76 percent in 1958–1962 to 21.71 percent in 1963–1967 to 16.95 percent in 1968–1972. During the same period the ratio of the corporate income tax to the individual income tax declined from 50.7 percent in 1958–1962 to 37.1 percent in 1968–1972. Even with the inclusion of social security contributions to personal and corporate taxes, the share of personal taxes in total Federal receipts increases by 12 percent over the period 1957–1973. Besides the regressiveness of the social security tax, it is obviously at odds with the rest of the Federal government's tax structure because of the effect of employer social security contributions as a deduction from corporate income. At the same time, since social security taxes collected by the Federal government are "committed" funds, they in no way alleviate the mounting dimensions of the government's fiscal problem.

Page 274

Tax "welfarism" and the ineffectiveness of subsidy programs are found in

Vanik, *op. cit.*, pp. 22–28 and pp. 14–15, respectively. Also see Charles Vanik, "Corporate Federal Tax Payments and Federal Subsidies to Corporations for 1972," *Congressional Record, op. cit.*

Page 275

The 1960 sales campaign of the oil companies is described in *Business Week,* Dec. 3, 1960, pp. 70–71.

Concerning who pays for the social costs of production, it should be added that there are significant inequities in the present system. If, for example, pollution costs were incorporated directly into the prices of goods, then buyers of these goods would bear the burden directly. Since the effective structure of the current U.S. personal income tax is at best proportional if not regressive, then to the extent that personal income taxes are used by the government to pay for social costs of production, this adds to the regressivity of the tax system. See also section 5 of this chapter.

Page 276

The problem of structural lag in changing tax laws is well stated in Vanik, "On Corporate Income Tax," *op. cit.:* "Our tax policy over the years has placed incentives and disincentives into the law hoping to correct specific problems. As the years roll on the problems come and go, the provisions of the tax code remain, with a constituency and effect that many times has little to do with the original intent of the legislation."

Concentration data on the Investment Tax Credit are from 118 *Congressional Record,* daily, July 19, 1972, p. H6709. Senator Bible's statistics on the Accelerated Depreciation Range are from 117 *Congressional Record,* April 22, 1971, p. S5372. In 1969 the 697 largest manufacturing corporations accounted for 71.1 and 77 percent of total claimed allowances under the provisions of, respectively, the depreciation allowances and the investment tax credits for all manufacturers. In the same year these corporations, however, accounted for only 63.8 percent of total manufacturing sales. See Charles Vanik, "Corporate Federal Tax Payments and Federal Subsidies," *Congressional Record, op. cit.*

Page 277

Former Treasury official on the negation of the market is quoted from an interview conducted by David Moore, Washington, D.C., November 1, 1973. Pierre Rinfret, a former economic adviser to the President and chief economic spokesman for Nixon's reelection campaign, like a growing number of other economists, has frankly conceded the negation of the market. "I think free enterprise is dead, I think it's finished." The U.S. economy is, he continued, "a system of large companies which, with the cooperation of the federal government, control the market." Rinfret concluded his testimony before the Senate Anti-Trust and Monopoly Subcommittee by saying "he 'shudders' at federal bailouts of companies that can't compete—he named Boeing—but are saved because of 'full-employment' arguments. Calling the system 'socialism for the rich and free enterprise for the poor,' he said, 'if you're big enough, the government bails you out; if you're small enough, you go under.' " *The Washington Post,* May 8, 1973.

Page 278

The underinvoicing case of Litton is currently in litigation. Limited information is obtainable from the Office of General Information, Bureau of Customs, Washington, D.C., and the U.S. Attorney's Office, San Diego, Calif.

Transfer pricing in the U.S.-Soviet wheat transaction is cited in *The Washington Post,* August 21, 1973, p. B-13.

Page 279
Financial technology of the global corporation is examined in Sidney Robbins and Robert B. Stobaugh, *Money and the Multinational Enterprise: A Study in Financial Policy,* New York: Basic Books, 1973; quote *op. cit.,* p. 41.

Pages 279–80
The multiple accounting systems were described in an interview conducted by Richard Barnet and David Moore, Washington, D.C., Nov. 13, 1973.

Page 280
The growth of foreign tax credit, its present level, and foreign before-tax profits are documented in Peggy Musgrave, "Tax Preferences to Foreign Investment," Part 2, 1972, *op. cit.,* p. 176. Discussion of the oil companies and the foreign tax credit are found in Philip M. Stern, *The Rape of the Taxpayer,* New York: Random House Vintage, 1973, Chapters 11 and 12; Vanik, *op. cit.,* pp. 14–15; and M. A. Adelman, *The World Petroleum Market,* Baltimore: Johns Hopkins University Press, 1972.

The bias of U.S. tax law in favor of foreign investment is found in the statement of Stanford Ross, Committee on Ways and Means, Hearings on Tax Reform, 1973, pp. 133–40.

Revenue loss due to allowance of a credit rather than a deduction for foreign taxes paid is found in Peggy B. Musgrave, statement before the Committee on Ways and Means of the U.S. House of Representatives, *Panel Discussion on Tax Reform,* No. 11, Washington: Government Printing Office, 1973, p. 177.

Page 281
Concentration of foreign source taxable income is taken from Musgrave, *op. cit.,* p. 108.

Quotes on tax havens, their characteristics, and the Syntex example are found in Tony Doggart and Caroline Voûte, "Tax Havens and Offshore Funds," QER, No. 8, The Economists Intelligence Unit, pp. 1, 45–70, and 16–17, respectively, 1972. The Fidelity Bank example is taken from Stern, *op. cit.,* p. 255.

Pages 282–83
Ross's statement on the ineffectiveness of the 1960's foreign tax reform is taken from an interview conducted by Richard Barnet and David Moore, Washington, Nov. 13, 1973. The anonymous statement on the IRS's 482 enforcement capacity is taken from an interview conducted by David Moore, Nov. 1, 1973.

Page 283
Stern's statement on the ineffectiveness of the 1962 reforms and DISC can be found in Stern, *op. cit.,* pp. 269 and 271, respectively.

Pages 283–84
On the use of intracorporate transactions rather than banks in making financial transfers, see M. Z. Brooke and H. L. Remmer, *The Strategy of Multinational Enterprises,* New York: American Elsevier, 1970, Part II; and Robbins and Stobaugh, *op. cit.*

Pages 284–85
U.S. monetary control, global corporations, and the Eurodollar market can be found in Brimmer, *op. cit.* (both), Budzeiki, *op. cit.,* pp. 59–60, and Mastrapasqua, *op. cit.,* pp. 27–38. Although the October 1969 and January 1971

increases in the fractional reserve requirements for Eurodollar borrowings coupled with the change in Regulation-Q of June 1970 on short-term certificates of deposit improved the Federal government's ability to control Eurodollars as they affect the domestic money supply, these regulations still did not cover medium- and longer-term maturities of C.D.'s, nor has there been an alignment of fractional reserve requirements for Eurodollar borrowings with those of C.D.'s. Noting this still-remaining gap in monetary policy, Frank Mastrapasqua, writing in January 1973, concluded that "the Federal Reserve system must certainly integrate into its decision making apparatus the most dynamic and expanding aspect of American banking, the foreign branch operations. Dollar denominated securities, both domestic and foreign, have now become the domain of the American financial system." *Ibid.*, pp. 65–66.

Page 285
Germany's "imported inflation" is discussed in P. B. Clark, and H. G. Grubel, "National Monetary Sovereignty Under Different Exchange Rate Regimes," *The Bulletin,* New York University Graduate School of Business, Institute of Finance, Nos. 78–79, January 1972, pp. 39–40; Michel G. Porter, "Capital Flows as an Offset to Monetary Policy: The German Experience," *IMF Staff Papers,* July 1972, and in Katz, *op. cit.,* pp. 18–32.

Pages 285–86
Quote from the 1973 study of the U.N. is *Multinational Corporations in World Development,* New York, 1973, pp. 62–63. The unrecorded transactions being picked up in the errors and omissions of balance of payments accounts are most notably those due to "leads and lags." The latter seem to account for the vast majority of the movements recorded in errors and omissions, although for the United States some $1 billion in 1969, increasing to $3 billion in 1973, were due to accounting problems in the recording of dividend out-payments of U.S. oil companies. The remaining portion of errors and omissions, some 80 to 90 percent, depending on the country, "are largely 'leads and lags' which usually respond to exchange rate expectations." Katz, *op. cit.,* p. 22. For a detailed treatment of global corporations' reasons for using "leads and lags," see M. Z. Brooke and H. L. Remmer, *op. cit.,* and Robbins and Stobaugh, *op. cit.*

Page 286
Estimates on short-term liquid assets controlled by global corporations come from Senate Finance Committee, *op. cit.,* pp. 536–40 (including the quote). The Finance Committee Study puts the estimate at $268 billion, while the lower figure of around $160 billion comes from private commercial bankers, most notably, the estimate of the First National City Bank.

How defensive the mysterious transnational money movements of global corporations are is still a debatable point. For example, the editors of *Harvard Business Review* introduce an article, on the techniques of avoiding risks and maximizing profit opportunities during the current period of international financial instability, in the following way: "In this setting, where the risks are riskier but the opportunities enormous, an MNC (multinational corporation) that wants to compete successfully had better sharpen its international finance function." (Introduction to J. T. Wooster and G. R. Thoman's "New Financial Priorities for MNCs," issue of May–June 1974, p. 58.)

Pages 286–87
On the increasing difficulty of central banks in defending their currencies given the large-scale ability of global corporations to utilize "leads and lags" for vast sums of short-term liquid assets, the German Bundesbank has said the following: ". . . complete neutralization of the liquidity inflows to domestic banks . . . prevents the banks from stepping up their lending to domestic

customers on the grounds of their additional liquidity, but it does not curb the expansive effects exerted by the inflows of funds from abroad to non-banks on the money stock." The latter, of course, refers to controlling nonbank liquidity, which is entering mainly via errors and omissions through the use of "leads and lags." *Monthly Report of the Deutsche Bundesbank,* March 1973, p. 3, as cited in Samuel Katz, *op. cit.,* p. 24. Michael G. Porter, in "Capital Flows as an Offset to Monetary Policy: The German Experience," *op. cit.,* pp. 395 and 415, found in his monthly econometric model that attempts by the German Bundesbank to control the domestic money supply via changes in required bank reserves "were substantially and rapidly offset in their effect on bank liquidity by capital inflows recorded mainly in the errors of omissions," i.e., within the period of one month the intended effects of changing reserve requirements would be offset by some 80 percent. For the German case, Katz (*op. cit.,* p. 22) concluded that these rapid shifts in capital flows were prompted not only by changes in German credit policies but, in addition, by anticipated exchange-rate changes.

Quote on Eurodollar market and dollar creation from H. S. Houthakker in "Policy Issues in the International Economy of the 1970's," *American Economic Review,* Vol. 64, p. 139. See also the articles cited earlier by Machlup, by Friedman, and by Klopstock, *op. cit.*

Concerning the control of the U.S. money supply, Arthur Burns has written, ". . . part of the present control problem stems from statistical inadequacies." The Commission of the European Community, however, was even more direct: ". . . in this area (monetary problems) the Commission considers that one of the principal measures should lead to a better knowledge of the financial flows accompanying companies' transnational operations," and "as regards company accounts . . . , the economic and social importance of which can no longer justify the degree of secrecy with which they surround themselves," Arthur Burns, Federal Reserve Press Release and Accompanying Letter (to Joint Economic Committee of U.S. Congress), Nov. 6, 1973, Washington, D.C.; Commission of the European Communities, *Multinational Undertakings and Community Regulations,* unrevised translation, Brussels, Nov. 7, 1973, pp. 8 and 15.

Page 287
The quote from *Fortune* and the price behavior of global oligopolies after the December 1971 devaluation is found in Carol J. Loomis, "New Questions About the U.S. Economy," *Fortune,* January 1974, pp. 73 and 163–66.

Pages 287–88
The analysis of the reasons for international convergence in domestic business cycles of advanced nations is our own and based on our study of global corporations' increasing use of transnational networks of subsidiaries engaged in complementary production ("worldwide sourcing"), centrally directed and timed from parent headquarters. See Brooke and Remmer, *op. cit.;* Gyorgy Adam, "New Trends in International Business: Worldwide Sourcing and Dedomiciling," and "Some Implications and Concomitants of Worldwide Sourcing," *Acta Oeconomica,* Vol. 7 (3–4), 1971, and Vol. 8 (2–3), 1972, respectively; and his "The Big International Firm and the Socialist Countries: An Interpretation," paper presented to The Growth of the Large Multinational Corporation, International Colloquium of the National Center of Scientific Research, Rennes, France, Sept. 28–30, 1972.

On the ineffectiveness of "policies or structural changes conducive to international stabilization," Geoffrey H. Moore has concluded that "the full implications of a more closely integrated international business cycle, or growth cycle, remain to be explored and projected." See his "Some Secular Changes in Business Cycles," *American Economic Review,* Vol. 64, May 1974, pp. 136–37.

For a Marxist interpretation on the importance of incorporating a theory of the state's role in understanding changes in business cycles, see Raford Boddy and James Crotty, "Class Conflict and Macro Policy," *Monthly Review* (forthcoming, 1974).

Page 289

The quote from George Schultz is taken from *Fortune,* January 1974, p. 61.

The question of instability in maintaining both internal and external equilibrium has long been a topic of conventional macro-economics. The famous "Tinbergen rule" (i.e., one policy for each policy objective, with subsequent modifications by Mundel) has failed because the real world political institutions of individual nation-states cannot implement it. At the same time the Keynesian-based theory upon which the institutions of the post-World War II international monetary system were derived has been equally inapplicable to the real world. The "prominence of large multinational firms," as Thomas Balogh has written, "profoundly alters the nature of international trade, payments and capital movements in a sense wholly ignored by conventional economics." Thus, he continues, "orthodox global methods of maintaining international balance have failed . . . for the reason that they have been based on the fallacious assumption that international trade is conducted by atomistically organized units in a framework of perfect competition, and is characterized by sub-units alternately expanding and contracting by means of which the system as a whole is kept in overall balance." Balogh with P. Balacs, "Facts and Fancy in International Economic Relations," *op. cit.,* pp. 93–94.

Page 290

Another aspect of instability deals with the institutions to which Balogh is referring. The globalization process was made feasible by the very institutions that today it has either destroyed or brought under the growing threat of destruction. Without the international monetary system of Bretton Woods, the GATT principles of free trade, and the stability of the U.S. dollar as the world's carrier currency, the ascent of the global corporation would have never reached the heights it has. However, Bretton Woods is now dead, the principles of free trade are now under renewed examination with the threat of regional trading blocks a reality, and the economic leadership role of the U.S. and its dollar is under challenge by the new economic power of Europe—with few signs of agreement between them. Reflecting on this current institutional vacuum and resulting lack of leadership in the international arena, Kermit Gordon, president of the Brookings Institution, has concluded that "the present situation is clearly unstable. The United States has lost . . . effective leadership in the creation of new institutions and arrangements, and other sources of leadership have not yet appeared." Charles Kindleberger, in likening the current vacuum in international economic leadership to a highly similar vacuum in the period 1929–1933, has noted that "when two major powers are unable to agree . . . the analog in the economic field is stalemate and depression."

Modern capitalism, of course, has always followed its growth and inflation spurts with recession and (less often but with equal historical predictability) depression (see, for example, Robert Lekachman, *op. cit.*). The reasons, however, have to do with more than just a vacuum in institutional leadership. Earlier in this chapter we referenced the studies pointing to the systematic similarity in money and financial indicators of the current period with that of the 1929–1933 period. Global interdependence, in turn, further explains why the growing probability of a major debt-liquidation crisis in the domestic financial system can be compounded or triggered by a similar event in the Eurodollar market. In looking at the difficulty of advanced countries such as Italy to refinance their oil- and inflation-induced balance of payments deficits, *The Economist* in April 1974 noted that "another sign of possible 1929-style international financial crisis is upon us. . . . Private Euromarkets may not be able to take the strain of oil-induced balance of payment deficits as smoothly as optimists had hoped." Whether further inflation or depression will be the outcome of the present situation of instability cannot be predicted at this time. However, once again we find that much of the cause of this instability can be traced to the globalization of the private industrial and financial sectors of national economies without a concomitant ability to adjust to these changes by the political institutions of these countries. Thus Helmut Arndt finds that "in some way and in some direction, therefore, the conclusion can be drawn that the management of a big multinational firm has more power or, at least, is less controlled than the President of the United States. Also anti-trust authorities like the American Federal Trade Commission or the German Bundeskartellamt have been relatively helpless against multinational corporations for two reasons: the practices within a multinational firm are mostly unknown and the practices outside of their own country are *beyond their competence*." (From his paper "Multinational Corporations and Economic Power," presented to The Growth of the Large Multinational Corporation, International Colloquium of the National Center of Scientific Research, Rennes, France, September 28–30, 1972, pp. 546–47 (italics his). Kermit Gordon is quoted from "Some Conjectures on Policy Problems of the 1970's," *American Economic Review*, Vol. 64, May 1974, p. 125. Kindleberger from his book *The World in Depression: 1929–1939*, Berkeley: University of California Press, 1973, p. 308. *The Economist* quote is from the Apr. 20, 1974, issue, p. 104, "If Italy Cannot Borrow Today What Happens to Britain Tomorrow?"

Ninety-five percent of the U.S. population had before-tax family incomes under $24,000, according to the U.S. Bureau of the Census, "Income in 1970 of Families and Persons in the United States," *Current Population Reports*, Series P-60, Washington, D.C.: Government Printing Office, 1971, pp. 1, 17.

Pages 290–91
Income distribution, revolution and counterrevolution, Samuelson quoted in Herman P. Miller, *Income Distribution in the United States*, Washington: U.S. Bureau of Census, 1966, p. 2; H. P. Miller quoted from Miller, *op. cit.*, p. 2; T. Paul Schultz is quoted from T. Paul Schultz, "Long Term Change in Personal Income Distribution: Theoretical Approaches, Evidence and Explanations," Santa Monica: Rand Corporation, 1972, pp. 11 and 29, respectively. Henle's data and quote are from Peter Henle, "Explaining the Distribution of Earned Income," *Monthly Labor Review*, December 1972; Rose quote is found in Stanford Rose, "The Truth About Income Inequality in the U.S.," *Fortune*, December 1972, p. 90.

Page 291
The structure of income redistribution in 1958–1970 is noted in Henle, *op. cit.*

Pages 291–92
The very rich, the top management, of 140 major corporations, according to the annual *Business Week* Survey, had an average increase in their *total* compensation of 13.3 percent in 1973 after a rise of 13.5 percent in 1972.

On the question of income inequality between average workers and the very rich of senior management, B. A. Okner and J. A. Pechman, in their new book, *Who Bears the Tax Burden?*, Washington, D.C.: The Brookings Institution, spring 1974, conclude that "the (U.S.) tax system is virtually proportional for the vast majority of families in the United States" under a reasonable set of assumptions that "if corporation income and property taxes are assumed to be shifted in whole or in part to consumers, the tax burden in the highest income level is about 30 percent or only five percentage points more than the average effective rate paid by most families." Quotes are taken from their article in the *American Economic Review,* May 1974, pp. 173–74. For an overview of an IRS report concerning major tax loopholes which benefit wealthy individuals, see "How Rich People Escape Taxes," *U.S. News and World Report,* June 3, 1974, p. 49.

Pages 292–93

Notes to Tables I and II: We wish to acknowledge the work of Bruce De-Castro, who was in charge of the study underlying the updating of the 1968–1972 data of Table 1. The procedures utilized in compilation of the data were first developed by Professor Wilbur Lewellen in his *Executive Compensation in Large Industrial Corporations,* New York: Columbia University Press, 1968; *The Ownership Income of Management,* New York: Columbia University Press, 1971; and "Managerial Pay and the Tax Changes of the 1960's," *National Tax Journal,* June 1972, pp. 41–131. Lewellen derived 1940–1963 figures in *The Ownership Income . . . , op. cit.;* and 1963 and 1969 figures (except as noted below) in the *National Tax Journal, op. cit.* The data not derived by Lewellen for 1969 (dividend income, capital gains, and market value of holdings) and all data shown in the table for 1972 are based upon our own study for the years 1968–1972 using procedures similar to Lewellen's. Lewellen's sample was for 50 large industrial corporations. Our sample was identical, minus 6 due to mergers by the 1968–1972 period. Ours and Wilbur Lewellen's (WL) data for before-tax salary and bonus overlap for the years 1968–1969. Because of differences in sample size and a few incomplete cells of information there was a slight variation in our totals compared with WL's for the overlapping years. Thus, we adjusted the 1972 before-tax salary and bonus data by deriving a coefficient based upon the difference between the WL figures and our own for the period of overlap. The adjustment resulted in a slight upward change (.84 of 1 percent) in our own chief executive officer's (CEO's) pretax salary and bonus estimate for 1972 and a slight downward change of 6 percent in our top-5 executives' pretax salary-and-bonus estimate for 1972. A tax rate comparable to that utilized by Lewellen was then applied to determine our 1972 after-tax salary and bonus figures.

For Table II all incomes except executives' are from U.S. Department of Labor, *Handbook of Labor Statistics, 1972,* Bulletin 1735, Bureau of Labor Statistics, Government Printing Office, 1972; real figures are in 1967 dollars; executive incomes are from Table I.

To be in the top fifth of family income in 1970 the minimum necessary income was $14,000, as reported in Census Bureau, *op. cit.,* pp. 1, 17.

Page 294

Concentration-in-wealth-ownership data are presented in Larry Sawyers and Jon D. Wisman, "Wealth Taxation for the United States," *The Journal of Economic Issues,* Sept. 1973. For data on individual trust holdings see J. D. Smith and S. D. Franklin, "The Concentration of Personal Wealth, 1922–1969," *American Economic Review,* May 1974, pp. 162–67. This article also reviews the debate on whether wealth concentration has been constant or increasing since World War II. Its conclusion of constancy, however, was based on an examination of only the richest ½ percent and 1 percent of the population. Extending the examination to the richest 5 or 10 percent of the population could well give different results; thus the debate is left still unresolved. Compare also Robert Lampman, *The Share of Top Wealth Holders and National Wealth, 1922–1956,* National Bureau of Economic Research, Princeton University Press, 1962.

Pages 295–96
Congressman Gaydos is quoted in Gyorgy Adam, "Some Implications and Concomitants of Worldwide Sourcing," *op. cit.*, p. 311.

Page 296
On the declining bargaining power of organized labor, a growing number of radical economists have documented a complementary explanation to the one outlined in the text. Their work has empirically verified an intensified trend toward further labor market stratification as large global corporations become more and more responsible for total value-added, in both home and host country economies. Stratification occurs by industry and occupation, by race, by ethnic groups, and by hierarchical differentiation, the latter due to the types of school system needed to support the current pattern of industrialization. The net effect is to divide labor along status lines, thereby mitigating their bargaining power. A good review of this work is provided by Howard M. Wachtel, "Class, Class Consciousness, and Labor Market Stratification" in the *Review of Radical Political Economics*, Vol. 6, No. 1, Spring 1974, pp. 1–32.

Labor's "fair return" is discussed in Lester Thurow's "Disequilibrium and Marginal Productivity of Capital and Labour," *Review of Economics and Statistics*, February 1968, pp. 23–31. The professional economist will note our use of the term "fair return" in place of the specialized economics terminology of "marginal product of labor [or capital]," in order to facilitate understanding of this concept for the general reader. Our use of the phrase "ideal fair return" refers, of course, to the marginal product of labor and capital as derived by Thurow through his application of his modified Cobb-Douglas production function. The term "actual returns" is used in the same manner as in Thurow. In explaining his results Thurow himself notes that "market imperfections and monopoly power may provide some of the explanation. . . . After labor's countervailing power reached its peak in the late 1940's, there were no further declines in the gap between actual and marginal returns to capital." On the labor side, "the change in the gap is not as dramatic as that for capital. This can be explained if labor bears the brunt of indirect business taxes" (p. 29).

Page 297
Data on net capital inflows are from *Economic Report of the President*, February 1974, pp. 45 and 29, defined as repatriated earnings plus royalties and fees minus new direct investment outflows.

On foreign trade impacts of global corporations, the U.S. Tariff Commission Study was prepared for, and is the same as noted earlier, the Senate Finance Committee, *op. cit.*, p. 35.

Page 298
Gilpin is quoted from "The Multinational Corporation and the National Interest," report prepared for Committee on Labor and Public Welfare, United States Senate," Washington, D.C.; Government Printing Office, October 1973, p. 18.

On changes in income distribution and employment: Our analysis focuses on structural changes in the demand for labor, i.e., changes in the composition of output as between different sectors (thereby changing the composition and level of demand for labor) and changes in the bargaining power of labor as between different industries over time. This approach does not negate but rather is complementary to aggregate-structural analyses of the supply of labor (e.g., the "natural rate" hypothesis of unemployment including changes in the composition of the work force and the role of women and younger workers, as well as the "search hypothesis" focusing on assumptions concerning perceptions of wage rates and unemployment). See the various analyses of these approaches in

E. S. Phelps, ed., *The Microeconomic Foundations of Employment and Inflation Theory,* New York: Norton, 1970, and the articles in the "Wage-Price
Dynamics, Inflation, and Unemployment" section of the May 1968 *American
Economic Review* and, for a critique of these approaches, the discussion papers
in this section. An example of the complementarity between our approach and
those cited concerns the role of women and young workers who, starting in the
1960's, entered the labor force to a greater degree than previously. These added
entries, largely into unskilled and semi-skilled jobs, came at the very time when
the relative demand for such jobs was being lowered owing to the shift toward
foreign investment in these industries. Thus during the 1960–1965 period the
wages of unskilled and semi-skilled workers were increasing less than those in
skilled categories, whereas after 1966 this pattern is reversed.

The studies of the employment impact of global corporations in the U.S.
are: "An American Trade Union View of International Trade and Investment,
AFL-CIO," Washington, D.C., in *Multinational Corporations,* a compendium
of papers submitted to the Subcommittee on International Trade of the Committee on Finance of the U.S. Senate, Washington, D.C.: Government Printing Office, 1973, pp. 59–86; "The Role of the Multinational Corporation in
the United States and World Economies," Emergency Committee for American
Trade, Washington, D.C., 1973; Robert B. Stobaugh and associates, "U.S.
Multinational Enterprise and the U.S. Economy," Harvard Business School,
January, 1972, in *The Multinational Corporation Studies on U.S. Foreign Investment,* Vol. 1, U.S. Department of Commerce, Washington, D.C.: Government Printing Office, 1972; quote is from pp. 30–31. See also the alternative
estimates made in Senate Finance Committee, *op. cit.,* pp. 645–72.

Page 299
Soma Golden is quoted from "Economists Plead Uncertainty on 1974 Outlook," *The New York Times,* Sec. 3, p. 5.

Pages 299–300
On disaggregation and long-term employment trends of U.S. global corporations: In the work done by its own staff in the first part of the Department of
Commerce Study, Vol. 1, *op. cit.,* disaggregation also makes one doubt the
conclusions of these findings. The Commerce staff analyzed various broadly
defined industrial classifications in which global corporations predominate for
the period 1965–1970. They concluded that "for those industries whose employment levels rose" there was a combined five-year employment increase of
16 percent or "nearly equal to the 17 percent rate for total U.S. employment,"
and that the basic employment trend "has been upwards." However, by dis-
aggregating the aggregate five-year percentage increase and looking instead at
the individual annual increases, a different picture emerges. This shows a
significant downward trend in the annual rates of increase in employment,
revealing a deteriorating employment impact. More importantly, their reported
overall five-year increase of some 16 percent did not include (for reasons not
mentioned in the report) those classifications which showed an absolute decline
in jobs between 1965 and 1970. When these are added in (but omitting automobiles because of the Canadian–U.S. Auto Pact), then instead of a five-year
increase of 16 percent, we obtain an increase of only 10 percent, far below
the 17 percent increase for overall U.S. employment.

Examination of the ECAT, Harvard Business School, and AFL-CIO, findings: Our examination of the ECAT findings, ECAT, *op. cit.* Table 12, was
through disaggregation over time. If additional disaggregation by industry
(see, for example, "Employment Changes in Selected Electronic, Electrical and
Other 'Technologically Advanced' Industries, Sept. 1969 to Sept. 1972,"
Congressional Record [daily], March 6, 1973, p. S3990) and the impact of

nonmerger concentration—e.g., bankruptcy—are considered, the ECAT findings become even more dubious.

Page 300
On export-related employment see also D. P. Eldridge and N. C. Saunders, "Employment and Exports, 1963–72," *Monthly Labor Review,* Bureau of Labor Statistics, August 1973, pp. 16ff. Their analysis shows export employment increasing its share of total employment from 3.8 to 4.1 percent in the period 1969–72; however, the "increase in agricultural exports was almost totally responsible for export employment's increasing its share of total private employment." In addition, agriculture was increasing its share in total value of exports at a much faster rate than it was increasing its share in total export employment because of the accelerating capital-intensiveness of food production in the United States. See also Lawrence B. Krause, "How Much of Current Unemployment Did We Import?," *Brookings Papers on Economic Activity,* No. 2, 1971, pp. 417–28.

Quotes from Harvard study are from Stobaugh, *op. cit.,* pp. 31 and 7 respectively. Independently of our own work, a Brookings Institution analysis (Horst, *op. cit.,* pp. 25 and 29–31) reached similar conclusions concerning the studies in question. Of the ECAT study and a similar Business International study Horst states, "Without some evidence that employment and exports were enhanced by the multinationality [sic], the ECAT and Business International claims are little more than *post-hoc-ergo-propter-hoc,*" p. 25. The Business International Study is Business International Special Survey, *op. cit.*

Page 301
Fritz Redlich can be found in his "New and Traditional Approaches to Economic History," *Journal of Economic History,* Vol. 25, December 1965.

Page 302
Arthur Burns is quoted from *The Washington Post,* May 27, 1974, citing an address given by him the previous day. On the same day as Burns made his address, economics professor David Meiselman of Virginia Polytechnic Institute and State University, wrote in his *New York Times* article, "Floating Rates as Inflation Deterrent," that "since 1965, worldwide inflation has tended to accelerate" and that it has emerged as "an intractable problem which, in the Western world, may well have been the single most important economic factor undermining democratic government and political stability" (p. F.10). This article was adapted from his paper presented to the Conference on the Phenomenon of Worldwide Inflation, American Enterprise Institute, Washington, D.C., May 1974.

11: The Obsolescence of American Labor

Page 303
The most comprehensive treatment of organized labor's problems vis-à-vis the global corporation, covering both industrialized and underdeveloped countries, and which we have drawn on throughout the chapter, is from the International Labor Office, *The Relationship Between Multinational Corporations and Social Policy,* prepared by the International Labor Office for the Meeting on the Relationship Between Multinational Corporations and Social Policy, Geneva, Oct. 26 and Nov. 4, 1972, and the Report of the meeting. Another rewarding work is Hans Günter, ed., *Transnational Industrial Relations,* London: Macmillan, 1973, covering a symposium of the International Institute of Labor Studies. For an excellent overview of good bibliographic sources see Robert W. Cox, "Labor and Transnational Relations," in Robert O. Keohane

GLOBAL REACH

and Joseph S. Nye, Jr., eds., *Transnational Relations and World Politics,* Cambridge, Mass.: Harvard University Press, 1972.

Employment statistics are from U.S. Department of Commerce, *Survey of Current Business,* October 1973, p. 37. For 1970, actual foreign-employment statistics are available for only a sample of 298 U.S. corporations which in 1966 accounted for 62 percent of the employment of all majority-owned foreign affiliates of U.S. firms. The total foreign-employment estimate for 1970 was derived on the basis of the 1966 percentage of the 298's employment in total overseas employment. Although there may be a bias in this estimation procedure, it is not clear in which direction. However, the bias is small, whatever its direction, and would not alter the percentage-of-domestic-employment figure cited in the text by more than one or two points.

A 1973 State Department *airgram* revealed impressive statistics on level of wages for the electronics industry in Hong Kong. The statistics indicated that in "Major Occupation" classifications of electronics-industry workers (including the higher-paid technicians) salaries averaged less than 50 cents per hour. Wages for lower-level occupations averaged much less. *Labor/Economic Survey of Electronic Industry,* Hong Kong, July 30, 1973. See also comparable results for South Africa and other countries in Helen Kramer, "Multinational Corporations and Working Conditions" (mimeo), United Auto Workers, April 1974. Also, for detailed comparisons, see tables in Chapter 6 above.

Nelson A. Rockefeller, *Quality of Life in the Americas,* Report of U.S. Presidential Mission for the Western Hemisphere, 1969.

Page 304

George Meany, testimony before the Subcommittee on International Trade, Senate Finance Committee, May 18, 1971, p. 6.

The "runaway shop" issue refers only to foreign investment in "export platform" operations and not to other investments—e.g., of the import-substitution type. For a detailed discussion, see *The Multinational Corporation and the National Interest,* a report by Professor Robert Gilpen to the Senate Committee on Labor and Public Welfare, Washington, D.C.: Government Printing Office, October 1973. The "runaway shop" phenomenon is a significant part of the growing problem known as "structural unemployment"—a theme covered later in the text. An illuminating survey article on the problem in New England is "New England: What Replaces the Old Industry?," *Business Week,* August 4, 1973, p. 38, which points out that "in the span of two decades the number of production workers in the textile, apparel, and leather goods industries . . . declined by more than 172,000 while the increase in jobs in such high technology industries as transportation equipment and instruments increased only 26,000." A significant part of this structural-unemployment problem of the region can be attributed to the globalization process of U.S. corporations. The other part is also due to the "transfer of production" outside the region, with the transfers going not overseas, but to the Southeastern United States. No one has yet measured the exact magnitudes of overseas versus interregional transfers of production. However, it is interesting to note that in an interview with a city planner of a major urban region of the Southeastern United States, he noted that his area was already experiencing, in its most labor-intensive industries, production transfers to Puerto Rico, Brazil, and Mexico. This is as was to be expected, given our analysis of the product-life-cycle theory in Chapters 6 and 8 above.

Page 305

The AFL-CIO testimony is in "An American Trade Union View of International Trade and Investment," Senate Finance Committee, *Multinational Corporations: A Compendium of Papers,* Washington, 1973, p. 62, and the

Report of the Executive Council, "World Trade in the 1970's," Feb. 20, 1973, p. 24.

For examples of the "runaway plant" phenomenon in the electronics industry, see the testimony of the president of the International Union of Electrical Workers (IUE), Paul Jennings, before the Joint Economic Committee, July 28, 1970. See also Nat Goldfinger, "A Labor View of Foreign Investment and Trade Issues," September 1970, for other union estimates.

Wright quoted in Goldfinger, *op. cit.*, p. 22, and Meany, quoted in *The Wall Street Journal*, *op. cit.*, p. 4.

For the strawberry case, see the testimony of Paul Jennings, president of the International Union of Electrical Workers, before the Joint Economic Committee, "A Foreign Economic Policy for the 70's," July 27–30, 1970.

For the Bulova case, see the research of Paul Ramadier and Jean-Pierre DuBois, *Vers l'Europe des Travailleurs: Difficultés et Contradictions,* Des Travailleurs aux Trises avec les trusts multinationaux, Paris: Edition Seuil, forthcoming. See also other publications of the Agenor Group, which is located in Belgium (Brussels), such as Bernard Jaumont, Daniel Lenegre, and Michel Rocard, *Le Marché Commun Contre l'Europe,* Paris: Edition Seuil, 1973.

Page 306
That the United States is becoming "a nation of hamburger stands" is a theme developed in *U.S. Multinationals—The Dimming of America,* a report prepared for the AFL-CIO Maritime Trades Department Executive Board Meeting, Feb. 15 and 16, 1973, in *Hearings—Multinational Corporations,* Subcommittee on International Trade, Senate Finance Committee, Washington, D.C.: Government Printing Office, 1973, p. 448.

See also Jonathan Galloway, "The Multinationalization of Labor: U.S. Perspectives" in Kurt P. Tudyka, ed., *Multinational Corporations and Labor Unions,* selected papers from a symposium in Nijmegen, May 17–19, 1973, pp. 199–208.

Meany discusses GE and the Japanese firms on pp. 4–5 of his May 18, 1971, testimony, *op. cit.*

Andrew Biemiller, AFL-CIO, testimony before International Trade Subcommittee of the Senate Finance Committee, March 7, 1973.

On Japanese production transfers see Chapters 6 and 8 above, particularly the findings of Gy Adam, "Some Implications and Concomitants of World-Wide Sourcing," *Acta Oeconomica,* Vol. 8. (2–3), 1972, pp. 309–23; "International Corporations in the Early Seventies," *New Hungarian Quarterly,* Vol. XVI, No. 49, Spring 1973, pp. 207–19; and Nomura Research Institute, *Investment Report,* 73G-1, June 25, 1973. The primary reasons for Japanese transfers are the same as for U.S. firms: labor, pollution, tax and tariff costs. For a more detailed discussion see Ronald Müller, "The Underdeveloped and Developed: Power and Potential for Change," in Papers and Proceedings of the World Conference of Sociology, August 1974; also "Japan: A Stepped-Up Search for Cheap Asian Labor," *Business Week,* March 31, 1973, p. 40.

Page 307
On foreign global corporations' investment in the United States, some managers interviewed felt that the prime motivation of firms like Volvo and Michelin was their fears of a forthcoming tariff war between more-developed countries, and therefore these investments are more of the "import substitution" and not of the "export platform" type.

Woodcock quotes Jefferson in *Hearings—Multinational Corporations, op. cit.*, Subcommittee on International Trade, Senate Finance Committee, Washington, 1973, p. 293.

464   GLOBAL REACH

Ford quoted in United Auto Workers, *Three Resolutions on International Trade, International Labor Solidarity, Peace,* International Affairs Department, May, 1972.

Shesky quoted by Goldfinger, *op. cit.*

Page 308
Statistics on employment and exports with regard to Mexico are available in *U.S. Multinationals: The Dimming of America, op. cit.,* p. 470.

The exports of Mexico and Taiwan are discussed in a statement by the AFL-CIO Executive Council, "Export of Jobs and Production," Atlanta, May 12, 1971.

In addition to lower wage costs, another prime reason for expansion of export-platform operations is the incentives provided such U.S. imports under Tariff Provisions 806.30 and 807.00. Basically these provisions permit U.S. corporations to pay a tariff on only the foreign value-added proportion of their imports from export platforms. Such imports increased by about 100 percent between 1966 and 1969 alone. Some 40 to 50 percent of these imports are due to U.S. global corporations alone. "According to the U.S. Department of Commerce, over 70 percent of total office machine sales by U.S. firms in the world market are produced by overseas subsidiaries of U.S. firms." *Economic Factors Affecting the Use of 807.00 and 806.30 of the Tariff Schedules of the United States,* Tariff Commission Publication 339, Washington, D.C., September 1970, pp. 100–104. The commission also reports similar findings for a host of other industries, including TV receivers and components, noting that "Producers state that without access to labor at costs comparable to those of foreign producers in the assembly functions, it would be virtually impossible for the U.S. industry to maintain a significant share of the U.S. market—a substantial part of which is already supplied by imports," p. 104. For a recent updating of these findings, see U.S. Tariff Commission, *Competitiveness of U.S. Industries,* Publication 473, Washington, D.C., 1972. See also D. W. Baerresen, *The Border Industrialization Program of Mexico,* Lexington, Mass.: Lexington Books, 1972. See also discussion in Chapters 6 and 8 above.

Watson quoted in Robert d'A. Shaw, "Foreign Investment and Global Labor Adjustments," paper presented to the Development Issues Seminar, Overseas Development Council, March 16, 1971, p. 9. Watson's conclusion is not necessarily correct, since it assumes perfectly competitive markets. Under the General Theory of Second Best for oligopoly markets, the final outcome (of more, less, or equal job trade-offs) is indeterminate. For discussion of Second Best Theory see J. M. Henderson and R. E. Quandt, *Microeconomic Theory,* 2nd ed., New York: McGraw-Hill, 1974, and C. E. Staley, *International Economics: Analysis and Issues,* Englewood Cliffs, N.J.: Prentice-Hall, 1970.

Henry Ford II is quoted in *News of the World,* March 14, 1971.

Page 309
For the Dunlop-Pirelli case, see Ramadier and DuBois, *op. cit.,* p. 30.

The Burroughs case can be found in Bernard Jaumont *et al., Le Marché Commun Contre l'Europe, op. cit.,* p. 17.

Similar to the Burrough's case but for the United States is a detailed case study of the manner in which U.S. global corporations have undermined the bargaining power of U.S. trade unions, documented in the work of Charles Craypo, "Collective Bargaining in the Multinational Conglomerate Corporation: Litton's Shutdown of Royal Typewriter," working paper, Department of Labor Studies, Pennsylvania State University, 1974. In this typical case, Litton met erosion of its U.S. market share by transferring typewriter production to low-wage areas, the Federal Trade Commission noted, as "an alternative to original research and to developing a suitable machine based on the present state of the art." *Ibid.*, p. 12. The incredible transcripts of the Litton–union negotiations reveal the almost complete powerlessness of organized labor to influence such decisions. See also Federal Trade Commission, *Initial Decision, In the Matter of Litton Industries, Inc.*, Packet No. 8778, Feb. 3, 1972. See other case studies involving such companies as Union Carbide and Monsanto.

The reader is also referred to papers and discussions presented at "Corporate Power" seminar at AFL-CIO Study Center, Washington, D.C., May 17–19, 1974.

For other surveys dealing with the avoidance of labor problems because of the existence of worldwide complementary production facilities, see Louis Turner, *Invisible Empires*, New York: Harcourt Brace Jovanovich, 1970; Ramadier and DuBois, *Vers l'Europe des Travailleurs, op. cit.*; Charles Levinson, *Capital, Inflation and the Multinationals*, London: George Allen & Unwin, 1971. See also Duane Kujawa, ed., *American Labor and the Multinational Corporation*, New York: Praeger, 1973.

Page 310
The *Times* quote is from Oct. 1, 1970.

On international union organization see Louis Turner, "Trade Unions and the Multinational Company" in Lisle Klein, *Fabian Industrial Essays*, forthcoming.

See Ramadier and DuBois, *op. cit.*

On a different occasion Maisonrouge had this to say about global mobility of companies versus the immobility of labor when a reporter asked him, "And what is the trade-union attitude toward multinational companies?" Answer: "They consider that the fact that a company can decide from one day to the next to transfer its production from point A to B, where labor is cheaper, is a menace to them. And it is true. The whole question is to know to what extent a company can transfer its production from A to B." From the French magazine *Les Informations*, April 1971.

Page 311
On ITT, see Anthony Sampson, *The Sovereign State of IT&T*, New York: Stein & Day, 1973.

Levinson is quoted in *The Wall Street Journal*, April 23, 1973.

Page 313
Meany quoted in Ramadier and DuBois, *op. cit.* For an excellent interpretation of the role of the bureaucracy in U.S. organized labor see Grant McConnell, *Private Power and American Democracy*, New York: Knopf, 1966.

For an extended critique of the labor bureaucracy, see Stanley Aronowitz, "Arthritic Unionism: Corporate Labor in America," *Social Policy*, May–June 1972, p. 40. See Len De Caux, *Labor Radical*, Boston: Beacon Press, 1970, pp. 449–54.

For a discussion of the American Institute for Free Labor Development, see Richard J. Barnet, *Intervention and Revolution*, New York: World Publishing Co., 1968, p. 240. See also Paul Jacobs, "American Unions," in *Memorandum*, Center for the Study of Democratic Institutions, Aug. 2, 1967, p. 28; Stanley Meisler, "Meddling in Latin America: The Dubious Role of the AFL-CIO," *The Nation*, Feb. 10, 1964, pp. 133–38. For a non–AFL-CIO union interpretation of organized labor's problems in the underdeveloped countries of Latin America, see Daniel Benedict, "Latin American and Caribbean Workers Face the Multinational Companies," report to International Metalworkers' Federation Regional Conference, Buenos Aires, Sept. 9–12, 1972.

466   GLOBAL REACH

Meany's anti-Communism is discussed by Wilfred Sheed, "Whatever Happened to the Labor Movement?," *Atlantic Monthly,* July 1973.

Exceptions to docile unions in Latin America, as already noted in Chapter 6 above, are those in the private extractive sector, such as those in Peru (copper) and Venezuela (oil) and public-sector employees' unions. Another exception is the banana workers' union in Honduras, to which the AFL-CIO cooperation was helpful.

The relative size of the skilled labor force (as a proportion of total labor force) in a given country can shrink if the rate of labor displacement, due to the introduction of new technology, is not offset by a sufficiently higher rate of new investment.

Page 314
Quote is from Galbraith, *Economics and the Public Purpose,* Boston: Houghton Mifflin, 1973, p. 118.

Interview with Herman Rebhan, director of the Department of International Affairs, United Auto Workers, conducted by Paula D. Echeverria, summer 1973.

The AKSO, N. V., dispute is given in *The Wall Street Journal,* April 23, 1973, p. 1. For a description of the sit-in, see Frans Drabbe, "Sit-in at Breda," *Free Labour World,* November 1972, page 14.

The Caterpillar strike is outlined in Ramadier and DuBois, *op. cit.*

For the union's interpretation of the Dagenham and other Ford-plant strikes in England, see John Mathews, *Ford Strike: The Workers' Story,* London: Panther Books, 1972.

Page 315
UAW's success in Venezuela is described in *Economic Intelligence Unit,* 1971.

For the Dunlop-Pirelli incident see Ramadier and DuBois, *op. cit.,* p. 30. Results of the Chrysler-plant survey can be found in Louis Turner, "Trade Unions and the Multinational Company," *op. cit.,* p. 8.

Levinson is quoted in "Multinationals: A Step Toward Global Bargaining," *Business Week,* Oct. 28, 1972, p. 52. See also *Capital, Inflation and the Multinationals, op. cit.*

On the Shell dispute, the ICF has also used this information to gain the support of conservation and ecology groups. See also *The Wall Street Journal,* Oct. 28, 1972, p. 1.

Page 317
See Victor Reuther, "Weltweite Gewerkschaftsgruppierungen in Zeitalter Internationale Grosskonzerne" (Unions in the Age of Large International Corporations) in *Freie Gewerkschafts Welt,* No. 183, September 1965.

See Rebhan interview, *op. cit.*

On the need for U.S. unions to have global relations, this is why Leonard Woodcock, in advocating import quotas on foreign cars because of unemployment in the auto industry during the winter of 1973–1974, emphasized the temporary nature of this policy until U.S. manufacturers retooled for small-car production.

Page 318
Interview with Irving Bluestone, director, General Motors Division of the UAW, conducted by Paula D. Echeverria, Washington, D.C., March 2, 1973.

The meeting of companies in New Jersey is in *Journal of Commerce,* April 6, 1973.

Regarding wage parity, the International Metalworkers' Federation (IMF), including the UAW, recognizing the difficulties in bringing about a move toward an international leveling of wages, has settled on a short-term strategy of promoting regional—e.g., Latin America—parity.' See Daniel Benedict, assistant general secretary of the IMF, "Multinational Companies: Their Relations with the Workers," report delivered to the Conference on Industrial Relations in the European Community, London, Oct. 4, 1973. This report gives an excellent overview of union perceptions of the problem, actions to date, and problems remaining. See also Daniel Benedict, "Trade Union Strategies on Multi-national Companies," paper presented to Conference on Multinational Corporations, Queen's University of Belfast, May 31–June 2, 1971, Newcastle, Ireland.

In fact the cost of capital investment for import-substitution purposes in poor countries is extremely low, because it is likely to have been paid off through its earlier use in the home country. This is probably not the case in export-platform operations, in which, increasingly, the technology has never been used in the home country. See the discussion of the product-life-cycle theory in Chapter 6 above.

Page 319
The AFL-CIO's position on the controversial Burke-Hartke legislation is expressed in "World Trade in the 1970's," *op. cit.,* pp. 27–32. The so-called Hartke-Burke Bill was introduced originally as the "Foreign Trade and Investment Act of 1972" (S-2591) on Sept. 28, 1971, and reintroduced on Jan. 4, 1973. For private industries' views on Burke-Hartke see the discussion and references in Chapter 10 above.

The tax findings are from the important study of Dr. Peggy Musgrave, "Tax References to Foreign Investment," in *The Economics of Federal Subsidy Programs: A Compendium of Papers,* Part II, International Subsidies, Washington: Joint Economic Committee of Congress, June 11, 1972.

On tax preferences for foreign investment see Peggy Musgrave, "Tax References," *ibid.* See also Arnold Cantor, "Tax Subsidies That Export Jobs," *AFL-CIO American Federationist,* November 1972, and *U.S. Oil Week,* Dec. 23, 1972, and Dec. 24, 1973.

Page 320
The UAW's position on the regulation of U.S. multinationals can be found in *Hearings, Multinational Corporations,* Senate Committee on Finance, Subcommittee on International Trade, 1973, pp. 277–78 and 289–98.

Page 321
Leonard Woodcock presented the United Auto Workers' position paper on adjustment assistance to the House Ways and Means Committee, May 15, 1973.

The Amtrak example is presented and analyzed on p. 5 of the *U.A.W. Resolution on International Trade* and Woodcock, May 15, 1973, *op. cit.* See also Woodcock's address before the National Foreign Trade Convention, Nov. 14, 1972. Other works on adjustment assistance are Charles R. Frank, *Adjustment Assistance: American Jobs and Trade with the Developing Countries,* Overseas Development Council, Paper 13, Washington, D.C., June 1973. For a critique of the inadequacies of the Administration's proposed revisions see *Trade Adjustment Assistance,* Report of Subcommittee of Foreign Economic Policy, House Committee on Foreign Affairs, Washington, D.C.: U.S. Government Printing Office, Aug. 29, 1972, which outlines the deficiencies of current adjustment aid to workers. The European Community approach is outlined in Commission of the European Communities, *Why A New Social Fund?*, Press and Information Directorate-General, Brussels, April 1972. For a business interpretation see Irwin Ross, "Labor's Big Push for Protectionism," *Fortune,* March 1973.

For a discussion of the Chrysler incident, see Woodcock's testimony before the House Ways and Means Committee, May 15, 1973, pp. 5–8. A detailed examination of the failure of current adjustment assistance and the reasons is found in Carl H. Fulda, "Adjustment to Hardship Caused by Imports: The New Decisions of the Tariff Commission and the Need for Legislative Clarification," *Michigan Law Review,* Vol. 70, April 1972, pp. 791–830. From 1962 to 1969, Fulda records, "no petitions for tariff adjustment assistance to firms or workers were granted," p. 795.

Woodcock's charges against the administration bill can be found on pp. 2–4 of his testimony of May 15, 1973.

The Chamber's position can be found in the Woodcock testimony of May 15, 1973, *op. cit.,* pp. 34–41.

Page 322

The Senate Finance Committee figures are quoted by Robert Shaw, *Columbia Journal of World Business,* July–August 1971, p. 10.

Data in the table taken from *Electronic News,* and quoted in *The American Federationist,* July 1972, and *The Dimming of America, op. cit.*

For global corporations' imports into the United States, see Chapter 10 above.

Nat Goldfinger, director of The Department of Research, AFL-CIO, "A Labor View of Foreign Investment and Trade Issues," September 1970.

On food imports and prices by U.S. global agribusiness firms, the reader is referred to the case study of Del Monte and the transfer of its pineapple-canning operations from Hawaii to an "export platform," the Philippines, where the cost of canning pineapple is 47 percent less than in Hawaii. Average wages of cannery workers in the Philippines are 20 cents per hour, while in Hawaii the average hourly wage for a cannery worker is $2.69. In addition, in 1950 Hawaii produced about 72 percent of the world's pineapple, while now it produces less than 33 percent. The average wage for field workers in Hawaii is $2.64 per hour, while for field workers in the Philippines the average hourly wage is 15 cents. Yet despite the substantial reduction in costs of producing pineapple, in the words of Senator James Abourezk, "the consumer pays the same." For these statistics and quotations, see the remarks of Senator James Abourezk, *Congressional Record,* Nov. 9, 1973, pages S20227–34. And, according to Abourezk, this is not an isolated phenomenon. To cite but another example, "Del Monte recently abandoned its white asparagus operations in California, Oregon and Washington and moved them to Mexico, where cheap labor has reduced the corporation's production costs by 45.1 percent. But the price of Del Monte's asparagus has not gone down. None of the corporate savings lightened the consumer's load." For additional information on the utilization of "export platforms" and pricing policies in the food industry, see the testimony of John Zuckerman of Zuckerman Farms of California, U.S. Tariff Commission Hearings, Oct. 31, 1972.

Page 324

See U.S. Department of Health, Education and Welfare, *Work in America,* December 1972.

"Who's Unhappy at Work and Why," by Neal Q. Herrick, *Manpower,* January 1972, pp. 3–7. For an extended discussion, see also Herrick and Harold L.

Sheppard, *Where Have All the Robots Gone?*, New York: The Free Press, 1972.

See, for example, the discussion of Lordstown in *Newsweek,* March 26, 1973; *The New York Times,* Jan. 23, 1972; see also Irving Bluestone's discussion of "Worker Participation in Decision Making," presented to Conference on Alternative Political Economy, Institute for Policy Studies (mimeo), March 1973.

Moreno and Morris quoted in *Newsweek,* March 26, 1973, p. 82.

Dance quote is from "Implications for Strategic Planning in the '70's," address delivered to Share Owners Information Meeting, Miami, Florida, Oct. 27, 1970.

For a spectrum of views on worker alienation see "Worker Alienation, 1972," Hearings before the Subcommittee on Employment, Manpower and Poverty of the Committee on Labor and Public Welfare, U.S. Senate, July 25–26, 1972, Washington, D.C.: Government Printing Office.

Page 325
UAW President Leonard Woodcock once referred to certain "Academics" concerned with the issues of worker alienation and job quality as proponents of "Elitist Nonsense." *Newsweek,* March 26, 1973, p. 82.

Foulkes quoted in *Newsweek,* March 26, 1973, p. 82. See also Foulkes's *Creating More Meaningful Work,* New York: American Management Association, 1969.

For a more detailed quantitative assessment, see Victor R. Fuchs, *The Service Economy,* National Bureau of Economic Research, New York: Columbia University Press, 1968.

Daniel Bell, *The Coming of Post-Industrial Society,* New York: Basic Books, 1973, pp. 129–42. See the critique of Bell's work by Professor Christopher Lasch in *The New York Review of Books,* Oct. 18, 1973.

Page 326
See Richard Bellman quoted in *Technology and the American Economy,* Report of the President's Committee on Technology, Automation and Economic Progress, Washington: Government Printing Office, 1966.

For this information on the character of work, see Bell, *op. cit.*

This quote taken from Bell, *op. cit.,* pp. 126–27.

Bell's treatment of the topic of alienation is quite similar to that of Karl Marx, except that the latter links it directly to a consequence of technology under capitalism. See Daniel Bell, "The Debate on Alienation," in Leopold Labedz, *Revisionism: Essays on The History of Marxist Ideas,* New York: Praeger, 1962. Bell, however, is wrong in arguing, as he once did, that Marx dropped the idea in his later writings. See Karl Marx, *Theories of Surplus Value,* trans. by G. A. Bonner and Emile Burns, London, 1951, p. 122; also Eric Zeitlin, *Marxism: A Re-Examination,* Princeton, N.J.: Van Nostrand, 1967, pp. 45–46.

Page 327
Johnson quoted in *Newsweek,* March 26, 1973, p. 81. Or, to cite another example, a Lordstown assembly-line worker: "Every day I come out of there I feel ripped off. . . . A good day's work is being tired but not exhausted. Out there all I feel is glad when it's over. I don't even feel useful now. They could replace me; I don't even feel necessary. . . . They could always find somebody stupider than me to do the job," in Stanley Aronowitz's *False Promises,* New York: McGraw-Hill, 1974, p. 21. This work is one of the most comprehensive recent syntheses of the alienation syndrome in modern industrial societies.

See R. Sennett and J. Cobb, *The Hidden Injuries of Class,* New York: Knopf, 1972.

Page 328
This quote from Sennett and Cobb can be found on pp. 258–59 of *The Hidden Injuries of Class, op. cit.*

See the work of Bell, *op. cit.,* and Alain Touraine, *The Post-Industrial Society: Tomorrow's Social History,* New York: Random House, 1971.

Page 329
The reference to Takeshi Hirano and Japanese workers is from Tom Braden, "Japan: A Nation of Company Men," *The Washington Post,* March 13, 1973, p. A23.

The quote of Niroshe Naruse is from *Newsweek,* March 26, 1973, page 82.

For a discussion of the implications of no-strike pledges, see A. H. Raskin, "Strike Surcease," *The New York Times,* June 12, 1973, p. 39.

For a description of the first steel-industry pact in history to replace the threat of a strike with voluntary arbitration, see "The USW's No-Strike Victory," *Business Week,* April 20, 1974, p. 62.

The "new docility" of American labor is evidenced by the negotiations between GM and the I.U.E. as well as the Shoe and Boot Workers and Stride Rite. For the negotiations and settlements see *The New York Times,* Nov. 22, 1971, p. 1; Nov. 23, 1971, p. 28; Nov. 24, 1971, p. 16; and Mar. 16, 1972, p. 42.

Page 330
David Sirota, "Job Enrichment: Another Management Fad?," The Conference Board, *Record,* Vol. X, No. 4, April 1973, and *The New York Times,* Sunday, May 6, 1973, Business and Finance Section.

Stanley E. Seashore and J. Thad Barnowe, "Collar Color Doesn't Count," *Psychology Today,* August 1972, p. 53.

Page 331
The *Newsweek* article is entitled: "The Job Blahs: Who Wants to Work?," March 26, 1973, p. 79.

These experiments are described in *Newsweek,* March 26, 1973, *op. cit.*

Page 332
Robert Rowthorn's views on the effects of multinationalization on domestic business can be found in *International Big Business 1957–1967,* Cambridge University Press, 1971, and Rowthorn and Stephen Hymer, "Multinational Corporation and International Oligopoly: The Non-American Challenge," in C. P. Kindleberger, *The International Corporation,* Cambridge, Mass.: MIT Press, 1970.

Taiwan's new foreign-investment policies are outlined in *The Washington Post,* June 24, 1973, p. F2.

12: The Ecology of Corporations and the Quality of Growth

Page 334
The Limits to Growth, Donella Meadows *et al.,* New York: Universe Books, 1972. Various criticisms and interpretations of this study can be found in H. S. D. Cole *et al.,* eds., *Models of Doom: A Critique of The Limits to Growth* (With a Reply by the Authors of *The Limits to Growth*), New York:

Universe Books, 1973. There is an extensive literature on the ecological and psychological consequences of economic growth and its composition in modern industrial society. One of the early studies that prompted the vigorous debate concerning economic growth was Ezra J. Mishan, *The Costs of Economic Growth,* New York: Praeger, 1967, later popularized in E. J. Mishan, *Technology and Growth: The Price We Pay,* New York: Praeger, 1970. For a debate between Mishan and his critics, including Robert Solow, see *Daedalus,* Fall 1973. See also *Economic Growth and Environmental Decay: The Solution Becomes the Problem* by Paul W. Barkley and David W. Seckler, New York: Harcourt Brace Jovanovich, 1972. For a good review of various U.S. political views on current rates and composition of economic growth and their environmental impacts, see Parts 3 and 4 of *Economic Growth vs. the Environment,* Warren A. Johnson and John Hardesty, eds., Belmont, Calif.: Wadsworth Publishing Co., 1971. For a balanced presentation of "The Problem of Environmental Quality as an Economic Problem Whose Resolution Requires Major Changes in Economic, Political and Legal Institutions," see the multidisciplinary approach of A. M. Freeman III, R. H. Haveman, and A. V. Kneese, *The Economics of Environmental Policy,* New York: Wiley, 1973. On the worldwide problem of ecology and the worldwide differences of opinion, particularly as between poor and rich nations and capitalist and socialist societies, see Tom Artis, *Earth Talk: Independent Voices on the Environment,* New York: Grossman, 1973. Also the important debates in the volume *The Economic Growth Controversy,* Andrew Weintraub, Eli Schwartz, and J. Richard Aronson, eds., New York: International Arts and Sciences Press, 1973.

Page 335

Quotations are from "A Blueprint for Survival," *The Ecologist,* January 1972, pp. 1–22.

Yale Professor William D. Nordhaus, long a critical analyst of the impacts on economic growth of the environmental crisis and potential resource shortages, now points out that historically "there had been no important resource constraints on growth. . . . We could afford to use our resource profligately; [however,] the new view of economic growth is that the closing of all our frontiers means that we are now operating in a spaceship economy. In a spaceship economy, great attention must be paid to the sources of life and to the dumps where our refuse is piled. Things which have traditionally been treated as free goods—air, water, quiet, natural beauty—must now be treated with the same care as other scarce goods." See W. D. Nordhaus, "Resources as a Constraint on Growth," *American Economic Review,* May 1974, pp. 22–26 (parenthesis ours).

Richard M. Nixon is quoted from First State of the Union Message, as quoted in Barry Commoner, *The Closing Circle,* New York: Knopf, 1971, p. 181.

David Rockefeller is quoted from his commencement address delivered at St. John's University, June 6, 1971. For a comprehensive review of the policies and perceptions of growthmanship by the advocates of growth themselves, see Walter Heller, *Perspectives on Economic Growth,* New York: Random House, 1968.

Page 338

Ramo quoted in Commoner, *The Closing Circle, op. cit.,* pp. 179–80. See also Ramo's address "Technology and Resources for Business," delivered at The White House Conference on the Industrial World Ahead: A Look at Business in 1990, Washington, Feb. 7, 1972.

Pages 338–39
Statistics and quotations from Commoner can be found in *op. cit.,* pp. 143–45. In addition to the *Closing Circle* Barry Commoner has published a number of articles dealing with the environmental crisis and its impact on the U.S. economy. Among these are Barry Commoner, Michael Corr, and Paul J. Stamler, *Data on the U.S. Economy of Relevance to Environmental Problems* (prepared for Committee on Environmental Alterations), American Association for the Advancement of Science, Washington, D.C., 1971; Commoner, Corr, Stamler, "The Environmental Cost of Economic Growth," *Environment,* April 1971. See also J. A. Edmisten, "Hard and Soft Detergents," *Scientist and Citizen,* October 1966. See also Commoner, Corr, Stamler, "The Causes of Pollution," *Environment,* April 1971, and Commoner, "Workplace Burden," *Environment,* July–August 1973.

Page 340
R. M. Stephenson, *Introduction to the Chemical Process Industries,* New York: Reinhold, 1966, p. 365.

Page 341
Statistics on profit rates are found in Commoner, *op. cit.,* p. 259. Commoner also includes a similar sketch of the relationship between "pollution and profits" in the (synthetic) fertilizer industry; see pp. 260–63. Although part of the reason why profits on sales have increased is the relatively more intense use of capital vs. labor in these new technologies, other data confirm what one would assume, that there is a higher rate of return on invested capital as well. As was noted in our discussion of the product-life-cycle theory in Chapter 6 above, the pioneer innovators of our technologies and products enjoy, during the initial years, a relatively stronger oligopoly (monopoly) position than the non-innovators, and thus oligopoly profits (rents) are higher. Cf. J. Blackman's evidence of this in the chemical industry in the next note below.

Jules Blackman, *The Economics of the Chemical Industry,* Washington: Manufacturing Chemists' Association, 1970, p. 215.

Fortune and Henry Ford II quoted in Commoner, *op. cit.,* pp. 263–64.

Page 342
For a detailed treatment of "holistic" methodology see Ronald Müller, "The Social Sciences and Society," in R. Müller, S. Arnold, and R. Felnel, eds., *Power and the World Political Economy* (forthcoming). On the lack of holism in scientific training and its social consequences see various essays by Abraham Maslow in his *Towards The Farther Reaches of Human Nature,* New York: Viking, 1971, and Arthur Koestler, *Ghost in the Machine,* New York: Macmillan, 1967. On the failure of psychology and psychotherapy to deal with socioinduced psychological problems of individuals see Seymour B. Sarason, *The Psychological Sense of Community: Prospects for a Community Psychology,* San Francisco: Jossey-Bass, 1974.

John Kenneth Galbraith discusses this in *The New Industrial State,* New York: New American Library, 1967, pp. 24–25.

Page 343
In reference to the absorption of cost increases by the companies instead of the customers, recent studies by Chase Econometrics Associates, a Chase Manhattan Bank subsidiary, estimate that anticipated pollution-control spending will retard productivity by 0.3 percent a year over the next four years. If the higher standards demanded by environmentalists were enacted into law, the effect would of course be greater.

Rockefeller's argument points, of course, to the social dilemma of global-oligopoly competition, for it is true if the global corporations of other advanced nations do not face similar pollution-abatement costs.

Rockefeller quote is from his St. John's commencement address, *op. cit.*

Page 344

Neil Fabricant and Robert M. Hallman discuss the energy requirements of commercial and noncommercial sectors in *Toward a Rational Power Policy: Energy, Politics and Pollution,* New York: Braziller, 1971.

John G. Welles quotes these figures in "Multinationals Need New Environmental Strategies," unpublished manuscript, September 1972. Later version of the manuscript published in the *Columbia Journal of World Business* under the same title, Vol. VIII, No. 2, Summer 1973.

Carl Gerstacker quoted in Welles, *ibid.* Occasionally, it is true, environmental improvements actually improve productivity. Hercules, Inc., according to *Business Week,* spent $750,000 for a recycling system that cuts pollution into the Mississippi River by 90 percent and saves $250,000 in water and material costs. But such cases are exceptional. The most that can be said of environmental recycling as a general proposition is that the new technologies may involve savings which somewhat offset losses in productivity.

Page 345

The News, Mexico City, March 15, 1973.

The discussion on this page can be found in Welles *op. cit.* The necessity for Japanese firms to find pollution havens is detailed in the Nomura research report cited in Chapter 8 above.

The National Industrial Pollution Control Council (NIPCC), Department of Commerce, Washington, 1973. Rockefeller was succeeded as chairman of NIPCC by Willard F. Rockwell, chairman of North American Rockwell.

Henry Steck, "Why Does Industry Always Get What It Wants?," *Environmental Action,* July 24, 1971, pp. 11–14. See also Steck's testimony before the Subcommittee on Budgeting, Management and Expenditures, Senate Government Operations Committee, June 17, 1971. See also Vic Reinemer, "Corporate Government in Action," *The Progressive,* November 1971, p. 28.

Page 346

Paul Ehrlich, "Where Do We Stand Now?" *The International Review,* October 30, 1972, p. 15. The Senate Select Committee on Nutrition and Human Needs quotes Michael Jacobsen, codirector of the Center for Science in the Public Interest, that "one-third of dog and cat food sold in ghetto areas is bought for human consumption," *Food Price Changes, 1973–1974, and Nutritional Status,* Part I, February 1974. See also "The World Food Problem" by F. M. Lappe, *Commonweal,* February 8, 1974, for a devastating comparison of consumption levels in rich and poor nations.

Page 347

John Kenneth Galbraith, *Economics and the Public Purpose,* Boston: Houghton Mifflin, 1973, Part 3. For critiques of this book compare Richard J. Barnet, *The New York Times Book Review,* Sept. 16, 1973, p. 1, and "Galbraith's Utopia" by Paul M. Sweezy, *The New York Review of Books,* Nov. 15, 1973, p. 2. It is from Veblen that Galbraith inherits the concept of the technostructure and the process of technology as well as the role of the technocrats versus the shareholders. From Schumpeter, *Capitalism, Socialism and Democracy,* he derives the basic ideas on the advantage of size for producing "systematized innovation" and planned growth, a condition that justifies the increase of corporate power over both consumer and producer.

"As ex-GM vice-president John DeLorean said recently: 'There is no forward response at GM to what the public wants today. It's gotten to be a total insulation from the realities of the world. From the standpoint of America it's frightening.' " As quoted in Bradford Snell, testimony before the Subcommittee on Antitrust and Monopoly, Senate Judiciary Committee, United States Senate, Feb. 26, 1974.

Joe S. Bain, *Industrial Organization,* New York: Wiley, 1968, p. 349. In addition, see Graham Bannock's discussion in *The Juggernauts,* New York: Bobbs-Merrill, 1971, Chapter 6. Also Edith Penrose, *The Theory of the Growth of the Firm,* Oxford: Basil Blackwell, 1959. See also the important recent studies of industrial concentration, efficiency, and competition in several key sectors—transportation, energy, and communication among them—undertaken by the Anti-trust and Monopoly Subcommittee of the Senate Judiciary Committee. For example, the Committee publication *American Ground Transport* by Bradford Snell; see also Senator Phillip Hart, *Industrial Reorganization Act* (S-1167).

Reference to 4,550 firms is from Morton Mintz and Jerry S. Cohen, *America, Inc.,* New York: Dial, 1971, p. 41.

Page 348
Galbraith, *The New Industrial State, op. cit.,* Mintz and Cohen, *op. cit.,* provide an interesting critique of the "technological imperative"; see pp. 43–45.

John M. Blair, *Economic Concentration, op. cit.,* Chapter 8, especially pp. 176–84.

See Blair, *ibid.,* pp. 184–85.

Weinberger quoted in Mintz and Cohen, *op. cit.,* p. 41.

Bjorksten quoted in Mintz and Cohen, *op. cit.,* p. 45.

Galbraith, *The New Industrial State, op. cit.*

In 1971, according to *Forbes,* May 15, 1972, p. 205, Harold S. Geneen, chairman of the Board of ITT, received $812,000 "total remuneration" (*excluding* dividend income) from the company, whereas in the same year, the "average [yearly] earnings of production workers on manufacturing payrolls," according to the Department of Labor (*Handbook of Labor Statistics, 1972*), amounted to less than $8,000. (It will be noted that these are wages paid to American workers and that the wages of most foreign employees of ITT are much lower.) See tables in chapters 6 and 10 above.

In fact, there is a precise statistical correlation between firm size and executive salaries. Bannock, *The Juggernauts, op. cit.,* pp. 108–109.

Page 349
On the American Tobacco Co. see pp. 100–101 of Bannock, *The Juggernauts, op. cit.*

On conglomerates and efficiency see *Economic Report on Corporate Mergers,* Bureau of Economics, Federal Trade Commission, Commerce Clearing House Edition, 1967, p. 248. Quoted in Mintz and Cohen, *op. cit.,* p. 43.

George J. Stigler quoted from "The Case Against Big Business," *Fortune,* May 1952.

Adams quote taken from *Planning, Regulation and Competition: Automobile Industry—1968,* Hearings before the Subcommittees of the Senate Select Committee on Small Business, pp. 12–13.

Page 350
McLuhan quoted in *Business Week,* June 24, 1972, p. 118.

Reference to the British Institute of Marketing is from L. W. Rodgers,

Marketing in a Competitive Economy, New York: International Publications, 1965 and 1969.

See "Inefficiency in America: Why Nothing Seems to Work Anymore," *Time,* March 23, 1970.

See Edwin Mansfield, *Industrial Research and Technological Innovation,* New York: Norton, 1968, and *The Economics of Technological Change,* New York: Norton, 1968. Jacob Schmookler, *Invention and Economic Growth,* Cambridge, Mass.: Harvard University Press, 1966, and *Patents, Invention and Economic Change,* Guliches and Hurwicz, eds., Cambridge: Harvard, 1972; John Jewkes, David Sawers, and Richard Stillerman, *The Sources of Invention,* New York: St. Martin's Press, 1959. See also Chapter 8 of Bannock, *The Juggernauts, op. cit.*

Arthur Koestler, *The Act of Creation,* New York: Macmillan, 1964.

Page 351

Watson quoted in Bannock, *The Juggernauts, op. cit.,* p. 185.

Papanek, *Design for the Real World, op. cit.*

On Chrysler see Mintz and Cohen, *op. cit.,* pp. 49–51.

Page 352

Levitt, *Advertising Age,* March 15, 1971, p. 55. See also Marion Stephenson, vice-president of administration, NBC Radio Corporation, "Blind People Do Not Fear Snakes," address delivered to Women's Advertising Club, Cleveland, Ohio, May 25, 1971. Reprinted in *Vital Speeches of The Day,* July 15, 1971, p. 584.

For the benefits of package redesign see Bannock, *The Juggernauts, op. cit.,* p. 211.

Page 353

Harry J. Skornia, *Television and Society,* New York: McGraw-Hill, 1965, p. 90.

Advertising Age, July 16, 1973.

L. W. Weiss, *Economics and American Industry,* quoted by M. A. Utton, *Industrial Concentration,* Baltimore: Penguin Books, 1970.

Page 354

While the FTC overlooked the fact that the "quarter-pounder" weighs less than 4 ounces at the time of the customer's purchase, the company pleaded guilty to advertising the product as a "quarter-pounder" when the meat weighed less than 4 ounces before cooking. (Information received from Ms. Ina Alcabes, Nassau County, Office of Consumer Affairs, Mineola, New York.)

Tomalin's investigation and the quote by the brewery executive are found in Bannock, *The Juggernauts, op. cit.,* pp. 212 and 213.

For information on the relationship between advertising and the environment see the Council on Economic Priorities, *Economic Priorities Report,* Vol. 2, No. 3, September–October 1971.

American Management Association Report, *The Changing Success Ethic,* 1973. For a review of the findings see *The New York Times,* June 3, 1973, Section 4, p. 12.

Page 355

Nevitt quoted in *Business Week,* June 24, 1972, p. 118. See also Marshall McLuhan and Nevitt, *Take Today: The Executive as Dropout,* Harcourt Brace Jovanovich, 1972.

Kenn Rogers, "The Mid-Career Crisis," *Saturday Review of the Society,* February 1973, pp. 37–38. See also Rogers' *Managers: Personality and Performance,* Chicago: Educational Methods, 1964.

Page 356
Jacques S. Gansler, "Social Responsibility and the Multinational Corporation Executive," unpublished graduate research paper, Department of Economics, The American University, Washington, D.C., 1973 (mimeo), p. 20.

This figure of 30 million can be found in Emma Rothchild, *Paradise Lost: The Decline of the Auto-industrial Age,* New York: Random House, 1973.

Weiss quote here is from *Advertising Age,* December 7, 1970, p. 1.

Page 357
Crawford H. Greenwalt, *The Uncommon Man,* New York: McGraw-Hill, 1959.

Personal interview with Ignacio Millán, June 1973. Millán's study will be published by Fondo de Cultura, Mexico, in 1975.

For an additional statement on the hierarchical structure of the multinational corporation and its implications see Stephen Hymer, "Is the Multinational Corporation Doomed?," *Innovation,* No. 28, 1972.

"I've Been Moved" is from Vance Packard, *A Nation of Strangers,* New York: David McKay, 1972, p. 278.

Page 358
See Robert Seidenberg, *Corporate Wives, Corporate Casualties,* American Management Association, 1973, and "Dear Mr. Success, Consider Your Wife," *The Wall Street Journal,* February 7, 1973.

"The Humanistic Way of Managing People," *Business Week,* July 22, 1972. See also the publications of the Organization Development unit of the National Training Laboratory, Washington, D.C.

Maccoby, *op. cit.*

Jules Cohn, *The Conscience of the Corporations,* Baltimore: Johns Hopkins Press, 1971, p. 4; and *Harvard Business Review,* March–April 1970, pp. 68 and 105–13.

Cohn, *op. cit.,* pp. 3–10, and Andrew Hacker, "When Big Business Makes Gifts (Tax Deductible)" in *The Corporation in the American Economy,* Harry M. Trebing, ed., Baltimore: Johns Hopkins Press, 1971, pp. 164–72. For an interesting analysis of corporate charity as it relates to large foundations see U.S. House of Representatives, Select Committee on Small Business, Subcommittee Chairman's Report, *Tax Exempt Foundations and Charitable Trusts: Their Impact on Our Economy,* Washington: Government Printing Office, 1968.

Page 359
Gansler, *op. cit.,* pp. 14–18.

Page 361
Victor Papanek, *Design for the Real World, op. cit.*

Marx's views on alienation are discussed by Erich Fromm in *The Revolution of Hope,* New York: Harper & Row, 1968, and *Marx's Concept of Man,* New York: F. Ungar, 1961. Another impressive discussion of Marx and alienation, with particular reference to the American experience, can be found in William Appleman Williams, *The Great Evasion: An Essay on the Contemporary Relevance of Karl Marx and on the Wisdom of Admitting the Heretic into the Dialogue About America's Future,* Chicago: Quadrangle, 1964.

13: The Transformation of Wealth and the Crisis of Understanding

Page 365
The phenomenon of "rootlessness" is discussed extensively in Vance Packard, *A Nation of Strangers*, New York: McKay, 1972.

On the necessity for constant growth and oligopoly expansion in modern capitalism see Robert L. Heilbroner, *The Human Prospect*, New York: Norton, 1974.

Page 367
Storey, Boekh & Associates quote taken from Storey, Boekh & Associates, *The Bank Credit Analyst, The Outlook 1974* (a supplement), December 1973, p. 25.

Page 372
For the Goldberg-Kindleberger proposal see Paul M. Goldberg and Charles Kindleberger, "Toward a GATT for Investment: A Proposal for Supervision of the International Corporation," *Law and Policy in International Business*, Summer 1970.

Ball quotes from "Cosmocorp: The Importance of Being Stateless," *Columbia Journal of World Business*, November–December 1967.

For an alternative position on international regulation, largely from the point of view of underdeveloped countries, see the Report of the secretary-general of UNCTAD to the secretary-general of the United Nations on measures adopted by UNCTAD III (U.N. Document TD/179, p. 10); and International Labour Organization, *Multinational Enterprises and Social Policy*, Studies and Reports, New Series, No. 79 (Geneva: International Labour Organization, 1973).

For an overview of the current literature dealing with the future of multinational enterprise and international regulation, see Robert O. Keohane and Van D. Ooms, *The Multinational Firm and International Regulation*, Department of Political Science, Stanford University, and Department of Economics, Swarthmore College, mimeo, 1974. The authors' essay "The Multinational Enterprise and World Political Economy" (in *International Organization*, Vol. XXVI, Winter 1971) is also helpful.

Kenneth Boulding *et al.* distinguish between the private market or "exchange economy" versus government expenditures in GNP or "grants economy" as follows: "Qualitatively, the grants economy represents the heart of the political economy, because it is precisely at the level of one-way transfers that the political system intervenes in the economic system. Quantitatively, a grant dollar tends to exert higher leverage on the economy than an exchange dollar, thus positioning the grants economy to act as a regulator of the exchange economy," in "Grants Economics: A Simple Introduction, *The American Economist*, Vol. XVI, No. 1, Spring 1972, p. 21. See also Kenneth Boulding, *The Economy of Love and Fear: A Preface to Grants Economics*, Belmont, Calif.: Wadsworth, 1972.

For the Gilpin study see Professor Robert Gilpin, *The Multinational Corporation and the National Interest*, Report to the Senate Committee on Labor and Public Welfare, Washington, D.C.: Government Printing Office, 1973.

Gilpin quotes are from *The Multinational Corporation and the National Interest, ibid.*

Page 386
Data on consumption of energy in the production of food energy is found in *Science*, Vol. 184, Apr. 19, 1974, p. 311.

Page 387
On the need for new knowledge, Robert Heilbroner, speaking at the 1974 meetings of the American Economic Association, reminded his colleagues that some twenty years earlier at those same meetings there were no organized sessions on theoretical problems of inflation, nor on the deterioration of the environment, and "no one had heard of the multinational corporation," while the "attitude toward economic growth in the less developed countries was one of encouragement, not to say enthusiasm." He then continued: ". . . much although not all of contemporary theory is of almost negligible importance for policy purposes. This is because it is built on assumptions with regard to behavior—both individual and institutional behavior—that are too far from reality to produce models in which we can place much confidence. . . . If I am correct in anticipating massive micro problems and mounting tensions over income distribution—in addition to the standard assortment of ills to which the economic body is heir—we will need a considerable advanced theory if we are to deal with these problems other than on a catch-as-catch-can basis" (pp. 121 and 123).

Index

479